D1561343

GREAT FISHING TACKLE CATALOGS
of the golden age

Edited by Samuel Melner and Hermann Kessler

Commentary by Sparse Grey Hackle

Crown Publishers, Inc. New York

To the boys we all once were.

H.K. and S.G.H.

To my father, who first taught me how, and still thinks he can outfish me; to my mother, who fosters this ridiculous idea . . . and to the Neversink River where it all began.

S.M.

Library of Congress Catalog Card Number: 72-84296
ISBN: 0-517-500221

Printed in the United States of America

Published simultaneously in Canada by General
Publishing Company Limited

CONTENTS

PREFACE

Shortly after gathering the first of the catalogs for this book, we began to be concerned with our ignorance about the tackle described in them—and the interest readers would have in the history and lore that surrounded many of the items. It was apparent that the material needed explanation and that such explanations had to be based on a knowledge we did not have. So we asked the remarkable Sparse Grey Hackle (Alfred W. Miller) to write a running commentary for this book, which is a selection of the more interesting pages from fishing-tackle catalogs dating back to the 1830s. He somewhat reluctantly agreed.

But his initial reticence turned into fascinated interest when he began to go through the old catalogs. I watched his eyes sparkle as he discovered old treasures as we pored over the pages together. I listened to his animated exclamations and groans, his recollections of bygone years, his lore and anecdotes of old fishing trips and friends. Those are hours I shall never forget.

Now we invite you to share this experience. In all but a few cases, the pages have been kept the same size as the original (the exceptions being a few covers, reduced in size to accommodate a caption), and whenever possible, Sparse Grey Hackle's commentary appears on the same page as the items discussed. So let's return to those wonderful days of the golden age of fishing, to the 1894 William Mills & Son catalog, with its original H. L. Leonard rods and Wood's "Improved Lollacapop"—"the greatest known antidote for mosquitoes, black flies, gnats in the world"; the 1917 Marshall Field, with Louis Rhead's "American Nature Flies"; the 1895 Foster's, with its dire warning, "Beware of vile imitations," in regard to its Acme lines, and its "steel ribbed rod" and the "Little David" with their "Challenge the World" slogans; the 1909 Abercrombie & Fitch for unusual items like "Matchless Prepared Foods in Self-heating Cans"; early Orvis catalogs for the childhood of one of our leading modern mail-order firms; the 1878 John Krider and the 1886 Thos. H. Chubb, with their items of historical importance; the 1894–95 Montgomery Ward and the 1902 Sears, Roebuck, with their 12-cent rods and 10-cent reels; and to catalogs with scores of fascinating items like "African Steel Vine" rods and Rube Goldberg gadgets, and the nostalgia of unbelievable prices and forgotten tackle and gear.

But see for yourself: Step into the waters of the past with us. Sparse Grey Hackle, your guide, is waiting to show you the best spots.

Samuel Melner

Croton-on-Hudson, New York
April, 1972

ACKNOWLEDGMENTS

We extend our warm thanks and appreciation to the following persons and firms, who were kind enough to provide us with catalogs from their collections, information of various kinds, and other assistance, without which this book would have been impossible:

Sewell N. Dunton and Son, Greenfield, Massachusetts, who were kind enough to lend us many of the catalogs from their collection; Frank Mele, of Woodstock, New York; Seth Rosenbaum, who, in addition to being generous enough to let us photograph many of the catalogs in this book, fed us while we took up an inordinate amount of his time, and exhibited an extraordinary amount of patience and understanding; Robert Boyle, fisherman, conservationist, and author of *The Hudson River;* William Mills & Son of New York City for permission to photograph some of their fine old catalogs; Baird Hall and the Orvis Co., Manchester, Vermont; The Museum of American Fly Fishing, Manchester, Vermont; the Rare Book Division of the New York Public Library, Astor, Lenox and Tilden Foundations; Mrs. Ethel Williams and W. E. Griffin, and L. L. Bean, Inc., Freeport, Maine; The Carl Otto v. Kienbusch '06 Angling Collection, Princeton University Library; and Gallery 19, New York City.

We are particularly grateful to Nick Lyons, consulting editor of Crown's Sportsmen's Classics Series and author of *The Seasonable Angler,* for his guidance, diplomacy, and patience.

Hermann Kessler is responsible for particularly diligent research that led to the uncovering of most of the rare catalogs represented in this book.

"ONLY YESTERDAY"

What fisherman cannot recall his boyhood excitement at the arrival of a new tackle catalog—the ecstasy of looking into a new Eden and the despair of beholding the angel barring the way with the flaming sword of penury?

What little boy of "only yesterday" did not beguile his rainy afternoons with pad, pencil, and the Sears "Roebook," compiling lists of "what I would buy if I had $50," then $25, then $10, and finally a mere $1, all fantasy because his allowance of pocket money, like mine, was five cents a week?

Frustrating? No, for the icy blast of economic reality was tempered by a divine providence to the scanty fleece of the forlorn lamb. After a catalog had been studied long enough, the hellfire flare of the fell figures faded into a rosy celestial glow as the opium of the copywriter bemused the senses of the little boy, lulling him into a blissful dream of owning all those magnificent gadgets and thereby becoming king of the water, the emperor of the fish.

From the days of the earliest settlements in America, men fished and hunted. But even on the frontiers, fishing and hunting provided no important sustenance for many or for long. No natural population of fish and game ever could support permanently any sizable human population, which likely is why the first explorers of North America found no more than a scattered, scanty population of aborigines. Notwithstanding the incredibly rich resources of this vast area, only those Indians who had been able to develop agriculture–the tribes on the Muskingum in Ohio, the Five Nations in the Finger Lakes area of New York, the pueblo-dwelling tribes of the Southwest–were able to create a population numerous enough to establish permanent communities.

The Puritan coming home from the woods in high-peaked hat and buckled shoes with a wild turkey slung on his flintlock is a myth. It took only a year or so for even a tiny settlement to kill or drive off game until it cost too much, in ammunition and time, to feed a family by hunting.

After that, hunting and fishing were mere diversions, and therefore considered to be not respectable. In 1847, the Reverend George Washington Bethune signed his fine, scholarly "biographical preface" to the first American edition of Walton and Cotton's *Compleat Angler* simply as The American Editor. He feared the wrath of his elite congregation if they were to learn that he countenanced and even engaged in the idle, trivial, frivolous, disreputable sport of angling. And "only yesterday," President Calvin Coolidge manifested honest surprise at being invited to go fishing. "A pastime for boys and loafers," this canny, hard-case politician called it, until his advisers pointed out the size of the "fishing vote."

"Only yesterday" the United States ceased to be predominantly agricultural and rural, when the last census disclosed that there are more people in cities now than on the land. Only now has fishing become a major sport, for actually, angling has always been primarily a sport of sophisticated city dwellers. For many years, the sporting goods industry dwelt on the number of millions of fishermen there were, including a horde of saltwater fishermen, and liberal estimates of the number of fishing landowners, none of whom required a license. But I can easily recall when the trade's own estimate of its annual sales volume was only about three million dollars.

Legend to the contrary, fishing was never the big thing for the country boy that hunting was. To be sure, he cut his pole, dug his worms, and went "trouting" in April, but the onset of spring quickly drove him back to the plow and the harrow, the cultivator, the hoe, and the mowing machine. By the time the bass season came in, the livelier, more gregarious pastime of baseball was in full swing. Only after the harvest could the country boy fire a couple of shells through his Montgomery Ward shotgun to clear the rust out of the barrels, and go hunting for rabbits, squirrels, quail, or grouse.

So there were no fishing tackle stores in the country; the hardware dealer and the general store sold tackle as a sideline. Only in cities of substantial size were there stores devoted exclusively to the sale of "sporting goods." It is the catalogs of such houses that are sampled in this look backward to yesteryear, before the glass rod and the fixed-spool spinning reel, the new leisure and the new affluence, doubled and redoubled and doubled again the ranks of well-read, sophisticated young recruits to the sport of angling.

As a boy who earned the 50 cents to buy his first rod by eating health-giving prunes at five cents for each eight prunes, and lived to refuse a $300 offer for a treasured wisp of bamboo less than seven feet long, I have run the whole course. So walk with me through the catalogs that my colleagues have assembled and permit me to add a few comments and explanations.

Sparse Grey Hackle

I

PRE-1890

J. CHEEK,

FISHING ROD AND TACKLE,

UMBRELLA, PARASOL,

WALKING STICK AND RIDING WHIP

MANUFACTURER,

THE GOLDEN PERCH,

No. 52, STRAND,

OPPOSITE THE BRITISH FIRE OFFICE.

LONDON:
HOWLETT AND SON, PRINTERS,
10, Frith Street, Soho.

1839.

IN consequence of the Extraordinary Patronage the Proprietor of the **GOLDEN PERCH** has received, since he reduced the extravagantly high prices of RODS and TACKLE, he is now enabled to make a still further reduction of upwards of 10 per cent. on the average, which will reduce them BELOW the prices which were two years since termed WHOLESALE, hoping by such reduction to meet with extra patronage and support. The Proprietor also pledges himself that if he meet with the support he feels himself entitled to, he will make still further reductions in the prices as soon and as often as the times and markets will allow.

CATALOGUE OF PRICES.

WALKING STICK RODS.

	£.	s.	d.
Three-joint Bamboo	0	2	6
Four ditto ditto	0	4	0
Three ditto ditto, screw ferrules	0	3	0
Four ditto ditto	0	4	6
Four ditto best ditto, spliced top	0	8	6
Four ditto ditto, and ringed	0	10	0
Three ditto ditto, very light and superior finish, for Ladies	0	14	0
Three ditto, ash butt	0	13	0
Four ditto ditto	0	16	0

Also a variety that have not the least appearance of a Fishing-Rod.

FLY RODS.

	£.	s.	d.
Four-joint best Hickory Fly-Rods, ringed	0	11	0
Five ditto ditto	0	14	0
Four ditto ditto, brazed	0	13	0
Five ditto ditto	0	16	0
Four ditto ditto, ringed, brazed, and winch fittings	0	15	0

6 J. CHEEK, GOLDEN PERCH.

	£.	s.	d.
Five ditto ditto	0	18	0
Four ditto best Hickory Fly Rod, with two tops, landing handle, ringed, brazed, winch fittings, socket, spear, and partition bag	1	0	0
Five ditto ditto	1	3	0
Six ditto ditto, butt bored instead of landing handle	1	6	0
Seven ditto ditto	1	9	0
Eight ditto ditto	1	12	0
Nine ditto ditto, for Pocket or Portmanteau	1	15	0
Ten ditto ditto	1	18	0

An Assortment with Screw Ferrules and Bayonet Joints.

GENERAL RODS.

	£.	s.	d.
Five-joint best Hickory general rods, with four tops, winch fittings, socket, spear, and partition bag . . .	1	5	0
Five ditto ditto, five tops . . .	1	8	0

Cheek is a bit unusual in that his rodmaking was part of the walking stick and umbrella industry. Most rodmaking in this era grew out of archery since bowyers were skilled at fitting and gluing strips of one or several woods into resilient staves.

Cheek's price of 15 shillings for a hickory flyrod was not low in 1839, when a skilled British workman made less than one pound sterling per week.

PRICE LIST OF FISHING TACKLE.

JOHN KRIDER,

Manufacturer and Importer of

AND

GENERAL

SPORTING IMPLEMENTS

Of Every Description,

N. E. COR. SECOND & WALNUT STS.,

Philadelphia.

PHILADELPHIA:

PRESS OF J. H. WESTON & SON, 438 WALNUT STREET.

1878.

Krider was the undisputed king of the sportsmen's outfitting business in Philadelphia all through the middle decades of the nineteenth century. Countless domestic safaris and numerous expeditions of titled and royal foreigners which passed through Philadelphia en route to the buffalo, grizzly, antelope, and other hunting of the western frontiers outfitted at Krider's.

9

FISHING RODS. *Net*

No.	Joints	Description	Price
3.	3	joint, single brass ferrules.	225
4.	4	" " " "	550
8.	3	" " " " ringed.	550
10.	3	" double " " "	750
12.	3	" " " " " capped butt.	900
18.	3	" single ferrule, ringed, light gudgeon.	550
20.	3	" " " " " "	700
25.	3	" " " " reel bands, capped butt.	1100
28.	3	" " " guides, capped butt.	1000
33.	3	" " " " " " reel bands.	1500
34.	3	" " " " " " full mounted	2500
40.	4	" " " " " "	1500
44.	4	" " " " " " 2 tips.	2400
47.	4	" " " " " " hollow butt.	3800
48.	4	" " " " " " full mounted, 2 tips.	3400
50.	4	" 15 ft. double ferrule, guides, capped butt.	3800
54.	4	" 16 ft. " " " " " 2 tips.	3000
72.	4	" bass " " " " " reel bands, 2 tips.	2400
74.	4	" " " " " " " full mounted.	3200

Bamboo, 4 joint, ringed. 1600
" 4 " " and reel bands. 1850.
" 4 " " " " " 1 tip in butt. 2500
3 " " " " " " 1350
3 " Plain 1050

Also on hand a full assortment of three and four joint extra-fine finished Rods, full mounted in brass or German silver.

KRIDER'S CELEBRATED SPLICED BAMBOO RODS.

3 joint, extra tip	in cases,	30 00	Ea
3 " extra 2d joint and extra tips	"	40 00	"
4 " " extra joint and tips	"	60 00	"

Krider knew how to charge. In 1878, when it was still argued that a workman should be able to support his family on a wage of $1 a day, Krider offered a fishing rod (material not specified) with hollow butt for $38, and a spliced bamboo rod with two spare joints for $60.

The catalog was printed blank so prices could be inked in, thus serving for either wholesale or retail use, for several years.

THIRD EDITION.

Dame, Stoddard & Kendall,

SUCCESSORS TO

BRADFORD & ANTHONY,

Importers, Manufacturers and Dealers in

FISH HOOKS,

FISHING TACKLE,

AND

ANGLING IMPLEMENTS.

374 WASHINGTON STREET,

OPPOSITE BROMFIELD STREET,

BOSTON, MASS.

Bradford & Anthony was a fine old Boston house for many years. A chance remark by one of their salesmen started Hiram L. Leonard on his rodmaking career over a century ago. The successor firm, Dame, Stoddard & Kendall, continued the business (as Dame, Stoddard & Co.) at least as late as 1930.

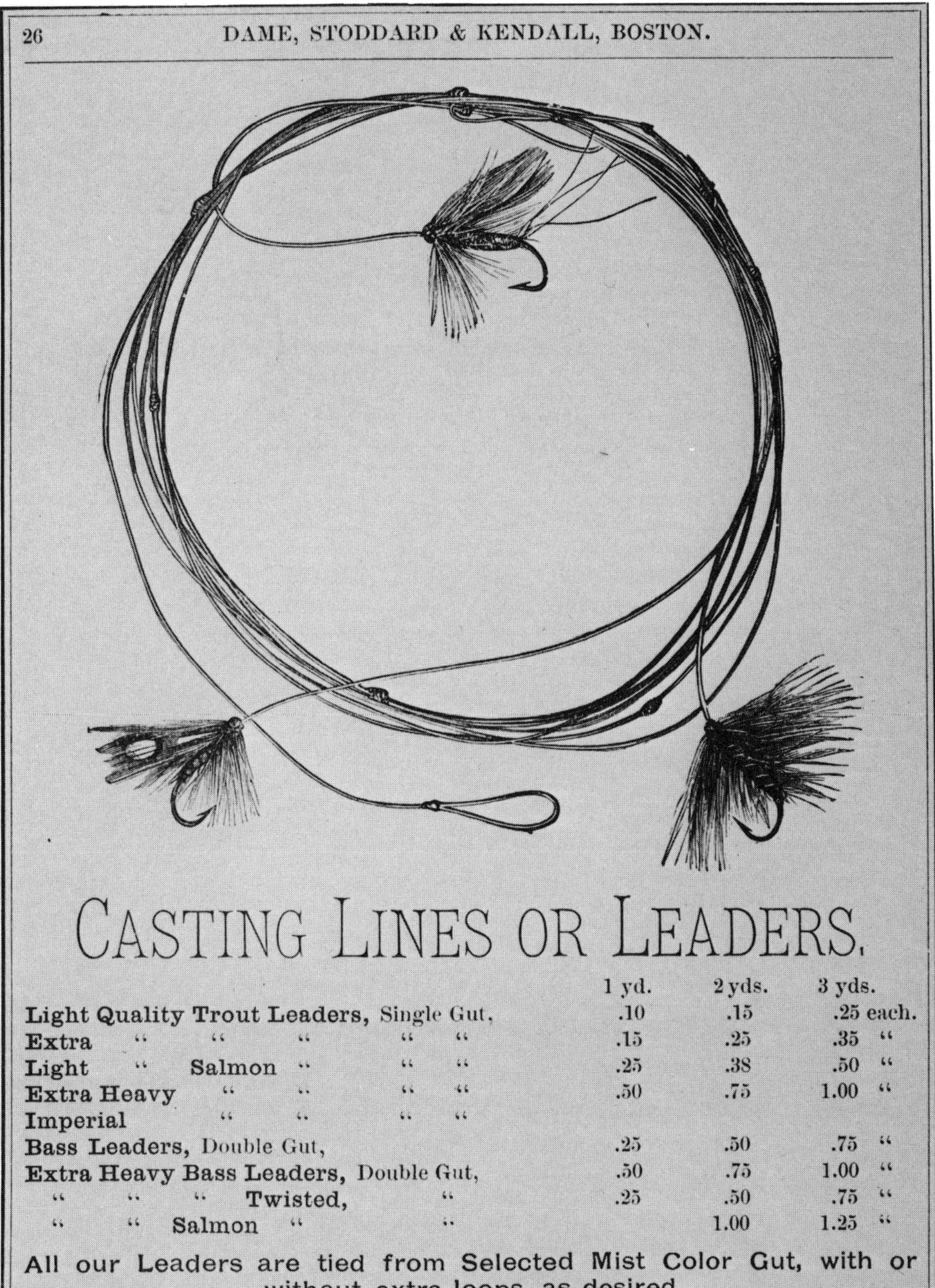

CASTING LINES OR LEADERS.

	1 yd.	2 yds.	3 yds.
Light Quality Trout Leaders, Single Gut,	.10	.15	.25 each.
Extra " " " "	.15	.25	.35 "
Light " **Salmon** " " "	.25	.38	.50 "
Extra Heavy " " " "	.50	.75	1.00 "
Imperial " " " "			
Bass Leaders, Double Gut,	.25	.50	.75 "
Extra Heavy Bass Leaders, Double Gut,	.50	.75	1.00 "
" " " **Twisted,** "	.25	.50	.75 "
" " **Salmon** " "		1.00	1.25 "

All our Leaders are tied from Selected Mist Color Gut, with or without extra loops, as desired.

BEST QUALITY BRAIDED FISHING LINES.

TRADE MARK.

BRAIDED SILK LINES.

Fac-simile of Sizes.

B
C
D
E
F
G

Nos.	B	C	D	E	F	G
On Boards of 50 yds.,	$3.00	2.50	2.00	1.65	1.35	1.00 each.
" " 100 yds.,	6.00	5.00	4.00	3.30	2.70	2.00 "

BEST OILED SILK LINES.

Nos.	C	D	E	F	G
In Coils of 50 yards,	$2.50	2.00	1.65	1.35	1.00 each.
" " 100 yards,	5.00	4.00	3.30	2.70	2.00 "

BRAIDED RAW SILK LINES.

Nos.	C	D	E	F	G
On Boards of 50 yards,	$2.00	1.65	1.35	1.10	.90 each.
" " 100 yards,	4.00	3.30	2.70	2.20	1.80 "

BEST BRAIDED LINEN LINES.

Nos. B, C, D, E, F, G, on Boards of 50 yards, ... .75 each.
" " " " " 100 yards, ...$1.25 "

HARD BRAIDED LINEN LINES.

Fac-simile of Sizes.

1
2
3
4
5

In Coils of 50 yards, all sizes, ... .75 each.

BRAIDED COD AND BLUEFISH LINES.

In Coils of 150 feet, ... No. 1, $1.00 each, No. 2, .75 each.
" " 250 feet, ...$1.25 "

30 DAME, STODDARD & KENDALL, BOSTON.

THE BRAY FLY BOOK.

MADE WITH GENUINE MOROCCO, OR GRAIN LEATHER COVERS.

MOROCCO,	2	leaves to hold	4	dozen flies,	....	$5.00	each.
	2	" "	8	"	....	5.50	"
	3	" "	6	"	....	5.00	"
	3	" "	12	"	....	6.00	"
GRAIN LEATHER,	2	" "	4	"	....	4.00	"
	2	" "	8	"	....	4.50	"
	3	" "	6	"	....	4.00	"
	3	" "	12	"	....	5.00	"

Bray's patent covered the use of a length of helical wire spring between the coils of which the gut snells of flies could be pushed to keep them from tangling. They're still sold today.

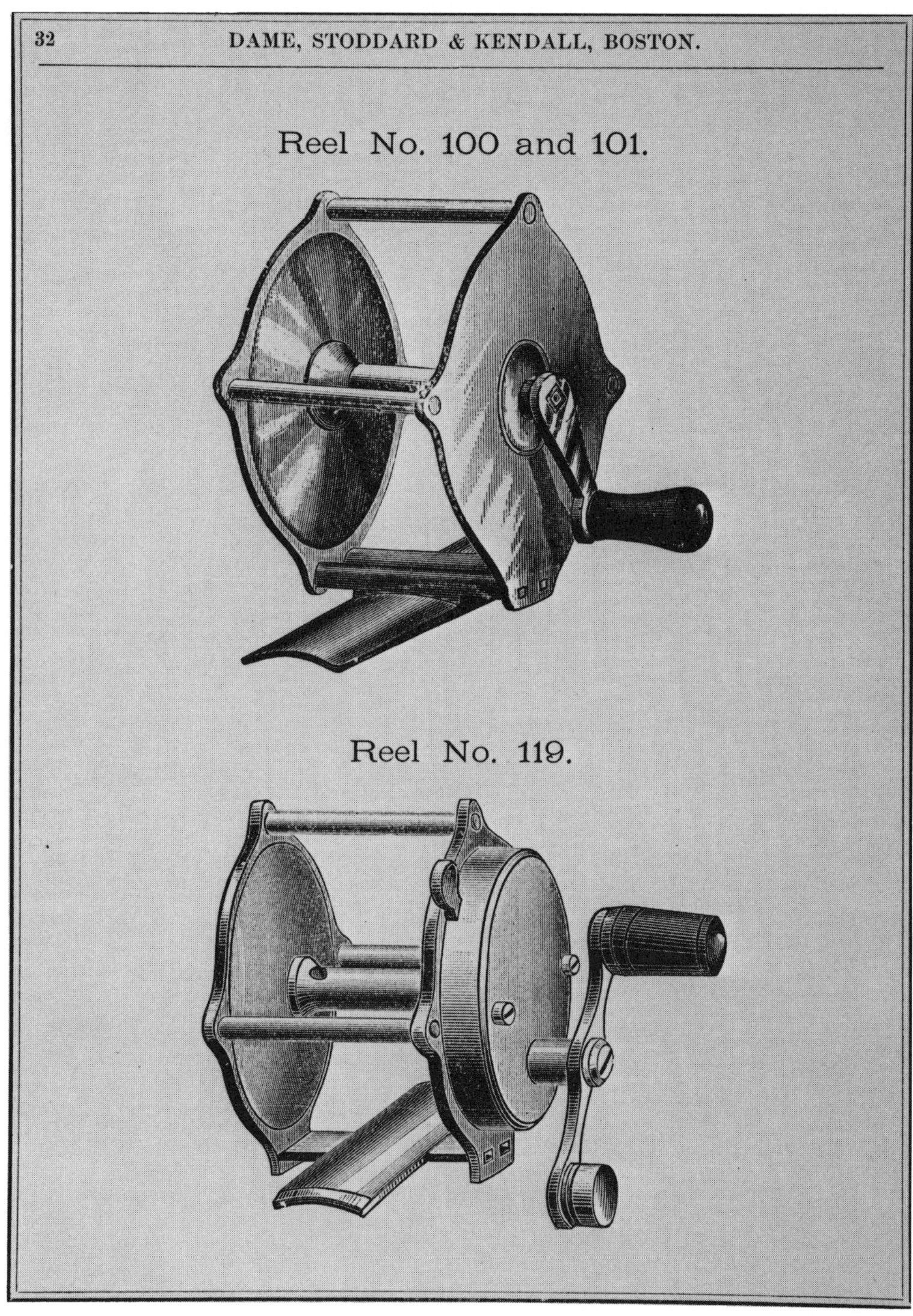

Reel No. 100 and 101.

Reel No. 119.

DAME, STODDARD & KENDALL, BOSTON. 33

FISHING REELS.

No. 100. Raised Pillar, Plain, Polished, with Plates.

	25	40	60	80	100	150 yds.
BRASS,	.35	.40	.50	.60	.65	.75 each.
NICKELED,	.50	.60	.65	.75	.80	.90 "

No. 101. Raised Pillar, Click, Polished, with Plates.

	25	40	60	80	100	150 yds.
BRASS,	.50	.60	.70	.75	.85	1.00 each.
NICKELED,	.65	.75	.85	.90	1.00	1.15 "

No. 102. Plain Single Brass Reel, Polished, with Stop.

25	30	40	60	80 yds.
.40	.45	.50	.55	.60 each.

No. 104. Brass Click, Safety Band.

	25	40	60	80 yds.
BRASS,	$1.00	1.15	1.25	1.40 each.
NICKELED,	1.25	1.40	1.50	1.65 "

No. 105. Fine Single Click, Polished.

	25	40	60	80	100 yds.
BRASS,	.90	1.00	1.10	1.20	1.25 each.
NICKELED,	$1.15	1.25	1.35	1.45	1.50 "

No. 106. Brass and Rubber Click Reel, Bushed.

	25	40	60	80 yds.
BRASS,	$1.15	1.25	1.50	1.65 each.
NICKELED,	1.40	1.50	1.75	1.90 "

No. 117. Rubber Click Reel, with Nickel Bands.

25	40	60	80 yds.
$1.75	1.85	2.00	2.25 each.

No. 108. Plain Multiplying Reel, with Drag.

	25	30	40	60	80 yds.
BRASS,	.85	.90	.95	1.00	1.15 each.
NICKELED,	$1.10	1.15	1.20	1.25	1.40 "

No. 118. Plain Multiplying Reel, with Drag. Balance Handle.

	25	30	40	60	80 yds.
BRASS,	.95	1.00	1.10	1.25	1.40 each.
NICKELED,	$1.20	1.25	1.35	1.50	1.65 "

No. 109. Raised Pillar Multiplying Reel, with Drag.

	40	60	80	100	150 yds.
BRASS,	.75	.80	.85	.90	1.10 each.
NICKELED,	$1.00	1.00	1.10	1.15	1.35 "

No. 119. Raised Pillar Multiplying Reel, with Drag. Balance Handle.

	40	60	80	100	150 yds.
BRASS,	.90	1.00	1.00	1.10	1.35 each.
NICKELED,	$1.15	1.25	1.25	1.35	1.60 "

Fine English Click Reel, Revolving Plate.

	$2\frac{1}{4}$ in.	$2\frac{1}{2}$ in.	$2\frac{3}{4}$ in.	3 in.
No. $30\frac{1}{2}$ B,	$3.25	3.50	3.75	4.00 each.

The Orvis Reel, ... $3.50 each

Those old brass and nickel-plated reels, single action or multiplying, are offered here for from 35 cents to $4.00.

DAME, STODDARD & KENDALL'S FINE CLICK REELS.

Reel No. 814 and 815.

No. 813. Fine Rubber Click, Rubber Safety Band.

40 yards,	$5.00 each.
60 "	5.25 "
80 "	5.50 "
100 "	5.75 "
150 "	6.50 "
200 "	7.50 "

No. 814. Fine Rubber Click, Nickel Plated Safety Band.

25 yards,	$2.75 each.
40 "	3.00 "
60 "	3.00 "
80 "	3.25 "
100 "	3.50 "
150 "	3.75 "

No. 815. Fine Rubber Click, German Silver Safety Band.

40 yards,	$5.00 each.
60 "	5.25 "
80 "	5.50 "
100 "	6.00 "
150 "	6.50 "

No. 817. Fine Rubber and German Silver Click, Raised Pillar.

Small Trout,	$7.50 each.
Large "	8.50 "
Grilse,	10.00 "

36 DAME, STODDARD & KENDALL, BOSTON.

SALMON REELS.

English Ebonite Reel, Bronze Revolving Plate,	4 in.,	$6.00 each.
" " " " " "	4½ in.,	7.00 "
" Bronze " " " "	4½ in.,	9.00 "
Good Quality Rubber Reel, Brass Finish,	4 in.,	10.00 "
Fine Rubber Salmon, with Nickel Plated Safety Band, No. 804,	4 in.,	12.00 "
" " " " " " 804,	4¼ in.,	13.00 "
" " " " " " 804,	4½ in.,	14.00 "
Finest Rubber Grilse Reel, with German Silver Safety Band, No. 805,	3½ in.,	18.00 "
" Salmon " " " " " " 805,	4 in.,	20.00 "
" " " " " " " " 805,	4½ in.,	22.00 "

But grilse and salmon reels went up to $22.

FINE MULTIPLYING REELS.

Reel No. 625.

No. 625. Fine Brass Multiplying Reel, Balance Handle, Click and Drag.

25 yards,	$2.25 each.
40 "	2.50 "
60 "	2.75 "
80 "	3.00 "
100 "	3.25 "

No. 625. Fine Nickel Plated Multiplying Reel, Balance Handle, Click & Drag.

25 yards,	$2.50 each.
40 "	2.75 "
60 "	3.00 "
80 "	3.25 "
100 "	3.50 "

No. 724. Fine Nickel Plated Multiplying, Patent Click.

40 yards,	$3.00 each.
60 "	3.25 "
80 "	3.50 "
100 "	3.75 "

No. 725. Nickel Plated Quadruple Multiplying, Click and Drag.

40 yards,	$5.00 each.
60 "	5.25 "
80 "	5.50 "
100 "	6.00 "

FINE FISHING RODS.

LANCEWOOD FLY ROD, No. 301.

No. 300.	Mountain Trout Rod, full Nickel Mounted, Reel Seat above the hand, 2 Tips, 9½ feet,	$3.50 each.
301.	3-piece Fly Rod, full Nickel Mounted, 10½ feet,	3.50 "
302.	All lance Fly Rod, full Nickel Mounted, Reel Seat below the hand, in wood form, 10½ feet,	4.00 "
312.	3-piece Lance Fly Rod, Nickel Trimmings, 10½ feet,	3.00 "
312.	Same Rod with 2 Tips,	3.50 "
402.	Greenheart Fly Rod, full Nickel Mounted, Reel Seat below the hand, 2 Tips, in wood form, 10½ feet,	4.50 "
303.	Henshall Black Bass Rod, Ash and Lance, full Nickel Mounted, Anti-friction Guides, 8½ feet,	3.00 "
304.	Henshall Black Bass Rod, all Lancewood, full Nickel Mounted, Anti-friction Guides, 8 ft. 3 in., in wood form,	4.00 "
404.	Henshall Black Bass Rod, Greenheart, full Nickel Mounted, Anti-friction Guides, in wood form,	4.50 "
306.	9 foot Black Bass Rod, all Lancewood, full Nickel Mounted, Anti-friction Guides, Raised Ferrules, in wood form,	4.00 "
307.	Same in every respect as No. 306, only 10½ feet in length,	4.50 "
305.	Lancewood Black Bass Rod, full Nickel Mounted, Reel Seat below the hand, length 10½ feet,	3.50 "
308.	10½ foot Black Bass Rod, 2 Middle joints, 3 Tips,	7.00 "
406.	Greenheart Black Bass, full Nickel Mounted, Anti-friction Guides, in wood form, 9 feet,	4.50 "
407.	Same as No. 406, only 10½ feet,	5.00 "
316.	3-piece Lance Black Bass Rod, Nickel Trimmings, 10½ feet, with 1 Tip,	3.25 "
316.	With 2 Tips,	3.75 "
309.	Lancewood General Rod, full Nickel Mounted, will make Fly Rod 10½ feet, or Bass Rod 9 feet, in wood form,	7.00 "
409.	Greenheart General Rod, full Nickel Mounted, will make Fly Rod 10½ feet or Bass Rod 9 feet, in wood form,	8.00 "

63.	5-piece Trunk Rod, Reel Bands, Guides, Lance Tips, 10 feet,	1.25 "
63¾.	" " " full Nickel Mounted, Hollow Butt, 10 feet,	3.00 "
64.	Trunk Fly Rod, full Nickel Mounted,	4.00 "
65.	" Bass " " " "	4.00 "

French Fishing Baskets.

No. 0,	.85	each.
1,	$1.00	"
2,	1.25	"
3,	1.50	"
4,	1.75	"
5,	2.00	"

TROUT BASKET.

Best Webbing Basket Strap,	.35	cents.
Best Russet Leather Basket Strap, 60 inch,	.35	"
Best Russet Leather Bait Box Strap, 48 inch,	.25	"
Russet Leather Belts,	40 to 60	"

SPORTSMAN'S BALANCES.

Parker's Pocket Scale,	to weigh	8 x ¼ lbs.,	.25	each.
Novelty " "	"	15 x ⅛ "	.50	"
English Brass Balance,	"	4 lbs. x 1 oz.,	$1.50	"
" "	"	7 x ¼ lbs.,	1.00	"
" "	"	12 x ¼ "	1.25	"
" "	"	25 x ½ "	1.50	"
" "	"	50 x ½ "	2.50	"
English German Silver Balance,	"	5 x ¼ "	1.00	"
" " "	"	10 x ¼ "	1.50	"
" " "	"	25 x ½ "	2.50	"
" " "	"	50 x ½ "	3.00	"

NOVELTY.

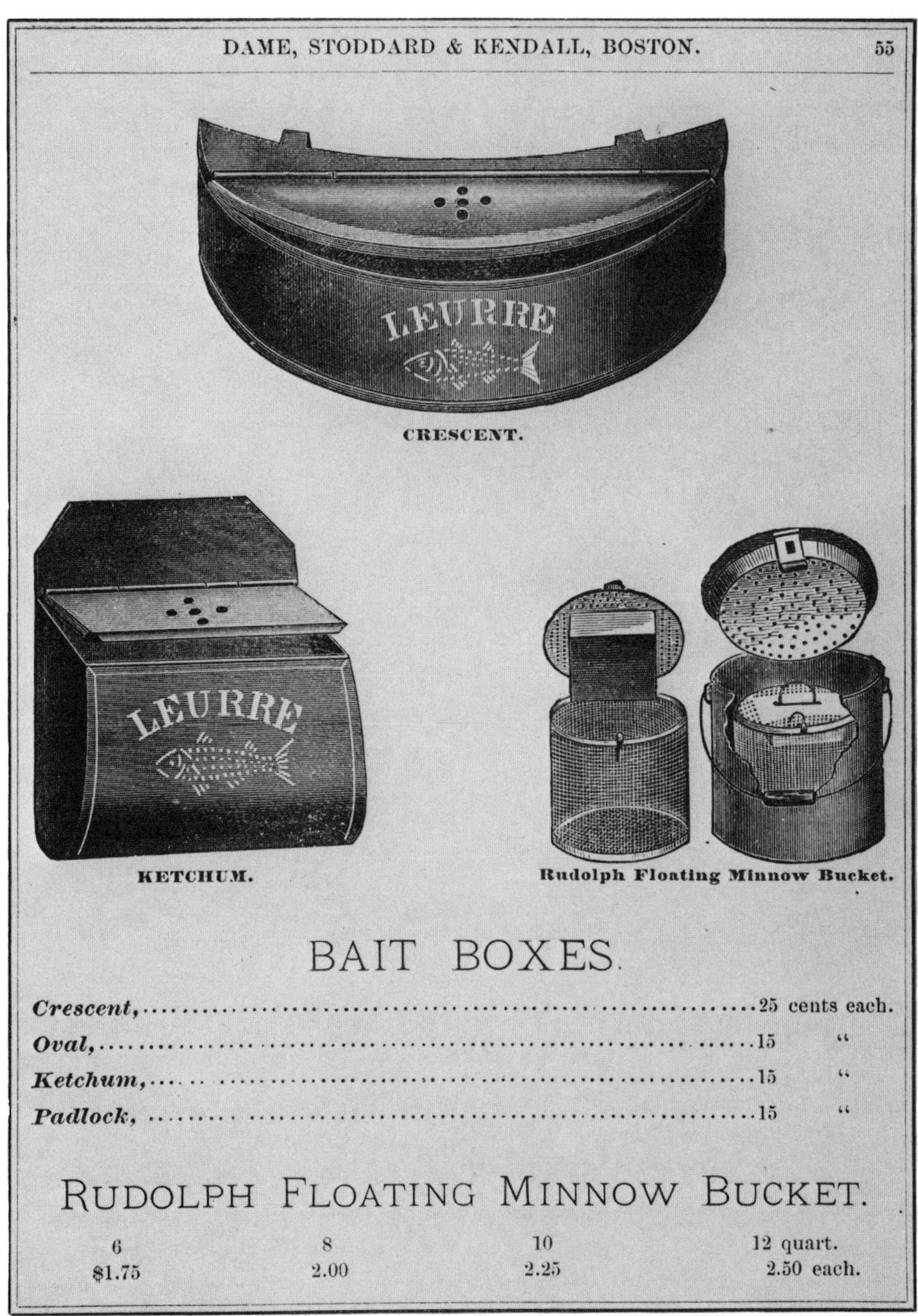

DAME, STODDARD & KENDALL, BOSTON. 55

CRESCENT.

KETCHUM.

Rudolph Floating Minnow Bucket.

BAIT BOXES.

Crescent,	25 cents each.
Oval,	15 "
Ketchum,	15 "
Padlock,	15 "

RUDOLPH FLOATING MINNOW BUCKET.

6	8	10	12 quart.
$1.75	2.00	2.25	2.50 each.

Worm boxes identical to these are still on sale. Why a fisherman needed to label his worm box, and in French at that, is one of the unsolved mysteries of angling.

62 DAME, STODDARD & KENDALL, BOSTON.

THE
Isaac Walton
FISHING SUIT.

Sizes, 34, 36, 38, 40, 42, 44 inch.

Coat, ... $4.00 each.
Vest, ... 2.25 "
Pants, ... 3.00 "

MACKINTOSH
ENGLISH WADING SOCKS,
$7.00 per pair.

SPORTSMEN'S OIL TANNED MOCCASINS, FOR HUNTING, FISHING, CANOEING.

No. 1. Regular **Shoe Pack.**
Price, ... $3.00 per pair.
No. 1. With English Tongue,
Price, ... $3.50 per pair.
No. 1. With extra Soles and Heels and English Tongue, .. $4.50 per pair.

No. 3. **Boot Moccasin.**
Price, ... $5.00 per pair.

Same, with extra Soles and Heels, ... $6.00 per pair.

Slippers, ... $1.50 per pair.

Even in those days, fishing coats had pockets on the sleeves.

THE ANGLER'S GUIDE

AND

TOURISTS

GAZETTEER

THE ANGLER'S GUIDE BOOK

AND

Tourist's Gazeteer

OF THE

FISHING WATERS

OF THE

United States and Canada,

1886.

COMPILED AND EDITED BY

WILLIAM C. HARRIS, Editor of "The American Angler."

THE ANGLERS' PUBLISHING COMPANY,
NEW YORK.
THE WESTERN ANGLERS' PUBLISHING COMPANY.
CHICAGO.

THE

Maine Central Railroad

IS THE

SPORTSMAN'S LINE TO THE EAST,

Leading as it does to

Moosehead and Rangeley Lakes, the Dead River and Mt, Katahdin Regions.

And all the Hunting and Fishing Resorts of Maine and New Brunswick.

It also operates the Portland, Bangor, Mt. Desert and Mechias Steamboat Co., and to many pleasure resorts offers choice of routes by land or water. Send for Summer Excursion Book detailing rates and time tables, and for "Open Season" description of all the sporting resorts of Northern New Brunswick.

F. E. BOOTHBY, General Passenger Agent. **PAYSON TUCKER,** General Manager, Portland, Me.

NEW YORK, PENNA AND OHIO R. R.,

IN CONNECTION WITH THE **ERIE RAILWAY,**

Forms the Great Through Route Between the East and West.

NO CHANGE OF CARS BETWEEN NEW YORK, CLEVELAND, CHICAGO, CINCINNATI AND ST. LOUIS.

3—Through Trains—3

Each way, daily, with Pullman Palace Sleeping Coaches, Pullman Hotel Coaches, New English Buffet Cars and Elegant Day Coaches.

ONLY
20 HOURS
26 ..
38 ..
Between New York and
CLEVELAND,
CINCINNATI,
ST LOUIS.

By taking the new Limited Train, without extra charge. For tickets and further information apply at all offices on line of road and of connecting lines, asking for ticket via NEW YORK, PENN. AND OHIO and ERIE RAILROADS.

A. E. CLARK, Asst. Gen. Pass. Agent, Cleveland, O.

FOR THE BEST SALT WATER FISHING

On the New Jersey Coast

Go to Beach Haven, N. J.

Leave New York via Penna. R. R., via C. R. R. of N. J. or via New Jersey Southern Railroad. Leave Philadelphia from foot of Market street. See notices on pp. 120, 122 and 124 of this book. For further particulars consult Penna. Railroad Summer Excursion Route Book, or address

H. N. GILSON, General Passenger Agent, Tuckerton, N. J.

SENECA LAKE.

Good Fishing, Fine Hotels Beautiful Scenery.

Can be reached via the AUBURN branch of the New York Central and Hudson River Railroad, fifty miles west of SYRACUSE, and fifty miles east of ROCHESTER. Can be reached from the Erie Railroad from WAVERLY, N. Y., via the Lehigh Valley Railroad; from ELMIRA on the Erie Railroad via the Northern Central and Syracuse, Geneva and Corning Railways via Himrods, and via Seneca Lake steamers from Watkins, N. Y.; from CORNING on the Erie Railroad via the Syracuse, Geneva and Corning Railway. From the main line of the New York Central and Hudson River Railroad from LYONS, N. Y., via the Lehigh Valley and Syracuse, Geneva and Corning Railways, twelve trains daily. Connects with the Erie Canal at Montezuma via the Cayuga and Seneca Canal. Steamers on Seneca Lake run all the year round, making six trips a day in summer and two in winter. New York State Experimental Farm located one and a half miles from village of Geneva, N, Y.

Established 1844.

GOODYEAR'S

India Rubber Glove

MANUFACTURING CO.

RUBBER GOODS OF EVERY DESCRIPTION.

503 and 505 Broadway

AND

205 Broadway, Corner Eulton St., NEW YORK.

P. O. BOX 1424.

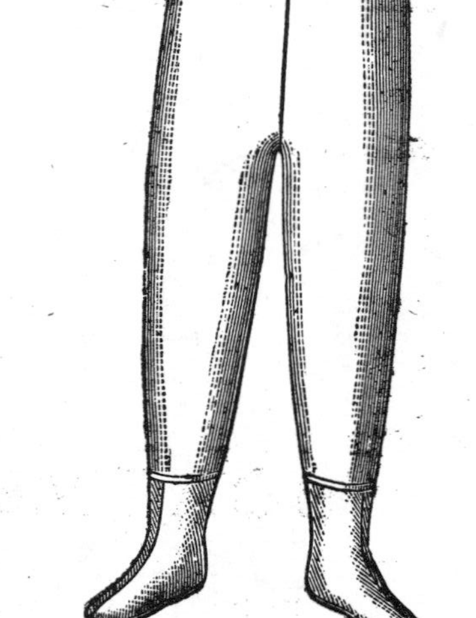

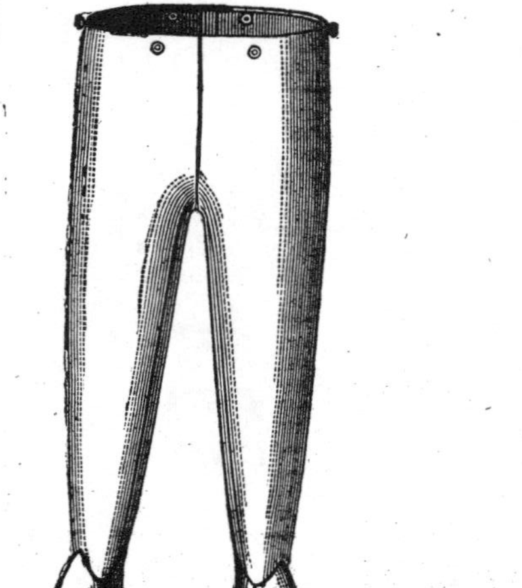

We give PARTICULAR ATTENTION to the manufacture of

RUBBER SPORTING GOODS.

☞ Send for full Illustrated Catalogue.

THE SPORTSMAN'S JOURNAL. 431

BOATS, CANOES, FISHING TACKLE, Etc.

Invented and Manufactured by
N. A. OSGOOD, Battle Creek, Mich.
Send for Circular.

OSGOOD'S FOLDING CANVAS BOAT. Weight, for trout fishing, with stretcher, side-boards and paddle, 25 lbs. With stretcher, side-boards, gunwale and paddle, 32 lbs. With stretcher, side-boards, gunwale, stools and oars, 40 lbs. With bottom board, side-boards, gunwale, stools and oars, 50 lbs. This cut shows twelve-foot boat.

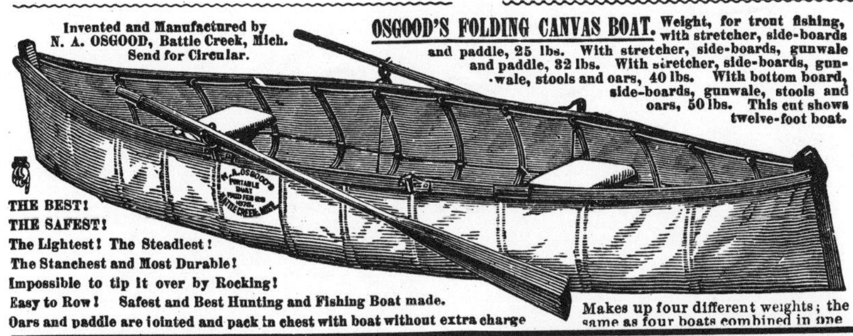

THE BEST!
THE SAFEST!
The Lightest! The Steadiest!
The Stanchest and Most Durable!
Impossible to tip it over by Rocking!
Easy to Row! Safest and Best Hunting and Fishing Boat made.
Oars and paddle are jointed and pack in chest with boat without extra charge

Makes up four different weights; the same as four boats combined in one

Size of Chest, 38 inches long, 17 inches wide, 18 inches deep.

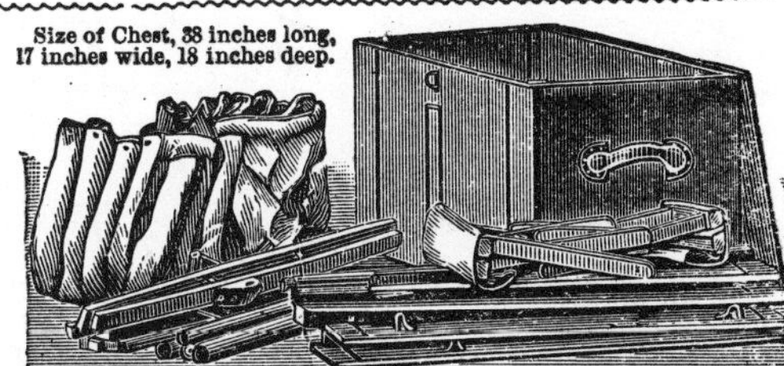

The above is a view of the Boat in its compact form, showing Boat folded, Bottom-Board, Camp-Stools, Gunwale, Stretcher, and Packing Chest. Oars and Paddles are jointed and packed with Boat in Chest.

The Radix Folding Centerboard

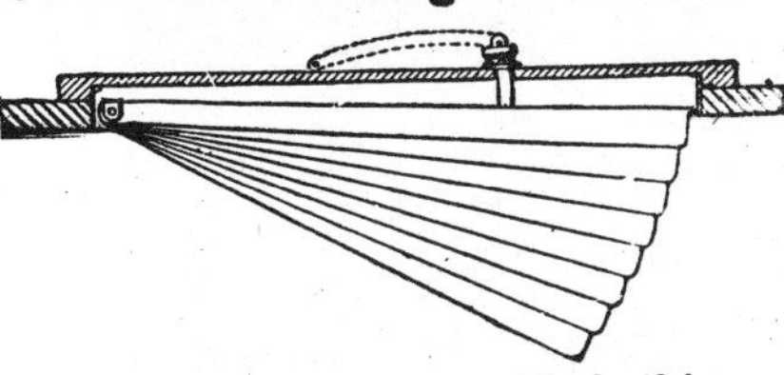

Two Sizes—30 in. by 15 in.; 36 in. by 18 in.
CONSTRUCTED ON AN ENTIRELY NEW AND SIMPLE PRINCIPLE.

For canoes and sailboats. Gives a flush floor and superior sailing qualities. Made entirely of brass. Indorsed by prominent canoeists, boat builders and others. Send for circular.

THE RADIX MANUFACTURING CO.,
25 6 26t 39 Old Slip, N. Y.

The Bow Facing Oars

For duck shooting and pleasure boating. Send for circular. Address
WILLIAM LYMAN,
25 14-3t Middlefield, Conn.

Hunting, Fishing and Pleasure Boats.

We build everything, from a Canoe to a Steam Yacht, either Clinker or Carvel, and have made a revolution in prices for strictly first-class work. A good Clinker built boat, 13 ft. long, 36 inch beam, weight 60 to 75 lbs., with oars, $20. We will make estimates on any kind of boat work. Send 10c. in stamps for illustrated catalogue. Chicago Headquarters, 115 Wabash Ave.

R. J. Douglas & Co., Waukegan. Il

CUT OF ALL LANCE WOOD FLY ROD.

Length, 10½ feet; weight, 8 oz.; 2 tips; has nickel-plated trimmings; metal reel seat; capped ferrules. Warranted first-class in every respect. Price $4.

Also same style rod for Bass, to weigh 12 oz., at same price. Can be sent by mail for 35c extra.

SEND FOR PRICE LIST OF ANGLER'S SUPPLIES.

TO THE TRADE.

Our Wholesale Catalogue for 1887 (sent to dealers only) will be ready for mailing November 1.

SEND FOR ONE AND EXAMINE PRICES.

Address **THOS. H. CHUBB,**
POST MILLS, ORANGE CO., VT.

Note that the 25-pound, 12-foot, canvas folding boat is "impossible to tip over by rocking." No Federal Trade Commission regulated advertising in those days.

The Lyman Gunsight Co. made and sold bow-facing oars well into modern times. Even today, guides in the Dismal Swamp and other constricted waterways still patch their old ones by brazing and welding, and wish they could buy new ones.

The Radix folding centerboard was used mostly on sailing canoes, a craft now seldom seen.

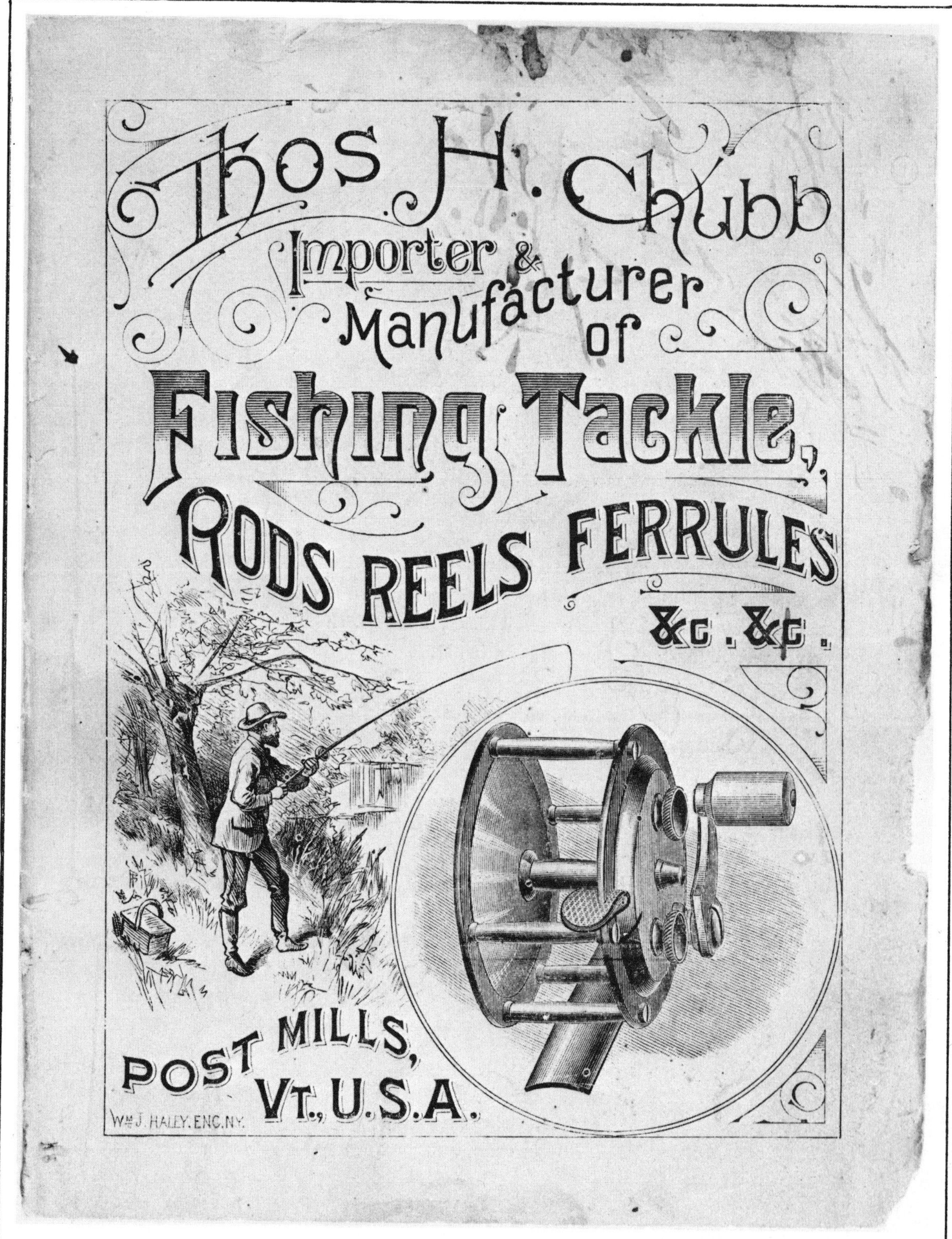
Thos H. Chubb
Importer & Manufacturer of
Fishing Tackle,
Rods Reels Ferrules
&c. &c.
Post Mills,
Vt., U.S.A.
Wm J. Haley. Eng. N.Y.

Captain Chubb had, by 1886, a substantial plant at Post Mills, Vermont, if the artist is to be believed, and was an important figure in the tackle industry for years. Although this was a relatively small industrial unit, it is unusual in having such adjuncts as a foundry and a machine shop to the main woodworking operation.

T. H CHUBB MANUFACTURER OF FISHING RODS.
POST MILLS, VT.
T.H.C.
T.H.CHUBB, MANUFACTURER OF FISHING RODS.
OFFICE
ESTABLISHED, 1869.

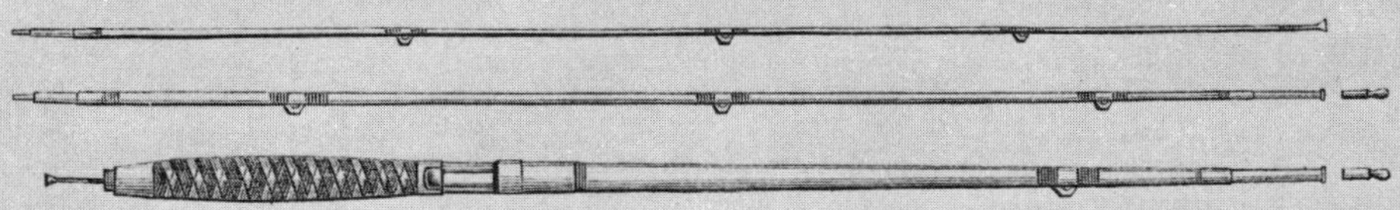

Cut of Rod I.

H.

Same rod as G, with German silver trimmings, waterproof ferrules, metal stoppers, grooved wood form, in cloth case.

Price, $6.00

Boxing and registered mail, .40

I.—Black Bass Bait Rod.

Three joint, either 9 or 10 1-2 feet, weight 14 to 15 oz.; ash butt and joint, lance wood tip and short inside tip, butt hollow for inside tip; butt and joint stained a rich, dark color, butt wound with patent whipping; nickel-plated trimmings, reel seat above hand, ferrules capped and welt, funnel tops and tie guides wound with silk, in cloth partition case.

Price, $4.00

Boxing and registered mail, .35

J.

Same rod as I, with German silver trimmings; lance wood joint, metal stoppers, butt wound with cane.

Price, $6.00

Boxing and registered mail, .35

These wooden rods had hollow butts to hold a short emergency tip. Apparently it was never a much-demanded feature. Who can remember seeing one?

T. H. CHUBB'S CATALOGUE. 21

"HENSHALL VAN ANTWERP" FOUR MULTIPLYING BLACK BASS REEL.

Designed and made expressly for the "Standard Henshall" Black Bass Rod, which has the reel above the hand. This reel has our new Lever Drag (patent applied for), as shown in the engraving, by which the line can be stopped when casting at any point in an instant, simply by the pressure of the thumb. And also, when the fish is hooked, the tension can be regulated by the thumb from a free running to a light drag, or a heavy drag to a complete stop. This reel also has an Adjustable Drag and an Adjustable Click. It is made of the very best of German silver, has steel gears and steel pivots throughout; is handsome, substantial and well made in every way. This reel is warranted just as represented, and if not satisfactory can be returned and the money will be refunded. Holds nearly 100 yards of line.

Price, $15.00

We have many testimonials from anglers, speaking in high praise of our rods, reels and trimmings, which we think it is needless to print here, as our goods are now well known; but as this reel is a new reel, placed upon the market by us within the last year we print a few of the many testimonials we have received from noted anglers.

It would be interesting to know just how a right-handed fisherman could use this thumb brake, and why he couldn't get the same result by merely thumbing the spool, as bait-casters always have done.

CYNTHIANA, KY., Sept. 22, 1885.

DEAR MR. CHUBB:—You may call the new Reel the "Henshall Van Antwerp." As now constituted it is the equal of any reel made. Congratulating you on your success in getting up so handsome and so excellent a reel, I am

Yours very truly, J. A. HENSHALL.

MT. STERLING, KY., Nov. 1, 1885.

MR. T. H. CHUBB, Post Mills, Vt. Dear Sir:—The long looked for Reel has arrived, and before I said anything more than admire the fine mechanical execution and complete running of it, I must test it, which I did to my own and companions' complete satisfaction in landing or bringing to gaff a jack pike, weighing 8 3-4 lbs., with a smallest size bass line. Now I have used all the fine reels I know of, at least six different ones, costing from $8 to $25 each, and when I say I never saw a better free-running, bait-casting reel, I do so from actual test and mechanical principles. Now this is not all; I carry my Fly Rod along on my fishing trips, as fish must be suited, as their taste runs different at times. I change my Reel to my Fly Rod, only adding my leader with flies attached, and I have with Variable Drag and Click, a most perfect Fly-casting Reel; now it is fashionable to add "I have no interest in the sale or manufacture of the Reel whatever, etc.," but I have. I want every follower of the famous apostle, when he says "I go a-fishing," to have one of Mr. Thos. Chubb's combined Fishing Reels with him, and to enjoy it as I have; and he will not feel he has lived in vain, for I now feel good all over when I go to rig my cast of flies or bait. Respectfully yours, WM. VAN ANTWERP, M. D.

GLENS FALLS, N. Y., Oct. 27, 1885.

CAPT. T. H. CHUBB, Dear Sir:—I take pleasure in saying that your new Reel is the best reel that I have ever possessed, and I have possessed most of the high grade reels of numerous makes. I know of no Bass Reel to surpass it, and its excellence does not cease with bass fishing. For trout trolling it is perfect; its free running qualities and rapid recovery altogether commend it for all fishing in which a multiplier is used. The Reel has a real, thoroughbred look, is compact, well balanced, and is thoroughly and honestly made. But I need not go into particulars, for as a whole it fills all my desires for a reel and seems as near perfect as man can make it. The Chubb Reel is a beauty as well as a perfect piece of workmanship, and I let it stand on my desk that I may admire it as I sit here writing.

Yours very truly, A. N. CHENEY.

TROY, N. Y., Oct. 5, 1885.

T. H. CHUBB, Dear Sir:—The Reel received; I think it is the most perfect Reel I have ever used; the finish is all that can be desired, but the most essential part to an angler is its durability of construction; nothing that I have used can equal it. I have many reels of many makes, and since procuring this new "Henshall" have resigned a few to the shelf. Very truly yours, H. P. SCHUYLER.

ERIE, PA., Oct. 26, 1885.

THOS. H. CHUBB, Esq., Post Mills, Vt. My Dear Sir:—I take pleasure in acknowledging the receipt of the Henshall Reel and I can truthfully say it is by far the best Reel I ever used, and I use it for all manner of fishing, both above and below the hand, in preference to any other reel I have, and I have nine different kinds. Under all circumstances the Reel can be regulated at will and kept under perfect control by use of the thumb piece alone. Altogether it is a great success, and I predict a larger sale for it than any other high-priced reel in the market.

I am, sir, yours very truly, F. B. WHIPPLE.

SIX STRIP SPLIT BAMBOO HENSHALL ROD.

This cut represents our "Henshall" Split Bamboo Bass Rod, length 8 feet, 3 3-10 inches, weight 8 oz. This rod has extra tip, light hand grasp whipped with cane. Metal reel seat, or reel bands as preferred. Hexagonal cap ferrules, with welt, no dowels, anti friction tie guides. Three ring tops, nickel-plated trimmings, fastened on these rods, all ready for use, with the exception of winding and varnishing, for $7.50. Above rod with German silver trimmings instead of nickel, $9.25.

SIX STRIP SPLIT BAMBOO RODS.

This cut represents our Six Strip Split Bamboo Bass Fly Rod, either 10 1-2 or 12 feet, weight from 10 to 12 oz., reel seat either above or below the hand. These rods have extra tip, light wood hand grasp, whipped with cane; trimmings nickel plated, with hexagonal cap, ferrules with welt. Metal reel seat; trimmings fastened on these rods all ready for use with the exception of ringing and varnishing, for $7.50 each.

Also, Trout Fly Rods of same style and finish, from 9 to 12 feet in length and from 6 to 10 oz. in weight, at same price.

Any of above rods, with German silver trimmings instead of nickel, $9.00.

THE "BOSS" LATHE.

Designed and made for Amateur Rod Makers. Suitable for turning, drilling and brass finishers' general use. This Lathe is made by practical machinists, is free running, but not loose or shaky, well made in all its parts, in a thorough and workmanlike manner.

Length of bed 30 inches. Distance between centers 17 inches. Swing 6 inches.

Hollow steel spindle with 3-8 inch hole. Hardened steel centers, hard bronze metal boxes with hardened steel cone step.

Price, $15.

Will furnish foot Wheel with Crank if desired. Price $5 to $6.

Fine Drill and Wire Chuck, all fitted to lathe, as shown in engraving.

Price, $7.

Centers, Spur Centers, Sockets, Burrs and all kinds of small tools furnished at reasonable price.

A lathe with no more than a ⅜-inch hole through the spindle wouldn't be of much use to even an amateur rodmaker since the butt joints of most rods of that era would have exceeded that measurement in diameter. It probably was intended mostly for finishing ferrules which had been rolled up out of sheet metal and the seam then brazed; or perhaps to turn ferrules out of bar stock.

OUR FACTORY.

OUR Fishing Rod Factory stands upon the bank of the Ompompanoosuc River, in the town of Thetford, VILLAGE OF POST MILLS (our post-office address), about six miles from Thetford and Lyme station on the Passumpsic River railroad, and about twenty miles north of White River Junction.

Early in 1869, our Mr. Chubb commenced manufacturing in a small way upon the site where the factory now stands; but the October freshet of the same year swept away the shop and all its contents. As quickly as possible another building was erected, and with push and energy he soon built up a flourishing trade; but on the night of February 14, 1875, the factory and its contents, to the value of $28,000, were consumed by fire, and there was but little insurance. Not discouraged, he set about repairing the mischief done by the fire, and by the autumn of 1875 he resumed business in the more extensive building now standing.

The factory is 120x32 feet, with an "L" 30x24 feet, three stories and a basement, giving a floorage of 15,360 feet. The work-rooms are all plastered, lighted by gas, and heated by steam, and are as comfortable as a dwelling-house. Order and neatness prevails. The work of the factory is divided into four departments:—

1st. The wholesale and finishing of rods.

2d. The retail and metalwork.

3d. The mill-room, where the sawing and turning is done.

4th. The shellac and varnish-room.

The heads of each department are held responsible for all work turned out by them, the whole being under the personal direction of Mr. Chubb.

We show in this catalogue a cut of the factory and a few rooms (the number entire is twenty-three), and will give a brief description of the work conducted in the same;—a full description would occupy too much space. The angler who sits at home and orders his fishing outfit, little dreams of the busy brains, toiling hands, and complex machinery that are at work to supply him with the means of his enjoyment, among the hills or on the shore.

OFFICE.

Here we find a force of clerks, busy from morning till night with office duties; writing letters, sending out circulars, etc. Here you will, also, generally find Mr. Chubb, who keeps the run of all branches of his business, and *who knows it because he has done it.*

MILL ROOM.

In this room are saws, turning lathes, stopper lathe, dowel machine, fitting machines, planers and moulders for shaping and turning wood into fishing-rods, camp chairs, landing-net frames, grooved wood forms, packing cases, etc. Adjoining is the drying-room, and near by the lumber-sheds, where a large stock of lumber is stored.

MACHINE ROOM.

In which are a great variety of machines for working metal, iron and brass, such as engine lathe, speed lathes, drill and other presses, milling machine, slitting machine, planer, drop-hammer, and in fact every machine that is usually found in a first-class shop. All the work for the factory is done here, making lathes and other machines, dies, mandrels, etc., the patterns of which were all made, and are owned, by the factory. Nearly all the machines that are now in use in the business were built here, and new ones are being constantly designed and made for this work.

REEL ROOM.

In which the famous "Henshall-Van Antwerp" reels are manufactured. Here are also lathes for turning, drilling, gear-cutting; screw machines, and all necessary tools for doing fine work.

BUFFING ROOM.

Where the metal is polished preparatory to plating.

NICKEL-PLATING ROOM.

Where the polished metal is plated in nickel.

FOUNDRY.

Where scrap and trimmings of brass are moulded into castings for landing-net frames, reels, etc.

BRAZING ROOM.

In which are made the guides, rings, tops, etc.; also where are prepared the reels, trimmings, etc., for the nickel bath.

SPLIT-BAMBOO ROOM.

This room has saws and special machinery for making split-bamboo rods, which requires more skill and complex machinery than any other department of the business. Nothing but the butts of selected Calcutta-bamboo poles are used. Often as many as half out of a bundle of 50 are rejected as unfit to make into split-bamboo rods.

FINISHING ROOM.

Devoted to metal and woodwork. A row of benches nearly encircles the room, in front of which, on one side, are lathes for brasswork, fitting of ferrules, making of reel-seats, funnel-tops, etc.; on the other are fitters and lathes for wood-turning where special work is done; through the center and at one end are cases of drawers filled with finished trimmings. At the benches are workmen who fit and fasten the ferrules on the rods; also the makers of fine lancewood rods, one of our specialties. Great care is taken in the selection of the wood; it is roughed out on the lathe, afterward balanced and finished with plane and file. Particular attention is given in selecting butt, joint and tips of wood of the same stiffness. These rods are put together, and thoroughly tested as to balance, workmanship, strength, etc., and each and every one is warranted to be first-class in every respect.

WINDING ROOM.

Where the silk lapping, rings and guides are put on rods. Keepers and cloth cases are also made here.

TACKLE ROOM.

Here, and in the store-room back of this, is kept a full stock of reels, hooks, lines, flies, leaders, and many articles of a fisherman's outfit, from which we are constantly supplying the anglers throughout the United States and Canada.

STAINING ROOM.

Where the rods are stained and filled preparatory to varnishing and shellacking.

SHELLAC AND VARNISH ROOM.

Where rods are coated and flowed with shellac or varnish, on some of which are put as many as five or six coats before they are ready to rub down or polish.

RUBBING DOWN OR POLISHING ROOM.

Where all the better class of work is smoothed by rubbing with pumice-stone and water.

STORE-ROOM.

For finished and unfinished work.

PAPER ROOM.

With machinery necessary for making paper bags, cardboard boxes, etc.

LEATHER ROOM.

Here are made the leather rod and reel cases.

CLOAK ROOM.

Designed expressly for keeping hats, wraps, etc., of the workmen.

In the basement is a seventy-five horse-power water-wheel, which is the motor that runs the machinery. Here we have also a twenty-five horse-power engine, an auxiliary in case of low water. The furnace, boiler, etc., are also here situated, for heating the rooms, etc. One mile from the factory is Fairlee Lake, three miles long

Finest
Rods: Reels: Flies:
Charles: F: Orvis
Manchester
Vermont

Manchester, Vermont, ..., 1884

To Mr. ....

Dear Sir:

I am desirous of collecting all the information possible relating to artificial flies as used in America. I have made many notes of my own observations, and I wish to add to these the knowledge and testimony of other fishermen. I should be glad of the privilege of printing the same, should circumstances favor, my intention being to publish a number of colored plates of artificial flies, to be bound in a convenient volume, supplementary to the plates already issued in "Fishing with the Fly," and to accompany these plates with brief descriptive notes giving name, origin and other knowledge regarding the flies. I shall, therefore, be most grateful if you will favor me with any facts suggested by the following questions. I shall wish to keep your reply, so if you will write on one side of the paper only I can then fasten the letter into a book.

Hoping most earnestly for your interest and aid, and assuring you of my gratitude for any response you may make, I am,

Yours truly, CHARLES F. ORVIS.

Manchester, Vermont.

QUESTIONS

Favorite fly or flies among those well known.

Testimony regarding the same, in connection with locality, time of day and season.

Facts relating to the origin of any fly; either those well known or new creations.

Incidents proving efficacy of above.

NEW FLIES.—Origin, time, name, place.

Theories regarding shape, color, size and kind of hooks and snells; whether they should be light or heavy, stained or clear.

Orvis, of Manchester, Vermont, is a legendary name in American angling. Charles F. Orvis invented the glass minnow trap and, in 1874, the reel with perforated side plates and spool—both in production today unchanged.

The oldest Orvis catalog we have turned up is No. 16, brave in embossed, gilded paper cover and hand-tied maroon silk binding cord and tassel. It is not dated, but it reprints a quotation published elsewhere in 1888, and does not mention *Favorite Flies and Their Histories,* an Orvis publication that appeared in 1892. Whether or not it came with the catalog originally one cannot now say, but tucked inside our copy is a printed sheet, a form letter dated 1889, reproduced here. It is a fair assumption that No. 16 came out after the publication of Orvis and Cheney's *Fishing with the Fly* (1883) and before 1892.

No. 16 is notable for only a few things. At the bottom of the index page in the front, there is a notation: "We ask special attention to articles on pages 4 to 56, as being very desirable." It is just a bit surprising to find that every item offered for sale in this catalog appears on pages 4 to 56. Hmmmm.

No. 16 is also the only one of our collected catalogs to offer a ladies' rod as such. These "elegant little" nine-footers apparently were intended for amazons; a nine-footer in lancewood would test many a man's casting arm. Somehow, this reminds me of an expression common in my youth, ". . . a nice figger of a woman, about 165 pounds."

It reminds me too of the wife of my ancestor John Hempsted, who "called to me pretty loud" as he rode down to engage in the Battle of Groton Heights. "I stopt my hors and ask'd her What She wanted. Her answer was Not to let me hear that you are Shot in the Back." (He stopped en route to help a kinsman hide a case of "holland Jinn" from Benedict Arnold's advancing Tories, but that's another story.)

Another unique thing about old No. 16 is that it offers the only rod made of hornbeam that appears in any of our catalogs.

It is noteworthy that one-fifth of all the tackle-listing pages are devoted to offering what for those days was a vast array of fishing flies. For many years, flies were an Orvis stronghold.

A hundred years ago flytieing was an occult and mystic art; remember how jealously Theodore Gordon guarded his tieing "secrets" even in 1915. Back in the 1870s and 80s, the fast-growing demand made an adequate supply of properly made, usable flies a problem. It was decided, legend says, to educate a member of the Orvis family as a tier, so Mary Orvis Marbury was initiated into the mysteries. Her encyclopedic work, *Favorite Flies and Their Histories,* published first in 1892, with its beautifully lithographed plates in true, vivid colors, is even today the classic reference book on the gaudy brook trout and bass flies of that era; it cost $5 then but you'll pay close to $100 for the same book today.

In the earliest days of the industry it was the custom of tackle dealers to identify merely by number, not name, the various flies of the great array they offered the customer. For one thing, this prevented a customer from switching dealers; one couldn't order Jones & Co.'s No. 8, for instance, from Smith & Co. without sending a pattern, which wasn't always possible.

Orvis (and this is still legend) changed all that. He began naming flies, which meant standardizing patterns. Tieing to standard was more difficult than varying the pattern according to what colors and materials were at hand; but Orvis could do it and the others couldn't, and to that extent were backed right off the boards. Mary O. was the first official tier to standard patterns; so hail Mary O.

One of her inspirations was putting a red belly-band onto the plump-bodied Coachman. "That's a beautiful fly, a regal fly," old Charles F. is said to have exclaimed. "Let's call it the Royal Coachman!"

Under that title it is Mary Orvis Marbury's monument. It is tied in innumerable variations: Hairwing, fanwing, leadwing, quack, california, McSneek, bivisible, wingless, parachute, hackleless, wet, and dry. What it represents no one knows. Preston Jennings opined *Isonychia* bicolor, in his *A Book of Trout Flies.* But Theodore Gordon speculated that the Royal might imitate a flying ant and for twenty-five years this commentator has agreed with him.

As well as his daughter, Orvis was also an author or, more strictly, a compiler. In 1883 he and Albert Nelson Cheney, an ichthyologist and once commissioner of the New York State Conservation Department, brought out a notable symposium, *Fishing with the Fly*. Like Mary's book, this one is coveted by collectors.

In time the Orvis hegemony came to be lightly accepted as a royal prerogative; one of Orvis's old catalogs airily explained that it was late because of the boss's preoccupation with his duties as tax assessor, first selectman, or something of the sort, of the community of Manchester. There was virtually nothing left of the Orvis business except a still honored name when D. C. Corkran bought it for a mere song—and Ducky wasn't a very good singer, either. But he was a good merchant. When the Bakelite Corporation's new patent on plastic-impregnated bamboo rods was issued, Ducky grabbed the exclusive American rights, and on that basis built Orvis into a thriving business.

Some years later, Leigh Perkins, a genius at direct-mail marketing, bought out Corkran and has made Orvis Co. the premier merchant in the direct-mail tackle industry.

ORDERS SOLICITED for any special kind of Fishing Tackle not mentioned in this Catalogue. Such orders will be carefully filled, and at the lowest price consistent with the quality of the goods.

In ordering from this list please designate by the name used in the catalogue, and the price of the article given. Refer to Catalogue **No. 16.**

PERSONAL ATTENTION given to each order.

All orders must be accompanied by P. O. Order, Postal Note, or Draft on New York or Boston for the requisite amount, or articles may be sent by express, C. O. D.

I prepay postage on everything in this catalogue except Rods, Landing Nets, Baskets, Rod and Tackle Cases, Crates, Bait Pails, Sinkers, Rod Holders, Hunting Knives, Fly Cases, Cushions and Pillows. Parties wishing their packages registered must inclose ten cents extra for each package.

Rods sent by mail are put up in the wood cases, and registered if desired; for rates. see Rod list.

INDEX

WE ask SPECIAL ATTENTION to articles on pages 4 to 56, as being very desirable.

4

Hexagonal Split-Bamboo Fly Rods.

WOUND HAND-PIECE.

No. 9.—This rod is 11 feet long, in 3 pieces, has two tips, sack and round wood case, and is, I believe, an improvement on any split-bamboo rod before offered to anglers. It is made with six strips, tips as well as other joints, is carefully constructed, has fine German-silver Mountings, with Banded Ferrules, Orvis' Patent Metal Reel-Seat. Is very finely finished, and is in every way as perfect as possible, and I am confident that fishermen will find that this rod will fill all requirements and in every way prove satisfactory.

WITH WOUND, FLUTED OR SUMAC HAND-PIECE, - - - - - - - - - **$20.00**
POSTAGE, including registration, 45 Cents.

SUMAC HAND-PIECE.

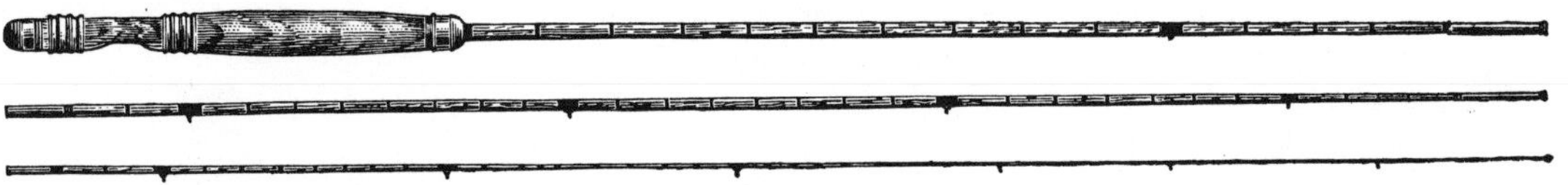

The Sumac Hand-Piece, as shown in the above cut, adds much to the beauty of a rod. Its extreme lightness, combined with the handsome color and fine finish which this wood takes, showing the grain, makes this a most desirable hand-piece.

Its entire length is 12 inches.

We recommend the short hand-pieces on rods as *allowing the elastic part of the rod to come quite near the hand, so giving them great sweep and uniform spring from tip to butt. All rods are in three pieces of equal length, made of best quality of stock, and joints perfectly fitted.*

No. 9½ Hexagonal Split-Bamboo Fly Rod.—Length 10 feet, in three pieces, has two tips, sack and round wood case. German-silver Mountings, with Banded Ferrules and Orvis' Patent Reel-Seat. This Rod is the same as No. 9, except that it is lighter. I feel sure that this will please those who desire a *light* 10-foot Split-Bamboo.

WITH SUMAC OR FLUTED HAND-PIECE, - - - - - - - - - - $20.00
POSTAGE, including registration, 40 Cents.

FLUTED HAND-PIECE.

The Fluted Hand-Piece, as shown in this cut, prevents the rod from slipping or turning in the hand (often so troublesome) and less grip is required to hold the rod securely. The wood is of selected black walnut, which makes a handsome contrast with the mountings. Entire length 12 inches.

Cork Hand-Piece.—We consider this a most desirable hand-piece for rods, it being extremely light, and very pleasant to hold when either wet or dry.

It is so constructed as to preserve the necessary strength and in no way to interfere with the perfection of the Reel-Seat.

Ladies' Fly Rods.

No. 16 Hexagonal Split-Bamboo Fly Rod.—Length 9 feet, in three pieces, CORK HAND-PIECE, German-silver Mountings, Banded Ferrules and Orvis' Patent Reel-Seat.

TWO TIPS, SACK AND ROUND WOOD CASE, - - - - - - - - - $20.00
POSTAGE and registration, 40 Cents.

No. 17 All Lance-Wood Fly Rod.—Same as No. 16, except this rod is made of Lance-Wood, - - - - - - - - - - - - - - - - $10.00
POSTAGE and registration, 40 Cents.

These rods are designed for the use of Ladies. They are elegant little rods, light but strong, and would be very serviceable for any angler. They are fitted with CORK HAND-PIECES that do not require as much strength to hold the rod firmly as do the other hand-pieces.

No. 7 "The Coming Bass Rod."—(For Black Bass.) Made according to suggestions by Dr. J. A. Henshall. Ash butt, Lance-Wood second joint and tips. German-silver Mountings. Orvis' Patent Reel-Seat. Extra tip, sack and round wood case. Length 8 feet, 3 inches. Reel-seat above the hand, and standing guides. Finished in finest style, - - - - **$10.00**

Postage, including registration, 40 cents.

"In February, 1875, I published an article entitled 'The Coming Black Bass Rod' in *Forest and Stream*, which gave a description of my idea of a proper rod for Black Bass Angling. * * * * Mr. C. F. Orvis, of Manchester, Vt., at once began the manufacture of a Black Bass rod from these suggestions, and they are to-day to be found in all parts of the country, he having been remarkably successful in introducing them, and they supplied a want long felt."

DR. J. A. HENSHALL, in "Book of the Black Bass."

No. 7½ Black Bass Rod.—This rod is just the same as No. 7, except that it is 9 feet in length, and is mounted with rings, with reel-seat back of hand, or guides and reel-seat above the hand, as preferred, - - - - - - - - - - - **$10.00**

Postage, including registration, 40 cents.

No. 12 All Lance-Wood, Hensnall Black Bass Rod.—Same as No. 7 rod in every respect, except it is all Lance-Wood. Length 8 feet, 3 inches, - - - - **$10.00**

Postage, including registration, 40 cents.

No. 12½ All Lance-Wood Black Bass Rod.—Same as No. 7½ rod, except it is all Lance-Wood. Length 9 feet, - - - - - - - - - **$10.00**

Postage, including registration, 40 cents.

No. 14 "The Cheney Bass Rod."—Made according to suggestions by Mr. A. N. Cheney. Length 11 feet; weight 13 ounces. Two tips, sack and wood case. Finest Nickel-plated Mountings. Reel-bands above or below hand; with standing guides or rings, as preferred. Wound hand-piece, and finished in finest style. Made of the best Hornbeam, - - - **$8.00**

Postage, including registration, 55 cents.

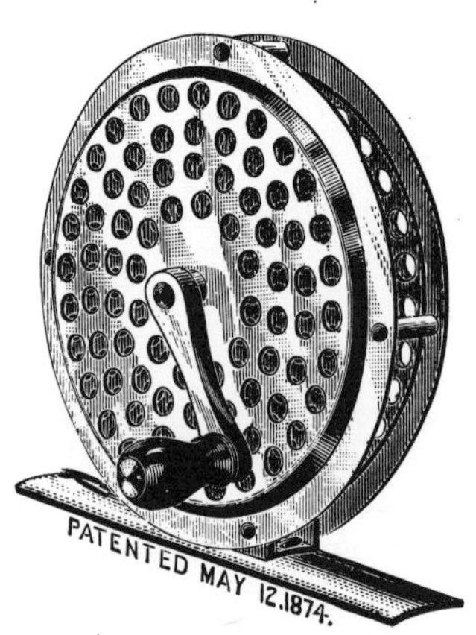

THE ORVIS REEL.

No. 1 This Reel is extra nickel-plated and finely finished. Is perforated, to make it light and keep it free from sand; also that the line may dry without removing it from the reel after use. Has a very perfect click. It is very light, very strong, and holds from 40 to 50 yards of line. It is more compact and less cumbersome than ordinary 20-yard reels. It is quite narrow, and takes up line rapidly. Sent by mail, postage prepaid, on receipt of price, or by express, C. O. D. Put up in neat Black-Walnut Case, - - - - - - - - - - **$3.50**

No. 2 Orvis Reel for Bass Fishing.—This is just the same as No. 1, except wider between plates, and will hold from 70 to 80 yards of line, - - - - - - - **$4.00**

Postage prepaid on all articles on this page.

No. 5.

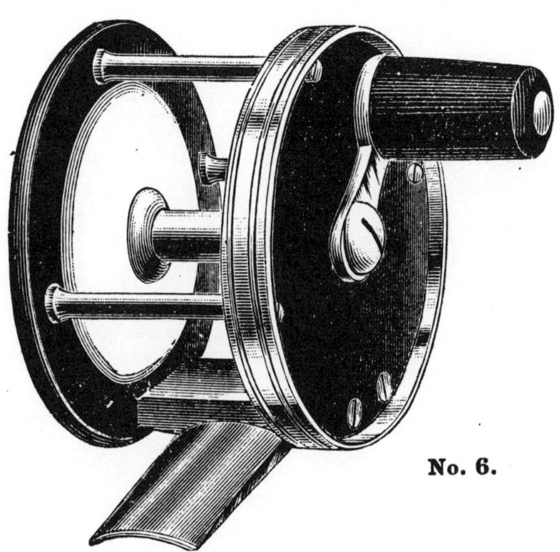

No. 6.

Rubber and Brass Click Reel. NICKEL-PLATED.		With Rubber Safety Band. NICKEL-PLATED.
PRICE, 25 Yards,	$ .75	
" 40 "	.85	$1.35
" 60 "	.95	1.45
" 80 "	1.05	1.65
" 100 "	1.15	1.85

Rubber and German-Silver Click Reels, with German-Silver Safety Band.

PRICE, 25 Yards,	$4.00
" 40 "	4.25
" 60 "	4.50
" 80 "	5.00

Postage prepaid on all articles on this page.

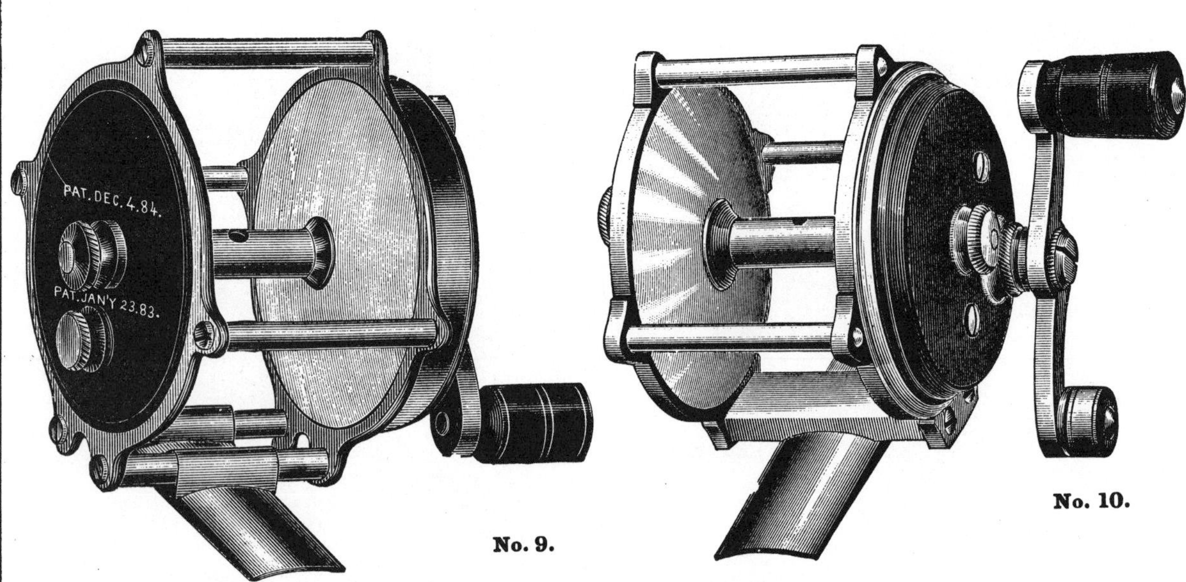

No. 9.

No. 10.

The New "Gem" Multiplying Reel, with Adjustable Click.

RUBBER AND NICKEL.

PRICE,	40 Yards, - - - - - -	$4.25
"	60 " - - - - - -	4.50
"	80 " - - - - - -	4.75

Finest Quality Rubber and German-Silver, Raised Pillar Multiplying Reels, Steel Pivot and Slide Click.

PRICE,	60 Yards, - - - - -	$12.00
"	80 " - - - - - -	14.00
"	100 " - - - - - -	16.00

Postage prepaid on all articles on this page.

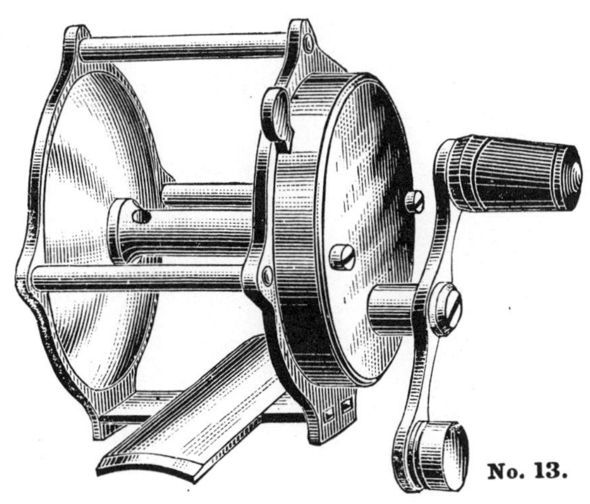

No. 13.

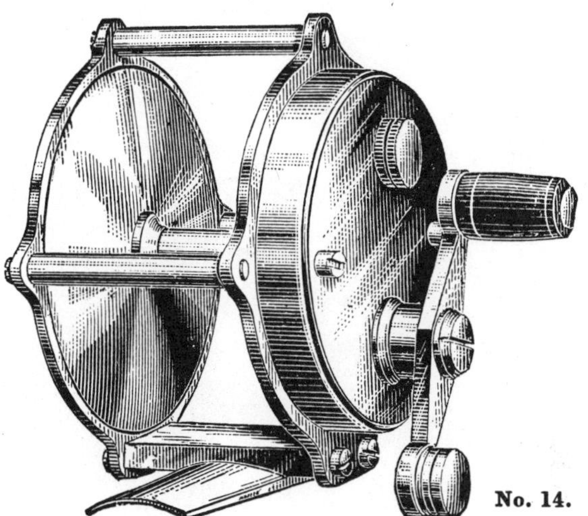

No. 14.

Multiplying, Raised Pillar, Balance Handle and Drag.

NICKEL-PLATED.

PRICE,	40 Yards,	$1.10
"	60 "	1.15
"	80 "	1.20
"	100 "	1.25

Best Multiplying, Raised Pillar, Balance Handle, Screw Click.

NICKEL-PLATED.

PRICE,	40 Yards,	$2.25
"	60 "	2.50
"	80 "	2.75
"	100 "	3.00

Postage prepaid on all articles on this page.

No. 15.

Best Multiplying Balance Handle, Slide Click.

NICKEL-PLATED.

PRICE,	25	Yards,	$2.25
"	40	"	2.35
"	60	"	2.50
"	80	"	2.75
"	100	"	3.00

No. 16.

Balance Handle and Drag.

NICKEL-PLATED.

PRICE,	25	Yards,	$1.25
"	40	"	1.30
"	60	"	1.35
"	80	"	1.40

Postage prepaid on all articles on this page.

No. 17.

Conroy's "Silver King" Multiplying Reels, Finest Quality Rubber and German Silver, Full Steel Pivots, Balance Handle, Screw-Off Oil Caps Patent Back Sliding Click.

Price,	60 Yards,	$ 8.00
"	80 "	10.00
"	100 "	12.00
"	150 "	15.00
"	200 "	18.00
Price,	250 Yards,	$21.00
"	300 "	24.00
"	350 "	27.00
"	400 "	30.00

22

"I shall bring you acquainted with more Flies than Father Walton has taken notice of in his 'Complete Angler.'"

TROUT-FLIES, (Reversed Wing). Price $1.50 Per Dozen.

LIST No. 1.

Local names and names of Flies alike in form and color, but differing in species or size, are placed under the same heading.

Sportsmen are invited to send to me for any special kinds of Flies not on Lists, that they may desire, in which case please send sample, if possible. I aim to fill all orders with exactness in every particular.

When an assortment of Flies is desired, and the selection left with me, I will use my best judgment to send the most desirable kinds.

Flies have names attached; are arranged on cards and packed in strong, convenient boxes.

TROUT FLIES tied on Superior Quality Spring Steel O'Shaughnessy or Sproat Hooks, with Single Gut Snells, 4 inches in length.

*Abbey.
Adirondack.
Alexandria, (St. Patrick).
*Alder, (Orl-Fly, Light Dun).
Bee.
Beaverkill.
Ben Bent.
Black Gnat, (Black Midge).
*Blue Professor.
Blue Jay.
Brown Hen.
Brown Coflin.
Blue Bottle, (Shad-Fly).
Black June.
Black Ant.
Blue Dun, (Cork Tail).
Bissett.
Camlet Dun.
Canada.
Captain.
Cinnamon.
*Caldwell.
Claret.
Cheney.
Cow Dung.
Coachman.
Coachman, Red Tip.
Coachman, Royal.

LIST No. 2.

Flies in List No. 2 can be made to order at short notice. Flies are placed on List No. 2 because not generally as well known, consequently not so often called for. We aim to keep in stock only those Flies for which there is constant demand, and thereby accumulate no old Flies. We endeavor to know of the merits of each Fly which we place on any of the lists. Many of the Trout-Flies can be made in Lake or Bass-Fly sizes.

Alice.
Ashy.
Ash Fox.
August Dun, (August Brown.)
Allerton.
Bright Fox.
Brown Ant.
Brown Adder.
Black Spider.
Cahill.
Caparer.
Carmen.
Dark Fox.
Dark Spider.
Dotterel Dun, (Yellow Dun).
Dun Spinner.
Egg.
Esmeralda.
Epting-Fly.
Furnace-Fly.
Fœted Brown.
Golden Spinner.
Golden Monkey.
Gauze-Wing.
Gosling.
Greenwell's Glory.
Hofland's Fancy.
Hamlin.
Hare's Ear.
Jewel.
King Fisher.
Lady Sue.
Lady Martha.
Lowrey.
Maurice.
Orange Dun.
Plum.
Prime Gnat.
Red Ash.
Red Spider.
Red Head.
Soldier Moth.
Sedge-Fly.
Stalkneck.
Water Cricket.
Willow-Fly, (Shamrock Fly, Little Pale Blue Dun).
Wyoming.

"*The trout-fly is a 'conventionalized' creation, as we say of ornamentation. The theory is, that, fly-fishing being a high art, the fly must not be a tame imitation of nature, but an artistic suggestion of it. It requires an artist to construct one; and not every bungler can take a bit of red flannel, a peacock's feather, a flash of tinsel thread, a cock's plume, a section of a hen's wing, and fabricate a tiny object that will not look like any fly, but still will suggest the universal conventional fly.*"—Charles Dudley Warner.

TROUT-FLIES MADE WITH GUT BODIES AND SCALE WINGS.

PRICE, $2.00 PER DOZEN.

We make these flies as a novelty, but doubt if they will ever take the place of the feathered flies, the use of which for several hundred years has proved their thorough efficiency.

They are close imitations of natural insects, and are extremely durable; although delicate in appearance they are practically indestructible. The wings are too tough to be torn, yet when in the water become pliable and offer to the fish no resistance, as do the quill wings and other wings of a similar character heretofore offered as a substitute for feathers.

We print an extract from a letter published, not long ago, in THE FISHING GAZETTE, headed,—

"*MATERIAL FOR WINGS OF ARTIFICIAL FLIES.*"

* * "*What is really required is a substance which combines the lightness and buoyancy of the feather in the air as well as in the water, with the toughness and power to retain its shape of the quill, together with the pliability, transparency and texture of the gold beater's skin, and the property of being easily stained or dyed, and this material, as far as I know, has yet to be discovered.*"—BITTERN.

We offer the scale wing (not a *pike*-scale wing) as the discovery which meets all the requirements mentioned in the above letter.

We suggest the following as the most desirable to be made with Gut Bodies and Scale Wings:—

Brown Coflin.	Deer Fly.	Gauze Wing.	Red Fox.
Black Ant.	Emerald Gnat.	Hoskins.	Red Spinner.
Black Gnat.	Emerald Dun.	Hawthorn.	Stone Fly.
Blue Dun.	Fiery Brown.	Morrison.	Scarlet Ibis.
Claret.	Green Drake.	Orange Black.	Soldier.
Cow Dung.	Grey Drake.	Pale Evening Dun.	Yellow May.

FLIES WITH CORK BODIES, FLOATING MAY-FLIES, CADDIS-FLIES AND CISCO-FLIES, MADE TO ORDER, ANY SIZE DESIRED, $2.50 PER DOZEN.

☞A discount of TEN per cent. from list prices of FLIES will be made on orders of SIX dozen or over, and TWENTY per cent. on orders of TWELVE dozen or over.

We are prepared to make the finest quality of Salmon-Flies. and shall take pleasure in giving careful attention to orders with which we may be favored. Flies not on list can be made to order from sample.

PRICES, according to pattern, ... $3.00 to $7.50 per dozen.

Baron.
Beaufort Moth.
Benchill.
Black Dose.
Black Fairy.
Black Ranger.
Blue and Brown.
Britannia.
Brown Eagle.
Brown Fairy.
Butcher.
Captain.
Champion.
Childers.
Colonel.
Curtis.
Dawson.
Dirty Orange.
Dunkeld.
Durham Range.
Dusty Miller.
Fairy.
Fiery Brown.
Gitana.
Gordon.
Greenwell.
Highlander.
Hill Fly.
Harlequin.
Infallible.
Jock Scott.
Lion.
MacNicoll.
May Queen.
Nepenthian.
Parson.
Phœbus.
Popham.
Prince Wm. of Orange.
Sailor.
Silver Doctor.
Silver Grey.
Spey Dog.
Taile's Fancy.
Thunder and Lightning.
Toppy.
Wasp.
White Miller.
Wilkenson.

"*The flies used for Salmon are more numerous and varied than those used for trout, and quite as uncertain and puzzling to those who use them.* * * * *There are, however, standard flies which experience has shown to be generally more 'taking' than others, and for this sufficient reason are always found in salmon angler's fly books; but no expert deems any fly, or any dozen flies, invariably adapted to all waters and all conditions of wind and weather. Without multiplying varieties indefinitely, it is yet necessary to have an 'assortment,' gaudy and sombre, large and small, but plenty of them. It is very unpleasant to run short when you are two or three hundred miles away from 'the shop.' Those who have had any considerable experience know just what they want, and the only safe thing for the novice do do, when ready to lay in his stock, is to seek advice of some one who knows something of what may be required in the waters to be visited.*"—GEO. DAWSON.

Postage Prepaid on Flies.

"*It is important that the size of the line should be adapted to the rod. A heavy line on a very light rod would be bad; a very light line on a heavy rod would be worse. I find many are inclined to use too light a line, supposing the lighter it is the less trouble there will be in casting it. This, I think, is an error. It is impossible to cast well against or across the wind with a very light line; and very light lines do not 'lay out' as accurately as do the heavier ones.*"

CHARLES F. ORVIS.

FINEST QUALITY FISHING LINES.

Braided Lines on Blocks.

G.

F.

E.

D.

C.

B.

Finest Quality Tapered Fly Lines.

TAPER F.

" E.

" D.

" C.

Enamelled Waterproof, Braided Silk Tapered Fly Lines; Finest Quality Made.

Size				
Size D.	50 yards, $4.00;	40 yards, $3.20;	30 yards, $2.40;	25 yards, $2.00 each.
" E.	40 " 2.80;	35 " 2.45;	30 " 2.10;	25 " 1.75 each.
" F.	40 " 2.80;	35 " 2.45;	30 " 2.10;	25 " 1.75 each.

Level Lines.—D. 8c., E. 7c., F. 6c., G. and H., 5c. per yard.

Level lines are in 25-yard lengths, 4 connecting.

Salmon Tapered Fly Lines.

Size B.	100 yards,	$11.00 each.	Size B.	120 yards,	$12.50 each.
" C.	100 "	9.50 "	" C.	120 "	11.00 "
" D.	100 "	8.50 "	" D.	120 "	10.00 "

"*The strain imposed upon a Leader by even the largest trout, is generally over-estimated. A Leader that will endure five pounds steady strain with a spring-balance will, when backed by the elasticity of a fair rod, resist the utmost effort of the largest trout that swims the Rangely Lakes.* * * * *See that the Leader never be bent when dry, and especially that no one step on it whether dry or not.* * * *I repeat, test your Leaders carefully, and be sure they are up to your work; but do not seek this result by using a cable where a thread is adequate, but by care in the selection of material, care in the manufacture, and care in preservation. If you do this, you will never lose a fish from this cause; if you do not, no matter how large the gut you may employ, it will sooner or later play you false.*"—HENRY P. WELLS.

"Mist Colored" Leaders, or Casting Lines, Very best quality, Tapered, with loops for "droppers," very convenient and durable.

Gossamer, - - - -	1 yard, 15 cents.	2 yards, 25 cents;	3 yards, 35 cents.
Trout, - - - - - -	1 " 15 "	2 " 25 "	3 " 35 cents.
Heavy Trout, - - -	1 " 20 "	2 " 37½ "	3 " 50 cents.
Bass, - - - - - -	1 " 25 "	2 " 45 "	3 " 65 cents.
Salmon, - - - - -	1 " 37½ "	2 " 75 "	3 " $1.00
Double Gut, - -	1 " 30 "	2 " 50 "	3 " 75 cents.
Treble-Twisted Gut, -	1 " 25 "	2 " 50 "	3 " 75 cents.

Postage prepaid on Leaders.

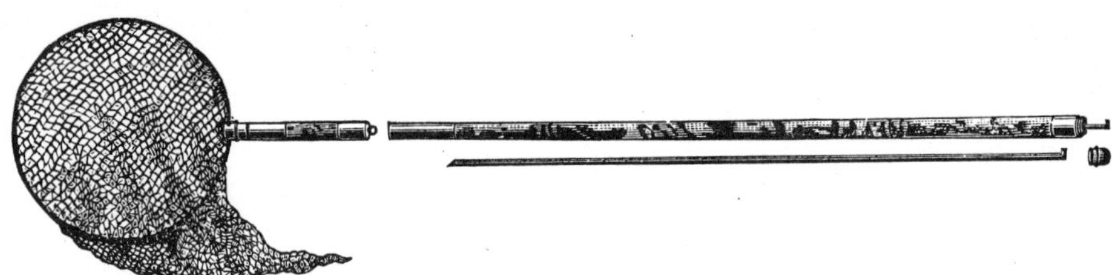

ORVIS' COLLAPSING LANDING-NET.

Light and strong; has two handsomely mottled bamboo handles—one long, for boat use, the other quite short, for wading. Ring in one piece, which goes into handle when not in use.

TROUT size, price complete with net, - - - - - - - - - - - - - $2.50
BASS size, price complete with net, - - - - - - - - - - - - - - 2.50

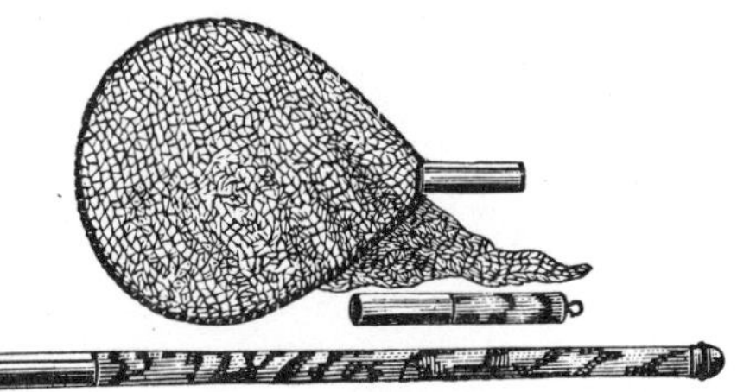

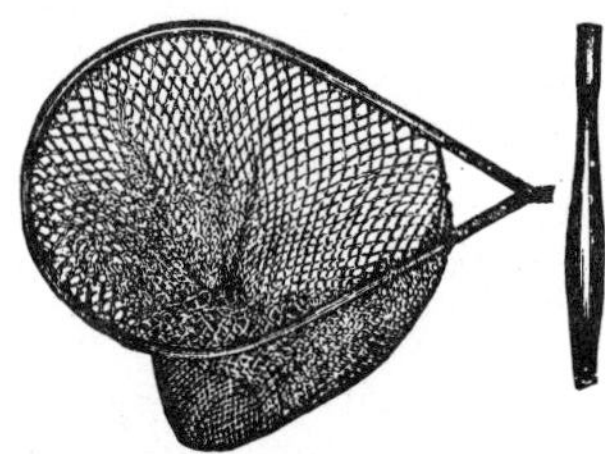

Orvis' Stationary Landing-Net.

Metal bow, nickel-plated mountings, long bamboo handle for boat use, short handle for wading.

Price, complete with net, - - - $1.50

Landing-Net Complete.

Wood bow, screw socket, 12 or 24 inch handle, as preferred.

Price, - - - - - - - $1.25

OILED SILK LANDING-NET, 24 inches long, - - - - - - - - - - $1.50 each.

OLRY'S PATENT POCKET FLASKS.

THE SCREWS ARE FASTENED WITH METAL INSTEAD OF CEMENT.

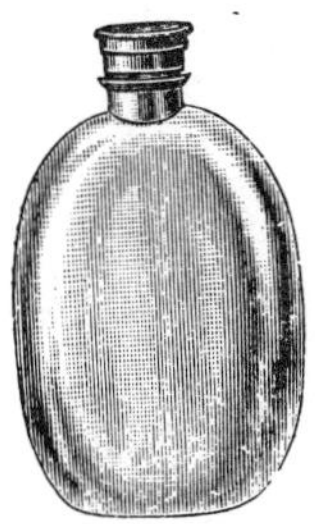

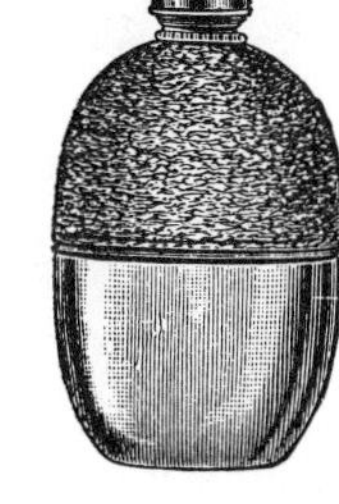

ALL METAL (BRITANNIA) WITHOUT CUP.	LEATHER-COVERED GLASS WITH BRITANNIA METAL CUPS.	HEAVY SILVER-PLATED INVERTED CUPS, VERY FINELY ENGRAVED. RUSSIA OR HOGSKIN LEATHER.
1-4 pint, - - - - $1.00	1-4 pint, - - - - $1.00	1-4 pint, - - - - $2.50
1-2 pint, - - - - 1.12	1-2 pint, - - - - 1.25	1-2 pint, - - - - 2.75
		3-4 pint, - - - - 3.00

SPORTSMEN'S TUMBLERS AND DRINKING CUPS.

Britannia Telescope Tumblers, enclosed in a Portable Box, .	20 cts. each.
Telescopic Goblets, Screw Case,	35 cts. each.
Companion Drinking Cup (small),	35 cts. each.
Niles' Hard Rubber Collapsing Cups,	$1.00 each.
Watch Case Collapsing Cups,	50 cts. each.
Soft Rubber Tumblers,	40 cts. each.
Soft Rubber Canoe Cups,	40 cts. each.
French Leather Canoe Cups,	35 cts. each.

Postage prepaid on all articles on this page.

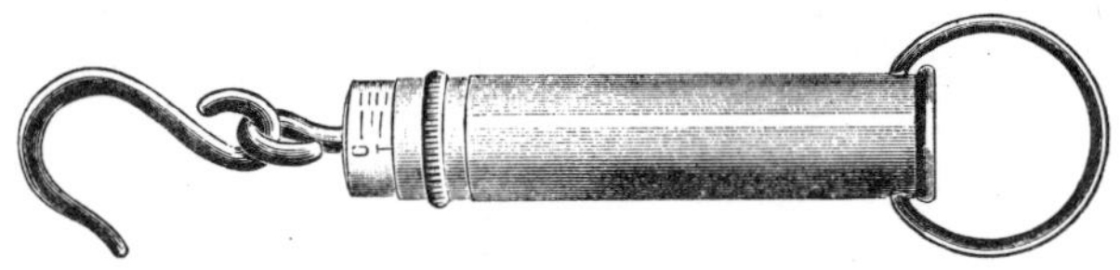

SPORTSMAN'S BALANCE.

Nickel-plated with loose hook, to weigh 15 pounds by 2 ounces, - - - 50 cents each.

OSGOOD'S FOLDING MINNOW AND FISH CRATE.

MINNOW CRATE.

Size 24x8x8, when folded 12x8x2,

Weight, - 12½ pounds.

Price, $2.00.

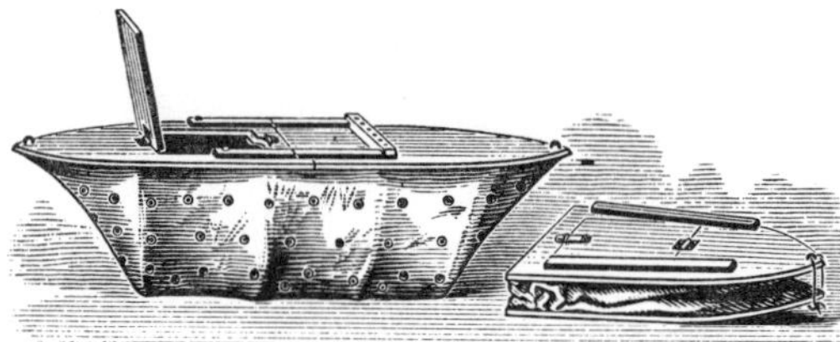

FISH CRATE.

Size 36x12x12, when folded 18x12x2.

Weight, - - 3 pounds.

Price, $3.00.

BASKET BAIT BOX.

15 cents each.

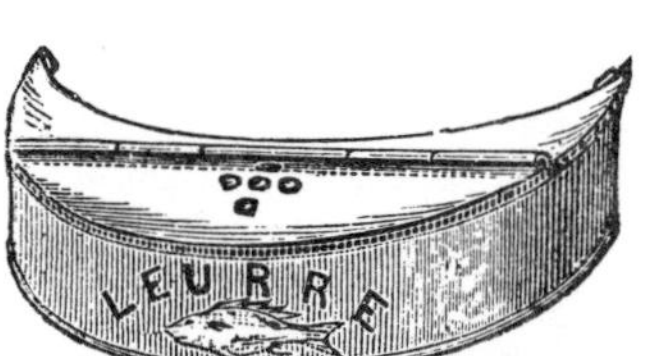

CRESCENT BAIT BOX.

25 cents each.

PADLOCK BAIT BOX.

15 cents each.

Bait Box Straps, 32 to 40 inch, - - - - - - - - 15 cents each.

Postage prepaid on all articles on this page, except Crates.

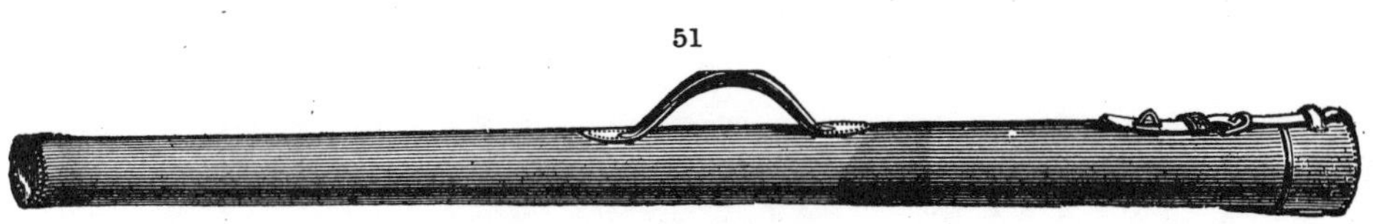

Leather Rod-Cases.

MADE OF HEAVY BRIDLE LEATHER, 48 INCHES LONG.

Price, each, - - - - - - -	$4.00	$5.00	$6.00	$8.00
Diameter at ends, - - - - -	1⅞x2	2⅜x3	3¼x3¾	4½x5½

The Orvis Rod-Case.

MADE OF WOOD. LENGTH 48 INCHES OR LESS.

This case is for a single rod, is round and tapered, very light and strong, and protects one rod much better than a leather case. Price, - - - - - - - - - - $1.00

Bamboo Tip-Cases.

Screw Top. Price, - - - - - - - - - - - - - - $1.00 each.

The Excelsior Bait Pail.

OUTSIDE.

This pail is strongly made of heavy tin, and handsomely painted. The inside pail has a perforated pan, which can be raised, bringing the bait above the water for easy selection.

Price each, 8-quart, $2.25; 12-quart, $2.75.

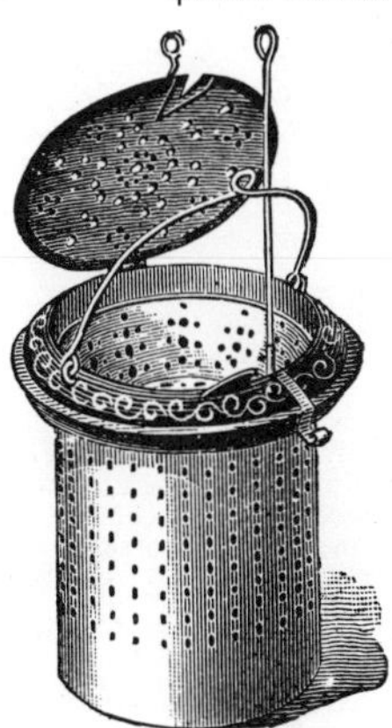

INSIDE.

53

Fishing with the Fly.

COLLECTED —BY—

CHARLES F. ORVIS —AND— A. NELSON CHENEY.

A Comprehensive Book on Angling, Beautifully Illustrated with

COLORED PLATES OF 149 STANDARD SALMON, BASS AND TROUT FLIES,

with names of each. These colored Illustrations are the most correct and the finest ever produced. A complete index will enable easy reference to each fly.

THE SKETCHES ARE TWENTY-ONE ORIGINAL ESSAYS, WRITTEN EXPRESSLY FOR THIS VOLUME.

and three reprints (the latter by special permission of the authors), making twenty-four articles contributed to the book by the best-known American writers on Angling.

Papers on Fly-Fishing in the Maine Lakes, by Mr. Henry P. Wells, and on the Nipigon, by Mr. H. H. Vail. With the latter article is given A COMPLETE MAP OF THE NIPIGON, which will be of advantage to all seeking information of this now celebrated fishing ground.

Accompanying the illustrations are Hundreds of Quotations from ancient and modern authors, of various countries, giving the sentiment and practice of almost every writer who has manifested an interest in the "gentle art." These quotations constitute a very remarkable and valuable part of the book.

Title-page design by Elihu Vedder. Cloth, Illuminated Cover, Gilt Tops, 334 pages, 8vo. Price $2.50, post-paid.

PUBLISHED BY HOUGHTON, MIFFLIN & CO., BOSTON AND NEW YORK.

COPIES CAN BE ORDERED OF

C. F. ORVIS, MANCHESTER, VT.

II

1890–1899

Compliments of
Thos. H. Chubb.

ESTABLISHED 1869.

RETAIL CATALOGUE FOR 1890.

—ISSUED BY—

THE FISHING ROD MANUFACTURER,

POST MILLS, VERMONT,

—MANUFACTURER OF—

—AND—

ANGLERS' SUPPLIES.

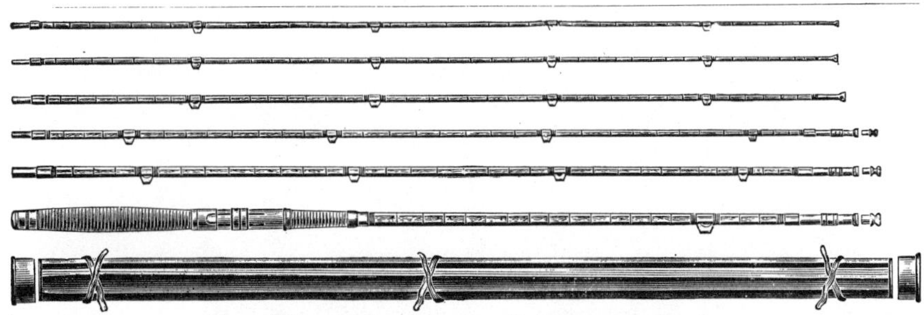

No. 30.—"Dr. Baxter" Salmon Rod.

This rod weighs from 24 to 26 oz., and is made in 8 strips instead of 6. Rod is 4-joint, 16 feet in length, has 2 tips, double hand-grasp wound with cane, metal reel-seat and stout welt ferrules with metal stoppers, anti-friction tie guides, all in grooved wood form, covered with cloth and in cloth case. This rod is made without dowels, and ferrules will be made water-proof, and also have heavy wide band shrunk on the outside of ferrules, so as to strengthen the ferrules where ends of joints come together, as shown in cut. Rod has *best* German-silver trimmings.

Price	$22.00
Price, Stout Tip to go in end of second joint, making 12 foot rod, extra	4.50
Price, Regular extra tips	4.00
Price, Extra third joint	4.50

The above cut shows rod with two regular tips and the extra stout tip.

No. 31.—"Union League" Fly Rod.

Four-joint Trout Fly Rod, 10½ feet in length; weight, 7 oz.; ringed; reel-seat below hand.

For style of this Rod, see cut of all lance-wood "Union League" Fly Rod.

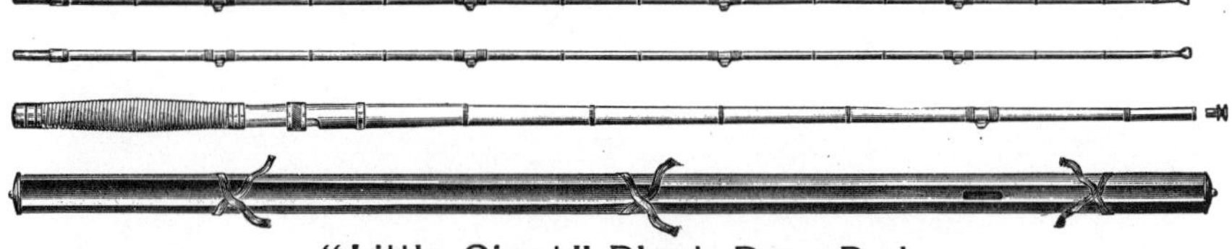

"Little Giant" Black Bass Rod.

This rod is made according to the dimensions furnished us by Dr. Henshall, and was designed for black bass fishing in Lake Erie and in Southern waters; also as a light rod for sea fishing. 2-joint; length, 7½ feet; weight 8½ to 9 oz.

Price, Ash Butt, Lance-wood or Greenheart Tips, Nickel-plated trimmings	$4.00
Price, German-silver trimmings	6.00
Price, All Lance-wood or Greenheart, Nickel-plated Trimmings	4.50
Price, German-silver Trimmings	6.50
Price, Six-Strip, Split-Bamboo, Nickel-plated trimmings	11.00
Price, German-silver trimmings	13.00
Price, Eight-Strip, Split-Bamboo, Nickel-plated trimmings	13.00
Price, German-silver trimmings	15.00

Made with Reel-Bands or Metal Reel-Seat, as preferred.

An eight-strip bamboo salmon rod for less than a dollar an ounce. The reinforcing sleeve shrunk over each female ferrule was an unnecessary novelty that never gained wide acceptance.

36 *THOS. H. CHUBB, POST MILLS, VERMONT.*

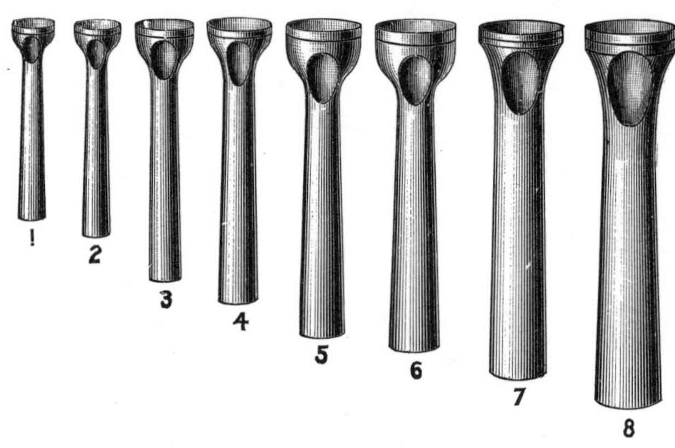

CHUBB'S PATENT FUNNEL OR TUBE TOP.

No. 1.

No. 2.

Cut No. 1 is a longitudinal or sectional view of my patent Funnel Top, which is put together without the use of solder, by cutting a deep annular groove or seat on the inner end of the head; the small end of dowel is inserted in this groove, and is secured thereto by driving swedging tool into the center hole, which forces the metal outward, thereby flanging or spreading the inserted end of the dowel and securely fastening or dovetailing it in the annular groove. This top being put together wholly without the use of solder, can easily be removed from the tip of a fishing-rod, when necessary, by heating, without danger of unsoldering the top. This top is secured by Letters Patent No. 277,230, granted May 8, 1883. All parties are hereby warned not to manufacture the same, under penalty of the law.

		Brass.		Nickel.	
No.	Size.	Each.	Per doz.	Each.	Per doz.
1,	3/32	$ .05	$ .50	$ .06	$ .60
2,	1/8	.05	.50	.06	.60
3,	5/32	.05	.50	.06	.60
4,	3/16	.05	.50	.06	.60
5,	13/64	.05	.60	.06	.70
6,	1/4	.05	.60	.06	.70
7,	17/64	.05	.60	.06	.70
8,	5/16	.05	.60	.06	.70
9,	11/32	.06	.70	.07	.80
10,	23/64	.10	1.15	.12	1.40
11,	3/8	.10	1.15	.12	1.40
12,	7/16	.10	1.15	.12	1.40

Chubb's diagram and description are incomprehensible. The sole value of the patent appears to be in reducing manufacturing cost.

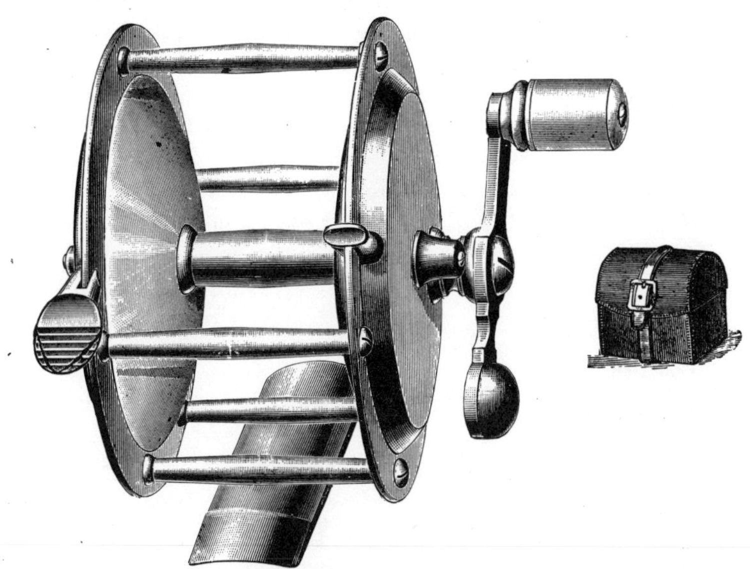

"HENSHALL-VAN ANTWERP" BLACK BASS REEL.

(Patented Sept. 27, 1887, No. 370,684.)

PUT UP IN LEATHER CASE, EITHER TWO OR FOUR MULTIPLIER.

Price.. $15.00

The following is what Dr. J. A. Henshall says about CHUBB'S "HENSHALL-VAN ANTWERP" REEL, in his description of Tackle used for Black Bass fishing, and is taken from his new book entitled "More About the Black Bass":—

MULTIPLYING REELS.

"The 'Henshall-Van Antwerp' reel is manufactured by Thos. H. Chubb, of Post Mills, Vermont. The reel was designed by Dr. Wm. Van Antwerp, of Mt. Sterling, Kentucky (one of the Fish Commissioners of that State), and myself. It is a perfectly symmetrical reel, the end plates being struck up so as to form, with the spool plates, a concavity at each end, in one of which is placed the gearing, and the adjustable click and automatic drag in the other.

"The automatic drag was designed to meet the requirements of those anglers who cannot educate the thumb to control the rendering of the line in casting the minnow. For my own use I prefer, as does any expert, a very rapid multiplier, without click or drag of any kind, in bait fishing; but there are good anglers who cannot, for some reason, successfully acquire the knack of thumbing the spool in a satisfactory manner, and the line will over-run and snarl, and the spool backlash in spite of their most patient and persistent efforts.

"To meet this difficulty the automatic drag acts in the place of the thumb, as the amount of pressure brought to bear upon the spool can be regulated, automatically, by a sliding button on the side of the reel, and

The thumb lever has been changed from the right to the left side, and made "automatic" by providing a movable button to hold it at any desired setting. It is one of a host of such devices, all largely ineffective for one reason—inertia.

62 *THOS. H. CHUBB, POST MILLS, VERMONT,*

REVERSED WING TROUT FLIES.—A.

Best quality, dressed after the natural, single gut, tied on Nos. 8 and 10 Sproat hooks. We have arranged these flies under the name of month in which they have been proved very killing, but they can be used successfully at other times, as they are all "Standard Flies."

These flies, both A and B quality, are put up in nice envelopes, each fly held separate, and name or number given.

Price, per dozen, $1.25. Price, each, 11 cents.

APRIL.

No.	Name.
103.	Cow Dung.
104.	Granum.
105.	Golden Dun Midge.
106.	Jenny Spinner.
107.	Gravel Bed.
108.	Cinnamon.
109.	Red Spinner.
110.	Stone Fly.
111.	Red Fly.

JUNE.

No.	Name.
121.	Gray Drake.
122.	Oak Fly.
123.	Orange Dun.
124.	Green Drake.
125.	Marlow Buzz.
126.	Alder.
127.	Blue Blow.
128.	Black Gnat.
129.	Dark Mackerel.
129½.	White Miller.

AUGUST.

No.	Name.
139.	Flaggon.
140.	Governor.
141.	Shad.
142.	Coachman.
143.	August Dun.
144.	Orange Fly.
145.	Land Fly.
146.	Green Camlet.
147.	Goslin.

MAY.

No.	Name.
112.	Iron Blue.
113.	Fern Fly.
114.	Sky Blue.
115.	Red Dun Fox.
116.	Little Dark Spinner.
117.	Turkey Brown.
118.	Hawthorn.
119.	Yellow May.
120.	Yellow Dun.

JULY.

No.	Name.
130.	Pale Evening Dun.
131.	Little Yellow May Dun.
132.	Silver Horn.
133.	July Dun.
134.	Red Ant.
135.	Wren Tail.
136.	Brown Palmer.
137.	Grizzly Palmer.
138.	Black Midge.

SEPTEMBER.

No.	Name.
148.	Red Palmer.
149.	Furnace Palmer
150.	Green Caperer.
151.	Spider Hackle.
152.	Black Palmer.
153.	Blue Bottle.
154.	Whirling Dun.
155.	Pale Blue Dun.
156.	Willow.

REVERSED WING TROUT FLIES.—B.

Tied on Nos. 6, 8 and 10 Sproat hooks.

Price, per dozen, $1.00. Price, each, 9 cents.

Name.	Name.	Name.
Montreal.	Ibis.	Coachman.
Professor.	Grizzly King.	Green Drake.
White Miller.	Black Gnat.	Spider Hackle.
Brown Hackle.	Cinnamon.	Cow Dung.
Red Hackle.	Black Hackle.	Red Fly.
Yellow May.	Grizzly Hackle.	Oak Fly.
Turkey Brown.	Gray Drake.	Governor.
Marlow Buzz.	Red Ant.	Shad.
Queen of the Water.	Beaverkill.	Seth Green.

In ordering the above flies, please to designate them as A or B.

It is surprising that almost all these patterns are still familiar, and still used in brook-trout country.

COMMON FLIES.

We have the following named flies, suitable for black bass and trout, tied on Nos. 2, 4, 6 and 8 Sproat hooks, which we claim to be far superior to many flies that are much higher priced. They are well tied on short but good gut. In ordering, mention size hook wanted. When ordering an assortment of a dozen or more, we place these flies in envelopes, made in the shape of fly book; each fly is held separate and name of fly printed on envelope; one of the handiest articles out for carrying flies.

Price per dozen, on No. 6 or 8 hook....... 50 cents. Price, each....... 5 cents.
" " " " " 4 " .... 60 " " " .... 6 "
" " " " " 2 " .... 75 " " " .... 7 "

Name.	Name.	Name.	Name.
Montreal.	Queen of the Water.	Green Drake.	Sand Fly.
Ibis.	Brown Hackle.	Beaverkill.	Cow Dung.
Coachman.	Red Hackle.	White Miller.	Gray Hackle.
Professor.	Yellow May.	Black Gnat.	Seth Green.
Grizzly King.	Royal Coachman.		

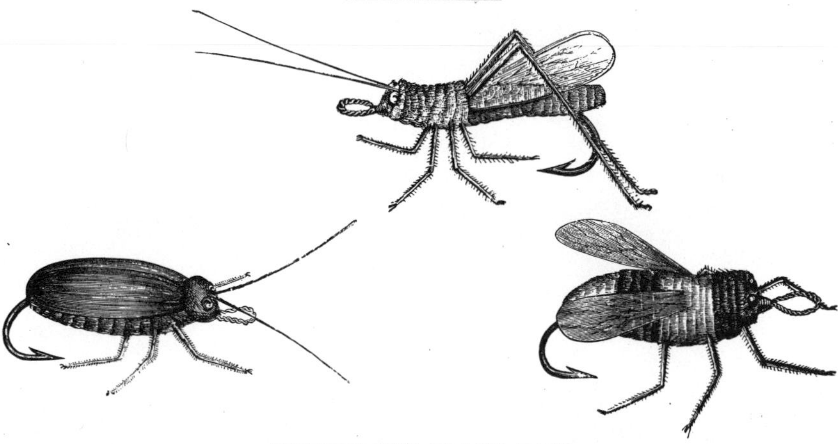

INSECTS FOR BLACK BASS.

These insects are made with scale wings, and are very durable. We keep only the following named varieties in stock:

Extra Fine.—A.

Price, each, 50 cents.

Name.	Name.	Name.
Bumble Bee.	Cricket.	White Moth.
Green Grasshopper.	Brown Beetle.	Green Dragon.
Yellow Grasshopper.	Yellow Hornet.	Red Dragon.

B.

Price, each, 25 cents.

Name.	Name.	Name.
White Moth.	Green Grasshopper.	Yellow Hornet.
Cricket.	Yellow Grasshopper.	Bumble Bee.

ACME (Improved).

Price $6.00

Size, 12 inches long, 8 wide, 5 deep, outside measurements. This case carries large and small reels; also a space for almost everything in the tackle line, separately, including flies and snelled hooks, tools for repairs, cigars, or pipe and tobacco. This case will carry all you will probably ever use. In cut, 6 and 7 are trays which fit into space marked 9; the bottom of this space 9 is fitted with cork for gangs, spoons, etc. No. 8 is a shallow tray for leaders, lines, etc., as desired. No. 10 is a removable division; both sliding doors are open in cut, showing arrangement for flies and hooks, similar to the Gem.

(BASKET.)

WILLOW TROUT BASKET.

Best Willow Baskets.

No. 1, to hold	6	pounds, price, each. ..	$ .75
" 2, "	9	" " "	1.00
" 3, "	12	" " "	1.25
" 4, "	20	" " " .	1.50
" 5, "	25	" " "	1.70

WEBBING BASKET STRAPS, PRICE, EACH, 25 CENTS.

SOLE LEATHER ROD CASE.

Fine Sole Leather Rod Case, made of heavy russet leather, with stout fancy handle, and cap on end, made up in fine, workmanlike manner.

Inside Diameter.	Inch.	Inch.	Inch.	Length. Inch.	Price, each.
1¾ inches............	35	39	45	50	..............$3.50
2 "	35	39	45	50	.... 4.00
2½ "	35	39	45	50	.... 4.50

LARGE SIZES MADE TO ORDER.

SILK WORM GUT.

Silk worm gut in hanks of 100 strands, 4 grades... ..	Nos. 1	2	3	4
Price, per hank................................	$ .50	$ .75	$1.00	$1.50

SILK.

Spool silk, enough for winding one split-bamboo rod, price... .... $ .25

PARTITION CLOTH CASE.

Partition cloth case, for 3 ft., 3½ and 4 ft. joints, price.......................... $ .25

Labor was cheap, materials were dear. Compare a handmade sole leather rod case—handle, cover, strap, and buckle—for a mere $3.50 with a little spool of silk thread for 25 cents.

Note that the best quality of gut cost *six times* as much as the poorest quality offered.

(SHOWING THE HOLDER IN USE.)

(PATENTED.)

FISHING ROD HOLDER.

Fishing Rod Holder is made of malleable iron, fastened with screw-clamp to the seat in boat, is adjustable so as to point in any direction; rod cannot be pulled out of the Holder by the fish, but can be easily taken out in a second by grasping the butt of rod with the hand; made substantial, durable, and is very handy.

Price $1.50

FISH HOLDER.

Is made of malleable iron; will grasp large or small fish. Length of holder, 9 inches.

Price $1.00

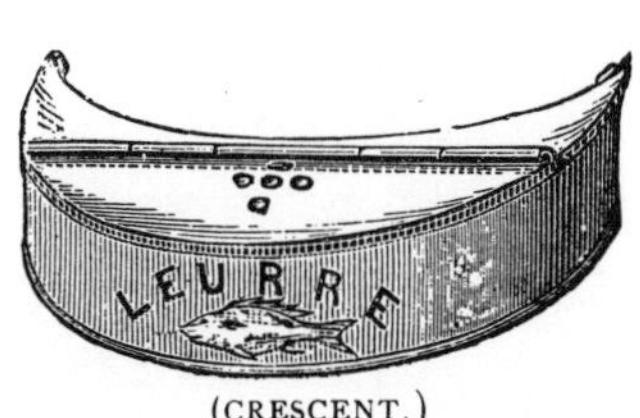

BAIT BOXES.

	Price, each
Basket	$ .15
Crescent	.20

(BASKET.)

(CRESCENT.)

With two lines in the water, this helmeted fisherman is reading, not a dime novel or a Laura Jean Libby paperback, but a tackle catalog. The perfect customer.

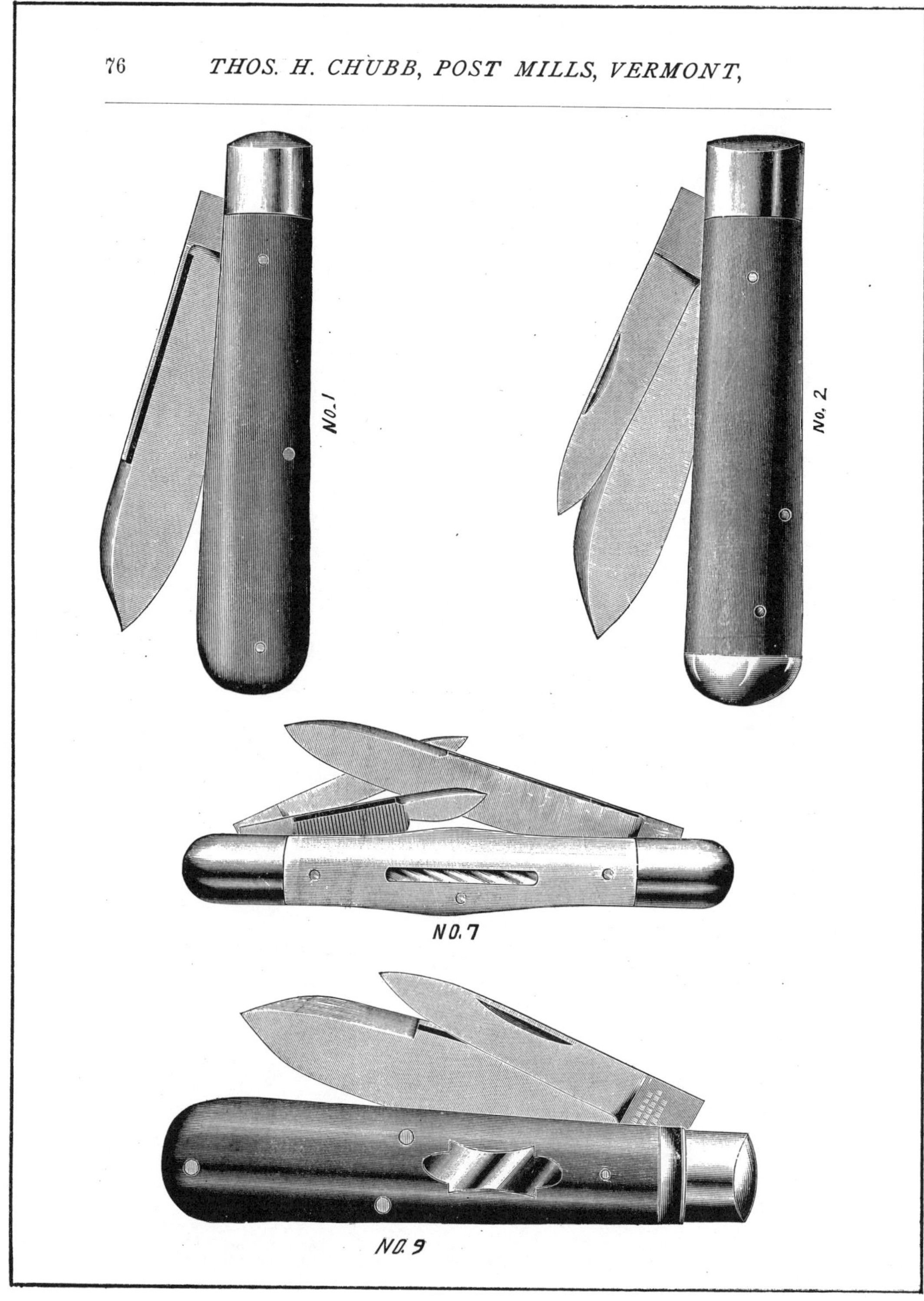

"Old Billy Barlow" (No. 1), the country boy's delight, for 20 cents; with two blades, 35 cents. You can buy the same knife today for about $5.

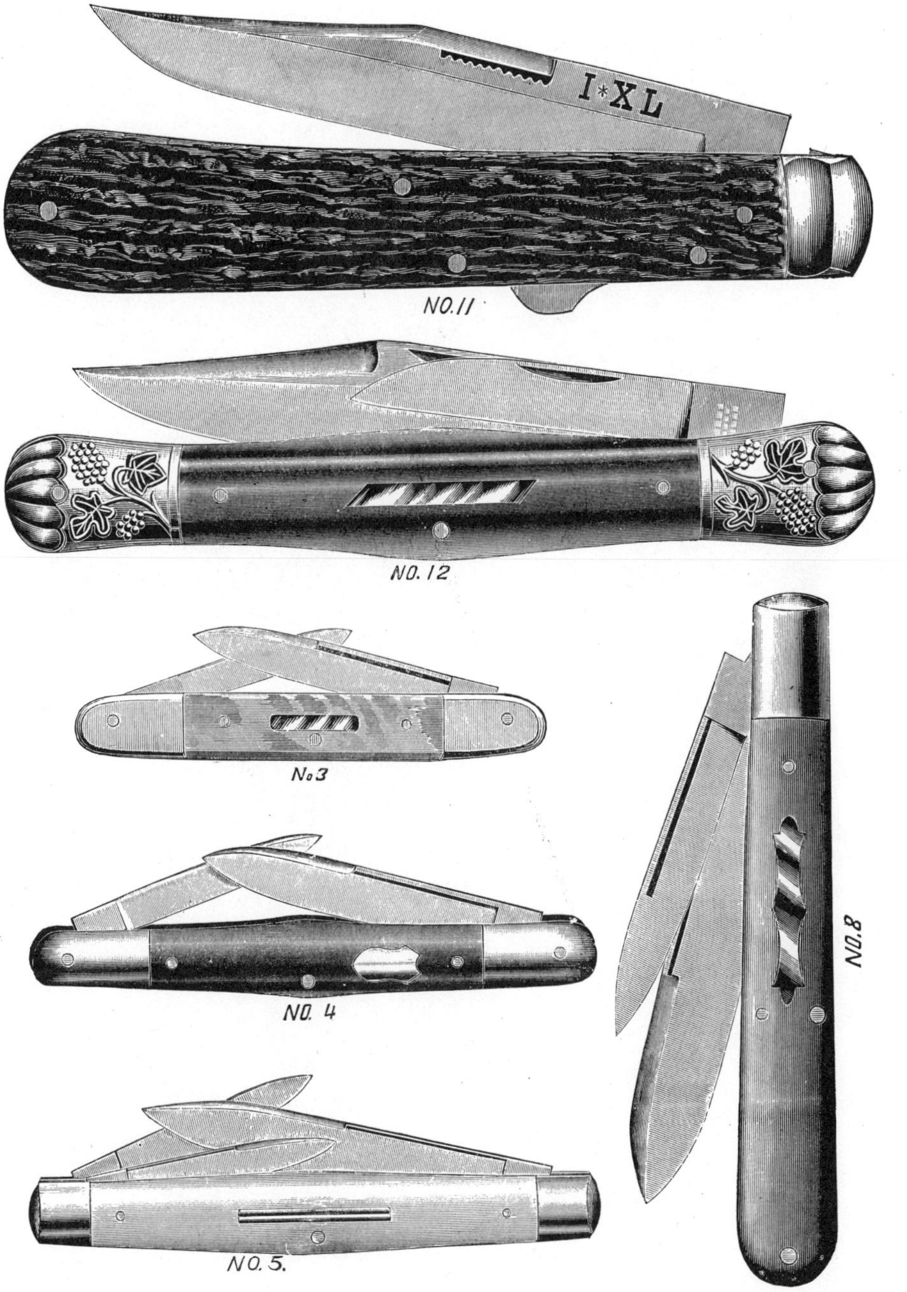

NO.11

NO.12

No3

NO. 4

NO.5.

NO.8

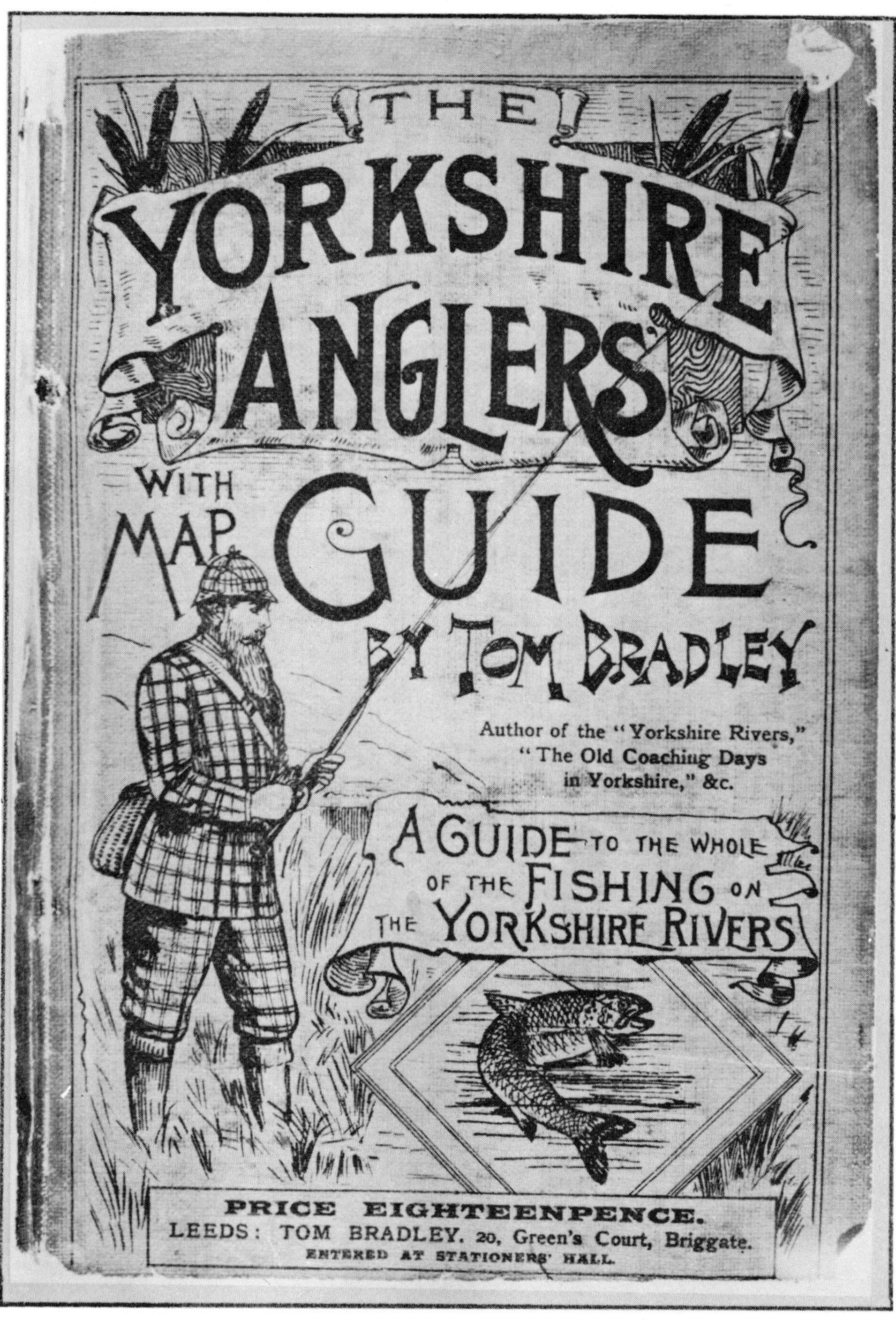
THE
YORKSHIRE ANGLERS' GUIDE
WITH MAP
BY TOM BRADLEY
Author of the "Yorkshire Rivers," "The Old Coaching Days in Yorkshire," &c.
A GUIDE TO THE WHOLE OF THE FISHING ON THE YORKSHIRE RIVERS
PRICE EIGHTEENPENCE.
LEEDS: TOM BRADLEY, 20, Green's Court, Briggate.
ENTERED AT STATIONERS' HALL.

Tom Bradley's booklet was but one of the numerous reprints of *Fishing Gazette* articles. The best and most famous was *The Trout Fly Dresser's Cabinet of Devices,* by Harry G. McClelland ("Athenian"). It contains about everything found in modern flytieing manuals and is the only one I recall that describes and pictures the right way to sharpen a hook.

The Oldest and Best Angling Paper in the World.

ANGLERS! READ

THE FISHING GAZETTE

ILLUSTRATED.

Established 1876. Every Saturday, price **2d.**

Entirely devoted to Angling, in all its Branches.

EDITED BY R. B. MARSTON,

(Hon. Treasurer of the Fly Fishers' Club; President of "The Anglers' Benevolent Society"; &c.)

MR. TOM BRADLEY'S capital work, "THE YORKSHIRE ANGLER'S GUIDE," was first published weekly in *The Fishing Gazette.*

The BEST MEDIUM FOR ALL ADVERTISEMENTS.

Addressed to well-to-do Anglers all over Great Britain and Ireland, and Abroad.

Proprietors:—

SAMPSON LOW, MARSTON, & COMPANY, LIMITED,

ST. DUNSTAN'S HOUSE, FETTER LANE, LONDON.

The unique and incomparable *Fishing Gazette* survived for some seventy years. Its founder and longtime editor, R. B. Marston, was also unique and incomparable. He wrote one of the best fishing books ever published, *Walton and Some Earlier Writers on Fish and Fishing*. In it, he disclosed, as the result of his research, that Izaak Walton was not, as then commonly supposed, a linen draper (milliner, Herbert Hoover said) but an ironmonger—a hardware dealer. Marston liked Americans, a rare thing in Britain in his time, and was for years an honorary member of The Anglers' Club of New York, a sort of American counterpart of the Fly Fishers' Club of London (of which Marston was the true founder). His name survives here in the Latin appellation of a rare Canadian salmonid, *Salvelinus marstonii*.

Ye Olde
Queene's Head Inne,
Bingley.

Ye House of Call for ye Brethren of ye Angle.

"And now let's go to an honest Alehouse, where we may have a cup of good Barley-wine, and sing and all of us rejoice together."—IZAAK WALTON.

Ye Hoste hathe rare accommodacion for Man and Beaste, eke for ye Wheelemenne.

Proprietor, WM. BRADLEY.

It is saddening to see that the phony antique "ye olde" has lived so long. Mr. Bradley's implication that "ye Wheelemenn"—he means bicyclists—are neither man nor beast was doubtless unintentional.

IMPORTANT.

If you want the BEST of Everything IN Rods, Tackle, Flies, Gut Casts, Reels, Baskets, Baits, Books, Cases, Lines, Brogues, Fishing Stockings, Trousers, Nets, &c., send for

HARDY'S ILLUSTRATED CATALOGUE, WITH OVER 200 ILLUSTRATIONS.

Before Cementing.

HARDY'S GOLD MEDAL CANE-BUILT RODS,

As made for H.R.H. Prince Albert Victor and leading Sportsmen.

With and without Steel Centres.

For Salmon, Trout, Grayling, Mahseer, &c.

After Cementing.

The GOLD MEDAL, "FISHERIES" EXHIBITION, LONDON, 1883.
Only PRIZE MEDAL, "INVENTIONS" EXHIBITION, LONDON, 1885.
Only GOLD MEDAL, LIVERPOOL, 1886.
Only PRIZE MEDAL, NEWCASTLE-ON-TYNE, 1887.
1889, AWARDS, PARIS and COLOGNE.

31 PRIZE MEDALS, &c., Largest Number held by any House in the World.

Only Makers of "Cholmondelz-Pennell's," "H. S. Hall's," "Marston," "Kelson," "Hi Regan," "Red Spinner," and "Major Turle's" Pattern Cane-built Fly Rods, &c.

The "PERFECTION," "GEM," "BADMINTON," & "PERFECT TEST" RODS.

THE CELEBRATED "ALNWICK" GREENHEART RODS.

"GUINEA" FLY ROD.—Three-piece 9 to 12 ft. Greenheart, 2 tops, cedar handle, Universal winch fittings, bronzed double-brazed cork stoppers, partition bag; if cork handle, 5/- extra.

"HOTSPUR" FLY ROD.—Two-piece, Greenheart, 1 top, cork handle, pat lock joint, Universal winch fittings, 25/-; if two tops, 35/-. Long bamboo top case, 10/- extra. Pat Bridge rings extra.

These rods, although so moderate in price, and only our second quality, are superior to any other make of "best." The great facilities we possess over all other makers enable us to do this. All balanced by our Mr. J. J. Hardy, who won the 16 ft. and 12 ft. Fly Casting Competition in Edinburgh, last year.

HARDY BROTHERS, The Practical Anglers, Inventors, and Manufacturers,

LONDON AND NORTH BRITISH WORKS,

ALNWICK, ENGLAND.

BLAKEY'S

Patent Noiseless BOOT PROTECTORS

The greatest boon ever offered anglers and other sportsmen. They are self-fixing, and boots fitted with them never want soling or heeling. **Sold at 1d. each.**

Agents wanted in every town.

JOHN BLAKEY, LEEDS.

WILLIAM MILLS & SON

Illustrated Catalogue ... OF

FISHING TACKLE

SALESROOMS . . .

No. 7 WARREN STREET, N. Y.

FACTORIES . . .

CENTRAL VALLEY, N. Y.

REDDITCH, ENGLAND.

· PRICE ·
TWENTY-FIVE
CENTS

The fine old New York tackle house of William Mills & Son was started there in 1822 by a representative sent over for the purpose by two brothers, Thomas and James Bate, who owned a needle and fishhook manufactory in Redditch, England. In 1828, Thomas came over to check up and liked it so well here that he stayed.

Brother James had a son, Thomas, and a daughter, Elizabeth; in 1843, son Thomas came over and joined with his uncle Thomas to form the tackle firm of T. & T. H. Bate. Ten years later, daughter Elizabeth came over with her English husband, William Mills, and their two-year-old son, Thomas Bate Mills.

William Mills became a partner in the Bate firm, and when the last Bate died in 1873, the firm became William Mills and Son. The infant Thomas Bate Mills had grown up in the company and he inherited it after his father's death in 1883.

Thomas Bate Mills—"old Mr. Mills"—lived into my time and I remember him well, a little, brisk, amiable man with a big reputation as a fisherman for the native speckled brook trout. A wet fly that he originated, the Mills Natural A, had a tremendous reputation among the old-time anglers for "speckles." He was a popular and active member of the Wyandanch Club on the Nissequogue, on Long Island. When he was an old man, he was knocked for a pinwheel by a speeding car while crossing the big concrete highway between the clubhouse and the river. But he was a tough old party and survived to the age of ninety, dying in 1941.

Three of Thomas Bate Mills's six children became active in the William Mills business—Eddie, the caster; "old" Arthur; and Chester, who because of delicate health established himself at Geneva, New York, in the beautiful Finger Lakes district and set up a flytieing project that supplied the firm with most of its American-made flies for some forty years.

Some time in the 1870s William Mills & Son had become the agents for the distribution of Hiram L. Leonard's split-bamboo rods; soon thereafter Mills bought an interest in the H. L. Leonard Rod Co., and eventually acquired that firm. Mills made both names, Leonard and Mills, famous throughout the angling world.

However, the real strength of the firm was always its tackle-jobbing and wholesaling business, which it once claimed had been for more than a century the world's largest. Until "only yesterday," there were more Americans living on farms and in small rural communities than in the cities, and except in a few large cities, fishing tackle was sold as a sideline by hardware dealers and general stores.

That was a Mills stronghold, and as each male scion reached manhood he served his apprenticeship "on the road" as a traveling salesman or "drummer." The little, dimly lit store at 21 Park Place, on the edge of New York's financial district, that has been William Mills & Son's home for seventy years, built up and still retains an amazing hard-core group of utterly loyal customers (of whom I have been one since 1922). But the real business of the firm has always been done on a wholesale basis, all across the country.

To return to the Millses: "Old" Arthur's son, "young" Arthur, and Eddie became the owners of William Mills & Son after buying out the other family interests, and eventually "young" Arthur became the sole owner and, after Chester and "old" Arthur died, the only surviving Mills in the management. Subsequently he retired to Florida after turning over the operation of the business to two of his three sons.

Note: At press time the fate of the Mills family business was uncertain.

LONDON, ENGLAND, 1883.

Exhibit of only Ten Leonard Rods

GRANTED FOR
GENERAL EXHIBIT.

SPECIAL MEDAL
FOR THE

PARTICULAR EXCELLENCE OF
Leonard's Catskill (Light) Fly Rods

SPECIAL MEDAL
FOR

BEST EXHIBIT OF
Split Bamboo Rods.

Other American Exhibitors received Awards of Silver and Bronze, but **LEONARD'S RODS** were the only ones receiving **GOLD MEDALS.**

Special Five Sovereign Prize for  Best Exhibit of Split Bamboo Rods.

Special Ten Sovereign Prize Awarded to our
"Standard" Braided Lines.

BERLIN, 1880.

AWARDED TO THE LEONARD RODS.

THE ONLY GOLD MEDAL
TO AN AMERICAN EXHIBITOR.

PARIS, FRANCE, 1889.

While we had no exhibit ourselves at this exposition, we loaned to a Florida Railway and Land Company, at their request, a Leonard Tarpon Rod, a W. M. & S. Imperial Tarpon Reel and a W. M. & S. Tarpon Line, which, by their superior excellence, attracted such universal attention and were so highly praised, that we were awarded a **SILVER MEDAL.**

Diploma and Large Bronze Medal Centennial Exposition, Philadelphia, 1876.

H. L. LEONARD'S

Celebrated Split Bamboo Fishing Rods.

THESE goods are so well and favorably known that it seems almost superfluous for us to call any special attention to their particular points of superiority. Nevertheless, we do wish to say that Mr. Leonard has for years made a study of this kind of work, and has succeeded in mastering it in every particular.

By his perfect method of fitting the strips of Bamboo, and the great care he gives to the proper balancing of all rods, he produces a rod that SURPASSES ANY OTHER ROD IN THE WORLD.

Particular attention is invited to the **Patent Ferrules** on the Leonard Rods, which are THOROUGHLY AND ABSOLUTELY **waterproof.** This, together with the additional advantages of the SPLIT FERRULE, both of which are more fully described further on, combine to place this rod AT THE HEAD OF THE LINE OF SPLIT BAMBOO RODS.

Mr. Leonard is most particular in his selection of material for his rods, and having, as he does, our entire importations of Bamboo to select from, he is enabled to secure poles that are entirely suitable to his requirements; and this, his THOROUGH KNOWLEDGE OF BAMBOO, together with his expertness in selecting, and his long and active experience, places him in a position to manufacture a rod that is

BEYOND COMPETITION.

Mr. Leonard is now located within 50 miles of New York, occupying a factory building erected expressly for him, and most perfectly appointed in every department, giving him increased facilities for producing his goods better and more promptly than ever before.

He wishes us to state, that he feels great pleasure that his efforts to place a perfect Fly Rod in the hands of Anglers are fully appreciated, which is daily made manifest both by an increase in the demand for Rods, and the satisfaction expressed, both verbally and by letter, from some of the oldest and most expert Fly fishermen in this country.

The fact is being constantly brought before us, both by Anglers whom we meet in person, and others writing to us from all parts of this country and England, that if a fisherman wishes **Perfection** in his Rods, and to be able to fish with the utmost accuracy and comfort, he **"must use a Leonard Rod,"** which is recognized both in this country and abroad as the highest standard of perfection and excellence.

These Rods are Hexagonal in shape, and six strips from Butt to Tip, each strip being a triangle of equal sides, which is the strongest and best form for the wood, this having been proven by Mr. Leonard by actual tests. A Rod with less than six strips sacrifices the enamel, and with more than six, the strength is diminished, there being too many glue joints, thus making them liable to twist at the Ferrules when taking the Rod apart, and in the tips the strips must be tapered to mere shavings, hence there is much more glue than wood.

The Patent Ferrule.

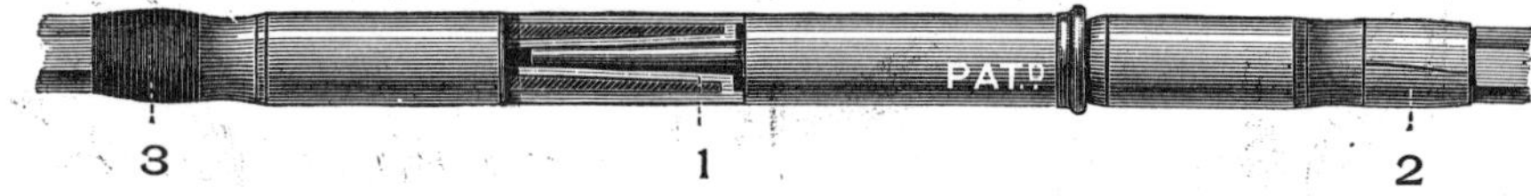

No. 1 Shows Waterproof Cup in Ferrule (Patented October 26, 1875.)

This prevents any moisture from reaching the wood, and the Ferrule from becoming loose. The constant wetting and drying of the Bamboo must rot the wood, and make other makes of rods less durable than Leonard's.

No. 2 Shows Split Ferrule (Patented September 3, 1878).

This split thoroughly strengthens where the ferrule is joined to the wood, which is the weakest part of a rod, and where so many of other makes of rods (bamboo especially) break. Mr. Leonard has yet to hear of a single instance of breakage at this point since the PATENT SPLIT FERRULE has been applied. We consider this the GREATEST IMPROVEMENT that has been introduced in rod-making since rods have been made.

No. 3 Shows Split Ferrule Whipped with Silk as it appears on the Rod.

LEONARD RODS—Continued.

A WORD IN REGARD TO ROUND RODS.

It has been made evident to us that parties, in considering this question of Round Rods, have in many cases quite overlooked the "**Maker**" in considering the "**Principle.**"

It should be borne in mind that the great bulk of Round Rods (we think we can safely say nine-tenths) were made by Mr. Leonard, and it was on the merits of Rods made by him that the excellence of Split Bamboos was established. But Mr. Leonard was the first to make a Six Strip Rod, and to leave the outside Hexagonal; in his increased experience on this work, and after severely testing the Hexagonal Rod, he has been manufacturing them almost exclusively for the past twelve years, and recommends **his** Hexagonal Rod as being far superior to any Round Rod, which recommendation we most heartily endorse.

However, to parties wishing these Rods, will say that we shall be pleased to furnish them Round or Hexagonal, as they may want. It is not our wish to induce them to purchase any but the style of goods they desire.

TOURNAMENT CASTING.

While recognizing the fact that this is not Angling, it must be conceded that in long distance casting a rod receives by far a more severe test and strain than it is possible to give it in angling.

Out of *Forty-two First Prizes, Thirty-seven have been taken* by contestants who have cast with the Leonard Rod: and in the instances where previous records have been broken it has invariably been done by parties using Leonard Rods.

We would also call attention to the wonderful increase in distance that has been shown at the tournaments where the Leonard Rods have been used.

Previous to 1883 there had been many tournaments held at the yearly meetings of the New York State Sportsmen's Conventions, and much interest and keen competition was displayed. Still 70 *to* 75 *feet* were the best records made by the most experienced casters, while 60 *to* 65 *feet* was the extreme length cast by the amateur classes.

In 1883 the Leonard Rods were first used in tournament casting, since which time the records have been very materially changed as compared with the above distances.

It now requires a cast of 80 *to* 85 *feet* in the AMATEUR CLASS to win a prize, while in the Expert, free-for-all, class, composed largely of winning amateurs of previous tournaments, records of from **92 to 102½ feet** have repeatedly been made.

The waterproof ferrule was a rather trivial thing and the application of the interrupted-thread principle to a locking reelseat was merely ingenious, but the split—serrated—ferrule is scientifically important and fundamental to good rod design.

Loud talk and sweeping statements were standard business practice in those days, and Mills held up their end. Probably all of the 37 out of 42 tournament-casting first prizes here mentioned were won by the company's own casting team—Rube Leonard and Hiram Hawes, nephews of old Hiram L. Leonard; and Eddie Mills. They were all topnotch performers.

The Mills' Patent Reel Lock.

IN USE ON THE LEONARD SALMON, TARPON AND SALT WATER RODS.

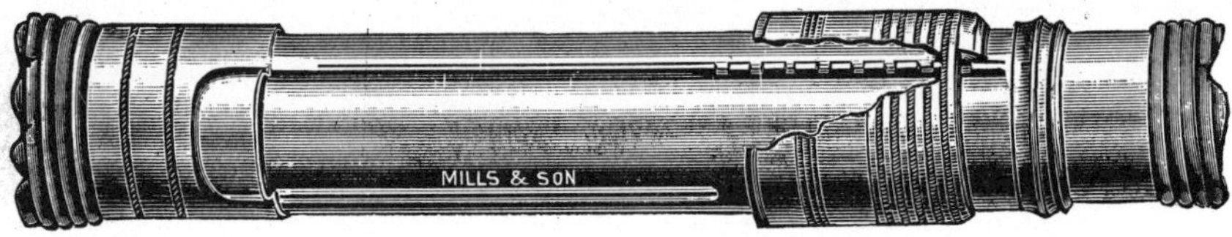

Makes a perfect and absolute Lock, and an impossibility of casting the Reel from the Rod when adjusted. Move the band down over Plate of Reel, and a simple turn to the left and the Plate is locked.

Leonard's Salmon and Grilse Rods.

	Each.
3 Piece, with Full Solid German Silver Plate and Extra Tip, length, 15 to 17 feet, with or without Patent Reel Lock (see above)........	$50 00
The New Calibre Salmon Rod, length, 15 feet 6 inches, weight about 24 ounces, is meeting with general favor and commanding a large sale.	
3 Piece, with Independent Handle, Full German Silver Reel Plate, 2 Butt Joints, 2 Middle Joints and 2 Tips, with or without Patent Reel Lock (see above)........	70 00
This is a new pattern of Rod; it is packed in convenient and compact form, and comprising, as it does, duplicate joints, it will do away with the necessity of carrying so many rods.	
3 PIECE, GRILSE, Full Solid German Silver Reel Plate and Extra Tip, length, 14 feet, with or without Patent Reel Lock (see above)........	40 00
3 PIECE, LIGHT GRILSE, also suitable for Black Bass, Full Solid German Silver Reel Plate and Extra Tip, length, 13 feet........	35 00

Leonard's Independent Handle Fly Rods.

	Each.
3 Piece, Extra Tip and Independent Handle, length, 9 to 10 feet, weight, 5 to 7 ounces, with Fancy Cork Handle	$35 00

The workmen who made these $30 to $50 Leonard rods probably earned about $12 a week. But the percentage of labor cost in today's $150 to $250 rods is higher than it was for the $30 to $50 rods.

Note that the rod cases shown are "hollow hard wood." The aluminum rod case did not appear until a good many years later.

LEONARD RODS—Continued.

Leonard Trout and Bass Fly Rods.

	Each.
3 Piece, with Solid German Silver Reel Plate, Extra Tip and Tip Case..	$30 00

Above Rods made in the following lengths and weights:

10 feet to 10 feet 3 inches..	weight from 6 ounces to 8 ounces.
10 " 6 inches..	" 7¼ " 9 "
10 " 9 " to 11 feet..	" 8½ " 11 "
11 " 3 " to 11 " 6 inches..	" 9 " 11 "

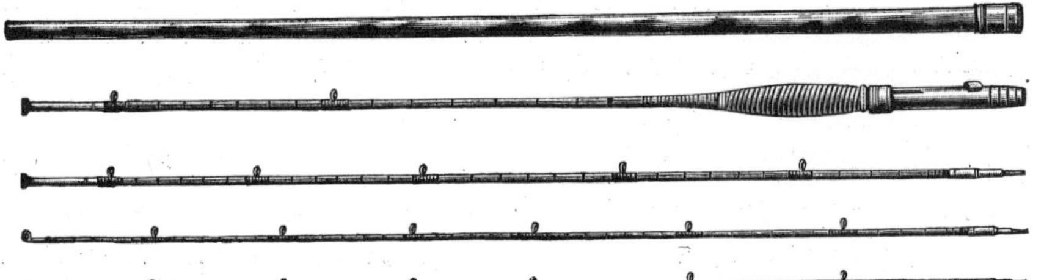

These Rods are generally finished with cane wound handles, but we usually have a few in stock with cork grasp, which are made in an improved manner and very durable.

The weights given are for Rods with Solid Reel Plates. 1 to 1½ ounces should be deducted for comparison, as the weights of Rods are usually given with Reel Bands.

The perfect distribution of material in these Fly Rods, each part of the Rod being proportionately balanced, and doing its relative part of the work, thus making the action true throughout, produces much pleasanter and more accurate Rods to cast with, in addition to their being more durable, and several ounces lighter for same length and strength of Rod, than any other make.

Catskill Fly Rod.

THIS ROD WAS AWARDED A SPECIAL GOLD MEDAL, LONDON, 1883.

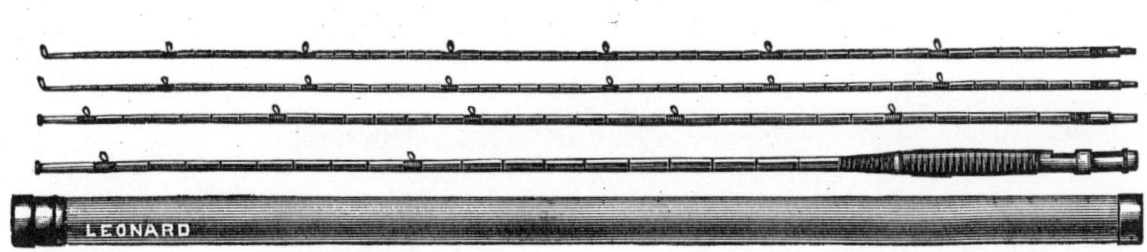

The Catskill was first made by Mr. Leonard, at our suggestion. Many of them have been sold, invariably giving perfect satisfaction (not a single complaint). EVERY Fly fisherman who wishes to use light tackle, and obtain the utmost pleasure from playing his fish (whether large or small), should own one of these Rods.

	Each.
3 PIECE FLY, with Reel Bands, length, 9½ to 10 feet, and weighs only from 4⅝ to 5¼ ounces, has Extra Tip, entire Rod inclosed in Hollow Wood Case..	$30 00

The "Petite" Catskill Fly Rod.

	Each.
3 PIECE FLY, with Reel Bands, length, 9½ feet, weighing only 3⅛ to 3¾ ounces, has Extra Tip, entire Rod inclosed in Hollow Wood Case..	$40 00

The "Fairy" Catskill Rod.

WEIGHT, 2 OUNCES.

	Each.
3 PIECE FLY, with Reel Bands, length, 8⅛ feet, has Extra Tip, and entire Rod is inclosed in Hollow Wood Case.......	$50 00

The lightest Rods ever successfully made; are thoroughly durable, and for a careful, experienced fisherman are very desirable. One of these Rods in the hands of a skillful caster has laid a fly 72 feet, and one angler used one for four days and killed two hundred (Long Island) trout, and finished with the Rod in perfect condition. **Rather a good record?**

Leonard "Tourist" Fly Rod

Consists of Independent Handles, 12 to 13 inches long, Duplicate Butt, and Middle Joints and three Tips. These Rods were first made at the suggestion of a well known angler and ardent admirer of Leonard's Rods. To anglers contemplating long trips, where reducing their rods to the minimum space is desirable, the advantages of these Rods are obvious. They are strong, durable, quick acting and extremely good and accurate Casting Rods. Additional Joints can be furnished, or two or more Rods can be made with interchangeable joints.

Made in two styles, see page 5.

LEONARD RODS—Continued.

The "Adirondack" Tourist.

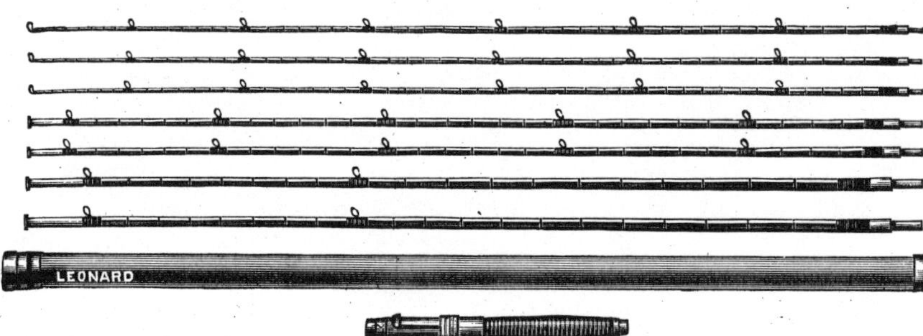

Each.

Length, 10 feet, weight about 6½ ounces........ $50 00

The "Parmachene" Tourist.

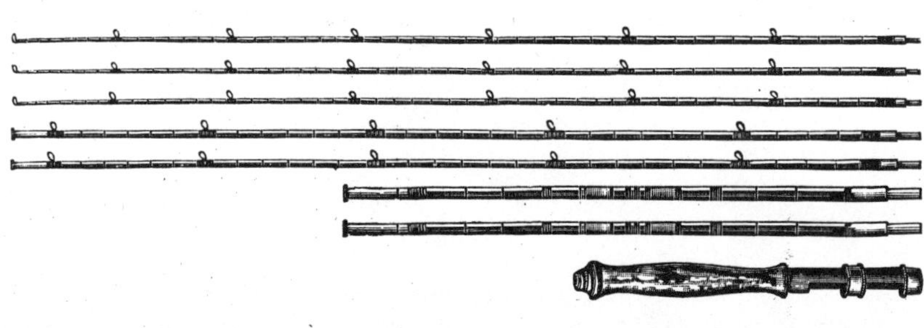

Each.

Length, 10 feet, weight about 7¾ ounces........ $50 00

These Rods, except Handle, packed in Hollow Hard Wood Case.

Extension "Tourist" Rod Cases.

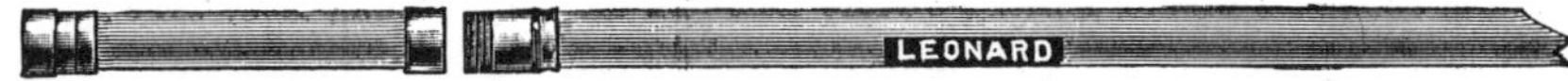

If desired, "Extension" ends, to hold Handle, can be made to screw on end of Hollow Cases, detachable for convenience in packing, at an additional cost of $2.00 each.

Black Bass Bait and Trolling Rods.

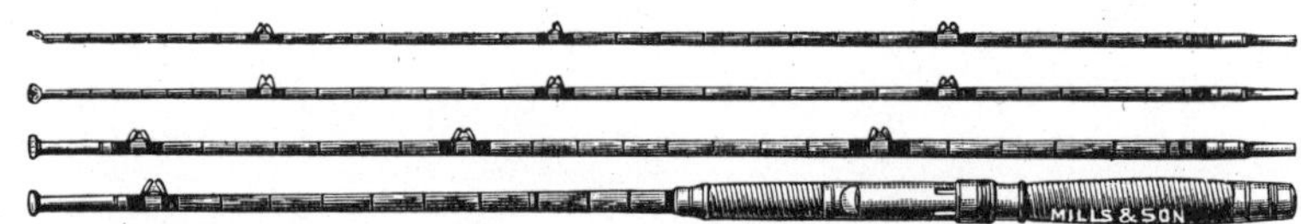

Each.

3 PIECE BLACK BASS BAIT OR MINNOW ROD, length, 8 to 9½ feet, weight, 9½ to 11½ ounces, Solid Reel Plate above the Hand-piece, Standing Guides, Extra Tip........ $30 00

3 PIECE "DR. HENSHALL'S FAVORITE" MINNOW CASTING ROD, length, 8½ feet, weight 7¾ to 8½ ounces, Standing Guides, Hand-piece above and below Reel Seat, Extra Tip........ 30 00

3 PIECE BLACK BASS BAIT AND TROLLING, length, 9½ to 11 feet, weight, 10 to 14 ounces, Solid Reel Plate above the hand, Extra Tip........ 30 00

3 PIECE HEAVY BLACK BASS BAIT, length, 9½ to 10½ feet, weight, 15 to 20 ounces, Solid Reel Plate above the hand........ 30 00

Weight given is for Rod with Reel Plate. Agate Tips or Guides furnished on any of the above Bass Rods, $1.00 each, additional.

RODS—Continued.

Superior Quality Split Bamboo Sea Bass or Trolling Rods.—Class 2A.

Having had an extensive demand for a really good and reliable Split Bamboo Rod of this style for a moderate price, we have manufactured and offer the following Rods :

All ferrules are of hard German Silver and very strong, but balance of Mountings are of Nickel, and the Rods are well finished, and make a strong, durable Rod.

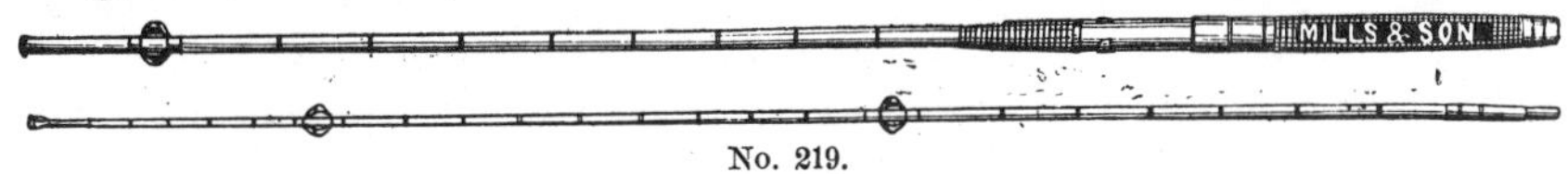

No. 219.

CANE WOUND HANDLES.

Nos.		Each.
219.	2 Piece, 8 feet, about 16 ounces, Solid Reel Seat	$8 00
	ALSO SAME ROD, HEAVIER.	
220.	3 Piece, 8 feet, about 16 ounces, Solid Reel Seat	9 00
	ALSO SAME ROD, HEAVIER.	

LANCEWOOD AND GREENHEART RODS.

Class 3.

In these Rods we offer a grade of Rods that we are convinced is unequaled at anything like the price. They are manufactured from well-seasoned material only, and are fitted with the most improved styles of Mountings. Particular attention is paid to the proper balancing of each Rod ; and they are of the most desirable patterns for the different styles of angling.

Fly Rods.

No. 0½.

Nos.		Each.
0½.	3 Piece Lancewood Fly Rod, Nickel Mountings, Solid Metal Reel Seat, Fancy Corrugated Wood Hand Grasps, 1 Tip, length, about 10 feet, in Bag	$1 50

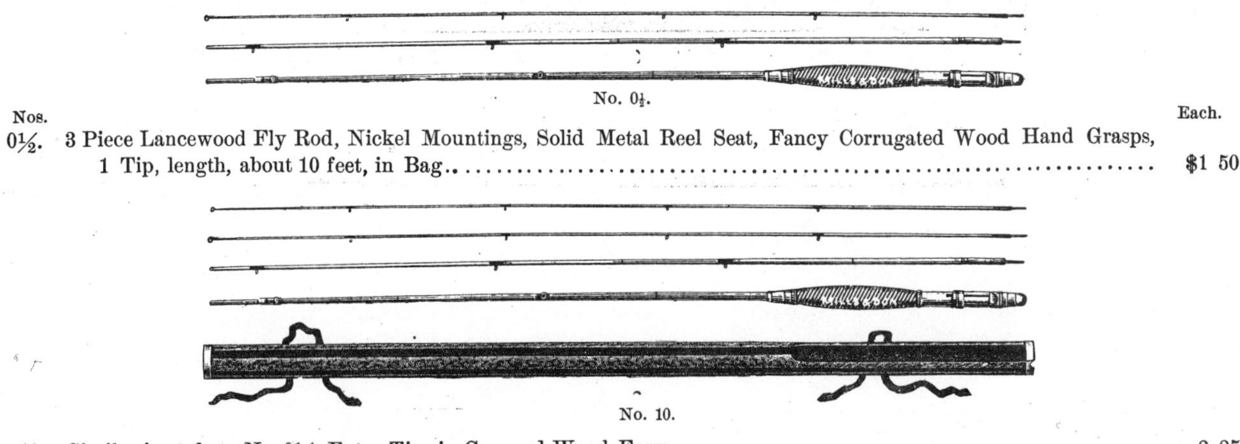

No. 10.

10.	Similar in style to No. 0½, Extra Tip, in Grooved Wood Form	2 25

No. A.

A Lancewood.	3 Piece Fly Rod and Extra Tip, about 10½ feet long, Nickel Mountings, Solid Metal Reel Seat, Rimmed Ferrules, Closely Wound, White Celluloid Handle, put up in Cloth Covered Grooved Wood Form	3 50
A Greenheart.	Similar in style to A, with Handle of Black Celluloid	3 50
A¼ Lancewood.	Similar in general style to "No. A Greenheart," but shorter and lighter weight, suitable for Light Brook Fishing	3 50

RODS—Continued.

The W. M. & S. "Standard" Split Bamboo Rod.

While we admit that the Leonard Rod is, without doubt, the Best Rod in the world, we claim that, with this exception, our "STANDARD ROD" is without a rival. We use only the best material in its construction, and the Ferrules, etc., are all hand made of the highest quality of German Silver. These Rods are manufactured in our own factory, by our own staff of experienced workmen, under our personal supervision, and are marvels of good workmanship. The calibre and style of the Rods are PERFECT, and they are infinitely superior to anything in the market, exclusive of a "Leonard."

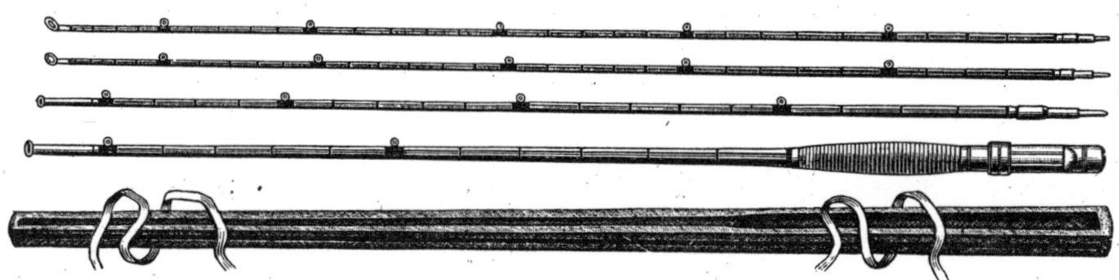

No. 110.

Nos.		Each.
110.	3 Piece Fly, with Solid German Silver Reel Plate and Extra Tip, lengths, 9 to 11 feet, weights, 6 to 10 ounces......	$15 00
111.	3 Piece Black Bass Bait, "HENSHALL PATTERN," Solid German Silver Reel Plate and Extra Tip, lengths, 8¼ to 9 feet........	15 00
112.	3 Piece Black Bass Bait, Solid German Silver Reel Plate, Extra Tip, lengths, 10 to 11 feet........	15 00
115.	Trunk Fly, lengths, 10 to 11 feet........	20 00
117.	Regular Combination Fly and Bait Rod, makes Bait Rod, 8 feet, Fly Rod, 10½ to 11 feet........	25 00

Our Special "Standard" Rods.

2 JOINTS.

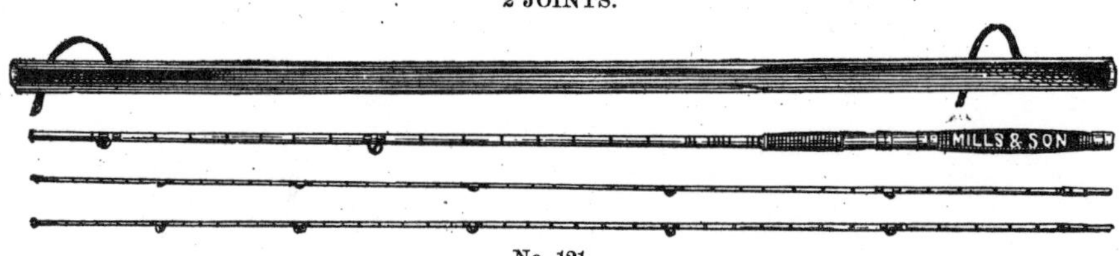

No. 121.

Nos.		Each.
120.	Salt Water Bass and Weakfish Rod, Double Guides, Reel Seat and Extra Tip........	$18 00
121.	Light Lake Trolling or Black Bass Bait Rod, Double Guides, Reel Seat, Extra Tip, an exceptionally fine Rod for Light Weak Fishing........	16 00

No. 121 is well suited for Light Striped Bass and Weak Fishing in vicinity of New York.

The strength and durability of the Ferrules on our "Standard" Rods, together with the great care used in their manufacture, make them a very desirable Rod, and anglers will do well to examine these Rods before making purchases elsewhere.

The Durand Patent Weighing and Measuring Attachment for Application to the Butt Joint of Fishing Rods.

PATENT APPLIED FOR.

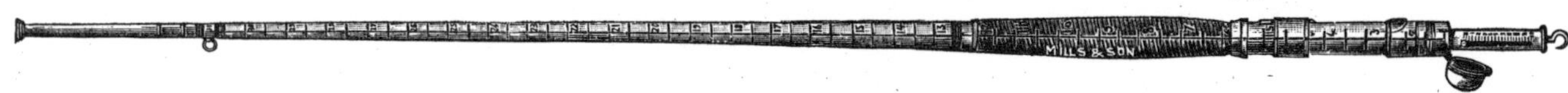

The above device consists of a light, specially made, accurate Sportsman's Balance, adjusted to and sliding in a metal tube permanently secured in butt of rod, and entirely concealed there by a neat hinged waterproof cap, when not in use. For measuring, the butt is divided by a straight line running its entire length, and accurately spaced off in half inch distances, and plainly marked at each inch. These attachments will be made and applied in an ornamental and substantial manner and will recommend themselves to those desiring to keep an accurate account of their catch.

Cost of applying to suitable rods........ $10 00 each

Page 92: (Durand Patent). This is a truly lighthearted affair, a real fun thing. Think of the mirth and curiosity it must have elicited in the clubhouse, hotel bar, or other fishermen's hangouts. One wonders how many they ever sold.

Page 94: William Mills really went overboard on this one, and took a licking on it. "Sure," said Eddie Mills when I queried him after finding an old picture of this "New Patent" reel about twenty-five years ago. "We've still got one," and he hauled it out. It is, of course, simply the planetary drive that was a scientific curiosity until Henry Ford used it in the transmission of his Model T "Tin Lizzie." (It is now used in the modern automatic transmission for motor cars.)

"We hired a professor at Massachusetts Institute of Technology to approve the design, and had the gears made by Brown & Sharpe, famous precision manufacturers," said Eddie indignantly. "Wasn't worth a damn; too much friction."

REELS, CLASS 5–Continued.

Our Finest Quality "Cutty Hunk" Reel.

For Tarpon, Beach and other styles of Salt Water Fishing.

WITH ADJUSTABLE CLICK.

	500	400	350 yards.
Size..	5/0	4/0	3/0
Price.	$38 00	$30 00	$27 00

New Patent Treble Multiplying Reel, with Automatic Drag and Protected Handle.

The following are some of its points of excellence:

LIGHTNESS AND COMPACTNESS, which makes this Reel from 2½ to 5 ounces lighter than any multiplier, and as light as any click reel of same capacity.

It has all the advantages of a single click reel, with a perfectly PROTECTED HANDLE, to which is added its value as a TRIPLE MULTIPLIER (it multiplying from the centre by an entirely new and superior principle). By this peculiar arrangement of the gear, we may say there is a GAIN OF SPEED without a corresponding loss of power, as in the old method.

THE SIMPLICITY of its Automatic Drag, which applies itself immediately (and only) when the line is running off, and instantly removes all pressure as the line is reeled in.

It is the most compact and light multiplier for use on a fly rod.

It is EXTREMELY free running, and yet impossible for it to overrun.

Prices with Drag.	Each.
TROUT, holding 35 to 40 yards..................................	$13 00

H. L. Leonard's Patent Click Reel.

HANDSOMER, STRONGER, LIGHTER, AND WILL HOLD MORE LINE THAN ANY OTHER REEL OF SAME DIAMETER.

ALL METAL (two colors), and **RUBBER AND GERMAN SILVER.**

Every reel warranted perfect in workmanship and quality, and all clicks are guaranteed against breakage.

2¼ inches diameter, weight about 3½ ounces, capacity 35 to 40 yards	$8 00
2½ inches diameter, weight about 4½ ounces, capacity 50 yards..	8 50
3 inches diameter, with Black Rubber Panels, very narrow Spool which winds the line very fast, Balance Handle, weight 6¼ ounces, capacity 60 to 75 yards..................	11 00

For Salmon and Grilse.

Grilse, with Balance Handle..................................	$12 00
Salmon, with Balance Handle, Rubber Panels, and our new Graduated Adjustable Drag. (See page 32)..........	23 00

REELS, CLASS 5—Continued.

The Automatic Reel.

Orvis Reel.

THE REEL IS MANIPULATED ENTIRELY BY THE HAND THAT HOLDS THE ROD.

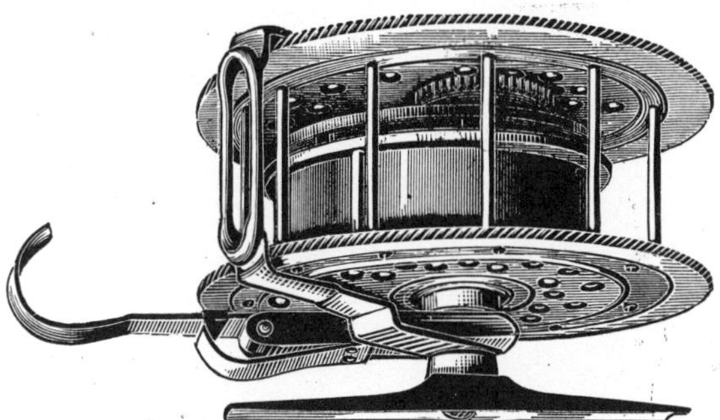

"THE LITTLE FINGER DOES IT."

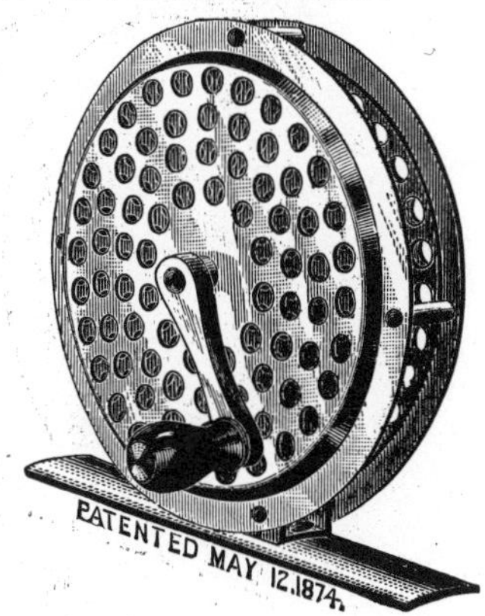

No. 1 Automatic Reel Carries 90 Feet of Line.

Brass	Weight,	7½	ounces,	$6 00
Nickeled	"	7½	"	7 00
Bronze	"	7½	"	8 00
Hard Rubber	"	6½	"	8 00
Aluminum	"	5¼	"	8 00

No. 2 Automatic Reel Carries 150 Feet of Line.

Brass	Weight,	11½	ounces,	$7 00
Nickeled	"	11½	"	8 00
Bronze	"	11½	"	9 00
Hard Rubber	"	10½	"	9 00
Aluminum	"	9¼	"	9 00

The "**ORVIS REEL,**" with Click and Nickeled.................. $3 00 each.

Wm. Mills & Son's "Standard" Braided Lines.

In our "Standard" lines it has been our chief aim to produce the highest grade of lines that it is possible to manufacture, and we offer them to anglers with confidence, knowing that there are no other lines made that are equal to them in quality and finish. These lines, when exhibited in the LONDON FISHERIES EXHIBITION, IN 1883, WERE AWARDED A

SPECIAL PRIZE OF TEN SOVEREIGNS.

Under examination they proved to be 25% to 30% stronger than most of the better known makes, while the finish was smoother than any others offered in competition. Special mention was made of our "**Imperial Waterproof.**" See that all of these goods bear "**Our Name and Trade Mark**" as per label shown.

William Mills & Son's "Standard Imperial" Waterproof Silk Line.

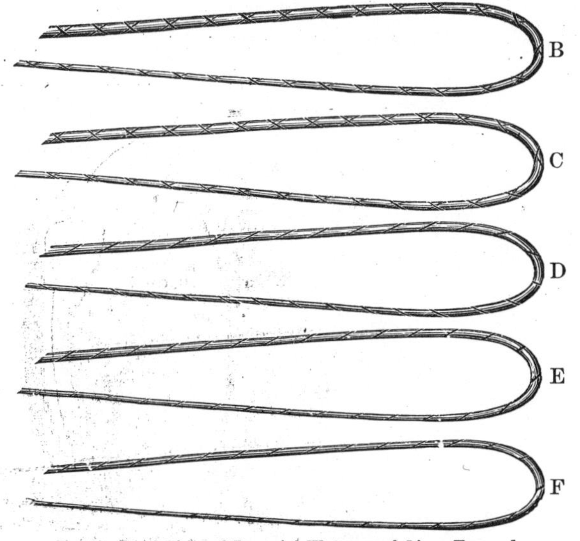

Fac-simile of Sizes of Imperial Waterproof Line, Tapered.

Tapered, size D, in 30, 40 yard lengths, double tapered, 10 c.; single tapered, 9 c. per yard.

Tapered, size E, in 30, 40, 50 yard lengths, double tapered, 9 c.; single tapered, 8 c. "

Tapered, size F, in 30, 40, 50 yard lengths, double tapered, 8 c.; single tapered, 7 c. "

Level, in 25-yard coil, 4 connected. D E F G H — 8, 7, 6, 5½, 5½ c. "

Our Imperial Waterproof Line still takes the lead; our special *water tint* is the popular color; and although numerous have been the imitations of our line since we received the London prize, it stands to-day unapproached for its excellence and durability. Our line runs the heaviest for its size of any in the market, which makes it a superior casting line to any. All the long distances at the tournaments in New York have been made with our Imperial Line.

Page 95: Heaviness was a virtue in a sinking line before the coming of the dry fly.

Page 97: Superior trout flies, 32 cents a dozen; wonder what the tiers were paid.

Page 99: These were later called Mills's Light Stream Flies. The Sneck hooks were much smaller, number for number, than today's Model Perfect, and they were the neatest, lightest, most delicate and deadly wet flies anyone could want. I used them up by the gross in my salad days.

Note that we have flies on eyed hooks and on barbless hooks, and "floating" (buoyant body) but not dry flies; and can tie "an exact imitation of any insect sent to us in good condition" for $5 a dozen. We keep up with the times!

ARTIFICIAL FLIES AND INSECTS.

Class 1.

ONE DOZEN

SUPERIOR TROUT FLIES

TIED ON CELEBRATED HOOKS.

Hook No...........

All Flies in this class, except No. 13, are packed 1 dozen in envelope or folder (neatly printed as above), and 1 gross in a box. We can furnish these Flies sewed on cards in all styles. Prices on application.

No. 10. Superior Trout Flies, all the Leading Patterns, on Sproat Hooks, Nos. 4 to 10......$3.84 per gross.

Alder.
Abbey.
Brown Adder.
Beaverkill.
Black Prince.
Black Gnat.
Black Hackle, orange body.
Black June.
Black Hackle, peacock body.
Brown Hen.
Brown Hackle.
Coachman.
Coachman Royal.
Cinnamon.
Cowdung.
Coch-y-bon-dhu.
Claret Gnat.
Canada.
Guinea Hen.
Golden Spinner.
Gray Drake.
Governor.
Grizzly King.
Gray Hackle.
Gray Fox.
Green Hackle.
House.
Ibis.
Jungle Cock.
March Brown.
Montreal.
Orange Miller.
Professor.
Polka.
Queen of Waters.
Red Spinner.
Red Hackle.
Red Ant.
Red Fox.
R. W.
Scarlet Ibis.
Scarlet Ibis and White.
Silver Black.
Sand.
Stone.
Wood Duck.
White Miller.
White Hackle.
Yellow Sally.
Yellow Professor.

No. 11. Superior Trout Flies, same patterns as above, tied with silk bodies on Sproat or Sneck Bent Hooks, Nos. 4 to 10............$5 40 per gross.

No. 11 grade of Fly tied to order in quantities only.

No. 12. Superior Bass Casting Flies, on Sproat Hooks, Nos. 2 and 3............$9 00 per gross.

Brown Adder.
Coachman.
Grizzly King.
Gray Hackle.
Governor.
Gov. Alvord.
Guinea Hen.
Jungle Cock.
Orange Miller.
Lord Baltimore.
Wood Duck.
Yellow Professor.

No. 13. Extra Superior Bass Casting Flies, patterns as below, tied on fine grade of Sproat Hooks, Nos. 1 and 2. These Flies are tied on double gut and each fly sewed on a card............$12 00 per gross.

Brown Hackle
Cheney.
Ferflueson.
Grizzly King.
Governor.
Gray Hackle.
Lord Baltimore.
Montreal.
Polka.
Parmachene.
Scarlet Ibis.
Seth Green.
Silver Doctor.

No. 14. Superior Bass Trolling Flies, on Sproat Hooks, Nos. 2/0 and 1/0............$13 44 per gross.

Brown Turkey.
Black Hackle.
Canada.
Coachman.
Cock Robin.
Gray Hackle.
Green Parrot.
Montreal.
Miller.
Professor.
Red Robin.
St. Lawrence.

Artificial Flies.—Class 2.

All Flies in Class 2 are packed 1 dozen in envelope. Prices for sewing on cards on application.

No. 30. Fine Quality Trout Flies, on best Spring Steel Sproat or Sneck Bend Hooks, Nos. 6, 8, 10, 12..$0 60 per dozen.

We can furnish this excellent grade of Flies in all the leading patterns, many of which are enumerated below:

Alder.
Brown Spinner.
Brown Hackle.
Beaverkill.
Brown Adder.
Black Hackle.
Black Prince.
Black Gnat.
Coachman.
Coch-y-bon-dhu.
Cinnamon.
Cowdung.
Claret Gnat.
Canada.
Dark Fox.
Dark Stone.
Downlooker.
Fern.
Green Hackle.
Green Drake.
GrayMiller.
Gold Spinner.
Grizzly King.
Governor.
Gray Hackle.
Guinea Hen.
Jungle Cock.
Jenny Lind.
King of Waters.
Light Stone.
Light Fox.
Montreal.
March Brown.
Orange Miller.
Oak.
Professor.
Queen of Waters.
Red Ibis.
Royal Coachman.
Red Spinner.
Red Hackle.
R. W.
Sand.
Scarlet Ibis.
Soldier.
White Miller.
White Moth.
Wood Duck.
Yellow Professor.
Yellow Sally.
Yellow Miller.
Yellow Coachman.
And many others.

No. 31. Same as No. 30, with Fancy Heads. To order in quantities only............$0 72 per dozen.

No. 32. Same as No. 30, with Jungle Feathers. To order in quantities only............1 25 "

ARTIFICIAL FLIES, CLASS 2—Continued.

No. 40. Fine Quality Black Bass Casting Flies, on Spring Steel Sproat Hooks, Tied with Helper Nos. 2, 4 .... $1 25 per dozen.

Alder.
Brown Hackle.
Beaverkill.
Black Hackle.
Black Prince.
Coachman.
Cinnamon.
Canada.
Dark Fox.
Dark Stone.
Green Hackle.
Green Drake.
Gold Spinner.
Grizzly King.
Governor.
Gray Hackle.
Jungle Cock.
King of Waters.
Light Stone.
Light Fox.
Montreal.
March Brown.
Orange Miller.
Professor.
Queen of Waters.
Red Ibis.
Royal Coachman.
Red Hackle.
R. W.
Scarlet Ibis.
Soldier.
White Miller.
White Moth.
Wood Duck.
Yellow Professor.
Yellow Coachman.

No. 42. Same as Quality No. 40, with Jungle Feathers .... $1 80 per dozen.

No. 50. Fine Quality Black Bass Trolling Flies, with Looped Gut and Tied on best Sproat Hooks Nos. 2/0, 1/0 .... 1 75 "

Coachman Royal.
Fergueson.
Gray Hackle.
Henshall.
Ibis.
Ibis and White.
Montreal.
Page.
Polka.
R. W.
Red Hackle.
Silver Doctor.
Seth Green's Favorites. { Seth Green. Seth Green Miller. Grizzly King. Gov. Alvord.

Insects.

Humble Bee. Lady. Grasshopper. Creeper.

Humble Bee, Beetles, Wasps, Grasshoppers, Crickets, Creepers, Lady .... $2 40 per dozen.

William Mills & Son's Extra Quality Flies.

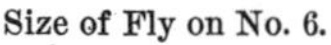

Size of Fly on No. 6.

Size of Fly on No. 8.

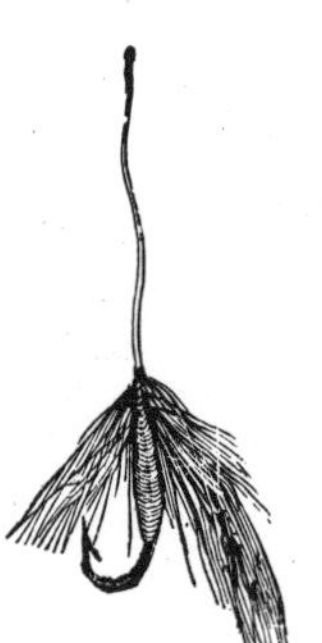

Size of Fly on No. 10.

Size of Fly on No. 12.

Size of Fly on No. 12 Sneck Hook.

These, OUR BEST QUALITY FLIES, have a wide reputation; they are very neatly and strongly made, with (excepting some of the Bass Flies) reversed wings, doubly tied, thereby giving them greater strength and durability.

We prefer to dress this grade of Fly on our celebrated *O'Shaughnessy Hook*, except the very small Flies, which are lighter and more desirable on the small Sneck Bent Hook, which is our favorite hook for small Flies, as the O'Shaughnessy is for the medium and large.

We usually have some of most of the patterns on Sproat Hooks for those who desire them.

We give a list of the leading patterns of Trout and Grayling Flies carried in stock, and are prepared to tie any pattern to order, from sample, at short notice, on any style or size of hook, at same price as from stock.

If parties who are unacquainted with names and sizes of flies, in ordering, will mention locality in which they are to be used, we can make selections suited to their wants.

On Hooks, 4 to 12 .... $1 00 per dozen.

Alexandria.
Alder.
Black Drake.
Brown Spinner.
Brown Hen.
Brown Hackle.
Brown Coughlin.
Beaverkill.
Brown Adder.
Black Hackle.
Black Prince.
Black Moose.
Black Gnat.
Blue Dun.
Blue Blow.
Cahill.
Cardinal.
Coachman.
Coch-y-bon-dhu.
Cinnamon.
Cowdung.
Claret Gnat.
Canada.
Dark Fox.
Dark Stone.
Downlooker.
English Pheasant.
Furnace Hackle.
Fern.
Green Hackle.
Green Drake.
Gray Miller.
Gold Spinner.
Grizzly King.
Governor.
Gray Hackle.
Great Dun.
Guinea Hen.
Gen. Hooker.
Gold-neck Stork.
Grannom.
Hawthorn.
Jungle Cock.
Jenny Lind.
King of Waters.
Light Stone.
Light Fox.
Lowery.
Montreal.
March Brown.
Orange Miller.
Oriole.
Oak.
Polka.
Professor.
Quaker.
Queen of Waters.
Red Ibis.
Royal Coachman.
Red Spinner.
Red Hackle.
R. W.
Silver-neck Stork.
Seth Green.
Sand.
Seehem.
Shoemaker.
Scarlet Ibis.
Soldier.
Van Patten.
White Miller.
White Moth.
Wood Dock.
Wren Tail.
White Hackle.
Willow Drake.
Yellow Professor.
Yellow Sally.
Yellow Miller.
Yellow Coachman.
Yellow Hackle.

EXTRA QUALITY FLIES—Continued.

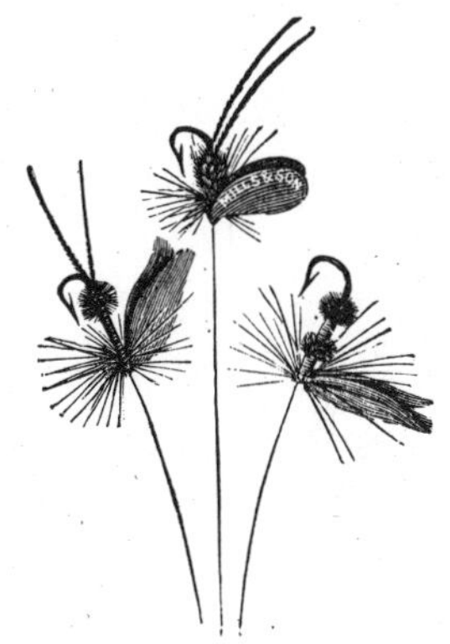

In addition to our regular Trout Flies, we are offering a line of patterns that are specially desirable for stream fishing. All of these have been successfully used by ourselves, and we confidently recommend them. These Flies are tied on light, bronzed Sneck Hooks, Nos. 8, 10, 12, 14, 16. Nos. 14 and 16 are tied on good drawn gut. Selected thin round gut is used for the others and graded according to the size of hook. On the larger sizes, Nos. 8 and 10, the gut is much lighter than usually used, but amply strong, and we consider by using the larger flies on light gut much better results are obtained in most cases than when using the very small sizes.

Price...$1 00 per dozen.

Coachman.
Cahill.
Golden Dun.
Grouse Spider.
Gray Marlow.
Grannom.
Good Evening.
Grizzy King.
Jenny Spinner.
Marlow Buzz.
Mealy Moth.
March Brown.
Oak.
Professor.
Queen.
Special Dun.
Stork.
Stone.
Van Patten.
Yellow Sally.
Wickham's Fancy.

Flies on Eyed Hooks.

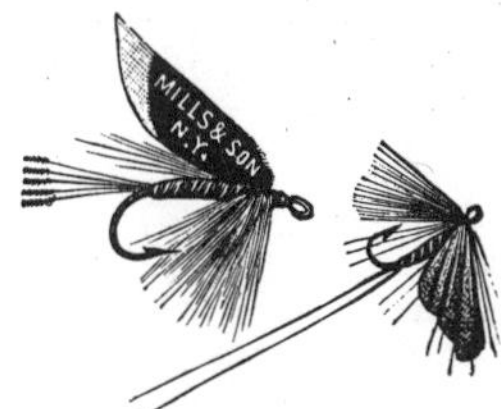

We are now carrying in stock a limited line of the best patterns of Trout Flies on Eyed Hooks.

Price .... $1 00 per dozen.

We can also tie any patterns to order.. 1 25 "

Black Bass Casting, or Maine Trout Flies.

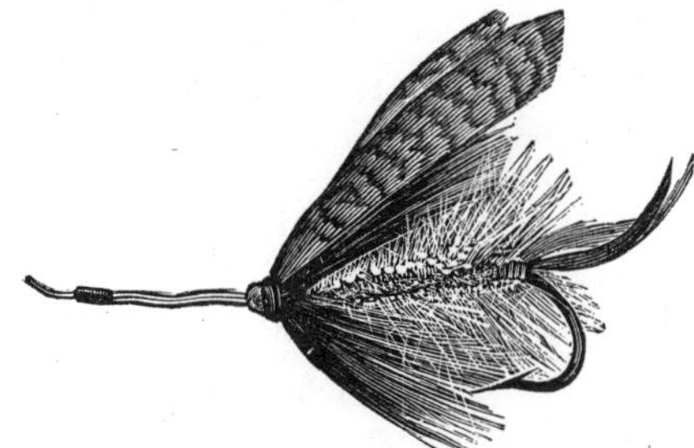

On Hook No. 4.

	Per dozen.
On Hooks, sizes 2 and 4....	$1 75
On Hooks, sizes 2 and 4, with Jungle Cock Feathers over wings..................	2 25

We give a list of the most approved patterns now in use.

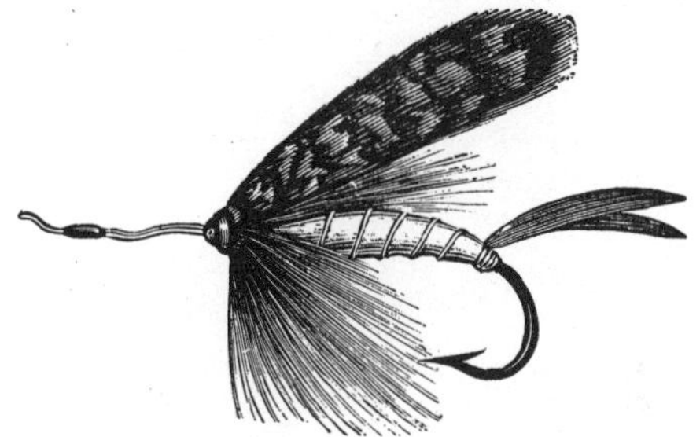

Shows size of Fly on Hook No. 2.

Flies most suitable for Jungle Cock Feathers, and which we have on hand, are marked with *

Alexandria.
Adder.
Alder.
Black Moose.
Brown Hackle.
Brandreth.
Beaverkill.
Black Prince.
Cheney.
*Coachman.
Ferguson.
Gray Hackle.
*Governor.
*Guinea Hen.
Gov. Alvord.
*Grizzly King.
Gen. Hooker.
Green Hackle.
Henshall.
*Ibis and White.
Jungle Cock.
J. H. Mann.
Kingdom.
La Belle.
McLeod.
Magpie.
*Montreal.
Mowry.
Oriole.
Orange and Black.
Page.
*Polka.
*Professor.
Parmachenee Belle.
Queen of Waters.
Quaker
Red Hackle.
*Reuben Wood.
*Royal Coachman.
Soldier.
Silver Doctor.
*Seehem.
Seth Green.
*Scarlet Ibis.
*Tootle Bug.
Wappinger.
*Wood Duck.
White Miller.
*Yellow Professor.

The above are tied on O'Shaughnessy Hooks, on heavy single gut, with double snell "guard" or "helper" at head of fly. Any style tied to order from sample. We are constantly adding new patterns. We cannot too strongly recommend these Flies.

Black Bass Trolling Flies.

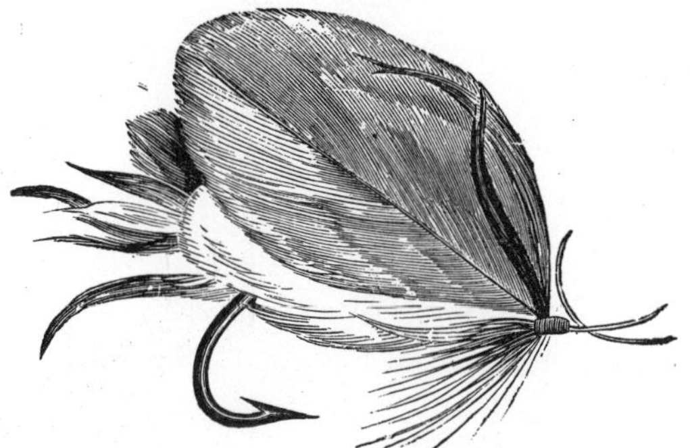

Shows size of Bass Trolling Fly on 2/0 Hook.

On Hooks 3/0, 2/0, Heavy Double Gut ....$3 00 per dozen.

These Trolling Flies are tied with very large, and some patterns have Fancy Jointed and Chenille bodies. Wings and Hackles are very full. They make an exceedingly showy Fly, even after long immersion in the water.

Coachman Fancy.
Cheney.
Daisy.
Ferguson.
Golden Duke.
Grizzly King.
Gray Hackle.
Montreal.
Morris.
Mistake.
Polka.
Page.
R. W.
Seth Green.
Silver Doctor.
St. Lawrence.
Scarlet Ibis.
Scarlet and White.
7. W.
Yellow Ferguson.

EXTRA QUALITY FLIES—Continued.

Our Celebrated Fine Lake Flies.

On O'Shaughnessy Hooks with snell guard or helper..$2 50 per dozen

Richardson.	Racquette.	Rangely.	Saranac.
Chateaugay.	Parson.	Fiery Brown.	Silver Doctor.
Magalloway.	Deacon.	Moosehead.	Oquassoc.
Cupsuptic.	Murray.	Black Jack.	Wood Duck.
Molechunkemunk.	Welokennebacook.	W. J. Cassard.	Volunteer.
Moosehead.	Mooselucmeguntic.	Round Lake.	Thistle.
Blue Jay.	Page.	St. Regis.	Lady Grey.

These fine Lake Flies are elegantly dressed with fancy feathers, and being tied in same manner as Salmon Flies, are very showy, strong and durable.

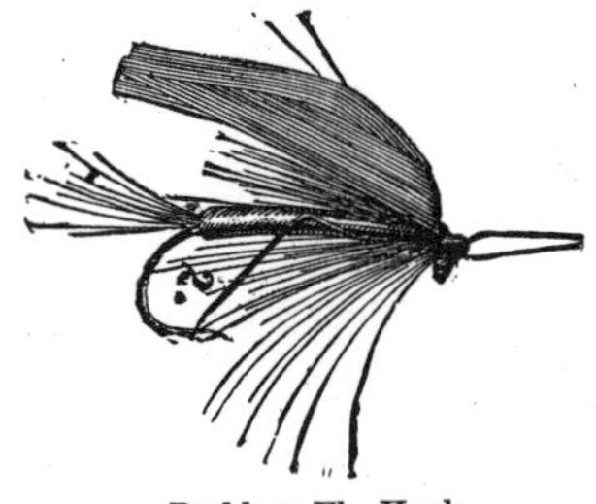

Barbless Fly Hook.

Flies on the Celebrated Barbless Hooks.

PATTERNS SAME AS ON ORDINARY HOOKS.

	Per dozen.
Trout and Grayling	$2 25
Bass Casting and Maine Trout	3 00
Bass Trolling	4 50

Salmon Flies.

We have a full line of the Celebrated Scotch Flies on double and single hooks.

PRICES ON APPLICATION.

William Mills & Son's "Floating" Flies, for Trout and Bass.

MADE IN ABOUT TWENTY BEST PATTERNS.

Trout size, assorted styles.............................. $1 25 per dozen.
Bass Casting or Maine Trout, assorted styles............ 2 25 "

These Flies are tied with heavy double wings and buoyant bodies, and are very natural and lifelike in motion.

New Insects for Trout and Black Bass.

These Insects are made with fish-scale wings which are almost indestructible; they are an excellent imitation of the insect they are tied to represent; they will be found very attractive to the fish, and at the low price charged, must become very popular.

For Trout, on medium and small hooks, on heavy single gut, see patterns below........................20c. each.
For Bass, on large hooks, with small, strong gut loop, see patterns below........................25c. "
For Trout, in fancy patterns, very showy........................20c. "
For Bass, in fancy patterns, very showy........................25c. "

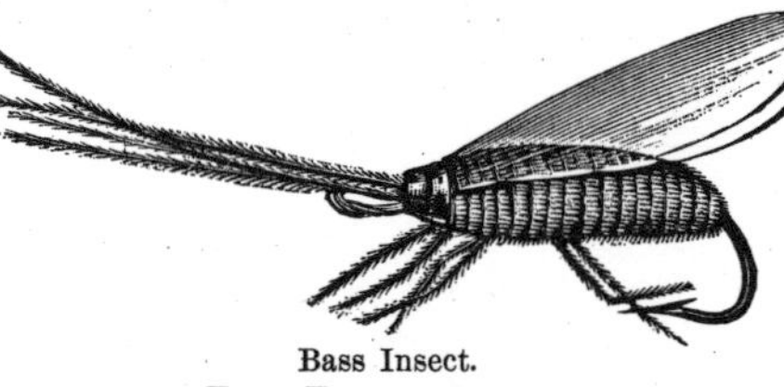

Bass Insect.

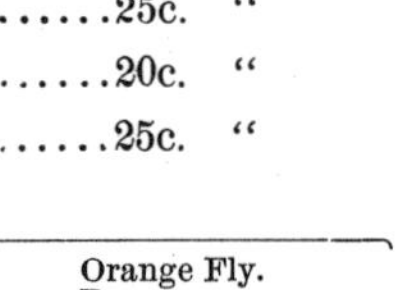

Trout Patterns.

Red Spinner.	White Moth.	Fern.	Orange Fly.
Water Cricket.	Black Gnat.	Green Drake.	Bee.
Golden Midge.	Downlooker.	Gray Drake.	Blue Bottle.
Stone.	Turkey Brown.	Dark Mackerel.	Yellow Grasshopper.
Jenny Spinner.	Little Dark Spinner.	Silver Horns.	Green Grasshopper.

Bass Patterns.

White Moth.	Gray Hornet.
Bee.	Brown Beetle.
Green Grasshopper.	Cricket.
Yellow Fly.	Yellow Hornet.
Yellow Grasshopper.	Black.

William Mills & Son's Fine Natural Insects.

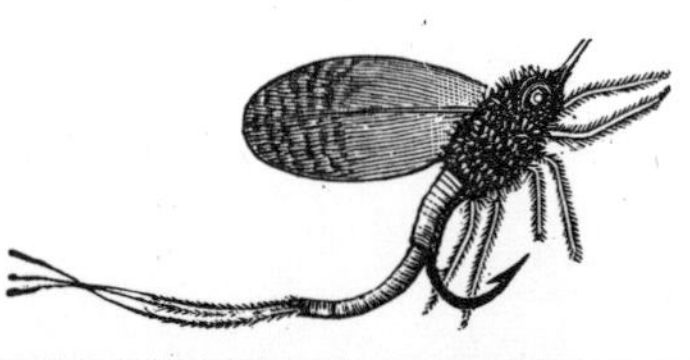

These are tied from live bugs and flies for patterns, and are a perfect imitation of the most killing trout baits known, having eyes, wings, legs, etc. Are very strong and durable, and are quite a work of art, $5.00 per dozen.

We can make to order an exact imitation of any insect sent us in good condition.

SILK WORM GUT LEADERS—Continued.

Class 3.

If sometimes a heavier leader is considered preferable, and perhaps necessary, particularly with a stiff, quick rod, we offer our Nos. 5 and 5½; which will meet all requirements. But we wish to say that the supply of Gut used in the manufacture of the Nos. 5 and 5½, is limited, and at times extremely scarce, so that we cannot always supply them.

		3	6	9 feet.	
No. 5.	Best Black Bass, Single	$4 80	$9 60	$14 40	per dozen.
" 5½.	Same as No. 5, with Extra Loops for Dropper Flies	4 80	9 60	14 40	"
" 8XX.	Heavy Cable Laid	6 60	....	....	"
" 8AA.	Double Cable Laid	4 80	....	....	"

SILK WORM GUT.

WHITE OR STAINED.

We have, through our correspondents in London and elsewhere, the best facilities for obtaining such Gut as we want, and although not claiming to use *nine-tenths* of the production, in our stock will always be found a sufficient supply of Fresh Gut, of a quality that will suit the most particular angler, and we very much doubt if there is any house in this country that uses more of the article (in the better grades) than we do.

		10	11	12	inches long.
No. 50.	Ordinary Trout	$3 75	$4 50	$5 15	per thousand.
		40	50	60	per hundred.
" 60.	Best Trout	4 75	5 50	5 80	per thousand.
		50	60	65	per hundred.
" 70.	Best Bass	5 50	6 80	7 80	per thousand.
		60	75	85	per hundred.
" 80.	Extra Bass	7 85	10 20	12 25	per thousand.
		85	1 15	1 40	per hundred.
" 90.	Heavy Salmon	24 00	34 00	40 80	per thousand.
		2 50	3 50	4 20	per hundred.

" 110. Special Extra Heavy Salmon, about 11½ inches, very scarce and cannot always be furnished. .$10 00 to $12 00 per hundred.

Above Gut quoted is *best quality*. We usually have a supply of most of the above grades and lengths in second quality, and also Gut in shorter lengths, 6½ to 8½ inches, and longer lengths up to 14 inches. Prices on application.

Selected Gut, Stained Mist Color.

For the past few years we have made a practice of keeping on hand, at all times, SELECTED GUT, ranging from 14 to 20 inches long, in the different grades. All the strands in each hundred are perfect and very uniform in size; of course, selecting the good and rejecting the worthless strands must necessarily make the price somewhat higher, but it is better value to the buyer. To those desiring Extra Choice and Long Gut, see description and prices below.

Very Fine Trout, about 15 inches, $1.50 per hundred; 20 inches	$2 00	per hundred.
Fine Trout, 15 to 16 inches	1 25	"
Heavy Trout, 15 to 16 inches	1 50	"
Bass, 15 to 16 inches	1 75	"
Heavy Bass, 15 to 16 inches	4 00	"
Extra Fine and Medium Drawn Gut, 14 inches, $1.75 per hundred; 16 inches	2 50	"

BEST QUALITY SILK GIMP.

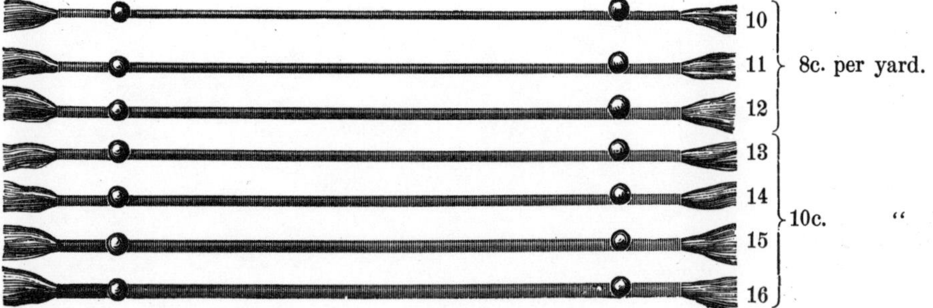

Gimp, in quantity, all sizes........ 60 cents per ounce.

ARTIFICIAL MINNOWS.

Caledonian, Size No. 6.

Caledonian Minnows.

Nos	2	3	4	5
Length of Minnow	1¾	2	2⅛	2½ in.
Per dozen	$5 76	$5 76	$5 76	$5 76
Nos	6	7	8	9
Length of Minnow	3	3¼	3¾	4¼ in.
Per dozen	$7 20	$8 76	$10 68	$11 64

Protean Minnow.

Nos	3	4	5	6
Length of Minnow	2	2⅜	3	3½ inches.
Per dozen	$3 72	$3 72	$4 68	$5 76

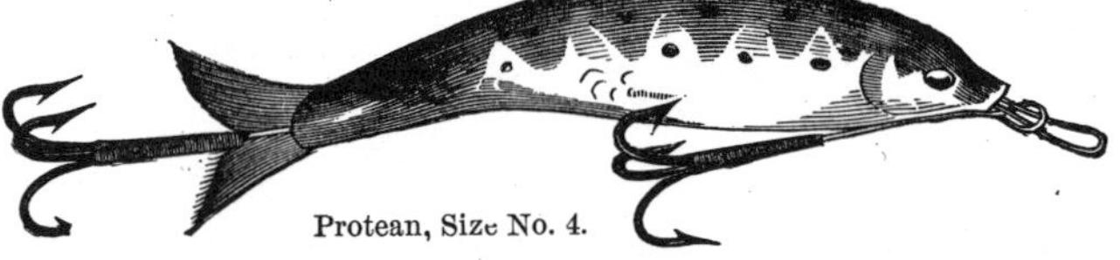

Protean, Size No. 4.

Metal Devon Minnow.

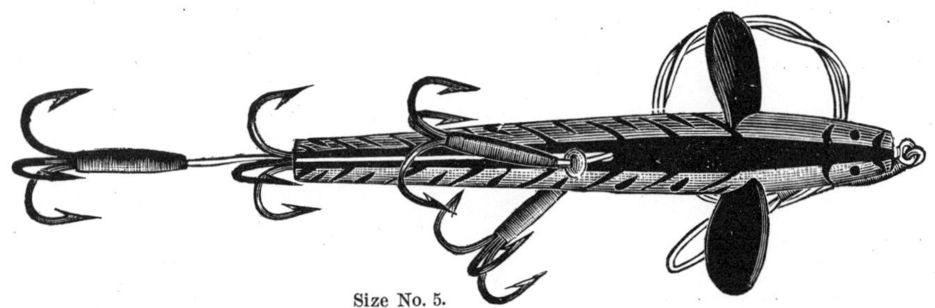

Size No. 5.

Nos	3	4	5	6
Length of Minnow	2	2½	3	3½ inch.
An Excellent Minnow for Bass.	$0 51	$0 54	$0 63	$0 72 each.

Celebrated Phantom Minnow.

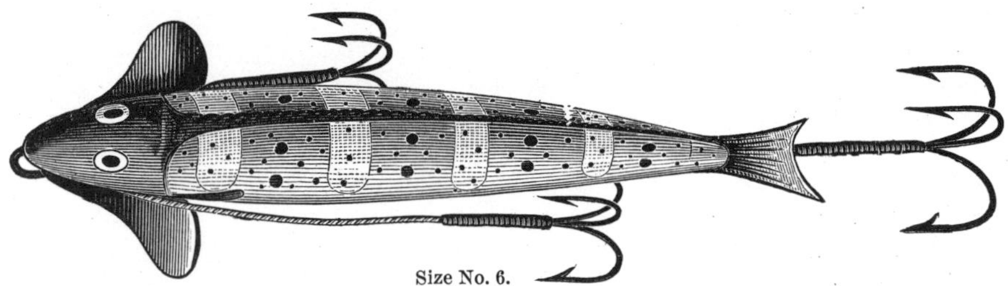

Size No. 6.

Made of Silk, coated with Rubber, very light, very fine for Black Bass and Pickerel.

Nos	00	0	1	2	3	4	5	6	7	8	9	10
Length of Minnow	1⅜	1½	1¾	2¼	2½	3	3½	4	4¼	4½	5	5½ inches.
	$0 60	$0 60	$0 60	$0 60	$0 60	$0 60	$0 60	$0 66	$0 78	$0 87	$1 02	$1 15 each.

"NEW" WHITE PHANTOM. Nos	3	4	5	6	7	8	9
Length of Minnow	2½	3	3½	4	4¼	4½	5 inch.
	$0 72	$0 72	$0 72	$0 84	$0 96	$1 04	$1 17 each.

SOLE SKIN PHANTOM. Nos	3	4	5	6	7	8	9	10
Length of Minnow	2½	3	3½	4	4¼	4½	5	5½ inch.
	$0 84	$0 84	$0 84	$0 96	$1 04	$1 17	$1 35	$1 50 each.

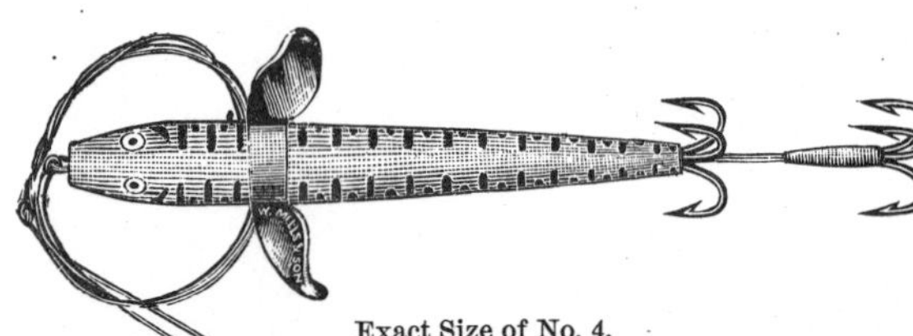

Exact Size of No. 4.

The New "Quill" Devon Minnow.

Nos	3	4	5
Length of Minnow	1¾	2	2¼ inch.
	$0 80	$1 00	$1 10 each.

Sand Eels.

Nos	4	5
Length	3½	4½ inches.
	$0 38	$0 40 each.

ARTIFICIAL SOFT RUBBER INSECTS.

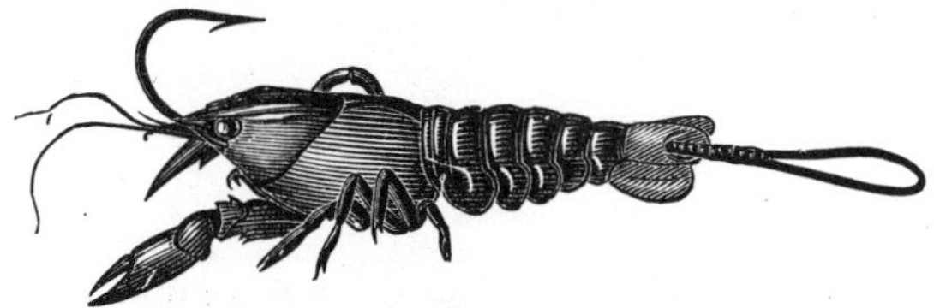
SOFT RUBBER CRAWFISH. Patented October 1, 1878, 40c. each.

SOFT RUBBER HELGAMITE OR DOBSON, Large (See cut) or Small, 30c. each.

Soft Rubber Frogs.

	Per dozen.
Large	$3 60
Small	2 40

Small.

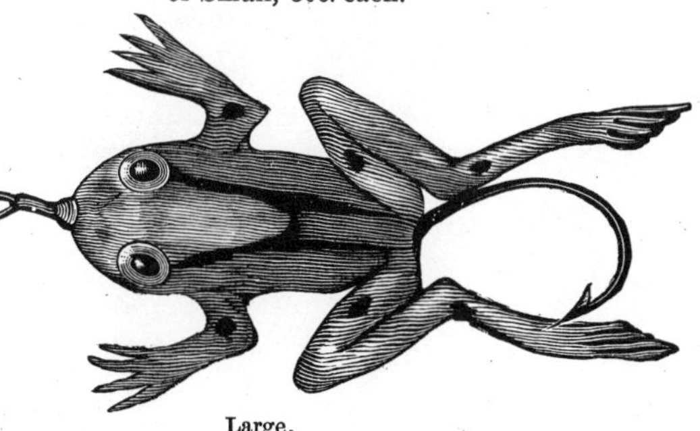
Large.

TROLLING SPOONS.—CLASS 1

Superfine Fly Spoons.

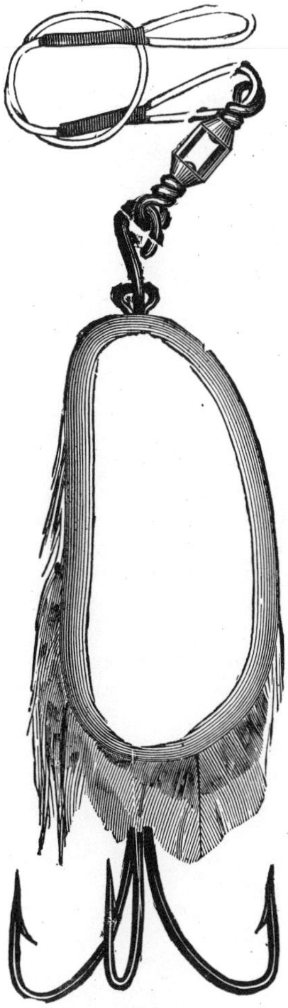

No. 1.  No. 2. 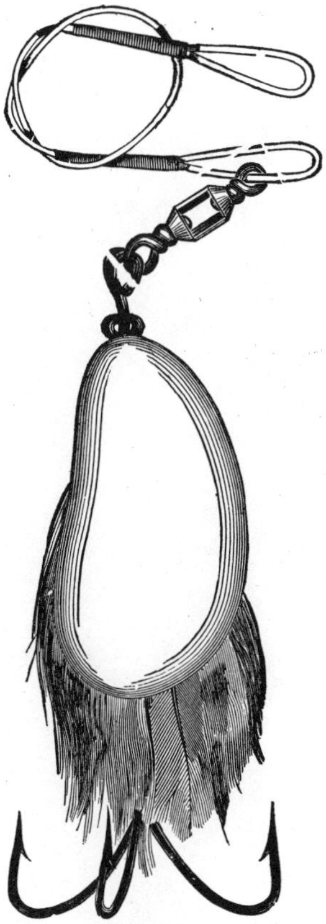 No. 3. 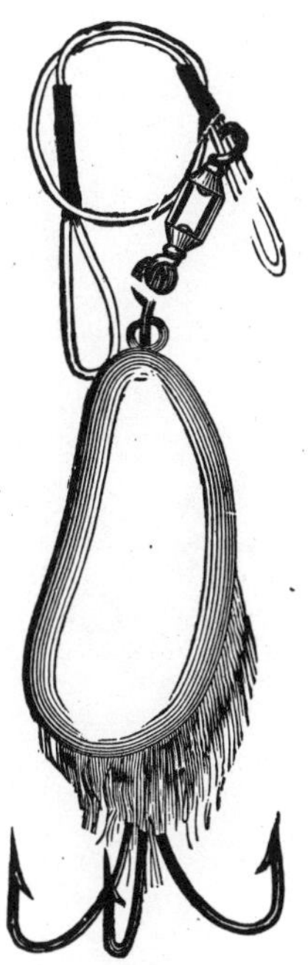 No. 4. 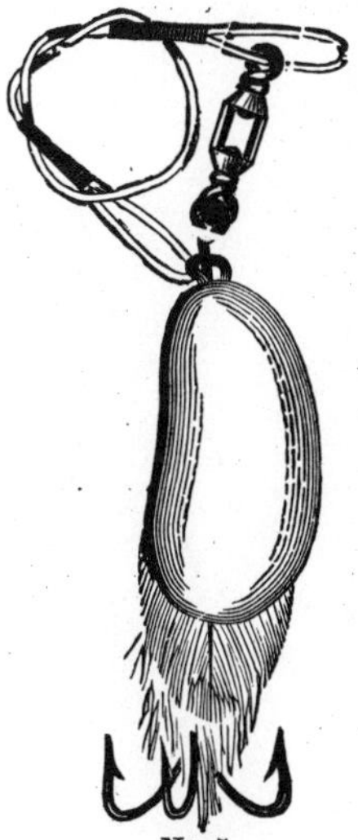 No. 5.

	Per dozen.
PIKE SPOONS, Polished Tin, Feathered, but no Swivel, sizes 1, 2, 3, 4, 5	$0 90
PICKEREL SPOONS, Polished Tin, Loose Treble Hooks, Feathered and Swivel, sizes 1, 2, 3, 4, 5	1 20
SUPERFINE FLY SPOONS, Nickel Plated, Loose Treble Hooks, Feathered Swivel and Gimp, sizes 1, 2, 3, 4, 5	1 50
SUPERFINE FLY SPOONS, Burnished Copper, Nicely Feathered, Swivel and Gimp, Nos. 1, 2, 3, 4, 5	1 80

HOOK AND TACKLE BOOKS.

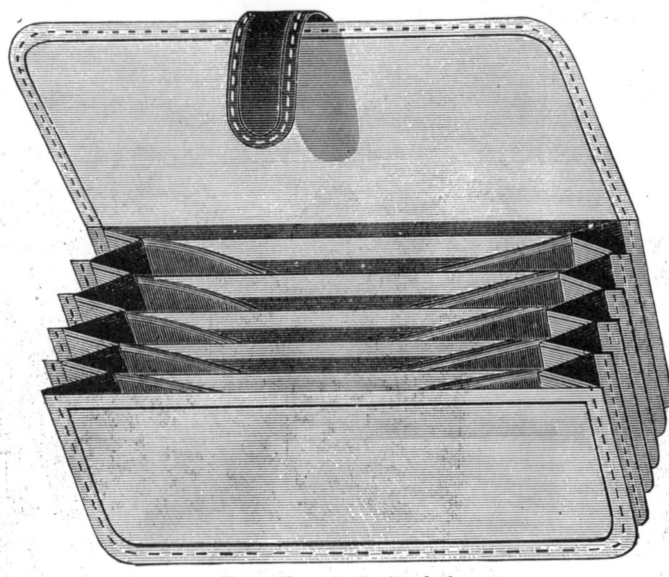

Shows Nos. 14, 15, 17 and 18.

LEATHER.

Nos.		Each.
14.	AMERICAN RUSSIAN COVER, 4 large and 3 small canvas pockets, 2 small pockets in cover, stitched and pockets bound, 6¼ inches long	$0 60
15.	SIMILAR IN STYLE TO No. 14. Length, 7½ inches	90
16.	AMERICAN RUSSIA COVER, 11 large parchment pockets, partitions in cover for carrying small tools, etc., nickel clasp 6¼ inches long	1 25
17.	IMITATION ALLIGATOR COVER, 6 large and 5 small canvas pockets, leather bound and stitched; fastens with straps: length, 6¾ inches	1 25
18.	SIMILAR IN STYLE TO No. 17. Length, 8 inches	1 75
43.	HANDSOME RUSSIA LEATHER, 8 inches long, lined with leather, sewed and bound, 9 large pockets, 8 small ones, with strap	2 25

CANVAS.

Nos.		Per dozen
56.	7 inches long, stitched and cloth bound, 4 large pockets and 3 small ones, with strap	$6 00
53.	8 inches long, slate colored, leather bound, 5 large pockets, 3 small ones, with strap.	10 20
1SW.	9½ x 3½ inches, stitched and cloth bound, 4 large and 3 small pockets	6 00
2SW.	12 x 3½ inches, stitched and cloth bound, 6 large and 5 small pockets. Takes snelled hooks at full length	7 20

The "Levison" Fly Book.

(PATENTED MARCH 11, 1884, MARCH 9, 1886.)

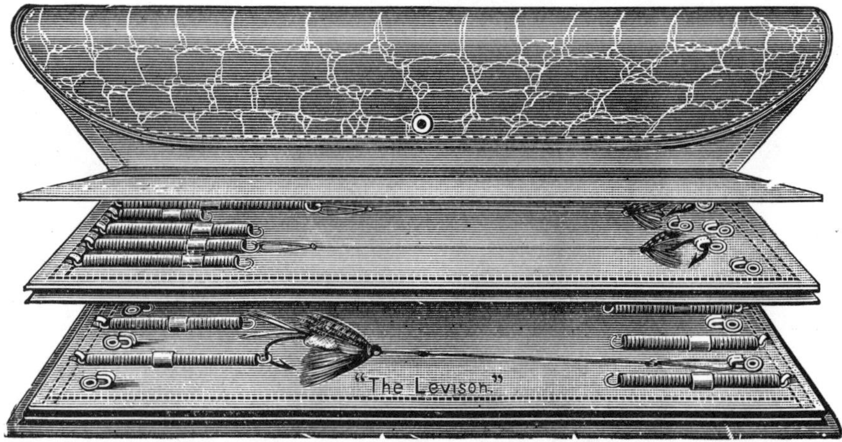

Our illustration shows one page arranged for Trout and one for Bass Flies. Small Flies as well as large can be held on the Bass arrangement.

In the "Levison" we have the PERFECT FLY BOOK. Each Fly is held in the book at full length and SEPARATELY by a spring and hook made especially for this purpose. Any fly can be taken out and returned readily without disturbing any of the others. The books are 7½ inches long and made in two widths, the regular width being about 4½ inches, the narrow being 3½ inches.

In our regular arrangement the above books of 2, 3, 4 leaves, contain one leaf arranged for Bass Flies. Either style will be arranged for all Trout or all Bass Flies, as purchaser may wish; mention in ordering how you wish them arranged.

The inventor of this book has also devised a means for holding knotted end dropper Flies, so much used. The device is simply a SLOTTED HOOK (Patented March 9, 1886) which holds the knotted end of gut perfectly secure, and which we put on the top row on the Trout leaf and on each end of Bass leaf.

SHOWS SLOTTED HOOK FOR HOLDING KNOTTED END DROPPER FLIES.

FISHING BASKETS.

Trout Basket.

Nos......	1/0	1	2	3	
Capacity..	6	9	12	20	lbs.
	$0 75	$0 90	$1 00	$1 25 each.	
Nos......	4	5	6		
Capacity..	25	30	35	lbs.	
	$1 50	$2 00	$2 50 each.		

Square Basket.

(With Single or Double Lid.)

Best.

Size about 14 inches,	No. 1B..	$2 75 each.
" 16 "	No. 2B..	3 25 "
" 18 "	No. 3B..	4 00 "

Second Quality.

Size about 14 inches,	No. 1....	$1 25 each.
" 16 "	No. 2....	1 50 "

The "Lody Smith."

(Made in 1 Size, No. 3, 30 lbs.)

Has composition cover, opening on end instead of centre. The opening is protected by metal spring hinged lid, closing automatically. The cover is hinged to basket by strong and ornamental metal hinges, and secured in front when closed by metal fastening. The basket is finished either with a durable coat of drab paint or two coats of best varnish, and is very strong and durable. $5 00 each.

Page 104: Chancellor Levison, a notable gadgeteer of this era, improved on Bray's patent by using a tiny coiled spring to stretch the snell of each fly. These books are no longer made—too expensive to make and too bulky to carry.

Old Chance posed, in derby hat and cutaway coat, for the casting pictures in Henry P. Wells's *Fly Rods and Fly Tackle*. He was an expert caster and fisherman.

Page 107: This picturesque old boy in his head net graced tackle catalogs year after year for half a century. This is one of about four different "stock cuts" the various manufacturers supplied to the tackle trade for catalogs. We'll see the others shortly.

Page 108: Rube Wood, a famous fisherman and tournament caster of this era, combined the pine tar and oil of pennyroyal in old Nessmuk's fly-dope formula with a heavy cup grease and sold tons of his compound over the years. Even today salmon fishermen sometimes beguile a long winter evening by putting on a flannel shirt, doping up with the tarry-smelling Lollacapop, and reading a fishing book before the blaze of an open fireplace. It puts them in the mood.

Page 110: Every fisherman has one of these cutters to hook over the high twig that has detained his fly. The rod tip is then withdrawn and a haul on the cord severs the twig—or would if the cutter were not in the angler's duffle bag, back at the cabin.

SWIVELS—Continued.

Brass Triple Action Swivel, No. 1.

Swivels.—Class 2.

Nos	2/0	1/0	1 to 5
BEST BRASS TRIPLE ACTION SWIVEL	$1 00	$0 80	$0 60 per dozen.

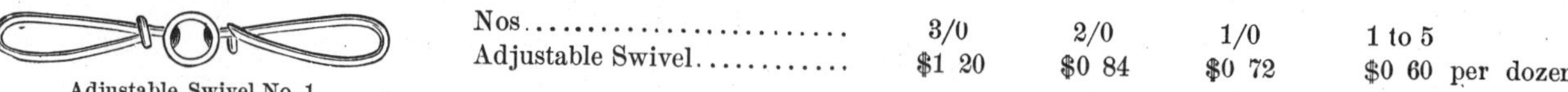

Adjustable Swivel No. 1.

Nos	3/0	2/0	1/0	1 to 5
Adjustable Swivel	$1 20	$0 84	$0 72	$0 60 per dozen.

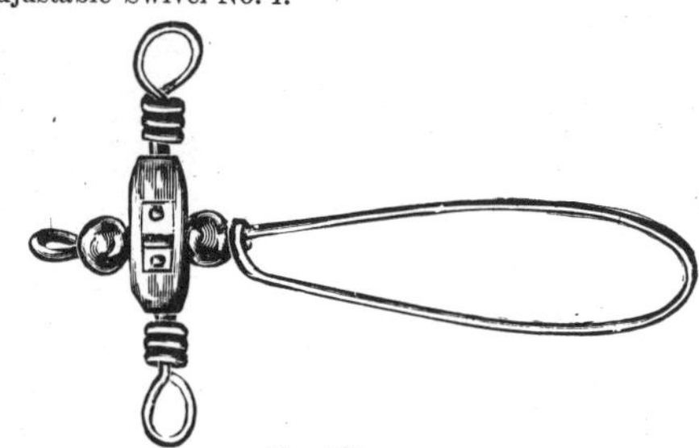

No. 101.

"T" Swivel with Adjustable Loop........ $1 00 per dozen.

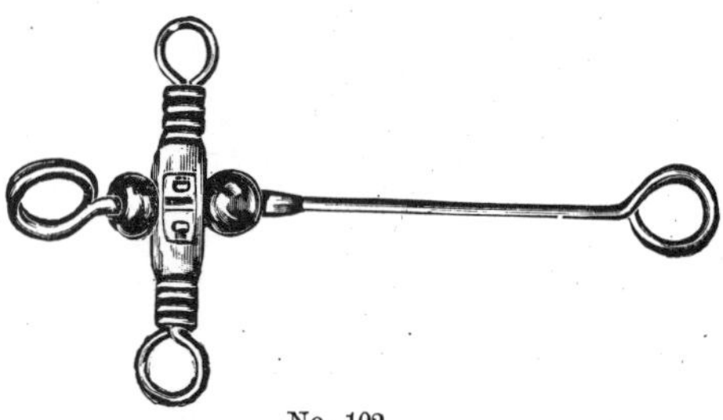

No. 102.

"T" Swivel with Adjustable Ring........ $1 00 per dozen.

C. L. Bollermann's Patent Rotary Leader Links.

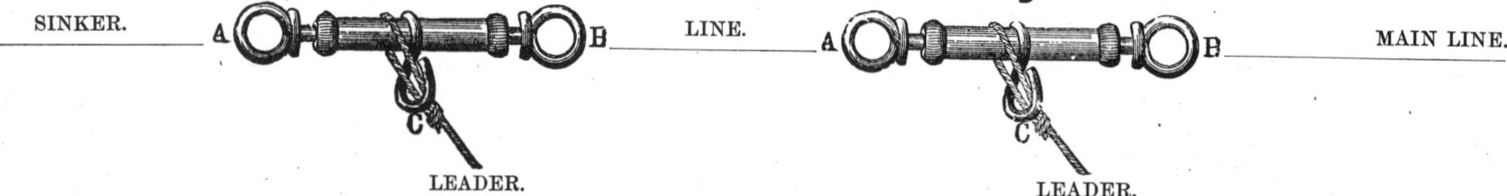

A simple and substantial device for the purpose of removing the cause of the entanglement of the leaders or hooks with the fishing line. C. L BOLLERMANN'S ROTARY LEADER LINKS render leaders and fishing line mutually independent as to their motions, turns and twists, and thereby do away with the cause for entanglement.

How to Apply.—Intersect the links to fishing line, at distance from sinker, to suit, by means of loops **A** and **B,** so that the links in position really form parts or sections of the main fishing line. Then attach your leader or hook to loop **C,** forming part of hollow revolving cylinder around spindle **A, B.** All motions, turns or twists, of the fishing line are thereby confined to the line itself, and leave the position of the leader or hook perfectly free or neutral, rendering entanglement with the line impossible.

$1.00 per dozen, or $0.10 each.

NOTICE.—There has been some difficulty in the past to obtain these goods. We can now supply them in any quantities, having recently purchased Mr. Bollermann's patent, and will always have a good stock of them on hand.

ROD MOUNTINGS.

Tips.

Three Ring Tips.

Nos. Large. Medium. Small.

Nos. 1 to 6.. $0 60 dozen.

German Silver.

Large German Silver Tips.

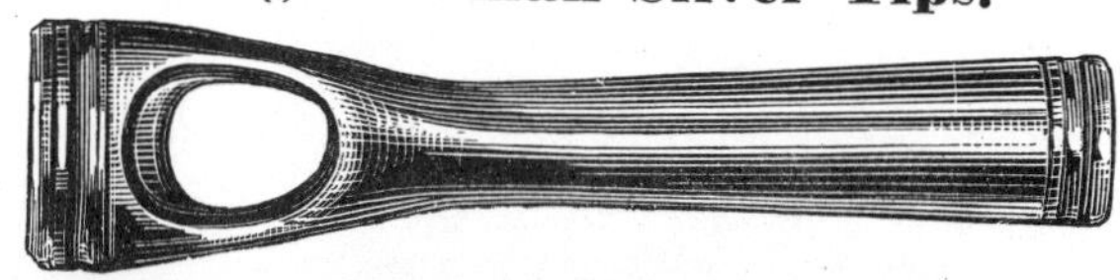

Large German Silver Tip No. 5/0.

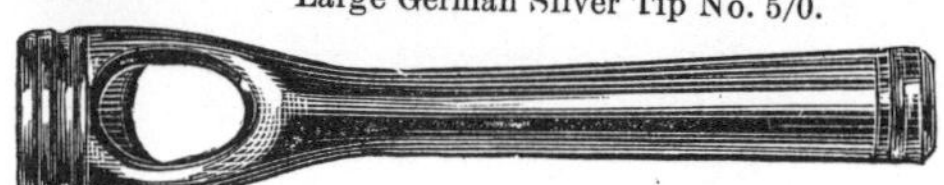

German Silver Tip No. 3/0.

Nos.	5/0	4/0	3/0	2/0	1/0	1	2	3	
Diameter of Tube	$\frac{14}{32}$	$\frac{12}{32}$	$\frac{10}{32}$	$\frac{8}{32}$	$\frac{6}{32}$	$\frac{5}{32}$	$\frac{4}{32}$	$\frac{3}{32}$	inch.
Nickel with Solid Tops	$0 20	$0 20	$0 20	$0 20	$0 20	$0 20	$0 20	$0 20	each.
German Silver with Solid Tops	40	40	40	40	40	40	40	40	"
German Silver with Screw Tops	60	60	60	60	60	60	60	60	"
German Silver with Agate Tops	1 25	1 25	1 25	1 25	1 25	1 25	1 25	1 25	"

ROD HOLDERS.

The "Dayton."

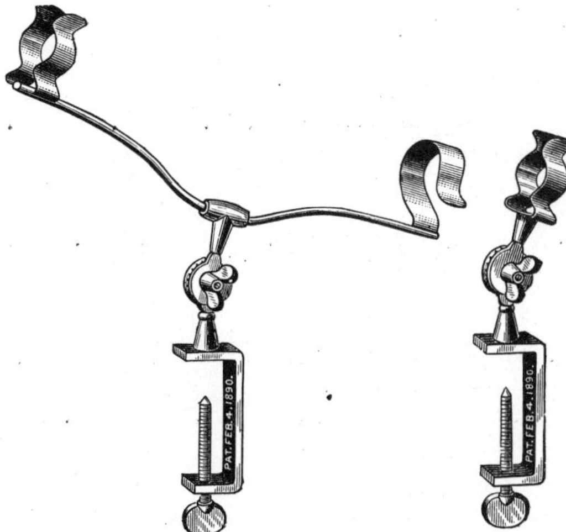
No. 1. No. 2.

We wish to call particular attention to the "**Dayton Rod Rest and Holder**" in its **simplicity, lightness** and **ease** of **adjustment** at **any angle.**

The light weight and compactness of the "**Dayton**" overcomes the hitherto most serious objection to the use of anything for this purpose.

While it is not practical for the angler to carry about with him an implement that weighs a pound, in the "**Dayton**" this objection is obviated.

WEIGHTS.

No. 1, 9 inches long, **Weighs only 5¾ ounces.**
No. 2, 7½ " " " **4¼** "

The former will readily pack in the larger size Tackle Boxes, and several of the No. 2 can be carried without inconvenience in **any** of the Tackle Boxes now offered.

It is made almost entirely of **Spring Brass,** which gives it sufficient **strength,** and is **handsomely Nickel-plated**, being a very attractive as well as useful article to the angler.

Every angler who does any boat fishing should have at least one of these holders in his outfit.

PRICES.

No. 1.. $1 50 each.
No. 2.. 1 25 "
No. 3 (1 and 2 combined, with single clamp).. 2 00 "

The Handy.

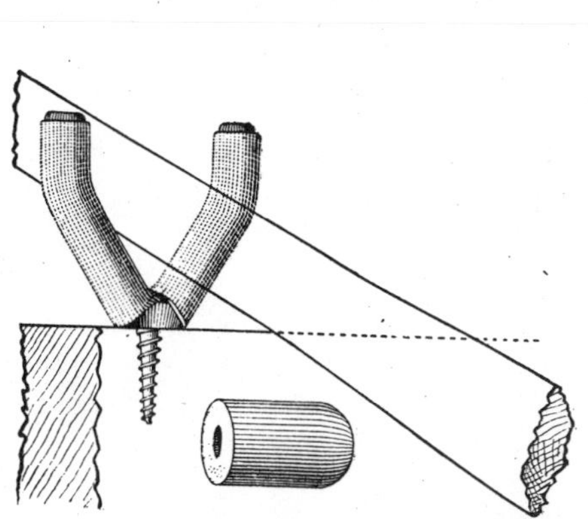
No. 1. Space between forks....¾ inch.
No. 1½. Space between forks...1¼ inches.

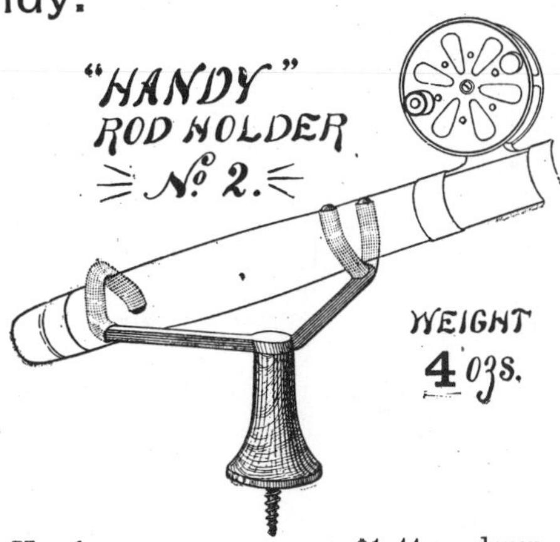

No. 1..................... $1 44 per dozen.
No. 1½..................... 1 92 "
No. 2..................... 4 80 "

DISGORGERS.

Plain.

PLAIN BRASS DISGORGER.. 5c. each.

Improved.

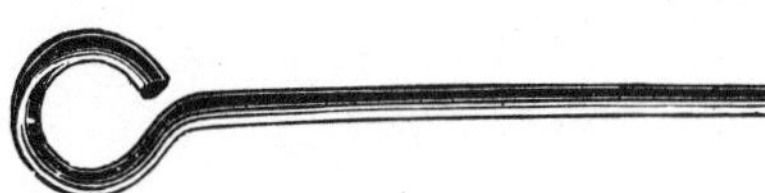

Nos.
1. For Trout, Perch and other small fish.. $0 20 each.
2. For Bass, Pike and Pickerel.. 30 "
3. For Muskallonge and large Bluefish.. 1 00 "

HEAD NETS.

A SURE PROTECTION AGAINST MOSQUITOES AND FLIES.

Tarlatan or Mosquito Bar, with case............ 75c. each.

INSECT REPELLANTS.

FOR PROTECTION AGAINST MOSQUITOES, BLACK FLIES, GNATS, ETC.

Hind's Fly Cream.............$3 00 per dozen.

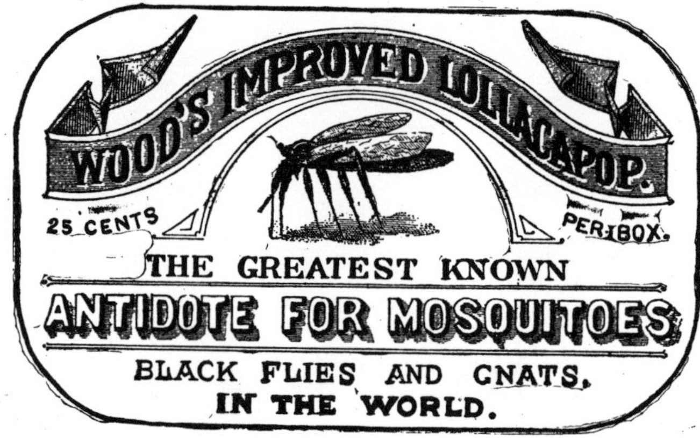

Lollacapop.................$3 00 per dozen.

WADING STOCKINGS AND PANTS.

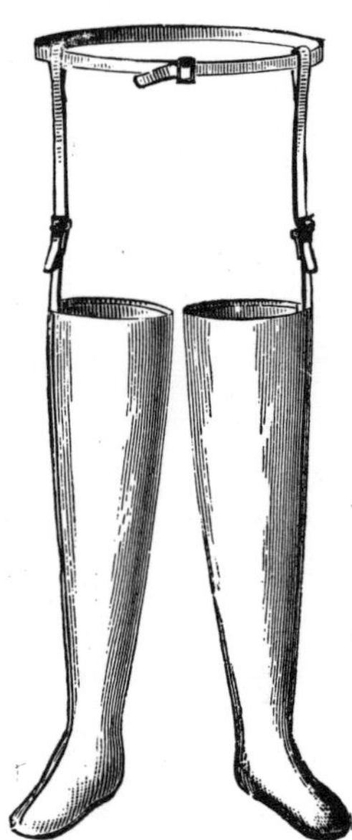

Wading Stockings.

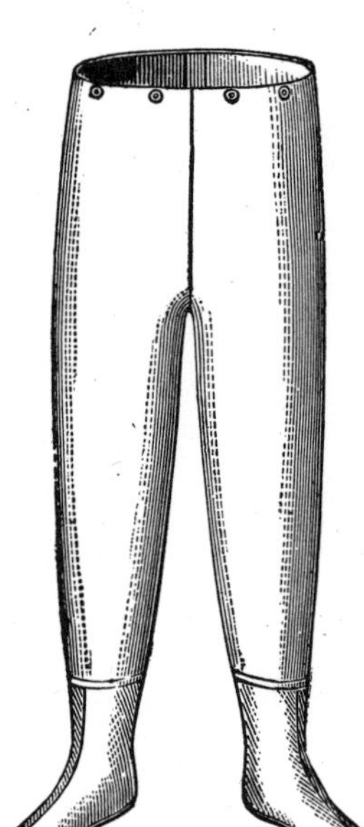

Wading Pants.

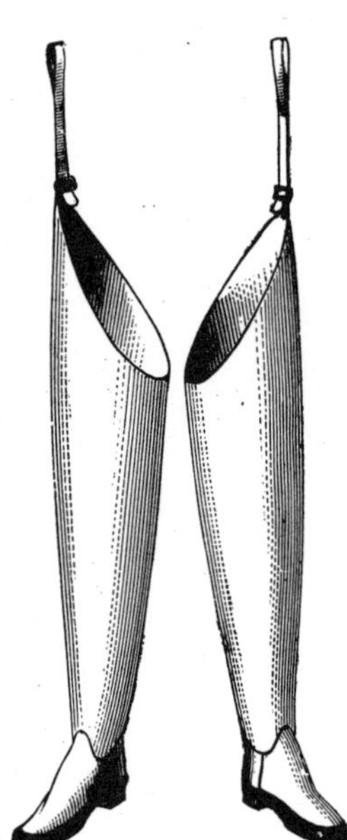

Stockings with Boots.

Nos.		With Stocking Feet.	With Rubber Boot Feet.
70.	Wading Stockings, Black Rubber, Best Make	$4 50	.... per pair.
71.	Wading Pants, Black Rubber, Best Make	6 00	.... "
72.	Wading Stockings, Double Texture, Medium Weight	7 50	$10 00 "
73.	Wading Pants, Double Texture, Medium Weight	10 00	14 00 "

The above medium weight goods we recommend as very desirable, having worn this kind for several seasons.

80. Wading Stockings with Boots, with Rubber and Cork Projecting Soles .... $10 00 per pair.
81. Wading Pants, with Boots, with Rubber and Cork Projecting Soles......... 14 00 "

Special attention given to selecting all Stockings and Pants to fit properly. Special sizes made to order at a slight advance in price.

RUBBER GOODS—Continued.

Rubber Camp Bags.

WITH HANDLE. FOR CARRYING CLOTHING, BLANKETS, SUPPLIES, ETC. ENTIRELY WATERPROOF.

Size.	Black Rubber.	Double Texture.
20 x 26 inch	$2 25	$4 50
22 x 30 inch	2 75	5 00
24 x 33 inch	3 25	5 50

Rubber Camp Blankets.

	Each.
Lustre, 52 x 72 inches	$1 50
Flannel Lined, 52 x 78 inches	3 50
Flannel Lined, 62 x 78 inches	4 00
Flannel Lined, 78 x 78 inches	4 50
Best Plaid, Lined, 72 x 78 inches	8 00
Poncho Blanket, 52 x 78 inches	2 25

Dunklee's Camping Stoves.

This is the best portable stove ever made. It broils, bakes or boils perfectly. It will add much to the camper's comfort.

No. 0 PACKED.

No. 1 PACKED.

No. 1.

The ware is so constructed that it nests and packs in the oven, and the oven and funnel pack inside of the stove, in which there is also room for Plates, Knives, Forks, Spoons, etc.

No. 0. Outside dimensions packed, 10x12x14; weight, about 20 pounds. Will cook for four persons. The ware consists of 8 quart Kettle, 6 quart Tea Kettle, 2 quart Coffee Pot, Fry Pan, Dipper, Broiler, Tent Collar, 8 foot Funnel and Oven. Price, complete $11 50

No. 1. Outside dimensions, 12x12x20; weight, about 30 pounds. Those desiring something light and durable, and in every way fitted for camping purposes, will find this stove exactly right. Will cook for 10 persons. The ware consists of 8 quart Kettle, 2 quart Tea Kettle, 2 quart Coffee Pot, Fry Pan, round Tin Pan, 2 square Pans, Dipper, Gridiron, Tent Collar, and 8 foot Funnel and Oven. Price, complete 15 00

Combination Pliers for Anglers.

Six tools in one, viz.:

1. Strong ordinary Pliers.
2. Shot Splitter.
3. Wire Cutter.
4. Extra strong Cutter for heavy wire
5. Screw Driver.
6. Counter Sink.

Made of highest grade steel .... $1 50 each.

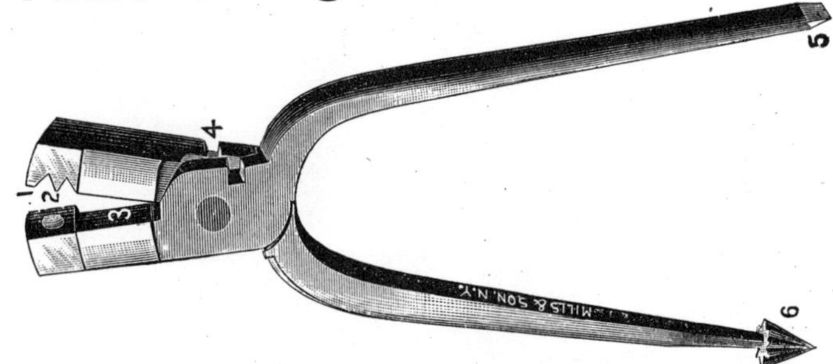

Cut two-thirds actual size.

Adirondack Pack Baskets.

Best Make, with Wide Strap, weight about 4 pounds .... $3 50 each.

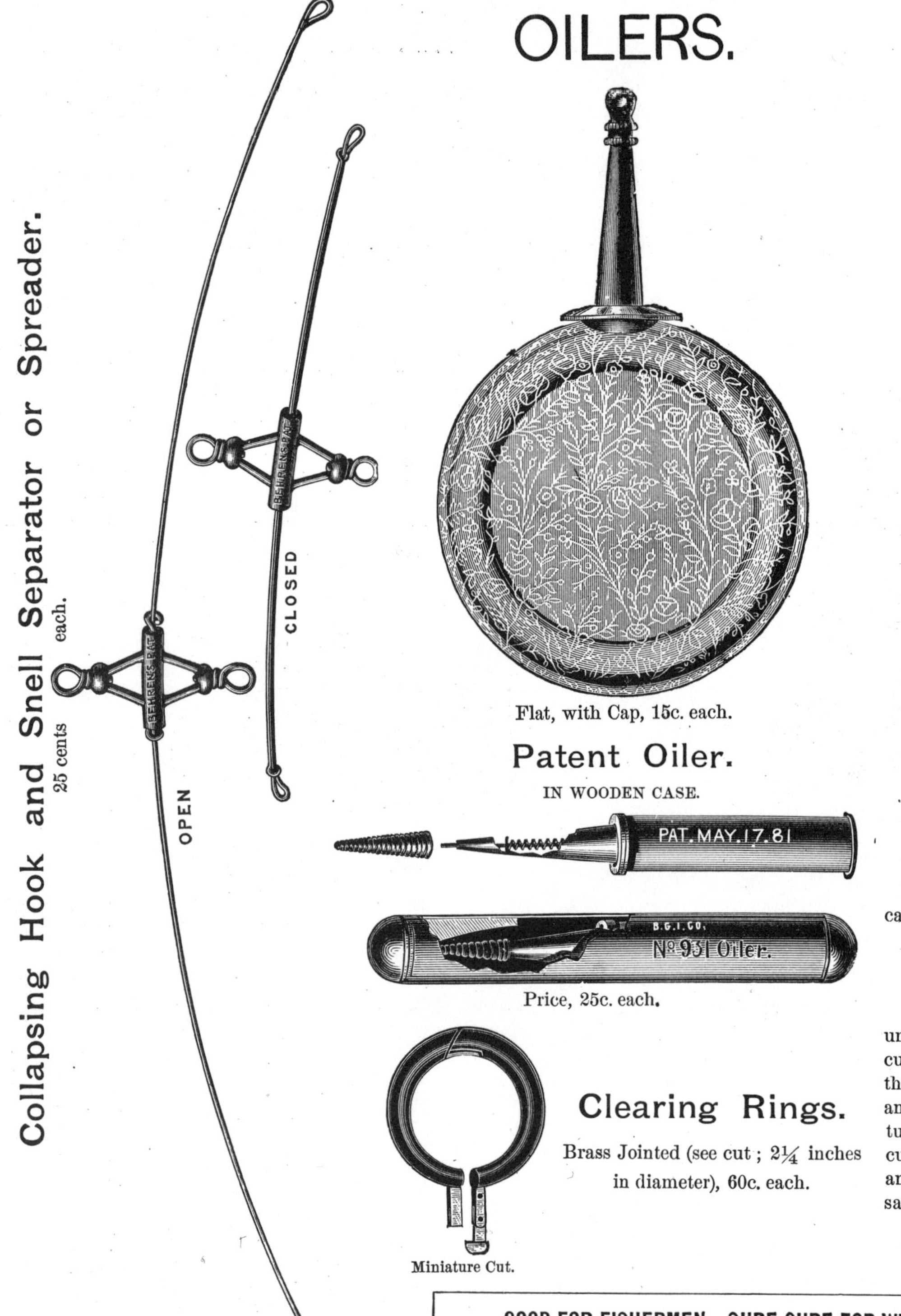

Collapsing Hook and Snell Separator or Spreader.

25 cents each.

OILERS.

Flat, with Cap, 15c. each.

Patent Oiler.

IN WOODEN CASE.

Price, 25c. each.

Clearing Rings.

Brass Jointed (see cut; 2¼ inches in diameter), 60c. each.

Miniature Cut.

THIS IS IT

Did you ever get your Flies caught up a tree? Well—

USE A

"Releaser."

Insert the tip of your rod under the rubber band (see cut), and with your rod raise the RELEASER to the twig and withdraw rod. A slight tug on the attached cord will cut the twig, down it comes, and your flies and leader are saved.

Price, $1.00 each

In Leather Case.

To remove the guard and hook, push up the slide, bend free end of wire loop outward **a very little,** and then force the guard round the corner. **Do not straighten out the loop.**

When live bait is hooked in the mouth, **the hook must pass downward through the upper jaw first,** as shown in the cut. This holds the bait right side up, and gives it the appearance of life even when dead. With other hooks, minnows and frogs will float belly up when dead or disabled.

It consists in a Weed Guard, having the weight of a Sinker and the attractions of a Lure, which is pivoted to the ringed eye of a fish hook in line with the point. It hangs below and forward of the hook, where it swings backward and forward automatically, actuated by its own gravity and the contact with water, weeds, snags, etc., leaving the hook fully exposed to fish, yet guarding it perfectly.

On an order for one dozen we send 2-2/o, 8-4/o, and 2-7/o, if not otherwise specified. The 4/o is the best selling size and the best for all round fishing.

GOOD FOR FISHERMEN. SURE CURE FOR WEEDS AND SNAGS.

Payson's Automatic Weed Guard, Lure and Sinker in one piece. Beats all for Bait Fishing.

POSITION TROLLING / OR STILL FISHING.

FIG. 1 — 4/0 Carlisle ½ Size — GUARD CLOSED — LINE LOOP — GUARD, LURE & SINKER — No Weed or Snag can touch the hook Lures by Form, Color and Oscillation.

FIG. 2 FRONT VIEW — LINE LOOP — GUARD, LURE & SINKER — HOOK

BAIT RIGHT SIDE UP ALWAYS.

Dotted lines show guard when closed. All three parts hinged together on cross pin, swing freely, in line, separately.

Hook always fully exposed to fish biting, and rarely fails to hook them and in the mouth. Is never swallowed. Will not foul in the thickest weeds. Will cast a long distance against wind. Will catch more fish than any other device, either in weeds or clear water, casting, trolling, or still fishing. WILL LAST FOR YEARS. HOOKS CAN BE REPLACED.

Three Sizes, 2-o, 4-o, 7-o Carlisle Hooks. *Mailed for 50 cents each.*

Patent issued January 16, 1894.

Pages 112, 113: The opticians certainly owed Montgomery Ward a medal for stimulating the demand for eyeglasses. In those days, farm advertising was crammed full of 6-point type, set solid, so as to give the farmer enough reading matter to last through the long winter evenings.

Here are fishing rods from 12 cents to $25 and reels as cheap as 10 cents. A farm boy could submerge himself for a week in just these two pages, and countless thousands of them did. After all, the best fishing is done not in water but in print.

FISHING RODS, TACKLE, ETC.

FISHING RODS.

In selecting the goods in this department it has been done with a view to get standard and reliable goods only, and we know of no single article in the following list that is not the best obtainable of its grade. Made of the best quality woods, warranted clear timber, free from knots and flaws. Weight given is for rods alone, and does not include cases. Any rod not found as represented can be returned at our expense and money refunded if returned as soon as examined.

Wood Rods.

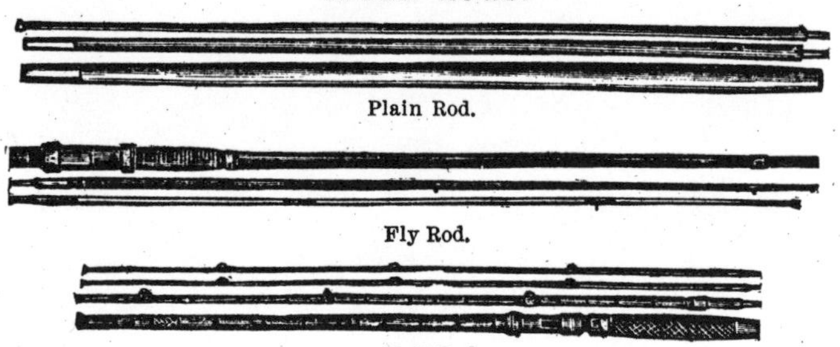

Plain Rod.

Fly Rod.

Bait Rod.

Our prices are lowest jobbing prices on fishing tackle. That is why the prices may seem low to you for Good goods.

No.	Description	Feet.	Each.
48410	Fish Rod, 3 pieces, jointed, single brass ferrule; about	10½	$0.12
48411	3-Piece Jointed Rod, single brass ferrule, ringed for line	10½	.15
48412	4 Piece Jointed Rod, varnished, single brass ferrule, ringed for line, natural color	12	.20
48413	3-Piece Light Bass, stained, double ferrules, rings and reel bands, brass capped butt	10½	.38
48414	Fish Rod, 3 pieces, fly or light bait, stained dark, double ferrule, brass butt cap, ringed for line, brass reel bands	10	.47
48415	4-Piece Bass or Bait Rod, stained lancewood tip, guides and reel bands, brass butt cap, double brass ferrules, finely finished	12	.75
48416	3-Piece Bait Rod, stained ash and lancewood tip, *brass mounted*, guides and reel bands	9½	$0.75
48417	3-Piece Light Bass Rod, varnished ash with lancewood, tip full mounted, in *nickel*. A good rod	10	1.20
48418	3-Piece Fly Rod, ash butt and second joint, nickeled lancewood tip, full mounted, a light, fine rod, covered dowels, 8 oz	10½	1.30
48421	4-Piece Fine Stained General Rod, covered dowels, reel bands, brass mounted, hollow butt, extra lancewood tip, braided butt	12	1.80
48422	4-Piece California General Rod, lancewood except first joint, ash butt, nickeled, full mounted, solid metal reel seat, silk wound, anti-friction tie guides and silk wound at short intervals, reel seat above hand, in cloth bag, 3 rods in one, good anywhere. One extra short tip and one extra heavy tip	12	3.00

Steel Rods.

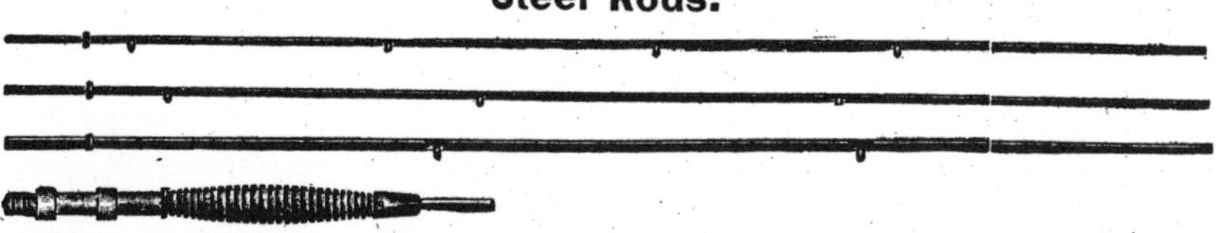

The Bristol Steel Fishing Rods. They are a marked departure from all rods of the past, and your fishing outfit is incomplete without one. Every rod guaranteed against breakage from reasonable use or from defects in manufacture.

48423 (1) Bass Rod, telescopic, 9 ft. 6 in., full nickel, mounted with solid reel seat above hand, line runs through the center of the rod; when telescoped the rod is 32 in. in length, all closed within the butt length, with celluloid wound handle. Weight, 12¼ oz. Price $4.25

48423½ (5) Fly Rod, 9 ft. 6 in., reel seat below hand, otherwise same style and description as No. 1. Weight, 11¾ oz. Price 4.20

48424 (8) Fly Rod, 10 ft., full nickel mounted, with solid reel seat below hand. This rod is jointed, has standing line guides on outside, does not telescope. Weight, 9¼ oz., with celluloid wound handle. Price 5.00

48424½ (13) The St. Lawrence Bass Rod, 7 ft. 6 in., full nickel mounted with solid reel seat above hand. This rod is jointed, has standing guides and 3 ringed tip. This is one of the best bait-casting or boat rods on the market. Weight, 9¼ oz., with celluloid wound handle. Price 5.00

Lancewood Rods.

Lancewood Bait Rod.

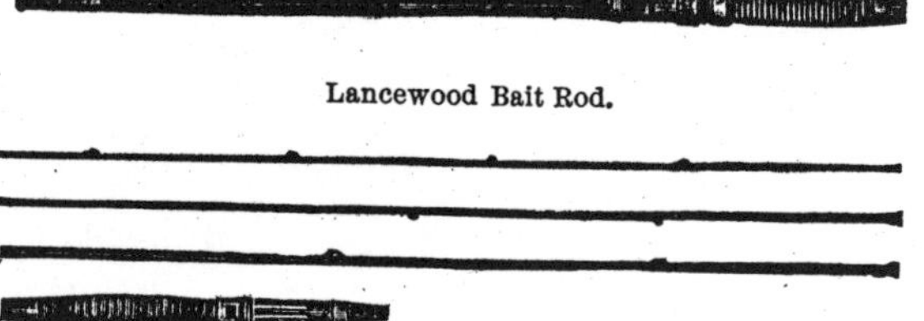

Showing Short Butt.

No.	Description	Length Feet.	Each
48425	3-Piece All Genuine Imported Lancewood Fly Rod, finely nickel plated, improved shoulder ferrules, silk wound tie guides, covered dowels, solid nickel reel seat below hand, fancy or corrugated hand grasp, with one extra tip, in cloth bag, partitioned, a BARGAIN. Fly rod, heavy	10½	$1.25
	Fly rod, light	10	1.35
48427	3-Piece All Genuine Imported Lancewood Fly Rod, in wood case or form, finely finished, full nickel plated shoulder ferrules, fancy silk wound tie guides, covered dowels, solid nickel reel seat below hand grasp, corrugated zylonite butt, with one extra tip. A good one	10½	1.95

Weights on rods may vary 1 to 3 oz.

No.	Description	Length Feet.	Each.
48428	3-Piece All Genuine Imported Lancewood Bass Rod finely nickel plated, improved shoulder ferrules, silk wound tie guides, covered dowels, solid nickel reel seat above hand, cane wound or zylonite butt, with one extra tip, in cloth bag, partitioned; a very fine rod (a bargain)	9	$1.25
48429	3-Piece All Genuine Imported Lancewood Bass Rod, in wood form, varnished and polished, nickel plated, solid reel seat, shouldered ferrules, covered dowels, metal plugs, fancy silk wound tie guides for line, wound or fancy butt stock, one extra tip (a bargain) Bass rod	9	1.95
	Bait rod	7½	2.00

48430 3-piece and extra tip, all best Jamaica lancewood carefully selected and thoroughly tested, patent hard rubber butt and extra fine finish, welt ferrules and metal plugs. Each rod in wood form, full nickel plated mountings, fancy silk winding between joints.

	Feet.	Each
Fly rod, reel seat below hand	10	$2.95
Bass rod, reel seat above hand	9	3.00
Bait rod, extra heavy	8	3.05

48430½ Trout or Black Bass Rod, best Jamaica lancewood, for bait casting, has rubber butt, full nickel plated mountings, fancy silk windings. Two piece, extra tip, in wood form, 6½ 3.00

Henshall Bass Rods.

48431 Henshall Bass Rod, all genuine Jamaica lancewood, solid rubber butt, German silver mountings, extra fancy silk windings. Each rod put up in lined wood form. The best lancewood rod in the market at any price. No better rod made. Generally retails at $8.00. 8 ft. 3 in. long. Our price 4.75

48431½ Jamaica Lancewood Short Bait Rod, genuine, 3-piece with extra tip, cork butt and aluminum reel seat, extra fancy silk windings, full German silver mountings, in lined wood form.
8 ft. bait 5.00
9¼ ft. very light fly 4.95

Combination Lancewood Rod.

48432 7-Piece Combination Lancewood Rod, corrugated black celluloid grip, shouldered and trimmed ferrules, nickel plated trimmings, silk wound tie guides, bass bait, trout bait and trout fly combination, 1 short butt, 1 long ash butt. When short butt is used will make a difference of 24 inches in length of rod, in any combination 7 to 10 feet; one of the best and handiest rods in the market. Will make 6 different rods. Each $2.75

48433 Florida Bass Rod, extra heavy, all lancewood, selected wood, rubber hand grasp, silk wound throughout, nickel plated mountings, metal plugs, 3-piece, extra tip; length, about 8¼ feet. Each .. $2.60

48434 Tarpon or Florida Bass Rod, combined rod, will make a 3-piece rod, 8½ ft., 18 oz., and a 2-piece rod 5¾ ft., 16 oz. Jamaica Dagame wood, double tie guides, solid nickel reel seat, nickel mounted corrugated zylonite butt. Heavy, strong and durable. The 2-piece rod is a good tarpon or gogebec trolling rod. Everything about this rod is finely finished, and the wood resembles lancewood very closely. Each .. $3.95

Jointed Bamboo Fishing Rods.

The Bamboo Rods are light, handy and strong, can be used with or without reels. The best trolling rods in the market.

No.	Description	Length, feet.	Each.
48435	2-Piece, Japanese bamboo, double ferrules, plain straw color	8 to 9	$0.15
48436	3-Piece, Japanese bamboo, double ferrules, plain straw color	14 to 18	.36
48437	4-Piece, Japanese bamboo, double ferrules, ringed, plain straw color	14 to 16	.44
48439	3-Piece, Calcutta bamboo, double ferrules, ringed, reel bands and capped butt	10 to 12	.55
48440	4-Piece, Calcutta Bamboo, double ferrules, ringed and capped butt	14 to 17	.65
48441	4-Piece, Calcutta bamboo, double ferrules, ringed, reel bands, capped butt	14 to 17	.80
48442	4-Piece, Calcutta bamboo, double ferrules, reel bands, capped and cane wound butt	13 to 16	1.10
48443	3-Piece, Calcutta bamboo, double ferrules, standing guides, reel bands, capped and cane wound butt, nickel mounted	10 to 12	.86

Bamboo 4-Piece Rod.

No.	Description	Length, feet.	Each.
48444	5-Piece Calcutta bamboo, double ferrules, standing ring guides, reel bands, and cane wound below hand, one extra tip in butt. This is a great favorite with the trade where an extra long, strong rod is wanted.	18 to 20	$2.20
48445	3-Piece, Calcutta bamboo, improved shoulder ferrules, wound tie guides, covered dowels, solid reel seat, nickel plated trimmings, capped and zylonite or cane-wound butt, extra lancewood tip, in cloth bag	9 to 11	1.90
48446	4-Piece, Calcutta bamboo, bass rod, nickel plated, improved shoulder ferrules, full mounted extra lancewood tip, standing guides, metal reel seat, cane-wound butt	14 to 16	2.00
48447	Jap Boat Rod, 2-piece Japanese Bamboo Boat Rod, with 14 in. corrugated black zylonite butt or grip, nickel plated mountings, solid reel seat, tie guides, tube tips. Length, 6½ to 8 feet		.75
48448	Oconomowoc Bass Rod, 1 corrugated short butt, with 1-piece Japanese bamboo, 7 to 8 feet long, brass mounted, tube tips, reel seat above hand. A big seller		.65

Split Bamboo Rods.

Our Split Bamboo Rods are the best in the market at anywhere near the prices we offer them, and are warranted as represented.

ALL OUR RODS ARE GUARANTEED *just as represented.* Any not found so can be RETURNED at our expense. Our "Split Bamboo" prices are 50 to 100 per cent. lower than regular retail prices.

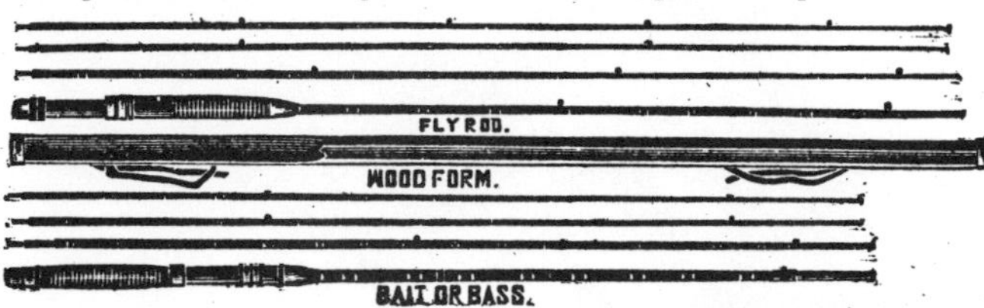

48448½ The "Baby Brook" Fly, the very best 3-piece all hand-made, six strip, split bamboo, polished orange wood butt, full German silver mountings, first-class in every particular, the equal to if not better than the best rods made by anybody. Each rod, with extra tip, in flannel lined wood form, with canvas case. Weight, 3 ounces, 7½ feet long. Price....................$25.00

48449 3-piece genuine six strip hexagonal split bamboo rods. Patent zylonite butts, full nickel plated mounting, welt ferrules, metal plugs, solid reel seat, fancy silk windings, 1 extra tip. Each rod in a wood form. Fly rod, reel below hand, 8 oz., 10½ feet.................. 3.50
Bait casting rod, reel above hand, 9 oz., 7½ ft.. 3.55
Long bait rod, reel seat above hand, 13 oz., 10½ feet.................................. 3 90

48450½ Three-piece hexagonal, six strip Bamboo Rods, welted waterproof ferrules, metal plugs, full nickel plated. fancy silk windings, fancy celluloid wound butt, inlaid with cedar, each rod in lined wood form. These rods are beauties. Fly rod, weight about 7 oz; length 10 feet.................................. 5 00
Bait rod, weight about 9 oz; length, 8¼ feet.... 5.10

48451 The very best 3-piece all hand-made six strip hexagonal split Bamboo Rods Patent hard rubber butts, full German silver mounted, waterproof welted ferrules, metal plugs, fancy silk windings, first class in every particular. Each rod in lined wood form, with canvas bag and extra tip. This is the rod that usually retails at $25.00, and is good value even at that price. It is the best rod that we can get made up. Fly rod, reel seat below hand, 7 oz., 10 feet..................................16.50
Bait rod, reel seat above hand, 10 oz., 8½ feet...16.55

48452 Three-piece split Bamboo Rods, genuine six strip hexagonal patent rubber butts, full German silver mountings, solid metal reel seats, welt ferrules, metal plugs, fancy silk wound. Each rod in a lined wood form, extra tip. The best rod offered by *anybody* for *anything* like the *price* we name.
Fly rod, reel seat below hand, 8 oz., 10½ feet... 6.00
Bait rod, reel seat above hand, 11 oz., 8½ feet.................................. 6.00

48452½ Trout Fly Rod, 3-piece split bamboo, six strip, cork butt, aluminum reel plate, full German silver mountings, with extra tip, fancy silk windings. Each rod in a lined wood form, the best rod for the price ever offered. Very light; 5 ounces; length, 9 feet. Each.................. 6.00

48453 Three-piece hexagonal six strip genuine Bamboo Rods. Welted waterproof ferrules, metal plugs, full German silver mounted, fancy silk windings between ferrules, inlaid cedar butt. Each rod in wood form, lined; extra tip. These rods we believe to be better than most $12.00 to $15.00 rods on the market. *They are good ones.* Fly rods, reel seat below hand, 6 oz., 9½ feet.................................. 8.90
Fly rods, reel seat below hand, 8 oz., 10½ feet.. 8.95
Henshall bass rod, 9 oz., 8 feet 3 in. long....... 9.00

48454 Three-piece genuine six strip hexagonal Split Bamboo Rods, full nickel plated mountings, silk wound tie guides, solid reel seats, metal plugs, corrugated zylonite butts, each rod in wood form; 1 extra tip. Fly Rod, reel seat below hand, 10 feet 1.25
Bait Rod, reel seat above hand, 9½ feet........ 1.30
Wood case weighs 10 oz., where rod is described in wood case or form.

48455 Three-piece, six strip, hexagonal split Bamboo Rods, full nickel plated mountings, silk wound tie guards, solid reel seats, metal plugs, corrugated zylonite butts, each rod in wood form, extra tip, selected stock. Fly rod, weight about 8 oz; length, 10½ feet.................... 1.80
Bait rod, weight about 12 oz; length, 9½ feet... 1.85

48456 Three-piece, six strip, hexagonal split Bamboo Rods, with cork grip, nickel plated mountings, solid metal reel seats and metal plugs in wood form. An extra tip. Fly Rod, weight about 8 oz; length, 10½ feet.............. 2.80
Bait Rod weight about 12 oz; length, 9½ feet.. 2.85

48457 Four-piece, six strip, hexagonal split bamboo rods, with zylonite grips, nickel plated mountings, solid metal reel seat and metal plugs in wood form, without extra tip. Bait rod only, weight about 13 oz; length, 10 feet........ 1.45

ALL OF OUR RODS ARE GUARANTEED *just as represented.* Any not found so can be RETURNED at our expense. Our "Split Bamboo" prices are 50 to 100 per cent lower than regular retail prices.

Our claim that this Catalogue opens the large markets to you is no idle boast. Where else can you find so much? As a genuine guide to prices it has no equal.

Trunk Rods.

	Feet.	Each.
48459 Five-piece Trunk Rod, varnished; long double nickel ferrules, covered dowels, nickel butt cap, one light, one heavy tip, making a good bass or bait, and also a light fly rod, ring guides, reel bands, lancewood tips, a very good, handy and cheap rod	11	$1.20
48460 Five-piece Trunk Rod, natural wood finish, varnished, double brass ferrules, lancewood tip, ring guides, brass butt, cap, fine little rod	10	.75
48461 Five-piece Bamboo Trunk Rod, plain brass-finished mounting, ring guides, 11½ to 12.		.90

48462 5-piece Bamboo Trunk Rod, improved and rimmed shoulder ferrules, covered dowels, silk-wound tie guides, metal reel seat, extra lancewood tip, a fine rod 2.00

48463 5-piece trunk rod, all genuine lancewood, butt varnished and polished, shouldered ferrules, fancy finish, nickel plated, whole rod made of lancewood, fancy silk windings and tie guides, solid metal reel seat, one extra tip; 10 to 13 oz., a good honest rod. Fly Rod, reel below hand, about 9¼ feet 2.50
Bait Rod, reel above hand, about 8½ feet.. .... 2.55

48464 Five-piece Trunk Rod, genuine hexagonal split bamboo zylonite butts, nickel plated mountings, solid metal reel seat, and metal plugs, fancy silk windings and a handsome rod. Each rod in a partition cloth bag. An extra tip with each rod.
Fly rod, reel below hand, about 8 oz., 10 feet.. 3.50
Bait rod, reel above hand, about 12 oz., 9½ feet. 3.55

Rod Cases.

48465 Round Rod Case, embossed russet leather, copper riveted, nickel trimmed, capped end, fastened with strap and buckles, 40 in., 2 inch diameter. Each..............................$2.85
50 in., 3 in. diameter. Each.................... 3.00
Cheaper quality leather neatly finished, 40 to 50 in. long, 2 in. diameter. Each.................. 1.80

48466

48466 Canvas Rod Cases, leather top and bottom, a dandy for the money. Weight, 6 to 8 ozs.—40 to 50 in. long. Each $0.60

48466½ Canvas Rod Case, plain, heavy canvas. Each 40

48467 The "Handy" Fish Rod Holder, can be carried in the vest pocket; screws on gunwale of boat; is covered with rubber. Ordinary size, each...$0.13
Large size, each .... .15

48468

48468 Fish Rod Holder, a good one for the money; screws on any part of the boat; forks covered with rubber. Each $0.35

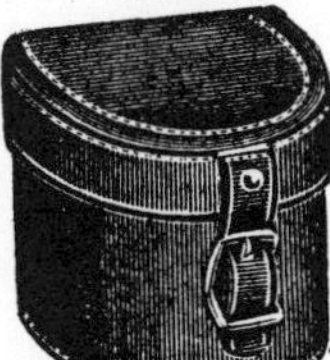
48469

48469 Leather Reel Cases are made of bleached oak, finest leather, felt lined, with leather covered buckles.

No. 11, to hold small single action reel............$0.75
No. 12, to hold large single action reel............ .88
No. 13, to hold small multiplying reel............ .88
No. 14, to hold large multiplying reel............ 1.00

The Universal Fish Rod Holder.

48510 For trolling and still fishing in a boat. It can be fastened either to the gunwale or seat. It enables a person, if he desires, to go fishing without a guide to row for him, or to have two or three rods in use without their being all over the bottom of the boat to be stepped on and broken. By means of a thumb-screw it can be adjusted to any angle or any direction, as it works on a ball and socket joint. It is neatly and strongly made, is tinned, and forks are covered with rubber; it will take any rod from ¾ to 2 in. diameter at butt. Weight, 26 oz. Each $1.10

Fishing Reels.

(Reels by mail, 10 to 15 cents extra.)

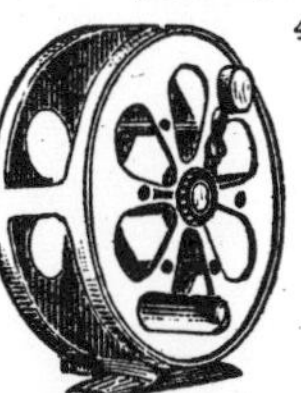

48511 The Expert Reel. This reel has an entirely new device for use in casting or "playing" a fish, whereby the angler may vary the reel from a free running to a delicate drag, heavy drag, or bring it to a complete stop, simply by the pressure of the thumb upon the guard. By this device the line may be stopped instantly at any desired point when casting. This guard is made of extra hard spring metal so that no matter how often used or struck by accident it will resume its original position. These reels, having a large diameter of spool, will reel in a line faster than the best quadruple multiplying reel. All finely polished, heavy nickel plated and well made; 40 yards, 2¼ in. diameter, with click. Each..$1.55
Extra by mail, 6c.
70 yards, 3 in. diameter, with click. Each...... 1.70
Extra by mail, 7c.

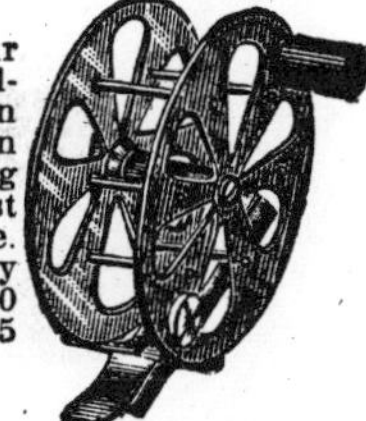

48512 The Famous Amateur Drag Reel, fine nickel plate, allowing line to dry quickly; can be changed to a free runner in an instant by simply pressing down on spring. Beats the best multiplier in reeling in the line. Very light weight, and fits any reel band. Small..........$1.10
Medium.................... 1.25
Extra by mail, 5c.

48513

48513 The Competitive Reel, brass finish, plain, no click or drag, light and strong. Plain, free runner. Each $0.10
Extra by mail, 3c.

48514 Brass Free Running Reel, with band to screw on rod, 25 yards. Each.......................$0.30

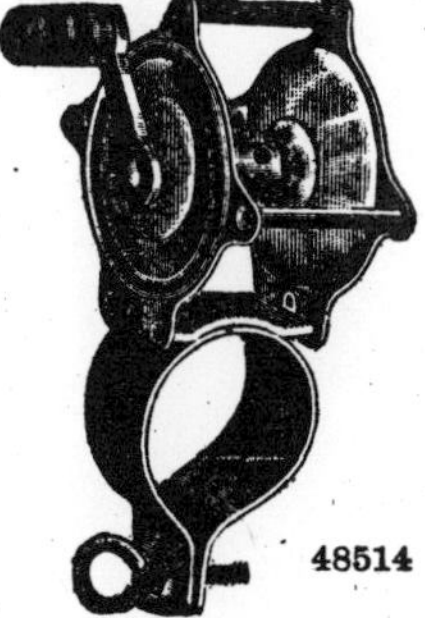
48514

48516 Rubber Side Plate Reel for light trout fishing, a good and strong reel.
25 yards, each..........$0.45
40 yards, each............ .50
60 yards, each............ .60
Extra, by mail............ .05

48517

48517 Polished Brass raised pillar, star pattern, with click, 25 yards, 1¾ inches diameter of plates.
Each............$0.20
40 yards, 2 inches diameter of plates.
Each............$0.23
60 yards, 2 3-16 in., diameter of plates.
Each............$0.30
Extra, by mail.. .04

48518 Raised Pillar, polished brass, free running, no click or drag.
25 yards, each..............................$0.20
40 yards, each.............................. .25
60 yards, each.............................. .30
Extra, by mail.............................. .05

Foster's of Ashbourne, England, wasn't the biggest British tackle house but it was the brassiest.

The Testing of Steel-Ribbed against Steel-Centred and other Rod Joints,

By R. Hoskin, M.I. Mech. E., and Thos. Nash, M.I. Mech. E.

"The 'Steel-Ribbed' Rod stands a maximum load of 14 lbs : the Steel Centre breaking at 7½ lbs."

CRITIQUE.—"Doubtless many of our readers never think of whipping for perch with anything but float tackle, paternoster, or ledger, but we can assure them there is infinite truth in Mr. Foster's advice—'that where perch are wary, fine sport may often be had by whipping (in fly-fishing manner, that is) with cad bait, fresh water shrimp, and other acquatic insects in nymphæ.'"—*Fishing Gazette.*

FOSTER'S PERFECT "K.D." DEVON.

The Devon is the most deadly of all spinning baits, and the "Kill Devil" Devon is the best of all Devons. This has been proved to the satisfaction of every minnow spinning client we have (and as we brought out the "K.D." Devon eight years ago, we have many). The following are samples of reports continually being received by us:—

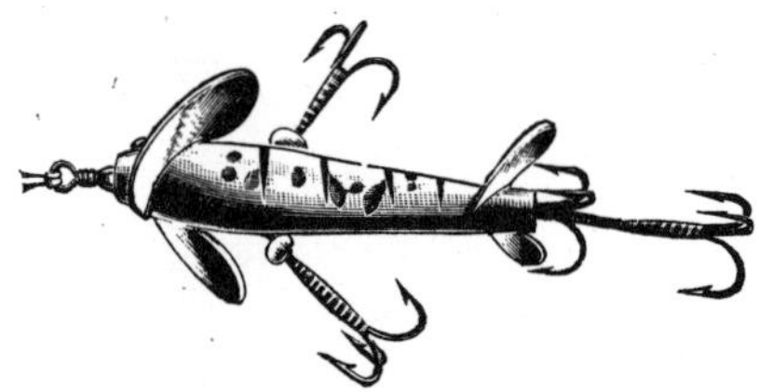

TROUT SIZE.

"Send by return one Perfect Kill Devil Devon for Trout. The old K.D. Devon I had has been the best bait I ever used."—From *Mr. W. G. Jones*, Gillar Street, Merthyr, Wales.

"Please send per return of post three Kill Devils 1½ inches, for which I enclose 8/6. These for a friend. They are the best artificial baits I ever spun."—From *Mr. George Wheatcroft*, 207, Orwell Road, Kirkdale, Liverpool.

"That spinning minnow (Heavy "K.D." Devon) was very effective. It was such a pity the gut got cut. I had caught lots of lake trout with it in Norway last August, but when that was gone nothing else was anything near as good."—From *H. F. T. Preston, Esq., M.D.*, Kidderminster.

"Please send me one each more of the trout Devons. I quite endorse the view expressed in your catalogue that they are the 'best killers of all baits in discoloured water.'"—*Sir Richard Barlow, Bart.*, Buckerell Lodge, Honiton.

CRITIQUE.—"This is a work originally prepared for English fishermen; yet Mr. Foster's work can hardly fail to excite the American reader's interest. Every line breathes a simple and genuine enthusiasm which never flags."—*New York Tribune.*

FLOATINE.

THIS

NEW FLOATING MIXTURE

For Dry Fly Fishing is a prepared

VASELINE OR PETROLEUM JELLY.

IT IS A GREAT ADVANCE ON PARAFFIN OIL.

IT FLOATS THE FLY BETTER.

It has no obnoxious smell, and is more handy to carry and use.

We refer our readers to the remarks made by Mr. Gedney in his able article on Dry Fly Fishing in the "Scientific Angler" (which we reprint in this list), *re* vaseline as a Dry Fly Floater.

We are indebted to Mr. Valentine Baker for the idea, which our knowledge of waterproofing chemicals has enabled us to make still more perfect.

NOTE.—

FLOATINE

bears the following Trade Mark on each tube, without which it is not the genuine thing.

Price 9d. per Tube.

76 FOSTER'S CATALOGUE.

CRITIQUE.—"The work, which is called the *Scientific Angler*, treats of every imaginable plan by which the finny tribe can be lured to the hook of the fisherman." *Bazaar.*

FLY DRESSING MATERIALS.

		s.	d.	
African Macaw Tail Feathers	... 8d., 1s. 6d., and	2	0	each.
Jay's Wings...	... ...	0	8	per pair.
Golden Pheasant Tail Feathers	... ... 1s. 0d. and	1	6	each.

From Henry P. Wells, author of "The American Salmon Fisher," and "Fly Rods and Fly Tackle," &c.

"New York City, U.S.A.,

"Gentlemen, "December 24th, 1885.

"My friend, Mr. A. N. Cheney (author of 'Fishing with the Fly,' &c.), advises me to write to you for a supply of material for Salmon Flies. He speaks in the highest terms of the quality of your material, as well as of the conscientious care with which you fill orders of those who cannot select for themselves."

OUR LATEST AT THE FLY-FISHERS' CLUB.

CRITIQUE.—"A copy of the fourth English edition of the above excellent work on 'Artistic Angling,' by the late David Foster, of Ashbourne, is to hand, and it gives us pleasure again to recommend it to our readers."—*Fishing Gazette.*

Using The Fly Fishers' to advertise their wares was a breach of good taste that couldn't have helped their sales to the members of that starchy organization.

"In unseasonable weather there are often a multiplicity of winged insects about, each species having but few representatives. In these circumstances, the sunk fly system may be practised with success."—*Scientific Angler.*

MALLOCK'S PATENT CASTING REEL, FOR SPINNING.

At Maker's Prices.

NO.	DIAM.	s.	d.	NO.	DIAM.	s.	d.
1026	$2\frac{3}{4}$ in.	18	6	1028.	4 in.	28	0
1027	$3\frac{1}{4}$ „	21	0				

BEST NOTTINGHAM REELS.

BEST WALNUT NOTTINGHAM REELS.

BEST BURNISHED BRASS MOUNTS.

NO.		Plain. Each. s.	d.	With Check (movable). Each. s.	d.
765A.	2 inch diameter...	1	9	6	6
765B.	$2\frac{1}{2}$ „ „	2	6	7	6
765C.	3 „ „	3	0	8	6
766.	$3\frac{1}{2}$ „ „	3	9	9	6
766A.	4 „ „	4	6	11	6
766B.	$4\frac{1}{2}$ „ „	5	6	13	6
766C.	5 „ „	7	6	15	6

The above may also be had with a star-shaped metal back at same price.

Note the brief space accorded to the Mallock reel, invented and made by a rival firm. The demand for it must have been terrific to force it into Foster's catalog.

The original David Foster apparently spent a lot of time on the water, fishing and mingling with his customers—a good salesman, an ingenious chap, and an indefatigable note-taker. In 1882, after his death, his sons D. and W. H. compiled from those notes a good, sensible little handbook polluted, however, with their blaring, blatant brag and bluster. They nicknamed old David "The Naturalist Angler of the Peak" and "The Amiable Angler of the Dell," thus covering the whole landscape, and named the book *The Scientific Angler*.

BEWARE OF VILE IMITATIONS.

No Metal Centred Line is genuine which has not our labels shown below.

OUR ENGLISH LABEL.

OUR AMERICAN LABEL.

Imitations, sir, are nothing less than Vile!

ASHBOURNE, ENGLAND. 131

CRITIQUE.—"It is no small proof of the intrinsic value of any work, more especially of a work devoted to one exclusive object, that in the course of a few years five large editions have been exhausted, and yet another is called for."—*Rod and Gun.*

So convinced are we, after three years' experience of it, that

THE BEST ROD IS THE

"STEEL RIBBED,"

For both lightness and relative strength, that we

CHALLENGE THE WORLD.

TO ENGLISH, CONTINENTAL, AND AMERICAN ROD MAKERS.

We are so confident of the superiority of our "Steel Ribbed," that we are willing, by way of an experiment, to produce a rod to be tested against a rod made by any contemporary, weight for weight, length for length, diameter for diameter. The maker of the rod roving inferior to defray all expenses incurred by the test, and to forfeit the modest sum (for we don't want to prevent the experiment from being made by naming a high figure) of Ten Pounds, which is to be paid to a public Charity, to be named by the winner.

If it is of Greenheart, a "Ribbed" Greenheart is superior to all other Greenhearts, whether steel centred or not, and the same result is found in the case of the Built Cane. A steel ribbed Built Cane broke at a maximum pressure of over 14lbs.; whereas a Non-Ribbed Built Cane broke at $7\frac{1}{2}$ lbs.; also on the score of stiffness the Ribbed Rod proved far superior. *See Engineers' tests* (by Thos. Nash, M.I.M.E., and R. Hoskin, M.I.M.E.) *See foregoing page.*

CRITIQUE.—"It is a fifth English edition, and there has also been a separate American edition. The fact is pretty good proof the work has been found attractive and useful by anglers."—*The Scotsman.*

Steel-centered and steel-"ribbed" rods are indubitably among the worst abominations that ever afflicted the rodmaking industry; they are worthless. Nevertheless, the Fosters' hard-sell of the fallacy that breaking strength had anything to do with casting efficiency set British rodmaking back a quarter of a century.

"When trout reach a more than ordinary size they disdain surface food. At twilight, and even later in the hot months, however, they will rise at the large moths, but are not to be allured to the surface by small flies."—*Scientific Angler.*

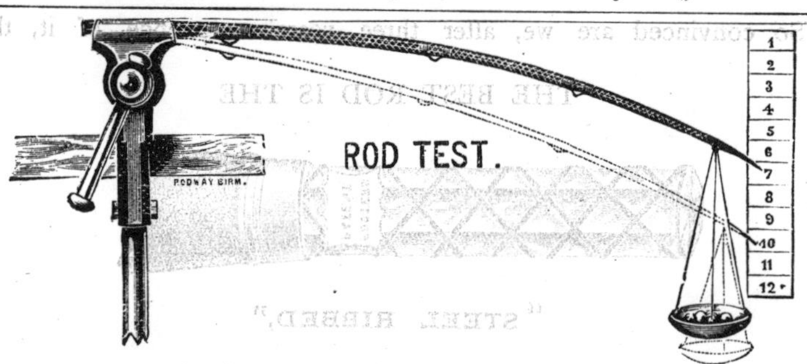

The above illustration gives the difference in stiffness of a Steel Ribbed and an Ordinary Rod, viz.:—The Ribbed Rod bending 7, and the Non-Ribbed 10 inches under the same weight!

Read the Reports (unsolicited) of habitual users.

Weakness transformed to Strength.

"Last Spring I sent you a rod, which was rather whippy, to be steel ribbed, which was a great success, and increased the power of the rod certainly twofold. It has given me great satisfaction."—MAJOR THE HON. F. TRENCH, Woodlawn, Co. Galway, Ireland, December 17th, 1893.

From same—Later.

"You have now ribbed three rods, one for a friend, and two of my own; all have given the most entire satisfaction, in fact in one case you have made a *very bad rod* into a real good one."—March 7th, 1894.

"The rod you have ribbed is very much improved."—Rev. G. R. PEAK, Bloxwich, near Walsall.

"I have given the greenheart rod you ribbed for me a fair trial lately on lake and river, and I am very pleased with it. It throws a long line, and requires very little muscular exertion. I also find I can strike fish better than before it was ribbed."—E. LLOYD MORRIS, Registrar, Llanelly, Carmarthenshire, August 4th, 1892.

"After spawning, trout linger by the edges of streams that flow into the throats of the pools, and at this period rise boldly and unsuspectingly for a time, and are then to be allured by the novice in a comparatively easy manner."—*Scientific Angler.*

CRITIQUE.—"The whole of these subjects are clearly and exhaustively treated, and we should say, to use a colloquialism, that what the author did not know about fish and fishing was not worth learning."—*Bell's Life.*

FOSTER'S "CHALLENGE THE WORLD" BRAND.

THE "LITTLE DAVID."

This rod has the identical "swing" or play of the celebrated rods made and used by our father, the late David Foster, of "Scientific Angler" fame. We call it the "Little David" because it is a modification. Were we to reproduce the exact length, weight, and power, he (our predecessor) used, the thing would prove too much for our clients. The tendency of the time is for a rod of 9½ to 10½ or 11 ft., which has power, lightness, and stiffness combined, and never were these characteristics combined more perfectly than in the case of the "Little David." The play is down to the hand, and not confined mainly to the top joint, as in the case of the "Darent."

No.	Description	s.	d.
671.	Cane-built, bronzed ferrules, 9½ to 11 ft., with the Devonshire rubber handle and reel fitting, steel ribbed	55	0

Cork handle same price. Screw lock joints, 4s. 6d. extra. Steel bound, 10s. extra. Steel centred, £1 extra. Rubber Button, 2s. extra. Extra top, 15s. extra. Roller end rings, 1s. extra each top.

"I may mention I have two rods of your make, one of which has been my companion for the last twenty-five years, and is as good as new now."—REV. EARDLEY W. MUHILL, Martin Vicarage, Salisbury.

CRITIQUE.—" Mr. Foster recommends casting into a floating walnut shell, for ourselves, a moderate-sized tub seems more educational . . . a handy little volume, easily carried in the pocket, it may well be added to the angler's library."—*Saturday Review.*

No.
1172C "OUR SPECIAL." Pigskin Fly Book; will wear everlastingly. Contents same as 1167. Prices, 5 in., 6/6; 6 in., 7/6; 7 in., 9/6.

1172D.	Fly and Tackle Book, in strong leather; best quality...	17	6
	" " Ordinary quality	8	6

" The late David Foster, of Ashbourne, was, I believe, the first to originate the plan of dressing flies similar to the above-named with wings, which would retain an almost upright position when wet, or subject to heavy usage."—*Theakstone's Angling Flies, New Edition.*

"When there is a good number of flies upon the water they quickly leave the deeps and will be found in the slow running streams."—*Scientific Angler*.

FOSTER'S TWIN SCREW DEVON.

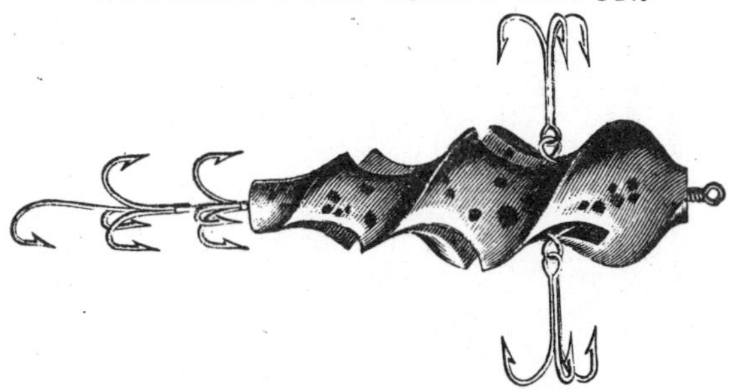

This bait has no flanges or outstretching wings, and therefore there is nothing to keep the fish from the hooks. In the case of the "Kill Devil Devon" the wings are shorter by almost one half, and in this case the principle is carried to its legitimate conclusion. The speed in spinning is maintained by the screw or spiral shape of the bait, thus, though without the usual spinning gear, the whole bait is a double screw spinner. On its first trial, six brace of trout were landed by it by the Rev. Fredk. Gutteries, of Nymet Roland Rectory, Lapford, North Devon, recently.

THE NEW TWIN SCREW SPINNER.

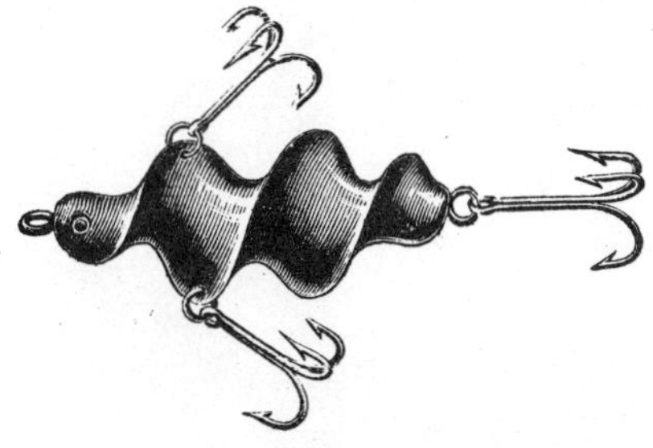

This and the preceding bait take a straight flight through the water, fewer fish being missed by it than any other spinning bait. We are protecting these baits, whether made in hard or soft substances. At the suggestion of the Editor of the *Fishing Gazette* we are getting them made in soft rubber.

"Whenever the grayling are not rising, unlike trout, they congregate in considerable numbers at the bottom of the deep holes."—*Scientific Angler.*

Twin screws were a recommendation for a ship, so why not for a bait? It's difficult to see the "twin" part of this screw.

"With regard to the vexed question of up or down stream fishing no distinct rule need be observed, a continuous resort to either is not desirable."—*Scientific Angler.*

THE "IMPERCEPTIBLE" SPINNER.

PATENT.

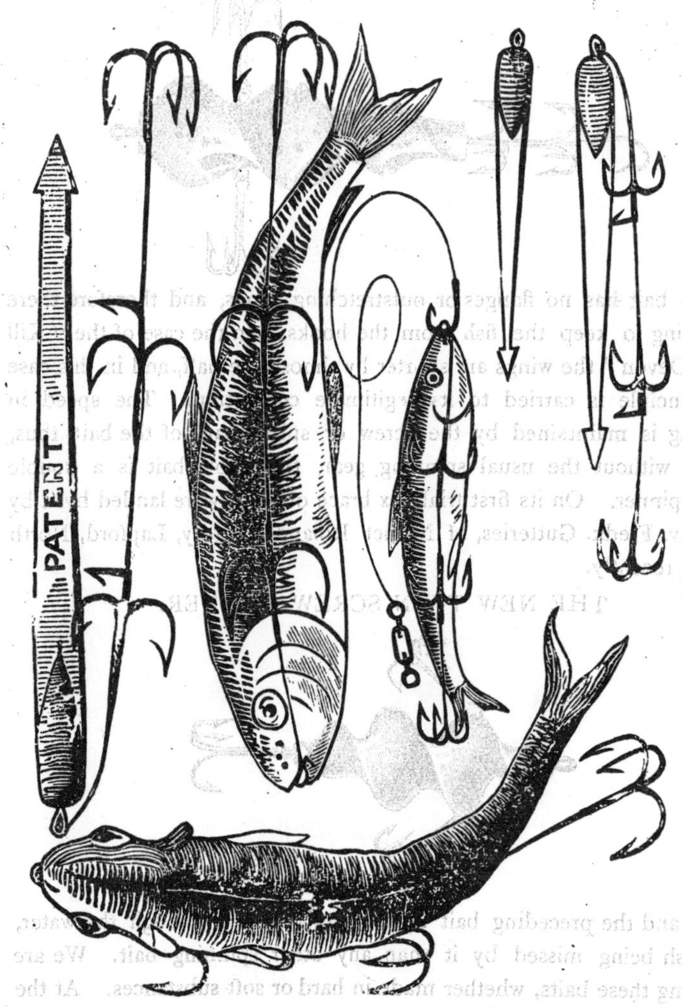

The top figure is the blade mounted with double hooks, with barbed shafts and a treble hook. Next below is a trout, with spinner inside and hooks fixed by barbed shafts. Next a minnow with spinner inside, &c. Next shows smaller sized blades. The figure to the left is a back view of the trout with spinner, after blade and trout being bent, showing the curve, and also how the double hooks (with shafts) stand off the bait.

"At this season of the year the fish leave the deep water, and sport on small streams is now good."—*Scientific Angler.*

216 FOSTER'S CATALOGUE,

THE "PARSEY" WADERS.

COMPLETE, WITHOUT THE ADDITION OF WOOL SOCKS.

A TEN AND A HALF POUND SALMON TAKEN WITH AN 11 ft. "DERBYSHIRE SWITCH."

This was taken by the Rev. T. W. Tomlins with a rod supplied to description given.

It's not often a 10 ½-pound salmon breaks into print.

OUR CREDENTIALS.

WE established our business in the year A.D. 1833, and have thus successfully catered for the angling public over sixty years.

During that length of time we have introduced the following improvements, now in general use everywhere:—

WATERPROOF PLAITED SILK LINES,
ERECT WINGED FLIES, STEEL CENTRED RODS,
PERFECT KILL DEVIL DEVONS,
STEEL RIBBED RODS.

The first three we did not patent, and the fruit of our brains went chiefly into the pockets of our trade contemporaries.

The response we have met with has been such as to cause us to be determined to force the superiority of our latest invention upon every trade contemporary concerned, and this we have done by our

"WORLD CHALLENGE,"

anent STEEL RIBBED ROD, which has now been publicly issued for nine months without thus far meeting with an acceptance.

We have exhibited on four occasions only, and the following awards are held by us:—

INTERNATIONAL FISHERIES, LONDON, 1883.
Seven Awards. A Prize Medal for Flies, a Prize Medal for Rods, a Prize Medal for General Exhibits, and Four Diplomas of Honour.

INTERNATIONAL SPORTS EXHIBITION, COLOGNE, 1889.
Silver Medal for Steel Centred Rods, Flies, Reels, &c.

PISCATORIAL EXHIBITION, BOLTON, 1889.
First Prize Medal for Flies, and the First Prize Medal for Lines (the only classes in which we exhibited).

INDUSTRIAL EXHIBITION, DERBY, 1892.
Highest Award for Rods. (This was gained by the Steel Ribbed).

Lastly, English Angling Literature is the richer, through efforts of ours, by a Work that has gone to six editions, and has been considered worth pirating by our transatlantic cousins.

ESTABLISHED 1872 INCORPORATED 1892

1896

THE WILKINSON CO.

MANUFACTURERS IMPORTERS
AND DEALERS IN

HAPPY THOUGHT

TACKLE

ALWAYS BELLY DOWN

....AND....

CAMP EQUIPMENTS

83 RANDOLPH STREET, CHICAGO

No. 65

SOLE AGENTS FOR
CLARK'S SPECIALTIES

Happy Thought Tackle. Always Belly Down. Advertising slogans in 1896.

Page 131: The Kosmic Company, for which the Wilkinson Company was a, or maybe the, distributor, is one of the least known and most intriguing of its time and trade. When the Mills interests broke off from the Leonard interest sometime in the 1890s, a number of the skilled workmen, including Thomas, Payne, Edwards, and the Hawes brothers, left and set up independent rodmaking shops. Edward F. Payne, originally a machinist, who was one of Hiram Leonard's original Bangor employees, and Frank Oram, who had been Leonard's superintendent at the Central Valley, New York, plant, formed the Kosmic Company in 1895, apparently with the financial backing of one of the Pratts of Standard Oil. Legend says their shop was in the plant of the Self-Winding Clock Co., also owned by Pratt, in Brooklyn, New York. Legend says further that Payne and Oram commuted to it daily from Highland Mills, New York, two miles above Central Valley, but that they found the traveling so arduous and the business so unremunerative that after a year or two the Kosmic Company closed down, and Payne and Oram set up the E. F. Payne Rod Co. in Highland Mills.

The illustration of the complicated and largely ineffective Kosmic ferrule indicates the length to which Payne and Oram went in an effort to circumvent Hiram Leonard's two ferrule patents, the trivial waterproofing disk and the fundamental serrated—split—back end.

A Six Strip Split Bamboo Rod.

Perfect in Action and Finish.

Patented May 6, 1890, and May 27, 1890. Registered March 18, 1890.

These rods approach as nearly an ideal standard as mechanical skill and a practical knowledge of an angler's needs can produce. The bamboo is of the finest quality. The patent ferrules used on these rods are absolutely non-breakable at the joints; they are made by hand of the highest grade german silver, re-enforced with celluloid.

THE KOSMIC RODS ARE GUARANTEED IN EVERY WAY.

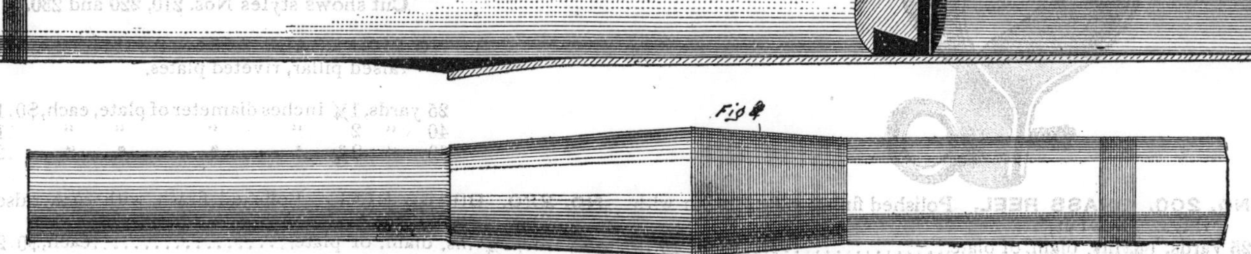

Illustrations show the construction of the Patent Ferrule.

Fig. 1. Elastic celluoid band re-enforcing the bamboo.
Fig. 2. German silver ferrule, patented March 6, 1890.
Fig. 3. Patent water-proof cap excluding all moisture.
Fig. 4. Showing Kosmic Ferrule in jointed rod.

KOSMIC FLY RODS.

No.	Length	Weight	Description	Price
No. 7.	9½ feet	5½ oz.	3-piece and extra tip; tips enclosed in Bamboo Screw Top Case	$25.00
No. 8.	10 "	6½ "	3 " " " " " " "	25.00
No. 9.	10½ "	7¾ "	3 " " " " " " "	25.00

The above rods have cork hand grasps and celluloid reel seats.

Sole Leather Case furnished gratis with each of the above rods.

THE KOSMIC FLY CASTING REEL.

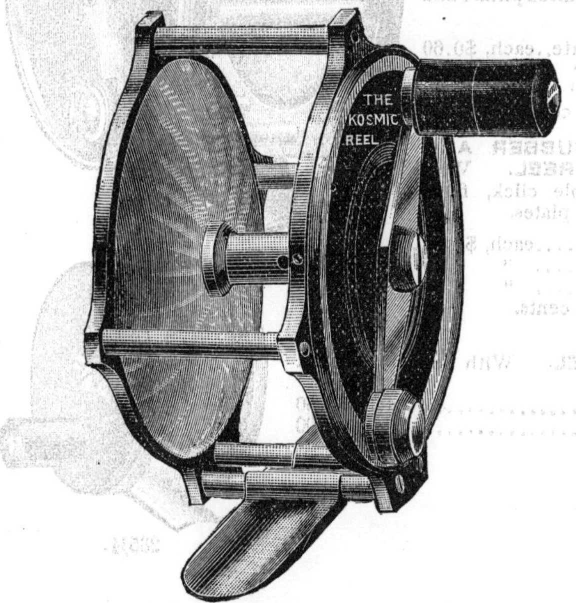

No. 926.

Best hard rubber and german silver; raised pillar; fine steel pivots in bushed, hardened bearings; adjustable back-sliding click, with steel cog, spring and ratchet; screw-off oil caps.

No. 925.	100 yards capacity, so as to build up the line	$6.00
No. 926.	150 " " " " "	7.00

Registered mail, postage 20 cts. extra.

THE KOSMIC FLY CASTING LINES.

The Kosmic Braided Enameled Silk Lines are designed to meet the demand for a fine quality.

TAPERED (BOTH ENDS).

D, 40 yards	$3.50	E, 40 yards	$3.25
F, 40 yards	$3.00		

LEVEL.

E, 25 yards	$1.50	F, 75 yards	$3.75
E, 50 "	3.00	F, 100 "	5.00
E, 75 "	4.50	G, 25 "	1.20
E, 100 "	6.00	G, 50 "	2.40
F, 25 "	1.25	G, 75 "	3.60
F, 50 "	2.50	G, 100 "	4.80

Any of the above lines sent by mail, postpaid.

Fishing Reels.

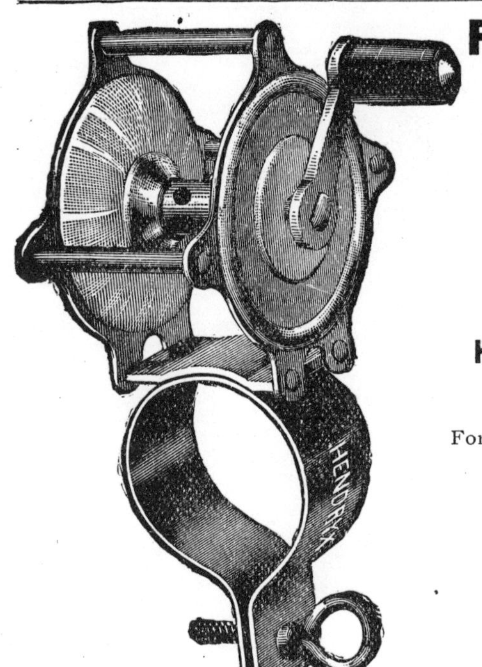

For price, see following pages.

Cut shows styles Nos. 210, 220 and 230.

NO 210. BRASS REEL. Polished finish, raised pillar, riveted plates.

25 yards, 1¾ inches diameter of plate, each, $0.10
40 " 2 " " " " .15
60 " $2\frac{3}{16}$ " " " " .20

NO. 200. BRASS REEL. Polished finish, raised pillar with rings. (See cut).

25 yards, 1¾ ins. diam. of plate..................... each, $0.15
40 " 2 " " .... " .20
60 " $2\frac{3}{16}$ " " .... " .25

Postage, 5 cents extra.

NO. 220. BRASS REEL. Polished finish, with *click*, raised pillar, rivited plates.

25 yards, 1¾ ins. diam. of plate..................... each, $0.20
40 " 2 " " .... " .25
60 " $2\frac{3}{16}$ " " .... " .30

Postage extra, 5 cents.

NO. 230. NICKEL PLATED REEL. With *click*, raised pillar and riveted plates.

25 yds., 1¾ ins. diam. of plate.. each, $0.25
40 " 2 " " .. " .30
60 " $2\frac{3}{16}$ " " .. " .35

NO. 230½. NICKEL PLATED REEL. With back sliding adjustable click, flush balance handle, raised pillars and screw plates.

40 yds., 2 ins. diam. of plate.. each, $0.60
60 " 2¼ " " .. " .65
80 " 2½ " " .. " .70

Postage extra, 5 cents.

NO. 235. HARD RUBBER AND NICKEL PLATED REEL. With back sliding adjustable click, flush balance handle, screw plates.

40 yards .... each, $1.30
60 " .... " 1.40
80 " .... " 1.50

Postage extra, 5 cents.

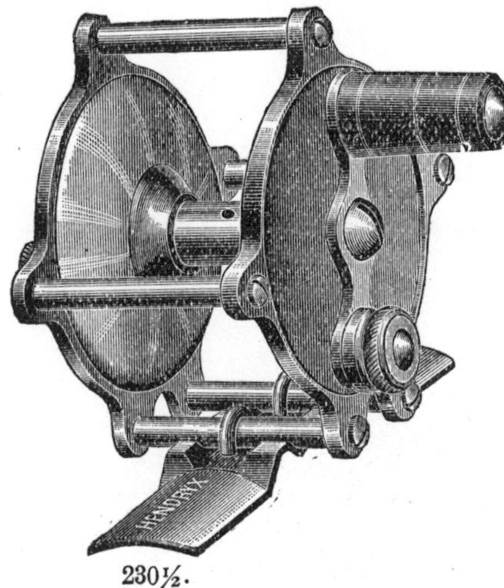

230½.

235

No. 235½. THE CELEBRATED ENGLISH FLY-CASTING REEL. With revolving disk and *extra fine* click. Made of ebonite bronze and hard rubber.

60 yards.. each, $3.50
80 " .... " 4.00

Postage extra 10 cents.

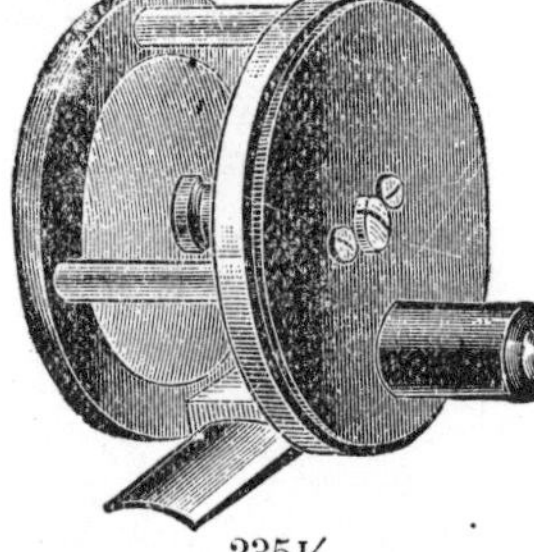

235½.

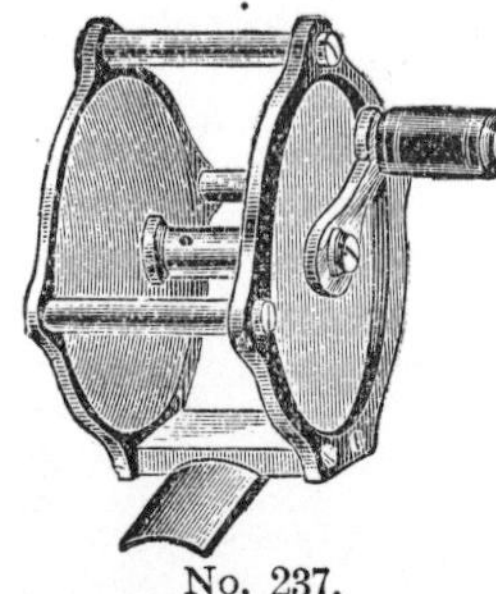

No. 237.

No. 237. HIGH QUALITY ALUMINIUM FLY-CASTING REEL. Adjustable click on rear plate, thereby making a free running reel when desired; raised pilla's, large ine capacity, handle revolving within and completely protected by the rim; very light, hence very desirable for using on light-weight fly rods.

40 yards.. $5.00
60 " 5.50
80 " 6.00

So light we can send by mail, postpaid.

FISHING REELS—CONTINUED.

No. 250. Nickel Plated Reel.—Double Multiplier, Balance Handle, Raised Pillar, Screw Plates, with *Adjustable Drag*.

40	yards, each	$0.75
60	" "	.80
80	" "	.85
100	" "	.90

No. 260. Nickel Plated Reel.—Double Multiplier, Balance Handle, Raised Pillar, Screw Plates, with *Back Sliding Click*.

40	yards, each	$0.75
60	" "	.80
80	" "	.85
100	" "	.90

Postage extra, 10 cents.

No. 270. Nickel Plated Reel.—Double Multiplier, Balance Handle, Raised Pillar, Screw Plates, with *Adjustable Drag and Back Sliding Click*.

40	yards, each	$0.75
60	" "	.80
80	" "	.85
100	" "	.90

Postage extra, 10 cents.

Our complete line of Reels comprise the gems of the market

No. 280. Fine Nickel Plated Bass and Muscallonge Reels.—Double Multiplier, Steel Pivots, Balance Handle, Heavy Adjustable Drag, and Sliding Click on Back Plate to save wear on main gearing. A well made, strong and durable Reel.

40	yards, Bass size, each	$1.25
60	" " " "	1.50
80	" Bass and Muscallonge size, each	1.75
100	" Muscallonge size, each	2.00

Postage extra, 10 cents.

No. 285. Fine Hard Rubber and Nickel Plated Double Multiplying Reel.—Raised Pillars, Balance Handles, Patent Adjustable Drag on front plate and Back Sliding Click on rear plate to save wear on main gearing.

40	yards, each	$1.00
60	" "	1.10
80	" "	1.25

Postage extra.

The No. 285 Reel is very light, compact, strong and durable. It is the cheapest and best rubber Reel in the market.

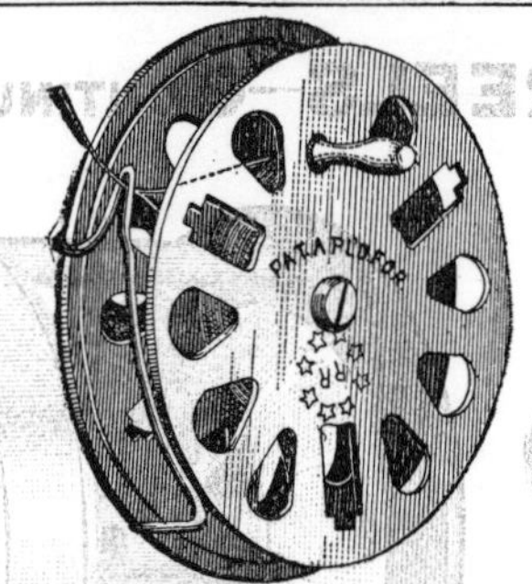

NEW IMPROVED EXPERT REELS, ETC.

THE R. R. REEL.

This reel is the simplest in construction of any yet made. The disk being perforated, the line drys readily. The spool being large, the line can be wound up quickly.

Price, Nickel Plated..........................each, $0.75

Postage extra, 5 cents.

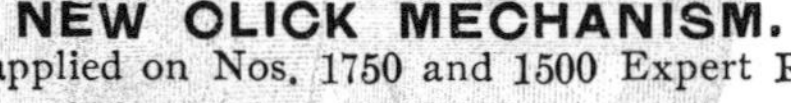

NEW CLICK MECHANISM.

As applied on Nos. 1750 and 1500 Expert Reels.

The click wheel, pawl or index snapper and click spring are made of hardened steel and tempered. This is a SLIDING click, and is so constructed that the pawl compensates any wear that might occur. The pawl can be used at either end by unscrewing the screw that holds the spring. It is very simple in construction and cannot easily get out of order, and will wear long. It is the BEST CLICK ever put on a reel and will no doubt increase the popularity of the "Expert" Reels.

No. 1700.

No. 1700. EXPERT REEL.

2¼ inches diameter, ¾ inch wide, 40 yards, upright, with drag (see cut).. 1.45

No. 1750. EXPERT REEL.

2¼ inches diameter, ¾ inch wide, upright, with click, (see cut No. 1500).. 1.45

Postage extra, 5 cents.

No. 1500. EXPERT REEL.

3 inches diameter, 1 inch wide, 100 yards, upright, with click, (see cut).. 1.75

No. 1600. EXPERT REEL.

3 inches diameter, 1 inch wide, 100 yards, upright, with drag, (see cut No. 1700).. 1.75

Postage extra, 10 cents.

No. 1500.

No. 2500.

THE EXPERT MUSCALLONGE TROLLING REEL.

3 inches diameter, 1½ inch wide, 150 yards upright, with drag 2.40

Postage extra, 10 cents.

The Expert Reels are finely polished and heavily nickel plated. They combine lightness, great strength and very fine running qualities.

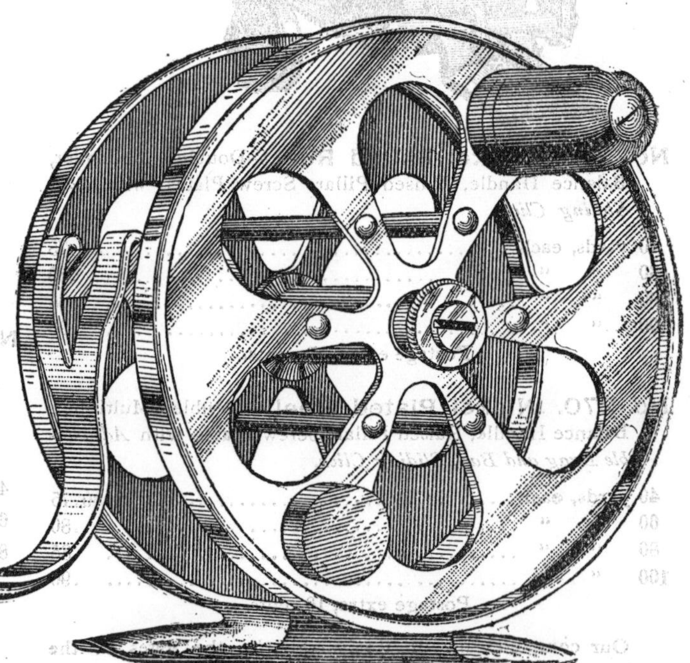

No. 2500.

FISHING REELS—CONTINUED.

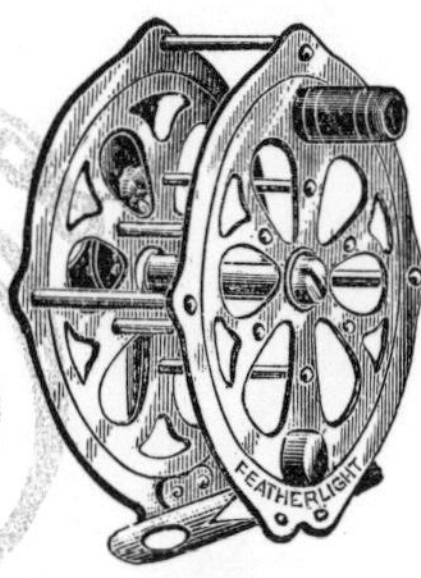

THE NEW "ALL RIGHT" REELS.

With Removable Spool and Back Sliding Adjustable Click.

No. 110. 60 yards, size spool, 1¾x1............Each, $1.50
No. 120. 80 " " " 2½x1............ " 1.75
No. 130. 100 " " " 2⅝x1¼............ " 2.25

Postage extra, 10 cents.

THE FEATHERWEIGHT REELS.

With Removable Spool and Back Sliding Adjustable Click.

No. 260. 50 yards, size spool, 1¾x¾............Each, $1.25
No. 270. 80 " " " 2¼x¾............ " 1.50

Postage extra, 10 cents.

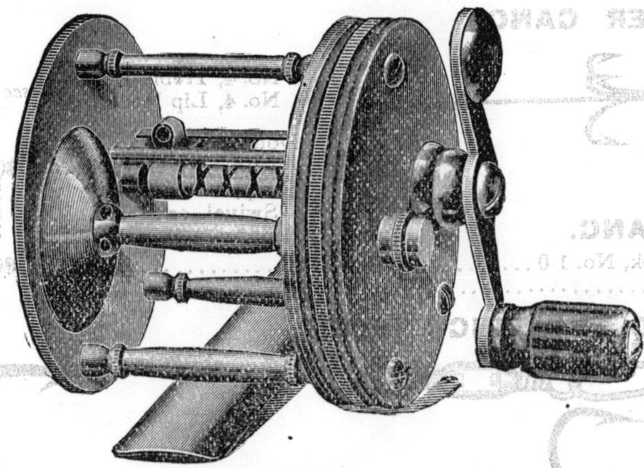

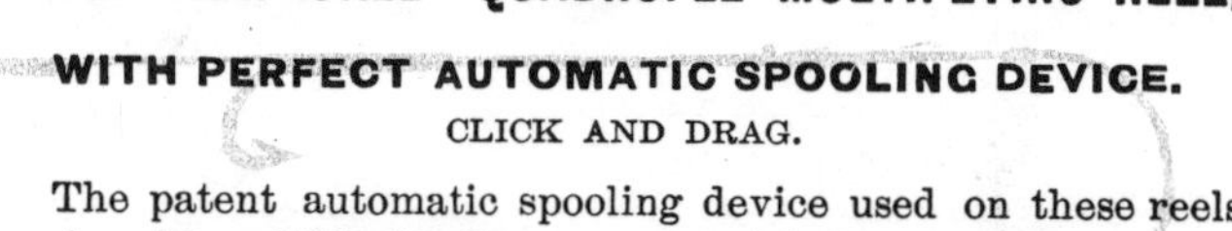

"THE MILWAUKEE" QUADRUPLE MULTIPLYING REEL,

WITH PERFECT AUTOMATIC SPOOLING DEVICE.

CLICK AND DRAG.

The patent automatic spooling device used on these reels works with so little friction as not to hinder the free running of the reel in casting. The reel is always in readiness for a successful cast, as the line is perfectly spooled, no matter with what haste or carelessness it may have been reeled in. The spooling attachment allows the fisherman to give his entire time and attention to his bait or fish. For muscallonge trolling they positively stand without a peer.

These reels are made in two sizes, Nos. 3 and 4, with a capacity for holding 60 and 80 yards of line. Hand-made, in hard german silver, of the finest workmanship and finish.

60 yards ....Each, $15.00
80 " .... " 16.00

Postage extra, 15 cents.

FOLDING FISHING HAT.

Made of dead grass color selecia; lined with green; Featherweight. Fits any head. When folded takes up about the same room in the pocket as an ordinary pocket handkerchief.

Price with case....................Each, $0.50

Sent by mail, post-paid.

LADD'S NEW FISH SCALER.

BEST STEEL.—GALVANIZED.

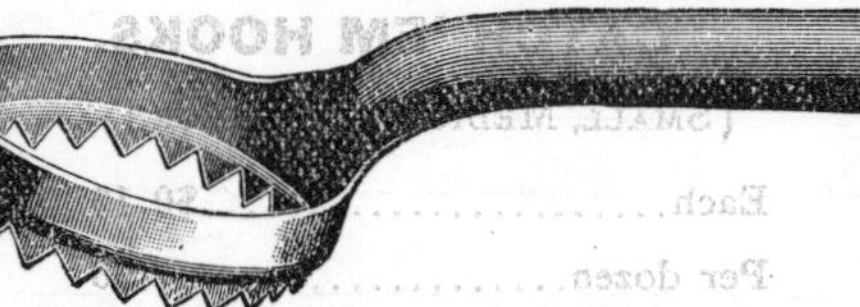

Compact, light and durable. It does the work and does it quickly and well. Each...$0 20

Postage extra, 5 cents.

The 50-cent folding sombrero is an old friend of every veteran fisherman; it was featured in all the catalogs for a generation or three.

The Milwaukee level-winder seems to have a particularly atrocious little hole in the distributing block through which the line must flow both coming and going. And even 80 yards of line seems little enough for a muskellunge.

GANG HOOKS, CASTING SNOODS, ETC.

THE ST. LAWRENCE GANG.

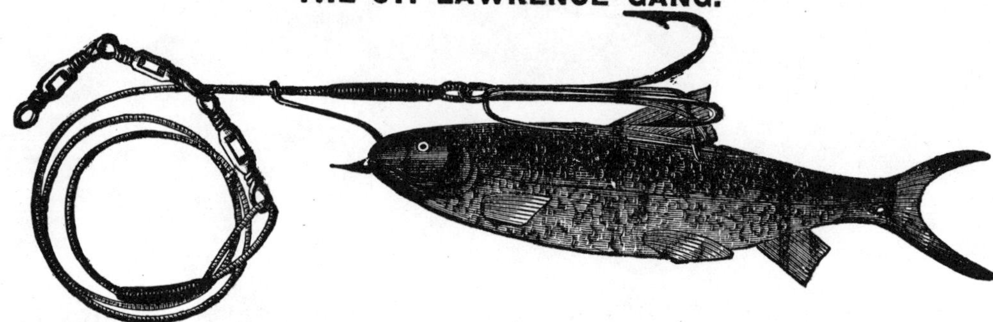

Patented in England and the United States.

All have patent Hooks with Baiting Needle, adjustable Lip Hook and Treble Swivel, best Silk Metal Wound Gimp. It can be adjusted to any size minnow instantly and perfectly. The Treble Swivel insures perfect revolution of bait, and reduces to the lowest possible point the liability of kinking the line.

Nos.	2	1	1-0	2-0	3-0	4-0	5-0	6-0	Sent by mail, postpaid.
Price each	.30	.30	.30	.35	.35	.35	.35	.40	

SETH GREER GANG.

No. 4, Treble Hooks } *see cut.*
No. 4, Lip Hook

Double Gut, 8 inches long with Swivel, each......$0.25
Gimp, 8 inches long with Swivel, each........... .25
Sent by mail, postpaid.

ADIRONDACK GANG.

Double Gut, 10 inches long, 3 Treble Hooks, No. 1-0. 1 Lip Hook, No. 1-0 .... Each, $0.35
Gimp " Same description .... " .35

MINNOW CASTING AND TROLLING SNOODS.

Impossible to lose minnows when casting.

No. 1. Wound on extra heavy double Gut, each..........$0.15

No. 2. Wound to Silver Gimp, each .... .15

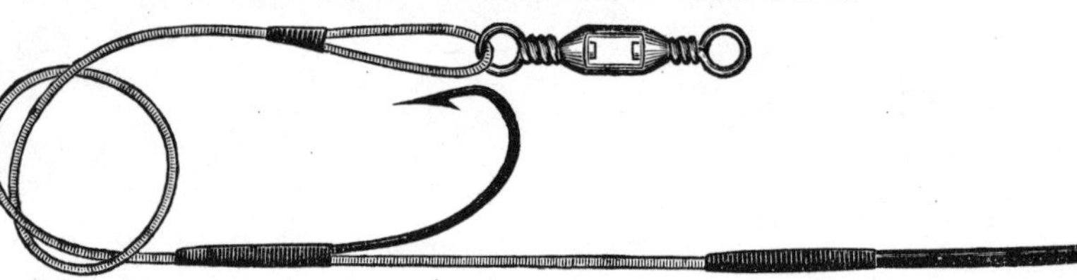

We make the following lengths between spears of hooks: 2¼, 2½, 2¾, 3 and 3¼ inches. Sent by mail on receipt of price.

SPRING, SNAP AND CATCH 'EM HOOKS.

(SMALL, MEDIUM AND LARGE.)

Each.......................$0.15

Per dozen.................. 1.50

Sent by mail on receipt of price.

GREER'S PATENT LEVER FISH HOOK.

Sprung

Set

The best fish hook on earth for lake and river fishing. No loosing bait, *nor coming home without your largest fish.* A dead-sure thing on getting your fish if it bites. It is simple and strong, being constructed on the principle of a lever, and the harder a fish pulls the stronger it holds him. It is easily adjusted to all kinds of fishing, by sliding the little clamp on the rod, which regulates the tension on the hook. Made on Carlisle Hooks. No. 3-0, price, each, 15 cents; per dozen, $1.50. Sent by mail, postpaid.

SOCKDOLAGER HOOK.

For Fish or Game.

Sockdolager.

Small. Each, 25c — Medium. Each, 25c — Large. Each, 25c

Sent by mail, post-paid.

BARBLESS HOOKS.

1 2 3 4 5 6 7

The celebrated "Edgar Barbless Hook" is now too well known to need a description.

Nos	1, 2, 3;	4, 5, 6;	7, 8, 9;	10
Per doz	.15	.18	.20	.25

Per dozen assorted, Nos. 1 to 10........................35 cents.

Sent by mail, postpaid.

MUNN'S NEW WEED HOOK.

With this device, the spring weed guard completely covers the point of the hook. A slight strike or twitch with the rod forces the guard down leaving the hook free to act.

No. 18. Cincinnati Bass Hook with swivel..Each, $0.15; Two for $0.25

Sent by mail, postpaid.

THE O. K. FISH HOOK.

HIGH GRADE.—BRIGHT FINISH.

This hook is very desirable for bait, such as crawfish, helgemmite, grasshopper, beetle, worm, clam and all manner of insects. Bait the needle or prong, then lock it over the shank of the hook. By this means it will securely hold the bait in a natural position. Fishermen who have attempted to keep grasshoppers and other delicate baits upon a plain hook will at once see the great utility of this device.

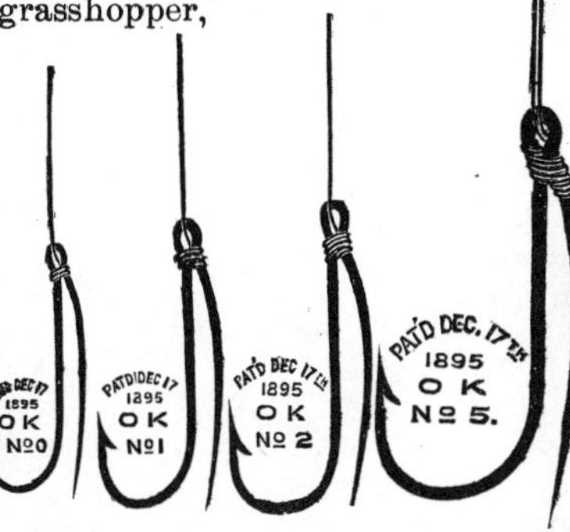

No. 0. Trout Size, Best Single Gut..........................Per Doz., $1.00
No. 1. " " " " " .... " " 1.00
No. 2. " " " " " .... " " 1.00
No. 4. Bass " " Double " .... " " 1.00
No. 4. Ringed only; Bass Size......................... " " .60
No. 5. " " " " .... " " .60

Sent by mail, postpaid.

THE REFLEX FISH HOOK.

HIGH GRADE. BRIGHT FINISH.

This hook is similar to the O.K. with the addition of the baiting needle or prong having a reflex bend at the end. By this means the prong can be passed under the gills of a minnow or lengthwise of a frog leaving the hook proper in both instances unincumbered with the bait.

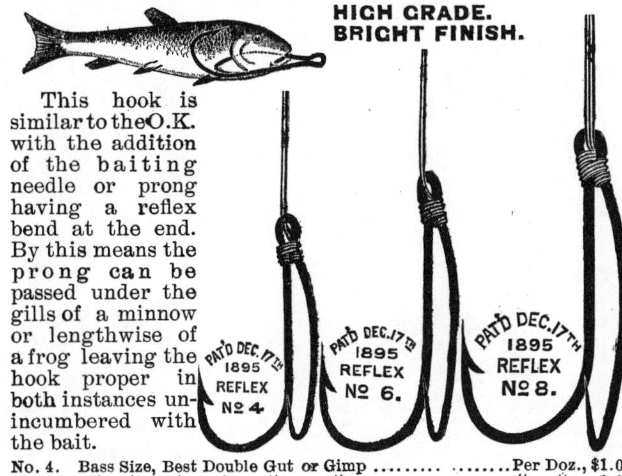

No. 4. Bass Size, Best Double Gut or Gimp ....Per Doz., $1.00
No. 6. " " " " " " .... " " 1.00
No. 8. Pike " " " " " .... " " 1.50
No. 4. Ringed only; Bass Size.................. " " .60
No. 6. " " " " .... " " .60
No. 8. " " Pike " .... " " 1.00

Sent by mail, postpaid.

THE PATENT "ARCHER" SPINNER.

This device is particularly adapted for using with the natural minnow, the needle passing lengthwise through the minnow, the hinge flukes or fins firmly grasping it through the gills. With this spinner, a very natural whirl and spin is given the minnow.

No. 1. Trout Size..Each, $0.50
No. 2. Small, Salmon and Bass Size.......................... " .50
No. 3. Large, " " " .... " .50
No. 4. Pike Size.. " .50

Sent by mail, postpaid.

PREVOST PATENT COMBINATION FROG HOOK.

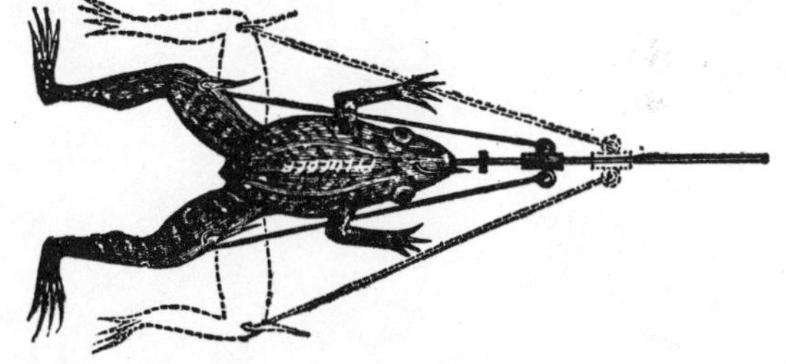

This new device is very desirable for frog casting. It allows free and natural action to the bait, takes a firm hold, and does not tear the frog.

No. 1. Small............Each, $0.20
No. 2. Medium.......... " .30
No. 3. Large............Each, $0.35

Sent by mail, postpaid.

Spring, snap, weedless, and other fancy hooks were a favorite playground for angling inventors in the good old days, but it's still too true that "weedless means fishless." Scores of such devices were patented between 1850 and 1900, some quite dangerous to set or handle.

Page 138: They're still made, guinea hen feathers and all.

PFLUEGER'S SUCCESS LUMINOUS SPOON.

"This spoon bait comprises more new features than any bait in the market. Five separate and distinct patents are incorporated into its construction."

It is a Perfect Working Spoon, under all circumstances.

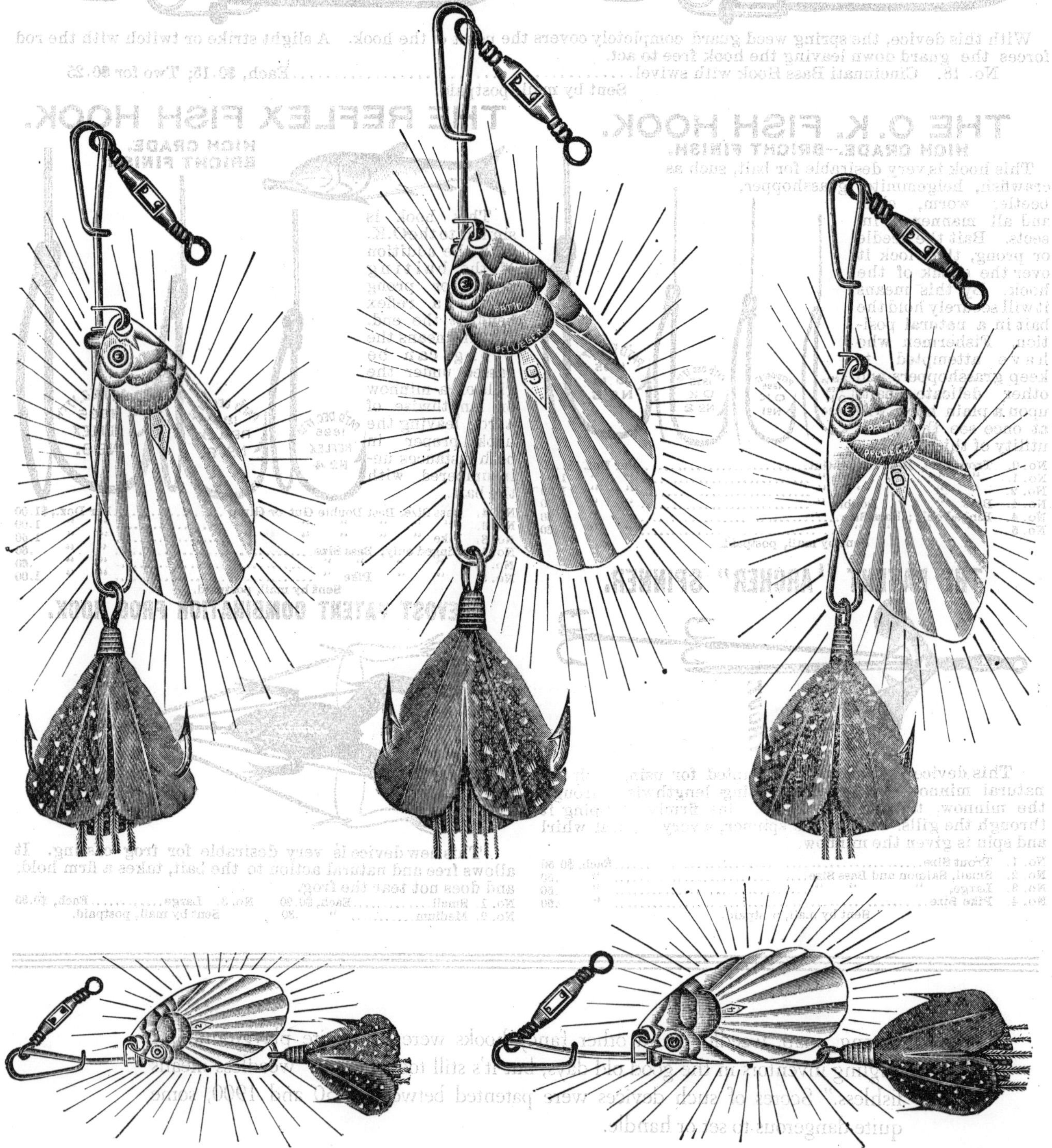

Extra heavy nickel plated Fluted Fish Head pattern, fitted with patent reversible hinge lug, inside painted with Pflueger's Celebrated Luminous Paint, tipped with red. In addition to the luminous features of these spoons, they are embellished with a gold flitter on the inside, which adds greatly to their attractiveness. Best hooks, very heavily and finely feathered.

BASS SIZE.
Nos. 2, 3, 4, 5, 6.... Each, $0.25

PIKE AND PICKEREL SIZE.
Nos. 7 and 8.... Each, $0.30

MUSKELLUNCE SIZE.
Nos. 9 and 10.... $0.35

Gimp Snoods on Nos. 2 to 7. Wire Snoods on Nos. 8 to 10,

Sent by mail postpaid.

PFLUEGER'S PATENT LUMINOUS INDESTRUCTIBLE BODY FLIES.

Effective, Morning, Noon, Evening and Night.

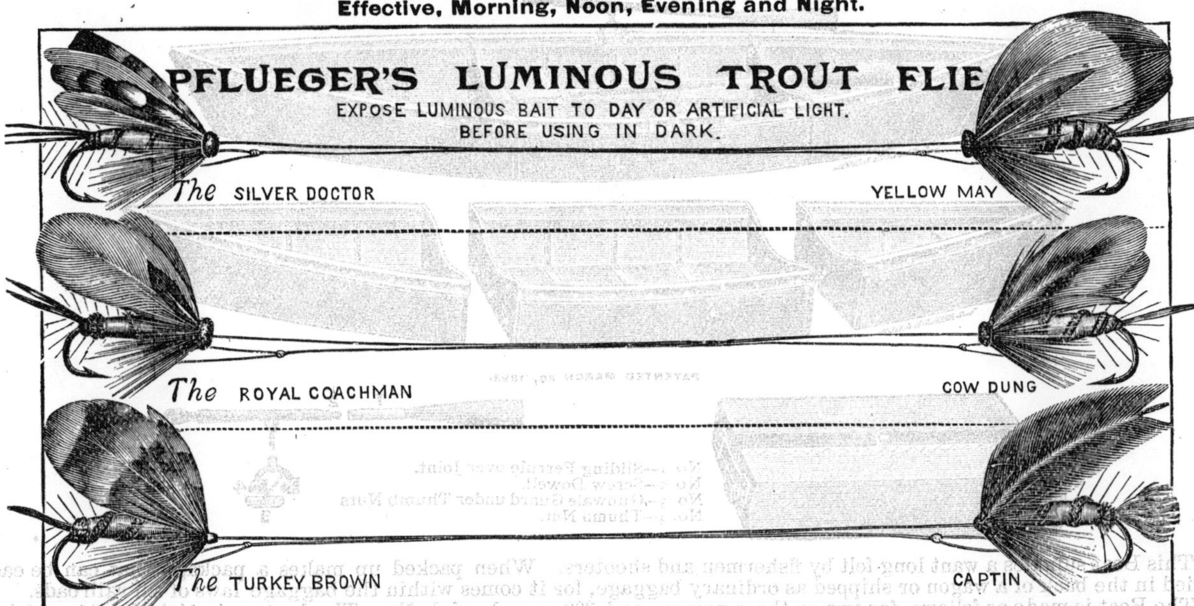

These flies are made with luminous indestructible bodies that throw off iridescent rays, which add greatly to the killing properties of the natural feather, of which they are made. The wings are also blended with Jungle Cock, Golden Pheasant and Wood Duck feathers.

LUMINOUS TROUT FLIES.

Harrison's Sproat Hooks. Best Single Gut. Nos. 4, 6, 8 and 10.

Grizzly King, White Miller, Yellow May, Black Gnat,
Professor, Coachman, Scarlet Ibis, Blue Bottle,
Queen of Water, Cow Dung, Hare's Ear, Brown Hackle,
Reuben Wood, Silver Doctor, Willow, Brown Stone,
Dusty Miller, Parmachenee Belle, Alder, Gray Hackle.

For Color of Wing Feathers see Specifications, page 57.

Per dozen..$1.00

LUMINOUS BASS FLIES.

Harrison's Sproat Hooks. Best Double Gut. Nos. 2 and 2-0.

Coachman, Silver Doctor, Seth Green, Yellow Butterfly,
Professor, Ibis, Oak, Brown Hackle,
Black June, Lord Baltimore, Parmachenee Belle, Polka.
Grizzly King, White Miller,

For Color of Wing Feathers see specifications, page 58.

Per dozen..$1.25

THE CELEBRATED HUGUNIN BASS FLY.

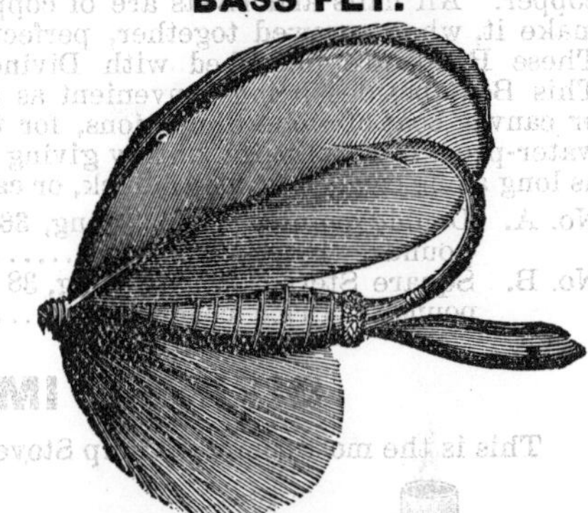

Wings tied so they cover point of hook and make a weed guard. Tied on 2-0 and 3-0 Harrison Sproat Hooks. Best Double Gut.

Montreal, White Miller, Ibis, Yellow May, Seth Green, Grizzly King, Jungle Cock, Royal Coachman, Professor, Lord Baltimore, Gov. Alvord, Black Gnat.

Per doz..$2.25

ABBEY & IMBRIE'S HIGHEST QUALITY BASS FLIES.

Also Desirable for Large Trout.

These Flies are tied with very best Single Gut and Helpers to No. 1 Harrison Sproat Hooks, per dozen $2.50

LORD BALTIMORE. Wings, black, with jungle cock shoulders; body, orange floss silk, ribbed with black silk; tail, black; legs, black hackle.

COACHMAN. Wings, white; body, peacock herl; legs, brown hackle.

SETH GREEN. Wings, female mallard, brown mottled feather; body, green silk and salmon plush; tail, mottled; legs, heavy brown hackle.

WHITE MILLER. Wings, white; body, white, ribbed with silver tinsel; legs, white hackle.

ROYAL COACHMAN. Wings, white; body, peacock herl, with band of red silk in middle; legs, brown hackle.

PROFESSOR. Wings, gray mallard; body, yellow, ribbed with gold; tail, scarlet ibis; legs, brown hackle.

BLACK JUNE. Wings, raven; body, peacock herl; legs, black hackle.

GRIZZLY KING. Wings, gray mallard; body, green, ribbed with gold tinsel; tail, red; legs, furnace gray hackle.

DONALDSON. Wings, white and yellow mixed; shoulder, golden pheasant; body, orange silk; tail, golden pheasant; legs, red hackle.

SCARLET IBIS. Wings, scarlet ibis; body, red, ribbed with gold tinsel; tail, scarlet ibis; legs, scarlet ibis.

MARTIN. Wings, black; body, yellow; tail, scarlet ibis and black; legs, orange hackle.

PARMACHENEE BELLE. Wings, mixed ibis and white; body, pale yellow mohair, ribbed with silver tinsel; tail, a stripe each, white and scarlet ibis; legs, bright scarlet and white hackle mixed.

DARK MONTREAL. Wings, wild turkey tail; body, dark claret, ribbed with gold; tail, scarlet ibis; legs, dark claret hackle.

RED BUTCHER. Wings, red ibis; shoulder, green peacock, golden pheasant; body, peacock herl; tail, red ibis; legs, brown hackle.

WHITE JEWEL. Wings, white; body peacock herl; tail, claret and white mixed; legs, claret and white hackle mixed.

BLACK TERROR. Wings, black, mixed with peacock swords; shoulder, green peacock, golden pheasant; body, peacock herl; tail, claret; legs, claret hackle.

GRAY DAWN. Wings, gray mallard; shoulder, green peacock and golden pheasant; body, peacock herl; tail, red ibis; legs, furnace gray hackle.

BROWN BUSH. Wings, turkey brown and peacock swords mixed; shoulder, golden pheasant tippet and green peacock; body, peacock herl; tail, red ibis; legs, brown hackle.

PEACOCK BEAUTY. Wings, peacock blue mixed with peacock swords; shoulder, red ibis and golden pheasant mixed; body, peacock herl; tail, red ibis; legs, brown hackle.

YELLOW SIREN. Wings, yellow; shoulder, red ibis; body, peacock herl; tail, red ibis; legs, yellow hackle.

YELLOW INVINCIBLE. Wings, yellow; body, yellow silk; tail, yellow; legs, yellow hackle.

BLUE BOTTLE. Wings, dark lead color; body, dark blue silk; legs, black hackle.

BROWN and RED PALMER. Body, red silk, with brown hackle wound the whole length of the body.

BROWN and PEACOCK PALMER. Body, peacock herl, with brown hackle wound the whole length of the body.

GRAY and YELLOW PALMER. Body, yellow silk, with gray hackle wound the whole length of the body.

YELLOW PALMER. Body, yellow silk, with yellow hackle wound the whole length of the body.

Any of the above flies sent by mail, postpaid.

THE CLARK-DIVINE PATENT NESTING CARRY BOAT.

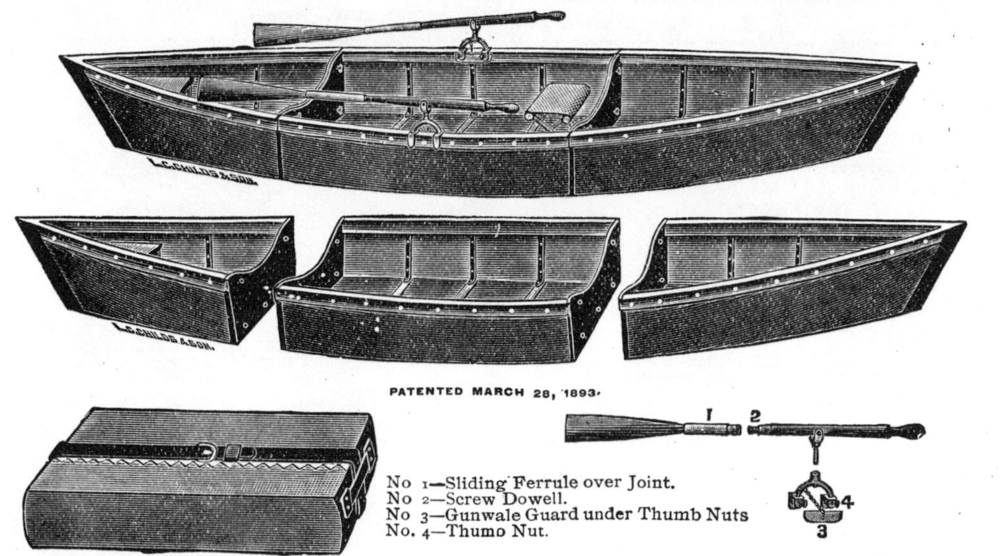

This Boat supplies a want long felt by fishermen and shooters. When packed up makes a package that can be easily carried in the back of a wagon or shipped as ordinary baggage, for it comes within the baggage laws of all railroads.

The Boat is made as follows, for two or three persons and 300 pounds of duffle: The bottom is ⅜ inch, sides ⅛ inch, bulkheads ⅝ inch pine; gunwales and keels are of oak riveted every six inches; ribs are ⅝ inch oval iron. The whole boat is covered with heavy army duck, put on with marine waterproof glue. All corners around bulkheads are bound with copper. All nails and rivets are of copper. The Boat is bound together with ten five-inch bolts and rubber washers that make it, when screwed together, perfectly water tight, the bulkheads making it stauncher than an ordinary boat. These Boats are furnished with Divine's Improved Adjustable Row Locks, Jointed Spruce Oars and Camp Stools. This Boat besides being convenient as a carry-boat, is one that will stand more rough usage than an ordinary wood or canvas boat of same dimensions, for the wood protects the canvas and the canvas the wood. Boat painted with a water-proof mineral paint, and by giving it a coat once a year a man has a boat that with any ordinary care, will last him as long as he can see to drop a duck, or cast a fly or bait. These Boats are guaranteed in every particular.

No. A. Double pointed, 12 feet long, 36 inch beam, 12 inch deep in center, 13 inch at bow and stern. Weight 75 pounds. Price complete.................................... $40.00

No. B. Square Stern, 12½ feet long, 38 inch beam, 12 inch deep in center, 13 inch at bow and stern. Weight 85 pounds. Price complete.................................... 42.00

DIVINE'S IMPROVED FOLDING CAMP STOVE.

This is the most compact Camp Stove ever made. It is made of Galvanized Iron, 2 feet long, 1 foot wide, 8 inches high two griddle holes, and has 10 feet of 3½ inch pipe. The joints are 2 feet in length, made so that one joint telescopes another, so that you can get 15 feet of pipe in a 2-foot length 3½ inches in diameter. The Stove when apart, consists of only ten pieces, and this includes the two griddle hole covers. The stove and pipe are put up in a heavy canvas cover, bound with two straps and buckles, with a handle, making a package 2 feet long, 1 foot wide, 1½ inches deep at the edges, and 5 inches in the center over pipe. Weight 20 pounds.

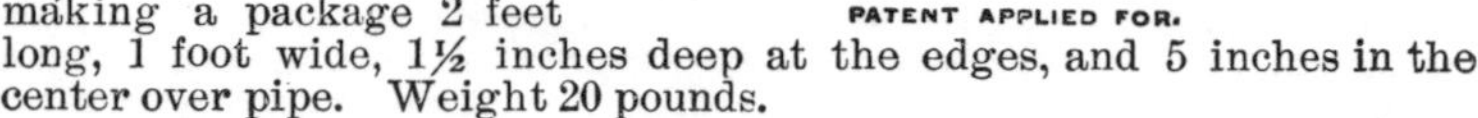

PATENT APPLIED FOR.

Price with 10 feet of pipe and tent collar.................................... $6.00

Price with Clark's folding oven (canvas case holds stove and oven).................................... 9.00

Oven takes a pan 7x15 inches.

CAMP STOVE. NOT FOLDING.

This Stove is made of Heavy Sheet Steel, is built the same as a cook stove in the flue, has a damper to run the heat into the oven or to give it a direct draught. Each stove guaranteed to bake perfectly. Dimensions: Length, 29 inches. Breadth, 16 inches. Height, 14 inches.

Price, with 8 feet telescopic pipe....................Each $6.00

Extra length of pipe 40 cents.

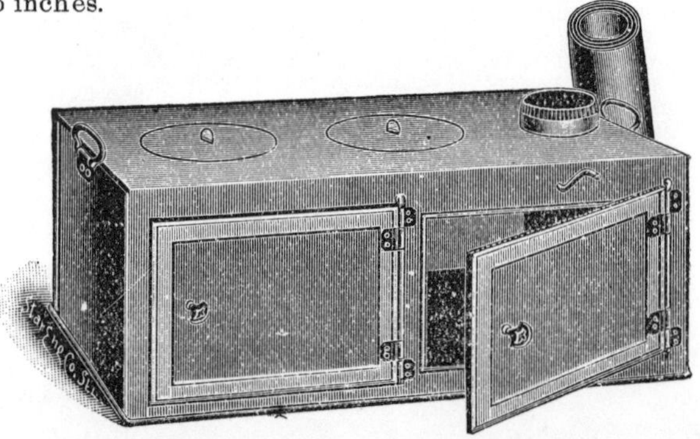

Page 140: Such folding boats were the only practical way to take a boat on a trip involving railroad travel; uncrated small craft were expensive to ship and very apt to suffer damage in the baggage car. This sectional job was more practical than most, and was on the market for years until the advent of the automobile; but it was not too strong (⅛-inch-thick sides) and developed leaks around the partitions that were difficult to stop.

Nessmuk called a camp stove "a little sheet-iron fiend" that was red-hot one minute and stone-cold the next. He was right; it takes one man to feed the campers and another to feed the stove. Folding stoves tend to stop folding after enough heat-warping.

Page 142: It's a bit startling to see a two-man tent selling for $4.18.

The hilarious "Star Reflecting Head Lamp" is a steal on the one old "Adirondack" Murray described in his book *Adventures in the Wilderness* in 1869—a headlamp made by setting a common kerosene lamp burner and reflector into the top of a fireman's leather helmet. He claimed that this ordinary burner would make an area 15 yards wide and *80 yards long* "bright as day," but Wilkinson says merely that their double burner "throws a strong light for quite a distance." All these lamps, particularly those that burned a mixture of lard oil and kerosene, produced more smoke, stink, and blisters than light.

PATENTED, U. S., JANUARY 13, 1891. PATENTED, CANADA, MARCH 11, 1891.

THE PROTEAN TENT.

A good all around tent for camping purposes. It is compact, roomy, easy to pitch, and suitable for both hot and cold weather. Only one pole required.

Fly can be used over roof, or as an awning in front, or as an addition, making the tent over 50 per cent larger.

It has other advantages too numerous to mention here. Has been on the market three seasons and fully tested.

PRICE OF PROTEAN TENTS, with Ash Pole and Pegs, but without Fly or Sod Cloth:

Size on Ground.	Height of Rear Wall.	Height of Pole.	8 ounce Best Duck.	10 ounce Best Duck.	Additional 3 Joint Pole.
6½x6½ feet.	2 feet.	6 ft. 9 inches.	$4.18	$4.80	$1.25
7 x7 "	2 "	7 " 3 "	5.26	5.90	1.25
8 x8 "	2½ "	8 " 5 "	6.50	7.30	1.75
9 x9 "	3 "	9 " 9 "	8.80	10.10	2.25

A Sod Cloth 9 inches wide all around bottom of tent will be furnished, when desired, at the following additional prices:

Size of Tent.	8 ounce Best Duck.	10 ounce Best Duck.
6½x6½ feet.	$0.60	$0.75
7 x7 "	.70	.80
8 x8 "	.75	.85
9 x9 "	.85	1.00

Flies will be furnished, when desired, at the following additional prices:

Size of Tent.	8 ounce Best Duck.	10 ounce Best Duck.
6½x6½ feet.	$2.13	$2.40
7 x7 "	2.17	2.48
8 x8 "	3.10	3.50
9 x9 "	3.70	4.00

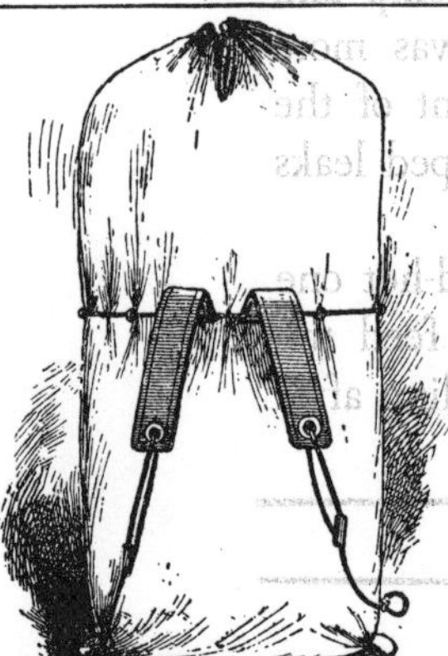

PATENT CARRY BAG.

A very simple and inexpensive bag for carrying either the Clark or Protean tent outfits, including tent, jointed pole and pegs, blankets, etc. It is light and convenient, and carries the load in comfortable position on the back. Bag can be instantly opened without removing the straps, and straps and cords can be instantly detached and stowed in the top of bag for shipment by rail.

Tent, jointed pole, etc., when packed in this bag, can be checked as baggage. Price, Patent Carry Bag..........$1.25

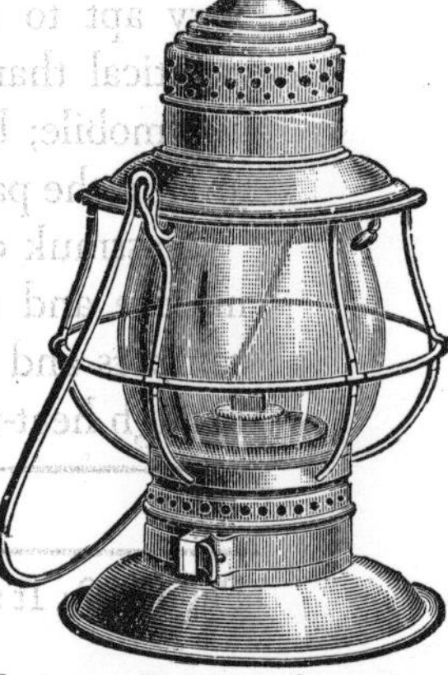

A good strong Lantern for camp use. Price, complete with Kerosene Burner..........$0.85
Price, complete with Lard Oil Burner.......... .90

STAR REFLECTING HEAD LAMP.

The above Head Light or Lamp is strongly made of the best tin-plate, has a concave semi-circular reflector, which is the most approved shape, and has two removable burners, which throw a strong light for quite a distance. It has no glass connected with it in any way to get broken in packing or while in use. It is used while rowing, fishing, hunting, driving, etc., and is adjustable, so as to fit any size or style hat or cap, in fact it is perfect in all its details and is the cheapest lamp on the market..........each, $0.90

OUT DOOR LAMPS.

GASOLINE TORCHES.

For lighting shops, factories, camps, construction work and for street vendors' use.

Each.......... $2.50

FERGUSON LAMP.

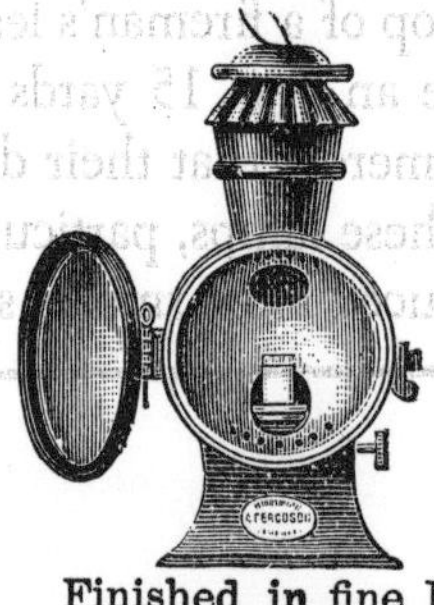

Finished in fine English Black Japan. It has no chimney. Burns signal oil, or lard or sperm oil mixed with kerosene. The wick is regulated from the outside of the lamp without opening the door. Combines Head Jack, Boat Jack, Fishing Lamp, Camp Lamp, Belt Lamp, Dash Lamp, Hand Lantern, etc. Height, 8½ inches; depth, 2¾ inches; face, 3¾ inches; weight, 17 ounces.

For the use of sportsmen, as well as for general use, this lamp is unquestionably the best Reflecting Lamp that has ever been brought to public notice.

Price, without Head Attachment, each, $6.50
" with " " " 8.25

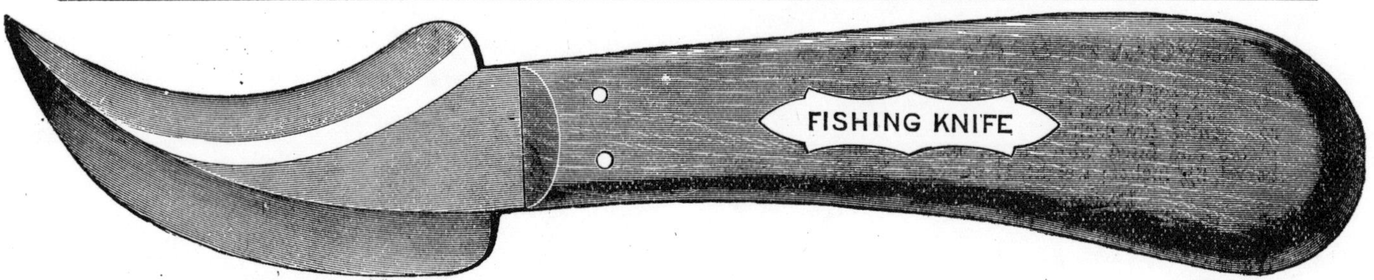

Cocoa Handle, Forged Steel Blade, Double Edge, Leather Sheath...Each, $0.75
Without doubt the best knife ever invented for cleaning and cutting fish. No fishing outfit complete without it.
Postage extra, 5 cents.

ENGSTROM'S SWEDISH KNIFE.

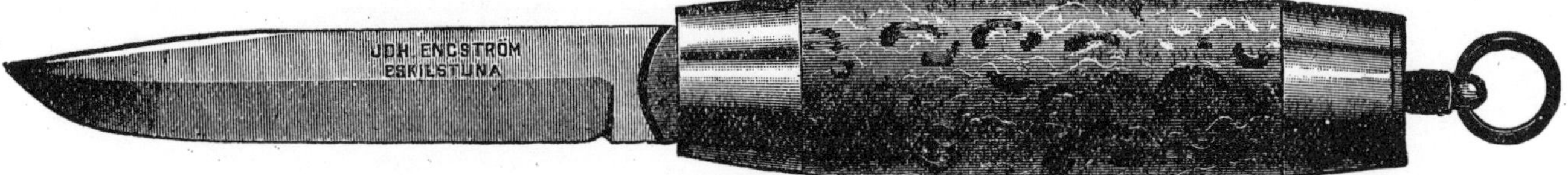

Made of the finest tempered steel. To close this knife press the spring on end of handle and draw the blade out of handle, then close the blade and put same back in handle. It is then convenient to carry in the pocket.
Price, with 3¼ inch Blade...Each, $0.90
Postage extra, 5 cents.

THE KRUSCHKE PATENT CLASP KNIFE.

The knife is simple in construction, and durable. Has genuine stag handle, made of best material and workmanship. Is warranted to give entire satisfaction.
Price each, postpaid, $2.50.

OPEN.

For Hunters, Fishers, Sailors, Linemen, One-Armed Men and Others.

This knife will be found very convenient, as it can be opened and closed with one hand, giving you the use of the other, while opening the knife. This knife locks its blade when open or closed.

CLOSED.

No. 25. Square Cushion Strop, extra fine, with paste box. Price, each.........$0.40
Postage extra, 5 cents.

THE ONLY AND GENUINE. THE STAR SAFETY RAZOR.

Beware of Cheap Imitations.

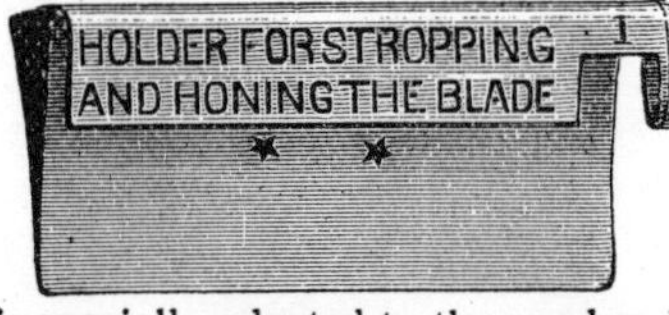

Cut shows one-half of Blade.

HOLDER FOR STROPPING AND HONING THE BLADE

A great invention, which renders shaving a simple, easy and convenient luxury, and positively obviates all danger of cutting the face. Warranted to shave clean. Time and money saved. It is specially adapted to the aged and the young; and is indispensable to travelers by land and by sea; to miners and persons camping out; to the man who wants a quick shave, and him whose skin is too tender to admit of the application of the ordinary razor. Once used, you will never be without it. Complete directions how to use accompany each outfit. Inclosed in compact and neat case.
Price, complete with holder for stropping, $1.50. Sent by mail postpaid.

This Swedish knife, the unhandiest clasp knife ever devised, has been on the market unchanged for almost a century.

Page 145: This manufacturer of filing cabinets and office furniture was among the earliest makers of that country boy's delight, the automatic reel. The gadget-minded and mechanically inclined American public received with delight a fish-catching machine from which no fish could break loose if the tension were correctly set for him. However, an automatic reel is the only one with which a one-handed man can flyfish.

Page 145: The bicycle craze was a city thing, mostly limited to larger communities that had smooth paving. Its duration was puzzlingly brief; it lost its American vogue (it never lost popularity in Europe) years before the automobile became more than a curiosity on the roads. One can only conjecture that the electric trolley car and interurban transit system (which had their own brief vogue) filled the American need for flexible, short-range transportation. By 1896, the date of this Wilkinson catalog, the bicycle was passing its peak of popularity. It made little impression on fishermen; the holsterlike rod cases for bicycles in the Abbie & Imbrie catalog (page 147) are one of the few bicycle-angling items.

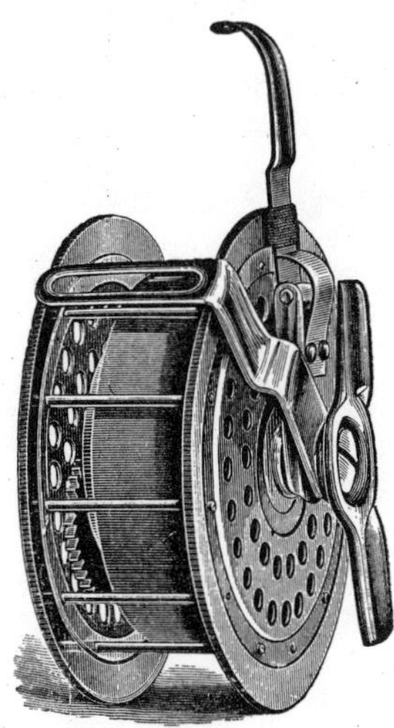

WHY NOT USE The Automatic Reel?

Please Read What Your Brother Anglers Have to Say:

THE WILKINSON CO., 83 Randolph St., Chicago.
Gentlemen: I value very highly the Automatic Reel purchased from you last year. With this reel and a 5½-oz. fly rod, I have handled many heavy fish, and have made high averages in fly-casting contests for delicacy and accuracy; and I now use it exclusively in fly-fishing, as it enables me to safely use the lightest of tackle.
Sincerely. F. B. DAVIDSON, Sec.-Treas. Chicago Fly-Casting Club.

MARION, O., Sept. 23, 1893.
Please accept these few words of praise in regard to your Automatic Reel. Along in 1886 I was induced by the late Reuben Wood, of Syracuse, N. Y., to try the Automatic. I did so, and since that time I have never used any other reel while whipping the streams. My 1886 reel has seen very hard service, but is still in good shape. On my next trip I shall try your new style reel, as it appears to be a great improvement over the one I have. Very truly yours, F. ARROWSMITH.

PARK CITY, UTAH, Sept. 12, 1894.
Have used your reel for five years and am compelled to say that it is the most perfect reel I ever used, and although I used it a great many times it always worked to perfection. Have discarded all my crank reels and shall always and only use the Automatic. For fly-casting it cannot be equalled. Yours, for sport, WM. BROTHER.

CHICAGO, ILL., March 7, 1895.
Have used your Automatic Reel for years, and I do not hesitate to say that it is the best reel made. I, in company with many other members of our fishing and gun club, use nothing else.
Yours very truly, JOHN GLENN COLLINS,
Of H. S. Rich & Co. (*The Western Brewer.*)

WASHINGTON, D. C., April 2, 1890.
Have used your reels for years and they are "dandies." I caught two of the largest black bass that have been caught in the Potomac for a number of years. The first one weighed six pounds and two ounces, the second six pounds and eight ounces; also caught two bass at one time, trolling with two hooks—one weighed four pounds four ounces, the other three pounds, a combined weight of seven pounds and four ounces. I had no trouble in bringing them to the net, as the reel worked like a charm. I can manipulate it with one hand and use lighter tackle than with any other reel and save more fish.
I am very respectfully yours, CHAS. H. LAIRD,
Room 11, P. O. Dept.

NEW HARMONY, IND., Oct. 11, 1894.
Have had splendid success with your Automatic Reel. On my last trip I landed quite a number of unusually large black bass. I am most pleased with my reel and I think that no lover of the rod should be without an Automatic, as they add immensely to the pleasure of fishing.
Yours truly, A. C. THOMAS.

CHICAGO, Aug. 15, 1894.
Have used your reels with splendid success in whipping the streams of the Wisconsin woods. I am delighted with the Automatic, and predict it is the coming reel. I would not use any other.
JOHN N. HILLS, 84 LaSalle St.

The foregoing are illustrations of the thousands of testimonials we have from fishermen regarding the merits of this reel.

YAWMAN & ERBE, ROCHESTER, N. Y.

WE ARE AGENTS FOR

THE REMINGTON

AND OTHERS.

Send Two Cents in Stamps for our Artistic Publication on this subject.

. . . . ADDRESS . . . .

THE WILKINSON CO., = 83 Randolph St., Chicago.

ESTABLISHED IN 1820.

1820 to 1897 = 77 HONEST YEARS.

Salesrooms....
18 Vesey Street, New York, U. S. A.

ILLUSTRATED CATALOGUE No. 155.

ABBEY and IMBRIE.

Succeeded Andrew Clerk & Co. in 1875.

Manufacturers of

FINE FISHING TACKLE.

Cable Address ....
Imbrie, Newyork,
P. O. Box 1294.

Fishing Rods—(Continued).

Class C½.

These Rods have extra fine nickel plated mountings. They all have FULL SOLID METAL REEL SEATS, with our PATENT ADJUSTABLE-LOCKING REEL BANDS. Joints as well as the tips are made of Lancewood. All have two tips.

Nos.		Feet long.	Each
379½	Three piece, "skittering," celluloid wound butt, fancy silk windings throughout rod, welted ferrules, metal plugs, entire rod finished in natural color	12	$4.50
380½	Three piece, "salmon fly," double handed celluloid wound butt, fancy silk windings throughout rod, welted ferrules, metal plugs, entire rod finished in natural color	14	6.00

Class D.

These Rods are all what are known as "Trunk Rods." By this is meant that they have joints not too long to be carried in an ordinary sized trunk or large sized grip-sack. The pieces, including plugs, are about 26 inches long.

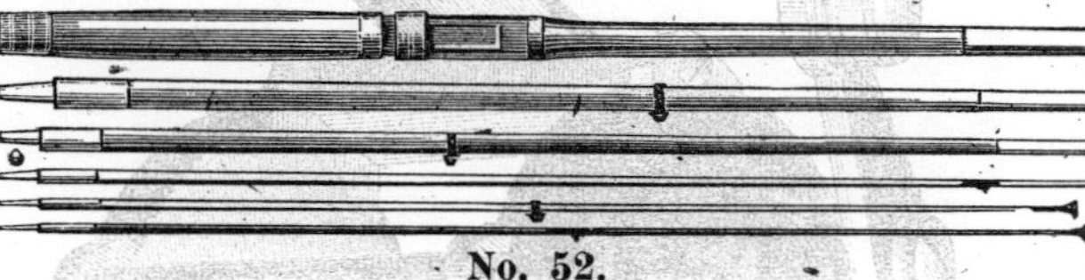

No. 52.

Nos.		Each
50D	Five piece, dark color, light bait, brass mountings, reel bands, rings, butt cap, solid butt, lancewood tip, 10 feet long	$0.75
52D	Same as No. 50D, extra finish in light color	.90
53D	Same as No. 52D, dark stained and nickel plated	1.15
54D	Five piece, light color, making 4 piece Trout rod with extra tip, reel bands, butt cap, guides, full nickel plated, 9⅓ feet long	1.25

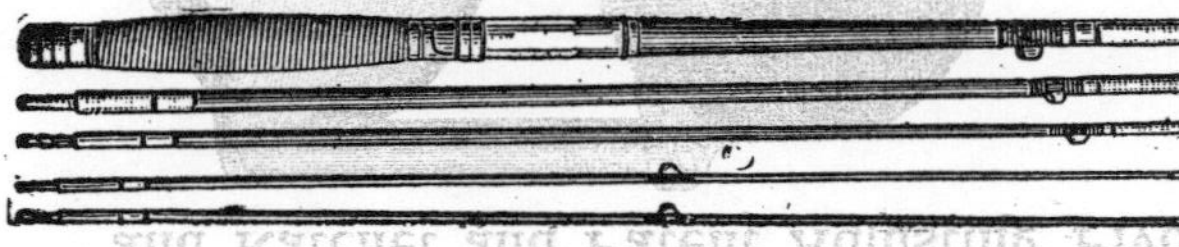

No. 56½.

Nos.		Each
55½D	Five piece, light color, zylonite butt, solid reel seat, full nickel plated mountings, all lancewood, making 4 piece Fly rod with extra tip, 9 ft. long	$1.75
56½D	Same as No. 55½D, making 4 piece Bait rod with extra tip, 9 feet long	1.75
65D	Five piece, Calcutta bamboo, double ferrules, guides and reel bands, 10 feet long	1.00

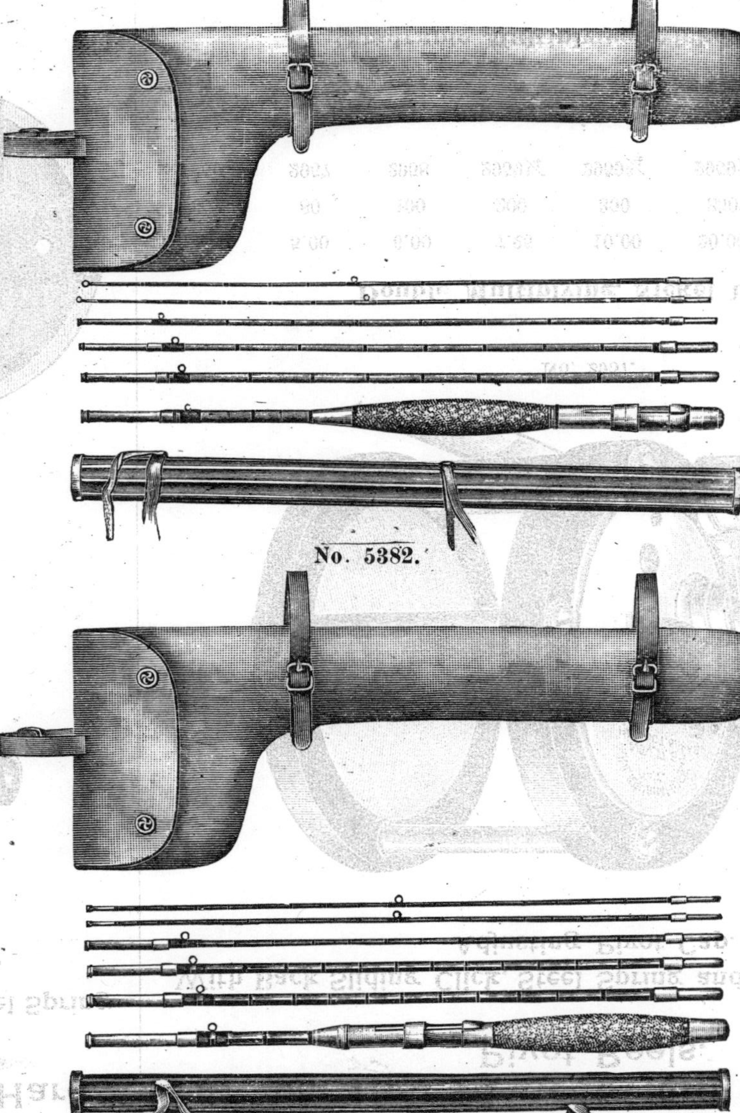

No. 5382.

No. 5045.

Bicycle Rods.

These Rods are intended, when used with the canvas cover, to fit between the frames of any bicycle. The cover contains a pocket which will hold a 100 yard multiplying reel. The Rods, including cover and wood case, measure 20 inches over all when taken apart. These Rods will also be found adapted to carrying in an ordinary grip-sack.

No. 5392. All Lancewood Bait Rod, with full nickel plated mountings, metal reel seat, cork butt, closely wound in red and green silk, length 8 feet, weight 9 ounces, each.......$3.00

No. 5382. All Lancewood Fly Rod, as 5392, length 8 feet, weight 6½ ounces, each...............$3.00

No. 5045. Six Strip Split Bamboo Bait Rod of good quality, with full nickel plated mountings, metal reel seat, cork butt, closely wound in red and black silk, length 8 feet, weight 9 ounces, each.......$4.00

No. 5040. Six Strip Split Bamboo Fly Rod, as 5045, length 8 feet, weight 7 ounces, each........$4.00

For Hexagonal Section Split Bamboo Trunk Rods see Class G, pages 64 and 65.

All Rods listed above with Solid Reel Seat have our Patent Adjustable-Locking Reel Bands. (See page 57.)

Fishing Reels—Double Multiplying.

"Abbey & Imbrie's" First Quality Hard Rubber Reels.

With Balance Handle, Back Sliding Click, Bushed, Steel Spring and Ratchet and Patent Adjusting Pivot Cap.

End View with Rubber Cap Removed. Inside View of Rubber Cap.

Nickel Plated.

$3.00	3.25	3.50	4.00	4.75	Each
40	60	80	100	200	Yards
2944	2946	2947	2948	2949¼	Nos.

J. vom Hoff's Patent Hard Rubber Steel Pivot Reels.

With Back Sliding Click, Steel Spring and Ratchet and Patent Adjusting Pivot Cap.

No. 2957.

Double Multiplying, Nickel Plated.

$4.50	5.00	6.00	7.25	10.00	20.00	25.00	Each
60	80	100	200	300	350	400	Yards
2956	2957	2958	2959¼	2959¾	2959 4/4	2959 5/4	Nos.

Quadruple Multiplying, Nickel Plated.

Same style and quality as No. 2956 series.

$6.25	7.00	8.00	Each
60	80	100	Yards
4956	4957	4958	Nos.

"Abbey & Imbrie's" Patent Compensating Steel Pivot Reels.

The vast superiority of these over all other Multiplying Reels will be manifest upon examination of the below cuts, showing the mechanical principles upon which the Reels are constructed. By this patent we are enabled to make STEEL PIVOT Reels that run with only about ONE-THIRD THE FRICTION heretofore necessary to all Reels. The Steel Pivots are so made that any wear can be adjusted in a few moments—so that the Reel is PRACTICALLY EVERLASTING. In addition to these advantages, the Reels ARE SO SIMPLE IN CONSTRUCTION that we can sell them AT PRICES much below what ordinary STEEL PIVOT REELS CAN BE MADE AT.

Out of the many thousands of these Reels which we have sold we have had returned to us for repairs less than one-quarter of one per cent. and in no case has a single Reel been found unsatisfactory to the purchaser. This fact, and the greatly and continuously increasing demand for them are PRACTICAL PROOFS that these Reels are incomparably the best Multiplying Reels on the Market.

ANOTHER IMPROVEMENT IN THEM.

H T

U

The latest patent secured by us (October 8th, 1889) on our Compensating Reels, makes the Reels absolutely perfect.

The sales of our Compensating Reels, both double and quadruple, have increased enormously every year. We have never received any complaints in regard to them. On the contrary, we are constantly receiving the most flattering letters from dealers and anglers complimenting us on the satisfactory way these reels act and the endorsement they are having from the public. Having secured such a good thing, we are constantly trying to make it better. The mechanical principles underlying the construction of these reels are easily seen by anyone to be true; but now and then we find that some men who are good anglers are poor mechanics, and are unable to adjust the bearings of our Compensating Reels after removing the cap M in order to oil the reel. Our last improvement enables anyone easily to oil his reel and readjust it perfectly in a moment.

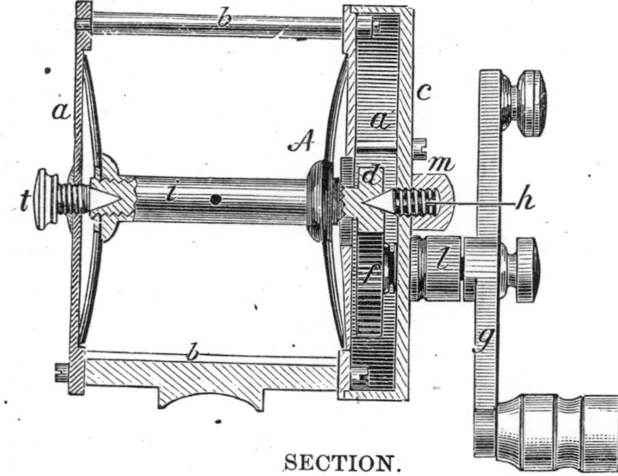

SECTION.

If you desire to oil a Compensating Reel, first unscrew the cap M, which protects the pivot screw H. Pour in the small oil hole, uncovered by the removal of the cap, the least possible bit of good reel oil. Then screw on the cap M. Then unscrew the pivot screw T. Be careful not to drop off and lose the spring washer U. Put the least bit of oil in the conical recess in which the point of the pivot screw plays. Then replace the washer U and screw in again the pivot screw T. Screw it in until the reel will hardly turn round; then unscrew it the least bit—just enough to let the reel revolve freely, but not enough to allow the axis (the spool of the reel) to wobble at all from side to side.

If you should happen to lose the cap M, the washer U, or the screw pivot T, we can always supply you with duplicates at a trifling charge. Let us know the number of the reel. It is always stamped on the bottom of the reel plate. If you are in the woods or any other place where you want a temporary washer U, you can use a small piece of leather, rubber, or even thick paper or cloth.

These reels as now made render it entirely unnecessary for the angler to carry with him a screw-driver to take them apart or put them together. There is no necessity of touching any part of the reel except the screw pivot T, the washer U and the cap M. Nothing but the thumb and forefinger are necessary to unscrew and screw these parts.

Sometimes the angler finds that, for some reason which he does not understand, the spool of his reel has too much side-shake; and sometimes he finds that it binds so much that it will hardly go round. In a badly made reel this may be attributed to many causes; but in a properly constructed reel it is owing to the expansion or contraction of the metal or rubber of which the reel is made. Our Compensating Reels are, we believe, the only reels in which any such difficulty can be removed instantly by the least bit of screwing or unscrewing the pivot screw T. Our patents on the reels, therefore, render end-wise shake or binding impossible; make (on account of the conical bearings) up and down shakes impossible, and provide for taking up all wear of bearings for a lifetime use of reel; and reduce the friction of the bearings to about one-third of what must exist in any other reel we have ever seen.

Leather Goods.

Sole Leather Butt Rests.

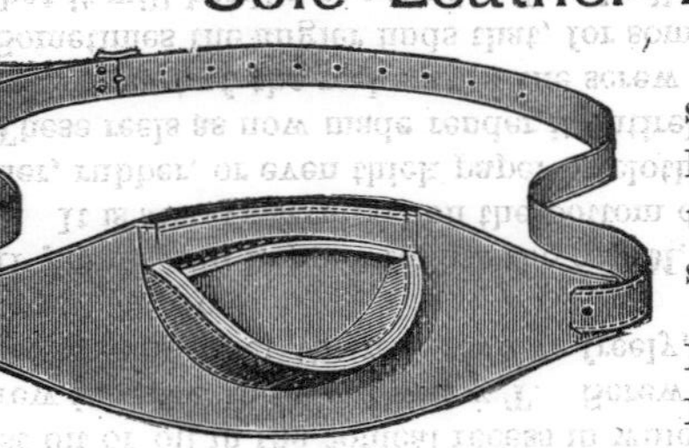

These Rests are almost a necessity for Bass, Salmon or Tarpon Fishing, to those who do not wish to tire themselves out with a day's sport.

No. 1. Extra Heavy......Each, $4.00
No. 3. Light Weight...... " 2.50

Heavy Solid Reel Cases.

First Quality.

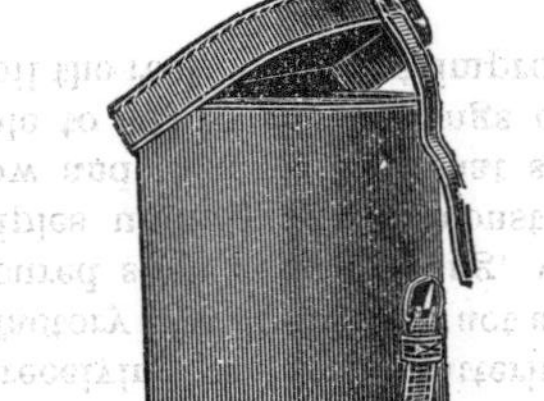

Second Quality.

"First Quality" are made of Bleached Oak finest leather, chamois lined, with leather covered buckles, name plate and handles.
"Second Quality" are made of heavy Russet leather, felt lined.

		First Quality.	Second Quality
To hold Small Single Action Reel.......	Each	No. 1, $1.25	No. 11, $0.75
" Large " " "	"	" 2, 1.50	" 12, .90
" Small Multiplying "	"	" 3, 1.50	" 13, .90
" Medium " "	"	" 4, 1.75	" 14, 1.00
" Large Salmon "	"	" 5, 2.50	
" Large Tarpon "	"	" 6, 2.75	

Stiffened Leather Fishing Rod Cases.

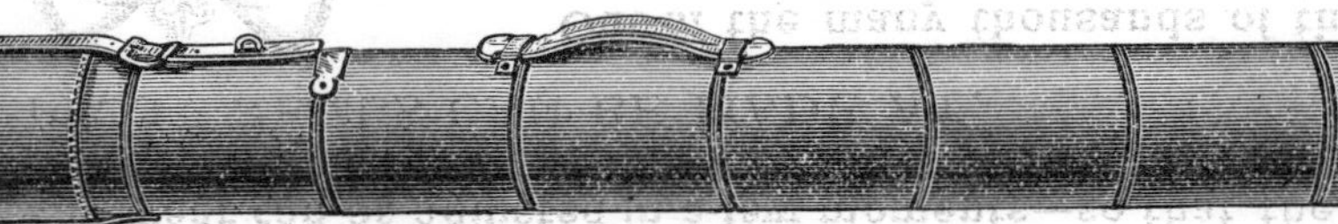

No. 6, of best Russet leather. Exceedingly strong and durable. A hard, stiff tube. A sliding handle, which lies flat when not in use.

44 inches long......	$4.10	4.50	5.00	5.50	6.25	7.00 Each
46 "	4.35	4.75	5.25	5.75	6.50	7.25 "
48 "	4.60	5.00	5.50	6.00	6.75	7.50 "
50 "	4.85	5.25	5.75	6.25	7.00	7.75 "
52 "	5.10	5.50	6.00	6.50	7.25	8.00 "
54 "	5.50	5.90	6.40	6.90	7.65	8.40 "
	2½	3	3½	4	4½	5 ins. diam.

Waterproof Goods.

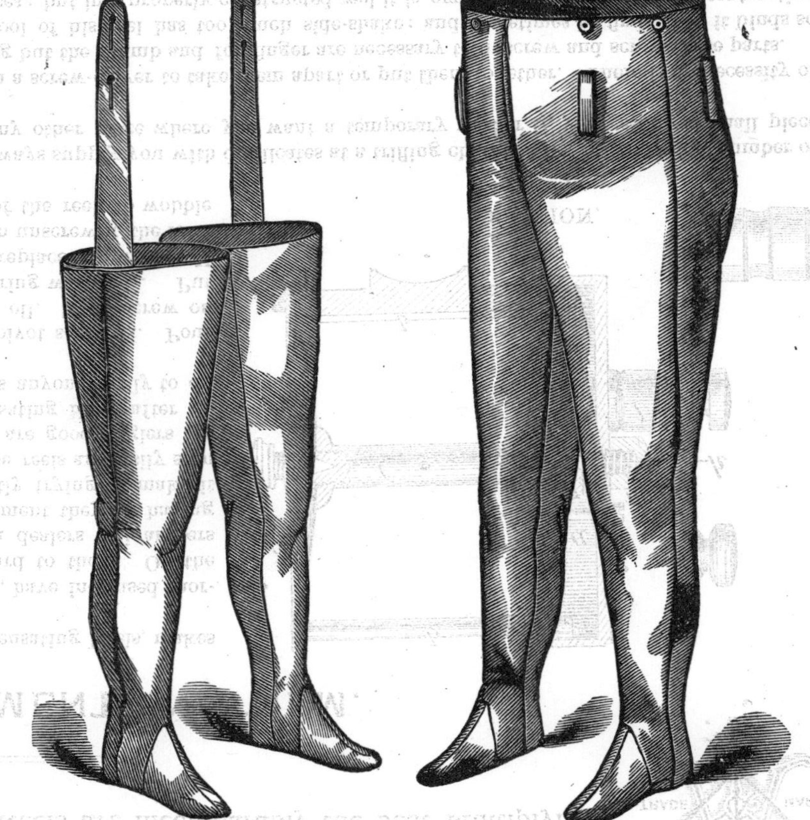

WADING STOCKINGS. WADING TROUSERS.

Stockings.

No. 50. Mackintosh ....per pair, $7.50
No. 55. Mackintosh, with boot feet .... " 10.00
No. 60. Empire Rubber............................ " 4.85

Trousers.

No. 70. Mackintosh..............................per pair, $10.00
No. 75. Mackintosh, with boot feet.......................... " 14.00
No. 80. Empire Rubber.............................. " 6.50

Wading Shoes.

Improved Canvas and Leather.

The price of these shoes is high, but they are worth the money...... per pair, $4.50

Gaffs and Shark Hooks.

The Automatic Pull Gaff.

Patented August 15, 1893.

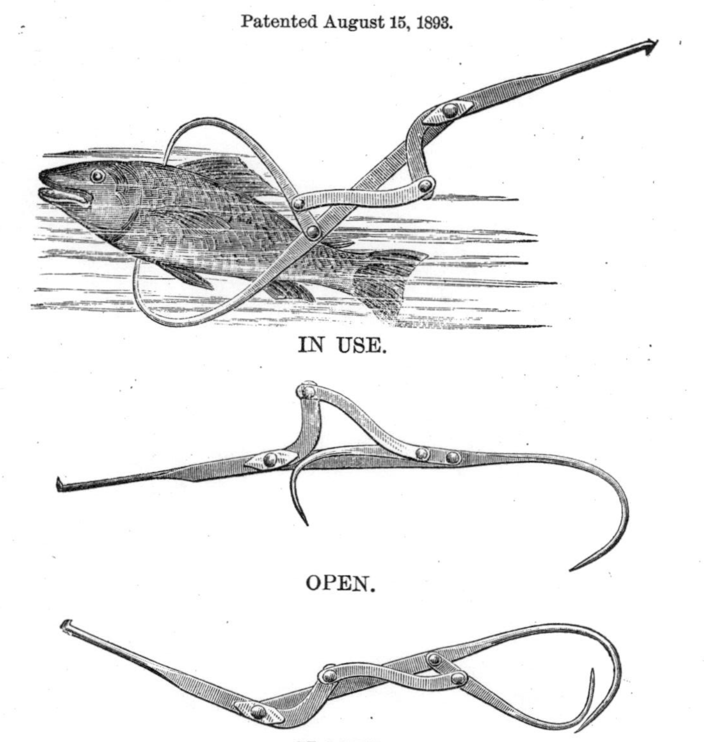

IN USE.

OPEN.

CLOSED.

All other gaffs are used by STRIKING the fish. The successful use of other gaffs requires both skill and experience.

This gaff is automatic by reason of a cam movement. This gaff performs mechanically and perfectly what no other gaff can do unless in the hands of the most experienced and skillful angler. It is NOT a spring gaff.

If the fish is gaffed from above, the angler has simply to HOOK, BEAR DOWN and PULL; if the fish is gaffed from below, the angler HOOKS, LIFTS UP and PULLS.

We make only one size. This size will lift any fish from 2 to 25 pounds. It is not mounted, and therefore may be carried in a tackle box. It is so made that it may be easily and quickly mounted on any handle by lashing. Rather fine copper wire is the best material to use in lashing.

The material and finish of this gaff is the very best.

Price...Each, $3.50

Steel Gaffs.

PLAIN WITH TURNED END TO DRIVE.

Nos.	1	2	3	4	5	
Length,	6½	7	9	10	13	Inches
Width,	1¾	2	2½	2½	2½	"
Each,	$0.15	.20	.25	.30	.40	

Fine Blued Steel Gaffs.

Nos.			Each.
9	To drive.	Length, 13 inches; width, 3¾ inches, usual size..........	$2.00
11	To drive.	Length, 12½ inches; width, 4 inches, for Salmon.........	2.50
12	To wind.	Length, 16 inches; width, 5½ inches, for Tarpon.........	2.50

Gaffs Complete.

Nos.		Each.
6	Plain Gaff No. 3, with 3 feet wood handle; nickel plated ferrule and butt cap....................................	$0.60
7	Same as No. 6, with 18 inch handle................................	.60
10	Fine Blued Steel Gaff No. 11, with screw socket and bamboo handle..	4.00

Shark Hooks with Chain.

Nos.	1	2	3	4	5	6	7	8	
Length of hook,	14	12½	12	10½	9	7½	6¾	5	Inches
Width of hook,	3¼	3	2¾	2½	2	1⅞	1¾	1⅝	"
Length of chain,	23	20	18	15	14	13	12	10½	"
Each,	$2.00	1.50	1.25	1.00	.85	.70	.60	.50	

III

1900–1909

Page 156: In 1902, a two-joint bamboo rod for 13 cents; with ring guides, 19 cents. Single action reel to match, 10 cents. Multiplying, 70 cents.

FISHING TACKLE DEPARTMENT.

Our Fishing Tackle Department for this season will contain the most complete assortment of high grade tackle on the market. We have dropped all the cheap grades and hereafter will not carry anything but **good tackle. We guarantee everything we sell in this department to be exactly as represented and of the best quality.** Do not compare our goods with the cheap grades. Descriptions of goods may be just alike, **but when you come to compare the goods themselves you will find great difference. ANY TACKLE BOUGHT FROM US MAY BE RETURNED AT OUR EXPENSE IMMEDIATELY IF YOU FIND IT NOT AS REPRESENTED, PROVIDED YOU RETURN IT IN PERFECT CONDITION.**

JAPANESE RODS.

We are offering our customers this season a line of Japanese jointed rods which we believe are better value than you can get from any other house in the United States, quality considered. We have departed from the regular rule of offering our customers common wood rods when we are able to offer them this season genuine Japanese rods at only a trifle more than common wood rods would cost.

We have endeavored to get most of this line of Japanese rods all fitted with solid reel seat and zylonite butt, which makes a very attractive and expensive looking rod, and by placing a large contract for these goods, we were able to get the cost of manufacture down to the lowest point, and by adding our one small percentage of profit we are able to give you such value as we believe you cannot get anywhere else in the United States.

Male Bamboo Two-Piece Rod, 7 to 8 Feet, 13 Cents.

No. 6R8595 Two-Piece Jointed Male Bamboo Rod, 7 to 8 feet. Price, each.......13c

If by mail, postage extra, 6 cents.

Male Bamboo Three-Piece Rod, 9½ to 10½ Feet, 22 Cents.

No. 6R8596 Three-Piece Jointed Male Bamboo Rod, 9½ to 10½ feet. Price......(If by mail, postage extra, 17 cents).....22c

Japanese Two-Piece Rod, 7½ to 8½ Feet, 19 Cents.

No. 6R8597 Two-Piece Japanese Rod, natural color, double telescope ferrules, ringed for line, about 7½ to 8½ feet. Price, each.......19c

If by mail, postage extra, 8 cents.

Japanese Two-Piece Rod with Zylonite Butt, 7 to 8 Feet, 45c.

No. 6R8600 Two-Piece Japanese Rod, about 7½ feet long, fitted with nickel plated telescope ferrules, solid reel seat above the grip, black zylonite butt, tie guides for lines made of mottled Japanese cane. One of the best rods on the market for the money. Weight, about 12 ozs. Our special price....**(If by mail, postage extra, 14 cents)**....45c

Japanese Three-Piece Rod with Zylonite Butt, 8½ to 9 Ft., 60c

No. 6R8602 Three-Piece Japanese Rod, about 8½ to 9 feet long, nickel plated telescope ferrules, solid reel seat above the grip, black zylonite butt, tie guides for the lines made of mottled Japanese cane, one of the best rods on the market for the money. Weight, about 13 ozs. Our special price.........**(If by mail, postage extra, 15 cents)**.........60c

Japanese Four-Piece Rod, with Zylonite Butt, about 14 Ft., 98c.

No. 6R8604 Four-Piece Japanese Rod, about 14 feet long, fitted with nickel plated telescope ferrules, solid reel seat above the grip, black zylonite butt, tie guides for lines made of mottled Japanese cane, the best long rod on the market for the money. Weight, about 24 ounces. A good rod to fish from the shore. Our special price only.......98c

If by mail, postage extra, 26 cents.

Four-Piece Calcutta Trunk Rod, about 8 Feet, 85 Cents.

No. 6R8606 Four-Piece Calcutta Trunk Rod, 7½ to 8 feet long, nickel plated telescope ferrules, strong tie guides for lines, solid reel seat above the grip; zylonite butt, made of genuine mottled Calcutta cane, nickel plated trimmings. Each piece is 24 inches long, so it may be carried in a trunk or grip. Our special price.......85c

If by mail, postage extra, 12 cents.

Calcutta Four-Piece Trolling Rod, 15 to 16 Feet, $1.08.

No. 6R8607 Four-Piece Calcutta Bamboo Rod, double telescope ferrules, ringed for lines, with butt cap and reel bands. Length, 15 to 16 feet. Weight, about 3 pounds. Price, each.......$1.08

LANCEWOOD RODS.

There are about thirty to fifty styles of Lancewood rods, manufactured by the various makers, and each style necessitates a change in equipment, machinery, etc., and by reducing the number of styles of our Lancewood Rods, we are able to save the expense of these changes, which expense is necessarily added to the rods when so many styles are handled by one house. We have decided to reduce the number of styles of Lancewood Rods in order to handle a few styles and manufacture them with the least possible expense. By doing this we were able to reduce the cost of our Lancewood Rods, and we give you the benefit of this reduction by pricing the following line of rods, based on our reduced cost, adding our one small percentage of profit.

St. Croix River Lancewood Fly Rods, 10 to 10½ Feet, $1.05.

No. 6R8616 Our St. Croix River Lancewood Fly Rod, made in three pieces, with an extra tip, genuine lancewood throughout, nickeled mountings and raised telescope ferrules. **Silk wound tie guides and silk whippings at each mounting. Solid reel seat below hand.** Zylonite corrugated grip. Length, about 10 to 10½ feet. Put up in neat partitioned cloth bag. Weight, about 9 ounces. A fine looking rod. Price, each..........**(If by mail, postage, extra 12 cents)**.........$1.05

Twin Lakes Lancewood Bass Rods, 8½ to 9 Feet, $1.00.

No. 6R8621 Twin Lakes Lancewood Bass Rod, made of genuine lancewood throughout; three pieces, with an extra lancewood tip, nickeled mountings, raised telescope ferrules, **silk wound tie guides and silk wrappings at mountings, solid reel seat above grip,** with corrugated zylonite butt. Length, about 8½ to 9 feet. Weight, about 14 ounces. Put up in neat partitioned cloth bag. A fine looking rod and one which will please you. Price, each.......$1.00

If by mail, postage extra, 18 cents.

Combination Bass and Fly Trunk Rod, $1.75.

No. 6R8624 This Rod is made of first quality lancewood, has four pieces when made into a bass rod and five pieces when made into a fly rod. It may be used as a fly rod as well as a bass rod. When the fly rod is assembled it makes the rod measure 9 feet, and when assembled as a bass rod, it measures about 7½ feet. The bass fly tip is interchangeable with the third joint of the fly rod, making it a **combination rod.** The pieces are about 25 inches long, the rod has the reel seat above the hand, is silk wound at short intervals, has shouldered ferrules, standing spiral line guides, nickel plated ferrules and trimmings, corrugated zylonite black and white butt, and one of the most convenient rods on the market. Weight, 13 ounces.

Our special price for this combination rod.......$1.75

If by mail, postage extra, 16 cents.

Two-Piece Lancewood Bass Rod, about 5½ Feet, $2.10.

No. 6R8625 Our Two-Piece Lancewood Bass Rods, about 5½ feet long, nickel plated telescope ferrules, silk wound at intersections, tie guides for lines, solid reel seat above the grip, zylonite butt, nickel trimmings, silk wound, put up in a neat cloth bag, with an extra tip. Weight of rod, about 7 ounces, for boat casting.

Our special price only.......$2.10

If by mail, postage extra, 12 cents.

The Beaverkill, a Very Fine Lancewood Fly Rod, $4.25.

No. 6R8626 Our Special Beaverkill Lancewood Fly Rod, made up with solid reel seat below the hand, German silver mountings all engraved or milled to make a very handsome appearance. It has solid anti-friction guides, windings of black and red, beautifully clustered. Put up in three joints with an extra tip on a wood form covered with velvet. We cannot recommend these rods too highly. **They are perfection.** Ordinarily retail at $10.00. Weight, 8 ounces. Length, 8½ feet.

Our price.......$4.25

If by mail, postage extra, 20 cents.

Lake George Special Lancewood Bass Rod, with Agate Tip, $4.65.

No. 6R8627 Our Lake George Fine Special Lancewood Bait Casting Rod, with solid reel seat above hand, German silver mountings, all engraved or milled to make a very handsome appearance. It has anti-friction trumpet guides, agate tip, windings of black and red, beautifully clustered. Put up in three joints with an extra tip on a wood form covered with velvet. We cannot recommend these rods too highly. **They are perfection.** Ordinarily retail for $10.00. Weight, 8 ounces. Length, 6½ feet. The short rod is the coming bait casting rod. Our price.......$4.65

If by mail, postage extra, 18 cents.

Our Celebrated Greenheart Rods, 6½ Feet, $1.90.

This Celebrated Greenheart Rod is made very much on the same principle as a split bamboo od, from a wood, known as Greenheart, which is usually imported from Spain and Italy, and is noted for its strength and durability. It is considered the strongest and best wood known for use in fish rods, and in color it is a greenish brown. They are having a large sale and are well liked.

No. 6R8628 Our Greenheart Bass Rod, nickel plated telescope ferrules, cork grip, alternate silk wrappings, nickel plated mountings, solid reel seat above the grasp, three pieces and an extra tip 6½ to 7 feet long.

Our special price.......$1.90

If by mail, postage extra, 20 cents.

OUR TERMS ARE **CASH WITH ORDER**

but we guarantee satisfaction or refund your money.

Stamped Sheet Steel Boats.

These boats are made of eight plates of galvanized sheet steel, riveted and doubly seamed, making them strong, light and durable. They have the advantage over wooden boats in that they do not become water logged when exposed to the sun, can be easily transported from place to place, are always ready for use and for hunting purposes have no superior.

They are modeled after the whaleback steamers of the Christopher Columbus type, the bottom is dish shaped, and can be used in shallow water, over grass, reeds, etc., and each boat has an air chamber sufficient in size to float four men on the upturned boat, should it happen to capsize, making it practically a perfect, non-sinkable boat. At each end there is a hole through the air chamber from top to bottom of the boat, which can be used either to anchor the boat with a pole or attach a temporary sail. The boats are all painted a dead grass color, and with an additional coat of paint from time to time the boats should last a good many years.

No. 6R8703 The "GET THERE" Sheet Metal Hunting Boat, 14 feet long, 36-inch beam, 14 inches deep at the top of combing. The cock pit is 9 feet long and the boat weighs about 80 pounds.

Our special price, with one pair of oars, one long or short paddle, one seat and one hickory slat bottom.......... **$17.50**

No 6R8704 "BUSTLE" Sheet Metal Hunting Boat is almost identically the same as the "Get There" except the air chambers are on the side of the boat instead of the ends, making it 10 inches wider than the "Get There," and is a little more steady in the water. Our special price, with one pair of oars, one long or short paddle, one hickory slat bottom and one seat.......... **$24.50**

Extra seats, each.......... .75

Our Special Folding Canvas Boat, at $19.50

and $24.60.

From the above illustration, engraved by our artist from a photograph, you can form some idea of our special canvas waterproof folding boats.

These boats are made from heavy duck, prepared by a flexible waterproof process, so they will not crack when folded, and are made in two sizes, 8 and 12 feet long. Our 8-foot boat is calculated to be a hunting boat, and for one person only. Our 12-foot boat is calculated to hold three persons safely; and as they draw only 4 inches of water, these boats can float in very shallow streams.

Our $19.50 and $24.60 canvas folding boats are constructed with bent wood ribs instead of common iron ribs, which rust easily, made of heavy army duck that will last a long time and not crack, and are built to our special order by a maker who has had twenty-five years' experience in canvas boat building—some boats which he built fifteen years ago being still in use. As these boats weigh only 35 to 45 pounds, they can be easily carried from one lake to another, may be shipped by express or freight at a very small expense, while a regular full length boat of any kind nearly always has a high classification of freight rate on account of it taking up so much room in a freight car.

No. 6R8706 Our 8-foot Canvas Boat. 36 inches wide, 11 inches deep amidship, with jointed bottom board, side boards, gunwale, one stool, one pair of 6½-foot copper tipped jointed oars. Designed for one person only. Weight complete, about 35 pounds.

Our special price.......... **$19.50**

No. 6R8708 Our 12-foot Canvas Boat. 33 inches wide, 12 inches deep amidship, 15 inches deep at stem and stern, with jointed bottom board, jointed side boards, jointed gunwale, one stool, one pair of jointed 6½-foot copper tipped oars. Designed for three persons, who weigh, all told, not over 600 pounds, and draws about 4 inches of water. Very steady in the water. Wgt. complete, about 40 lbs. Price.. **$24.60**

Each boat comes put up in a cloth bag so that it may be easily handled.

The Genuine Feather Light Reel, $1.36.

This Reel has a removable balance spool, as shown in illustration, which **makes it very handy for cleaning same. Has drag steel click and steel spindle** and is made in fine oxidized finish. The reel is 2¾ inches in diameter and ⅜ inch wide, for trout or bass fishing.

No. 6R8722 60 yards. Price, each.......... **$1.36**

If by mail, postage, extra, 10 cents.

Our Mascot Multiplying Reel, 65 Cents.

No. 6R8730 This is one of the very best double multiplying reels on the market. It is full nickel plated, with balance handle, double screw-off oil cap, one of the easiest and smoothest running reels on the market, the bearings being of steel. They have back sliding click and drag. Every reel is stamped Mascot.

No. D, 80 yard reel. Our special price.......... **65c**

If by mail, postage extra, 15 cents.

No. 6R8736 Our Chicago Single Action, raised pillar, riveted brass reel. A strong and durable reel, without click. 25 yards. Price.......... **10c**

If by mail, postage extra, 4 cents.

Our Orleans Reel, single action, raised pillar, riveted brass reel. **A very strong and durable reel with click.**

No. 6R8737 25 yards, Price.......... **15c**

No. 6R8738 60 yards, Price.......... **20c**

If by mail, postage extra, 6 cents.

Double multiplying raised pillar, balance handle, **screwed connections,** lacquered brass reel, with patent **adjustable slide drag and back sliding click,** polished bearings.

No. 6R8740 40 yards, **45c**
No. 6R8741 60 yards, **55c**
No 6R8742½ 80 yards.......... **65c**

If by mail, postage extra, 9 cents.

Our double multiplying raised pillar, balance handle, screwed connections, full nickel plated reel, with patent adjustable slide drag and back sliding click, polished bearings.

No. 6R8743 40 yards. **60c**
No. 6R8744½ 60 yards.......... **70c**
No. 6R8745 80 yards. **80c**

If by mail, postage extra, 9 cents.

Our Polished Rubber Cap Reel, double multiplying **raised pillar,** balance handle, screwed connections, **nickel plated reels,** with patent adjustable slide drag and back sliding click.

No. 6R8746 40 yds., **65c**
No. 6R8747 60 yds., **75c**
No. 6R8748 80 yds.. **85c**

If by mail, postage extra, 9 cents.

Our Quadruple Reel has round disc, balance handle, screwed brass connections, **with fine steel pivots in bronzed bushed bearings,** patent adjustable slide drag, back sliding click, and nickel plated.

No. 6R8750 40 yards.......... **$1.25**
No. 6R8751 60 yards.......... **1.40**
No. 6R8752 80 yards.......... **1.65**

If by mail, postage extra, 13 cents.

Our Acme Trout Reel is single action, extra fine quality screwed **hard rubber reels with** flush balance handle, bushed bearings and back sliding click, **nickel plated.** For trout and fly fishing.

No. 6R8753 40 yards... **75c**
No. 6R8754 60 yards.. **85c**

If by mail, postage extra, 10 cents.

Our Genuine Pennell Reel made especially for us. Each reel is carefully tested for smooth running and careful adjustment before leaving the factory. Don't buy imitations when you can get genuine goods at the same price or even less. We guarantee these to be the genuine Pennell quadruple reels, the best reels for bass fishing or trolling.

Our Quadruple Pennell Round Disc Reel is fitted with adjustable sliding click and drag steel pivots, bridge over cogs; **one of our leaders.** This is a high grade reel, and one that we are offering at a very low price; and made of the best material possible, handsomely nickel plated, balance handle and constructed for all fishermen who are looking for a **fine looking reel at a low figure.**

No. 6R8755 40 yards size.......... **$1.75**
No. 6R8756 60 yards size.......... **2.00**
No. 6R8757 80 yards size.......... **2.25**
No. 6R8758 100 yards size.......... **2.40**

If by mail, postage extra, 15 cents.

The Celebrated Pennell Rubber Plate and Nickeled Quadruple Reel, $2.75.

The Celebrated Pennell Patent Compensating Quadruple Reel, finest quality throughout, one of the best reels made, **with steel pinion and pivots. Rubber plate and nickel plated metal bands incasing the rubber, which protects same** from any **breakage.** It has **steel pivots in bushed bearings, bridge over pinions, balance handle, back sliding click, front drag, screw-off oil cap.** These reels have the finest reputation for perfection and smoothness of action. **They are strictly high grade reels** and cannot be purchased at retail for double our price. They positively compare with the finest quadruple reels made.

No. 6R8759 80 yards. Our special price, each, **$2.75**
No. 6R8760 100 yards. Our special price, each. **3.00**

If by mail, postage extra, 15 cents.

The above reels sell on this market at from $5.00 to $7.50 each.

Our Celebrated Tournament Agate Cap Quadruple Pennell Reels for $3.00.

We offer you for the first time in the history of the fishing tackle business a 60-yard Quadruple Agate Cap Reel with balance handle, round disc, wide spool fitted with click and drag, all parts made true, to run with the least possible friction. The discs and agate caps are milled, making a very handsome appearance, handsomely nickel plated, screw connections, adjustable slide click and drag. **These celebrated reels have the genuine agate caps, which makes them smooth and free running,** and by reason of a large contract we were able to obtain a price which admits of our selling the 60-yard reel at the exceptionally low price of **$3.00.** Many people have said that we could not place a reel with genuine agate bearings upon the market at three times the price we are asking you, but we give you our **binding guarantee** that these reels have the genuine agate bearings or money refunded.

No. 6R8762½A Our 60-yard agate bearing Pennell reel, only.......... **$3.00**
No. 6R8763½A Our 80-yard agate bearing Pennell reel, only.......... **3.25**

If by mail, postage extra, 15 cents.

Our Celebrated Rubber Cap, Agate Quadruple Pennell Reels for $3.90.

At $3.90 we offer you an 80-yard Rubber Cap Quadruple Genuine Agate Reel, with balance handle, round disc, wide spool fitted with click and drag, all parts made true, to run with the least possible friction. All are handsomely nickel plated, screw connections, adjustable sliding click and drag. **These celebrated reels have the genuine agate caps, which makes them smooth and free running,** at the exceptionally low price of **$3.90. OUR BINDING GUARANTEE.**—We guarantee these reels to have the genuine agate bearings or money refunded.

No. 6R8765½A Our 80-yard agate bearing Pennell reel, only.......... **$3.90**
No. 6R8766½A Our 100-yard agate bearing Pennell reel, only.......... **4.15**

If by mail, postage extra, 14 cents.

Our Round Plate Multiplying Reel, 70 Cents to $1.00.

We offer for the first time a Round Plate Reel at a popular price. This reel is excellent value and must be seen to be appreciated. Every reel is carefully tested before leaving the factory. Our round disc reel is fitted with balance handle, round plate, screw oil cups, adjustable sliding click and drag and all are handsome nickel plated. Double multiplying and nicely finished. Order by number and state size wanted.

No. 6R8768 40 yards size. Price, each.... **$0.70**
No. 6R8769½ 60 yards size. Price, each.... **.80**
No. 6R8770 80 yards size. Price, each.... **.90**
No. 6R8771 100 yards size. Price, each.... **1.00**

If by mail, postage extra, 12 to 18 cents.

Our Pennell-Vom Hofe Quadruple Reel, $2.25.

This is the latest high grade reel on the market, combining all the good points of the Vom Hofe and Pennell reels. Each and every reel is tested to gauge, accuracy and smooth running qualities before leaving the factory, and for casting or trolling these reels have no equal. Our Pennell-Vom Hofe reel has the new 1¼-inch wide spool, is quadruple multiplying, fitted with accurate steel pivots, handsomely nickel plated and knurled adjustable click and drag, special handle and adjusting pivot cap. Made in 80 and 100-yard size only.

No. 6P8772 80-yard size. Price, each.. **$2.25**
No. 6R8773 100-yard size. Price, each..... **2.50**

If by mail, postage extra, 12 to 18 cents.

ILLUSTRATED CATALOGUE

WILLIAM MILLS & SON

FISHING TACKLE

Salesrooms, 21 Park Place, New York

FACTORIES:

Central Valley, N. Y, Redditch, England.

Large Wooden Reels for Salt Water Fishing.

The Spools of these Reels are made of selected wood and are about one inch wide. They are made of large diameter so that they will reel in line as rapidly as a Multiplying Reel. The Spool revolves on a steel spindle which is attached to brass plate by which the Reel is fitted to Rod. The Reels are very free running.

		Per Dozen.
No. 1.	Spool of Selected Maple, Natural Color, size, 4½ to 6 inches in diameter	$3 00
No. 2.	Spool of Selected Maple, Stained, size, 6 inches in diameter	4 00
No. 3.	Spool of Selected Maple, Stained Dark, Handles on Metal Cross-bar, size, 6 in. in diam. $6 00, 7 in..	9 00
No. 4.	Spool of Extra Quality Mahogany, Fancy, Extra Strong Cross-bar for Handle, Reel Extra Strongly Bushed, size, 5 inches, $13 50; 6 inches, $18 00; 7 inches	22 80

THE "GOOD LUCK" WOOD REEL.

Patented March 9, 1897.

Made in Two Styles.

LIGHT,

HANDSOME,

FREE RUNNING.

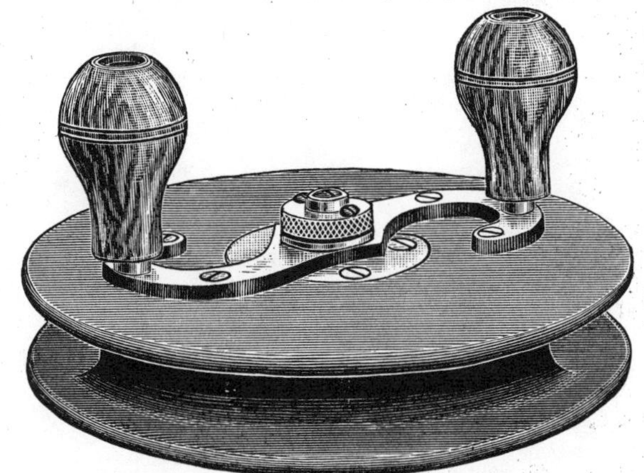

"Ball Bearing" and "Straight Spindle."

	5	6	7	8 inch.
Ball Bearing,	$2 47	$2 67	$3 13	$3 67 each.
Straight Spindle,	15 25	16 50	18 75	21 25 dozen.

ALUMINUM CLICK REEL WITH REVOLVING PLATE HANDLE, FANCY MILLED EDGES AND SIDES.—Class 4.

Size No. 623½.

Yards	40	80
Nos	625	623½
	$3 00	$3 50 each.

EXTRA FINE ALL ALUMINUM, RAISED PILLAR, CLICK REEL, WITH PERFORATED SPOOL.

Yards	200
No	581
	$8 00 each.

EXTRA FINE RUBBER AND ALUMINUM CLICK REEL.—Class 4.

Size No. 541.

Sides of Reel are made of very fine grade of rubber. The Revolving Plate, Bearing Handle, and also the Spool are made of Aluminum. The Reels are of large diameter and made narrow.

Yards	100	200
Nos	543	541
	$6 00	$7 00 each.

The "Martin" Standard Automatic Fish Reel.

These Reels are made of Aluminum with Brass Bearings, German Silver Trimmed.

	each.
No. 1—Creek Whipper, Line Spool is $2\frac{3}{4}$ inches in diameter with $\frac{7}{8}$ hub and 5-16 wide, will hold 25 yards of medium line. Price....	$6 00
No. 2—Fly Casting, has the same diameter of line spool and hub, but is $\frac{5}{8}$ wide, having a capacity for 25 yards of casting line. Price	7 00
No. 3—Bass Reel. Line spool is $2\frac{3}{4}$ in diameter, hub $\frac{7}{8}$ and width $\frac{7}{8}$ inches, holds 50 yards. For "Bass," this is the "real" thing. Price	8 00
No. 4—Salmon Reel. Has line spool $2\frac{3}{4}$ inches in diameter, hub $\frac{7}{8}$ inch, and the width is 13-16, giving space for 50 yards of large line. Automatic for 100 feet. Price......	9 00

Has all the latest improvements. The ENDLESS SPRING making it both desirable and durable Has capability of main spring being readily and easily adjusted to greater or less tension at any time during the operation of landing a fish.

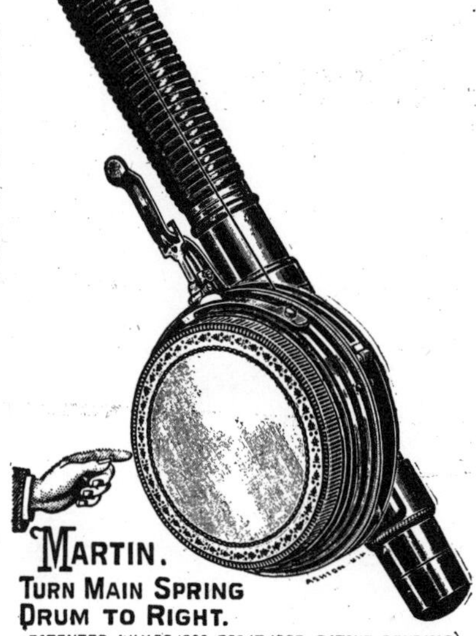

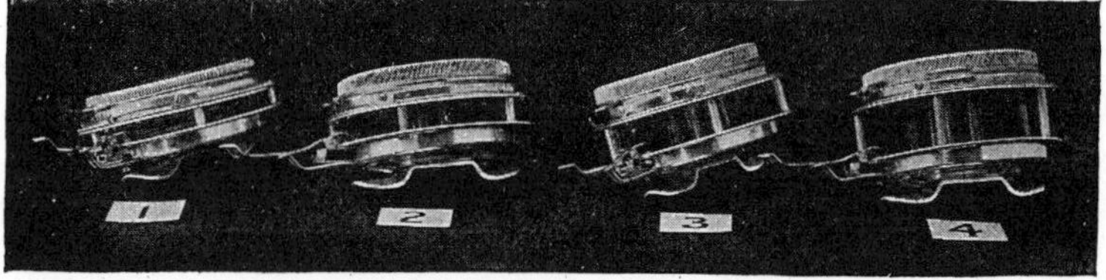

Martin Pat. July 26, '92; Dec. 17, '95; Nov. 30, '97.

WE ARE SPECIAL AGENTS FOR THE "MARTIN" REELS.

Amateur.

Expert.

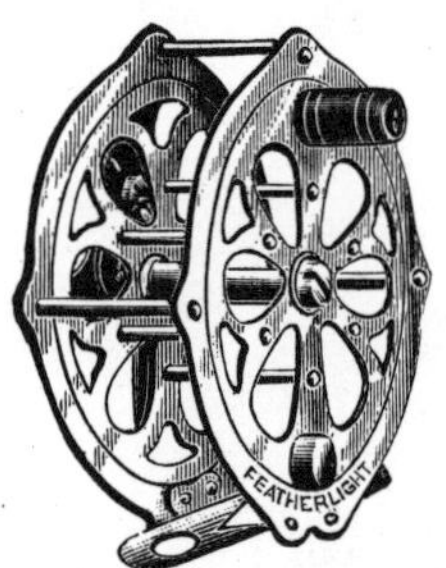

Featherlight.

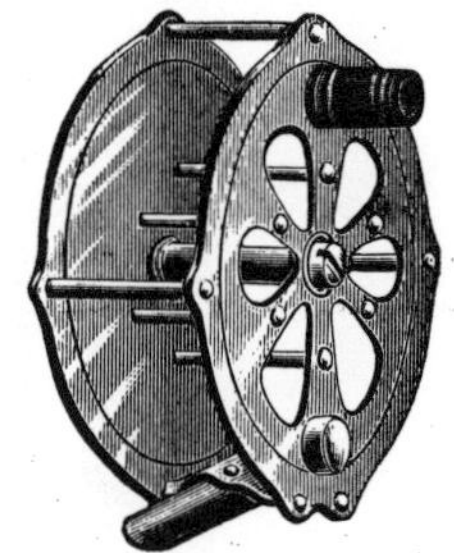

Alright.

No.	Capacity.	Spool.	For	Has	Per Dozen.
Amateur 1.	150 yards.	$4\frac{5}{8} \times 1$ inch.	Trolling.	Drag.	$21 00
" 10.	40 "	$2\frac{1}{4} \times \frac{3}{4}$ "	Trout or Bass Fly.	Drag.	15 00
Expert 17.	100 "	3×1 "	Bass or Trolling.	Click & Rim Drag.	30 00
" 19.	40 "	$2\frac{1}{4} \times \frac{3}{4}$ "	Trout or Bass Fly.	" "	24 00
" 22.	200 "	$3 \times 1\frac{1}{2}$ "	Trolling or Salt Water.	" "	39 00
Alright 120.	80 "	$2\frac{1}{4} \times 1$ "	Bass Casting.	Click.	24 00
" 130.	150 "	$2\frac{5}{8} \times 1\frac{1}{4}$ "	Trolling.	"	30 00
Featherlight 270.	70 "	$2\frac{1}{4} \times \frac{3}{4}$ "	Trout or Bass Fly.	"	24 00
" 280.	80 "	$2\frac{1}{4} \times 1$ "	Bass Casting.	"	24 00

William Mills & Son's "Intrinsic Phantom" Minnow.

Only the very best of materials used throughout in the construction of these Minnows, and the highest quality of Hollow Pointed Spring Steel Treble Hooks are used. We believe that there are Anglers desiring the best Minnows they can get, and as such a Minnow we offer this grade. One of these Minnows will outlast several of the cheaper grade. Each Minnow has Improved Swivel in head. Carried in stock in Blue, Speckled and Silver.

Nos.	1	2	3	4	5	6	7	8	9	10
Length of Minnow	$1\frac{3}{4}$	$2\frac{1}{4}$	$2\frac{1}{2}$	3	$3\frac{1}{2}$	4	$4\frac{1}{4}$	$4\frac{1}{2}$	5	$5\frac{1}{2}$ inches.
	$7 20	7 20	7 20	7 20	7 20	8 40	9 60	10 80	12 60	14 40 per dozen.

PATENT "ARCHER" SPINNERS.

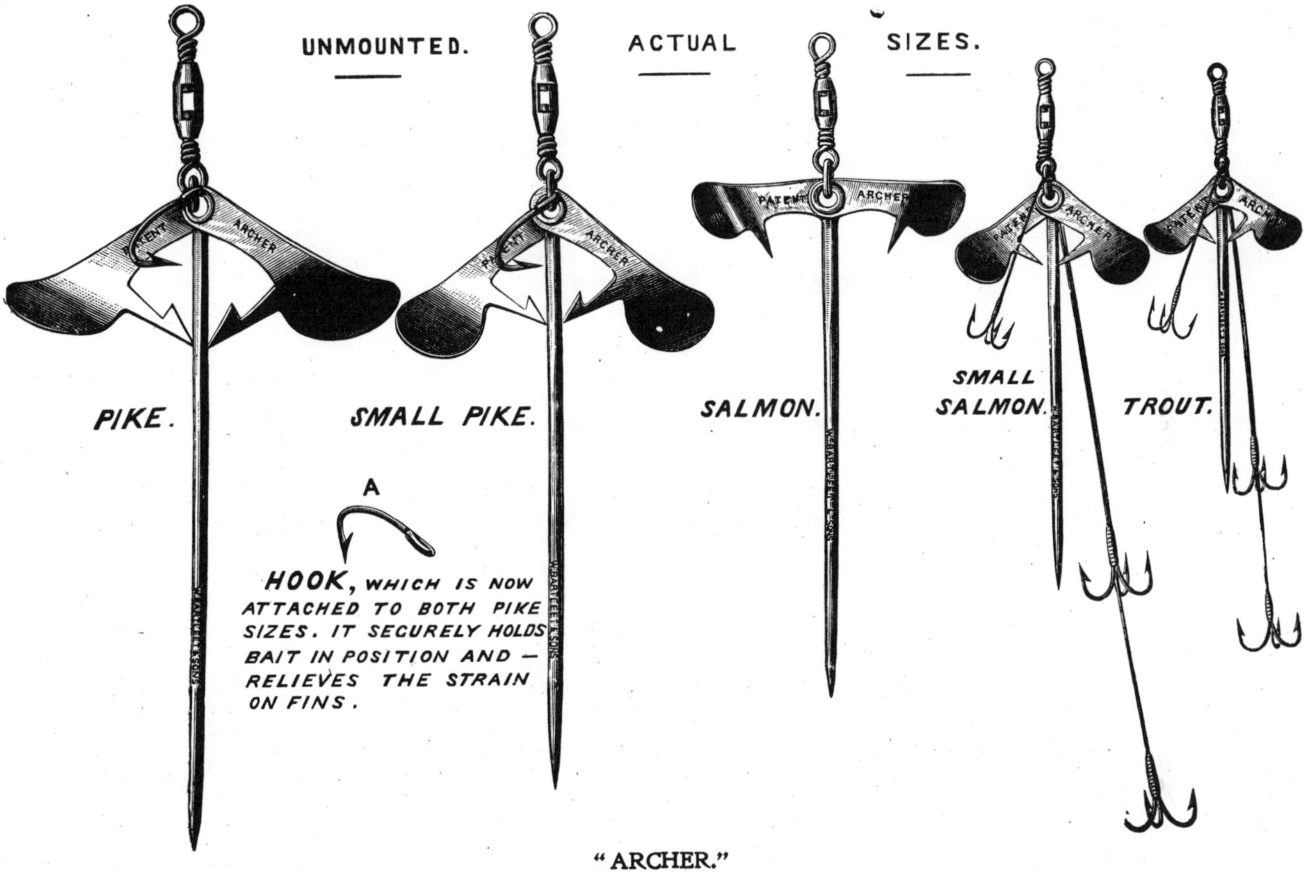

UNMOUNTED. ACTUAL SIZES.

PIKE. SMALL PIKE. SALMON. SMALL SALMON. TROUT.

A

HOOK, WHICH IS NOW ATTACHED TO BOTH PIKE SIZES. IT SECURELY HOLDS BAIT IN POSITION AND — RELIEVES THE STRAIN ON FINS.

"ARCHER."

Pike.	Small Pike.	Salmon.	Small Salmon.	Trout.
$6 00	6 00	6 00	6 00	6 00 per dozen.

"ARROW."

The "Arrow" Spinner is American made and is lower in price than the "Archer."

Nos.	11	12	13	14	15
	Pike.	Small Pike.	Salmon.	Small Salmon.	Trout.
	$4 20	4 20	3 60	3 60	3 60 per dozen.

TWO NEW SPINNERS.

INDIAN ROCK SPINNER.

With fine Salmon Fly. Best Trolling device for Landlocked Salmon and large Trout

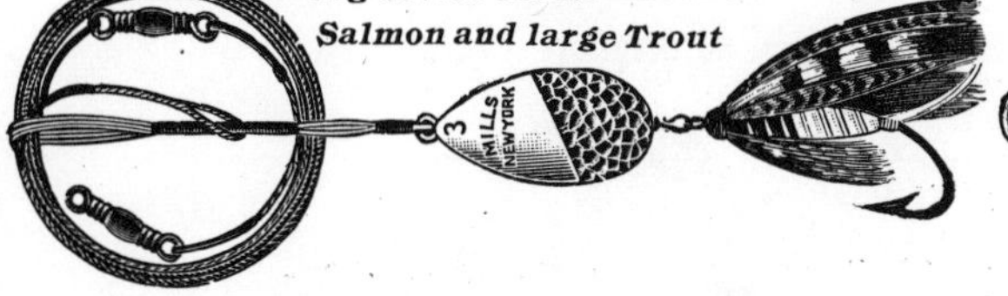

Miniature cut $\frac{5}{8}$ size. hows design of blade used on No. B. Has 3 ft. twisted gut trace with 2 swivels.

Furnished with either Jock Scott or Silver Doctor.................. $15 00 per dozen.

Parmachene, Montreal, &c......... 12 00 "

Shows full size of spoon blade used on these spinners, and design of blade used on No. E.

THE "DIRIGO" SPINNER.

Miniature cut $\frac{5}{8}$ size, handsomely made, with attractive and durable fly. A splendid lure for Landlocked Salmon, large Trout and Black Bass.

Price.............................. $4.20 per dozen.

Furnished with either Parmachene Belle, Brown Hackle, Montreal, Royal Coachman. } Flies.

Sunshade Pocket Hat.

Patented 1892.

This is something quite new and novel. It has a very wide brim and shades the face and neck perfectly; weighs but ½ to ¾ ounce, and as it has a flexible adjusting band it can be worn either over or in place of the ordinary hat. It is perfectly rigid when in use, but can in an instant be folded to carry in small bag 6 inches in diameter and ½ inch thick. Price............................$3.75 per dozen.

Same with mosquito netting to use as a protection against black flies and mosquitoes.............................. $8 40 per dozen.

Perfection Disgorgers.

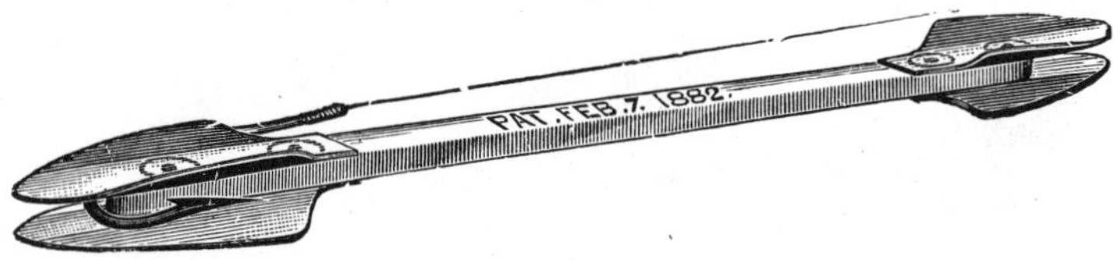

No. 1.

No. 1. Brass, Nickel Plated.. $3 00 per dozen.

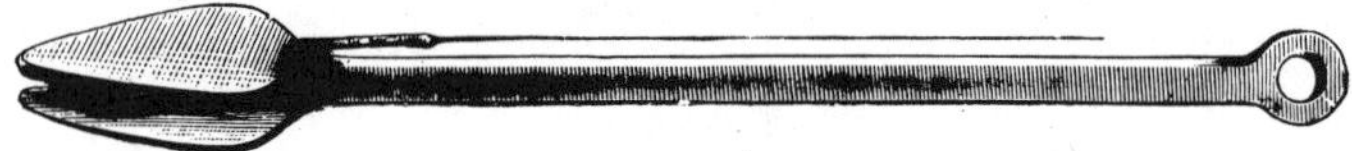

No. 2.

2. Malleable Iron, Nickel Plated.. $1 80 per dozen.

Glass Minnow Trap.

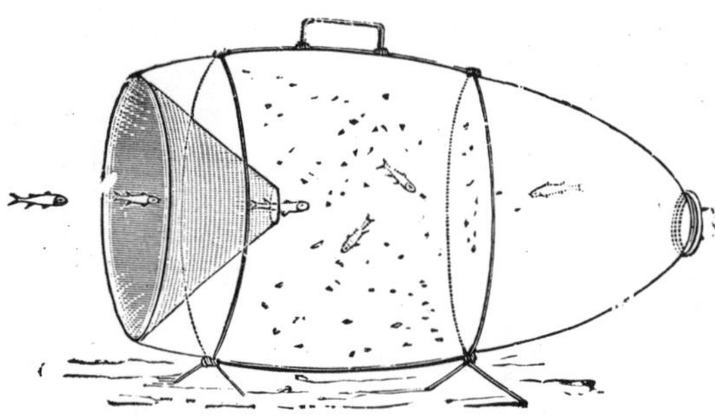

Each.
Each Trap securely packed in convenient box, $3.00

The "Bonanza" Fish Stringer.

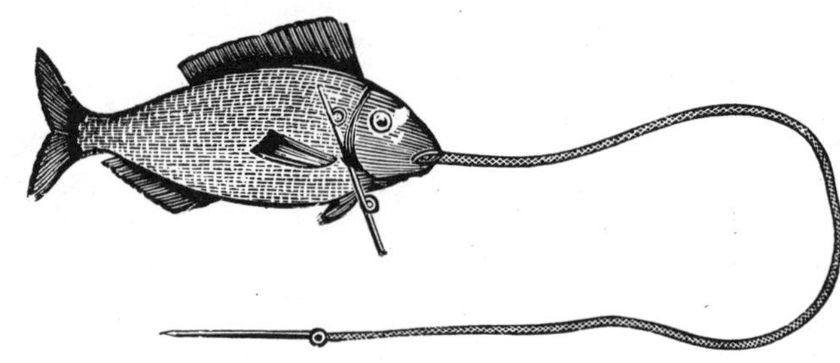

Price, $1.20 per dozen.

A simple device for stringing and carrying the fish. The needle may be slipped through two openings which form a part of the bar (see cut), and the loop thus formed offers a convenient handle by which to carry the fish.

SCAT.................................. $3 00 dozen.

Clearing Rings.

Miniature Cut.

Brass Jointed (see cut; $2\frac{1}{4}$ inches in diameter), $7.20 per dozen.

DRINKING CUPS.

White Rubber Canoe Cup.

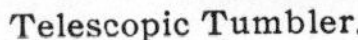

Telescopic Tumbler.

White Rubber Tumbler.

Hard Rubber Telescopic Cups . . $9 00 per doz.
Best Metal Telescopic Cups. . . . . 2 40 "
Best Metal in Screw Top Box. . . 3 60 "
White Rubber, Folding, for
Pocket, Tumbler or Canoe. . . . 1 90 "

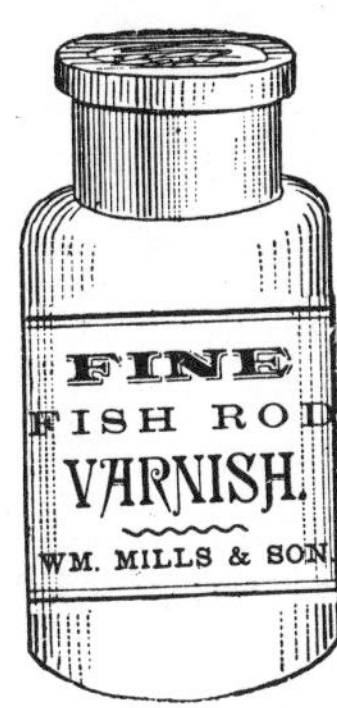

One-half Size.

2 oz. Bottles Best Varnish, $4 20 per dozen.

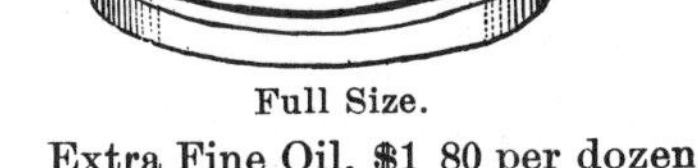

Full Size.

Extra Fine Oil, $1 80 per dozen.

THIS IS IT.

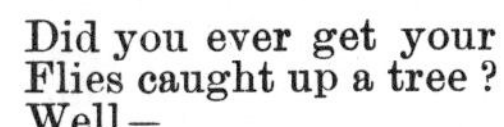

Did you ever get your Flies caught up a tree? Well—

Use a

"RELEASER"

Insert the tip of your rod under the rubber band (see cut), and with your rod raise the RELEASER to the twig and withdraw rod. A slight tug on the attached cord will cut the twig, down it comes, and your flies and leader are saved.

Price, $1.00 each.
In Leather Case.

MILLS' LIVE BOX.

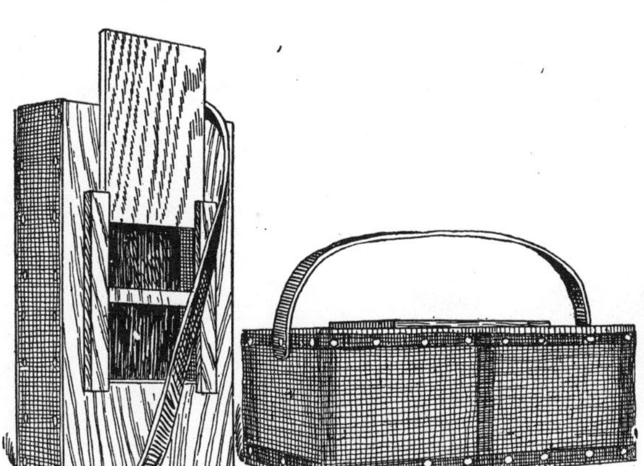

13 × 6½ × 5 inches.

Has 2 separate compartments for carrying and keeping frogs, crawfish, helgramites and crickets for bass bait. It is strongly made, and netting is galvanized. $1.00 each.

POCKET FILTER.

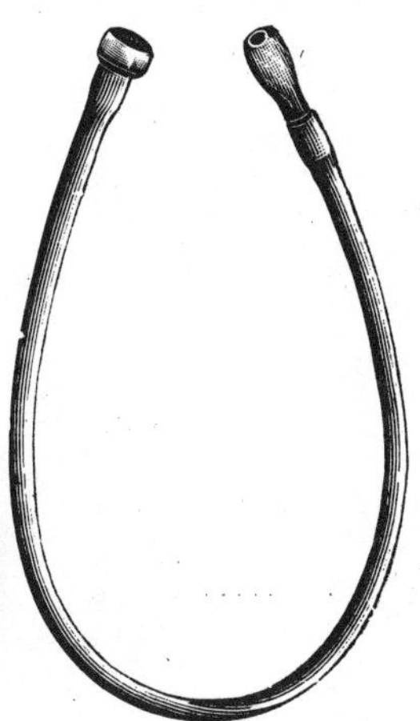

Very useful to anglers, cyclists and tourists. Absolutely prevents the drinking of any impurities in spring water.

$3.00 per dozen.

Page 162: The hat is cheaper here, only $3.75 a dozen. With mosquito netting, $8.40. In other words, $3.75 for the hats, $4.65 for the netting. There must be a catch in this somewhere.

These old friends, the double-ended disgorger, the glass minnow trap, and the brass clearing ring, haven't changed to this day.

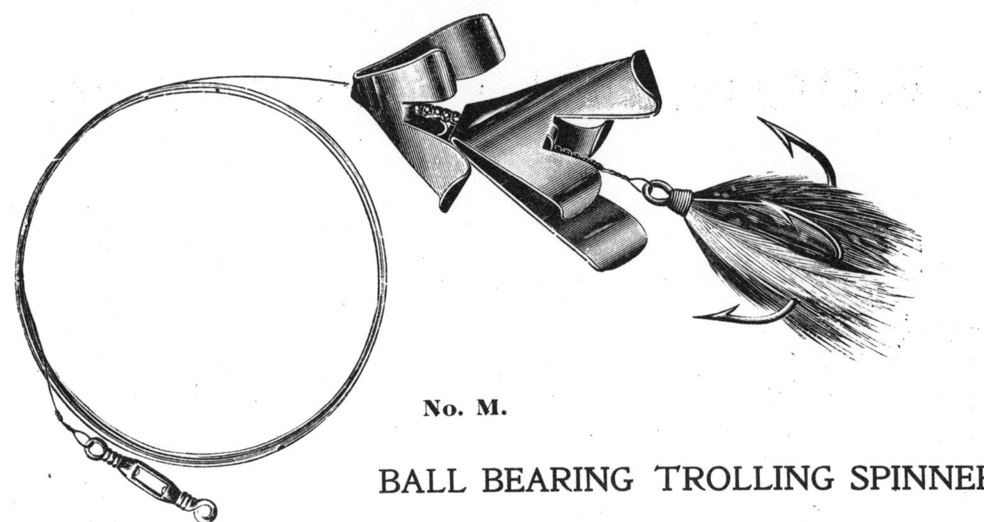

No. M.

BALL BEARING TROLLING SPINNERS.

Spinner with Single Hook, and Baiting Wire.............Nos. BN, $6.00 B, $4.80 C, $4.80 R, $4.80 per dozen.
Spinner with Single Hook, Baiting Wire, and 4 ft. Wire Leader..................................No. D, 5 40 "
Spinner with Feathered Treble Hook.........Nos. F, $5.40 N, $5.40 G, $5.40 AF, $6.60 T, 7.00 "
Double Spinner with Feathered Treble Hook..............Nos. SH, $10.00 NH, H, E, E½, X, 6.60 "
Spinner with Feathered Treble Hook, and 4 ft. Wire Leader..............................Nos. O, P, 6.00 "
Double Spinner with Feathered Treble Hook, and 4 ft. Wire Leader..........Nos. M, M½, AX, S, 7.80 "
Double Spinner with Feathered Treble Hook, and short Wire Leader.......................Nos. PB, 7.20 "
Spinner with Flies, on card............... Bass, A, $8.60 AB, $8.60 Trout, AA, $8.60 OK, 15.50 "

LEATHER BOAT SEAT BUTT REST

WITH CLAMPS.

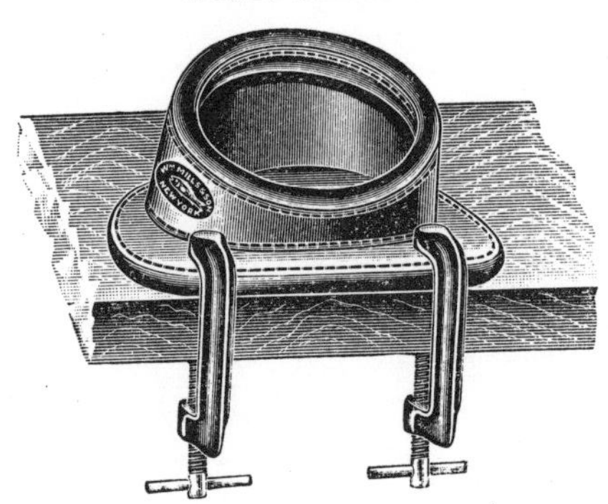

Price.......................... $3 50 each.

WILLOW BASKET,

With Single or Double Lid.

Nos.	High.	On Top.	Dozen
1.	8 inches.	15 x 9½ inches.	$15 00
2.	9 "	17 x 10 "	18 00
3.	9½ "	19½ x 12 "	21 00

Those with Double Lids are preferable.

OUR "SIMPLEX" ROD BELT.

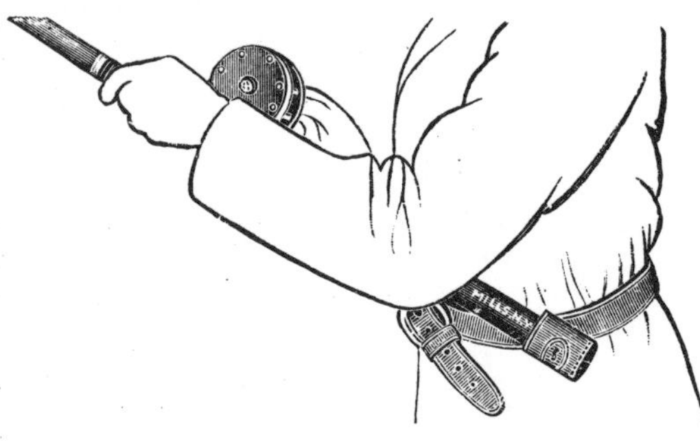

For use as shown in cut. Very light and in many styles of angling is preferable to the heavier belts, though we do not recommend them for the heaviest fishing. Specially good for Salmon angling. Price, $1.25 each.

"PERFECTION" FISH STRINGER.

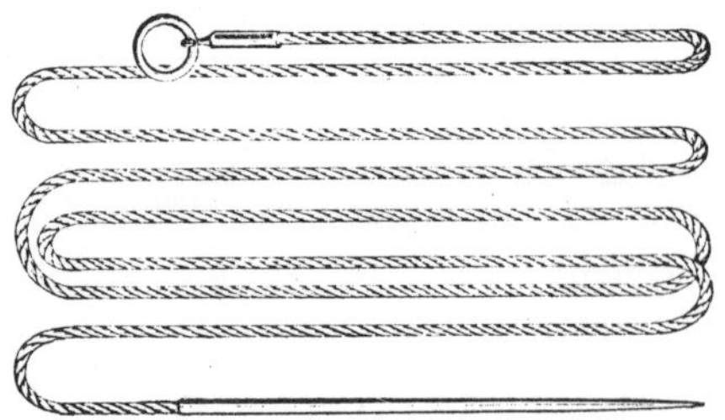

Six feet of Hard Braided Cord with Ring on end, Solid Brass Needle.

Price......................... $3.00 per dozen.

WHOLESALE PRICE LIST
OF
FISHING TACKLE
AND
HUNTING OUTFITS
ESTABLISHED 1875
The H. H. KIFFE CO.
523 BROADWAY - NEW YORK
COPYRIGHT 1903

TRANSFER AND DRYING REEL.

LIGHT, COMPACT, CHEAP, STRONG, SIMPLE, CONVENIENT.

It can be taken apart or set up in one minute. It weighs only 3½ ounces. It takes very small space in tackle box. It costs only one-quarter the price of other reels for the same purpose. It takes up nearly a yard of line at each turn and will hold two lines at once.

DRY YOUR LINES AND SAVE YOUR MONEY.

Lines keep their strength three times longer if fully dried after use. This reel saves its cost ten times over each season in economy and convenience. It avoids all the vexations of tangling and twisting in transferring lines to and from the fishing reel. No more breaking of lines stretched on tree trunks or fences. No more walking fifty times around a chair to take up a line left there to dry. No more snarled coils on floor, table or ground. Sent by mail on receipt of price..................50c.

WOOD REELS.

No.		Price Each	Extra by Mail
1.	Maple, Diameter 5 inches..	20c.	10c.
2.	Mahogany Finish, 6 in....	25c.	10c.
3.	Same as No. 2, with S Handle..................	35c.	10c.
4.	Same as No. 3, 7 inches...	50c.	12c.
5.	Mahogany Finish, French Polish with brass S shaped handle plate and bushed bearings, Diameter 6 inches.....	$1.00	15c.
8.	Fine Mahogany Finish, French Polished, bushed bearings, heavy Brass S shaped handle plate with extra large handles, Diameter 5 inches..	1.35	20c.
9.	Same as No. 8, 6 inches...	1.50	25c.
10.	Same as No. 8, 7 inches...	1.75	30c.

BALL BEARING REELS.

See Illustration Below.

No.		Price Each	Extra by Mail
13.	Same as No. 8, 5 inches...	2.35	20c.
14.	" " 6 " ...	2 50	25c.
15.	" " 7 " ...	3.00	30c.

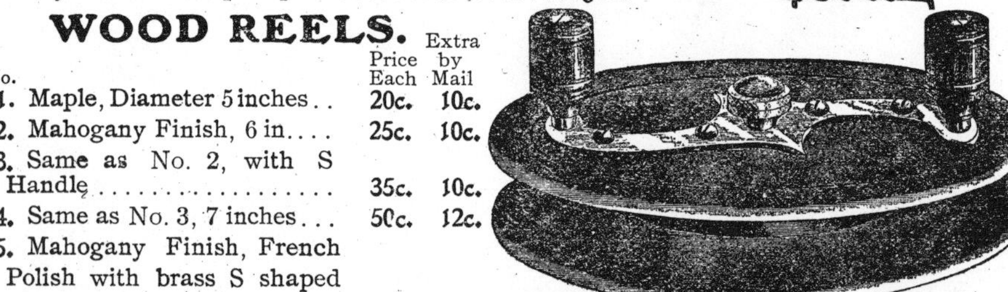

Nos. 3, 4 and 5.

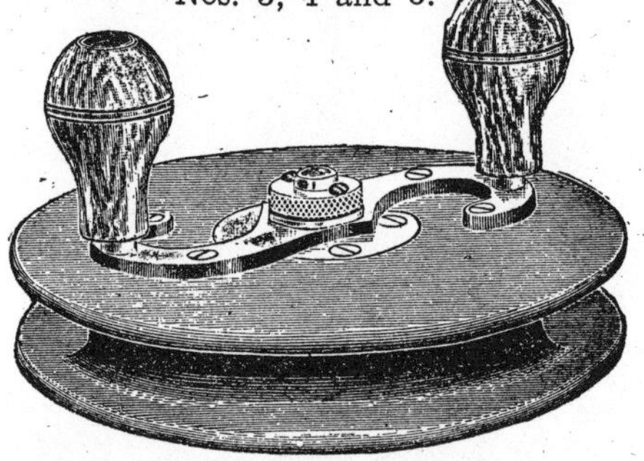

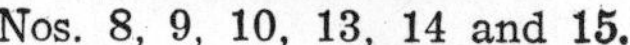

Nos. 8, 9, 10, 13, 14 and 15.

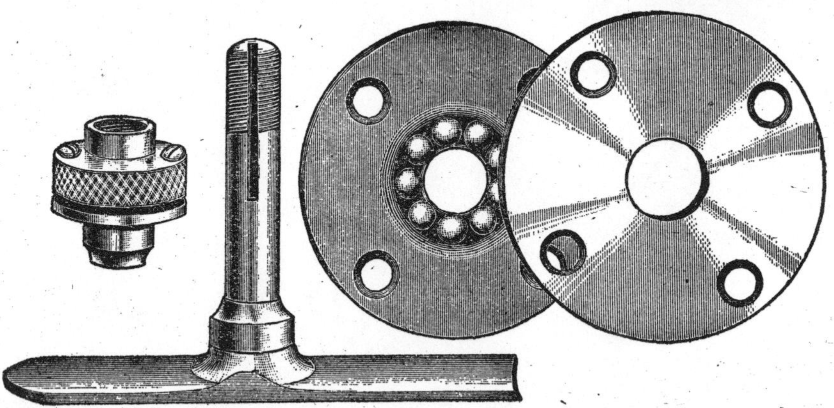

A fine old New York tackle house in its day. It's still in business handling army surplus items.

SHAKESPEARE BAITS.

The Shakespeare Revolution Spinner.

The Shakespeare Bucktail Spinner.

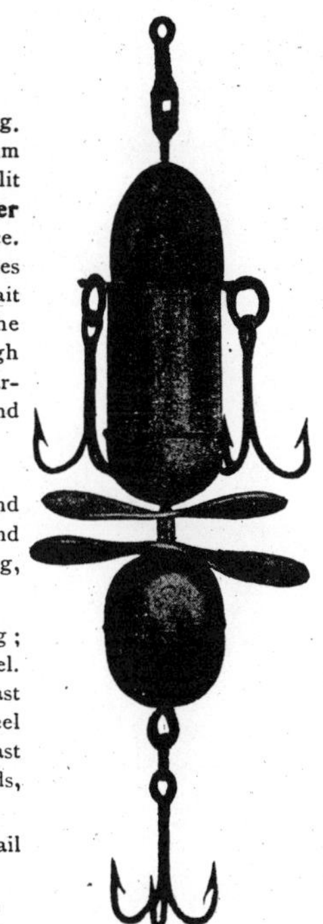

The Revolution Bait. A new departure in Fishing. Made entirely of Aluminum with First Quality Treble Hooks attached with Split Rings. **It catches fish.** It catches **more** and **larger** fish than live Bait when used at the same time and place. Adapted for trolling, casting and splashing. It does away with the troublesome task of catching live bait before going fishing. The peculiar construction of the revolving blades allows the bait to be drawn through rushes and weeds without snagging the hooks. It is particularly good bait for bass, pickerel, muskalonge and every fish that takes a live bait.

Instructions to Fishermen.

Trolling.—Attach the **Revolution Bait** to a line and troll close to the edge of the rushes and lily pads, and just between deep and shallow water. In the morning, evening and after dark is the best time for trolling.

Bait-Casting.—Use a short Rod from 5 to 7 feet long ; a fine smooth line and a free running quadruple reel. Wind the line until the bait is close to the rod ; then cast the bait from 50 to 75 feet from the boat, allowing the reel to run free. Keep your boat in deep water and cast toward the shore to the edge of the rushes and weeds, trolling the bait to the boat by reeling in the line.

Sizes,..................	1	2	3	Bucktail
Length of Body, inches..	2¾	3½	4½	3½
Price, each.............	50c.	60c.	75c.	65c.

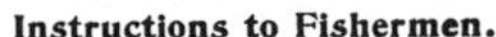

THE FAYETTE BAIT. ONCE TRIED ALWAYS USED.

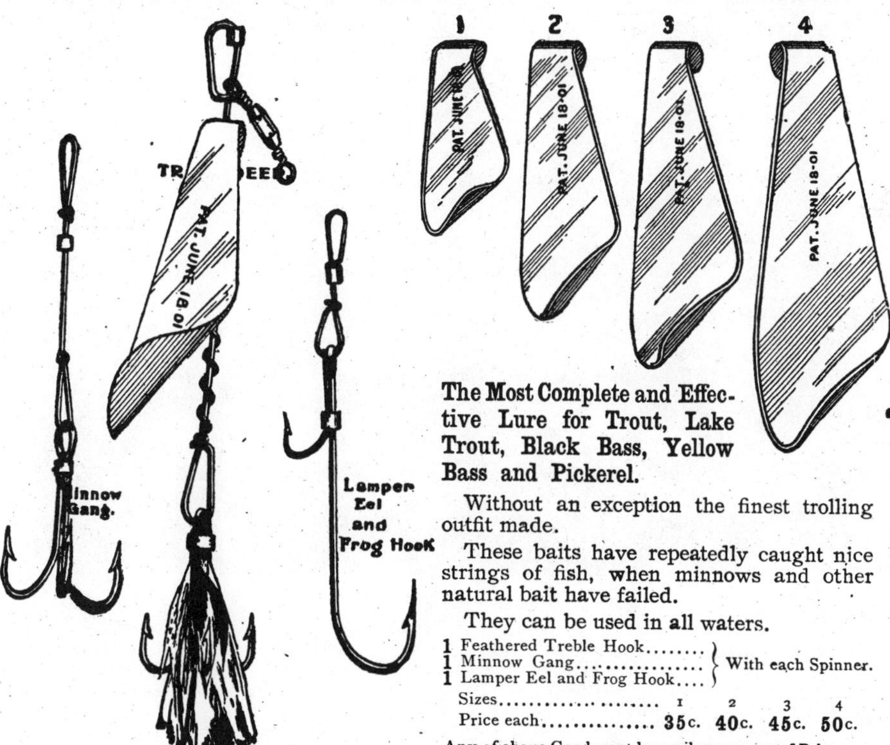

The Most Complete and Effective Lure for Trout, Lake Trout, Black Bass, Yellow Bass and Pickerel.

Without an exception the finest trolling outfit made.

These baits have repeatedly caught nice strings of fish, when minnows and other natural bait have failed.

They can be used in all waters.

1 Feathered Treble Hook.......
1 Minnow Gang.................. } With each Spinner.
1 Lamper Eel and Frog Hook....

Sizes....................	1	2	3	4
Price each...............	35c.	40c.	45c.	50c.

Any of above Goods sent by mail on receipt of Price.

The first aluminum lure? This one catches more and larger fish than live bait; and it can be "drawn through rushes and weeds without snagging the hooks." It says so, right here. No Federal Trade Commission then, obviously.

92 THE H. H. KIFFE COMPANY, NEW YORK.

FLY CREAM.

It is founded upon an entirely new principle, which will *at once* distinguish it from *all* other preparations for the same object, Its efficacy does not depend upon Oil of Pennyroyal alone, and would be quite as effective without it. **It contains no Tar or Animal Fats,** leaves no stain, is neat and cleanly, easily applied, *washes off readily without the necessary use of soap,* and leaves the Skin Soft, Smooth and free from Irritation. It is very soothing and healing in its nature, and relieves the inflammation and pain of Sunburn, and if used in season, prevents the burning. **Price, 20c.**

COMBINATION TOOL HAFT.

Made of Cocobolo, finely polished, with Nickel Plated Metal Cap.

Each Haft contains twelve tools made of the best Tool Steel, tempered and finished in the most workmanlike manner.

ONE REAMER	ONE TACK PULLER	ONE PEGGING AWL	SIX BRAD
ONE CHISEL	ONE SCREW DRIVER	ONE MARKING AWL	AWLS, ASSORTED

The complete tool is 4 inches in length and can be easily carried in the pocket. Being made of solid wood, it is not liable to split.

The tools stand upright in holes under the metal cap, facilitating selections.

Besides being very useful as an angler's repair kit and a household article, it is also, by reason of its compactness and quality most valuable for mechanics' use.

Price each, 55c. By mail, 5c. extra.

ANGLERS TACKLE
REPAIR OUTFIT
H H KIFFE C°
NEW YORK

DODGE'S ... CEMENT!

ANGLER'S REPAIR KIT.

TOOL HAFT.

This is an article which no angler can afford to be without. Every fisherman knows the disappointment which attends the breaking of a rod while in use, at a great distance from a convenient place for repairs. Possessing this useful equipment you can repair your rod on the spot and go on fishing. The Outfit is put up in a neat little case convenvenient for the pocket. **Price, by mail, $1.00.**

CONTENTS—One Bottle Best Shellac, One Brush, One Spool Scarlet Winding Silk, Two Spools Heavy Black Silk, One Knife-Edge File, One Piece Wax, One Package Assorted Needles, One Box Guides, Ring Tips, etc., One Stick of Ferrule Cement, One Oiler, One Screwdriver, One Box Split Shot.

These smug city fellows with their *perfumed* cream.

160 THE H. H. KIFFE COMPANY, NEW YORK.

PAT. MARCH 10.96.

Packed for shipment, 14⅛x10⅛x8. Weight Kit only, 15 pounds. Kit and Table Ware, 20 lbs.

Kamp Komfort Tent Heater,

$5.50.

Size, 15½x12x15. 9 feet of pipe. Weight 24 lbs.

KAMP KOOK'S KIT, (21 Pieces), $5.50.

1.—Wrought iron fire jack, riveted, with hasp for padlock. 2.—8-quart heavy steel combined camp boiler and dish pan. 3.—5-quart heavy steel camp boiler, with lifting clips, riveted. 4.—Heavy tin cover, fits Nos. 2, 3 and 5. 5.—Combined frying and baking pan, riveted clip and ring. 6.—Adjustable wrought handle for Nos. 3 and 7. 7.—3 quart coffee pot, riveted handle and bail. 8.—Heavy retinned corrugated folding wire broiler and toaster. 9 and 10.—Heavy wrought retinned ladles. 11 and 12.—Heavy retinned cake turner and basting spoon. 13 and 14.—Three-tinned retinned flesh fork and can opener. 15 and 16.—Large wire ring pot cleaner and dish towel. 17, 18, 19 and 20.—Match box, flour dredge, salt and pepper boxes. 21.—Eldnac (candle) lantern frame, for No. 2 fluted chimney.

Table Ware—33 Pieces—(will pack inside "Kamp Kook's Kit") **$1 50**

6 each steel knives and forks; 6 silver finish embossed heavy tea spoons and 2 table spoons; 6 heavy retinned open-handle cups and 6 tin plates; one butcher knife, redwood handle, in copper-riveted leather case.

KIT AND TABLEWARE, COMPLETE (54 pieces) packed for shipment.............**$7 00**
KAMP KOMFORT TENT HEATER, (with pipe and tin collar)...................... **5 50**

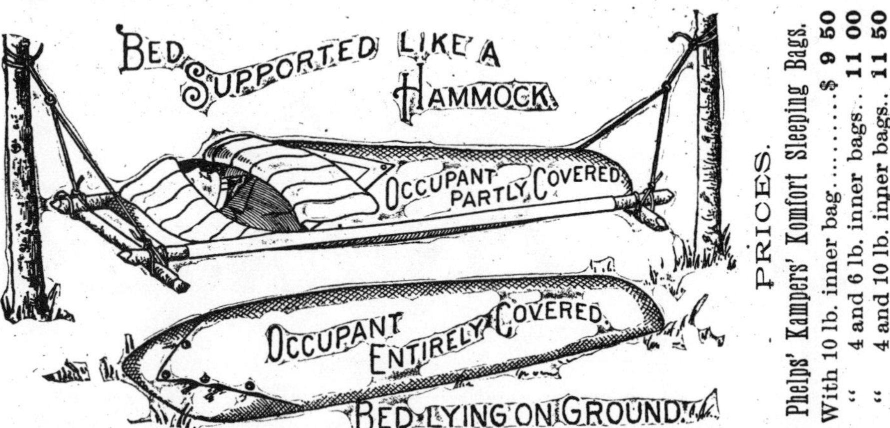

PRICES.

Phelps' Kampers' Komfort Sleeping Bags.

With 10 lb. inner bag........**$ 9 50**
" 4 and 6 lb. inner bags.. **11 00**
" 4 and 10 lb. inner bags.. **11 50**

PHELPS' "KAMPERS' KOMFORT" COMBINATION SLEEPING-BAG AND SPRING-BED.

The use of this sleeping-bag insures a warm, dry, and comfortable bed in or out of doors in all seasons. Any degree of warmth. No damp bedding. No stumps to make life miserable. Rubber blankets are unnecessary. The total saving in weight of bedding from that ordinarily carried into the woods is considerable. The poles used are cut wherever convenient, allows the bed to be rolled up into a small bundle for transportation and avoids carrying of unnecessary weight. It takes but a few minutes to adjust them—lash them together at the corners— and support the bed either by ropes tied to trees, or by stakes, logs, or rocks placed under the corners. Any number of inner bags (each separate) may be used according to the season. In the summer or early Fall the **outer bag with two light-weight inner bags** will be found sufficient and most convenient. In colder weather, **heavier inner bags** are recommended. All the bags are nested together, and the user gets under as many thicknesses as desired. The less over him the more under. The outer bag may be buttoned up from the inside (snap buttons being used) or left open to any extent.

COQUINA SLEEPING BAGS...Each, **$12 50**

These trees that grow so straight, just the right distance apart—in catalogs.

Finest Rods Reels Flies
Charles F. Orvis
Manchester
Vermont
AND
No. 26
FISHING TACKLE.

IN PRESENTING to my patrons this No. 26 Catalogue, I take pleasure in bringing to their notice such fishing and camping appliances as will meet their approval should they contemplate purchasing

HIGH GRADE FISHING TACKLE

The pleasure of fishing largely depends on the selection of the rod to be used; to enjoy fishing one should cast a good line, to cast a good line one must have a good rod.

Now to construct a properly balanced rod is my aim, and the reputation of the **ORVIS ROD** signifies how well this has been accomplished. In the construction of my rods the greatest care is used that they are properly balanced to cast the line with accuracy and ease and that the material used is of the very best, and every detail of construction from butt cap to ring tip most carefully made.

The **SOLID CORK HAND PIECES** are used in preference to all others and are as durable as they are agreeable to the hand.

BANDED FERRULES OF MY OWN MAKE are made of German silver and most carefully fitted their entire length. No long metal joint with non-elasticity breaks up the action of my rods. No dowels are used, as they weaken a rod and tend to throw the joints apart.

THE ORVIS PATENT REEL SEAT is simple in construction and convenient, without troublesome slide rings, and is adjustable to any reel, which can be easily placed in position or removed.

SPECIAL RODS MADE TO ORDER

Customers are invited to intrust me with the execution of their ideas for any special rods.

REPAIRING RODS

The greatest care given to the repairing of any make of rods and all work done at very reasonable prices.

REFINISHING, REWINDING AND VARNISHING.—Complete redressing of rod.

Split Bamboo Rods, first quality	$2 50
Lancewood Rods, first quality	1 50

Cheaper rods in proportion to work required.

NEW JOINTS

Split Bamboo Tips, finest quality	$2 50 each	Good quality	$1 75
Split Bamboo Joints, finest quality	3 00 each	Good quality	2 50
Split Bamboo Butt, finest quality	5 00 each	Good quality	4 00
Lancewood Tips, finest quality	1 25 each	Good quality	75
Lancewood Joints, finest quality	2 00 each	Good quality	1 00
Lancewood Butts, finest quality	3 50 each	Good quality	2 50

GOODS SENT BY MAIL.—Notice carefully goods upon which I pay postage; all other articles require postage at one cent per ounce or the amount specified.

REGISTERED MAIL.—10 cents extra for each package.

The man who has just paid $40 to have a rod refinished, rewound, and revarnished must be saddened to see that he could have had the same job for $2.50 in 1905.

Finest Quality Hand-Made

Hexagonal Split-Bamboo Fly Rods

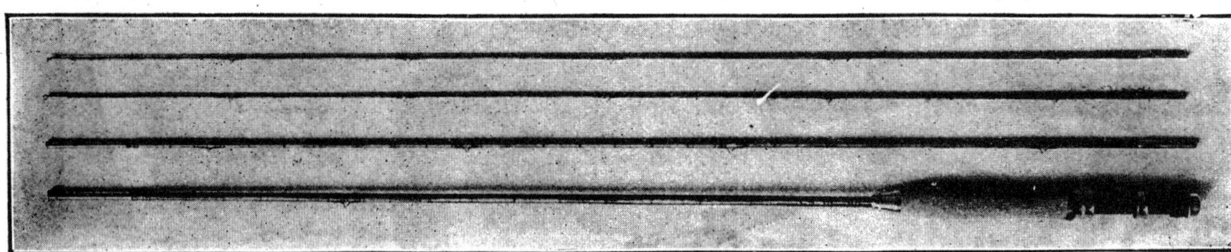

THE PERFECTION IN ROD BUILDING

Ease in Casting. Durability and Finish

THE ORVIS ROD is made in three pieces, has two tips, sack and Orvis round wood Rod case. German Silver Mountings, with Banded Ferrules, Snake Guides, and whipped with silk.

These Rods are very finely finished with solid cork hand-pieces that will not loosen, crack or come off.

I am confident fishermen will find that these rods will fill all requirements and in every way prove satisfactory.

No. 4.— **FOUR OUNCE FLY ROD,** "A Perfect Beauty."

Made from the choicest selected stock, is not a toy but a practical rod with which to fish.

Length of rod 8 feet, 3 inches; actual weight 4 ounces Price $15 00

Postage and Registration, 40 cents.

And how earnestly Mr. Orvis insists that an 8-foot 4-ounce flyrod is "not a toy but a practical rod with which to fish." Today, Orvis is saying much the same thing about its rods weighing less than 2 ounces.

Split-Bamboo Fly Rods

Three pieces, extra tip. Full nickel-plated mountings; solid metal reel plate and metal plugs; silk wound rings and keepers, and whipped between rings. Cork Grip. Put up in wood form and cloth bag. Made in lengths of 9½, 10 and 10½ feet. Price $1 00

No. 490—FLY ROD. Lengths, 10 and 10½ feet, weight, 7 and 7½ ounces. Cork Hand Piece. Nickel Plated Mountings; extra tip, sack and grooved wood form; silk whippings. Price $1 75

No. 400 C—FLY ROD. Length, 10½ feet, weight, 6½ ounces. Cork Hand Piece. Nickel-plated Mountings; extra tip, sack and grooved wood form; whipped throughout with silk $2 50

No. 514½ C—FLY ROD. Length, 10 feet, weight, 6½ ounces. Cork Hand Piece. Nickel-plated Mountings; extra tip, sack and cloth-covered wood form; whipped throughout with two colors silk.
Price $3 50

Postage and Insurance on each of these, 25 cents.

Orvis Split-Bamboo Rods

TEN DOLLAR GRADE

All of these Rods are of six strips throughout; have three joints of equal length, extra tip, partition sack and Orvs Rod Case, German Silver Mountings, Banded Ferrules, Orvis Patent Reel Seat and Cork Hand Piece. Equally well balanced as highest grade rods.

No. 9x—FLY ROD. Length, 10 feet; weight 6¾ ounces $10 00
No. 9x—FLY ROD. Length 10½ feet; weight, 7 ounces 10 00
No. 9x—FLY ROD. Length, 11 feet; weight, 7¼ ounces 10 00
No. 9½x—FLY ROD. Length, 10 feet; weight, 6 ounces 10 00
No. 16x—FLY RODS. Length, 9 feet; weight, 5 ounces 10 00

Postage and Insurance, 40 cents.

FIVE DOLLAR GRADE

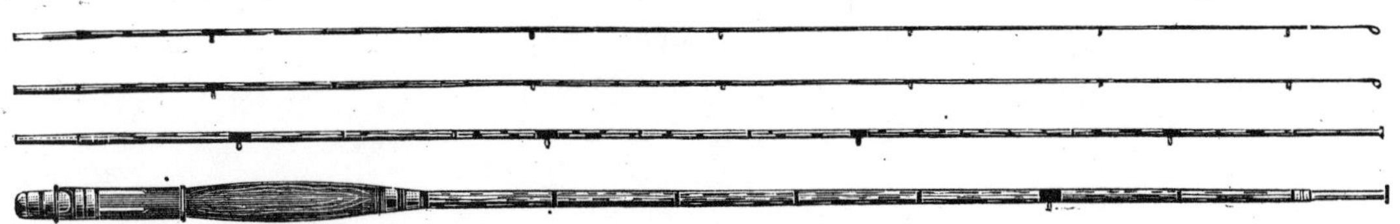

A very durable Rod at a low price and equally well balanced as our best grade of Rods. Has Nickeled Mountings, Solid Metal Reel Seat, Solid Cork Hand Piece and partition sack.

Length, 9 feet, weight, 5 ounces. Price $5 00
Length, 10 feet, weight 6 ounces. Price 5 00
Length 10½ feet, weight 6¾ ounces. Price 5 00

These $5.00 Rods do not have the Orvis Rod Case.

Postage and Registration, 40 cents.

18 *CHARLES F. ORVIS, MANCHESTER, VERMONT*

Bristol Steel Telescopic Rods

FULL LENGTH.

CLOSED.

When telescoped the entire rod is enclosed within the butt length. In use the line runs through the center of rod—a great convenience in brush fishing.

No. 1.—BASS ROD.—Length, 9½ feet. Nickeled Mountings. Length when telescoped, 32 inches; weight, 11¾ ounces.

With Plain Maple Handle	$3 50
With Celluloid Wound Handle	4 00

No. 6.—FLY ROD.—Length, 10 feet; weight, 10 ounces; Nickeled Mountings. Length when telescoped, 37 inches.

With Plain Maple Handle	$3 50
With Celluloid Wound Handle	4 00

Combination Reel and Handle for Steel Rods

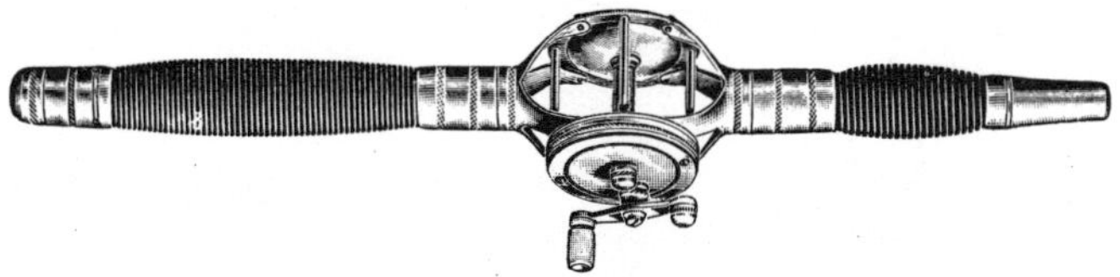

This Combination Reel and Handle brings the weight in the center of the rod so that the rod will not turn in the hand. Reel is quadruple action, has adjustable click and drag or free running, holds 80 to 100 yards of line.

With Maple Handle. Price	$6 00
With Celluloid Wound Handle. Price	6 50
With Cork Handle. Price	7 00

Ordered with a new rod adds $4.50 to the catalogue price of the rod.

The telescoping steel rod with outside guides is still made, but the original model, with the line running inside the rod, was the genuine sagwa, the pure quill, the inventor's dream; the old patent records are full of them. When I was twelve I dreamed of owning such a treasure, with which a worm could be poked through the alders without snagging the line. The trouble was that a big night-walker and even a few split shot did not provide enough weight; it took a hearty haul from a good-sized trout to drag the line down the center of the rod against all that friction.

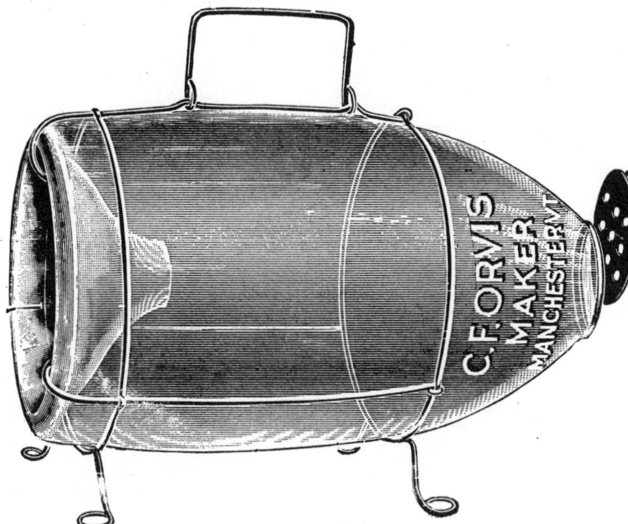

THE ORVIS MINNOW TRAP

Has maker's name blown in the glass

THE BEST DEVICE FOR CATCHING MINNOWS

Try one, it will save you both time and money. Great success past seasons has proved its worth

A delay in procuring live bait has spoiled the pleasure of many a fishing expedition. The ease, rapidity and certainty of securing live bait with this trap has placed it far ahead of the old method of using a minnow seine. Anglers are assured that with the ORVIS MINNOW TRAP they may be certain of supplying themselves easily and promptly. Once possessed, this trap is found to be indispensable to an outfit.

This trap is made of heavy "flint" glass, and is not easily broken. Handle and legs of galvanized metal. Size of trap, 13 inches in length and 24 inches in circumference.

Place a handful of cracker crumbs inside the trap (cracker crumbs are the best because they are light and float well when the trap is filled with water), attach a cord to the handle and lower the trap where minnows frequent.

When lowering the trap into deep water fasten the end of the cord to a float of some kind, so that you can readily regain the trap.

Each trap is packed in a hinged wood box, convenient for transportation. Price complete.... $2 25

THE IMPROVED ORVIS REEL

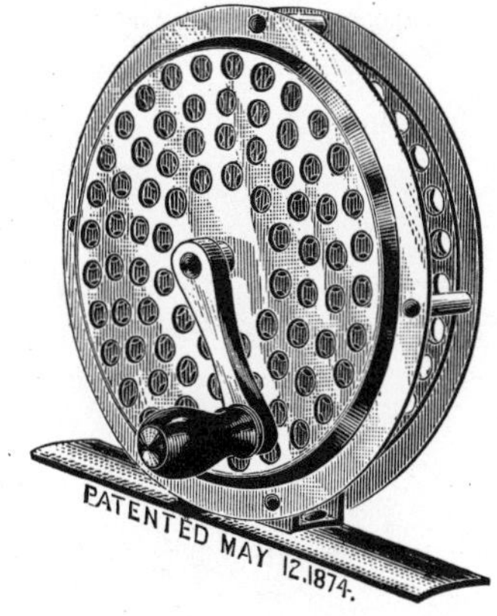

No. 1.—The improvements on the Orvis Reel make it the best click reel in the market for the money. It is now put together with screws instead of rivets—has bushed bearings and screw-off oil cap, reel bar improved in shape, click perfected and placed between plates.

The reel is nickel-plated and finely finished. It is perforated to make it light and keep it free from sand; also that the line may dry without removing it from the reel after use. It is very light, very strong, and holds from 40 to 50 yards of No. 4 waterproof line. It is more compact and less cumbersome than ordinary 25-yard reels.

Regular style, see cut .... $2 50 each
With Safety Band .... 3 00 each
Aluminum .... 3 50 each

No. 2.—IMPROVED ORVIS REEL FOR BASS FISHING—Has balance handle, safety band and back sliding click, making either a free running or click reel; holds from 70 to 80 yards of No. 4 line.
Price, post-paid $3 00

Postage Prepaid.

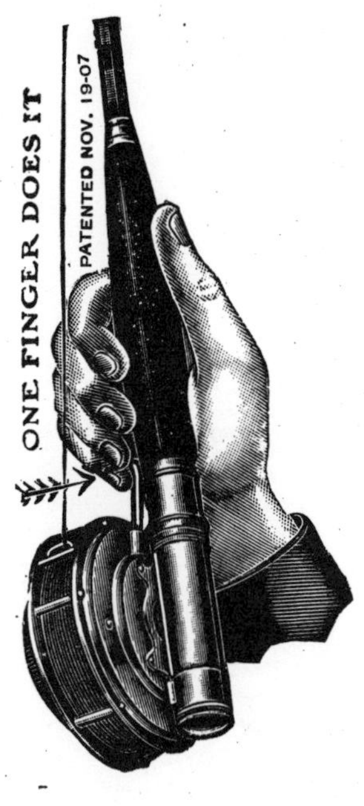

Kelso Automatic Reel

This new automatic reel cannot get out of order, as it has friction relief action at both ends of spring.

It is automatic in its action, reeling in the line upon a slight pressure of the controlling lever, keeping the line taut at all times after fish is hooked.

Capacity, 100 yards H. or No. 6 line. Will take in 150 feet of line without rewinding.

Case of aluminum, satin finished, weighing 7½ ounces.

The steel wearing parts of this reel are enclosed in the aluminum case in such a manner that it is impossible for the reel to get out of order, and with ordinary care it should last a lifetime.

No. F. $4 00

"Ideal" Perforated Click Reel

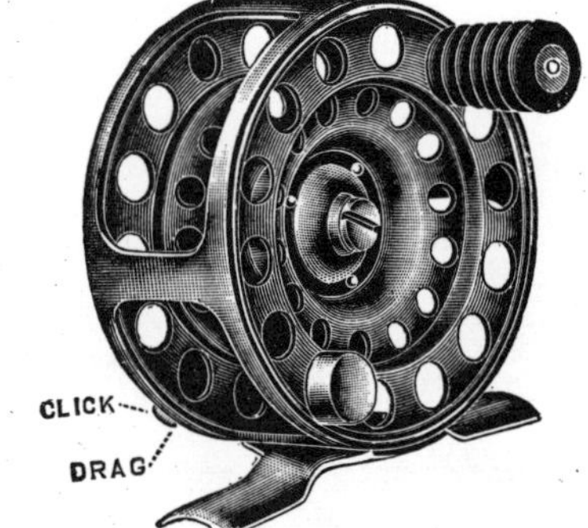

The **IDEAL** Reel is a very nicely made click trout reel and will please any angler. The reel has adjustable click and drag or can be made free running by a simple movement of lever. Weight, 4 ounces, and holds 35 yards No. F. enameled waterproof line. The open sides permit line drying without removing from reel.

Made of German Silver. Price, postpaid:

No. 1, Trout size, 80 yards $1 25
No. 2, Bass size, 120 yards 1 75

Another automatic reel. With spring enough to take up 150 yards of line, the chance of a smashed tip was good if the line wrapped around the top guide or presented a knot in its homeward flight. Note another appearance of the rare new metal, aluminum.

Meek German Silver Kentucky Reel No. 2M

Standard

CAPACITY: 80 yards of No. 2 Braided Silk Line. A most excellent size for light bait casting for both angling and tournament casting. The engraving is three-quarter size and shows handle forward, Aluminum Spool, and Cork Arbor.

DIMENSIONS: Diameter End Plate, 1¾ inches. Lenght Spool, 1⅝ inches. Diameter Spool Head, 1¼ inches.

NET PRICE.

No. 2 M. German Silver Reel, Click, Balance Handle forward, Screw off oil caps. Each $26 00

No. 2 M. J. Same as No. 2 M. except made with Jeweled pivot bearings. Each..... 32 00

The above reels will be furnished with either Aluminum or German Silver Spools as ordered without extra charge

Cork Arbors $1.00 each extra.

Reels made to order with Spools longer or shorter than standard or with handle at the top or bottom $2.00 extra.

Meek German Silver Kentucky Reel No. 3M

Standard

CAPACITY: 100 yards No. 2 Braided Silk Line. If you can afford but one reel take this one. This is the most popular reel we make for angling and tournament casting and is the size used by nine-tenths of our customers.

DIMENSIONS: Diameter End Plate, 2 inches. Length Spool, 1½ inches. Diameter of Spool Head, 1½ inches

NET PRICE.

No. 3 M. German Silver Reel, Balance Handle forward, Click or Click and Drag, Screw off oil caps. Each........ $26 00

No. 3 M. J. Same as No. 3 M. except made with Jeweled pivot bearings. Each.... 32 00

The above reels will be furnished with either Aluminum or German Silver Spools as ordered without extra charge

Cork Arbors $1.00 each extra.

Reels made to order with Spools longer or shorter than standard or with handle at the top or bottom $2.00 extra.

It is astonishing to discover that as far back as 1905 aluminum spools were available, *without extra charge,* in Meek reels. Bait-casters of my generation do not recall Meek reels with aluminum spools until fairly recent times, near the demise of the company; we always believed that the company's conservatism in respect to the aluminum spool and the level wind made the Meek and Milam reels, once the standard of the industry, obsolete.

Legend says that Meek and Milam were watchmakers—and bass fishermen—who migrated from Pennsylvania to Kentucky. The superb reels they made for themselves soon got them out of watchmaking and into the reel business. They were originally, legend says, Meek & Milam but later split into separate companies. Owners of Meek reels delighted to tap the handle and invite attention to the length of time the reel would spin, not realizing that the inertia of the indestructible, beautifully made spool was the mother of backlashes, more and more so as the weight of popular types of casting plugs dropped from an ounce to half of that. Incredibly enough, one could get a Meek reel to his preferred dimensions and handle position for a mere two bucks extra—in 1905.

Kingfisher Highest Quality Enameled Silk Lines

These lines are very strong, invisible in color and carefully enameled especially for fly fishing. Lines are carded in lengths of 25 yards, four connecting.

Length	25 yds.	50 yds.	75 yds.	100 yds.
Size F..............	$1 00	$2 00	$3 00	$4 00
Size G..............	90	1 80	2 70	3 30
Size H..............	80	1 60	2 40	3 20
Size I..............	75	1 50	2 25	3 00

Postage Paid on Lines.

(3)

42 CHARLES F. ORVIS, MANCHESTER, VERMONT

ORVIS FLY CASE

For Flies on Eyed Hooks

A perfect metal pocket fly-case that is finished in nice style. Has hinged cover and all corners rounded.

The cork strips to which flies are attached are firmly held in position by metal on three sides.

Price, each, postage prepaid .... 35 cents

Size 5½ x 3 x 1.

Repairing Outfit

Packed in Metal Case with Hinged Cover

Contains Wax, Ferrule Cement, Varnish, Brush, Rod Rings Keepers, Ring Tips, Silk, Thread, Assorted Needles, File, Screw Driver, Scissors, Pocket Oiler and Cork Screw.
Price, postage prepaid .... $1 50 each

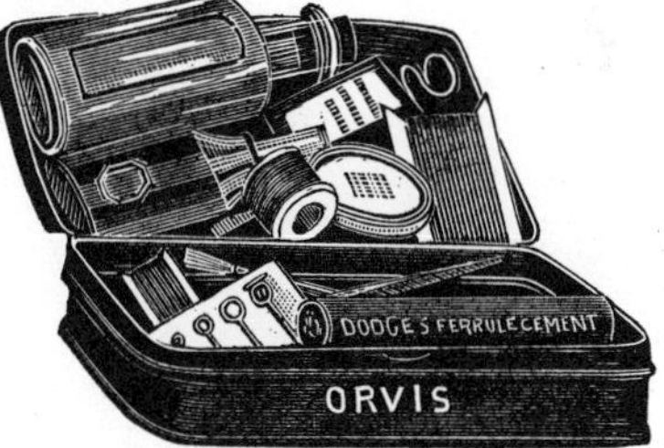

Size 5½ x 3 x 1¼.

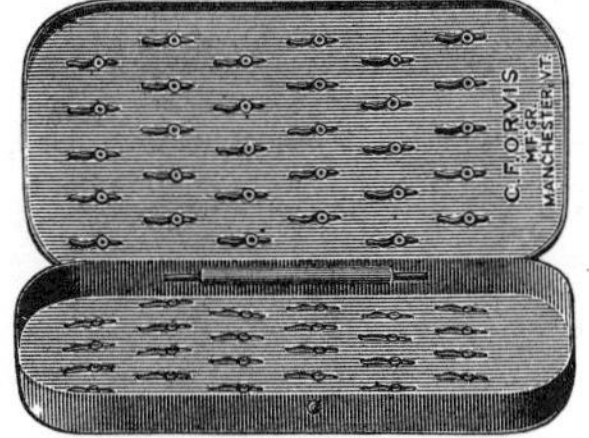

Size, 6¼ x 3¼ x ½.

Orvis Eyed Hook Fly Case

Aluminum

Holds 4½ dozen Flies. A perfect metal pocket fly case that is finished in nice style. Has hinged covers and all corners rounded.

Price, postpaid .... $1 25 each

These fly boxes are on the market, unchanged, today. And in the "repairing kit," only the corkscrew is now obsolete.

"I shall bring you acquainted with more Flies than Father Walton has taken notice of in his 'Complete Angler.'"

ORVIS TROUT FLIES

(Reversed Wing, i. e. Double Fastened)

Price .... $1 50 per dozen

On Hooks from Smallest to No. 5 Inclusive

☞ A discount of **TEN** per cent. from list prices of **FLIES** will be made on orders of **SIX** dozen or over, and **TWENTY** per cent. on orders of **TWELVE** dozen or over.

Local names and names of flies alike in form and color, but differing in species or size, are placed under the same heading.

Sportsmen are invited to send to me for any special kind of Flies not on Lists that they may desire, in which case please send sample, if possible. I aim to fill all orders with exactness in every particular.

When an assortment of Flies is desired, and the selection left with me, I will use my best judgment to send the most desirable kinds.

Flies have names attached, are arranged on cards, and packed in strong, convenient boxes.

TROUT-FLIES TIED ON SUPERIOR QUALITY STEEL SPROAT OR O'SHAUGHNESSY HOOKS WITH SINGLE GUT SNELLS FOUR INCHES IN LENGTH.

FLIES TIED ON PENNELL LIMERICK EYED, PENNELL SNECK EYED, OR SPROAT EYED HOOKS TO ORDER.

Trout Flies for Dry Fly Fishing

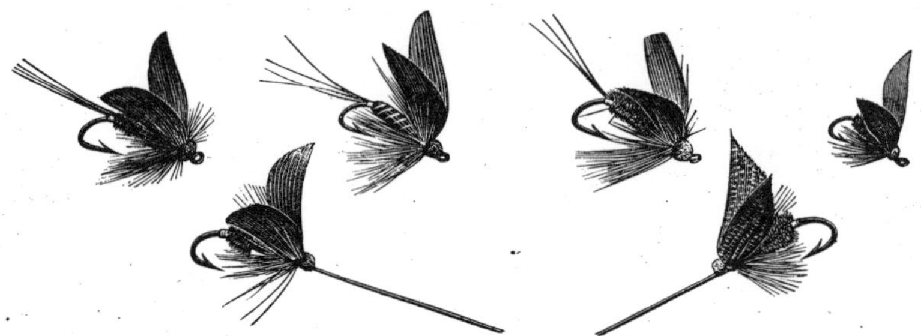

The Streams in some parts of this Country becoming depleted and the fish more shy, there is a demand for smaller flies, delicately tied in colors less gaudy than needed for flies used on wild, unfrequented rivers and lakes.

Experienced Anglers have generally advocated using extremely small flies tied on Eyed hooks. The following patterns are the most desirable:

Made on Hall's Eyed Hooks or on Hooks with Snells. Price..................... $1 50 per dozen

Adjutant Blue.
Alder.
Artful Dodger.
Autumn Dun.
Badger Quill.
Black Ant.
Black Gnat.
Blue Dun.
Blue Quill.
Brown Badger.
Cinnamon Quill.
Claret Bumble.
Claret Spinner.
Coachman.
Cork-Screw.
Cow Dung.
Dark Sage.
Drake's Extractor.
Fisherman's Curse.
Flight's Fancy.
Furnace.
Ginger Quill.
Golden Dun.
Gold Ribbed Hare's Ear.
Goose Dun.
Governor.
Grannom.
Grannom Larva.
Green Insect.
Half Stone.
Hammond's Adopted.
Hare' Ear Quill.
Harlequin.
India Rubber Olive.
Indian Yellow.
Iron Blue.
Jenny Spinner.
Large Wickham.
Little Chap.
Little Marryat.
Needle Brown.
Orange Bumble.
Orange Sedge.
Orange Tag.
Pink Wickham.
Red Ant.
Red Quill.
Red Spinner.
Red Tag.
Rough Olive.
Saltoun.
Sanctuary.
Silver Sedge.
Welchman's Button.
Wickham.
Yellow Bumble.

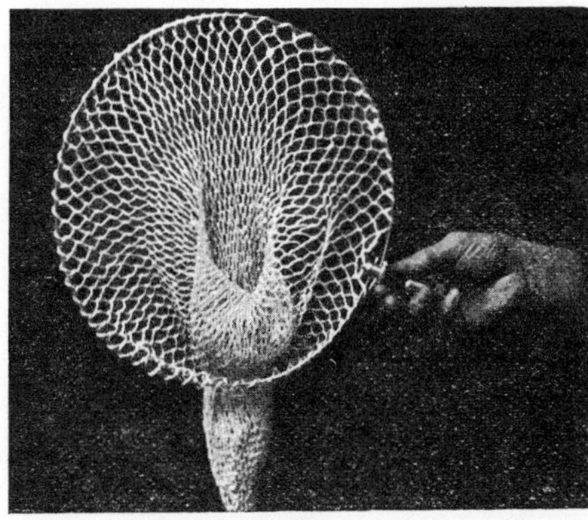

The Angler's Friend Landing Net

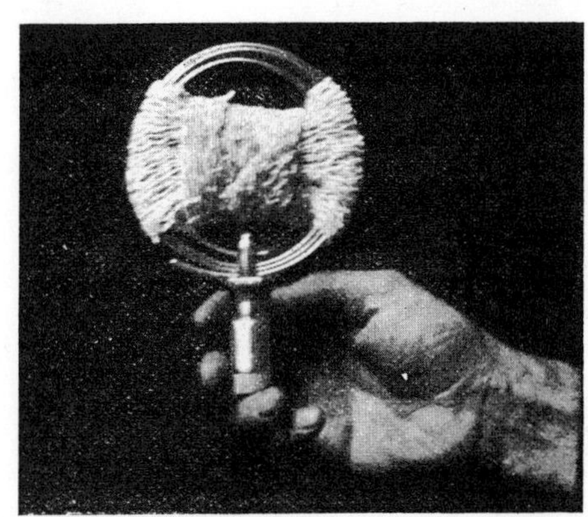

A Pocket Take-Down Landing Net that can be reduced from a 12-inch ring to a 4-inch size. Compactness a great feature.

Has socket with inside screw for attaching any handle that may be cut in the woods.

PRICES POSTPAID.

With 20-inch dark colored Braided Linen Net.......... $2 00
With 20-inch dark colored Twisted Linen Net.......... 1 75
With 20 or 24-inch Linen Gilling Net.......... 1 50

The New Century Telescopic Landing Outfit

Comprises a three-piece telescopic handle with cork grip, 34 inches long when extended without gaff hook. With gaff hook it is 40 inches long. When telescoped with hook removed it is 16 inches long.

A handsome steel, nickel-plated gaff hook and a steel collapsing landing net frame, with strong small mesh linen landing net.

Price, complete.......... $6 00
Landing Handle and Net Frame only.......... 5 50
Landing Handle with Gaff only.......... 5 00

RODS, REELS, FLIES AND FISHING TACKLE 87

BAIT BOXES

Padlock, 10 cents. Crescent, 20 cents. Oval, 10 cents.

Postage cn Bait Boxes, 5 cents each.

BAIT BOX STRAPS... 15 cents

Grasshopper Box

A live box for insects. Has a sliding cover to admit of one grasshopper or cricket to come out at a time. Right size for the pocket. Postpaid...........25 cents

Floating Live Net

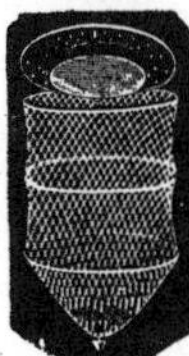

Cover has an Air Compartment to float net when placed beside boat or at dock to keep fish alive.

Size, 14 x 20; collapses to 1½ inch.

Price $1.00

Cricket and Grasshopper Holder

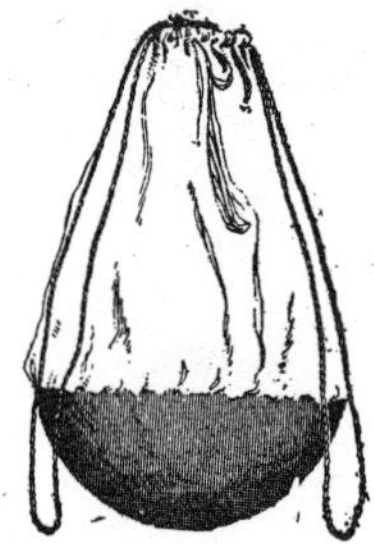

Has wire case, cloth top with shir-strings. Size, 6 x 3.........................25 cents

The worm boxes are still labeled to remind French-speaking fishermen where they put their worms.

Page 183: A dozen or so of these books are still classics and sought by collectors; several are currently available in reprint.

FAVORITE FLIES and THEIR HISTORIES

BY

MARY ORVIS MARBURY

With Many Replies from Practical Anglers to Inquiries Concerning How, When and Where to Use Them.

Illustrated by Thirty-Two Colored Plates of Flies (nearly 300 Flies), Six Engravings of Natural Insects, and Eight Reproductions of Photographs, making Forty-six Full Page Illustrations.

In One Volume, Size 7½ x 9½. Price, Postpaid, $5.00.

THE COLORED PLATES OF 300 FLIES ARE ALONE WORTH THE PRICE OF THE BOOK.

CONTENTS

PART I.—Insects, Natural and Artificial; History of the Red Hackle.

PART II.—Prefatory; Histories of the Favorite Flies, accompanied by letters relating to their use in—Canada; Maine, Vermont and New Hampshire; Connecticut, Massachusetts and Rhode Island; New York; Pennsylvania, New Jersey and Delaware; Virginia and West Virginia; Ohio; Missouri; Iowa; Indiana and Illinois; Michigan; Minnesota and Wisconsin; Maryland, Tennessee, Kentucky, Georgia and Mississippi; Florida; Louisiana, Texas, Arizona and Nevada; Colorado, Wyoming, Utah and Idaho; Montana; Washington; California; Oregon; "Hic Habitat Felicitas;" Index of Plates and Flies; List of Correspondents.

Accompanying the histories of the flies depicted in colors, are letters from two hundred practical fishermen giving advice regarding the use of these flies in all parts of the United States and Canada.

ANGLING AND CAMPING BOOKS

The following books sent, postpaid, on receipt of price: "Hunting," "Fishing," "Camping," "Guide," or any book sent at lowest price possible.

		Price
American Fishes	By G. Browne Goode	$3 50
Angler's Secret	By C. B. Bradford	1 10
Angler's Annual	By C. B. Bradford	50
Book of the Black Bass, and supplement	By James A. Henshall	3 00
Brook Trout and the Determined Angler	By Charles Bradford	65
Canoe and Camp Cookery	By "Seneca"	1 00
Determined Angler	By C. B. Bradford	65
Domesticated Trout	By Livingston Stone	2 50
Favorite Flies	By Mary Orvis Marbury	5 00
Fishing in American Waters	By Genio C. Scott	2 50
Fishing Tourists	By Chas. Hallock	2 00
Floating Flies and How to Dress Them	By Frederick M. Halford	12 00
Fly Rods and Fly Tackle	By Henry P. Wells	1 75
Fish Hatching and Fish Catching	By Roosevelt and Greene	1 50
Forest Runes	By George W. Sears (Nessmuk)	1 50
Hints on Camping	By Henderson	1 25
How to Tie Salmon Flies	By "Captain Hale"	5 00
I Go A-Fishing	By W. C. Prime	2 50
In the Wilderness—Adirondack Essays	By Charles Dudley Warner	1 00
Lake Champlain and Its Shores	By W. H. H. Murray	1 00
Log Cabins: How to Build and Furnish	By Wm. S. Wicks	1 00
Modern Fish Culture	By Fred Mather	2 00
Paddle and Portage	By Thos. Sedgwick Steele	1 50
Pictures from Forest and Stream		2 00
Sam Lovel's Camps	By Rowland E. Robinson	1 00
Speckled Brook Trout	By Louis Rhead	3 50
The Basses	By Louis Rhead	3 50
The Complete Angler	By Walton and Cotton	2 75
The Game Fish	By R. B. Roosevelt	2 00
Uncle Lisha's Shop	By Rowland E. Robinson	1 00
Woods and Lakes of Maine	By Hubbard	3 00
With Fly, Rod and Camera	By Edward A. Samuels	5 00
Wild Fowlers	By Charles Bradford	1 00
Ye Gods and Little Fishes	By James A. Henshall	2 00

William Mills & Son

Fine Fishing Tackle

21 PARK PLACE

NEW YORK, U. S. A.

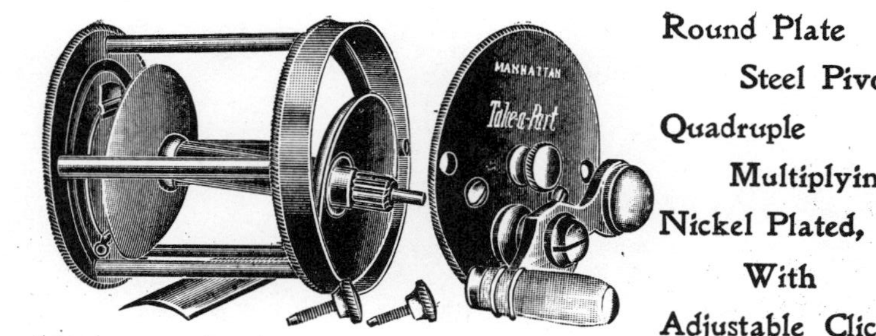

Round Plate
Steel Pivot,
Quadruple
Multiplying,
Nickel Plated,
With
Adjustable Click.

MANHATTAN "TAKE-A-PART" REEL.

One size only, 80 yards.................................. $3 25 each

A Very Popular Pattern.

Patent
Quadruple
"TAKE-A-PART"
Reel.
Round Plate with
Cross Bars,
All Metal.

No. **3-60**, Spool $1\frac{7}{16}$ in. diam., $1\frac{5}{8}$ in. long, Plain Click..... $3 15 each

No. **3-61**, Spool $1\frac{7}{16}$ in. diam., $1\frac{5}{8}$ in. long, Automatic Click 3 70 "

Blue Grass
Simplex Quadruple
"TAKE-A-PART"
Reel.

Patented July 5, 1904.

One size only, that of No. 3 Kentucky Reel.

No. **33**.. $7 50 each

The frame being tubing enables the spool to be made of larger diameter and therefore of larger capacity.

Patent
Quadruple
Tubular Frame
"TAKE-A-PART"
Reel.

Spool $1\frac{3}{4}$ inches diameter
$1\frac{5}{8}$ inches long.

No. **4-80**, All Metal, Plain Click........................ $6 00 each

No. **4-81**, All Metal, Automatic Click.................... 6 50 "

No. **4-82**, Rubber Veneered, Plain Click................ 7 00 "

No. **4-83**, Rubber Veneered, Automatic Click........... 7 50 "

4

Mills' "Intrinsic" Tarpon and Tuna Reel.

Shows ⅝ Size.

The "Intrinsic" Tarpon and Tuna Reel is extra **large size,** being $4\frac{1}{2}$ inches in diameter; it is most modern in both design and workmanship, and **is a very handsome and beautiful model.** It has been our aim to construct a **durable and simple** reel which would be suitable **for the heaviest angling.** All parts of this reel are made in the best possible manner and only the very **best** of **materials enter into its construction.**

The **strength of the reel** is very much **increased** by the introduction of two **German Silver rings or plates** between the rubber side-plates and the bars or pillars which hold the reel together. These plates **take the strain entirely** off the rubber, and while they add only a few ounces to the weight of the reel, **they strengthen the reel very materially** and make it much superior to any reel which does not have these plates.

The click, which is made in the strongest manner, is on the handle side of the reel, and the pall works against a specially made and hardened ratchet wheel, which is used for this purpose only and is set under the pinion wheel.

The drag is one of the principal features of the reel; it is the **simplest, surest and strongest drag ever applied to a fishing reel.** It can be readily thrown on or off by a convenient push button on back plate of reel. When set for use **it works only against the fish** when taking line and **not against the angler** when winding in the line. The drag **does not work** through or **on the gearing,** but does work on the left-hand plate of spool, which is made amply heavy to withstand the slight wear to which it will be subjected. The **construction** of the drag **is very simple** but it does its work accurately and well and is just **the drag which Tarpon and Tuna anglers are looking for.** When the reel is sent out by us the drag is set at about $5\frac{1}{2}$ lbs. strain, but it **can be set, readily and surely, to any strength desired** by simply removing the back plate of reel and tightening or loosening the lock nut which keeps the drag in place.

The handle is **long** and **very strong,** with a good generous grasp, it furnishes **good winding-in power.**

It is a fine example of first-class reel making. Diameter of plates, $4\frac{1}{2}$ inches; width of barrel, $2\frac{1}{16}$ inches; capacity, about 600 feet of 30-thread line or 900 feet of 21-thread line. The Handle Drags (see pages 56 and 57) can also be applied to this reel.

Price, $40 00; in fine leather case, $43 00.

55

As reels grew in size and loading, the fragility of hard rubber side plates became increasingly a problem. It is difficult to understand why the industry clung so long to this unsuitable material.

Methods of Fastening Eyed Hook Flies.

"Jam Knot" Attachment for Turn Down Eyed Trout Hooks.

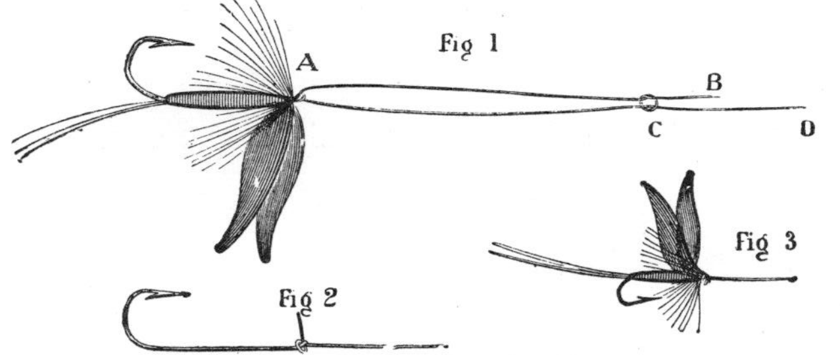

FIRST. Take the fly by the bend in the position shown, with the eye turned upwards (**Fig. 1**); pass 2 or 3 inches of the end of the gut casting line (**B**) (previously well moistened) through the eye (**A**) *towards the point of the hook*, and then letting go the fly, double back the gut and make a single slip knot (**C Fig. 1**) round the centre link (**D**).

SECONDLY. Draw the slip knot tight enough only to admit of its just passing freely over the hook eye (**A Fig. 1**), and then run it down to, *and over*, the said eye—when, on gradually pulling the central link tight, the "jam knot" is automatically formed, as shown on the bare hook (**Fig. 2**), and in the fly complete, actual size (**Fig. 3**). FINALLY. Cut off the superfluous gut end to within from about $\frac{1}{8}$ to $\frac{3}{16}$ of an inch, according to the size of the hook.

The "Turle Knot" Attachment for Bare Hooks.

1 — 1st Stage; 2 — 2nd Stage; 3 — 3rd Stage (knot complete)

"*1st Stage*": Pass the end of the line (**A**) through the hook eye (**B**), and run the hook a few inches up the line out of the way, then make a "running noose" (**C**) with the slip knot (**D**), and *draw the said knot as tight as possible.* "*2nd Stage*": Run down the hook again (to the position shown in **Fig. 1**), and passing the noose (**C**) over it, pull the line (**E**) quite tight—cutting off the spare end. This completes the knot—*vide* "*3rd Stage.*"

The "Jam Knot" Attachment is suited to artificial flies tied on the foregoing hooks, sizes up to No. 2 inclusive; above that size, the "Double Slip Knot," illustrated in the diagram, is that recommended by Mr. Cholmondeley-Pennell.

"Double Slip Knot" Fastening for Salmon and Grilse Hooks.

(*Complete in 40 Seconds.*)

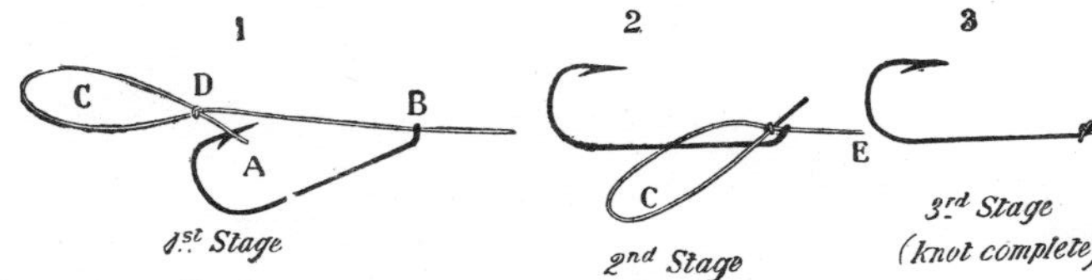

Take the hook by the bend between the finger and the thumb of the left hand, and with the eye turned downwards in the position shown in the diagram; then—the gut being first thoroughly well soaked—push the end, with a couple of inches or so, down through the eye (**B**) towards the point of the hook; then pass it round over the shank of the hook, and again, from the opposite side, downwards through the eye in a direction away from the hook's point (the gut end and the central link will now be lying parallel); make the double slip knot (**A**) round the central link (**C**) and pull the said knot itself perfectly tight; then draw the loop of gut, together with the knot (**A**), backwards (towards the tail of the fly) until the knot presses tightly into and against the metal eye of the hook (**B**), where hold it firmly with the forefinger and thumb of the left hand, whilst with the right hand—and "humoring" the gut in the process—the central link is drawn tight, thus taking in the "slack" of the knot. When finished cut the superfluous gut end off close.

[To tie a Double Slip Knot: Make a single slip knot (*a*) and, before drawing it close, pass the gut end (*b*) a *second time* round the central link (*c*), and then again through the loop (*a*), when the knot will be like (**A**) in the larger diagram. To finish, pull the end of the gut (*b*)—gradually, and at last very tightly—*straight away*: in a line, that is, with the central link (*c*).]

"PONCE PARK" PHANTOM.

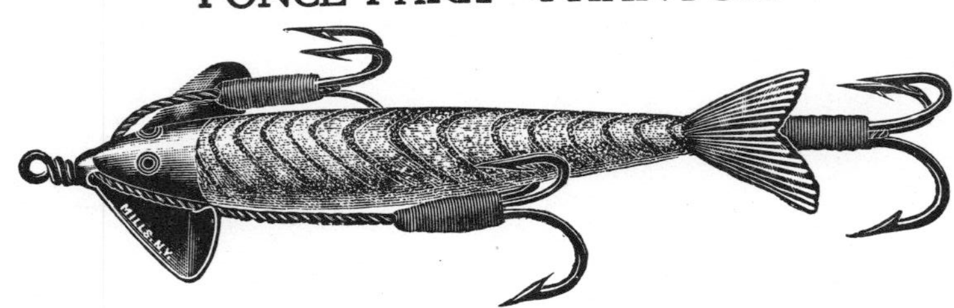

Above we illustrate a phantom, which we believe will be a very popular one, for trolling for sea trout and pickerel. It is made of extra strong canvas, the hooks, which are extra strong, are mounted on twisted wire gimp, and the snelling is closely wound with fine copper wire. Taking it all together it is a phantom calculated to withstand the teeth of these fish as well as many hard knocks which would destroy the regular weight phantom. Made only in one color, silver striped, light green.

Nos.		Each
296	Minnow, 3¾ inches long	$0 90
297	" 4¼ " "	1 15
298	" 4¾ " "	1 25

"STERLING" PHANTOM.

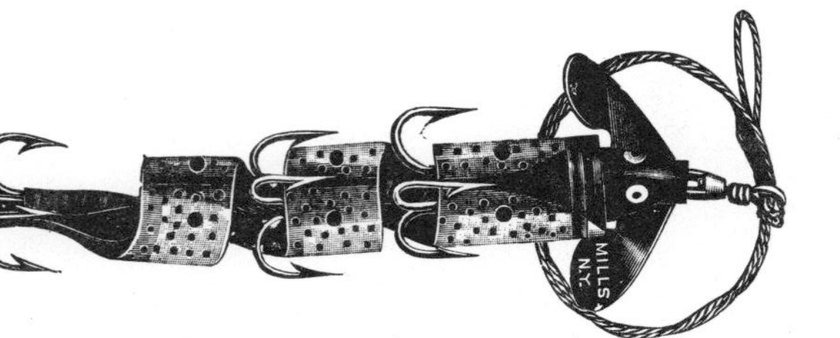

This phantom is used quite extensively abroad but it is little known in this country. It is suitable to use either trolling or casting for large trout, black bass, or Oswego bass, it is very lifelike and "fishy" in its motions. We carry it in two sizes and two colors.

Nos.		Each
196	Minnow, 3 inches long, either blue or brown spotted	$0 65
196½	" 3½ " " " " "	75

"ROXBURY" PHANTOM.

This phantom also is very little known in this country; it is, however, a very successful minnow both for trolling and casting. On being drawn through the water it not only revolves but the tails fly back and forth and renders the motion very natural.

197 Minnows 3 inches long, either blue or brown spotted above, silver underneath.................................$0 60 each

WILLIAM MILLS & SON'S "INTRINSIC" CASTING SPOONS.

These, like our "Intrinsic" trolling spoons are the very highest quality throughout. The hooks are very high grade and are made especially for these casting spoons.

The above cut shows the spoon with auxiliary hooks; we also carry them in stock with one hook. They are very successful either with or without bait, for casting from a fly rod. They add quite a good deal to the effectiveness of a minnow if they are used for trolling instead of a plain hook.

With auxiliary hooks, either silver or enamel finish, on double gut or gimp, Nos. 1 to 3................................$0 25 each

With one hook only, either silver or enamel finish, on double gut or gimp, Nos. 1 to 3................................20 "

Blades are same size as "Intrinsic" trolling spoons, page 84.

88

Worden Bucktail Specialties.

BUCK TAIL CASTING SPOON

A sure killer for Bass, Pickerel and other game fish.

Size	1	2	3	4	5	
With Bucktail Treble Hook	$0 35	$0 35	$0 35	$0 40	$0 40	each
With Bucktail Single Hook	35	35	35	40	40	"
With Bucktail Weedless Single Hook	....	....	40	40	....	"

Nickel Fluted Bucktail Minnow Spoon.

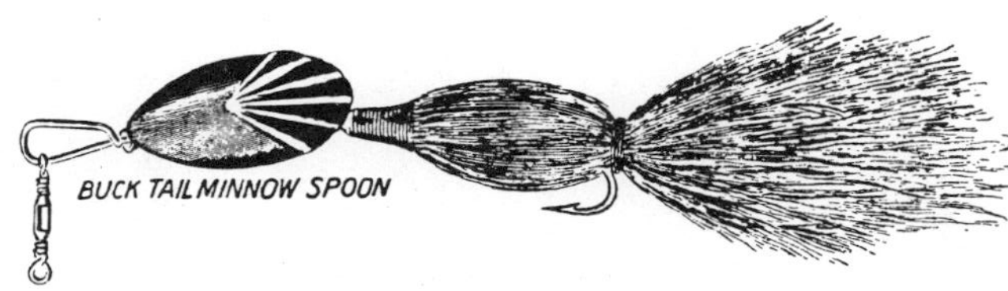
BUCK TAIL MINNOW SPOON

This arrangement of the Bucktail on the Hook is an excellent imitation of a live Minnow.

Sizes, 3 and 4 .... $0 50 each

Bucktail Treble Hooks.

These are far more alluring than the ordinary feathered Treble Hooks.

Size....	1	1/0	2/0	3/0	4/0
Each..	$0 25	$0 25	$0 25	$0 25	$0 25

Worden Wooden Minnows.

These Wooden Minnows are made of red cedar, finely finished in the following colors; Green and Red with "cracked back," Green and White with "cracked back," Red, White, Yellow. All are fitted with new Patent Spinner, the strongest and best spinner ever attached to any wooden bait.

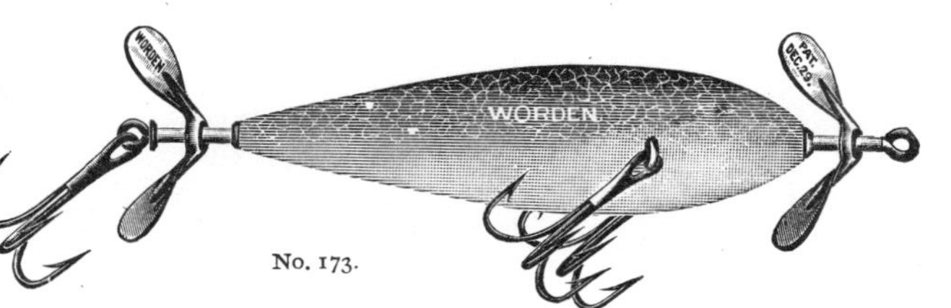

No. 173.

Nos.		Each.
173	Wooden Minnow; length 3 inches, 3 Treble Hooks	$0 50
75	Wooden Minnow; length 5 inches, 5 Treble Hooks	60

Worden Combination Minnow and Bucktail.

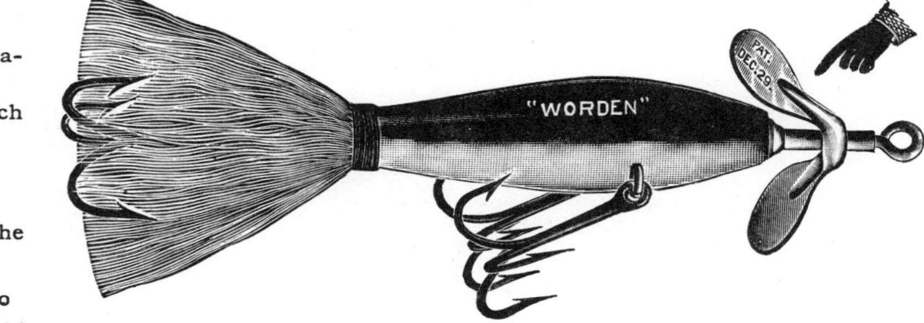

No.		Each.
73	Wooden Minnow; length 3 inches, 3 Treble Hooks	$0 50

89

"Manco" Casting Lures.

These "Manco" lures are quite well known and have proven very successful wherever used, they are among the most popular casting baits. They are made of wood, handsomely and durably decorated in most attractive colors and are mounted with the best quality hooks. The minnows are loaded and balanced so that they travel level and a proper distance below the surface. Nos. 104 and 204 are the famous floating lure, they can be used in ordinary trolling if desired, but if used for that purpose Nos. 104 and 204 would require a small sinker placed on the line several feet from the lure.

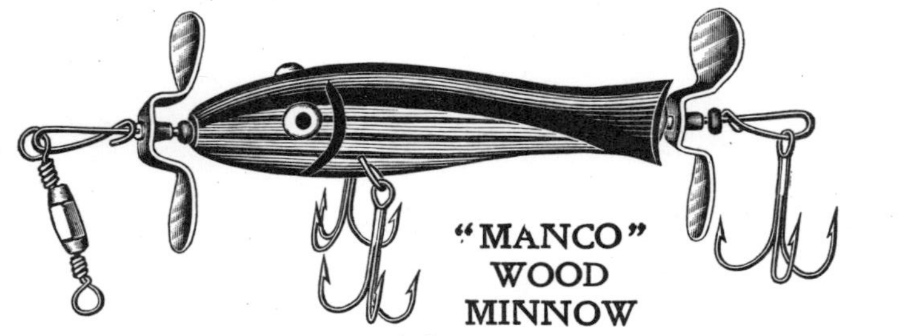

"MANCO" WOOD MINNOW

⅔ size.

No.		Each.
103.	Wood Minnow, Length 3¼ inches, 3 Treble Hooks	$0 65
203.	Wood Minnow, Length 3¼ inches, 3 Single Hooks	65

"MANCO" FLOATING FROG

⅔ size.

No.		Each.
104.	Floating Frog, Length 2½ inches, 3 Treble Hooks	$0 75
204.	Floating Frog, Length 2½ inches, 3 Single Hooks	75

"Mills" Yellow Kid.

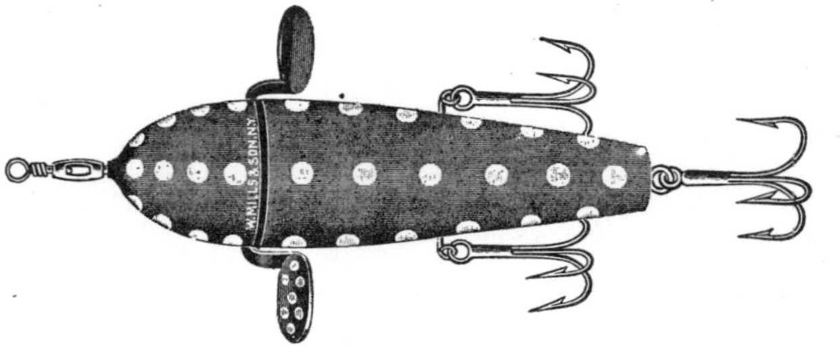

⅔ size. Also furnished with 3 Single Hooks.

One of the best known surface casting baits. Made of copper, and is absolutely watertight. Far superior to the ordinary metal casting baits (which are made of aluminum and therefore not so strong or watertight as the Yellow Kid).

	Each.
Furnished in Yellow, White, or Red, Spotted	$0 75

"Jersey Queen" Casting Baits.

Similar to the "Yellow Kid," only made of Red Cedar.

Made in three sizes; the medium size is same size as "Yellow Kid." All sizes furnished with either the treble hooks or three single hooks.

	Each.
Large, Enameled Yellow, White or Red, Length 2¾ inches	$0 75
Medium, Enameled Yellow, White or Red, Length 3¼ inches	60
Small, Enameled Yellow, White or Red, Length 3¾ inches	50

The above lines are particularly desirable for fishing in New Jersey and other near-by waters.

90

The Yellow Kid, drawn by R. F. Outcault, was an enormously popular character in the Sunday "funny papers" of the Gay Nineties. This lure, and the Jersey Queen, copied the old Anson Decker "Lake Hopatcong" plug of the surface-disturber type. It always was and still is an excellent one.

"Expert" Wood Minnows.

Shows No. 2 (⅔ Size).

Furnished in Green, Aluminum, Red and White Enamel.

Nos.		Each
1	Length, 3½ inches; weight, ¾ ounce; 5 Treble Hooks..........	$0 75
2	Length, 3 inches; weight, ⅝ ounce; 3 Treble Hooks..........	75
3	Length, 2½ inches; weight, ½ ounce; 3 Treble Hooks..........	75

"Dowagiac" Casting Baits.

Minnow.

Nos.		Each
100	Regular Casting Minnow, 2¾ inches long. This is a sinking minnow, and as such is very successful; furnished either rainbow, fancy back, red or white..........................	$0 75
150	Larger Minnow, 4 inches long, otherwise same as No. 100...	1 00

"Manhattan" Wood Minnows.

We offer these Minnows to meet the demand for a lower priced Wood Casting Bait. They are well made, nicely finished and good value for the price.

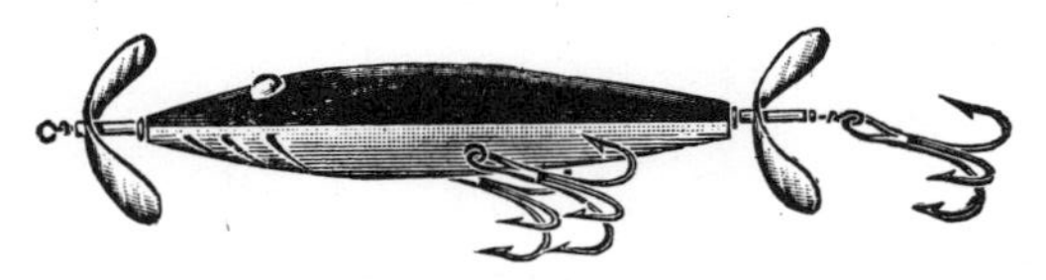

Nos.		Each
30	Length, 3¼ inches, 3 Treble Hooks, Green..............	$0 35
35	Length, 3¼ inches, 3 Treble Hooks, White..............	35
40	Length, 3¼ inches, 3 Treble Hooks, Yellow..............	35

"Coaxer" and "Teaser."

These baits are quite striking as to color and design, the bodies are made of cork and are enameled white, the wings are made of red felt, the tail is composed of a number of red feathers. The baits are heavy enough to cast very nicely from a free-running reel, they will always float right side up.

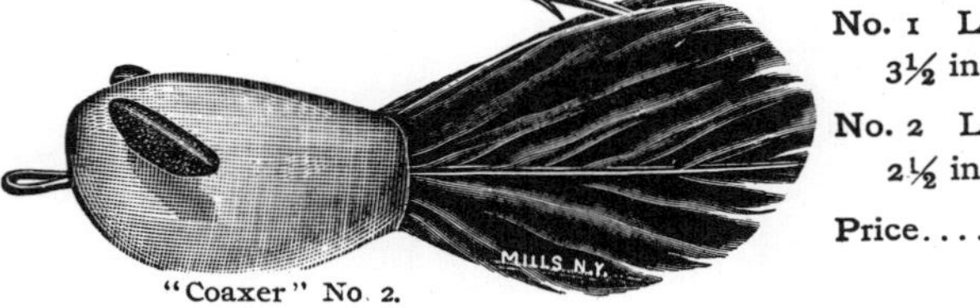

"Coaxer" No. 2.

No. 1 Length over all 3½ inches.

No. 2 Length over all 2½ inches.

Price......$0 50 each

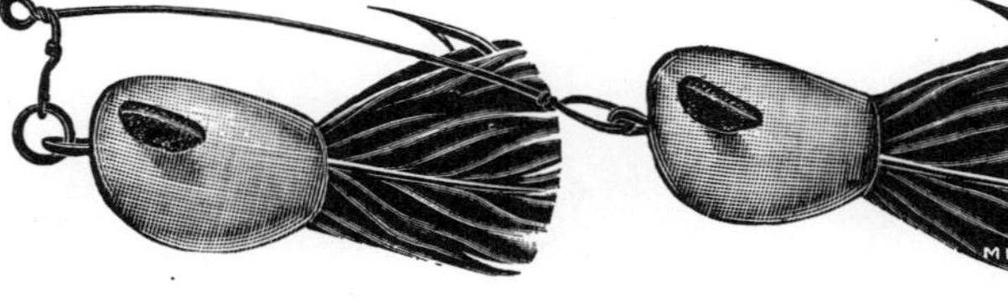

Shows "Teaser" (3-5 Size).

"Teaser"..$0 75 each

91

The Heddon "Dowagiac" lures were standard for many years; out in Kansas the country boys called all casting plugs "dowjacks." This Injured Minnow is still the basic sinking-type plug. Before you buy it, blow on the blades to make sure they spin in opposite directions, to avoid twisting your line.

Manhattan Company's Electric Tackle Box.

No. 97 Large commodious box, handsomely japanned green and decorated, 12⅜ inches long, 8½ inches wide, 6⅛ inches high; box is divided into three compartments, one large enough to hold two large reels, other two will hold fly books or other large articles. Small tray has three compartments for gangs, spoons, minnows, etc.; large tray extending full length of box, with one long compartment for snelled hooks at full length, and seven other compartments. Will hold a large quantity of Tackle. **It is a box well suited for Salt Water Tackle....$2 25**

131

Talcott's Fly Lotion. 2 sizes, large, 50c.; small, **25c.**

Price, 25c. per box.

Electric?

Here's another city slicker who can't draw flies.

Rubber Goods for Anglers.

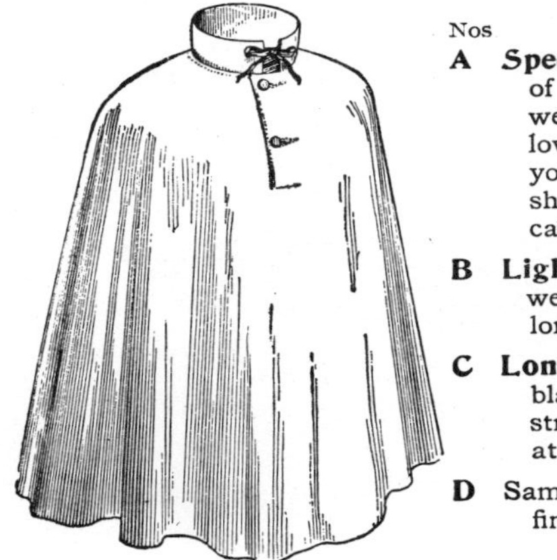

Nos		Each
A	**Special Trouting Cape,** made of gossamer rubber cloth, weight 9½ ounces reaches below top of waders, will keep you dry through many a shower, packed in neat case and can be carried in pocket	$3 00
B	**Light Weight Cape,** heavier weight than No. A, 37 inches long, packed in neat case	3 50
C	**Long Light Weight Cape,** black rubber surface, has draw string at neck and elastic cord at wrists	5 50
D	Same as No. C, but surface of fine **Tan** Rubber	7 50

BOAT SEAT CUSHION, WITH BACK.

Nos.	Seat	Back	Covering Tan Duck	Fine Corduroy
11B	12 x 12 in.	12 x 12 in.	$4 75	$6 25
12B	12 x 14 in.	12 x 20 in.	5 75	7 50
13B	12 x 15 in.	15 x 28 in.	6 75	8 50

CUSHION WITHOUT BACK.

10	12 x 12 inches	$2 50	$3 25
11	12 x 14 "	2 75	3 50
12	12 x 16 "	3 00	3 75
13	12 x 20 "	3 50	4 50

CAMP BLANKETS AND PONCHOS.

	45x72	52x78	62x78	78x78 inches	
Black rubber, flannel lined,	....	$3 75	$4 50	$5 50	each
Black rubber, drill lined,	$2 00	....	....	....	"
Poncho, sheeting lined,	1 75	....	....	....	"

Deflated and Rolled Up.

A mattress 6 ft. 3 ins. x 2 ft. 1 in., makes a bundle 7 x 14 ins., and weighs 10 lbs.

PNEUMATIC CAMP MATTRESS.

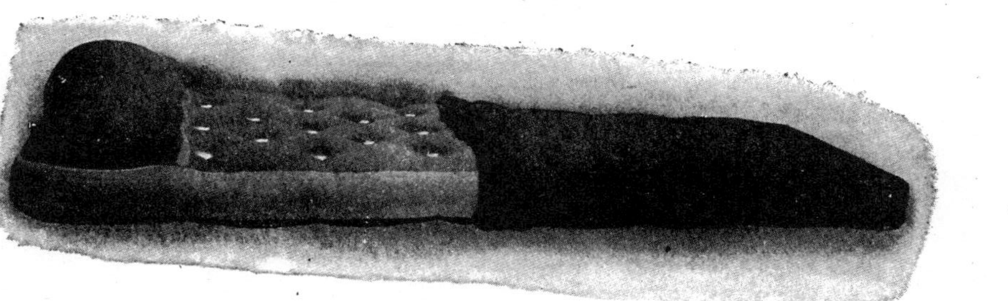

Shows Camp Mattress, with Pillow.

These mattresses have a good brown duck covering, which is shown in cut pulled partly off. When rolled up they take up very little room and can be carried very conveniently with other camp goods. The No. A weighs about 10 pounds.

No. A	Length 6 feet 3 inches, width 2 feet 1 inch	$18 00
" **B**	" 6 " 3 " " 2 " 8 "	21 00

If they are required with pillow, as shown above, add $2 00 to price quoted.

142

RUBBER GOODS FOR ANGLERS.

Haversack or Carry-all.

Sizes	8x11,	10x14 inches
Black Rubber	$1 50	$2 00 each
Tan Mackintosh	2 50	3 50 "
Canvas	1 25	1 50 "

Camp Clothing Bags.

Sizes	20x26,	22x30 inches
Black Rubber	$2 00	$2 50 each
Tan Mackintosh	4 00	4 50 "

Round Air Boat Cushion.

Sizes 12 in. $1 75, 16 in. $2 25 each
" 14 in. 2 00, 18 in. 2 50 "

Boat Cushion, Air Pillow and Life Preserver, Combined.

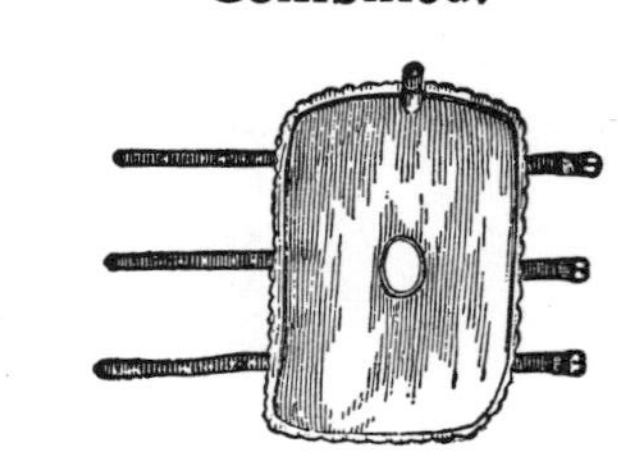

Tan Mackintosh........$3 25 each

Square Air Boat Cushions.

Size	Each
12 x 16 inches	$2 50
14 x 16 "	2 75
16 x 16 "	3 00
15 x 18 "	3 25

Above covered with Tan Cloth.

Air Pillows.

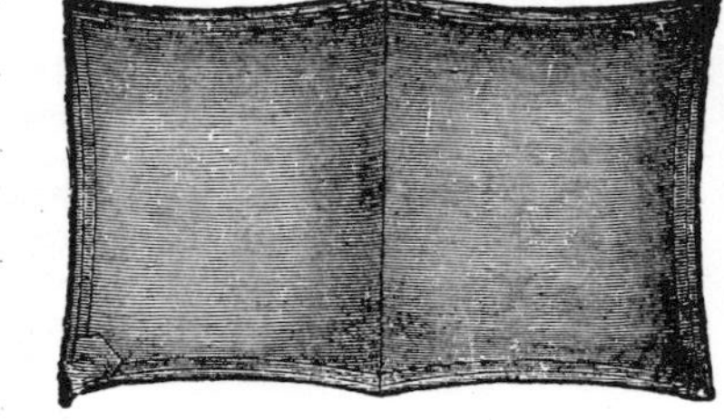

Size	Each
9 x 13 inches	$1 60
10 x 16 "	1 85
12 x 18 "	2 50
14 x 23 "	3 00

New Pattern Life Preserver.

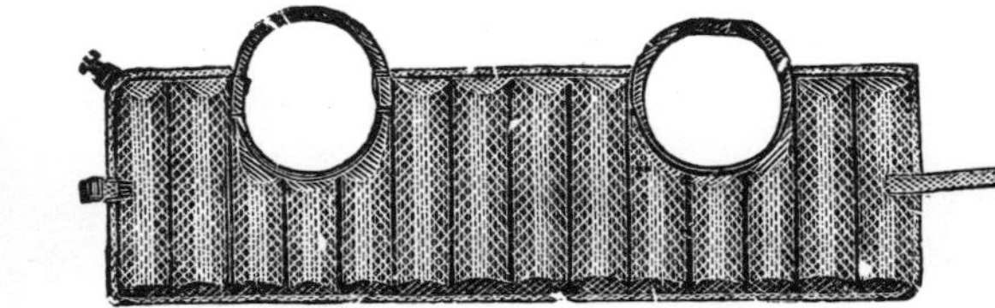

	Each
Length, 29 inches	$2 50
" 33 "	2 75
" 37 "	3 00
" 41 "	3 50

These being made with shoulder and body straps when attached remain firmly in position, and cannot move down or off the body, thus giving complete safety and great buoyancy.

Kelso FISHING TACKLE SPECIALTIES 3

"Senate" Steel Vine Rods

Senate steel vine is the strongest material obtainable for making rods. It grows similar to a grape vine but the fibre runs all the way through the stock giving it a toughness and elasticity found in no other material.

Showing Fibre of Senate Steel Vine Stock Which our Senate Rods are made from

Our Senate rods are made of six strips of this steel vine glued together and we make them round, a finish impossible to secure in a split bamboo rod.

They are attractively wound with silk and fitted with nickel plated mountings.

Every Senate rod is fitted with Frost's patent locking reel seat. With this reel seat it is absolutely impossible for a reel to work loose. A description will be found on page 24.

These rods are put up in a substantial partition bag and enclosed in an "Otter" waterproof black case. This case has screw-off ends, protects the rods when laid away and is a mighty convenient way of carrying.

We take special pride in the Senate rod and recommend it as the best balanced, best finished and most serviceable rod for the money.

"Senate" Fly Rod, Nickel Plated

Three-piece with extra tip, snake guides.

No. 3000.	Midget, 8 ft., 4¼ oz.....	Each $6.65
No. 3001.	Light Trout, 9 ft., 5½ oz.	
No. 3002.	Medium, 9½ ft., 6¼ oz..	
No. 3003.	Heavy, 10 ft., 7 oz......	

"Senate" Bait Rod, Nickel Plated

Three-piece with extra tip, two-ring guides, and three-ring tips.

No. 3005.	Bass Casting, 6 ft., 5½ oz.	Each $6.65
No. 3007.	Short Bait, 8½ ft., 8 oz..	
No. 3009.	Long Bait, 10 ft., 9½ oz..	

"Senate" Fly Rod, German Silver

Three-piece with extra tip, snake guides.

No. 3010.	Midget, 8 ft., 4¼ to 4½ oz.	Each $10.00
No. 3011.	Light Trout, 9 ft., 5½ oz.	
No. 3012.	Med. Trout, 9½ ft., 6¼ oz.	
No. 3013.	Heavy, Trout, 10 ft., 7 oz.	

"Senate" Bait Rod, German Silver

Three-piece with extra tip, two-ring guides.

No. 3015.	Bass Casting, 6 ft., 5½ oz.	Each $10.00
No. 3017.	Short Bait, 8½ ft., 8 oz.	
No. 3019.	Long Bait, 10 ft., 9½ oz.	

22 Kelso FISHING TACKLE SPECIALTIES

The Jungle Mosquito Shield

The most practcal, durable and convenient Mosquito Shield that is made. It affords absolute protection from all kinds of insects.

The front is made of hair cloth and it is sufficiently stiff to remain perfectly flat and it holds the netting away from the face. While the mesh is small it does not obstruct the view.

In front of the mouth there is a hinged metal ventilated door. This enables the wearer to smoke or even eat without removing the head net. When the opening is not being used, the door swings down and entirely closes the opening, while the perforations in the door itself afford ventilation. There is no rubber to deteriorate; no hoops to get out of way—in fact, this new net is without a doubt the simplest and most efficient protector made. Are packed one in a flat envelope and can be carried in the pocket.

No. 100. Made from superior quality imported lace with fine mesh, positively midge proof. This is held in position by straps which tie under the arm, fully protecting the neck. Easily and quickly removed. Each........ **$1.00**

No. 101. Made from a fine grade of mosquito netting. This is held in place by a puckering string round the neck. Each.. **.75**

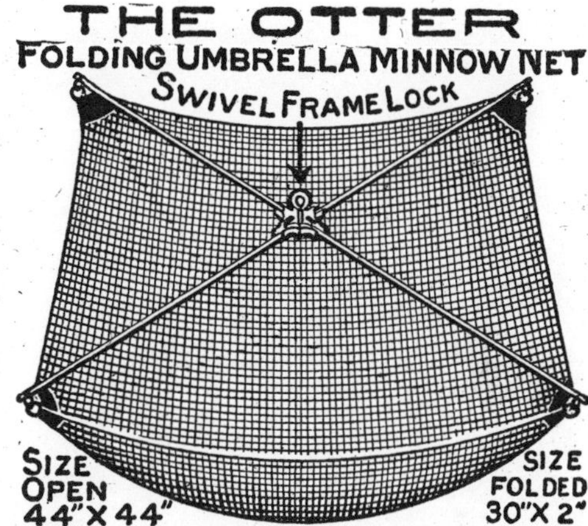

This Net will catch Minnows when everything else fails. It is dropped in the water and cracker crumbs thrown in or over; it is brought up with a quick action and takes in fish of any kind that is above the net.

Steel Frame, 3½ feet square, can be folded in a moment's time. The Net is heavy, ¼-inch mesh, reinforced with cloth at the corners, fitted with brass rings at each corner to attach frame. Cord is supposed to be attached to the Steel Frame, and if necessary a Fishing rod or Bamboo pole can be used to lower and take in the Net. $1.50 Each.

Steel vine was the classic fishing fake of the ages. It never existed except in the imagination of larceny-minded copywriters. It actually was Calcutta cane worked up into a six-strip rod that was then turned down to the roundness of a pencil. The hoax went undetected for almost twenty years.

Here's a newcomer to the headnet set. His has a metal door in front through which he can smoke or even, it says here, eat. That would be worth watching.

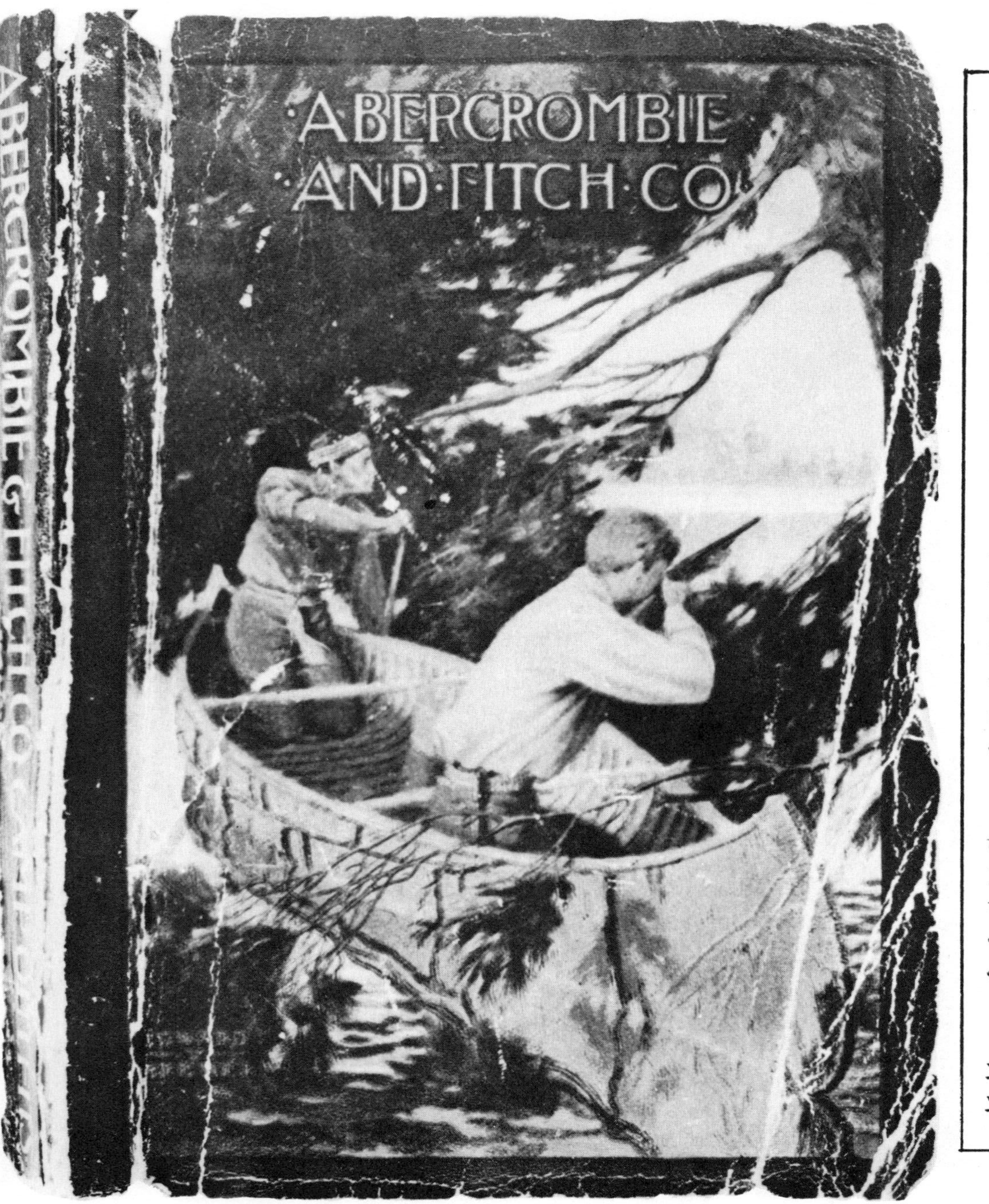

That is how and why we have grown to be the Mecca of Sportsmen throughout the world. A man who has spent months in one Wilderness has us build to his order, and after his own invention, the things he finds best suited to that soil or climate, the camp accessories needed for protection against insects, reptiles or fever. He gets us to build something which he has to have for that particular country. Then that accessory is a part of our stock, to supply other travellers in that part of the world, and we are the only people who do have it.

If the man from Australia or the man who has walked a respectable portion of the trails in India wants to penetrate the Arctic circle, he knows that his Antipodean or Tropic experiences will be nearly useless. He comes to us for information as to the outfit he will need in the frozen North and he gets it, for we know. We have reviewed, digested and tabulated the experiences of the Arctic explorers—not merely one, but nearly all of them—not merely of some Northern sections, but of every one.

Do you want to know the best guide to take you through the Everglades of Florida? We can tell you. Do you want to know just what game or what fish you may expect to find there? We can tell you. Do you want to know what equipment others have found to be the best for that trail? We can tell you.

The point of it all is that we want to tell you. We want you to write us and ask us questions about the place to which you are going. We have no end of little side lights on it

"MATCHLESS" PREPARED FOODS. IN SELF-HEATING CANS.

An innovation in canned goods which will be appreciated by all who must prepare meals with little or no fire. The foods are excellent and are made piping hot in a few moments by merely puncturing the outer can at points indicated and pouring in a little water. The food is sealed in an inner can which is inclosed by an outer case partly filled with quick-lime. The addition of water to the lime generates a terrific heat, which warms the inner receptacle to the boiling point almost at once. These cans are invaluable for fishermen, yachtsmen, balloonists, motorists and for hunters for use in duck-blinds, run-ways and where fire is either impossible or undesirable. Full directions with each can.

SOUPS.

Tomato, Mock Turtle, Ox-Tail, Consomme, Bouillon, Julienne, Mutton Broth, Vegetable, Beef, Pea, Clam Chowder, Clam Broth. .... Price, per can, 25 cents
Chicken, Chicken Gumbo, Mulligatawny. Price per can .... 30 cents

FOODS.

Pork and Beans............................Price per can, 20 cents
Irish Stew—Beef and Vegetables.......................... 30 cents
New England Boiled Dinner—Sauerkraut and Sausage...... 35 cents
Vienna Sausage, Braised Beef, Burgundy Beef, Hungarian Goulash, Veal and Green peas........................... 40 cents
Chicken Curry Indienne, Chicken Saute Marengo........... 50 cents

"DITMARS" SNAKE-BITE KIT.

In certain localities the camper or traveller is often exposed to the bite of venomous reptiles. Such cases, in the absence of prompt and proper treatment, always result most seriously and often fatally. Realizing the need of and demand for such a kit, put up in compact form and containing the necessary accessories, we have devised this perfect little outfit.

Indorsed by Prof. Ditmars, of the New York Zoological Society, the well known authority on reptiles. **Contains rubber tourniquet, lancet, artery** clamps, surgeon's scissors, surgeon's needle, surgeon's silk, tube of sterilized cat-gut, hypodermic syringe in pocket case, clinical thermometer, absorbent cotton, antiseptic gauze, adhesive plaster, bandages, safety pins, tube of Pasteur Anti-Venom Serum, Strychnia and Potassium Permanganate hypodermic tablets, Corrosive Sublimate tablets for antiseptic dressings. Put up in neat black morocco case of best quality, with instruments on removable tray.

Size, 6¾x4x2½ in.; weight, complete, 20 oz. Price........... $15.00

We include with each kit pamphlets by Prof. R. L. Ditmars and Dr. H. Plympton, giving full instructions for the treatment of snake bite by both the anti-venon or potassium permanganate methods.

"MIDGET" HYPODERMIC SYRINGE.

The most compact and convenient hypodermic outfit on the market.

Fine quality syringe with graduated piston and cap. Has two needles which screw into protecting guard, and three medicine vials. All fitted in spring-clip removable tray and inclosed in nickel-plated hinged box with slide lock.

Size, 3¼x1⅛x½ in.; weight, 2⅝ oz. Price............ $2.50

162

"N E P I G O N"

Norfolk Fishing Coat. Knickerbockers with button cuff.

"C A S T A L I A"

Fishing Coat with Stanley pockets, military collar.

The dude in necktie and stiff white collar could be found occasionally on the stream. But the hussy in knee pants, exhibiting her *legs?* Not in 1909! In 1912, a chap confided in hushed tones that "my wife puts on a pair of my pants and goes duck hunting with me *just like a man!* Of course, no one else sees her." And I thought privately that she was evidently a good sport, but not very nice.

Copyrighted.

AUTOMOBILE CAMPING OUTFIT.

As an aid in the selection of an automobile camping outfit we herewith give a list that may easily be carried on the running boards and baggage rack of a five-passenger touring car, sufficient to give perfect comfort and protection against all conditions on an extended trip.

1	large Tanalite Automobile Tent (if party of men)........	$36.40
2	small Tanalite Automobile Tents (if party of women and Men). See p. 40..............................Each,	31.90
	If trip is made through country infested with mosquitos, bobbinet front should be added. See p. 46	
5	Fitch Combination Sleeping Bags (for moderate weather, Model B). See p. 51...........................Each,	23.00
5	No. 1 Air Beds. See p. 56.........................Each,	21.00
5	Air Pillows, 11x16. See p. 55....................Each,	2.75
1	Automobile Cooking and Lunch Outfit, see p. 131, or 1 No. 6 "Aluminol" or "Armorsteel" Cooking Outfit, see pp. 124 and 129.	
1	No. 3 Folding Aluminum Baker, bread board, and case. (For baking bread, roasting meats, fish, etc.) See p.136.	7.00
1	Tanalite Automobile Cover, if car is used without top. To be used as dining fly in rainy weather. See p. 297.	
2	¾ axes in leather sheaths. See p. 67................Each,	1.60
1	India or Carborundum Axe Stone. See p. 68.	

Copyrighted.

AUTOMOBILE OUTFITTING.

Our Motor Car outfits are a revelation to those who have depended for their needs on the automobile supply houses or department stores.

We have automobile outfits that are "different," most of which you have probably never seen, the majority being our own make and design and exclusive with us. We know what every man should have on his car in the shape of proper equipment and can intelligently advise you in the selection of many accessories which go to make touring or cruising a pleasure and comfort, no matter where you go, the time of year or the state of weather. We are not aiming to run the whole gamut of automobile supplies with its attendant "junk," but a selected line of specialties which are not generally known and often difficult to obtain.

Of course we can sell you anything in the automobile line you want, from a tire chain to a crank shaft. If you are a customer of this house and find yourself in a broken down car on the road to Mandalay or in a suburb of Kamchatka, you can send to us for anything movable that motes or helps to mote and we'll get it to you quick.

In 1909, the boss drove and the chauffeur was just a lackey to keep the car running. There were people in those days who actually enjoyed driving and were proud of their skill. Incredible!

57 READE STREET, NEW YORK 351

THE DARLING-FLEGEL TOURNAMENT REEL.

This wonderful reel, we confidently believe, marks a new era in long distance bait casting. Designed by Messrs. Lou S. Darling and B. F. Flegel after long and careful experiment and its superiority for distance casting has been proven beyond question. Casts of over 240 feet have been made in practice—this during cold weather—and in the coming season we expect to see all records go to this reel. It is fitted with the Redifor "throw-off" attachment for free-spool casting and is entirely automatic in its action, requiring no attention from the caster and no buttons or levers to operate. The gears are always in mesh and the line is reeled up in the regular way, the cast made in the ordinary manner, the spool being automatically released by the forward motion of the rod. The main feature of this reel, however, is the double spool. Its great advantage is that the line runs from the right hand spool and the caster thumbs on the other spool. The thumb never touches the line, which is impeded in no way in its free outrunning, and there is no pressure upon it to pull back on the spool and induce "back-lashes."

If the line be accidentally broken it may be knotted and makes little or no difference in the casting, while in the old style reel it would be necessary to put on a new line. Absolutely perfect control of the cast is possible with this reel as the position of the thumb never changes throughout the cast.

Another unique feature is the thumb rest at side of reel which is a double pillar, built out from the back plate to center plate, and which affords a perfectly steady and secure rest for the thumb and insures even thumbing.

The barrels or cores of the spool are made larger in diameter to induce quick starting of the reel and it is not necessary to wind the spool with extra line or apply cork drums to bring it up to the proper size for the fine tournament line. The thumbing spool, however, should be wound with a little silk line to give the proper amount of friction. Made of "Redifor metal" and weighs only 4½ ounces. Finest bronze bearings. Price, $25.00

THE FLEGEL TOURNAMENT REEL.

Similar to the Darling-Flegel model but has single spool only and no thumb rest. Price, $20.00

This earthshaker was merely a free-spool reel with an extra-long spool, one half for the line and the other for thumbing control—twice the weight and hence, inertia, to cause backlashes. This one sank without a trace.

IV

1910–1919

1910 Edition Fifty Cents

THE ANGLER'S GUIDE

HOW WHEN and WHERE TO FISH

Including Latest U. S. and Canada

Fish and Game Laws

Published by

The Field and Stream Publishing Co.

Like To Fish?

You'll have more fun and catch more fish if you use a Reel that always works

THE "TAKAPART" $4 REEL

(CAPACITY 100 YARDS)

Never Fails. Test it under the severest conditions. Put it in competition with reels of the highest price. ¶ Note its perfect construction. See how light it is—how small for its reel capacity. Most reels of the same capacity are about a quarter larger and heavier. ¶ See how delicately and noiselessly the spool spins around. How perfectly RIGID the frame is, because drawn from ONE SOLID PIECE of brass tubing. ¶ How fine and true the BEARINGS are, and how impossible it is for anything to work loose, owing to the absence of screws and bolts. ¶ Note the FRICTION DEVICE, which prevents back-lashing. ¶ ANOTHER THING—the head and end plates can be adjusted so that the HANDLE and CLICK can be placed in FOUR different positions. In this way the crank handle can be so arranged that it cannot hit the fingers or foul the line. ¶ The "Takapart" Reel can be taken apart instantly without tools, simply by unscrewing the ring at either end.

No increase in price could possibly improve the "Takapart" Reel in these respects.

Guarantee: We positively guarantee every reel to be perfectly satisfactory in every respect—to work every time.

Our "Tripart" Reel, capacity 80 yds., carries the same guarantee as the "Takapart" Reel. **Costs $3.00.**

SOLD BY DEALERS EVERYWHERE.

Made by A. F. MEISSELBACH & BRO., 17 Prospect St., Newark, N. J.

May we send you (free) a series of the best short fishing-stories ever written? "Leaves from an Angler's Note book,"—"A Day with the Brook Trout," and four others. Write for them to-day.

When you write Home about that Big Mess write with an

The Fountain Pen that Fills Itself and Cannot Leak

The $3 size (Style D) is particularly suited for a Sportsman's use, as it is only 4½ inches long and can be carried in the pocket of your Khaki trousers or coat.

In fact, you can carry it sideways, endwise, upside-down, any old way, it cannot leak!

Three other sizes, $2.50, $4 and $5. Fifteen style points in each size.

Sold on a Guarantee of "Satisfaction, New Pen or Money Back" by live dealers everywhere. If no dealer near you handles the Onoto, write us for Catalog 25, and order direct.

ONOTO PEN COMPANY

261 BROADWAY NEW YORK

CAMPING, SHOOTING, FISHING, CANOEING

"NEAR ENOUGH TO BROADWAY FOR CONVENIENCE
FAR ENOUGH FROM BROADWAY FOR ECONOMY"

NEW YORK SPORTING GOODS CO.

15 and 17 WARREN STREET

NEW YORK SPORTING GOODS CO

NEW YORK, N.Y., U. S. A.

P. R. Robinson, *Pres.* James E. Murray, ***Treas.***

Fishing rods like most other goods have a wide range as to value, and yet, a high price does not necessarily mean superior quality. The construction of a properly balanced rod for fly casting is a work of art; the maker should be an expert fly fisher and a man of mechanical accuracy. The bamboo must be selected with conscientious care as there is a great difference in the strength of stock. In the Orvis rods only the very best is used as the aim is for quality rather than quantity, and we are frank in saying that we do not believe a better rod can be produced even if the makers ask $25 or even $30. Strength and ease of casting can be proven by practical test in use. Just try one or ask any angler who has used an Orvis rod what he thinks of their merits.

All rods are made hexagonal, in three pieces, two joints; have an extra tip and solid cork handles. They are put up in cloth partition sack and round wood rod case with screw top.

ORVIS HAND-MADE SPLIT BAMBOO FLY RODS, FINEST QUALITY, $15.00

Made in three pieces, has two tips, sack and Orvis round wood rod case. German silver mountings with banded ferrules. Snake guides. Orvis patent metal reel seat, and whipped with silk. These rods are very finely finished with solid cork hand pieces that will not loosen, crack or come off.

No.				
No. **164.**	Fly Rod	Length	$8\frac{1}{4}$ ft.	Weight 4 oz.
No. **$16\frac{1}{2}$.**	"	"	9 "	" $4\frac{1}{2}$ "
No. **16.**	"	"	9 "	" 5 "
No. **$9\frac{1}{2}$.**	"	"	10 "	" 6 "
No. **9.**	"	"	$10\frac{1}{2}$ "	" 7 "

TOURIST'S, OR FOUR JOINTED FLY ROD.

For those who wish a fine quality fly rod of four joints which will economize space in packing, this rod will please. It is Orvis' very best make. Length, 10 feet; length of each joint, 31 inches. Made of split bamboo with German silver mountings. Banded ferrules and Orvis patent reel seat, sack and rod case.
No. **T.** Weight, 6 ounces.......................... **$15.00**

ORVIS FLY RODS, $10.00 GRADE

For those who prefer a less expensive rod but equally well balanced, with German silver mountings, solid cork hand piece and all respects a fine rod, we suggest "The $10.00 Orvis."

All of these rods are of six strips of split Bamboo throughout; have three joints of equal length, extra tip, partition sack and wood rod case, German silver mountings, banded ferrules. Snake guides. Orvis patent reel seat and cork hand piece.

No.				
No. **16 x.**	Fly Rod.	Length,	9 feet	Wt. 5 oz.
No. **$9\frac{1}{2}$x.**	"	"	10 "	" 6 "
No. **9 x.**	"	"	$10\frac{1}{2}$ "	" 7 "

Postage on above rods including registration, 40c.

UP-TO-DATE

Fishing Tackle

for BLACK BASS
MUSKELLUNGE
PICKEREL
PIKE AND
TROUT FISHING

MANUFACTURED BY

THE W. J. JAMISON COMPANY

736?S. CALIFORNIA AVENUE
CHICAGO, ILL.

The largest trout shown above (a three pounder) and several of the others was caught on a Jamison Trout Spoon, shown on page 21 of this catalogue. The rest were all caught on a Coaxer Trout Fly.

From DR. C. S. NEISWANGER, Marshall Field Building, Chicago, Ill,

Dear Sir:—In purchasing my fishing and hunting outfit last September from Mr. Al. Berg of Bullard & Gormully, he insisted that I include some of your little "Coaxer" Trout Flies, but I declined to do so, so he gave me one and said. "You will catch your largest trout with that fly." The morning after making camp at the head of Battle Creek in Owyhee Co., Idaho, I concluded to try the "Coaxer," and caught with it 19 speckled beauties averaging 12 inches in length, before breakfast. In one day's fishing in Jack's Creek, my brother and I caught 117 fine trout, over 75 of which were caught on the little "Coaxer." We drew cuts that day to see who would fish with it; as luck was against me, I lost, and although I had quite an assortment of good flies I caught only 39 of the 117. As the "Coaxer" is practically indestructible I suppose my brother, who lives in Idaho, is fishing with it yet.

Yours very truly,
C. S. NEISWANGER.

Mr. Neiswanger's brother has since reported that he caught over 400 trout on this one Coaxer Trout Fly and was still using it.

From M. FROELICH, Prop. Lost Lake Resort, Sayner, Wisconsin.

"The little Coaxer made a new record here August 28th by taking a 15-inch brook trout in Stella Creek. This is the largest brook trout ever taken in this section. The Coaxer was the only thing that could get this big fellow, as he lay so far back under over-hanging brush that the bait had to be floated about 10 feet in order to reach him. Next day another one of almost the same size was hooked, but it got away." (See photograph of trout on this page.)

From S. J. WALPOLE, Masonic Temple, Chicago.

"When preparing for my annual fishing trip last summer I bought a large assortment of domestic and foreign flies and four of your Coaxers. Had very good luck and am pleased to inform you that 90 per cent of my catch was made on the Coaxers, and three of them are as good as ever. Hereafter 90 per cent of my flies will be Coaxers, as they are all that is needed to lure the trout."

"Please send six assorted by first mail. All the boys here are using the Coaxer and think it is the only thing."

"The little Bass Coaxer is certainly fine. I never could get a bass fly before that would make enough of a showing to attract bass to do any good."

"Have caught both bass and pickerel on No. 1 and No. 3 Coaxer Fly. They take it fine."

The "Coaxer" Underwater

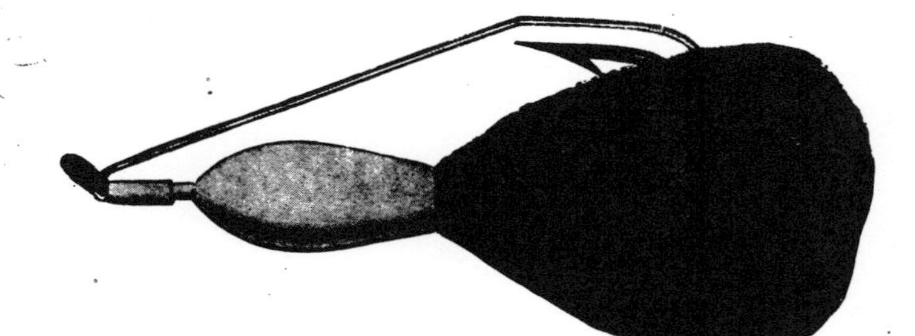

Above illustration is exact size and color of the "Coaxer" Underwater, which is composed of a combination metal and wound body and feather tail. This bait is designed especially for deep fishing, although it may be used near the surface by rapid reeling. It has no equal for ease of casting, is absolutely weedless and is a dead sure killer. When cast the head goes first and the fluttering of its feathers gives the bait a very life-like appearance. For casting or trolling.

The "Coaxer" Underwater Bait, put up in handsome box, each....40 cents Postage, 2c

The Night "Coaxer" Underwater

Same as above, except that it glows at night or in deep, dark water.

Price each, 50 cents: postage 2 cents.

CLIPPED FROM
The Chicago Daily Tribune

HERE'S INDIANA'S RECORD FISH

It's a Pickerel, and When Dragged from Wawasee Lake Weighed Twenty-five Pounds.

Wawasee, Ind., May 8.—(Special.)—A record breaking pickerel was caught last week in Wawasee Lake by H. Cory of Syracuse, Ind. The fish weighed twenty-five pounds and was forty-six inches in length and twenty-one inches in circumference.

Mr. Cory was casting about the lake when he got a terrific strike and after hooking the fish played it half an hour before he could land it. The fish was caught on a lure manufactured by a Chicago firm, who afterwards bought the fish from Mr. Cory. The fish is now on exhibition in Chicago.

The cut shows this big pickerel and it was caught on the "Coaxer" Underwater.

The Weedless Struggling Mouse

Surface or Underwater at Will
Weedless, but a Sure Killer

Patented

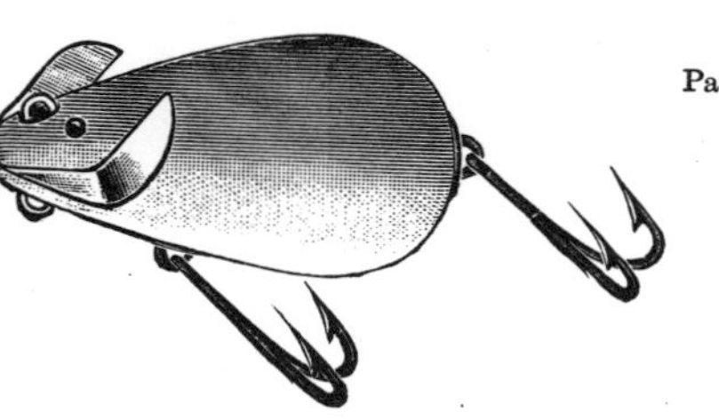

Weedless Struggling Mouse

Treble Hook Struggling Mouse

It struggles and labors through the water like a badly crippled living creature trying desperately to escape, and its resemblance to a live mouse is truly remarkable. The most prominent authorities in the world have endorsed it as the most life-like imitation of a natural live food of game fish ever produced and predict that it will be the most successful and popular bait for casting and trolling.

It is a well known fact to all anglers that game fish will attack any crippled or helpless creature in preference to others that are all right. The sight of this most perfect imitation struggling and wobbling along evidently trying to escape is too much for them to resist and they strike it instantly and viciously. The natural result is that many big catches are made where other less attractive and natural looking baits absolutely fail to bring even a strike.

We also make this wonderful bait in a Crab color that is so natural in appearance and action that it will deceive the wisest old bass when he sees it scuttling along and he is bound to strike it, as every fisherman knows that the crab is a favorite food of the black bass. We recommend the "Crab" style for deep water fishing and the "Mouse" style for surface or near-surface fishing, although either style can be used for all purposes.

Another nature color is the "Frog Back," which is a close imitation of the meadow frog. This is for use among or near lilies, where frogs are apt to be found. The weedless style can be cast right into the thickest lilies, and as this is a favorite hiding place of all game fish when feeding good catches nearly always result.

In addition to the above colors we make these baits in the very popular Red Head and White Body style, which is pronounced by all authorities the most successful combination of colors known for all-round fishing. If you are uncertain as to what color to use then we advise the "Red Head," as it is a sure fish getter under nearly all circumstances. Also made in all Red, all Yellow and all White.

These baits are enameled with the finest celluloid enamel and finished with pure clear celluloid and are waterproofed by our own special process, which insures them against splitting or peeling. Your money back if they do, but they don't. All metal parts, including hooks, are nickel plated and polished. The body of the bait is 2¼ inches long. It weighs about two-thirds of an ounce, which is heavy enough for good casting, yet light enough that it does not injure either rod, reel or line. It reels easily and works with the slightest movement so that it is good for trolling as well as casting. The double hook style is extremely weedless and can be used freely in the thickest weeds, rushes or lilies. The treble hook style is also weedless to a large degree, owing to the hooks being protected by the body of the bait. Both styles are sure killers. A very desirable bait and guaranteed to give entire satisfaction in every way.

DIRECTIONS: For Underwater use attach line to upper screw eye. For Surface use unscrew upper screw eye, turn wing over, and attach line to lower screw eye.

Mouse Color, Crab, Frog Back, Red Head with White Body, All White, Yellow or Red, each..........**75c; postage 2c**
New "De Luxe" Style, Superfine Fish Scale Finish with Improved Glass Eyes, each................**90c; postage 2c**

The New "De Luxe" Style has natural minnow colors, dark olive green back, silver scales on sides fading into pure white on the belly, and a wonderful, changeable red stripe running full length of each side that constantly changes from a brilliant red flash to a pink glow, just as you see on a red-side minnow, making an extremely attractive and effective bait. It is the absolute limit in artificial bait finish and is to be found only on Jamison Baits. We also supply it on our Mascot, Humdinger and Chicago Wobbler baits.

Sure Catch Grasshopper Hook

For baiting with Grasshoppers, Small Minnows and Frogs, Worms or Bugs, for Trout, Bass, Perch, Croppies, etc.

This is the greatest trout hook ever devised. With it every grasshopper means a trout. No trout or other fish ever lived that can steal the bait off of this hook. Every trout fisherman knows that the grasshopper is a great bait for trout. There is no better. But the trouble has been that the trout got them off too easy. It generally took about a dozen hoppers for each trout. Now you get a trout for each hopper, and often two or three can be taken on the same bait. Also this hook keeps the bait in absolutely perfect shape, making it much more attractive. See illustration. It is also very nearly snag proof, as the bait protects the points of the hooks. You never lose a bait, and you get practically every fish that takes it. You cannot afford to be without a few of these hooks. We give them our personal recommendation, and will cheerfully refund your money if you wish it. Order now while you think of it so you will be sure to have them on your next trip. Cut shows exact size of hooks.

No. 8 No. 6 No. 5 No. 4 No. 4LS No. 2 No. 1

Above sizes 10 cents each, postage 1 cent. $1.00 per dozen, postage 2 cents.

The Sure Catch Minnow Hook

Size	Length	Price each	Postage	Per dozen	Postage
Size 1-0,	2¾ inches long,	15 cents each,	postage 1 cent;	$1.60 per dozen,	postage 2 cents.
Size 2-0,	3¼ " "	15 " "	" 1 "	1.60 " "	" 2 "
Size 3-0,	4 " "	20 " "	" 1 "	2.00 " "	" 3 "
Size 4-0,	4⅜ " "	20 " "	" 2 "	2.00 " "	" 3 "
Size 5-0,	4¾ " "	25 " "	" 2 "	2.50 " "	" 5 "
Size 6-0,	5⅜ " "	25 " "	" 2 "	2.50 " "	" 5 "

Jamison's Weedless Frog Tandem

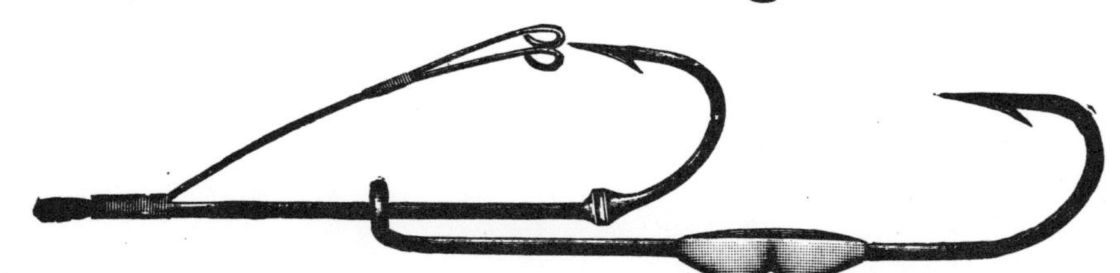

Adjustable to any size frog. Made of hollow point, extra stout, 5-0 Carlisle hook. Extra long rear hook. Weedless and a sure killer.

Jamison's Weedless Frog Tandem, each..........................25 cents. Postage 2c

Jamison's Weedless Pork Tandem

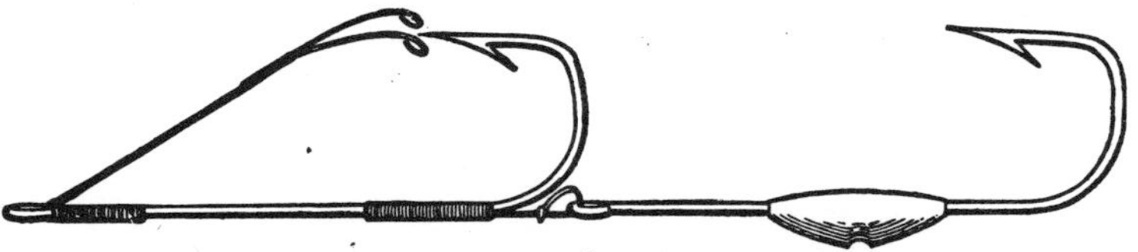

This tandem is exact size of cut and is intended for pork chunk or small frog. Made of 4-0 hollow point, extra stout, sneck-bend hooks. You don't miss any strikes with this tandem.

Jamison's Weedless Pork Tandem, each..........................25 cents. Postage 2c

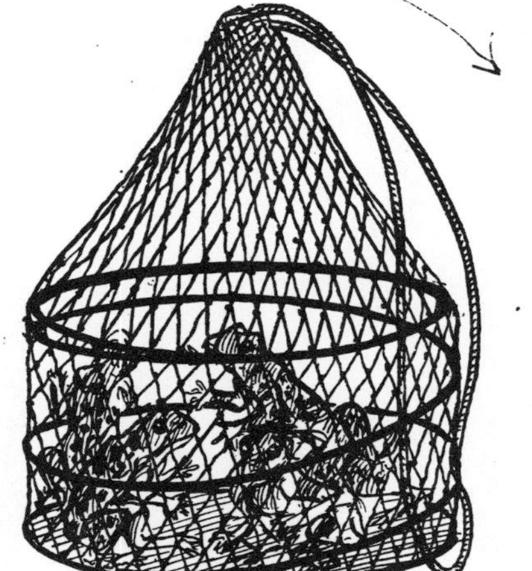

Pyott's Ideal Frog Carrier

The Pyott Ideal Frog Carrier is such a great improvement over all other methods of carrying live frogs that there is no comparison. It is light, compact and sanitary. After being used it can be compressed into a space of five inches wide and one-half an inch deep and can be slipped into the coat pocket if desired. It is no bother to carry and will last for years. It will soon save its price in frogs as they do not die in this carrier like they do in the ordinary basket or bag, as they always have plenty of air, light and water and the carrier is always clean. It is very easy to take the frogs from the carrier as the space is small and you can see what you are doing, enabling you to take any particular frog desired without trouble. It is impossible for frogs to escape from this carrier. Placed under the seat of the boat with a little water in the pan the frogs will be just as lively at the end of a hot day as at the beginning. In a basket or bag they are often dead on account of a lack of air and bad sanitary conditions. The Ideal is not only a perfect frog carrier, but can be used as a minnow bucket by simply hanging it in the water. It is made in two sizes, the small one, 5x7 inches high, will carry two dozen frogs. The large one, 8x8 inches high, will carry 5 dozen frogs.

The Pyott Ideal Frog Carrier, small size, each..........................50 cents. Postage 5c
The Pyott Ideal Frog Carrier, large size, each..........................75 cents. Postage 10c

The Johnson Rain Cape

Fills a long-felt want. No matter whether you wade the streams or fish the lakes **from a** boat, you will find this little cape very convenient. The hunter, or any other **outdoor** man will also find use for it. It is so small that you can stick it into your pocket **without** the slightest inconvenience. No use carrying a heavy, unwieldy raincoat along. **This little** cape will keep you dry just as well and with no bother, and the cost is very **small.** No fisherman or hunter can afford to be without it. Made in three grades as described below.

Grade B-A reversible cape. A fine article. Sheds water perfectly and gives long service. **Price $2.00.** Postage 5c.

Grade C-A silk lined reversible cape, made from finest material. Folds into somewhat smaller package than others. Sheds water perfectly and gives long service. **Price $2.50.** Put up in box 2x2¼x5¾ inches. Postage 5c.

Address all orders to THE W. J. JAMISON COMPANY, 736 S. California Avenue, Chicago, Ill.

No. 30
FISHING TACKLE
& A FEW TIPS ON FISHING
A&F Co.
ABERCROMBIE & FITCH Co.
EZRA H. FITCH. PRES.
57 READE ST.
NEW YORK. U.S.A

USEFUL DATA.

If the fisherman will take a copy of the following table, he will be able to ascertain the weight of a trout he takes, very closely, without weighing:

9 inches long.......	¼ lb.		18 inches long......	2½ lbs.
11¼ " "	½ "		19 " "	3 "
13 " "	¾ "		20 " "	3½ "
14 " "	1 "		21 " "	4 "
15. " "	1¼ "		22 " "	4¾ "
16 " "	1⅝ "		22½ " "	5⅛ "
17 " "	2⅛ "		23½ " "	6 "

SHRINKING OF FISH AFTER DEATH.

The shrinkage in weight of any fish after it has been out of water 6 to 12 hours can be figured very closely by using this table:

Just Killed	Dead 6 hours	Dead 12 hours
1 lb.	15¼ oz.	15 oz.
2 lb.	1 lb. 14½ oz.	1 lb. 14 oz.
3 lb.	2 lb. 13¾ oz.	2 lb. 13 oz.
4 lb.	3 lb. 13 oz.	3 lb. 13 oz.
5 lb.	4 lb. 12¼ oz.	4 lb. 11 oz.
6 lb.	5 lb. 11½ oz.	5 lb. 10 oz.
7 lb.	6 lb. 10¾ oz.	6 lb. 9 oz.
8 lb.	7 lb. 10 oz.	7 lb. 8 oz.
9 lb.	8 lb. 9¼ oz.	8 lb. 7 oz.
10 lb.	9 lb. 8½ oz.	9 lb. 6 oz.
12 lb.	11 lb. 7 oz.	11 lb. 4 oz.
15 lb.	14 lb. 4¾ oz.	14 lb. 1 oz.
20 lb.	19 lb. oz.	18 lb. 12 oz.
30 lb.	28 lb. 9½ oz.	28 lb. 2 oz.
40 lb.	38 lb. 2 oz.	37 lb. 8 oz.

This shrinkage table is a remarkable tabulation since it is universally believed that the trout is the only fish that keeps on growing after it is dead.

30 ABERCROMBIE & FITCH CO.

DIVINE RODS

We are the New York agents for The Fred D. Divine Co., one of the oldest firms manufacturing *Hand Made Rods Only.* These Rods are so well known that it is not necessary to write about them. Any of their goods not listed in this catalogue we can furnish in a reasonable length of time.

All Rods in the following list are *Hand-Made* and *Warranted Perfect,* in both Material and Workmanship, and will be made good to purchaser, free of charge, in case of breakage from either poor material or workmanship.

SPLIT BAMBOO RODS.

These split Bamboo Rods are one of the best makes in the market and are sold at reasonable prices. We can make up any special Rods to order.

All Split Bamboo Rods are made from carefully selected Calcutta Reed, in six and eight sections, from butt to tip, glued with the very best elastic waterproof glue. The varnish used is guaranteed to be the very best there is for fishing rods. We have given it very severe tests and find it will not crack under strain, being very elastic and waterproof. All Fly rods have open reel seats and English steel snake guides. All rods are mounted with solid drawn seamless German Silver Ferrules, banded with solid welts. Solid Cork Grasps. All rods are wound with silk made especially for this purpose.

IF YOU ARE A HUNTER—YOU NEED OUR CATALOGUE ON FIRE ARMS, AMMUNITION AND ARM SUNDRIES.

Fred Divine (sometimes "Devine") was one of the second-grade rodmakers who preferred mass production for the trade to fine custom work for an elite clientele. Legend says his business was eventually absorbed into Horrocks-Ibbotson Co.

Divine was a great hand for novelties with sales appeal. Here are listed an eight-strip rod which isn't as good a design as six strip; and that abomination, a rod wound solidly from end to end. The weight of that varnished-soaked silk sleeve was enough to break the heart of any flyrod. Not listed here is his famous

57 READE STREET, NEW YORK 31

EIGHT-STRIP FLY RODS.

Eight-strip Rods are considered by some fishermen to possess many superior qualities. Being constructed of eight, instead of six strips of Bamboo, making them nearer round, hence a very fine action.

Price, $20.00 Each

No. 0.	10 ft.,	3 pieces, extra tip,	8 oz.
No. 1.	10 ft.,	3 pieces, extra tip,	6½ oz.
No. 2.	9½ ft.,	3 pieces, extra tip,	6¼ oz.
No. 3.	9 ft.,	3 pieces, extra tip,	6 oz.
No. 4.	8½ ft.,	3 pieces, extra tip,	5 oz.
No. 5.	8 ft.,	3 pieces, extra tip,	4½ oz.

All of the above Rods are put up in a Tube holding the two tips in a partition bag.

THE DIVINE SILK-WRAPPED FLY ROD.

These Rods are of selected Split Bamboo. Being wrapped the entire length with an especially made and prepared silk, they are so finished that the grain of the wood can be seen through the silk wrappings. They are absolutely water proof and much stronger than the ordinary Split Bamboo Rod.

3 piece extra tips. Tips carried in Tube in partition bag.

9½ ft., about 6¼ oz.......... $30.00
9 ft., about 5¾ oz.......... 30.00
8 ft., about 3¾ oz.......... 30.00

SIX-STRIP FLY RODS.

The Rods are made from Six strips of choice, selected, well seasoned Calcutta Bamboo, carefully prepared and glued with an elastic waterproof glue. Made in the following regular lengths and weights, but can be made in any length and weight desired to suit the customer.

Price, $16.00 Each

No. 1.	10½ ft.,	3 pieces, extra tip,	8¼ oz.
No. 2.	10 ft.,	3 pieces, extra tip,	7½ oz.
No. 2½.	10 ft.,	3 pieces, extra tip,	6⅝ oz.
No. 3.	9½ ft.,	3 pieces, extra tip,	6¼ oz.
No. 4.	9 ft.,	3 pieces, extra tip,	5¾ oz.
No. 5.	8½ ft.,	3 pieces, extra tip,	4⅝ oz.
No. 6.	8 ft.,	3 pieces, extra tip,	3½ oz.

Extra Lengths for above Rods, finished:

Butts, $5.50; 2nd Joints, $4.50; Tips, $3.00

All of the above Rods are put up in a Tube holding the two tips in a partition bag.

spiral rod, twisted after gluing but before the glue set. It was thereby made stiffer, naturally; when you twist anything you shorten it, so a twisted 8-foot Divine simply had more wood in it than an untwisted 8-footer. Note that Divine was still using Calcutta cane in 1911 although the custom rod industry had started going over to "Tonkin"—Chinese—cane in 1910 when its importation began.

TRAVELING MAN'S FRIEND.

This Rod is the Perfection of a Trunk Rod, making six distinct Rods.

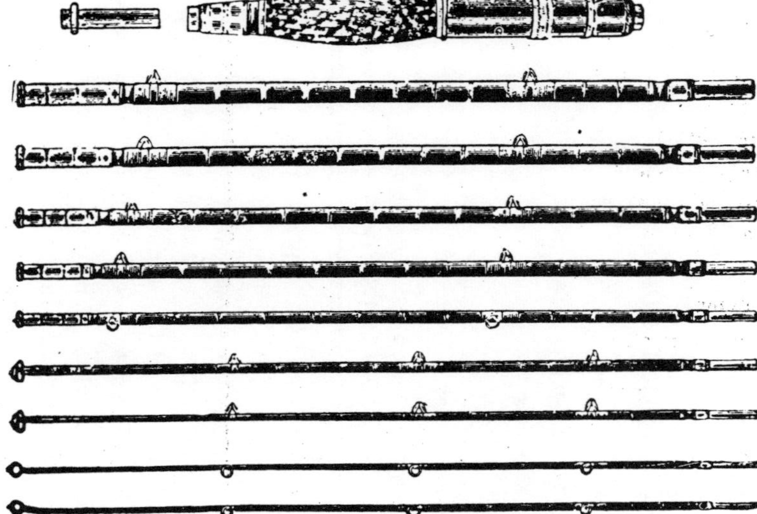

This Rod is composed of nine joints, 17 inches long, with reversible butt.

(1) Take six joints, together with the butt, make a 9 foot Fly Rod, weighing 7 to 8 ounces.

(2) Remove the lower joint and use the reducing ferrule and you have a 7½ foot light Fly Rod, weighing 4½ to 5 ounces.

(3) Remove the two upper joints and put in the lighter of the two Bass tips, and you have a 6⅓ foot Bass Casting Rod, weighing 5 to 6½ ounces.

(4) Add to this the first joint and you have a 7½ foot Bass Rod, weighing 7 to 8 ounces.

(5) Remove the two upper joints and put in the heavy Bass tip, and you have a 6½ foot heavy Bass or light Trolling Rod, weighing 6 to 7 ounces.

(6) Remove lower joint and use the reducing ferrule, you have a 4¾ foot stiff Bass or light Trolling Rod, weighing 5 to 6 ounces.

The Butt is reversible, so you can have Reel above or below the hand, on any of the Rods. This makes a combination of six good practical Rods in one.

Prices:

Split Bamboo $20.00
Bethabarra 15.00
Lancewood 10.00

BETHABARRA BEACH SURF CASTING ROD.

Planed out of straight grained timber and rounded by hand, 5½ foot tip, Independent 22 inch cord wound or 27 inch Plain Hickory spring butt. Double German silver reel seat Double German silver hand made bell guides and agate casting top. The 5½ foot tip is standard, but we will make any length tip to order.

Price..........$15.00

Fitted with trumpet guides and agate casting top:

Price..........$12.75

With 1 set agate, 1 set of trumpet guides and agate casting top: Price..........$16.50

All agate guides and top:

Price............$17.50

NICHOLS COLLAPSIBLE SPRING BUTT.

Without doubt, the "long or spring butt," will be the butt of the future for surf anglers.

Heretofore its main object has been the long reach to the handle of the reel, which interfered greatly in handling a fish.

In the new Nichols Collapsible Spring Butt, this objection is entirely done away with, as, after making the cast, it can be telescoped to half its original length, giving the angler the regulation 20 to 22 inch butt.

Its operation is extremely simple, being regulated by a slight turn of thumbscrew. It is very strong, having been thoroughly tested by the inventor, a surf angler of 20 years' experience.

All mountings are of German silver and its general appearance adds greatly to the looks of any rod. Its easy action is solid comfort to the angler.

Price..........$5.00

Plain hickory spring butt (not collapsable) $3.50

Any of above rods with adjustable spring butt: $1.50 Extra.

LINES

"AYANEFCO" SOFT ENAMEL LINES.

Fly Fishing.

(Vacuum Dressed.)

Finished by the Halford Process.

These lines, which are made for and imported by us exclusively are absolutely without equal for finish, flexibility and wear. They positively will not kink, the enamel will not chip or strip and the line comes from the reel evenly and smoothly. In casting they are perfection as the long tapers and correct balance carries true. The fisherman who employs the "slack line" cast will find they render smoothly and without snarling. Their wonderful flexibility and ease of floating makes them especially valuable to the "dry fly" fisherman as this line carries out and lies upon the water straight and true. As to durability, they will stand several seasons' hard use with no appreciable wear and the longer they are used the softer and smoother they become.

They are braided solid from the very finest silk, carefully enameled by the vacuum process and dressed down by hand. As the finishing of these lines is all hand work, and by a secret process, we are only able to secure a few lines at a time, the supply by no means equals the demand. We endeavor, however, to keep in stock a few lines each of the sizes listed and new stock is constantly being received. This line is one of our greatest specialties and cannot be duplicated or obtained elsewhere.

Made in double tapered styles only and finished in a brown color. No. 1 is for rods of 3 ozs. or less. No. 2 for rods from 3 to 4 ozs. No. 3 for rods 4 to 5 ozs. No. 4 for regular fly rods and No. 5 for very heavy fly rods or grilse rods.

DOUBLE TAPERED TROUT LINES.

All Sizes, 30 yards long................................Each, $6.00
All Sizes, 40 yards long................................Each, $8.00

DOUBLE TAPERED SALMON LINES.

Light, Medium or Heavy.

All Sizes, 40 yards long, (For splicing)........................$12.00
All Sizes, 100 yards long.......................................20.00
Splicing salmon lines (in addition to cost of "backing")........1.00

IF YOU ARE INTERESTED IN WINTER SPORTS, SEND FOR OUR SPECIAL CATALOGUE ON THESE GOODS.

Actually, there was no "secret process" about this line, which apparently was, under an A & F "house" brand, the famous British "Halford" line with which so many of us started dry-fly fishing. Aside from its dark brown color, which was a bit difficult to see on the water, there was nothing whatever wrong with the old Halford line and I just wish I had a few in D taper, right now. Halford's patent covered the immersion of the undressed, braided silk in a mixture of boiled linseed oil and kauri gum varnish in a closed vessel. When air pressure in the vessel was reduced with a pump, air bubbled out of the line, to be replaced with the oil mixture when the pressure was allowed to return to normal. A smooth coating was built up on this foundation by repeated coating and drying, and was then rubbed down with rottenstone or pumice and polished, usually with talcum powder.

TROUT REELS.
IMPROVED ORVIS FLY REELS.

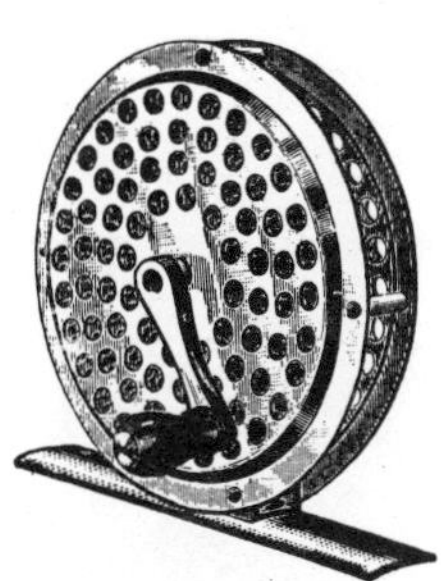

No. 1. It is put together with screws instead of rivets—has bushed bearings and screw-off oil cap, reel bar improved in shape, click perfected and placed between plates.

The reel is perforated to make it light and also that the line may dry without removing it from the reel after use. It is very light, very strong, and holds from 40 to 50 yards of No. 4 waterproof line.

Regular style, with crank handle............Price, $2.50
With Safety Band 3.00
Aluminum 3.50

No. 2 Improved Orvis Reel for Bass Fishing—Has balance handle, safety band and back sliding click, making either a free running or click reel, holds 70 to 80 yards of No. 4 line. Price, $3.00.

NEW GEM No. 2 GERMAN SILVER (80-YARD).

The Gem reel is particularly adopted for Fly casting, its advantages being its light weight and free running qualities.

Owing to the large shoot it takes up the line quickly as a double multiplying reel.

The open or perforated spool permits the line to dry quickly. Can be taken apart by removing one screw. The click is made on an adjustable frame so that it cannot get out of order.

Gem No. 2. Price, $ .75

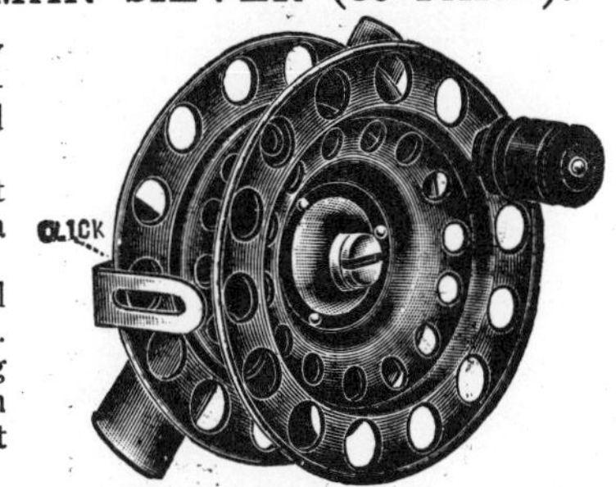

NEW GEM No. 1 60-YARD

The reel is made with the same kind of spool as the No. 2, only of brass, nickel plated.

This reel has a click, which is made on an adjustable frame so that it will not get out of order. Price each, 50 cents.

NEW MODEL IDEAL. German Silver.

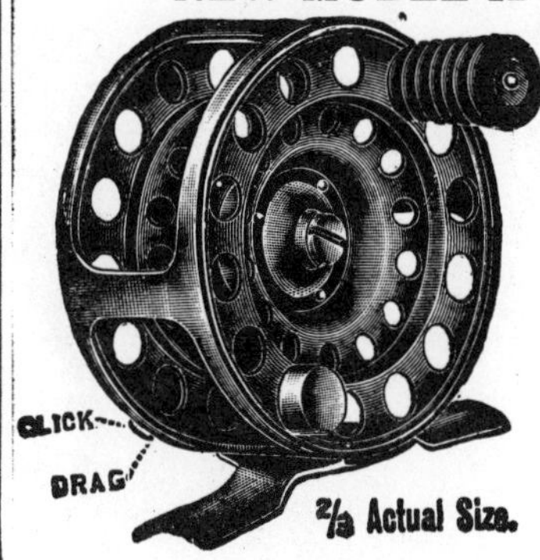

The bearings are reinforced at wearing points, perfectly centered and balanced. Adjustable click and drag, phosphorous bronze spring and large open spool. This reel may be taken apart by simply removing one screw. German Silver makes it perfectly rigid; will not dent or get out of order.

No. 1 Spool measures 2¼x1 in 80 yards, ...$1.00 each.
No. 2 Spool measures 3¼x1⅛ in 120 yards, ... 1.50 each.

ENGLISH "ROACH" BAIT.

A particularly effective bait for black bass, pike, pickerel, etc. Colored by hand true to life and beautifully mounted with three treble hooks and best quality trace. Spin fast and easily and are very durable. A fine lure for bait casting.

Length, 3¼ inches; each $0.60

ENGLISH "DACE" BAIT.

An especially taking bait for all styles of bait casting and trolling with artificial minnows. Beautifully colored by hand and finished true to life. Mounted with three fine quality treble hooks and trace.

Length, 4 inches; each $0.80

THE "RAINBOW" FLEXIBLE MINNOW.

Soft, flexible bodies. Beautifully colored true to life, in brown and green. Mounted with treble hooks and trace and swivel. Very finest quality and a most deadly bait for large trout in either stream or lake fishing. Very light in weight and can be easily cast by rod. Spins fast and easily.

Style A, 1½ inches long, 1 treble hook........Price, $0.30
Style B, 2¼ inches long, 2 treble hooks........ " .45

MOUSE BAIT.

Soft rubber, covered with real skin. A splendid bait for black bass. Mounted with single hook.

Gray Mouse, black tails, body, 2 inches long........Price, $0.60
White Mouse, pink tails, body, 2 inches long........Price, .60

THE CELEBRATED "PHANTOM' MINNOW.

Finest quality pure silk bodies, beautifully colored. Mounted with 3 fine quality, bright treble hooks. Fine swivel in head. Furnished in blue and silver, brown spotted or silver.

Number.	0	1	2	3	4	5	6	7	8	9	10
Inches..	1¾	2	2¼	2½	2⅞	3¼	3⅞	4¼	4¾	5½	6
Each...	35c.	35c.	35c.	35c.	35c.	35c.	45c.	55c.	65c.	75c.	85c.

THE "PORPOISE" MINNOW.

Same style as above, but made from fine porpoise hide, with metal head and fins. Hooks mounted on heavy six-ply twisted gut, and has 10-inch six-ply gut leader with two swivels. Made expressly for the heavy fishing and practically indestructible. Finished in blue and silver or plain silver.

Number	5	6	7	8	9	10
Inches	3¼	3⅞	4¼	4¾	5½	6
Each	$0.90	$1.00	$1.10	$1.20	$1.35	$1.50

MECHANICAL SWIMMING FROG.

ALWAYS ALIVE AND SWIMS. NEVER DIES AND NEVER TIRES

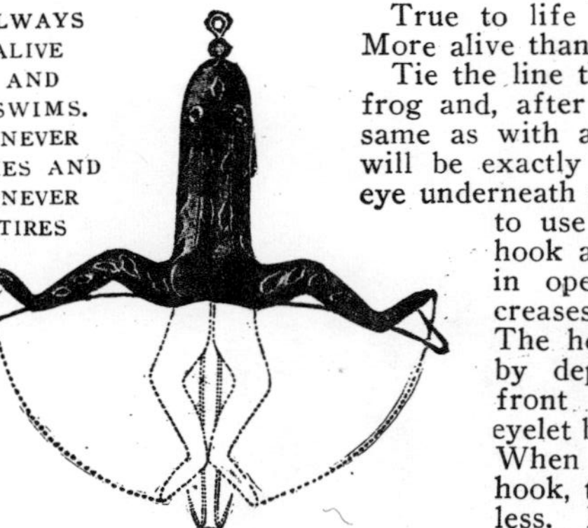

True to life in action and appearance. More alive than a live frog.

Tie the line to the eyelet at the head of frog and, after making the cast, jerk the same as with a live frog and the results will be exactly life-like. The brass open eye underneath the belly enables the angler to use an extra double or treble hook at will, when using the bait in open water, and greatly increases its fish-catching qualities. The hook can be easily removed by depressing belly of frog in front of eyelet, the opening in eyelet being shielded by the rubber. When used without the under hook, this bait is absolutely weedless. Price ....Each, $0.75

'MEADOW" FROGS.

Made of finest quality soft rubber, beautifully finished and painted true to nature. Mounted with bright treble hooks and gimp loop. Length, 2½ inches..........$0.30 Length, 3½ inches..........$0.35

"YELLOW BELLY" GREEN FROGS.

Same quality as "Meadow" Frogs.

Mounted with best treble hooks and gimp loop.

Frog, 1¾ inches long........$0.25 Froggie, 1 inch long......$0.20

PEARL MINNOW.

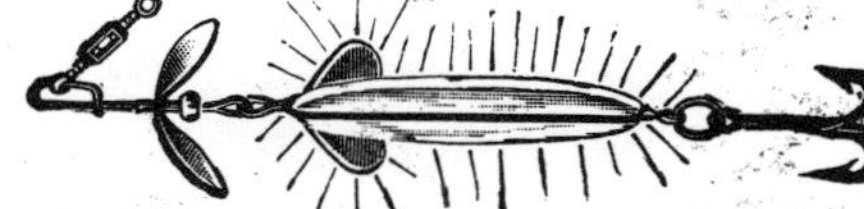

The bright, iridescent pearl is very attractive, either for casting or trolling. These minnows are an improved form, mounted with German silver fins and wire running lengthwise of the bait. Jointed at head with fine spinner and swivel.

Length of pearl, 2¾ inches..............................Price, $0.50

HELGRAMITES OR DOBSONS.

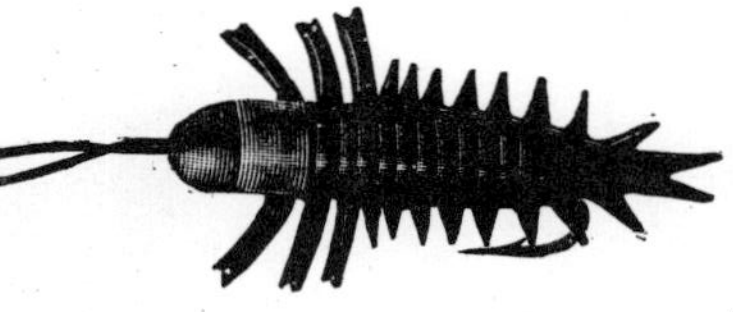

Fine quality soft rubber. Black bodies with bronze heads. Mounted on single hooks of proper size for Black Bass, with gimp trace and swivel.

No. 1, 1 in.; No. 2, 1¾ in.; No. 3, 2½ ins..Each, $0.25

ENGLISH WORM TACKLE.

Soft rubber, hand painted. The closest possible imitation of the natural worm. Mounted on gut with three fine quality single hooks and swivel. A fine bait for brook fishing and very durable.

No. 1 Small size, 1½ inches long ....Each, $0.25
No. 2 Medium size, 2 inches long ....Each, .25

PORK RIND BAIT.

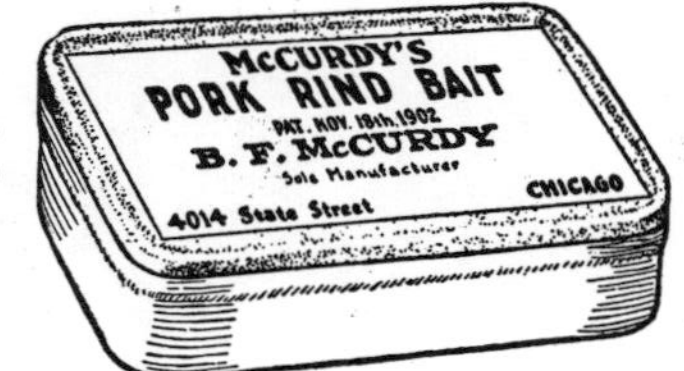

A most effective bait for Bass and Pickerel, especially for casting in connection with enameled casting spoons. Cut minnow shape and packed 8 in a box.

Price per box, 15 cents.

"YOPTECADLE" FISH LURE.

A vegetable compound made from a combination of aquatic plants by Ans. B. Decker, of the famous Decker family of fishermen. It is the result of 50 years' careful study of fish habits and the maker claims that a few drops placed upon the bait will infallibly attract the fish. Price per bottle, $1.00

TOURNAMENT CASTING "PLUGS."

For tournament and practice casting. Size and shape correct. The official weight for all tournaments held under rules of National Association of Scientific Angling Clubs. Made of aluminum and exact weight.

Half ounce or quarter ounce ....Each, $0.10

LIVE MINNOW FLOAT.

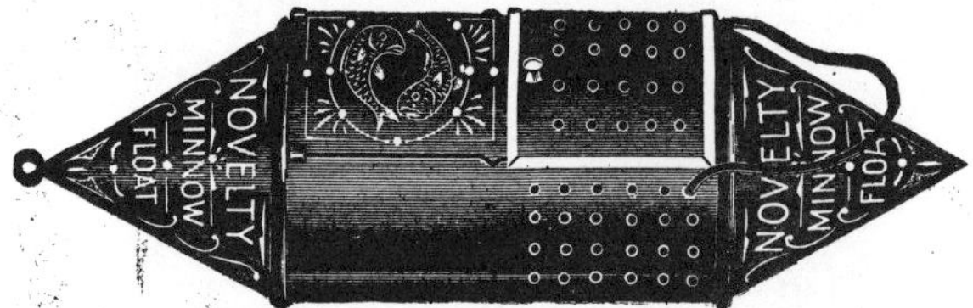

A new model which will commend itself on sight. It will keep minnows alive and fresh and is easier handled than the regulation bait pail. The water is always fresh and no changing is necessary. It leads easily through the water. As it is only perforated for half its length it can be carried the same as the regular pail. Made of heavy galv. iron finished in best baked enamel. Has self-locking sliding cover. Strongly made throughout and will last for years.

Length, 24 in. Dia., 7½ in. Capacity, 10 qts.............Price, $1.75

"KETCH-UM" TRAP

Made of steel wire netting, heavily galvanized. Diameter, 10 inches. Length, 16 inches. Breaks in the center and one piece packs inside the other.

Price, 75 cents.

THE "ORVIS" TRAP.

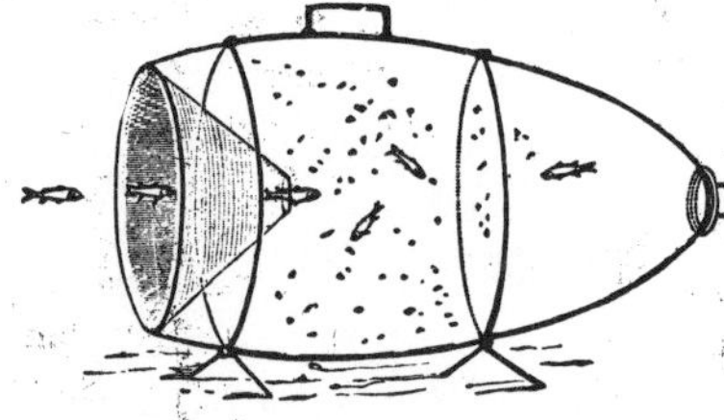

Made of heavy "flint" glass, and is not easily broken. Handle and legs of galvanized metal. Size, 12 inches long, 24 inches circumference.

Place cracker crumbs inside trap, attach cord with float to handle and lower trap where minnows frequent. Price, $2.25.

"HOPPER-COOP" LIVE BOX FOR INSECTS.

This box for carrying live insects is superior to anything of the kind made.

The size just fits the pocket, and, as all corners are rounded, there are no sharp points. Made of heavy tin plate, enamel finish, all seams and joints are machine clamped. Has patent sliding top for releasing the bait. This bully little box will appeal to the angler using such baits as crickets, grasshoppers, beetles, June bugs, grubs, helgramites, crawfish, lampreys, small frogs.

Size 3½ inches high, 3½ inches wide, 1¼ inches thick....Each, 15c.

142 ABERCROMBIE & FITCH CO.

"NATARE" DRY-FLY OIL.

Imported English.

The very finest preparation of the kind on the market and far superior in every way to paraffine oil or others of a like nature. "Natare" will positively float any fly and, even when freshly applied. Its greatest advantage, however, is that the flies may be treated months in advance and will, when used, float like thistle down and positively will not become sodden. "Natare" in no way injures either the gut, hooks or feathers and is quite odorless and clean to handle.

Dry-fly fishermen will at once recognize its wonderful qualities and we cannot recommend it too highly. Put up in strong glass bottles, flattened for convenience in carrying, fitted with screw top, hard rubber corks and rubber washer.

Price, per bottle, 40 cents.

DRY FLY OIL.

An American preparation similar to "Natare" Oil and quite satisfactory for general use. Put up in glass vials with metal screw-cap.

Price, per vial, 25 cents.

DRY FLY BOTTLE.

A neat, handy and practical device for the dry-fly fisherman. Bottle is fitted with brush and wood-topped stopper in one piece, secured by pigskin strap and snap-button. A second strap has button hole which is slipped over the coat button and so carried—always convenient.

Price, 30 cents.

PARAFFINE OIL IN TUBES.

For dry-fly and floating-fly fishing. Put up in the "One Drop Oiler," a solid metal tube which cannot leak. When the cap, which has a wire attached is unscrewed and withdrawn, just enough oil adheres to dress the fly.

Best Paraffine Oil and Tube ....Each, 20 cents.

IMPORTED ENGLISH DEER FAT.

Unequaled as a line dressing, especially for enameled lines, rendering them soft, smooth and flexible. A great preservative and lines dressed with this preparation will not become sticky. Invaluable to the dry-fly fisherman for floating the line and leader, for which purpose it is unexcelled. Put up in 2½-ounce round tins, handy for the pocket.

Price per box, 25 cents.

POCKET LINE GREASER.

Invaluable for the dry-fly fisherman. Fine pigskin case with best felt pad for rubbing line with deer fat. Pad is removable and has lead foil back to prevent grease working through—fastens with snap button.

Size 3½x1¾. Price, 35 cents.

English "paraffine" was, and is, just kerosene, a fair fly flotant especially if carelessly refined so that it still contains a little mineral wax. Theodore Gordon used it, hence his reference in one of his published letters to "Standard Oil."

Red deer fat (usually just mutton tallow) was never a good line flotant and soon gave way to Mucilin—low-melting-point paraffin wax and mineral oil—that virtually monopolized the British market for many years.

FINE REEL OIL.

In the care of fine reels the quality of oil should not be overlooked. The famous "Ezra Kelley" oil needs no introduction. It has long been acknowledged the best, and is the oil used by the Swiss and American fine watch factories.

The "Monarch" is also a standard watch and clock oil, and is largely used. A few drops of fine oil occasionally applied to clean bearings will double the life of any reel.

"Ezra Kelley" Oil, per vial $0.45
"Monarch" Oil, per vial .... .25

GRAPHITE.

Specially prepared for smoothing and polishing enameled casting lines, Imparts a smooth, glassy finish and prevents the line from kinking and snarling. Put up in tight fitting friction-top tins.
Price, 25 cents.

FERRULE GREASE.

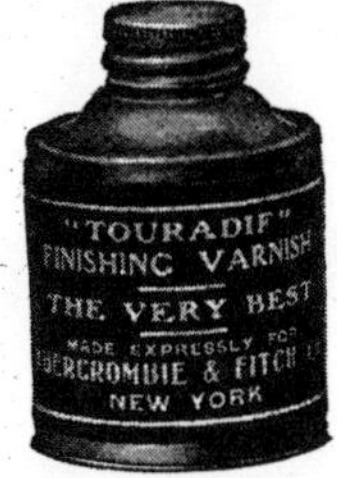

Made especially for greasing and lubricating ferrules and reel seats. Positively prevents pitting and corrosion of all metals. The best preparation of the kind made and highly recommended. Put up in 2 ounce friction-top tins. Price, 20 cents.

"TOURADIF" ROD VARNISH.

The finest and best varnish it is possible to make and guaranteed superior to any other on the market. It is the same varnish we use on all our best rods and is extremely hard, elastic and durable. Our regular varnish gives a good, durable body and is satisfactory for ordinary purposes but to procure the best results the finishing varnish should be used as a last coating, which gives a smooth, glassy finish. Put up in 2 ounce screw top tin cans. Full directions on each can.

No. 1 Body Varnish ....Price, per can, $0.25
No. 2 Finishing Varnish ....Price, per can, .25

"KINGFISHER" LINE DRESSING.

Prepared Especially for Oiled and Enameled Lines.

The Kingfisher Line Dressing is the same as we use ourselves in finishing and polishing our highest quality lines and is the best preparation for preserving new lines and refinishing old ones.

Lines treated now and then with this dressing will keep in perfect condition for years, even when in everyday use, and we recommend its use regularly on all oiled or enameled lines.

Put up in handy screw-top cans. Full directions for using on each can. Price, 25 cents.

Anyone who graphites a greased line will be startled by the tremendous enhancement of his line-shooting capability. He will be startled again when he looks in a mirror, for it is impossible to handle graphite without blackening everything, including one's hands, face, and clothing. Graphite is an old tournament caster's trick now, I believe, outlawed in competition.

WILLIAM MILLS
& SON
FISHING
TACKLE
LEONARD
RODS
21 Park Place, New York

DRY FLY ANGLING

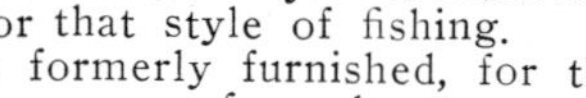

MR. R. C. LEONARD, SALMON CASTING

In England, the home of dry fly fishing, anglers, until quite recently, considered the heavy rods more suitable for that style of fishing.

We formerly furnished, for this purpose, many of our heavy tournament rods (see page 27, Nos. 56 and 57), and while we have never had any fault found with these rods by the users, we think that these very powerful 10½ and 11 foot rods (they are much more powerful than English rods of similar weights) must in many cases have proven too strong for the thin gut that is used in dry fly fishing. These rods are so powerful that an angler of ordinary strength cannot get all there is in the rods out of them, but it is also a fact that with them anglers, who have the required strength, can cast and dry a fly at a very long distance.

MR. E. J. MILLS, TROUT CASTING.

During the past two or three seasons our shorter and lighter rods have been very much used in England, and on the Continent, by many of the most prominent anglers on many of the best known dry fly streams. It is now only a question of how short and how light a rod can be used and give perfect satisfaction to the dry fly angler.

The prevailing opinion at the present time is that the proper rods for dry fly fishing are our **Light Tournament** patterns on page 27, Nos. 51, 52 and 53. These we make for the English and Continental anglers, with somewhat longer and larger handles. The 9 foot rod is known as the Enz.; the 9½ foot as the Itchen No. 2; the 10 foot, as the Itchen No. 1.

MR. F. M. HALFORD ON RIVER ITCHEN, 1903.

In every case, parties using the above-mentioned rods claim that they can cast the heavy dry fly lines better, farther and in a more satisfactory manner, than they have formerly done with their English rods of ten ounces or more in weight. To those who have never used the **H. L. Leonard** rods, we would say that the casting power of these rods is wonderful, compared with the heavy

2

Sound doctrine, fairly expounded. R. C. ("Rube") Leonard was the son of a brother of old Hiram L. Leonard; he was the only Leonard who remained with the rod company after the big split-up in the 1890s. E. L. ("Eddie") Mills was a son of old Thomas Mills. Rube and Eddie were both strapping six-footers who

DRY FLY ANGLING—(Continued)

FOUR ITCHEN TROUT, SEPTEMBER, 1903

rods they have been using, and that there is a pleasure in store for them if they elect to try our rods. The selection of a rod for dry fly angling should not depend so much on the size of the fish to be killed as on its ability to cast flies properly. Any rod that casts well will kill any fish. It is the continual casting that wears on a rod.

Just a word in regard to the extremely light rods. We do not recommend a 2 or 2⅛ ounce fly rod for promiscuous fishing, but we would state that during August, 1904, one of the above-mentioned rods was put in the hands of a doubting angler on the Itchen River, near Winchester, England. He was asked to proceed and catch a fish in the weediest parts of the stream and fish in his usual manner. He caught a trout of 2⅛ pounds and landed him quickly without a net (see illustration taken at the time). We mention this to show that there is strength even in the very lightest of our rods, and would say that the English and American anglers who would like to see what there is in really light rods should order one of our special Catskill rods (page 26, No. 45).

FISHERMAN'S REST ON ITCHEN

Dry fly angling, as practiced abroad, is stalking a fish. The streams in England and on the continent, where this style of fishing prevails, are rather sluggish streams where trout can readily be seen, when feeding on flies, on the surface. The angler does not cast until he sees a fish feeding near either bank (those rising in mid stream are usually small fish). He then secures as good a position on the bank as he can find available, and casts up stream, a few feet above the fish and allows his fly to float quietly down to, or over, the rising fish.

TROUT $2\frac{1}{8}$ LBS. CAUGHT ON THE ITCHEN (DRY FLY) WITH $2\frac{1}{16}$ OZ. LEONARD ROD

We know of very few streams in this country that are available for this sort of fishing—most of our streams being rapid and wooded to the water's edge. But, if the trout angler will substitute one of the new dry flies (of rather large size) for his usual wet fly, and fish it at times dry fly style (up stream), his catch will be more fish and larger fish than in the old style of sunk fly (down stream) angling.

3

were powerful and superbly skillful tournament casters; with Hiram Hawes, a son of H. L. Leonard's sister, they constituted a formidable casting team that did a lot to advertise Leonard rods in the heyday of tournament casting.

William Mills & Son's "Crescent Reel."

Extra Quality, Raised Pillar, Rubber and German Silver, Steel Pivot Multiplying Reel.

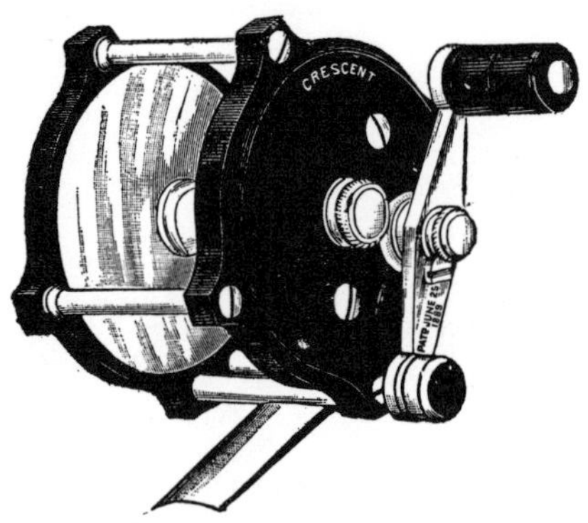

We call particular attention to our **Crescent Reel.** It is very strong, and yet is **the lightest multiplying reel** made. It has an **extra long handle,** which is of great service in winding in a long line. The reel has an **adjustable click** and is **extremely free running.** Its **lightness** makes it a most desirable multiplying reel for **use on a fly rod.** No. 2 size will hold 100 yards of medium trolling line.

Yards	150	100
Nos.	**2**	**3**
Price ....each	**$11.00**	**$11.00**

Fine Leather Case, **$1.75** each additional

THE SOUTH BEND ANTI-BACK-LASH CASTING REEL

Is the first and only **"Anti-back-lash Reel"** which works just as if it were thumbed by an expert, the spool being free when the bait is going out and the brake automatically applied with just the proper force as the line slackens at the end of the cast.

One size only, 100 yards........**$7.50**

66

Here is a curious, transitional stage of product development. The line passed under the wire bail, which it kept raised as long as the plug pulled out line. When the plug slowed down at the end of its flight, the bail dropped, applying an internal brake to the revolving spool.

The South Bend antibacklash, level-wind reel was heavily advertised all through the years between the two world wars at a high price, up to $35. It was a highly popular item. But the reel shown in this 1912 catalog *has no level-wind attachment,* although that was an old invention even then.

I never saw or even heard of this version of the antibacklash reel and wonder how many collectors have one now.

MARTIN AUTOMATIC REEL.

These reels have been on the market for a number of years and have given satisfaction. Spring which winds in line can be readily and easily adjusted to greater or less tension at any time during the operation of landing a fish. They all have a lock which allows of keeping the reel in condition to take in line without keeping the finger on the lever continually. Made of aluminum, trimmed with German silver.

No.		Each
1.	Trout Reel, size of spool is 2¾ inches in diameter and 5/16 inch wide, will hold 25 yards of medium weight line..............................	$5.00
2.	Large Trout Reel, same diameter spool, but it is ⅝ inch wide, holds 30 yards of medium weight line..............................	6.00
3.	Bass Reel, same diameter spool, but it is ⅞ inch wide, holds 50 yards of medium weight line..............................	7.00
4.	Salmon Reel, same diameter spool, but it is 13/16 inch wide, holds 50 yards of heavy line..............................	8.00

MEISSELBACH AUTOMATIC REEL

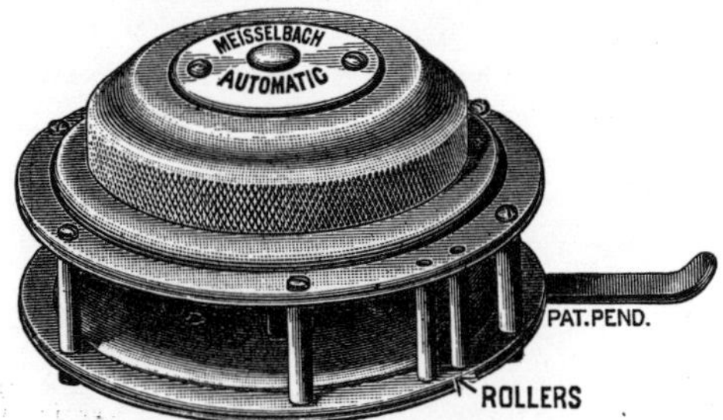

MECHANICAL FEATURES

Mechanism is very simple, and not likely to get out of order. Main shaft is of carbon steel, substantial in size and runs in German silver bearings.

Spring is of the finest tempered steel. All working parts are of hard brass and tempered steel, working in German silver bearings. All working parts are enclosed.

Anyone can take this reel apart and put it together in less than five minutes.

Reel fully guaranteed.

DESIRABLE FEATURES

This reel has an exclusive feature in a Safety Winding Spring, which allows the spring to be wound up at any time when line is in or out, by turning the milled spring box, without any danger of overwinding.

Spool has friction release which allows stripping of spool under all conditions.

Spool is fitted with a safety release which allows the spool to be run in at any speed without any fear of injuring the mechanism.

The line is guided by two revolving rollers. This prevents the line from being injured and worn, as is the case of all other reels.

Size of Spool, 3 inches; with of Spool, ¾ inch.......................each $3.50

William Mills & Son's
EXTRA QUALITY TROUT AND OUANANICHE FLIES.

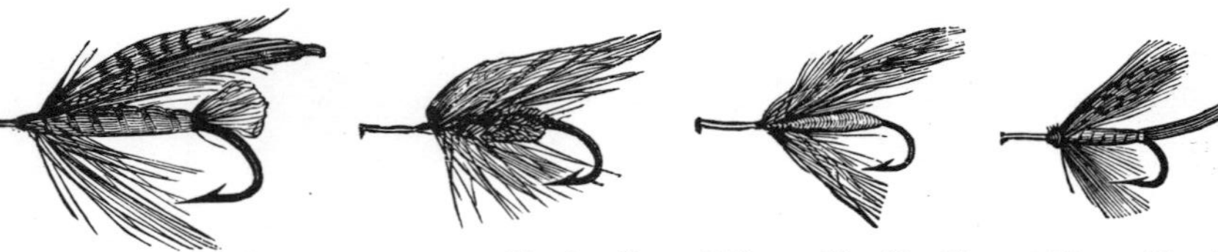

Size of Fly on No. 6 Size of Fly on No. 8 Size of Fly on No. 10 Size of Fly on No. 12

These Extra Quality Flies are the ones usually used throughout the country for general stream and lake fishing. They comprise all the well-known patterns.

They are beautifully made, true to pattern and the best materials only are used in their construction.

The flies are tied on our celebrated O'Shaughnessy Hooks which are the strongest and best hooks for this class of strong fly.

We have them in stock tied on hooks Nos. 6, 8, 10 and 12, but not all patterns on all sizes, for some of the patterns are only used in two or three sizes. While we have most of the patterns on Nos. 8, 10 and 12 we only stock the leading patterns on No. 6 hooks.

On Hooks sizes 6, 8, 10 and 12 ....per dozen **$1.00**

Alder
Alexandra
Babcock
Barrington
Beaverkill
Bee
Black Gnat
Black Hackle
Black June
Black Moose
Black Prince
Blue Jay
Blue Professor
Brown Adder
Brown Hackle
Brown Hen
Cahill
Canada
Cinnamon
Claret Gnat
Coachman
Coch-y-bon dhu
Cowdung
Critchley Fancy
Dark Fox
Dark Stone
Dark Coachman
Downlooker
Dr. Breck
Feted Green
Furnace Hackle
Gold Stork
Gold Monkey
Gold Spinner
Gordon
Governor
Gray Hackle
Gray Miller
Great Dun
Green Drake
Green Hackle
Grizzly King
Guinea Hen
Hackstaff Hackle
Hawthorn
Jenny Lind
Jungle Cock
Katy-did
King of Waters
Lady Beaverkill
Light Fox
Light Stone
Lowery
March Brown
Markham
McGinty
Mills No. 1
Montreal
Montreal Yellow
Montreal Silver
New Page
Oak
Orange Miller
Pale Yellow
Parmachene Belle
Preston's Fancy
Professor
Quaker
Queen of Waters
Red Hackle
Red Spinner
Royal Coachman
Rube Wood
Scarlet Ibis
Seth Green
Shoemaker
Silver Doctor
Silver Stork
Swift Water
Van Patten
White Hackle
White Miller
White Moth
Wickham's Fancy
Widow
Willow
Wilson
Wood Duck
Yellow Coachman
Yellow Hackle
Yellow May
Yellow Miller
Yellow Sally
Yellow Professor
Zulu

GAUZE WING FLIES.

These flies are made with wings made of a waterproof gauze to imitate the wings of Ephemera flies.

They have proven very killing, especially when the May flies are on the water. They are tied on pennell eyed hooks with gut passed through the eye and tied in with the body of the fly. Made in the following patterns:

Coachman
Cowdung
Fern
Governor
Hawthorn
Ibis
Red Ant
Red Quill

With rubber body, sizes 8, 10 and 12...per doz. **$1.50**
With regular body, following style: Sizes 8 10 and 12 ....per doz. **1.25**

96

TARPON PHANTOM.

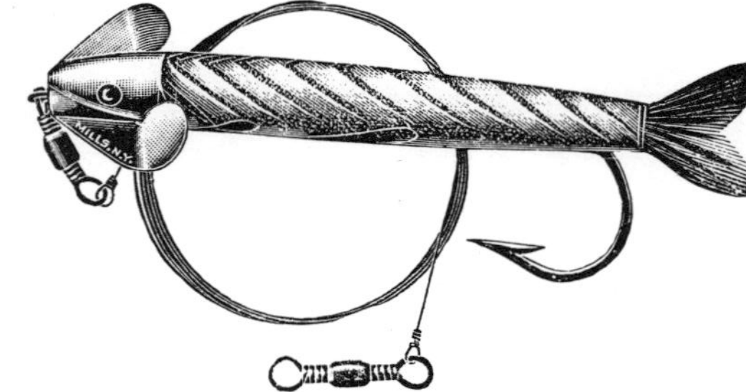

For several years it has been difficult, and at times almost impossible, to get proper bait to use for tarpon. This phantom is made of extra strong canvas, and they have proven very successful and durable.

The hook is our Captiva, mounted in the usual style, with one extra swivel. Made only in one color, silver, striped light green. Length, 6¼ inches.

Price, mounted complete ....each **$2.00**
Price, without trace ....each **1.75**

GEEN COMBINATION BAIT

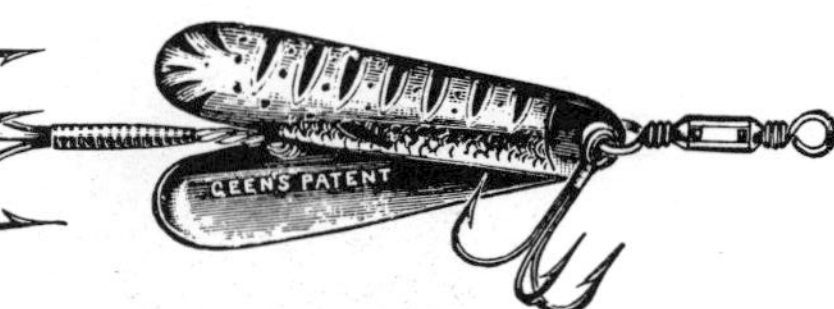

These are a combination of a revolving spoon and a phantom. They are double concave. The concave sides burnished bright gold like a spoon and the convex sides painted like blue phantom. The treble hook at head is detachable.

Nos.	3	4
Length, inches	2	2¾
Each	**$0.60**	**$0.65**

RED DEVIL SQUID.

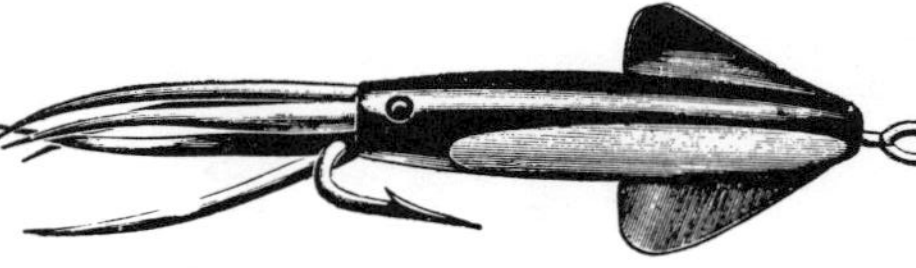

These have proven most successful for a great variety of Florida salt water fish, they are quite durable and have very strong hooks.

One size, 4¾ inches long..each **$0.75**

110

"JERSEY QUEEN" CASTING BAITS

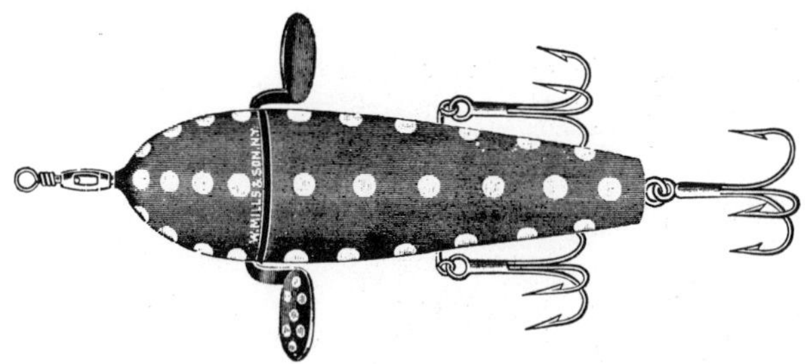

Also furnished with 3 Single Hooks

One of the best known surface casting baits. They are made of wood, nicely enameled, white or yellow, and yellow with gold spots. They are made in three sizes: large, 3¾ inches; medium, 3¼ inches; small, 2¾ inches. All sizes are furnished with either three treble hooks or three single hooks.

Size		Each		Each
Large,	Yellow or White	**$0.55**	Yellow, gold spotted	**$0.60**
Medium,	Yellow or White	**.50**	Yellow, gold spotted	**.55**
Small,	Yellow or White	**.45**	Yellow, gold spotted	**.50**

The above lures are particularly desirable for fishing in New Jersey and other nearby waters.

THE MICHIGAN LIFE LIKE MINNOW

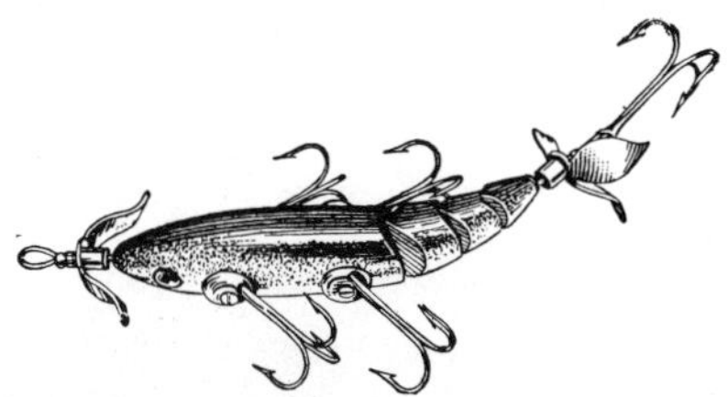

The improvement on this minnow over other makes is the Jointed Tail portion, which is flexible, and when being drawn through the water the Three-Blade Propeller wiggles the Jointed Tail portion and makes an excellent imitation of a live minnow while swimming.

It has been pronounced to be the most perfect casting and trolling bait ever put on the market.

FIVE TREBLE HOOK MINNOW

Length of Body, 2¾ inches. Made in the following colors:

No.		Each
1.	Light Green, Speckled Back, White Belly	**$0.75**
2.	Dark Green, Speckled Back, White Belly	**.75**
7.	Brook Trout	**.75**
9.	Dark Back, Yellow Belly	**.75**
14.	Perch	**.75**

THREE HOOK TREBLE MINNOW

Length of Body, 2¾ inches. Made in the following colors:

No.		Each
4.	Light Green, Speckled Back, White Belly	**$0.65**
5.	Dark Green, Speckled Back, White Belly	**.65**
8.	Brook Trout	**.65**
10.	Dark Back, Yellow Belly	**.65**
15.	Perch	**.65**

William Mills & Son's "Intrinsic" Repair Kit

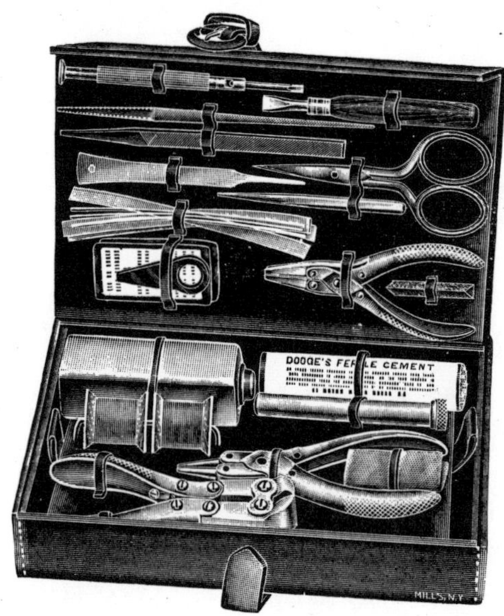

The tools in this kit are specially selected for their adaptability for use in making repairs "on the field."

The tools and materials are the very highest quality that it is possible to procure and must not be compared with those usually marketed for this purpose.

They are housed securely, yet in a very get-at-able manner in a fine leather carrying case with strap and buckle.

Size, 7½ inches long, 5 inches wide, 1 inch thick, with articles as below: Flat-nosed parallel plyers, round-nose parallel plyers, cutting plyers, jeweler's screw-driver, special pattern reel screw-driver, oil can and oil, varnish, and can, ferrule cement, tweezers, flat file, round file, pin punch, scissors, hook stone, wire and sheet metal for splicing, silk wire and linen for winding, wax, needles, emery cloth.

Price, complete..............**$12.00**

William Mills & Son's Spare Line Carrier

This article was gotten up to fill a long felt want for a safe, convenient and get-at-able way to carry spare salmon and tournament lines. The line holders are beautifully made of aluminum; both sizes are sufficiently large for the largest and heaviest salmon line. The container is a hand-sewn leather box with convenient **handle**.

Price, complete, container and two line carriers..........................**$4.50**
Large size carrier, diameter 7⅜ inches, 1 inch thick........................ **1.10**
Small size carrier, diameter 5⅜ inches, 1 inch thick........................ **.90**

160

The compound-lever wire cutter in the repair kit was an excellent idea; it could handle tempered piano wire, or cut right through the brazed shank of a treble hook—very handy when a man gets hooked. Of course, $12 was a week's pay for me in 1912.

Winding line off a carrier spool like these onto a reel was easy; one simply hung the spool over a doorknob. But getting the line back onto the carrier was a tough job if one wanted to avoid a twist in the line on each turn.

FLY TYING REQUISITES

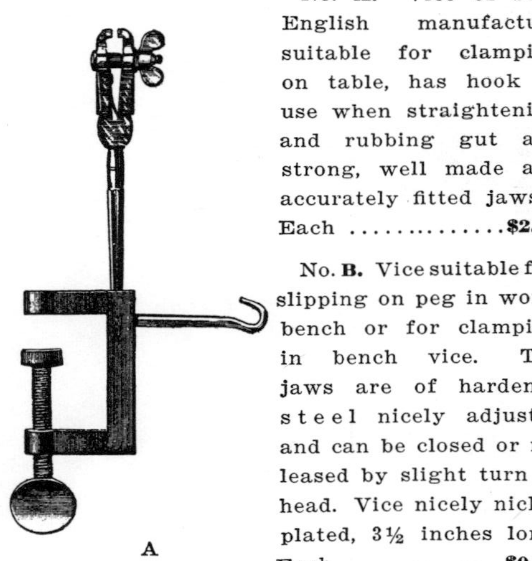

A

No. **A.** Vice of best English manufacture suitable for clamping on table, has hook to use when straightening and rubbing gut and strong, well made and accurately fitted jaws. Each **$2.00**

No. **B.** Vice suitable for slipping on peg in work bench or for clamping in bench vice. The jaws are of hardened steel nicely adjusted and can be closed or released by slight turn of head. Vice nicely nickel plated, 3½ inches long. Each **$0.75**

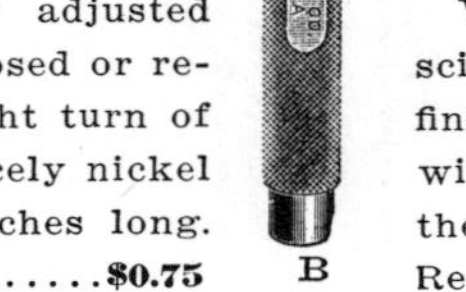

B

SCISSORS

Very best quality scissors points are very fine and nicely adjusted, will cut well even at the point **$0.60**
Regular quality ... **.30**

Hackle Plyers, brass, small **$0.30**
Hackle Players, large, German silver .... **.40**
Stiletto, ivory handle .... **.50**

BODY MATERIAL

Floss Silk, all colors, per skein.... **$0.05**
Mohair, per package, all colors... **.10**
Chenille, per hank, all colors...... **.20**
Silver or Gold Tinsel, flat, per spool .... **.35**
Silver or Gold Tinsel, round, per spool .... **.35**
Winding Silk, all colors, per spool. **.15**
Wax, per piece .... **.10**

FEATHERS

Hackles, natural ....dozen **$0.15**
Hackles, dyed ....dozen **.20**
Mallard, gray ....dozen **.10**
Mallard, brown ....dozen **.15**
Teal ....dozen **.15**
Widgeon ....dozen **.20**
Scarlet Ibis ....dozen **.25**
Peacock, sword feathers.....each **.08**
Peacock, Herl ....bunch **.20**
Turkey feathers ....each **.07**
Wood Duck, barred..........each **.07**
Swan plumes, natural........each **.08**
Swan plumes, dyed, all colors.each **.10**
Jungle Cock, spotted.......dozen **.50**
Golden Pheasant crests.....dozen **1.25**
Golden Pheasant neck feathers, dozen **.35**

HOOKS

Taper Shank Hooks for tying flies with gut leaders. See page 132 for sizes.

Per doz.
Sproat or Sneck, sizes 1 to 12.....**$0.15**
O'Shaughnessy, sizes 1 to 12...... **.20**

Turn-Down Eyed Hooks

Highest Quality Hooks, for sizes see page 133.

Per doz.
Limerick shape, sizes 1 to 12......**$0.20**
Sproat shape, sizes 1 to 12........ **.20**
Sneck shape, sizes 1 to 12......... **.20**

Turn-Up Eyed Hooks

Limerick shape for sizes see Turn-Down Eyed Hooks, page 133.

Per doz.
Long shank, sizes 8, 10, 12........**$0.30**
Medium shank, sizes 8, 10, 12, 14.. **.30**
Short shank sizes 8, 10, 12, 14..... **.30**

Gut, see page 129; Gut Tippets, page 98.

165

DRY FLY REQUISITES

Pocket Gut Cutters and Tweezers

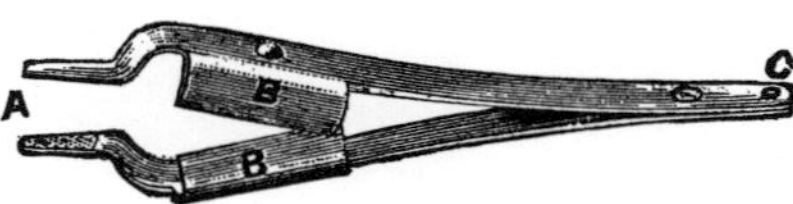

Most useful for the eyed fly user for picking flies from box and for cutting the superfluous ends of gut.
Made of high quality steel, polished............pair **$1.00**
Tweezers alone, without cutter............pair **.30**

William Mills & Son's "Floatine."

A clear, colorless, odorless liquid which when applied to the fly either by brushing on with brush provided for that purpose, or by dipping the fly in the liquid will render it waterproof and the fly will float quite some time. It is also useful on Dry Flies when fishing in very rough water. Complete with brush and packed in handy wooden case............each **$0.25**

POCKET ATOMIZER

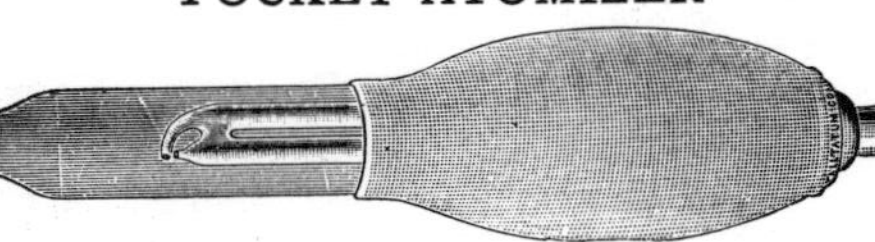

Useful for spraying floating flies with "Floatine" or other substance so as not to mat down the wings and hackles.
The glass tube collapses into the bulb and cork goes in the end of tube. Size collapsed, 4 inches long, 1¼ inches diameter............each **$0.75**

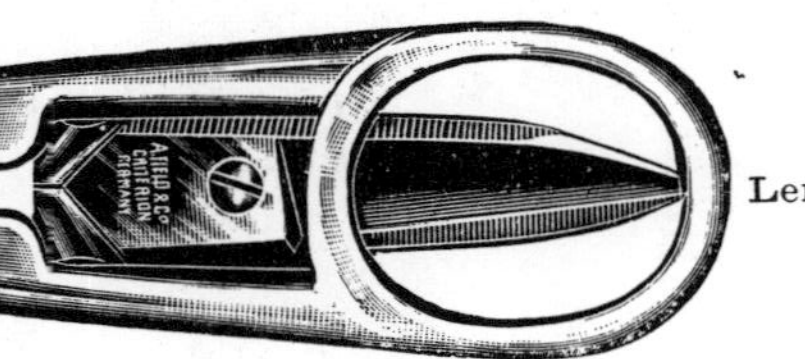

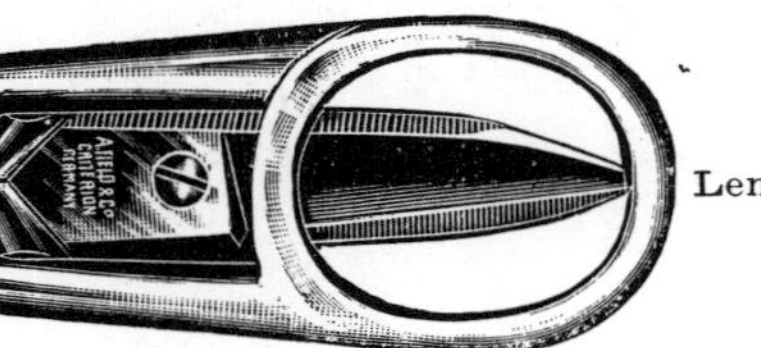

FOLDING SCISSORS

Length extended, 3¼ inches, folded 2 inch x 1 inch...........each **$0.50**

LINE GREASER

Made of pigskin, with thick felt attached to cover, suitable for applying paraffine to sticky line or grease to line to make it float.

No.		Each
484.	3¾ inches long, 2 inches wide	**$0.40**
458.	5¼ inches long, 3¾ inches wide	**.50**

205

William Mills & Son's Special Wading Sox

These Sox are made expressly to wear between the stocking feet wader and the canvas shoe. They are extra heavy wool and will obviate the abraiding of the wader by the sand or gravel that may work in. Being made expressly for wading, they are shorter in the leg, just long enough to come above shoe top..............pair **$0.50**

Regular length sox, made same material and weight............pair **$0.50**

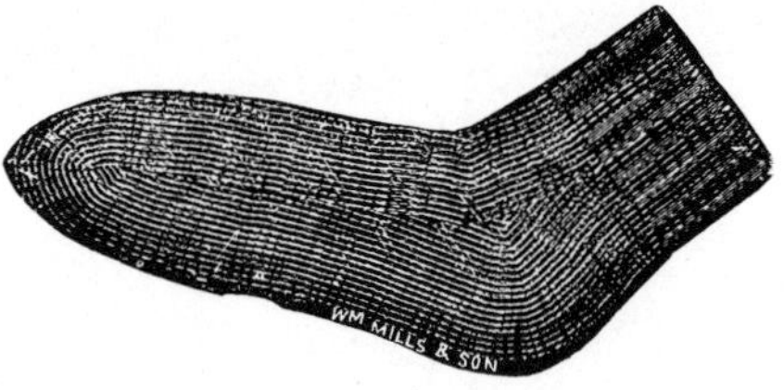

William Mills & Son's Canvas Wading Shoes

No.		Per Pair
1.	Made of good canvas, with hob nails	**$4.60**
2.	Made of heavy brown canvas, with heavy extension sole and soft iron hob nails	**5.50**

William Mills & Son's Best English Hob Nails

½ Gross in Box

No. 13

No. 16

These are a superior quality of soft iron hob nails and are infinitely better and more efficient than the ordinary cast hob nails.

Nos.	13	16
Per box	**$0.25**	**$0.30**

WING SCREW CALKS

No 00

No G

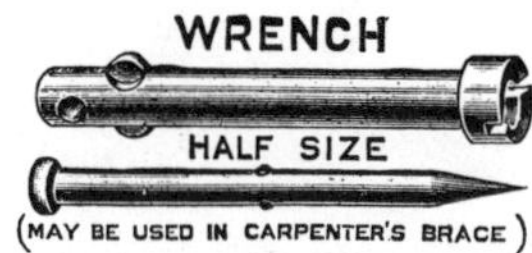

Made of toughened steel, the shape is designed for durability, they will screw into hard leather and will also hold in soft. May be inserted and removed as desired. Wrench to screw them in with comes in each box.

Price per box of 50, either size, with wrench..............................**$0.50**

188

Drop a tear, brother angler, for dear old Mills No. 16, the very best soft iron, wading-shoe hobnail ever made. It went off the market during World War II, and today neither it nor any other soft wading or mountaineering type is made anywhere in the world.

BAIT CHOPPER.

This Chopper is made expressly for chopping Menhaden, etc., for chumming. It is strong, well made and well tinned.

Size 12½ inches long, 8 inches high, 7 inches wide, with handle detached .... each **$5.00**

THE "ANGLERS FRIEND" LINE DRYER.

The base is made of wood and the arms, which when extended are 10 inches diameter, fold down on the base and the dryer collapsed is 9½ inches long, 3 inches wide and 1¼ inches thick.

Each **$2.00**

FISH KNIVES.

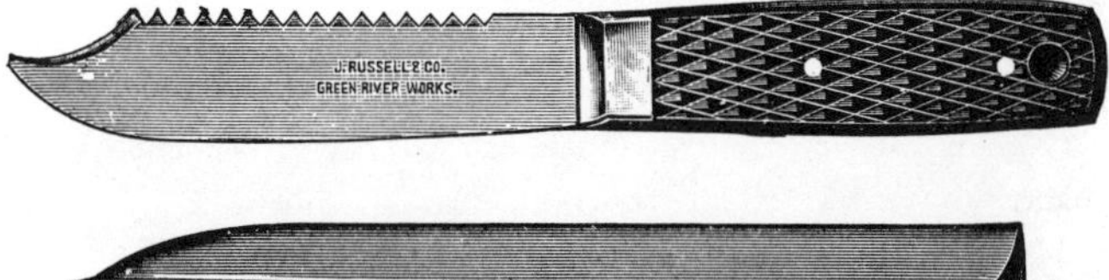

Good quality steel knife with notched back for scaling; length of blade, 4½ inches; length of handle, 3 inches.

Without sheath .... each **$0.35**
With leather sheath .... each **.50**

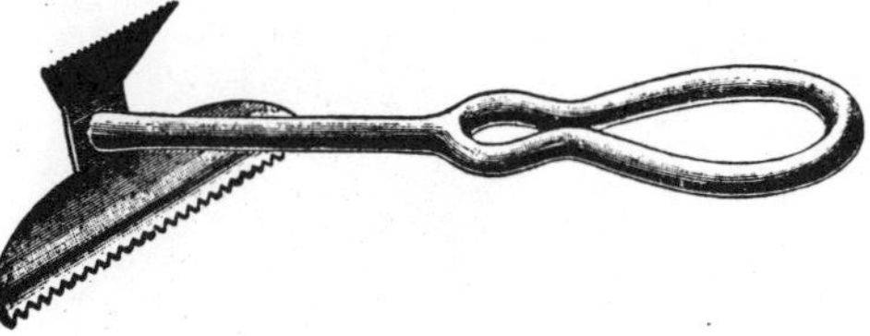

FISH SCALER

Cast iron handle with stamped steel scraper, width of wide scraper blade, 3 inches; length over all, 6½ inches.

Each **$0.10**

200

SUNSHADE HATS AND HEAD NETS.

These have a very wide brim and shade the face and neck perfectly; weighs but ½ to ¾ ounces and as it has a flexible adjusting band, it can be worn either over or in place of the ordinary hat. **It is perfectly rigid when** in use, but can in an instant be folded to carry in small bag, 6 inches in diameter and ½ inch thick.

Price ....each **$0.35**

Same with mosquito netting to use as a protection against black flies and mosquitoes.........each **.65**

PATENT HEAD NET.

Fine mesh cloth to keep out even punkies. Eyes, nose and mouth exposed so one can eat, drink and smoke. No obstruction to sight, adjustable to all faces, suitable for lady or gentleman.

Price ....each **$1.00**

IMPROVED HEAD NET.

This mosquito protector fits over hat and around shoulders. It is made of best Egyptian cotton, is strong and durable, will not stick to face in case of rain or perspiration. The horsehair window allows one to see clearly and self-closing valve permits the smoking of pipe or cigars.

Price ....each **$1.25**

Same style, made of tan cloth........each **1.00**

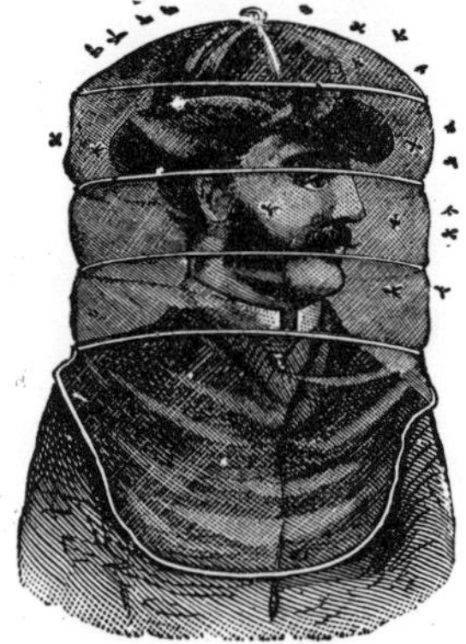

HEAD NETS.

A SURE PROTECTION AGAINST MOSQUITOES AND FLIES

Tarlatan or Mosquito Bar, with Case 75c. Each

202

A whole page of old friends—"stock cuts" that went unchanged for at least a quarter century. One wonders how the pipe-smoker got the smoke out of his little enclosure, or what he did about spitting.

Those folding hats are still 35 cents; with mosquito netting, 65 cents.

Quite possibly the earliest established (1820) of the fine old tackle firms of yesteryear.

Suit Case Fishing Rods.

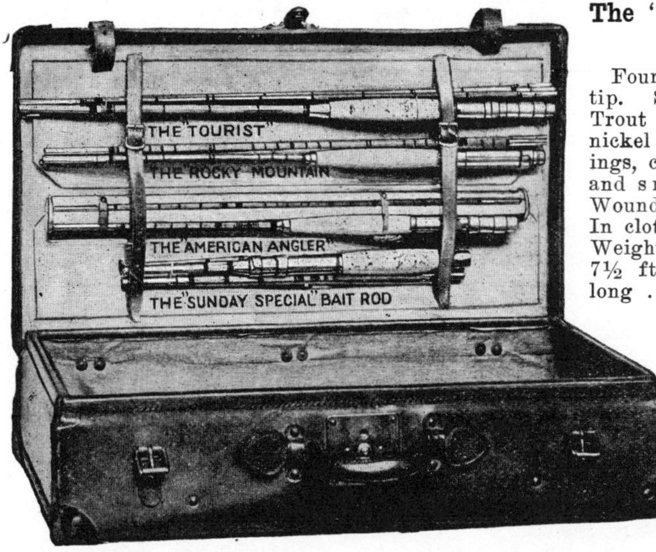

The "Tourist" Fly Rod.

Four-piece and extra tip. Split Bamboo Trout Fly Rod with nickel plated mountings, cork hand grasp, and snake guides. Wound with red silk. In cloth partition bag. Weight, 6 oz.; length, 7½ ft. Joints 23 in. long ...... Each, $2.25

The "Sunday "Special" Fly Rod.

Made in five pieces, with extra tip, in cloth partition bag. All joints 18 in. long. Rod is 7 feet long and weighs 5 ounces; has broad purple silk windings, well shaped cork grip and full nickel mountings. **Snake Guides. A splendid little rod for brook or "brush" fishing**............................Each, $2.75

The "Sunday Special" Black Bass Bait Rod.

Made in five pieces, with extra tip. In cloth partition bag. All joints 15 inches long. Rod is 6 feet long and weighs 7 ounces; has broad purple silk windings, short cork grip, bait-casting guides and tips, and full nickel mountings. **The busy man's bait casting rod**..................................Each, $2.75

The "Rocky Mountain" Fly Rod.

Four-piece and extra tip Split Bamboo Trout Fly Rod, with nickel-plated mountings, cork grip, reinforced ferrules, and snake guides. Closely wound with red and black silk wrappings. In cloth partitioned bags. Weight, 5½ ounces; length, 7 feet; joints 21½ inches long....Each, $3.50

The "American Angler" Fly Rod.

Five-piece and extra tip Split Bamboo Trout or Bass Fly Rod, with reinforced ferrules and snake guides, cork grip, nickel plated mountings. Beautifully wrapped with broad clustered purple windings. Each rod packed in a cloth covered wood form and bag. Weight, 6 ounces; length, 8 feet; joints 20 inches long .... Each, $4.00

See page 36 for our new "DUPLEX" Suit Case Rod.

The Sunday rod was so called because it was short enough to conceal inside a trouser leg, so that the truant angler could not be spotted by disapproving churchgoers.

84 *Abbey & Imbrie, N. Y.* *"Fishing Tackle that's Fit for Fishing."* *Catalogue for 1912*

Reel Attachments.

The Flegel Spooler.

Patent applied for.

Light, strong and durable. Made of German silver. Can be attached to any reel without cutting or marring it. The only spooling device that does not run when making a cast. The motion of the cast swings the device down to a position where the line does not touch the pulley. One single move of the finger, before reeling in, swings it into place; it then spools the line perfectly, thus avoiding the necessity of changing the hand to the position above the reel. It allows the angler to hold the rod by the cork grasp when playing a fish.

It contains no gears. The line running over the little aluminum pulley, turns it and makes the pulley travel on a rod which contains an endless thread.

Made in four sizes. When ordering give the measurements of the reel between the side plates, which will probably be 1⅜ inches (No. 0), 1½ inches (No. 1), 1⅝ inches (No. 2), or 1⅞ inches (No. 3)............**Price, $3.00 each.**

The "Governor" Drag. May be Fitted to Any Reel.

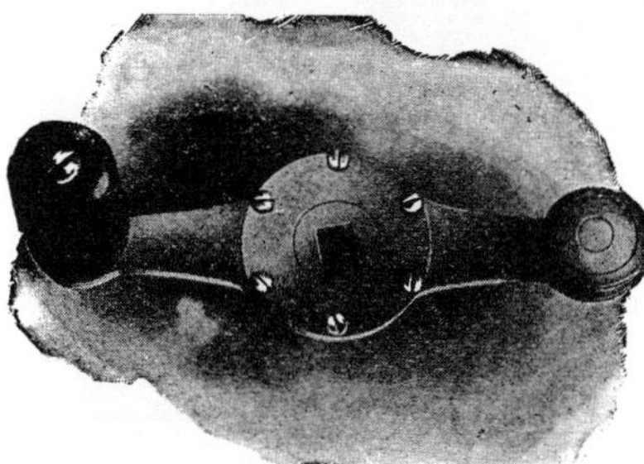

The "Governor" is a friction device placed inside of a balanced handle which may be fitted to any reel. It may be adjusted to give friction just within the breaking strain of the weakest point in the tackle. The reel with a "Governor" attached is entirely under the control of the angler's right hand, while the left hand is free to grasp the rod above the reel while playing a fish, or to guide the line upon the spool while reeling in. The angler merely holds the handle, and the friction discs do the rest. A rush which would ordinarily break the line is taken up by the retarded slipping of the discs under well regulated friction. When the fight relaxes, the angler turns the handle and the line is recovered at the full speed of the reel.

Made in Two Sizes.

	Nickel Plated	German Silver	
No. 2. Length 3 9/16 in. (For salt water or large fresh water reels)	**$2.00**	**$2.50**	each
" 3. " 2 7/16 " (" small multiplying reels)..........	**1.50**	**2.00**	"

The following sizes are kept in stock: .250, .235, .230, .202, .195, .187 inch diameter.
The No. 3 "Governor" is also made with a round hole for our "Take-Apart" Reel.

(For Rabbeth Handle Drag, suitable for large salt water reels, see page 75.)

The Huffman Attachment.

Combines a Hand Rest, a Finger Hook, and a Reel Lock.

Made of German silver. Makes bait casting easy. Relieves the tiresome, awkward gripping of the rod when guiding the line upon the reel. Fits any rod and holds fast the reel so that it cannot work loose. No tools required. With it a reel may be clamped on a common cane pole. Strong, light, and perfectly fits the hand.

Each........**$1.00**

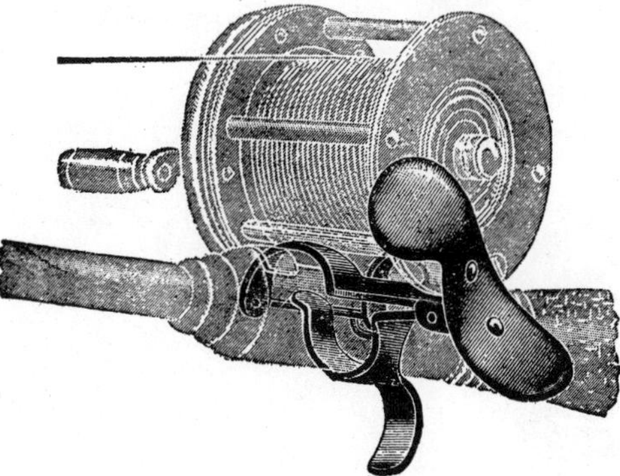

A page of toothsome gadgets. The Flegel device would spool, all right, but would it cast? Experience teaches that to permit line to peel smoothly off a wide spool, the spooling device *must* run on the cast unless it automatically disengages itself from the line, as in the old Beetzel reel.

The "Governor" was the famous Williams patent, a slipping clutch self-contained in a replacement reel handle. The forerunner of the star drag, it was widely marketed in several conformations, mostly for surf and other heavy-duty reels.

Fishing Tackle Assortments.

For the merchant who wants to display attractively a small and well selected stock of fishing tackle.

Contents of "Empire City" Assortment—$3.60 Each.

Size of box, 10½ x 16½ inches. Weight, complete, 3 lbs.

600	Fish Hooks	**Retail**	2 for 1 cent	$3.00
12	Eureka Lines	"	1 cent each	.12
12	Eureka Lines	"	2 cents each	.24
12	Braided Lines	"	5 cents each	.60
12	Best Trout Lines	"	5 cents each	.60
24	Ringed Sinkers	"	1 cent each	.24
4	Boxes Split Shot	"	5 cents each	.20
18	Furnished Fish Lines	"	1 cent each	.18
12	Furnished Fish Lines	"	3 cents each	.36
8	Furnished Fish Lines	"	5 cents each	.40
36	Snelled Hooks	"	2 cents each	.72
12	Adjustable Floats	"	5 cents each	.60

Total retail value for which assortment can be sold...... $7.26

Fishing Tackle Assortments (Continued).

(For illustration of box see opposite page.)

This assortment should appeal strongly to the Boy's Camp Director for the promotion of angling. This collection of tackle is especially appropriate for camps situated on small lakes and rivers, and is an ample supply for a camp of 40 boys. We will be glad to make up assortments including rods, reels, lines, etc., suitable for camps in any locality. Prices will be governed by the quality as well as the extent of the assortment selected.

Contents of "Imperial" Assortment—$7.20 Each.

Size of box, 16¾ x 18½ inches. Weight, complete, 6 lbs.

8	Furnished Fish Lines	**Retail**	5 cents each	$ .40
4	Furnished Fish Lines	"	10 cents each	.40
10	Furnished Fish Lines	"	3 cents each	.30
6	Furnished Fish Lines, with Float	"	5 cents each	.30
30	Furnished Fish Lines, with Float	"	1 cent each	.30
8	Adjustable Floats	"	5 cents each	.40
6	Adjustable Floats	"	10 cents each	.60
12	Braided Fish Lines	"	5 cents each	.60
24	Eureka Lines	"	2 cents each	.48
72	Eureka Lines	"	1 cent each	.72
12	Trout Lines on Cards	"	5 cents each	.60
54	Ringed Sinkers, Assorted	"	1 cent each	.54
36	Snelled Hooks	"	2 cents each	.72
200	Hooks	"	1 cent each	2.00
600	Hooks	"	2 for 1 cent	3.00
100	Hooks	"	2 cents each	2.00

Total retail value for which assortment can be sold......$13.36

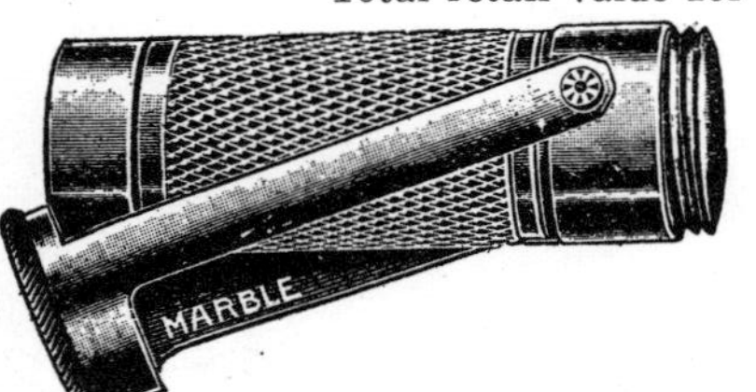

Waterproof Match Box, $ .50.

It can be quickly opened and closed in the dark and is absolutely water and moisture proof. Made of seamless drawn brass, heavily nickel plated.

The "Abbey" Reel-Handle Grip.—Each $ .10.

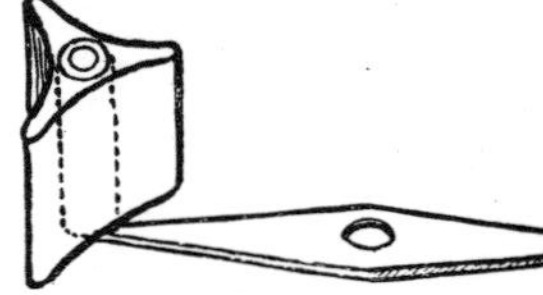

Illustration shows the "Abbey" grip attached to the ordinary reel handle.

A three sided, soft rubber grip that is designed to slip over the handle of a reel. When in place, the three sides accommodate naturally and comfortably the thumb and two fingers of the hand used in manipulating the reel. The "Abbey" Reel-Handle Grip gives the fisherman complete control of his reel. The handle **can not slip from the fingers. Grips of hard rubber of the above description can be put on any reel for 50 cents.**

The Riverside "Coat Pocket" Steel Rod $3.00

FOR BAIT CASTING

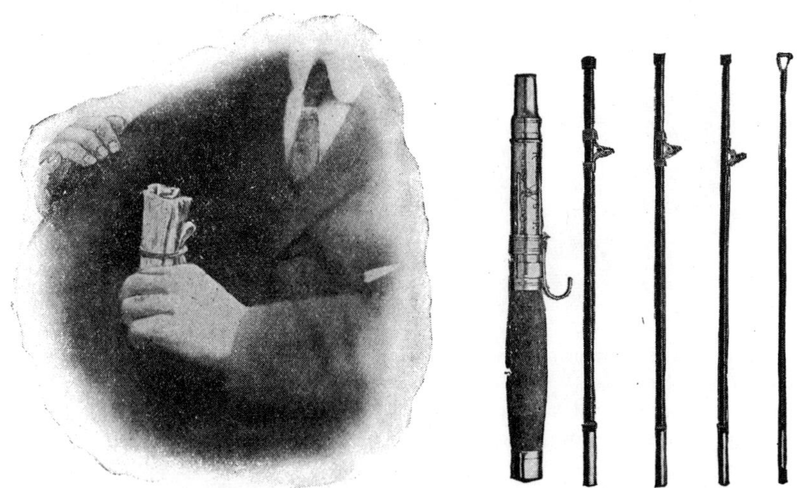

"Ye may walk and there is no man shall wist whereabout ye go."– Izaak Walton.

Do you ever want to talk business with a man without letting him know you're going fishing?

Have you ever taken a horseback or bicycle trip to a place where you could have caught fish if you'd only had your rod?

Do you ever travel with just a handbag?

Then YOU need a Riverside "Coat Pocket" Steel Rod.

DESCRIPTION.

Best Quality tubular steel enameled black.
Four joints and detachable cork grip.
Nickel plated mountings. Detachable "trigger" or "finger hook."
"One-ring" Casting Guides. (Inside diameter of rings 5/16 inches.)
Length of rod 4½ feet.
Length of joints only 12 inches.
Weight of all parts in bag, ready to carry in pocket or valise, 6¾ ounces.

The "Imbrie Deep Sea" Reel

The simple mechanism and rigid construction of the new 1913 model "Imbrie Deep Sea Reel" will commend it to the anglers who delight in the invigorating sport of surf casting. Its *automatic drag* acts only when the fish runs—*never* while you are reeling in your line.

Its *adjustable tension* screw gives any degree of pressure on the spool. That helps you counteract the tendency of the line to "over-run" when making a cast.

To *take it apart*—just push the button and twist your wrist. In *two seconds* you can get at the mechanism to clean or oil it.

Its rigid German Silver rims (*stamped*—not cast) are riveted to the strong *one-piece* cross-plate.. All the strain is on the metal; none upon the hard rubber plates.

A better salt water reel in design, construction, and practical usefulness cannot be made.

Width of Spool, 1 15/16 *Inches.*

	Comfortable Capacity	
No. 9 Cuttyhunk Line................	300 Yards	Each $12.00
No. 12 " "	225 "	
No. 15 " "	180 "	
No. 18 " "	150 "	

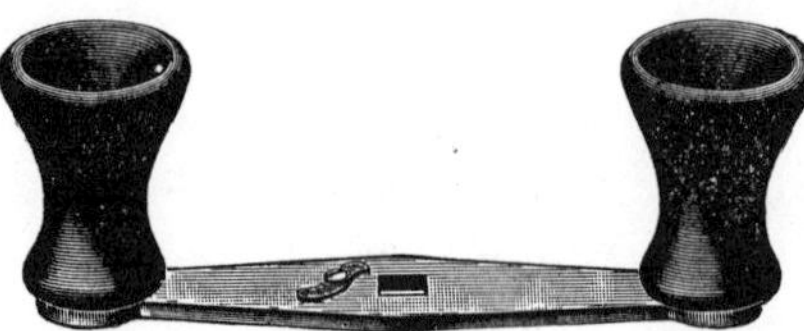

Double Grip Handle

We prefer to furnish this reel with the double grip handle, as with this handle vibration (or wobble) is eliminated and a perfect balance, at all speeds is attained. The ordinary handle may be supplied to order, if desired.

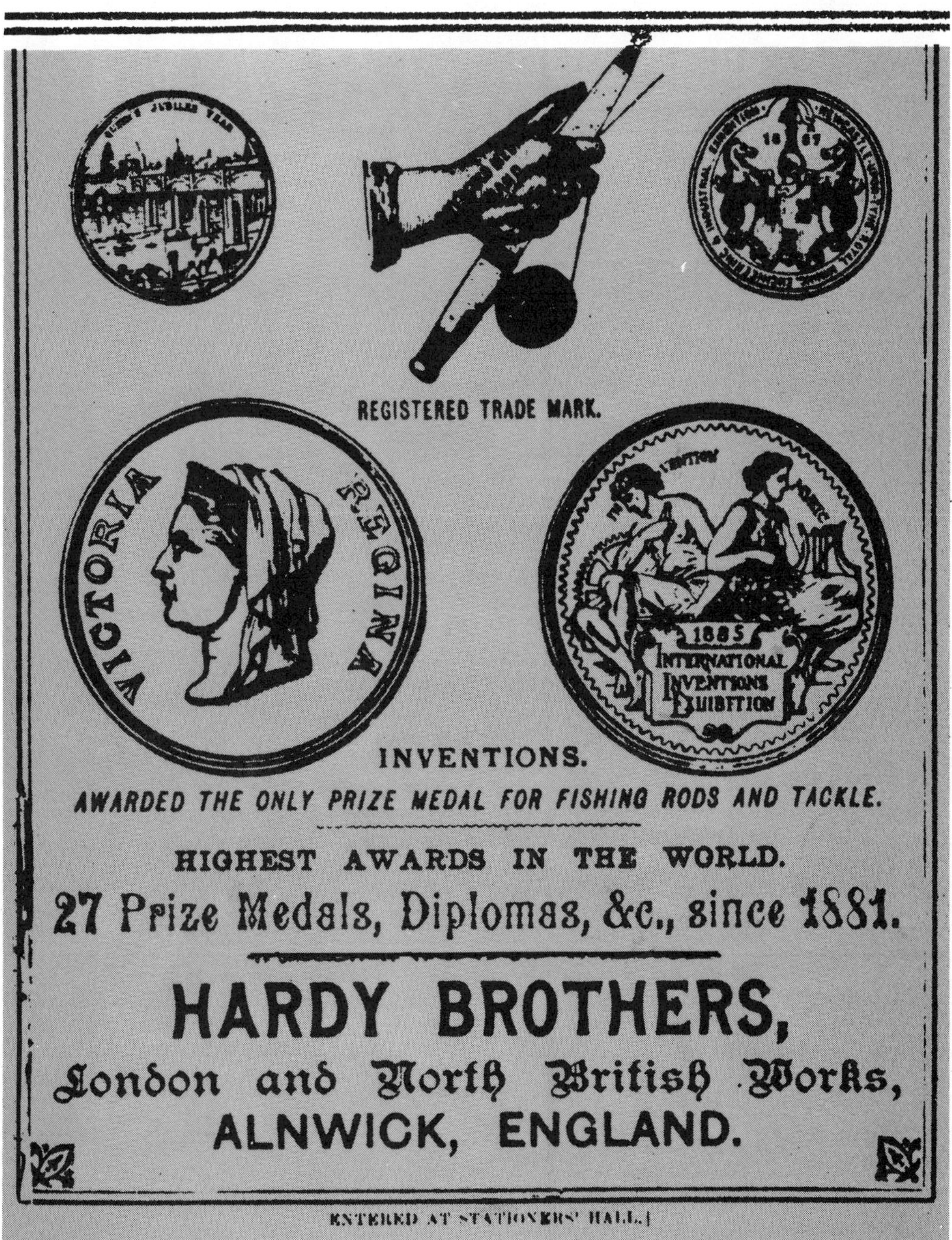
REGISTERED TRADE MARK.
VICTORIA REGINA
1885
INTERNATIONAL INVENTIONS EXHIBITION
INVENTIONS.
AWARDED THE ONLY PRIZE MEDAL FOR FISHING RODS AND TACKLE.
HIGHEST AWARDS IN THE WORLD.
27 Prize Medals, Diplomas, &c., since 1881.
HARDY BROTHERS,
London and North British Works,
ALNWICK, ENGLAND.
ENTERED AT STATIONERS' HALL.

REPORT FROM "FISHING GAZETTE."

OLYMPIC GAMES

ELEVENTH INTERNATIONAL

Fly and Bait Casting Tournament

FRANCO-BRITISH EXHIBITION, LONDON, 1908.

(The last International Casting Tournament, held in Great Britain, in which makers of Fishing Rods and Tackle were allowed to compete.)

Harold John Hardy. John James Hardy. Laurence R. Hardy.

A SKILFUL TRIO

From "FISHING GAZETTE."

There is an old saying that " the man who drives fat oxen should himself be fat," and, by parity of reasoning, the man who makes first-rate fishing tackle should himself be able to use it in first-rate fashion. This certainly holds true of the " Hardys." Mr. J. J. Hardy's portrait, flanked by those of his two nephews, Messrs. L. R. Hardy and H. J. Hardy, is here reproduced.

Fly Makers' Tools

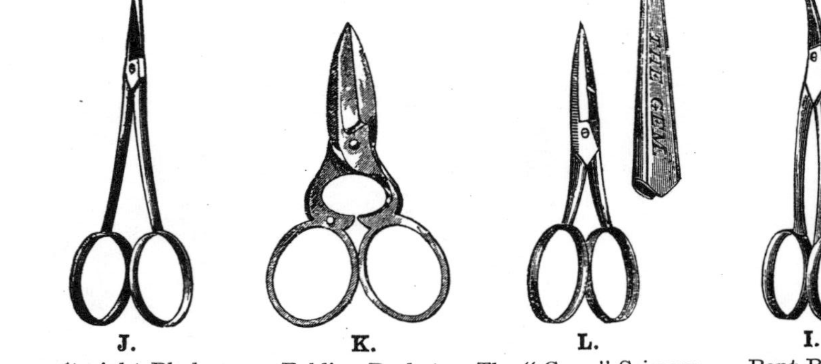

J. Straight Blade Scissors, **1/9** pair.

K. Folding Pocket Scissors, **2/3** pair.

L. The " Gem " Scissors, in case, **2/9** pair.

I. Bent Blade Scissors, **3/-** pair.

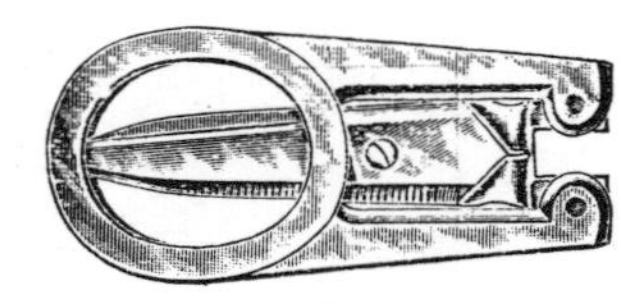

M. Folding Scissors, best quality, **3/-** 2nd Do., **1/6** per pair.

N. Telescopic, best quality, **3/6** per pair.

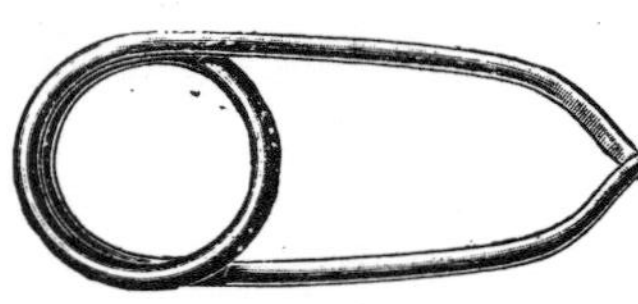

Q. Fly Vice, to screw in table or use on thumb, as illustrated, **7/6** each.

O. Fly Tweezers, **1/6** per pair.

P. File for Pointing Dull Hooks, **1/-** each.

Ditto, to screw on table with hook for looping, **6/-** ; larger size, **12/6** each.

The best Guide and Instructor for Salmon Fly Dressing is " Salmon Fishing," by J. J. Hardy, 20/- post paid. Only a few copies left.

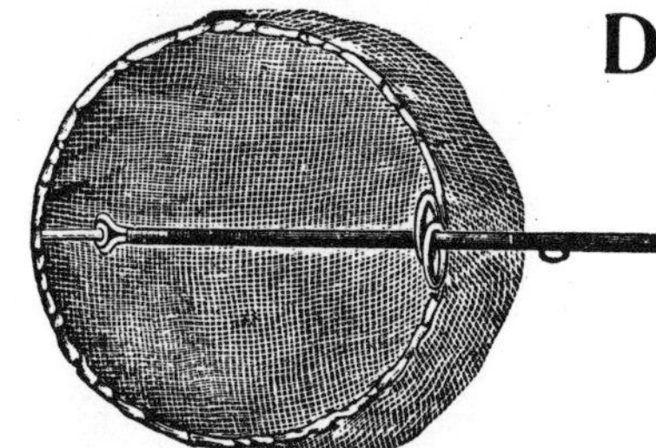

Dry Fly Requisites

FLY CATCHER.

A useful little net, 3¼ in. dia. Can be quickly attached to the rod top to pick a fly from the water.

Price **10**d. each.

RED DEER FAT.

A specially prepared fat for rubbing the reel line. Will float the line a considerable time.

Price **6**d. per tin.

See also "Cerolene" (page 122). **9**d. per tin.

POCKET LINE GREASER.

For fatting the reel line. Price **1/-** each.

KNEE PAD.

Made of grained cowhide, with pad and two straps for buckling on. A great protection when kneeling on wet grass, gravel, or loose sand.

Price **6/-** each.

The "Curate." Regd. 557672.

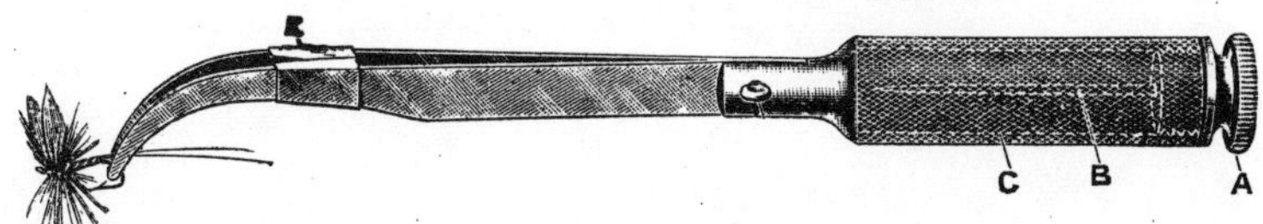

The "Curate" is an ingenious combination of angler's tools, comprising (1) Tweezers, useful as a disgorger or fly holder; (2) Gut Cutter E; (3) Reservoir C, to hold oil for dry flies or reels; (4) Stiletto B, used to apply oil or clean the eye of the fly. The handle is milled as a match striker or small "priest." **Price 6/- each.**

FLY PAD.

A green felt pad (Size, 4½ in. × 2 in.), with leather back and leather pocket to carry Stiletto, fitted with two clip hooks to attach to coat. A handy arrangement for carrying flies, **1/-** each. Stiletto, **1/-** extra.

A luscious spread of British goodies. Tons of the "Curate" were sold for Christmas and "thank-you" gifts and always gladly received for they were easy to lose.

Dry Fly Oil Bottles

EXACT SIZE

WAISTCOAT POCKET FLY OIL BOTTLE

A convenient form for the waistcoat pocket. The interior is fitted with a long sleeve, which prevents the oil flowing back when filled to line mark.

PRICE **1/6** each.

THE "ZEPHYR" POCKET BOTTLE

Specially designed for anglers who use "Zephyr" (see page 99) and similar preparations, which only require the fly to be dipped in the liquid. The stopper is easily detached with one hand, by gripping the glass bottle at the shoulder with the first and second fingers (one on each side of bottle) and pressing the bottom of metal holder with the thumb.

The bottle is thoroughly protected by the metal holder and can be safely carried in the pocket.

PRICE, **1/9** each.

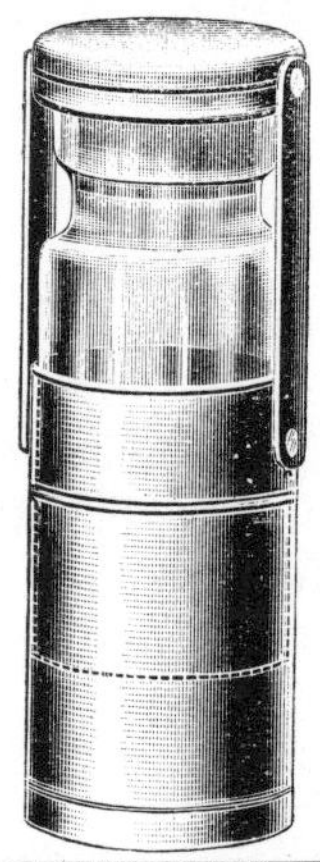
EXACT SIZE

FIG. 1. FIG. 2.

POCKET DRY FLY VAPOURIZER

This vapourizer is of a convenient size, 3 ins. overall, when closed as Fig. 1. In this form the glass reservoir is thoroughly protected by the rubber bulb and the vapourizer can be carried in the pocket. When required for use, hold the bulb firmly in the hand and press against the metal valve, this will start the glass reservoir, when it can be easily grasped and pulled out as far as the stop on its end will allow (see Fig. 2). The glass reservoir should never be filled more than one-third of its capacity.

PRICE **5/-** each.

Refills, Hardy's "Zephyr" Preparation
1/- per bottle
(See page 99).

Hardy's Tweezers, Gut Cutter and Disgorger

(Nickel plated.)

ACTUAL SIZE.

A most useful article for cutting off gut ends and extracting flies from the box. The handle end is formed as a disgorger and turn screw.

Price **2/-** each.

MAGNIFIER

A BOON TO THOSE WITH DEFECTIVE SIGHT.

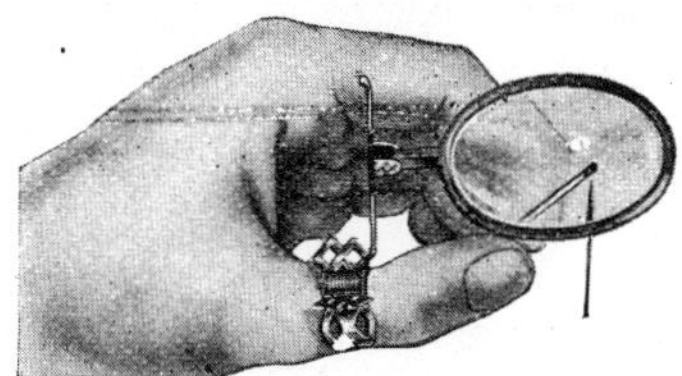

FIG. 1.

A handy form of magnifier fitted with neat clip for attaching to the thumb, whilst threading the gut through the eye of a hook and making the knot.

PRICE, Fig. 1, **2**/- each.

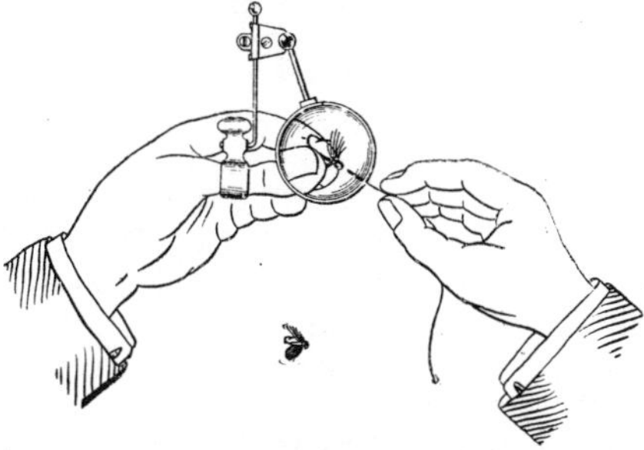

FIG. 2.

Fig. 2, with high power lens, superior finish, **6**/- each.

The thumb clip magnifier is still made, as crude and primitive as ever. On a sunny day one can ignite a cigarette with it—or a thumbnail.

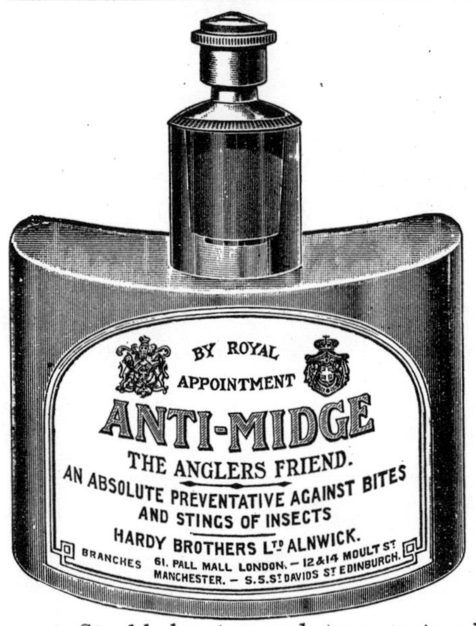

A most excellent compound of essential oils, which we have proved effective on many a midge-infested riverside. It is a clean, healthy preparation, not unpleasant in odour, and has no deleterious effect on the skin. Some form of midge preventative is a necessity for anglers, and this compound does all that is required in most parts. The bottle is of a convenient form to fit the waistcoat pocket, and has a sprinkler stopper. Price **1/-** each.

NOTE.—Where blackfly or mosquitoes abound, it is necessary to have something extra strong, we recommend a mixture of one part Stockholm tar and two parts olive oil. With this we have defeated hosts of mosquitoes. It is not so bad as it seems, and although it naturally browns the face, it is easily washed from the skin.

A New Dry Fly Preparation.

A New Dry Fly Preparation.

This new preparation is made from a secret scientific formula given us by one of the most eminent analytical chemists of the age.

It is perfectly clean, harmless to feathers and wax, and is sweet to use—has no stickiness like the usual dry fly oils, and is an absolute perfect preparation for floating flies. It does not discolour the flies in any way, so that when using this preparation the flies are presented as they should be, giving full effect to all colour instead of, as is the case with all other dry fly preparations, with the colour changed. We recommend all dry fly anglers to give it a trial.

Price **1/-** per bottle.

I have used your new dry fly preparation and find it admirable.

MONMOUTH. B. G. HARVEY.

LONDON AND NORTH BRITISH WORKS, ALNWICK. 111

Silkworm Gut Department

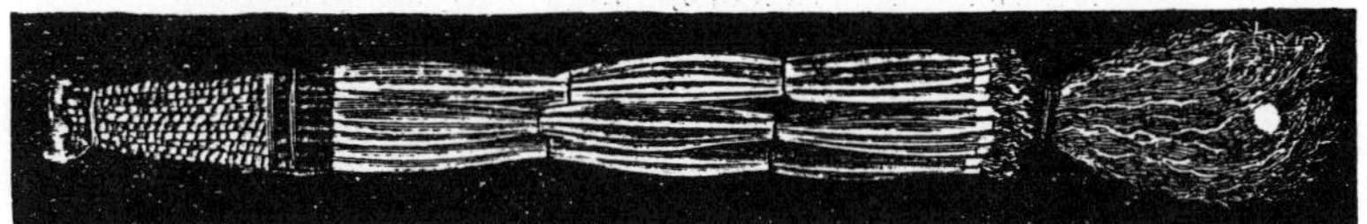

GUARANTEED PURE UNBLEACHED SPANISH "SELECTO" GUT.

Diagram showing the actual Thickness of NATURAL GUT.

Grade	Thickness
"REFINA"	7 to 9 / 1.000
"FINA"	11 to 13 / 1,000
"REGULAR"	13 to 14 / 1,000
PADRON 2ND	14 to 16 / 1,000
PADRON 1ST	15 to 16 / 1,000
MARANA 2ND	16½ to 17½ / 1,000
MARANA 1ST	18 to 19 / 1,000
IMPERIAL	18½ to 19½ / 1,000
ROYAL	20 to 22 / 1,000

As the largest retail importers of Spanish gut in Europe, and actual gut workers in drawing, twisting, plaiting, cast making, etc., we fear no competition either in price or quality. This will be at once apparent when our prices are considered; in doing this, it should be remembered that only the finest Spanish "Selecto" is offered. In casts and drawn gut, quality is our object. We cannot make better. We guarantee that only SPANISH gut is used in our works, and that of the highest quality only.

FOR MOUNTED FLY CASTS, SEE PAGES 104 TO 106.

Hardy's drawn silkworm gut always had a high reputation for strength, partly because their "X" designations were one step larger than those of their competitors; thus, 3X was .007 inch diameter for everyone but Hardy's. Their 3X was .008 inch diameter.

Diagram showing Actual Thickness of our "Diamond" Drawn Gut

Description.

XXXX

XXX

XX

X

½ drawn

¼ drawn

Mounted Sample Cards, showing all thicknesses free.

Good drawn gut can only be produced from clean strands of best Spanish, **and we use no other.** Drawn Gut cannot be expected to last as long as perfect "Refina." The great difficulty in getting perfect fine gut has been overcome by the production of xxx and xxxx, which is drawn by us through **Jewelled** plates. All gut of this class sold by us is our own make, and of the highest possible quality.

453—10 in. long **4/6** per 100.
455—12 ,, **5/6** ,,
449—14 ,, **7/-** ,,
451—16 in. long **8/6** per 100.
452—17 ,, **9/6** ,,

In ordering please state whether x, xx, or xxx is required.

Extra Superior Long Fine "Maravilla" Gut Strands

30 inches, **2/6**; 33 inches, **3/-**; 36 inches, **4/-** per dozen.

Picked "Perfectos" Gut

Selected from the very finest long "Refina" gut, trimmed and stained.

445½—12 in. long **7/-** per 100.
446½—14 ,, **9/-** ,,
445—16 in. long **12/6** per 100.
447—18 ,, **15/6** ,,

Substitute for Gut.

There is no real substitute for gut. A supposed substitute is sold in this country under different fancy names. This material is Japanese twisted silk, dressed with a gum. When the gum washes out, as it is bound to do in use, the real character, "Twisted silk," is seen. In self-defence we stock this material as follows :

	3 yard casts.	1½ yard traces.
Extra Heavy No. 1	**2/6**	**2/6** each.
Heavy No. 2, ,, ,, 3	**2/-**	**2/-** ,,
Medium No. 4, ,, ,, 5	**1/6**	**1/6** ,,
Light No. 6	**1/-**	**1/-** ,,

Hardy's Celebrated Double Taper Trout Fly Lines.

THE "CORONA SUPERBA."

Size at point.	Size at centre.	Size at point.
16	No I.E.I. 21	16
18	No I.D.I. 22	18
18	No I.C.I. 24	18
18	No I.B.I. 25	18

A beautiful soft and pliant line of the highest quality, suitable for either wet or dry fly fishing, made in 35 yard lengths only.

	Size.	Weight.	Price.
Ex. Fine I.E.I.	16 to 21 to 16	0 oz. 9 drms.	**14/6** each.
Fine I.D.I.	18 to 22 to 18	0 oz. 13 drms.	**15/6** ,,
Medium I.C.I.	18 to 24 to 18	0 oz. 15 drms.	**17/6** ,,
Heavy I.B.I.	18 to 25 to 18	1 oz. 3 drms.	**21/-** ,,

Exact sizes and thicknesses are not guaranteed as the dressing sometimes varies.

I have fished a considerable number of your "Corona" lines, and think that the one you sent me last is the best I have used. Kindly send me a second exactly like it.

LONDON. FREDERIC M. HALFORD.

The "Filip" (1911 Model).

Special Tapered Salmon and Trout Fly Lines.

This is an attempt to help the Angler,—to make casting easier and more accurate. These are desirable objects, and we are glad to say that with the kind co-operation of the late Philip F. Ch. Trench, Esq., of Dublin, we evolved *this* the latest thing in fly lines.

Roughly, the idea is, that a longer foreline can be thrown when "shooting," owing to the special form of back taper, and the fact that the principal weight of the line is nearer the fly. Thus a longer line can be "shot," with a comparatively short casting line; a consideration when in difficult places, with bushes, etc., behind.

The same idea has been carried out in trout *dry fly* lines. Here accurate casting is absolutely necessary. For this work they are a great help, as they "shoot" most perfectly, and make continuous casting less tiring.

The quality of silk, dressing and finish is the same as the "Corona" and "Corona Superba" lines, beautifully soft and supple.

No. 1. Salmon,	40 and 50 yds.	suitable for rods,	16 to 18 ft.	**25/-** each.
No. 2. ,,	40 ,, 50 ,,	,,	15 and 16 ft.	**25/-** ,,
No. 1. Trout,	35 ,,	,,	10 ft. 3 in. to 11 ft.	**15/-** ,,
No. 2. ,,	35 ,,	,,	9 and 10 ft.	**15/-** ,,

Level "Corona" Salmon Fly Lines.

No. 3.

No. 4.

No. 5.

No. 6.

No. 7.

Beautifully soft and supple. Made of the very best silk, dressed and finished similar to the "Corona" double tapered fly lines. Made in 50 yard lengths only.

No. 3.	Suitable for 17 ft. rods, ...	**25/6** each.
No. 4.	,, 16 ft. ,, ...	**22/-** ,,
No. 5.	,, 15 ft. ,, ...	**19/6** ,,
No. 6.	,, 14 ft. ,, ...	**17/6** ,,
No. 7.	,, 13 ft. ,, ...	**12/6** ,,

The "Reliance" Waterproof Spinning Line

These lines are dressed in an entirely new preparation of our own invention; they are second only to our "Alnwick."

Price per Score Yds.	No.		B.W.G.
2/6	1.		22
3/-	2.		21
3/3	3.		20

Made in 60, 80 and 100 yard lengths. The Nos. 2 and 3 are most suitable for salmon, pike, etc. The No. 1 for fine spinning or bottom fishing.

The "Solidae," Best Plaited Undressed Silk Lines.

No. 000.	Gossamer	**6**d.	per score yards.
No. 00.	Ex-fine	**7**d.	,, ,,
No. 0.	Fine	**9**d:	,, ,,
No. 1.	For Roach	**1/-**	,, ,,
No. 2.	For Bream and Chub... ...	**1/4**	,, ,,
No. 3.	For Barbel and Pike	**1/6**	,, ,,
No. 4.	For Pike, Salmon, Mahseer, etc.	**1/8**	,, ,,

DAPPING LINES.

Extra loose plaited undressed silk, specially made for Blow Line Fishing, **1/6** per score yards.

☞ The most perfect preparation for spinning and dry fly lines. It is non-adhesive, clean to handle, keeps the line pliant, in good order, and has great floating power.

This preparation may be melted and undressed lines steeped in it for half an hour, then drawn through a cloth to remove the surplus dressing, when they are ready for immediate use.

PRICE,
9d. PER TIN.

The "Cerolene" has made my sticky line work most satisfactory; it has a wonderful waterproofing quality.
F. M. WAINWRIGHT, Kistna.

Pocket Line Greaser, **1/-** each. See page 96.

128 HARDY BROTHERS LTD.,

Hardy's Patent "Perfect" Fly Reel

MADE OF "ALUMIN."

Without doubt the lightest and most perfect Fly Reel the world has ever seen—Ball Bearings and Regulating Check.

No.	Sizes. in.	Prices. £	s.	d.	Approximate Weights. ozs.
416	3	1	10	0	6¼
417	3¼	1	12	6	7½
418	3½	1	15	0	8¼
419	3¾	2	2	6	11¾
420	4	2	6	0	13½
421	4¼	2	12	6	17

No.	Sizes. in.	Prices. £	s.	d.	Approximate Weights. ozs.
422	4½	2	15	6	18½
423	4¾	3	0	0	20
424	5	3	5	0	22
425	5¼	3	15	0	24
425A	6	5	0	0	28

For 2⅞ size see page 132.

Illustration shows the patent revolving line guard as applied to salmon reels ; for trout reels with this guard see page 133.

Patent Revolving Line Guard to Salmon Reels, 3½ ins. and upwards, **7/6** extra.

All the Hardy Perfect reels sent into the U.S. market that I have ever seen had beautiful, big, hand-cut agate line guides that were, however, fragile. A proud customer who boasted of Hardy's workmanship—"the four pieces of the line guide are fitted so closely you can scarcely see the joints"—was downcast when the clerk at Folsom's told him the guide was supposed to be just one piece.

Hardy's New Compensating Check

Pat. No. 24245.

Most anglers have experienced annoyance, by the check work of a reel sticking at some time or other. This has hitherto been due to the absence of **elasticity** in the arrangement, the tongue being a fixture. The possibility of sticking is now happily overcome by our new method, which is perfectly elastic, and allows the tongue to move freely in any direction.

The above diagram shows the tongue, or pawl, held under a strong steel bridge, on the under side of which is a steel peg, on which the check works. The pawl is slotted as shown by the interior dotted lines. The outer dotted lines show the path of the check, while working in the direction of E or D. It will be clearly seen, that the slot allows the check to move at any angle from C to B, while at the same time it can rise or fall, under pressure of spring F, and so take up wear and tear; or may rise away from the wheel in case of any irregularity, and so **prevent any possibility of locking**. The spring F keeps the pawl to its work, but allows it to rise should any excessive pressure be applied. The form of the spring gives a pleasant light and fine check when winding in. When the drum is turned in the direction of the arrow D (as when a fish takes line), the check can be regulated to almost any stiffness, by turning the screw of the regulator H, which forces arm G to compress spring F, and give the required pressure.

This important improvement calls for no comment, as the immense advantage is at once apparent, and must appeal to all.

The illustration shown is the exact size of the interior of our $4\frac{1}{4}$ in. "Perfect" salmon reels. We fit all our fly reels, down to and including the "Uniqua" quality (which latter, however, has not the regulator), with this improved check work.

HARDY'S
Patent No. 2 "Silex" Casting Reel

Illustration shows the No. 2 "Silex" reel which is now acknowledged to be the climax and perfection of all reels used for bait casting.

Since its introduction, we have received hundreds of testimonials from clients, expressing the greatest satisfaction.

The great ease and comfort with which even the most moderate performer may (with the aid of this reel) place his bait wherever his fancy may direct, must be seen to be appreciated.

CAUTION.— Imitations of our original "Silex" now being offered by dealers under various fancy names.— As the "No. 2 Silex" is so vast an improvement on our old "Silex" (now discarded), we need hardly caution purchasers against these inferior imitations of an obsolete article.

I tried the 4 in. "Silex" No. 2 reel yesterday, and after about two or three casts could easily send all the line out. I never had an overrun. It is just what I wanted.

York, *Dec. 4th*, 1913. J. MELROSE.

Hardy's "Eureka" Reel

FOR ALL KINDS OF BOTTOM FISHING; ROACH, CHUB, PERCH, BARBEL, GRAYLING, &c.

This reel has been designed to meet the requirements necessary for the up-to-date Bottom angler, and is pronounced by several experts who have used it to be the most perfect reel yet devised for the work.

It is made of our Alumin, the outside diameter being $3\frac{1}{2}$ inches, the width between plates $\frac{13}{16}$ inch. The form is "contracted," the drum being specially designed for very quick recovery of the line. The bearings are of phosphor bronze, the spindle being of finest tool steel with latch fastener. The check-work is our new patented design, similar to the new "Nottingham" reel on page 148. The ratchet is carried on a lever which rises and falls, and so overcomes any possibility of locking in the wheel, as on the least irregularity the lever rises and frees it. The action of throwing the check out of or into gear is effected by the lever A projecting from the rim, which can be operated by the forefinger without altering the position of the hand in fishing.

The rim is cut away for about half the circumference, so that the drum may be governed by the forefinger or thumb when casting direct from the reel, or trotting a float. The drum is exceptionally light and permits a small float to draw line and travel without causing the slightest drag.

All Bottom anglers who like the best gear should provide themselves with one of these, which will greatly enhance their sport.

Size $3\frac{1}{2}$ in. Price, **25**/- each.

This reel is also made specially for roach fishing, without the lever check, at **5**/- less.

Plain "Nottingham" Reels

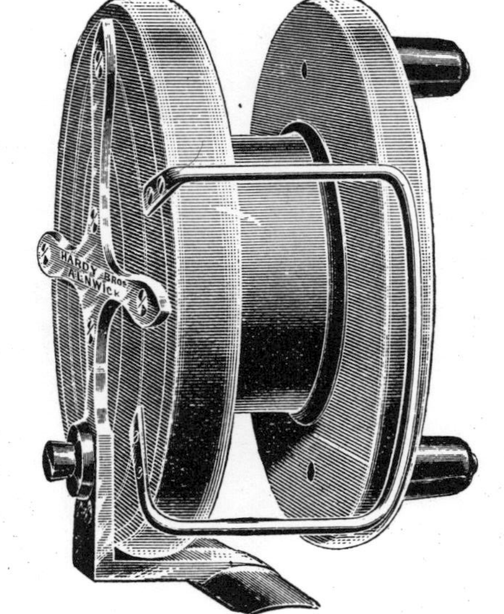

These are good sound reels at a low price. They are made of seasoned wood with brass star back, steel optional check worked with knob on back; steel spindle, ratchet wheel and tongue. The handles are horn with brass bearings.

The sizes up to $4\frac{1}{2}$ inches are suitable for river work, spinning from the reel in the usual "Nottingham" style. The $4\frac{1}{2}$ in. and 5 in. make good cheap trolling or sea reels.

Sizes	3 in.	$3\frac{1}{2}$ in.	4 in.	$4\frac{1}{2}$ in.	5 in.
Prices	**6/6**	**7/6**	**8/6**	**9/6**	**11/6**

I have delayed writing to acknowledge the receipt of the 1912 pattern "Nottingham" reel, as I wished to try it first and let you know the result. I was fishing on Saturday, and I was astonished and delighted at the ease with which I was able to cast quite long distances with a light "Swallowtail" bait. After a few minutes I felt quite at home with the reel, and astonished my two fishing companions who had seen my previous poor efforts at casting from the reel. The finish and workmanship are perfect, and I must thank you very much for adding so greatly to my pleasure. I need hardly say I shall have great pleasure in recommending it to all and sundry, as it fully deserves.

I hope one day to be the proud possessor of one of your metal "Silex" No. 2 reels.

Dublin. E. PALMER.

Best Solid Leather Reel Cases

LINED WITH VELVET.

FOR "PERFECT" REELS.

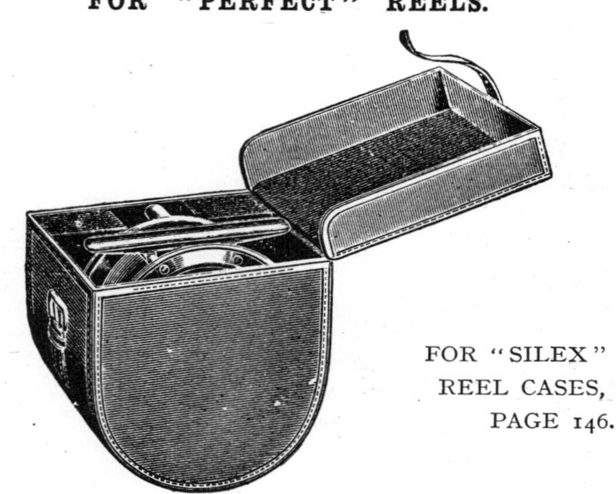

FOR "SILEX" No. 2 REEL CASES, SEE PAGE 146.

For $2\frac{7}{8}$ in. Reel	...	**9**s. **6**d.	For $3\frac{3}{4}$ in. Reel	...	**11**s. **6**d.
,, 3 in. ,,	...	**9**s. **6**d.	,, $3\frac{7}{8}$ in. ,,	...	**12**s. **6**d.
,, $3\frac{1}{8}$ in. ,,	...	**10**s. **0**d.	,, 4 in. ,,	...	**12**s. **6**d.
,, $3\frac{1}{4}$ in. ,,	...	**10**s. **0**d.	,, $4\frac{1}{4}$ in. ,,	...	**13**s. **0**d.
,, $3\frac{3}{8}$ in. ,,	...	**10**s. **6**d.	,, $4\frac{1}{2}$ in. ,,	...	**13**s. **6**d.
,, $3\frac{1}{2}$ in. ,,	...	**10**s. **6**d.	,, $4\frac{3}{4}$ in. ,,	...	**15**s. **0**d.
,, $3\frac{5}{8}$ in. ,,	...	**11**s. **6**d.	,, 5 in. ,,	...	**16**s. **0**d.

SELVYT REEL BAGS.

Where a case is not used these are indispensable.

Prices:

For reels $2\frac{1}{2}''$ to $3\frac{3}{8}''$	-	**2/6**
,, $3\frac{1}{2}''$ to $3\frac{3}{4}''$	-	**2/6**
,, $4''$ to $4\frac{1}{2}''$	-	**2/9**

Mr. Geen's Patent "Corkscrew" Sand-Eel Spinners

(SOLE MANUFACTURERS.)

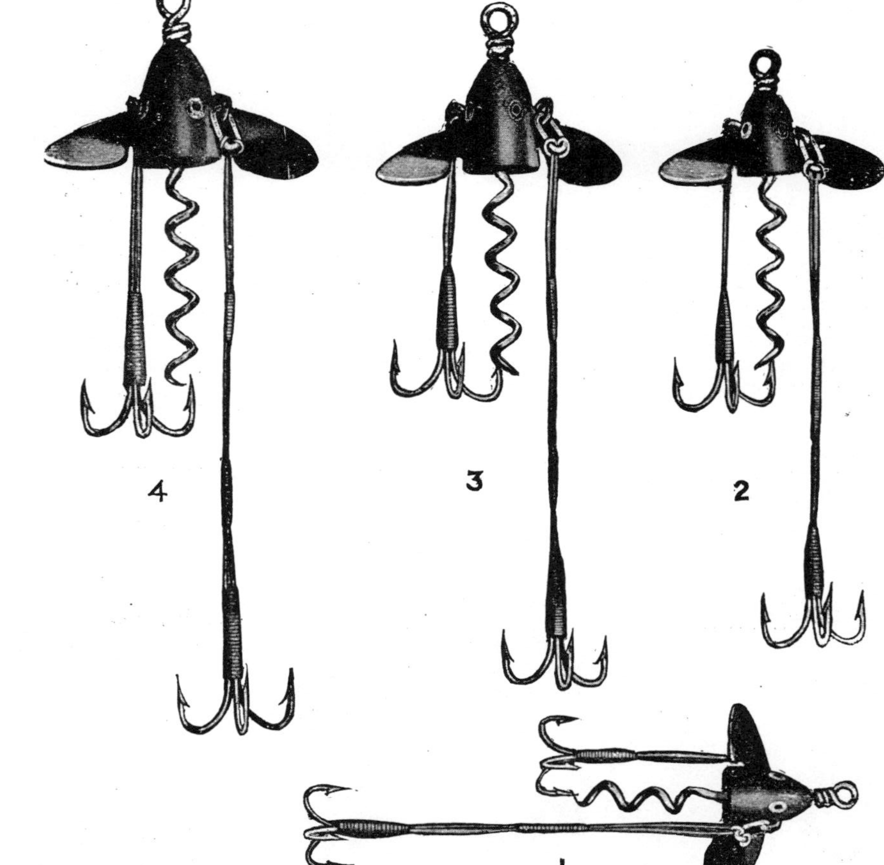

These Spinners, the invention of Philip Geen, Esq., are an excellent idea. The Sand-Eel, after cutting, is turned on the screw until it comes up against the head with back up. The hooks are tied down and all is ready.

Prices, No.	1.	2.	3.	4.
	1/6	**1/9**	**1/9**	**2/-**

All mounts for use with Sand-Eels are worthy of note, as during the close season, March 15th to June 15th, when fresh water baits may not be sold, Sand-Eels cut to proper length make an excellent substitute for minnows, and kill well.

FOR PRESERVED SAND-EELS SEE PAGE 169.

170 HARDY BROTHERS LTD.,

Worms (Pinktails)

IN BAGS, SCOURED AND PACKED IN MOSS.

One Gross, **1/9**; 2 Gross, **3/-**; Post Paid.

One day's notice is required if ordered from Alnwick, London, or Manchester, as these are procured from our Edinburgh House. They may be had by return, if ordered direct from our Edinburgh House, 5 South St. David Street.

Exact size of tin.

These sprats are procured abroad, where they are fatter and better than those procured in this country. They are preserved in a special manner, and will keep bright for years in any climate.

The tins contain 9 to 12 of the large sized sprats, and from 15 to 24 as the sprats get smaller.

This manner of packing makes them more suitable for carrying, as there is no fear of broken glass or leakage.

From our experience with trout, salmon, pike, and sea fish, we believe these sprats to be one of the very best baits when mounted on suitable tackle.

Clients who have used them in India speak very highly of them as Mahseer baits.

SPRATS FOR SALMON AND SEA TROUT—3 to 3½ ins.
SPRATS FOR SALMON AND PIKE—4 to 4½ ins. } Price, **1/3** per tin.

So Hardy's once sold live worms! Well, Halford's autobiography reveals that he once wrote a stirring defense of worm fishermen for some magazine.

The "Hardy" Phantom

Pat. No. 22,000.

FIG. 1.

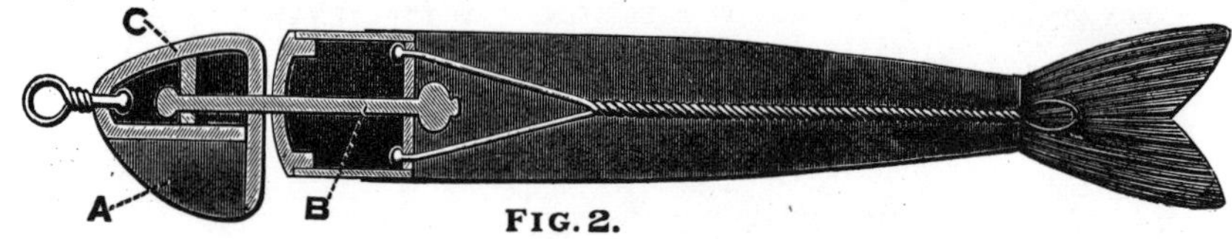

FIG. 2.

As far back as we can remember, anglers have exercised their minds in the difficult task of how to prevent *kink* and *twist* in spinning lines, due to the revolution of the bait.

Swivelled traces are not all they seem, as a very light tension, produced by a heavy bait, or one with large flanges in a quick stream, soon locks the swivels.

" Anti-kink " leads have been devised, and although excellent, they only tackle the trouble after it has been produced. " Prevention is better than cure," and our method in this bait is to *prevent the creation of* this twist, and is most effectual.

The head is not an integral part of the bait, but is only attached to it by the strong swivel pin B, as may be seen in Fig. 2, which is a section of the arrangement. B, the pin referred to, holds the head to the body. C is the metal frame work of head. A, the lower lead part of the head, is virtually the KEEL. When the bait is drawn through the water, this keel A comes into position as shown on illustration and remains so.

KINK, the " Bete Noir " of the spinner, does not exist, while the appearance of the bait is very natural.

The construction of the body is the same as the " Ideal " phantom, page 197, *i.e.* lead centre with cork and silk covering.

We are only able to produce these Phantoms in the following sizes :

Sizes in inches,	2½	3	3½.
Price - -	**3/6**	**3/6**	**4/6.**

COLOURS.—Blue and Silver, Brown and Gold, and Gudgeon Colour.

LONDON AND NORTH BRITISH WORKS, ALNWICK. 211

Fig. 8.
SECTION OF BAMBOO.

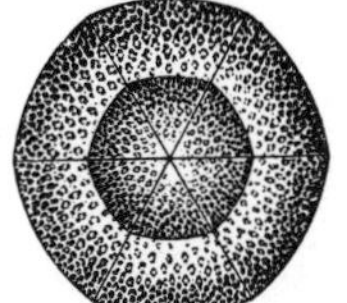

Fig. 9.
SINGLE BUILT.

Fig. 10.
DOUBLE BUILT.

Fig. 11.
DOUBLE-BUILT STEEL CENTRE BEFORE CEMENTING.

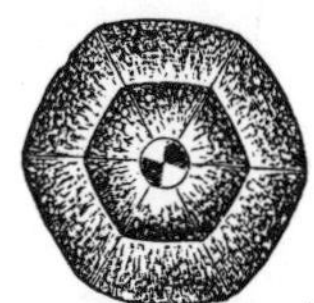

Fig. 11.
DOUBLE-BUILT STEEL CENTRE AFTER CEMENTING.

Fig. 12.
SINGLE-BUILT OCTAGONAL BEFORE CEMENTING.

Fig. 12.
SINGLE-BUILT OCTAGONAL AFTER CEMENTING.

Fig. 13.
DOUBLE-BUILT STEEL CENTRE NONAGONAL BEFORE CEMENTING.

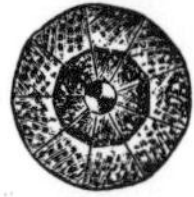

Fig. 13.
DOUBLE-BUILT STEEL CENTRE NONAGONAL AFTER CEMENTING.

SECTIONS OF RODS.

NOTE.—Hitherto it has been our custom to call split-bamboo rods " Cane-built rods." This is an error, as bamboo is not cane : it belongs to the family of grasses. In future they will be called " Split-bamboo."

In 1914 the British began "muddling through" a world war at frightful cost; but these pages show them already muddling through the technical problems of rod-building, with closed minds and mutton-headed obstinacy. Double-building adds nothing but weight and labor. The center of a rod does no work and the rod would be better without it; when better adhesives became available, highly successful hollow bamboo rods were made—in America. Double-building, steel centers or ribbing, and eight- and nine-strip construction were worse than worthless "selling points."

The "Halford" Rod Joints

(MODEL 1913.)

Patent applied for.

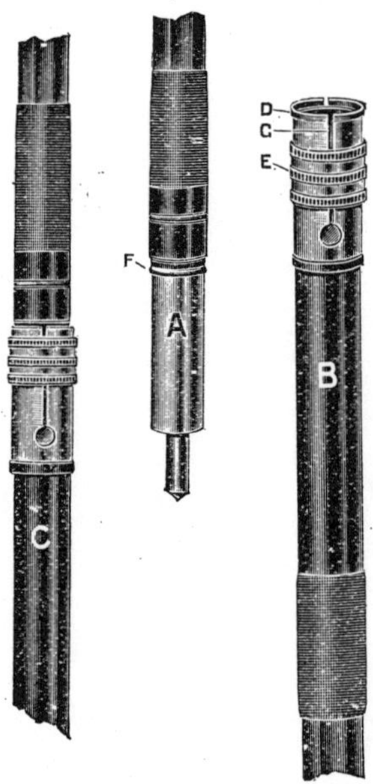

These joints are fitted only to the "Halford" 1912 model Dry Fly Rod for stock. They are simple, light and a perfect lock. Fig. C is the joint closed, and shows the two portions locked together for work. Fig. A shews the male and B the female portions. It will be noticed that on A there is a raised ring F. On B the sleeve E is drawn back to show slot G and curved lip D. When A is pushed home, the spring portion of the outer ferrule jumps over the ring F, when E should be pushed up to receive it.

These joints may be had fitted to any of our split bamboo rods at the following prices extra to the "Lockfast" joint prices as listed: 15 to 18 ft., 3-pce. rods, 2 tops, **10/-**; 10 to 14 ft., 3-pce. rods, 2 tops, **8/6**; 2-pce. rods, 1 top, **5/-**; with 2 tops, **7/6**.

EXTRACT from "The Dry Fly Man's Handbook," by F. M. HALFORD:

I have tried this arrangement for some days, and consider it is the best lock-fast fitting I have ever used. I cannot see any weak point in it, and think it should prove a decided boon to the dry fly man.

216 HARDY BROTHERS LTD.,

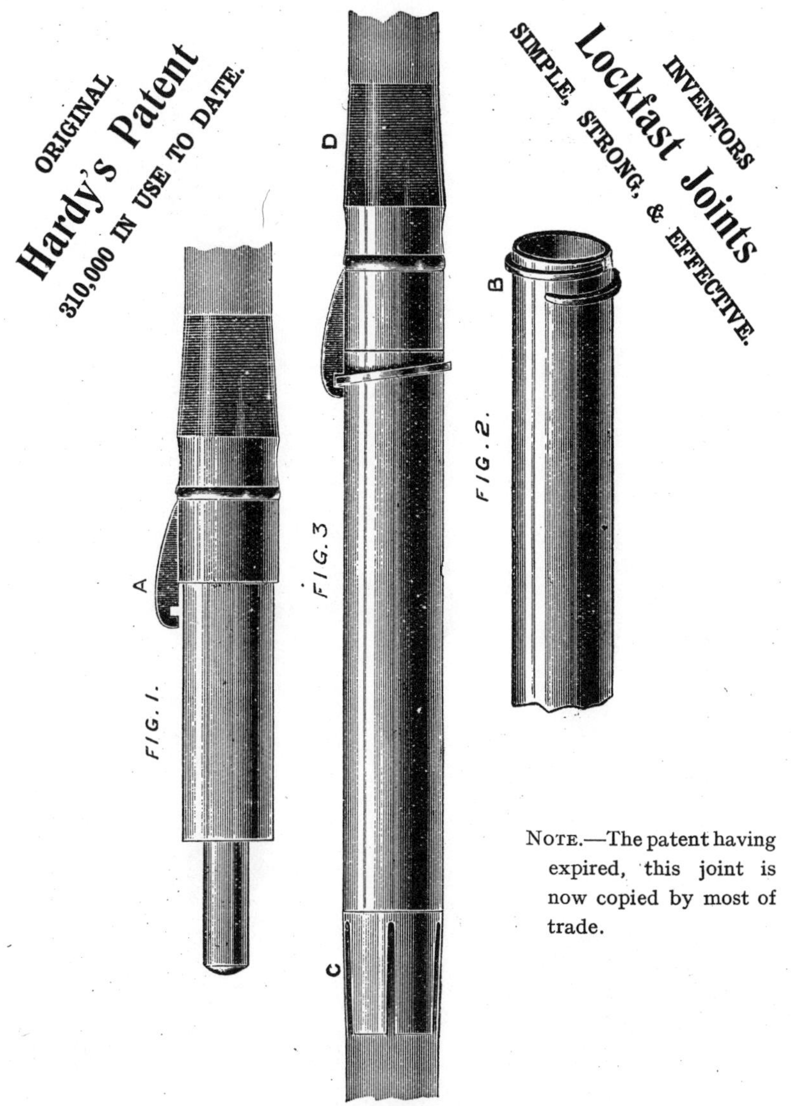

Fig. 3 is the joint fixed, the continuation and splint ends of ferrule are shown at C before binding, and at D as finished. Fig. 2 is the female part of joint before fixing, showing spiral B. Fig. 1 being the male part, showing hook at A.

To fix the joint Fig. 1 is pushed into B, when A engages with B and half a turn closes. The reverse action forces the joint apart.

The joints are metal lined and thoroughly waterproof.

" HARDY'S Special Lockfast Ferrule is the best fastening yet invented, in our opinion."—*Fishing Gazette.*

" These joints are undoubtedly an excellent invention, and as Messrs. HARDY BROTHERS fit them to their rods our readers cannot do better than apply to this well-known Northumberland firm."—*Land and Water.*

Dozens of screw-thread, snap-catch, latch, and other types of "lockfast" mechanical fastenings to keep British ferrules from coming apart were the price paid by this stolid British refusal to learn to make and fit a simple, light, efficient friction ferrule. Even today they don't entirely trust the miscalled "suction ferrule."

Hardy's Original
"Weeger" Universal Winch Fitting

(Now copied by all the trade.)

This fitting has great strength, extreme simplicity and adaptability. They have now been in use for thirty years, and have given every satisfaction. This is the original " Universal " Winch Fitting, given us by the late Dr. Weeger, of Brünn.

For New "SCREW GRIP FITTING," see page 218.

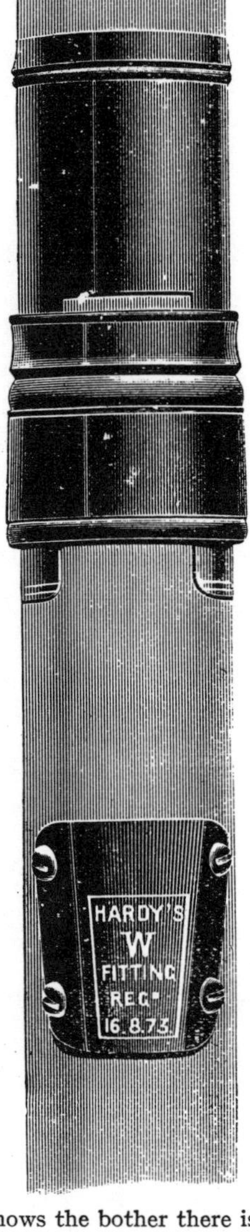

HARDY'S PATENT

Combined Spear and Butt Cap

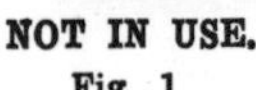

NOT IN USE.
Fig. 1.

IN USE.
Fig. 2.

Every fisherman who uses a rod with a spear to it, knows the bother there is often with the ordinary screw in spear. Left in the bag, or in the drawer at home—in fact, not there when wanted—and when there, always a chance of losing the part which is out of use. This simple plan, as shown above, completely solves the problem.

Fitted to any new rod ordered, 5/- extra.
,, to old rods .. .. 8/6 extra.

Fishing Gazette.—" An ingenious and useful arrangement."

Well over a century ago, the classic British chalk streams were fished with live insects on gossamer silk, wind-carried "blow lines." So the trees were cut back from the riverbank a hundred feet or more to give the wind full, even sweep. Today, the typical chalk stream bank has only an occasional low bush behind which the angler must kneel for cover; hence the kneepad. And since the angler may have to wait hours for a rise to develop, and no tree handy against which to lean his rod, the removable or collapsible butt spear enables him to stand his rod upright and safe on the turf. It is not intended, as some light-minded American types insist, to repel the charge of an infuriated trout.

233 HARDY BROTHERS LTD.,

Important Testimonial

Dear Sirs,

Some eight years ago, when fishing at Inchnadamp, as we were starting off from the place where the Boats are moored, which is in the River Loanan, the ghillie having laid my rod with the point projecting over the stern, the butt on the middle seat, with the reel downwards, a gust of wind caught the boat and sent her quickly across the narrow river, the point of my rod going into the bank, the butt being held fast by the reel against the seat. The bank was hard and the result was that the rod top was doubled backwards upon itself, into approximately the above condition. Of course I thought the rod was "done," but upon examination I found that the cane was uninjured and even the varnish uncracked. I straightened it out as best I could and for a time it had a bit of a "kink" but this gradually disappeared, and it is quite straight now. I am still using the rod, a "Palakona" Split-Bamboo of 11 ft., and I do not think you have ever had it back even for revarnishing. At the time I thought of sending you a description of the incident, but was afraid of being put down as an inventor of yarns, but "a fact is a fact for all that."

You are quite at liberty to use this as a testimonial of the undoubted quality of your "Palakona" Split-Bamboo Rods. Pontefract, Nov. 22nd, 1912. Yours very truly, T.B.

N.B.—ILLUSTRATION IS EXACT SIZE OF POINT OF TOP PIECE.

Some might say that such a rod was worthless. Still it was once a popular American fallacy that a good rod should permit bending until its ends touched, without breaking. W. C. Prime, W. H. H. Murray, and other fishing writers of their era told about "giving the butt" to a big fish until the tip guide rattled against the bars of the reel.

The "Fairchild" Rods

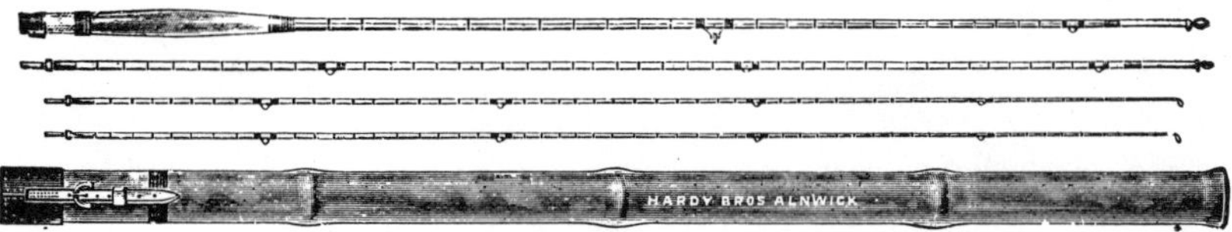

In three pieces, "**PALAKONA**" split-bamboo, with two tops, cork-covered handle, plain suction joints. "Snake" intermediate, with Agate butt and end rings. In bamboo protector, which carries the whole rod.

Weights—	$3\frac{1}{4}$ ozs.	4 ozs.	$4\frac{3}{4}$ ozs.	PRICE **£5 5**s. **0**d.
Lengths—	8 ft.	9 ft.	9 ft. 6 ins.	

These rods were originally designed and made for S. W. Fairchild, Esq., of New York, where they are in great favour. They are very light, at the same time powerful enough to kill large trout.

The rods which you have made for me have given the very greatest satisfaction. I have taken at one cast two one-pound Rainbows and had no trouble in landing them both. There is so much pleasure in using a light rod in casting for trout, as you need only use your wrist. *You make the best rods in the world.*

New York, U.S.A. S. W. FAIRCHILD.

The "Casting Club de France" $2\frac{3}{4}$oz. Rod

THE LIGHTEST PRACTICAL FISHING ROD IN THE WORLD.

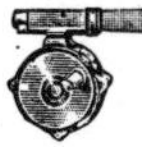

7 feet in two pieces, "**PALAKONA**" split-bamboo with one top, cork-covered handle suction joint, snake intermediate, with Agate butt and end ring. Price £**3 3**s. **0**d.

8 feet, weight $3\frac{3}{4}$ ozs.; 9 feet, weight, $4\frac{3}{4}$ ozs. PRICE £**3 3**s. **0**d.

PRINCE PIERRE D'ARENBURG writes: "I tried the little 'C.C.F.' rod yesterday in a gale of wind. It worked beautifully, and I am quite pleased with it. I do not think it possible, to build a rod with more power of such light weight."

REMARKABLE FLY-CASTING.—WORLD'S LIGHTEST FISHING ROD.

(*Extract from "Fishing Gazette."*)

Some extraordinary fly-casting was witnessed yesterday morning at the Tir aux Pigeons in the Bois de Boulogne, Paris, where a tournament is being held under the auspices of the Casting Club of France. Mr. John James Hardy, British champion salmon and trout fly caster, gave an exhibition of fly-casting, for which he used what is probably the *lightest fishing rod in the world.* It is made of "Palakona" bamboo, 7 ft. in length, and weighs only $2\frac{3}{4}$ oz. With this rod Mr. Hardy cast *twenty-five yards*, which is much further than the average cast of an expert fisherman using a rod three times this weight.

Hardy's "New Zealand" Gaff

The gaff is elongating, and when fully extended measures over 4 feet. To bring it into use, the wire clip A is pushed over the hook towards the point, the gaff withdrawn from the carrier and thrown out sharply, when it will fully extend. The hook cannot turn in the handle, as the shank is square. One hand only is necessary to manipulate it. The end is leaded, and may be used as a "Priest."

PRICE - 20/-.

With Sling complete.

Weight about 18 ounces.

Hardy's "Lash On" Gaff

WITH IMPROVED CARRIER.

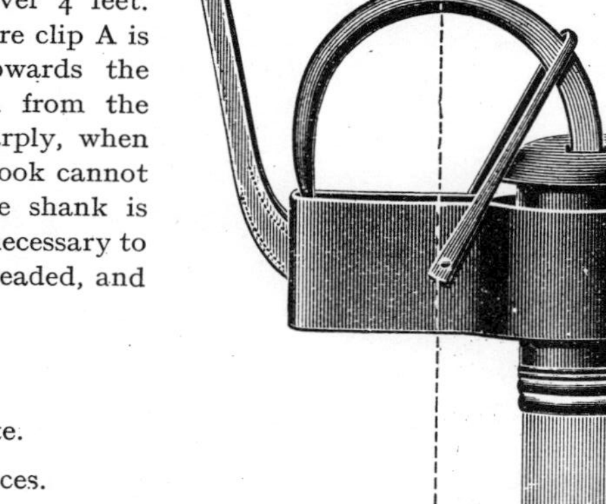

Illustration shows a long handled "Lash-on" gaff with a very simple and secure method of carrying. The gaff can be carried in position as illustrated, or upside down. In this latter position the shaft is passed through ring at B and the strap wound round shaft at A. To release the gaff when in position, as illustrated, pull strap at A off button and push gaff upwards, when it will release at clip B. When in second position, pull strap at A off button, and gaff handle will slide down out of ring at B.

The gaff consists of a best quality steel fluted hook attached to a 4 feet handle.

Price, complete with carrying attachment, **14/6** each.

Hardy's Combined Gaff and Wading Staff

A most useful article, originally designed for our own use. It is indispensable when wading on rough ground, or where the angler, after hooking his fish, requires to leave the water quickly, as it acts as a third leg. It may be carried in the hand as a staff, when fastened by the leather strap over the shoulder (as shown in dotted lines). After wading into position, it should be allowed to hang by the strap, until that part of the cast is fished, when it can be taken in the hand to make the next step, and so on. The staff is also useful to gauge the depth in coloured water. The strap can be adjusted, so that the gaff may also be worn over the shoulder, as shown in illustration A to B, when it is quite out of the way. In either position it can easily be detached with one hand by pressing the scissor clip at A or C.

Very strongly made, with a well-shaped hook, fitted with spring steel point protector. The shaft can also be used as a landing net handle. Length over all 4 ft. 9 in.

PRICE **21/-**.

TELESCOPIC SALMON GAFFS.

Best Tempered Steel, with Brass Slides and Rosewood Handles.

644—Three Joints ... ... square **17/-**.
645—Two ,, ... ,, **13/-**.

STEEL GAFF HOOK (Salmon) to screw into Handle **3/6** each.
,, ,, (Plated) ... **4/6** ,,
,, to lash on Handle ... **6/-** ,,
,, ,, (Plated) ... **7/-** ,,

For Trout and Pike (small size with screw) **3/-** each.
,, ,, (Plated) ... **4/-** ,,

LONDON AND NORTH BRITISH WORKS, ALNWICK. 372

Hardy's "Sensitive" Boom

(PATENT.)

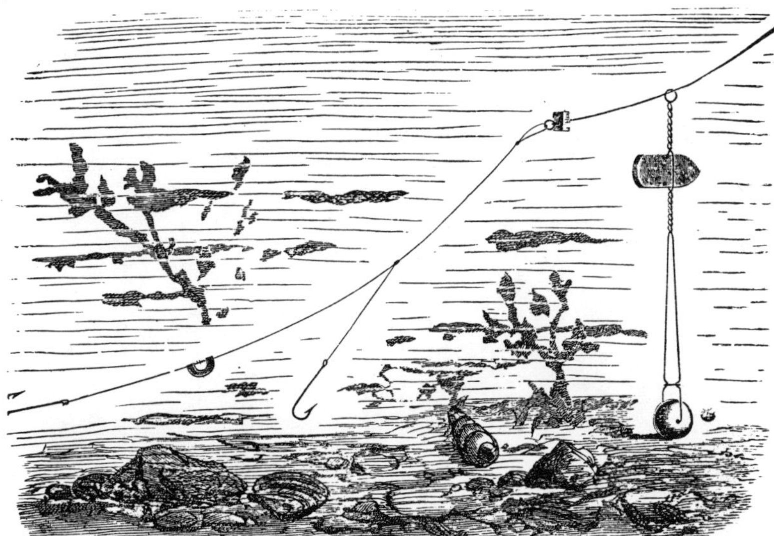

This tackle is suitable for all kinds of bottom fishing in River, Lake, or Sea. By an ingenious arrangement the leads can be exchanged in a moment, and a light one substituted for a heavy one, or *vice versa*, according to the weight of the tide or stream. It is the simplest and quickest thing of the kind ever devised. The cork float always keeps the hooks clear of the bottom, so that the baits may be seen, instead of being buried in the sand as in most ledgers.

F. G. Aflalo says: "It is a very clever tackle."

No. 1.—Light Boom with wire and strong gut cast mounted as in diagram, for river work, carries leads $\frac{3}{8}$ to $\frac{1}{2}$ oz. **1/1**

,, 2.— Do., heavy, river or light sea fishing, carries leads $\frac{3}{4}$ to 1 oz. **1/1**

,, 3.—Med. do., Sea Leads, $1\frac{1}{2}$ to 2 ozs. **1/3**

,, 4.—Large do., Sea, 3 to 4 oz. **1/4**

Spare Gut Cast, mounted with two hooks and lead, as in diagram ... ... **6**d. each.

Drilled bullets—

Weight,	$\frac{1}{4}$ oz.	$\frac{1}{2}$ oz.	$\frac{3}{4}$ oz.	$1\frac{1}{2}$ oz.	2 ozs.	3 ozs.	4 ozs.
Price,	**9**d.	**10**d.	**1/-**	**1/3**	**1/6**	**2/-**	**2/6** per doz.

IN ORDERING FROM THIS LIST PLEASE QUOTE LETTER X.

There are ferocious tidal currents along some British coasts and ingenious rigs are required to fish them. And in inland waters, bottom fishing for coarse fish is more highly developed than dry-fly fishing for trout.

The "Squire" Rig

FOR SANDY BOTTOMS.

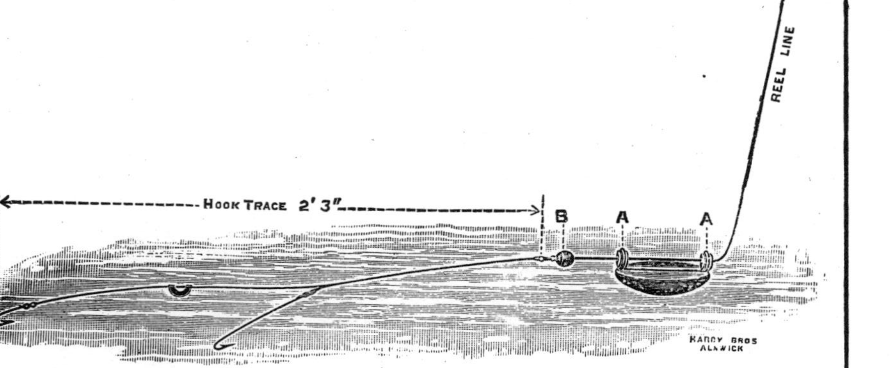

The advantages are: (1) the smallest nibble is at once indicated; (2) the lightest tackle can be used; (3) the hooks never get entangled with the lead in casting; (4) the hook trace does not twist in casting; (5) it permits instant striking without moving the lead.

TO MOUNT.—Thread the reel line through porcelain eyes A A on lead, then through the rubber buffer B, and attach to swivel on trace.

In fishing, the lead anchors in the sand, leaving the baits free to thoroughly search the bottom, as they move about with the current, line being let out as may be required.

PRICES.—Complete rig, including lead, buffer and 2 ft. 3 in. gut trace, with two hooks and "Simplex" lead, as per illustration.

2 oz., **1/2**; 4 oz., **1/3**; 6 oz., **1/4**; 8 oz., **1/5**; 10 oz., **1/6** each.

Leads only } 2 oz., **5**d.; 4 oz., **6**d.; 6 oz., **7**d.; 8 oz., **8**d.; 10 oz., **9**d. each.

Buffer and Trace only, **9**d. each.

704 S. **THE "NEWHAVEN" CREEL.**

Strongly and neatly made of green willows, with strong cross bar, hand hole and lid.

SMALL.	LARGE.
7 in. × 8 in. × 15 in., **5/6**.	9 in. × 11 in. × 20 in., **7/6**.

LANDING NET.

970—Oval Hickory Head, 22 in. × 16 in. inside, fitted with suitable net and stout fixed shaft, **15/-** each.

515½—Gaff Hook, wood shaft, as illustration, **3/6** each; with bamboo handle, **1/6** each.

Patent Sensitive Spreaders

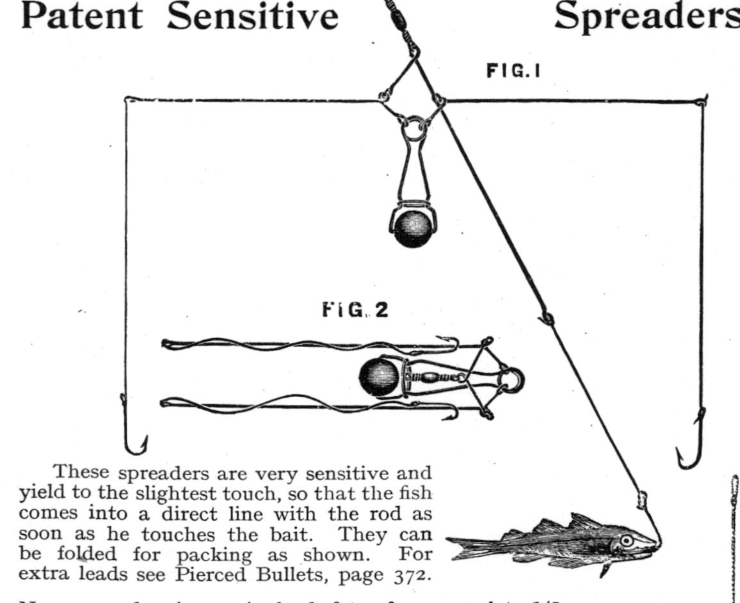

These spreaders are very sensitive and yield to the slightest touch, so that the fish comes into a direct line with the rod as soon as he touches the bait. They can be folded for packing as shown. For extra leads see Pierced Bullets, page 372.

No. 1	spread 14 in.	carries leads $\frac{3}{4}$ to $1\frac{3}{4}$ oz.	complete	**1/8**
No. 2	,, 17 in.	,, 2 to 4 oz.	,,	**1/9**
No. 3	,, 20 in.	,, 3 to 7 oz.	,,	**2/-**

St. Leonard's Sea Tackle and Special Anchor Lead.

The illustration shows the form of tackle which is in use at St. Leonards-on-Sea. It is there used by throwing out from the shore or pier. The two traces C B and A B form one continuous line of four hooks. The special shape of the lead D causes it to anchor in the sand. When used from a boat, the two portions of the trace are as shown in the sketch, and in this way the bottom baits take the bottom feeding fish, and the upper ones the mid-water fish. The arrangement of the clip for holding is of such a nature that leads of varying weights can be exchanged quickly.

Prices complete—

With 4 oz. lead, **1/3**; 6 oz., **1/4**; 8 oz., **1/6**.

Leads separate with Attachment:
4 oz., **4**d.; 6 oz., **5**d.; 8 oz., **6**d.

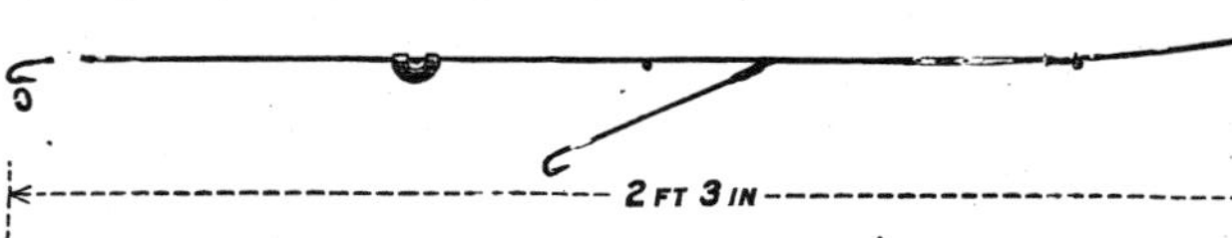

647½—The "Royde" Landing Net for Trout

ORIGINAL PATTERN.

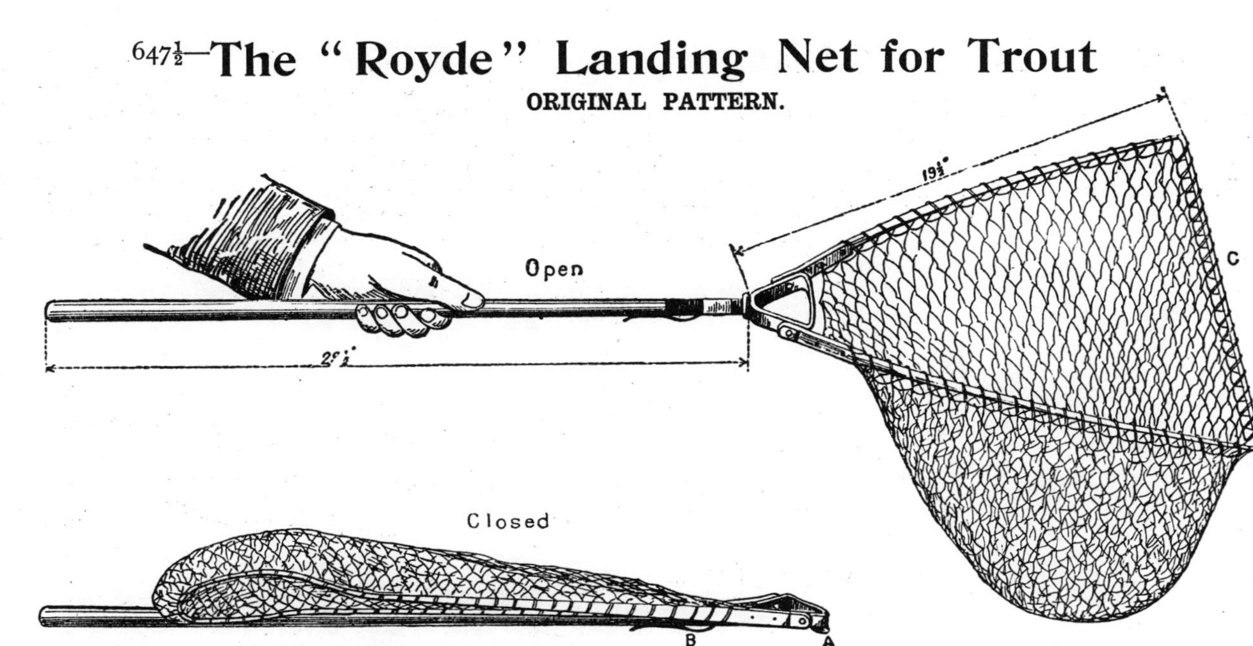

This is a very convenient form of landing net. The arms close up and the net is carried quite out of the way on the creel or shoulder strap. It is easily brought into play with one hand, as by simply throwing the head over, the net is ready for use. The reverse action closes it again. A particularly handy and easily carried net. Best quality only, price **16**/- complete. With solid waterproof plaited silk net **2/6** extra.

BARNSLEY.

I am much pleased with the flies and casts. I have given your "Royde" Net three seasons' hard work, and I consider it far away the best net I ever had, as it is very handy and strong, and for boat work excellent. W. SPENCER STANHOPE.

The original form of the flopover landing net, but without the automatic catch to hold it open. A good net except for quite heavy fish.

The "Suirvale" Landing Net

HARDY'S PATENT NOS. 16611 AND 23961.

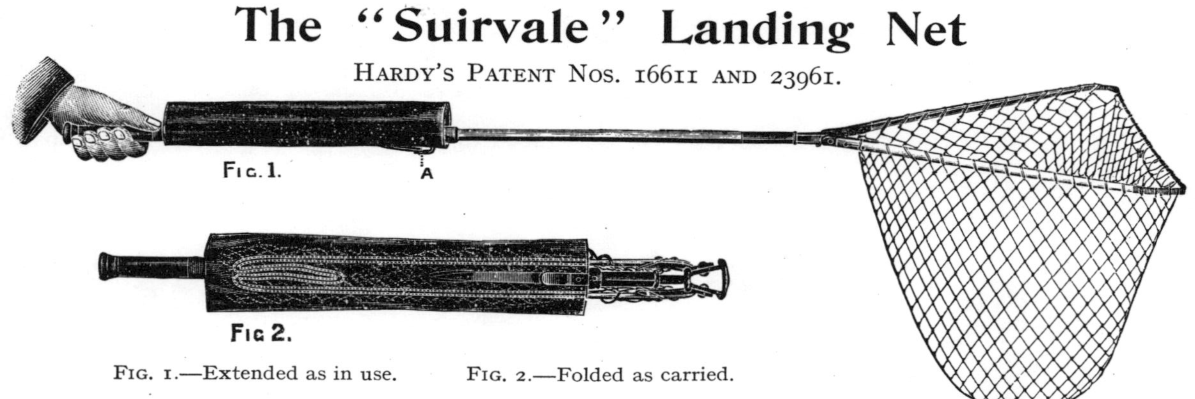

FIG. 1.—Extended as in use. FIG. 2.—Folded as carried.

The great feature of this landing net is the protection against briars, thorn-hedges, and all manner of trouble-some things one meets in fishing, which may be called " wait a bits." Not only do they compel you to " wait a bit," but very often tear the net to pieces. It is light, portable, easily handled, and the net proper is fully protected.

Anglers who use this net speak very highly of it.

The fittings are made of " Aluminium " and similar in construction to the " Royde," page 314. The handle is telescopic and made of Aluminium, the sliding portion being well-seasoned Greenheart. Fixed to the handle is the sheath, into which the net and head are enclosed when not in use, see dotted lines, Fig. 2.

The net can be brought into action with one hand by simply throwing out the telescopic portion and turning the head over, see Fig. 1. The reverse action closes it, when the net folds and slides into the sheath as shown in Fig. 2. The net proper is waterproof solid plaited silk. When folded the net complete measures 26 inches. When extended, 58 inches. Weight 24 ozs. Price **47/6** each. If fitted with self-locking arrangement as the " Improved Royde," page 315, **52/6** each. The button at end of handle can be unscrewed at any time to remove sand or grit, or for oiling.

CATALOGUE OF

Fine Fishing Tackle

MADE BY

Horrocks-Ibbotson Co.

UTICA, N. Y.

HEXAGON SPLIT BAMBOO FLY RODS

Split African Steel Cane Rods

No. 2353

No. 2353.—Made from selected **African steel cane,** 6 strips cemented together, as in a split bamboo rod, and **rounded.** This is a strong fibre rod with a beautiful action. Fly or trout rod, three-piece with extra tip, silk whipped at close intervals, nickel mountings, snake guides, **locking** reel seat below hand, cork grasp, finished with flowing varnish. Lengths 8¼, 8½, 9, 9½ and 10 feet; weights 5, 5½, 6½ and 7 oz. In flannel covered form and flannel bag ---------------------- **Each, $ 5.00**

No. 2753.—Bait rod with reel above hand; 7½ to 10 feet; weight 7½ to 8½ oz.; otherwise same as 2353 -- **Each, 5.00**

No. 2354.—Three-piece, split **African steel cane** fly rod with extra tip, full nickel mountings, hand welted ferrules, cork grasp, **locking reel seat** below hand, **closely whipped in red and green silk,** with **broad solid green winds** on butt and second joint, snake ring guides. Same length and weight as 2353. Put up in **velvet covered** form and flannel bag -- **Each, 6.00**

¶ Sometimes we are asked "What is African Steel Cane?" **African Steel Cane is a light colored, close grained, strong fibered variety of bamboo.** Has great tensile strength and much elasticity, making a very durable rod. The **rounding process** gives the rod a better action.

Combined Split Bamboo Fly Rod and Landing Net.

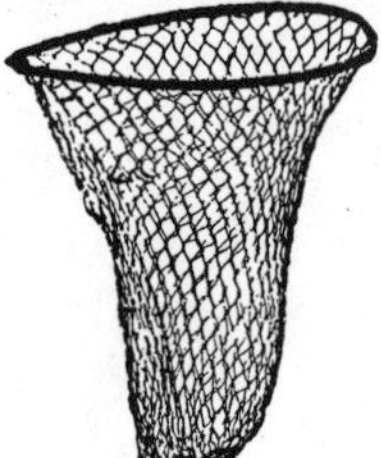

No. 2338.—To meet the demand for a **rod and net combined,** for stream or for boat fishing, we have brought out this new rod. The net bow is collapsible, 11¼ x 13½ in., fitted with tanned landing net, and **screws on the handle,** which is 42 inches long and contains both tips. The rod is made from good quality split bamboo, three pieces and extra tip. Closely wound with light green silk. **A very popular novelty-Each, $6.00**

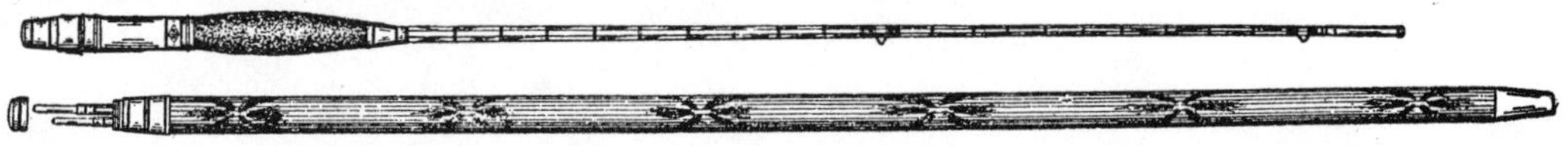

No. 2338

Special Extra Light Fly Rod

No. 2350

No. 2350.—Special light weight split bamboo fly rod, three-piece, extra tip, made from selected stock, closely wrapped in three colors of silk with cluster and border winds. This rod is made especially for the fisherman wishing a very light, strong rod. **Locking reel seat.** 8¼-foot weighs 3¾ oz.; 9-foot, 4⅛ oz. Put up with extra tip in velvet covered form and flannel bag --------------- **Each, $ 6.00**

Another of the old, established houses. It specialized in modestly priced grades of tackle.

"African steel cane" again. Theodore Gordon said it resembled bamboo—Calcutta —with the outside cut off, and that's just what it was.

Page 273: Note the disarming comment that "our cuts are old but our stock fresh."

HEXAGON SPLIT BAMBOO BAIT RODS—Continued

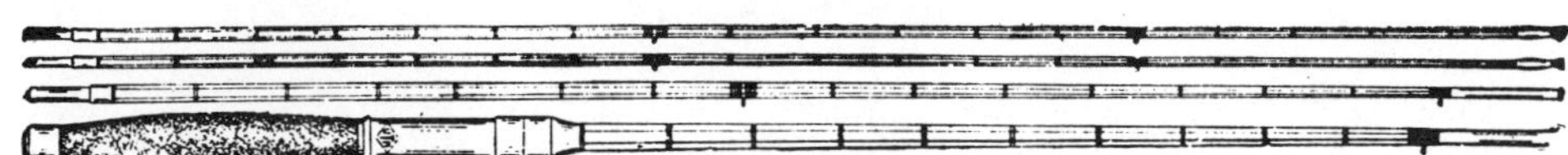

No. 2714.—Three-piece, split bamboo bait rod with extra tip, nickel mountings, water proof improved welted ferrules, cork grasp, reel seat above hand, closely wound in green silk. Lengths 7, 7½, 8, 8½, 9 and 10 feet; weight 7½ to 11 oz. In silesia covered form and cloth bag — **Each, $ 2.00**

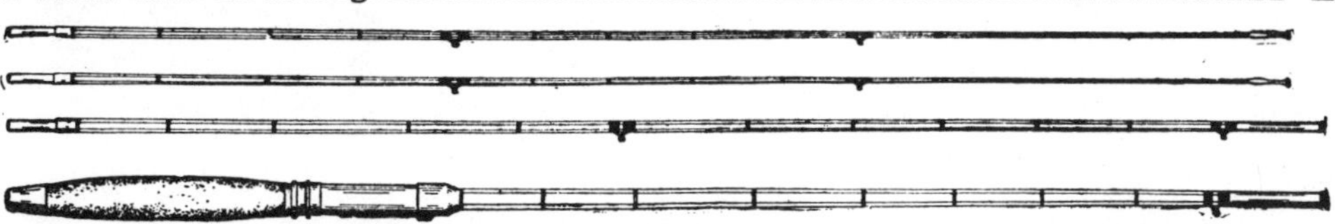

No. 2713.—Three-piece, split bamboo bait or bass rod with extra tip, solid nickel mountings, standing ring guides, extra winds in red and black, cork grasp, reel seat above hand. Length 7, 7½, 8½, 9, 9½ and 10 feet; weight 7½ to 11 oz. In wood frame and cloth bag — **Each $ 1.75**

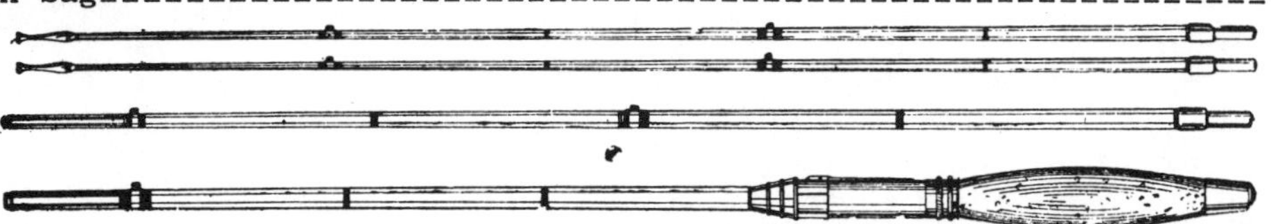

No. 2712.—Three-piece, split bamboo bait or bass rod, with extra tip, solid nickel mountings and standing ring guides, red windings, cork grasp, reel seat above hand. Length 7, 7½, 8, 8½, 9 and 10 feet; weight 7½ to 11 oz. In wood form and cloth bag — **Each, $ 1.25**

No. 2711.—Same as 2712, with ebonized wood grasp. In wood form and cloth bag — **Each, 1.00**

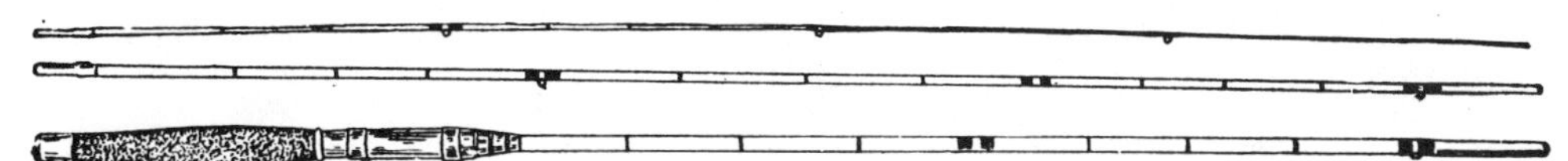

No. 02712.—Same as 2712, but with one tip. In cloth partitioned bag — **Each, $ 1.00**

No. 02711.—Same as 02712, with ebonized wood grasp. In cloth bag — **Each, .90**

GENUINE LANCEWOOD BAIT RODS

A WORD ABOUT LANCEWOOD

For nearly a century fishing rods of highest grade have been made from Lancewood. Other kinds of wood and bamboo have been tried, but many expert fishermen, both in this country and England, still cling to the Lancewood rods as being the strongest, most durable and best, both for fly casting or bait fishing.

Because of its close, straight grain, its springy, tenacious fibre and great strength, Lancewood still maintains its place as one of the best materials for fishing rod manufactured.

The best Lancewood grows in Cuba, in forests back some distance from the coast. During the past few years, especially during the Cuban revolution and the Spanish war, this was so difficult to procure that many imitations have been used and placed on the market. A certain prejudice against the genuine has arisen, from the use of these imitations, as they in all cases have been far inferior to the genuine.

We put up all our Lancewood Rods regularly in cloth bags, being more compact and convenient to carry. Forms will be supplied when ordered, at the following prices:

Plain Wood Form	Each, $	.25
Silesia Covered Form	"	.35
Flannel Covered Wood Form	"	.40
Velvet Covered Form	"	1.00

No. 08712.—8½ to 10 feet bass, Cuban Lance, three-piece, standing guides, nickel mounting, reel seat above hand, scored grasp, 8½ to 10½ oz. Designed especially for boat fishing. In cloth partitioned bag — **Each, $ 1.00**

No. 08711.—Imitation Lancewood, 8½ to 10 feet bait rod, three-piece, standing guides, nickel mountings, reel seat above hand, imitation celluloid grasp. Good rod for boat fishing. In cloth partitioned bag — **Each, .85**

No. 8712.—Same as 08712, with two tips. In cloth bag — **Each, 1.35**

¶ Our cuts are old, but our stock fresh—as we are the manufacturers.

"Y and E" Reels

Their Distinct Advantages Over Old-style Reels

IF you have experienced the full joy of a fight to the finish with a gamey member of the Finny Tribe you know also the one cloud that lurks in the background, and that is—the chance that all your skill may be nullified by the clumsy mechanism of your reel—because your fish is quicker than you are, naturally, and can MAKE slack QUICKER THAN YOU CAN TAKE IT UP with the old-style reel. So, then, we may come quickly to the great feature of the "Y and E" Automatic Reel, which may be defined exactly thus:

Skykomish River, Wash., where "El Comancho" (W. S. Phillips) caught the 15 lb. (Record) Rainbow trout

Automatically to so control the tension of the line that no slack will be given no matter how swiftly your fish may turn

That's the idea—just to take in the slack automatically—not to reel in the fish, or, in the slightest degree, lessen the sensation of fighting every minute, if you are to win out.

So gently does the reel respond to the pressure of the little finger on the brake that its use soon becomes simply a matter of instinct: You apply the tension automatically, just as quickly as you would check a horse that tried to bolt.

"Y and E" Automatic-Combination Reels

The moment you make your cast you press the slide with your finger and at once your Reel is automatic instead of free-running. The change requires no muscle and but a fraction of a second of time

OF our two styles of Automatic Reels, the great favorite is the Automatic-Combination—because—you can make your cast free-running, and the instant slipping of a catch applies the tension—either to re-wind your line for another cast, or to prevent Mr. Fish from dropping your hook, in case you get a "strike." The Automatic-Combination has also the key-winding feature which enables you to apply more tension instantly in case you have a lot of line out—or to vary the tension according to your requirements.

Tension is also supplied (same as with the plain automatic reel) by the drawing off of the line, thus winding up the automatic spring.

These Reels are in no sense toys, or experiments. They have received the highest praise from the crack fishermen of this country and of Europe. A multitude of expert fishermen use "Y and E" Reels exclusively, and their record of famous catches would alone make an interesting book.

Use a "Y and E" Reel and you will know and realize that "A trout in the basket is worth two in the brook."

"Y and E" Reels have been imitated, copied but never equaled.

"Y and E" is the only automatic reel that has stood the test of time.

"Pardner" (Mrs. W. S. Phillips) and the Biggest Bunch of trouble that ever wore Gills.

Old Reliable "Y and E" Automatic Reels

(Made of Aluminum, with Tool Steel Bearings)

"Y and E" Automatic Reels are made in the following sizes:

No. 1—Carries and rewinds automatically 90 feet of No. 5 silk line; diameter 3 1-32 inches; weight, 8 ounces. Price------$5.00

No. 2—Carries and rewinds automatically 150 feet of No. 5 silk line; diameter 3 3-16 inches; weight, 12 ounces. Price------$6.00

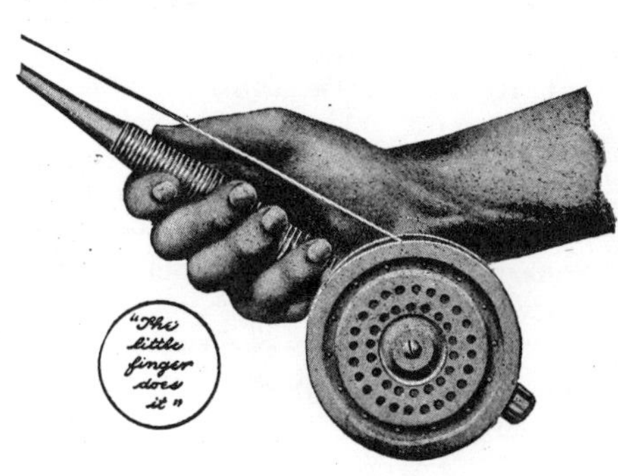

New Style "Y and E" Automatic-Combination Reels

(Made of Aluminum with Tool Steel Bearings)

(One-half actual size)

STYLE A

Diameter, 2 7-16 inches.
Weight, 7½ ounces.
Capacity, 125 feet No. 5 silk, winding automatically 50 feet without rewinding.
Price $7.00.

(One-half actual size)

STYLE B

Diameter, 3⅜ inches.
Weight, 11 ounces.
Capacity, 300 feet No. 5 silk, winding automatically 90 feet without rewinding.
Price $8.00.

This is the favorite size for all-around use.

We make the Automatic-Combination in these three sizes, to afford perfect selection to suit the kind of fishing proposed.

(One-half actual size)

STYLE C

Diameter, 4⅛ inches.
Weight, 16 ounces.
Capacity, 600 feet No. 5 silk, winding automatically 150 feet without rewinding.
Price $9.00.

HORROCKS-IBBOTSON CO.

Successors to Reel Department of

Yawman & Erbe Mfg. Co.

UTICA, N. Y.

HIGHEST GRADE WOOD MINNOWS

These minnows are the most perfectly shaped, most workmanly made, most beautifully finished of all wooden minnows. The body is so shaped and weighted that it rides at the proper depth under all speeds. Their appearance when cast or trolled is so animatedly life-like that the wariest of game fish are deceived. Just why these fish attack these baits so savagely will probably remain a matter of dispute, yet the fact remains that whether their appetite is stimulated or their fighting instinct aroused, the Wooden Minnow gets the "strike" and lands the fish. They cost slightly more than numerous imitations, a difference which is more than justified by the difference in quality. They have come into such general use for casting and trolling for Bass and other fresh water game fishes as to require no further claims for their successful killing qualities. Their beautiful and **durable decorations** and finish and **perfection of mechanical detail** have given them an envied place in the affections of artistic anglers everywhere. They are best in shape, weight and balance; have the best hook presentment; **detachable hooks; perfection of spinner action** and **strength** and **durability.**

Hollow Point Nickel Plated Treble Hooks. Each in Separate Box.

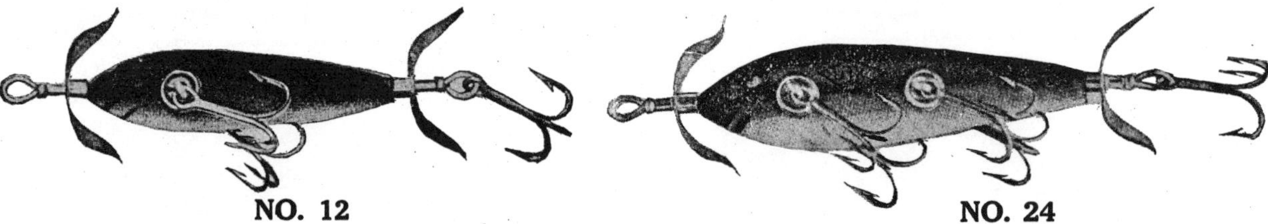

NO. 12

Body 3 inches long, 2 Spinners, 3 Treble Hooks. Made in Following Colors:

No. 12-200—Fancy green back, white belly, blended colors ---------------------**Each, 50c**
No. 12-201—Green back, white belly--**Each, 50c**
No. 12-202—White, solid color-------**Each, 50c**
No. 12-204—Red back, yellow belly---**Each, 50c**
No. 12-205—Green back, yellow belly, blended. **Each** ------------------------------**50c**
No. 12-206—Shaded yellow perch----**Each, 50c**
No. 12-211—Solid aluminum color----**Each, 50c**
No. 12-212—Red back, aluminum belly-**Each, 50c**
No. 12-213—Solid red color---------**Each, 50c**
No. 12-214—Red back,yellow belly---**Each, 50c**
No. 12-215—Solid yellow color-------**Each, 50c**

No. 12 Assortment—For the convenience of our customers we have put up 12 assorted of above best sellers. Price assorted 12 No. 12 Minnows -------------------------**$6.00**

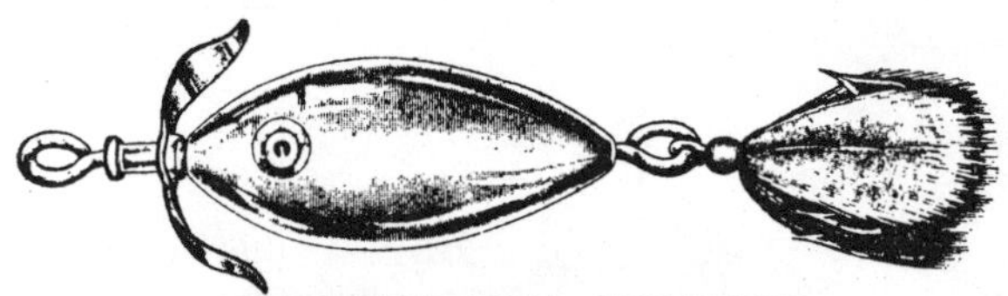

PUMPKINSEED MINNOW

Made with Feathered Treble Hook.

No. 12-208—Red back, aluminum belly **Each, 50c**
No. 12-208½—Green back, aluminum belly--**50c**
No. 12-208A—Green back, white belly-**Each, 50c**

WHIRLWIND SPINNER

No. 12-209—Total length 4 inches----**Each, 50c**

NO. 24

Body 3⅜ inches long, 2 Spinners, 5 Treble Hooks.
No. 24-250—Fancy green back, white belly--**60c**
No. 24-251—Green back, white belly--**Each, 60c**
No. 24-252—White, solid color-------**Each, 60c**
No. 24-254—Red back, yellow belly---**Each, 60c**
No. 24-255—Green back, yellow belly-**Each, 60c**
No. 24-256—Yellow perch, shaded---**Each, 60c**
No. 24-261—Solid aluminum--------**Each, 60c**
No. 24-263—Solid red color---------**Each, 60c**
No. 24 Assortment—Best sellers and most popular of above 5 Treble Minnows put up 12 assorted in carton. Per box of 12 minnows------**$7.25**

METAL PLATED MINNOWS

Same size as No. 12, only made with a thick deposit of metal over the entire minnow.

No. 12-210—Solid copper-----------**Each, 85c**
No. 12-216—Solid nickel------------**Each, 85c**
No. 12-217—Solid gold-------------**Each, 85c**

For the convenience of our trade we are prepared to supply this famous assortment:

SOUTH BEND ASSORTMENT NO. 358

Bodies are of Red Cedar, beautifully blended in a variety of Standard Colors. **Will not crack or peel.**

This assortment of one dozen Minnows, varied as to style and color blendings, mounted on easel back "Silent Salesman," as illustrated, is a business getter —a very attractive display.

To facilitate sales, this "Silent Salesman" has printed opposite each bait, description and retail price. Retail value, $7.75.

No. 358—Minnow Assortment----Per Card, $7.75

COMPLETE FISHING OUTFITS FOR THE DEALER
THE BOYS' OWN OUTFIT, NO. 500

This Fishing Outfit complete, containing the following:

1 Fancy Bamboo Fishing Rod.
1 All Brass Click Reel
2 Doz. Split Shot Sinkers
9 Fishing Lines Assorted
6 Trout and Bass Flies
6 Snelled Hooks
2 Doz. Assorted Fish Hooks
1 Trolling Spoon Bait
3 Trout and Bass Leaders
1 Float or "Bobber"
1 Adjustable Sinker
3 Swivels

Everything in this outfit is of high quality, practical and each item will give perfect satisfaction.

If bought separately the price would be $2.48. Put up in Strong Cardboard Carton and can retail complete ready to use at **$2.00**

SILENT SALESMAN FISH ROD DISPLAY STAND

Holds 24 Rods

A Permanent Store Fixture

Each Rod can be easily taken from Stand and shown.

Takes up but a few square inches of floor space. Height, 5 feet; diameter at base, 16 inches.

Price, Japan Finish, $5.00 net
Shipping weight, 20 lbs.

Send at once for one of these Stands to the old reliable Fishing UTK (TRADE MARK REG. U.S. PAT. OFF.) Tackle Factory.

The Celebrated YANKEE DOODLE or Sockdolager FISH HOOK
The Hook That Holds.
$2.50 per dozen, or 25c each.

SPORTSMAN'S DELIGHT OUTFIT, NO. 150

This Fishing Out fit is complete, containing the following:

1 FANCY SPLIT AND GLUED BAMBOO FISHING ROD—3-piece, split bamboo bait rod, with extra tip, nickel mountings, water-proofed ferrules, standing guides closely wound in red silk, ebonized grasp, reel seat above hand. Weight, 8 oz. Length, 6 to 8½ feet.
1 All Brass Click REEL, 40-yard size.
10 Split Shot SINKERS, buck size.
6 Trout and Bass Flies, assorted.
6 SNELLED HOOKS, Double Gut.
100 Assorted FISH HOOKS, Ringed.
1 Monarch Silk Finish FISH LINE.

Everything in this outfit is of highest quality, practical and each item will give perfect satisfaction.

If bought separately the price would be $2.60. Put up in strong Cardboard Carton and can retail complete ready to use at **$2.00.**

No. 175 OUTFIT—Same as above with 1 BASS STEEL Rod, full nickel mounted, with solid reel above hand, standing guides and three-ring tip, cork grasp, furnished in the following lengths: 7, 7½, and 8½ feet, in place of Split Bamboo Rod.

ADVERTISING CUTS FURNISHED FREE

Fishing is the Sport!

There is nothing more restful or rewarding than a day's fishing. This is doubly true when the tackle used is the Famous UTK Brand.

We are showing a very complete line--and at attractive prices.

For example

No. 9—Single Column

THE UTK BRAND

BEST FISHING TACKLE

No. 2

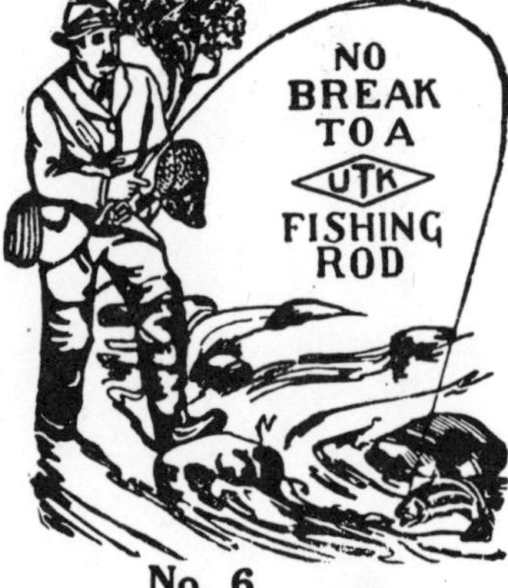

No. 6

No. 3

Camp Life and Fishing

Has a touch of realism

That is most fascinating. When on a Fishing Trip there is nothing to equal the rest, the care-free feeling, the glory of the out-of-doors.

In our stock you'll find everything for outdoor sports, and the highest grade

Fishing Tackle

For we sell the Famous UTK Brand, made by Horrocks-Ibbotson Co. Utica, N. Y.

This Cut is No. 15. Takes Double Column, 7½ inches lonfi. Is mortised all in the center here for special prices and any matter dealer wish, together with name.

This is Cut No. 16, Single Column, 3½ inches long, mortised here for special printing and name.

Cut No. 17, Mortised for full printing of special goods and name.

FIELD and STREAM TWENTY YEARS OLD THIS MONTH
MAY 1915
PRICE, 15 CENTS
FIELD AND STREAM
OFFICIAL ORGAN of the CAMP FIRE
Osborne Mayer.

CASTING DOWN WIND—A FINE STRIKE!

All advertisements are indexed—See page 2A

All advertisements are indexed—See page 2A

Our Expert Casting Line

Hard Braided, of the Highest Grade of Silk. The Strongest Line of its size in the World. Used by Mr. Decker in contest with Mr. Jamison. Nuf sed. Every Line Warranted. 50 Yard Spools $1.00

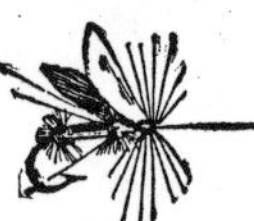

Trout Flies

For Trial---Send Us

18c for an assorted dozen. Regular price....24c. Quality A
30c for an assorted dozen. Regular price....60c. Quality B
60c for an assorted dozen. Regular price....84c. Quality C
65c for an assorted dozen. Regular price....96c. Bass Flies
75c for an assorted dozen. Regular price...$1.00 Gauze Wing
2.00 for an assorted dozen. Regular price...$3.50 English

Steel Fishing Rods

FLY RODS, 8 or 9½ feet....................$ .80
BAIT RODS, 5½, 6½ or 8 feet............ .70
CASTING RODS, 4½, 5½ or 6 feet........ 1.25
BAIT RODS, with Agate Guide and Tip.... 2.25
CASTING RODS, with Agate Guide and Tip 2.75
CASTING RODS, full Agate Mountings.... 3.50

ORIGINAL and GENUINE

OLDTOWN CANOES

Introduced and made famous by us.

16 to 19 ft.

$25 TO $50

The H. H. Kiffe Co., *521 Broadway, New York*

Illustrated Catalogue free on application

Fish Bite

like hungry wolves and keep you busy pulling them out, whenever, or wherever, you use our

Wonderful Fish-Luring Bait

Best fish bait ever discovered for nets, traps, and trot lines. No poison. Not unlawful to use. We guarantee satisfaction. Write to-day and get a box to help introduce it. Agents Wanted.

Walton Supply Co., Dept. 45, St. Louis, Mo.

CANADIAN MOCCASINS

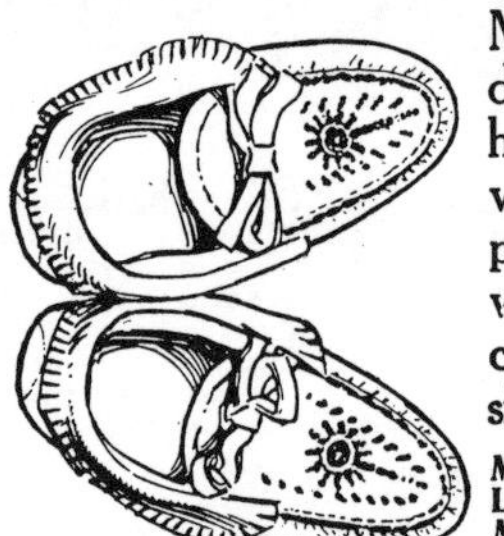

Made of genuine Indian tanned Moose hide. Ornamented with beads or Porcupine quills. A long wearing, serviceable, comfortable Moccasin.

Men's Sizes,	8 to 12	$2.00
Ladies' "	3 to 7	1.50
Misses' "	11 to 2	1.00
Child's "	7 to 10	.75

Guaranteed Eskimo-made waterproof Mucklucks, knee length, all sizes, $4.00.

Send 2c. in Stamps for our New Illustrated Catalogue —Showing the largest collection of Indian Souvenirs on the Coast, typical of Alaska and the Northwest.

HUDSON BAY FUR CO., Inc.
918 First Avenue Seattle, Wash.

The Rod of Quality

This phrase is certainly substantiated by the record of my rods in the Prize Fishing Contest. One landed the First Grand Prize brook trout, 1914—a 6 5/16 pound one at Upper Dam, Me.

My hand-made, split-bamboo rod bears my name and behind this stamp of my approval and supervision stands many years' accumulation of experience and reputation—and I'm not fearing the loss of this by heartily and conscientiously recommending the rod to you.

The finest bamboo in the world perfectly united and finished with a guarantee of satisfaction.

F. E. THOMAS
117 Exchange St. Bangor, Me.
Ask for my booklet

THE EXCELSIOR SPORTSMEN'S BELT SAFE

Just what I have been looking for —has been the expression of every man we have shown it to—Made of Brass, Nickel Plated, Gun Metal or oxidized and furnished complete with fancy Canvas Belt for $1.00.

Will keep money—jewels—watch—cigarettes or matches perfectly safe and dry. **HYFIELD MFG. CO., 48 Franklin Street, N.Y. City**

Advertising was a rare thing among the old custom rodmakers but Fred Thomas, Hiram Leonard's first employee in the rod business, speaks his piece here. Fred went back to Bangor after the big Leonard Co. bust-up in the 1890s and set up for himself. Some of his rods were heavy and stiff for his Maine customers, who lifted three-pound fish out with the rod; but he made any number of flyrods that money simply would not buy from their owners today. After Fred died his son, Leon, ran the business, but eventually it became bankrupt and its few assets, principally a fine old name, were sold by the receiver at auction.

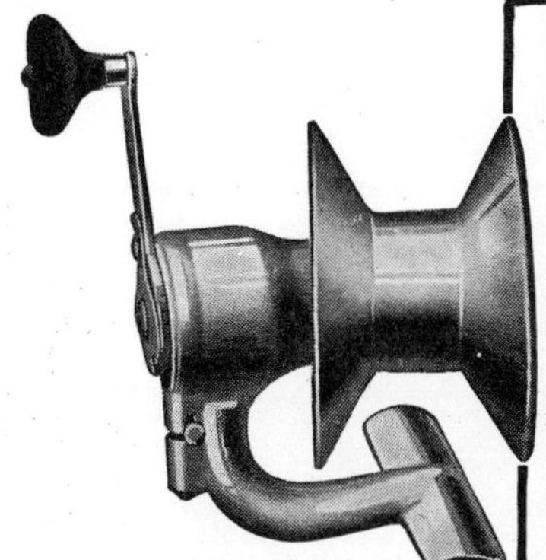

Another apparently good idea that didn't succeed. Such an oscillating mechanism is simple and rugged; and the open spool certainly would be conducive to longer casts and far, far fewer backlashes. One can only conjecture that perhaps the very openness of the spool was its undoing—that "working" a plug in little jerks and tip manipulations would produce alternate tightening and slackening of the line so that a coil or two might slip off the spool. Just the same, I wish I had one to try. There has to be a better way than that little hairpin running back and forth in the conventional level winder.

When that Marble gaff came out, it revolutionized the ancient art of poaching.

THE "MASCOT" WEEDLESS BAITS

Wobble, Dive, Float, Surface or Underwater

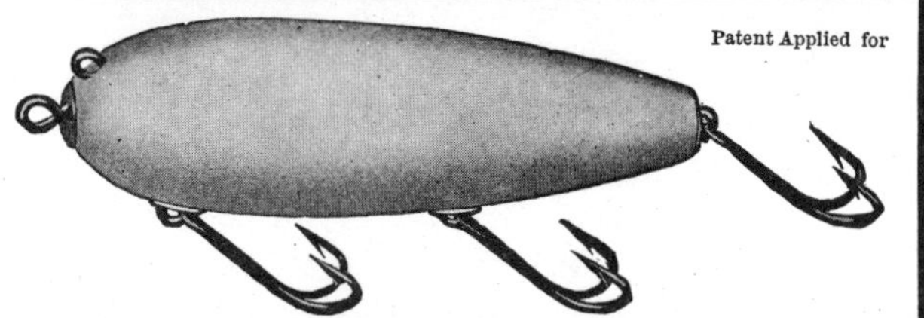

THE WEEDLESS "MASCOT"
NEAR SURFACE OR SURFACE BAIT

We guarantee that you can cast this bait among thick lilies, rushes, underwater weeds, logs, stumps, snags, etc. Also that it is a sure killer. It runs at varying depths from the surface to two feet deep and will either Wobble or swim straight as desired. Is also reversible. Made with Red Head and White Body or all Red, White or Yellow.

PRICE EACH, 75 CENTS, Postage 3 Cents

THE "ICE TONGS" Principle of the hooks on the "Mascot" Baits automatically hooks the fish instantly if he even touches the point of the hook. Get our circular and let us explain all about this greatest of all artificial bait inventions. We guarantee every claim made. Money refunded if not satisfied. Order one and see for yourself.

WEEDLESS No. 1 WINGED "MASCOT"
DEEP WATER OR SURFACE BAIT

This bait is also very weedless and a deadly killer. It can be used as a strict surface bait, throwing a spray of water, or as a deep water bait, running five feet deep or more. It "Wobbles," dives and floats when at rest. Fully guaranteed in every respect. Made with Red Head and White Body or all Red, White or Yellow.

PRICE EACH, 75 CENTS, Postage 2 Cents

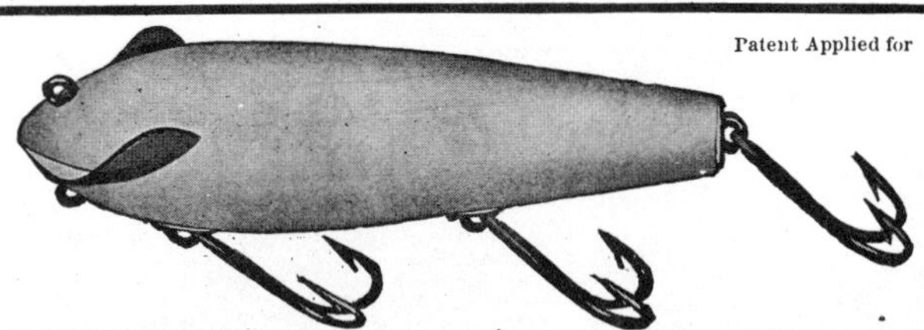

OUR TACKLE CATALOG in colors shows "Coaxer," "Mascot" and "Nemo" Baits, "Coaxer" Floating Trout and Bass Flies, Trout Spoons, Imported Flies, Fly Dressing Materials, Weedless Hooks, Frog Harnesses, Anti-Back Lash Reels, Jamison Famous Casting Lines, Leaders, Sinkers, etc., etc.

THE W. J. JAMISON COMPANY, Dept. F - - - 736 S. California Avenue, Chicago, Ill.

PERFECTION LINE GUIDE FOR FISHING RODS

CASTING MADE EASY AND SURE

For sale at dealers or direct from

F. L. RUMBLE, 250 W. Wyoming Ave., PHILADELPHIA, PA.

B. C. MILAM & SON

BUILD REELS

For 76 years we have built, on one spot, the Milam Frankfort Kentucky Reel. Ask your dealer to show you our New $5.00 Reel. If he can't, write us.

At FRANKFORT, KY.

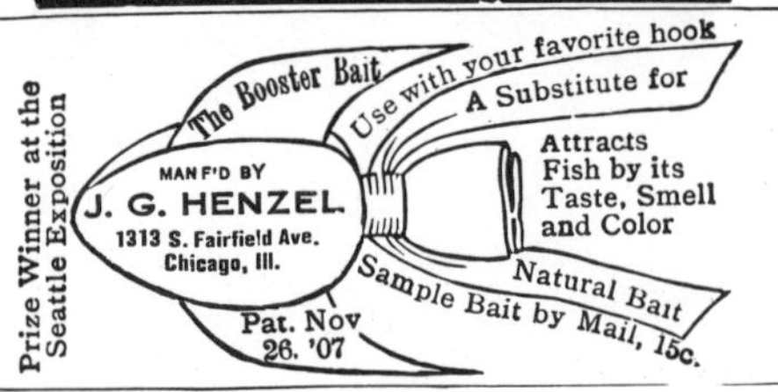

CATCH BIG BASS
With the
ANS. B. DECKER
Genuine Topwater Casting Bait

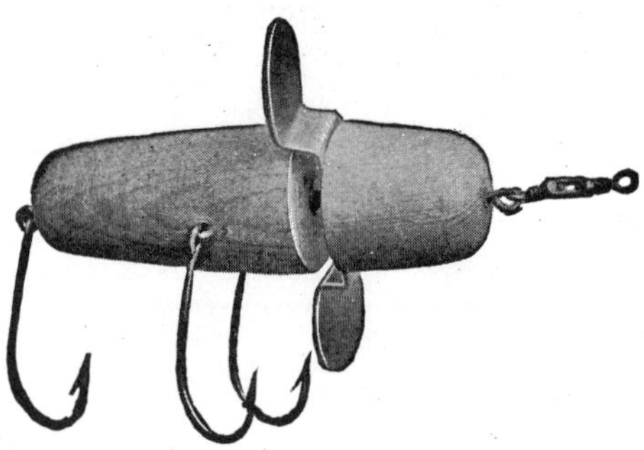

This floating bait was invented and is made at Lake Hopatcong, N. J., by the original Decker. Put up in YELLOW Boxes and must show the Decker signature on box to be the right one—look out for the imitation. For sale by all first-class dealers, or fifty cents by mail, postpaid.

ANS. B. DECKER
Lake Hopatcong, N. J.

Try one of my Famous Ans. B. Decker Casting Lines, fifty yards, $1.00. We also make the famous "Decker Wobbler" for pickerel, thirty-five cents each.

According to this 1915 ad, the Milam reel business goes back to 1839.

EVINRUDE + ROWBOAT = MOTORBOAT
EVINRUDE
DETACHABLE ROWBOAT & CANOE MOTORS
If you want the whole family to have a good time this summer — Get an Evinrude!
The Evinrude is a powerful little marine motor that enables you to instantly convert any kind of craft—rowboat, sailboat, house-boat or canoe—into a power boat. It drives a rowboat seven to eight miles an hour — a canoe ten to twelve miles — and runs four hours on less than a gallon of gasoline.
Think of what it means to be able to take with you to lake, river or sea-shore, a portable power plant that relieves you of the hard work of rowing and enables every member of the family to enjoy the pleasures of motor boating — without the expense. The Evinrude is used by thousands of sportsmen and pleasure seekers the world over. The 1915 model has Waterproof Magneto built into the flywheel, Maxim Silencer, and Automatic Reverse. You'll be interested in our new catalog. Just say: "Send me a copy of your catalog and tell me where I can see an Evinrude."
Evinrude Motor Co., 15 Evinrude Block Milwaukee, Wis., U.S.A.
Distributing Branches: 69 Cortlandt St., New York, N. Y. 218 State St., Boston, Mass. 436 Market St., San Francisco, Cal. 182 Morrison St., Portland, Ore.
1130-7122

1916 CATALOG Nº 66 1917

SPORTSMAN'S HANDBOOK

NEW YORK SPORTING GOODS CO. NEW YORK. U.S.A.

WOMEN'S "KAMP-IT" OUTING CLOTHING

The fine twill, soft texture and attractive olive green color of "Kamp-it" material makes it particularly suitable for women's outing clothing. The tailoring is much better than is usually furnished in garment at so moderate a price.

On golf-links, in summer camps, for hill-climbing, horseback riding, cycling and tramping you will find "Kamp-it" garments at their best. They are light and comfortable in hottest weather, and are made ample to give perfect freedom of motion.

WOMEN'S NORFOLK JACKET

No. **W1.** Norfolk Jacket. Is made of a single thickness of material. Cut on very graceful lines with plaits extending to the shoulder. Two set-in pockets with flaps **$3.50**

WOMEN'S RIDING COAT AND BREECHES

It combines stylish appearance and perfect freedom when in the saddle. The length is long enough to serve as an outside garment when walking, if worn in connection with riding breeches and leggins. Fitted with three pockets.

No. **W7.** Riding Coats, 38 to 40 incles long **$5.00**

No. **W9.** Breeches, for riding or outdoor wear. Fashioned after men's pattern, two large pockets, lace below the knee **3.00**

No. **W24.** Leggins, well shaped and neat appearing, to button **1.25**

RIDING SKIRT

The front of this skirt is fastened with a row of buttons on the left and buttons over on the right which may be partly unbuttoned while riding and when walking completely closed. Can be worn with or without bloomers or breeches.

No. **5.** Combination Skirt **$4.50**

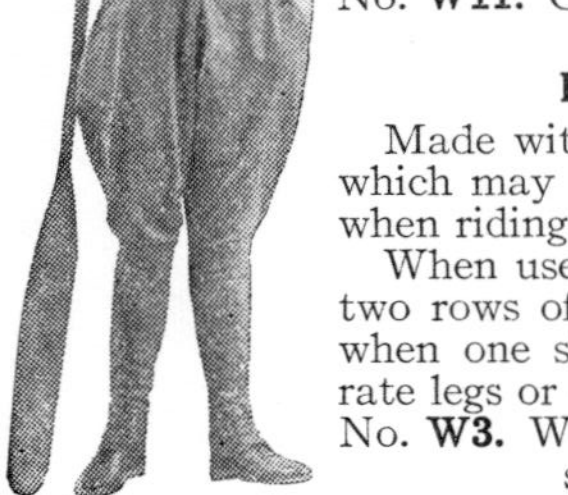

WOMEN'S BLOOMERS

A new model this year. Fits comfortably under the skirt, or can be worn without skirt.

No. **W11.** Cuff and Buckle at knee. **$2.25**

DIVIDED SKIRT

Made with a detachable panel in front which may be removed or buttoned over when riding.

When used for walking the skirt shows two rows of buttons down the front and when one side is unbuttoned two separate legs or divisions are formed.

No. **W3.** With pockets on either side **$4.50**

Delivery Prepaid in U. S. if Cash is Sent with Order at Above Prices

MARBLE'S SAFETY POCKET AXES

The Marble safety axe is made with a guard that protects the blade and allows you to slip the axe into hip or coat pocket, or carry it in a sheath at the belt. They are large enough and strong enough for any except the heaviest work expected of an axe, and so small and light that the added weight is not noticed. A perfect axe for "blazing," clearing a trail, making camp, etc. All blades are made of one piece of tool steel. The nickel-plated guard is lined with lead and is hinged on a spring in a manner that either open or closed it is firmly held in position.

STEEL HANDLE MODELS

The metal handles are nickel-plated and side plates black hard rubber.

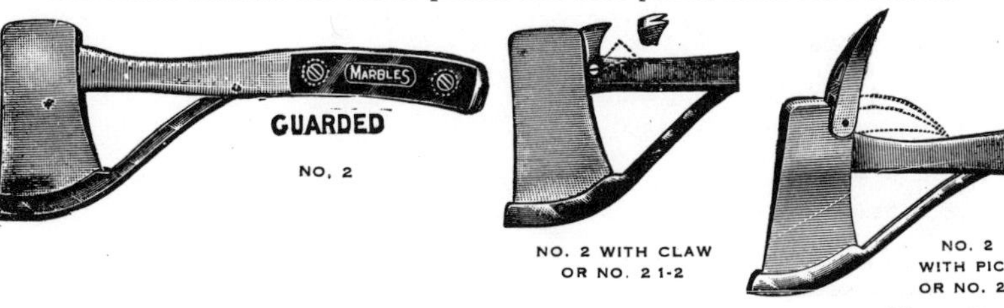

NO. 2

NO. 2 WITH CLAW OR NO. 2 1-2

NO. 2 WITH PICK OR NO. 2P

		List	Net
No. **2.**	Weighs 20 ozs., 11 ins. long, solid steel blade 2⅜x4 ins....	$2.50	**$2.25**
No. **2½.**	Same size and style as No. 2, but fitted with claw.......	2.75	**2.50**
No. **2P.**	In size and style the same as No. 2, but made with pick.	4.00	**3.50**
No. **3.**	Weighs 27 ozs., 12 ins. long, solid steel blade 2½x4⅜ ins...	3.00	**2.75**

WOOD HANDLE MODELS

The handles are of hickory with steel lined groove and folding nickel guard.

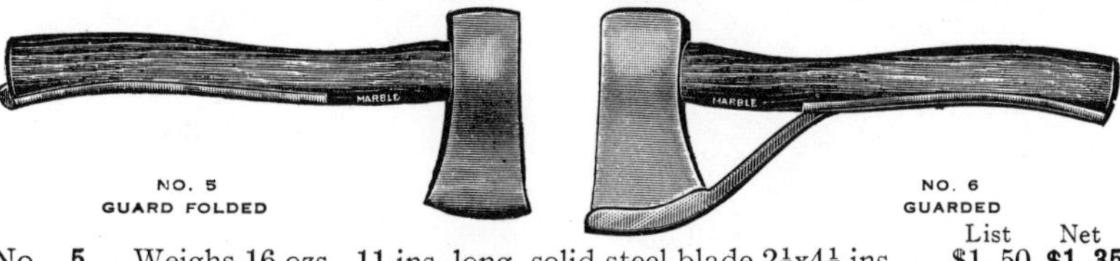

NO. 5 GUARD FOLDED

NO. 6 GUARDED

		List	Net
No. **5.**	Weighs 16 ozs., 11 ins. long, solid steel blade 2½x4½ ins...	$1.50	**$1.35**
No. **6.**	Weighs 22 ozs., 12 ins. long, solid steel blade 2⅞x4¾ ins...	1.50	**1.35**
No. **19.**	Leather sheath, full length...........................	1.00	**.85**
No. **20.**	Leather sheath, half length..........................	.75	**.65**

MARBLE'S NEW CAMP AXE

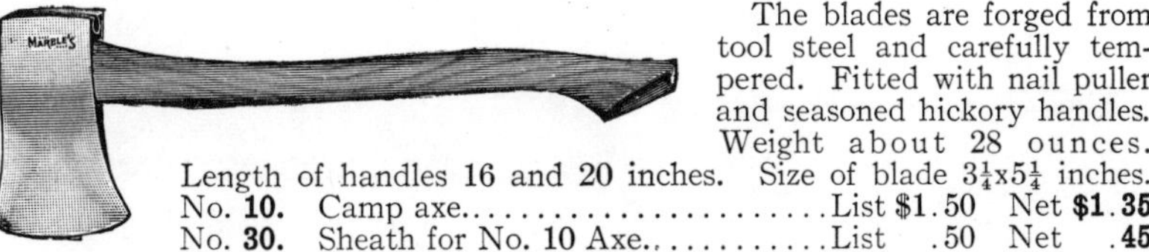

The blades are forged from tool steel and carefully tempered. Fitted with nail puller and seasoned hickory handles. Weight about 28 ounces.

Length of handles 16 and 20 inches. Size of blade 3¼x5¼ inches.

No. **10.** Camp axe.......................List $1.50 Net **$1.35**
No. **30.** Sheath for No. 10 Axe...........List .50 Net **.45**

Delivery Prepaid in U. S. if Cash is Sent with Order at above Prices and 15c. addition is sent for delivery of an axe and 5 cts. for delivery of a sheath

The pocket ax was made famous by old Nessmuk, who designed and had made for him a double-bitter that weighed a pound according to Colclesser, a famous old time Pennsylvania ax maker who produced duplicates for the trade. Whether or not this weight included the handle is not stated, but it probably did. The handle couldn't have been more than 10 inches long, judging from the drawing in Nessmuk's *Woodcraft*. The wood-handled Marble Safety Pocket Ax shown here therefore must be a virtual duplicate of Nessmuk's ax in weight and length.

Though famous, the Nessmuk ax was never very popular because a double-bitted ax has a sinister, wicked look that repels most people. But the single-edge Marble version, either steel- or wood-handled, enjoyed decades of widespread popularity until the cheaper, simpler Boy Scout Hatchet came into use.

In strong, skilled hands, a pocket ax with a head weighing between eight ounces and a pound is capable of astonishing performance.

SAMSON STEEL RODS, UNGUARANTEED

This style of reel fastener is furnished without extra charge.

These steel fishing rods, though unguaranteed, are made by a reputable manufacturer, and while they are not claimed to be the equal of higher priced rods they will, nevertheless, give a reasonable amount of satisfaction. These rods are regularly made with cork handles, nickel-plated trimmings on the butts, and reel seat either above or below the handle as described. The rod proper is finished in dark enamel, in order, as far as possible, not to reflect the light, which is a recognized advantage. The trimmings of the rods are nickel-plated. Good material is used, but they are in no way guaranteed.

FLY RODS, UNGUARANTEED

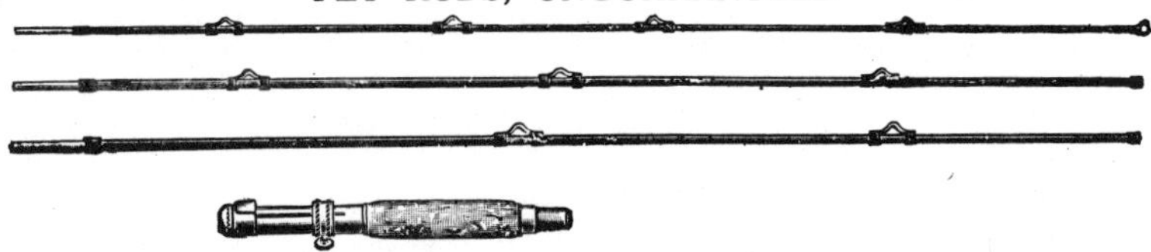

They are made with three joints, cork grip and in general makeup are similar to the bait rods except that they are lighter and the reel seat is placed below the handle. The line guide is of the "snake" pattern and the top of the small tip is fitted with a single ring.

No. **F86.** Length 8½ feet..........................
No. **F96.** Length 9½ feet.......................... } **$1.25.** Delivered $1.35

BAIT RODS, UNGUARANTEED

Three joints and butt, cork grip, regular style reel seat with sliding band placed above the handle. Regular standing two-ring guides with three-ring top.

No. **B7.** Length 7 feet..........................
No. **B8.** Length 8 feet..........................
No. **B9.** Length 9 feet.......................... } **$1.25.** Delivered $1.35

This rod is only supplied with regular guides and agates cannot be furnished.

EMERGENCY TOP

To be used in case of accident to the regular tip joint, or in place of the tip joint to make a very stiff trolling rod. Above cut shows ¾ size; it can be carried conveniently in a vest pocket. Being slightly tapered it will fit practically all steel rods.

No. **E.** Each. Postage paid...**$ .15**

STEEL ROD SHORTENER

A device for converting a steel rod into a short boat rod. Remove the first joint and seat the shortener in the handle, and the second joint in the shortener.

No. **S.** Each. Postage paid...**$ .20**

Delivery Prepaid in U. S. if Cash is Sent with Order at Above Prices.

FISHING TACKLE
MARSHALL FIELD
& COMPANY Annex
The Store for Men

48 MARSHALL FIELD & COMPANY

Louis Rhead's American Nature Flies

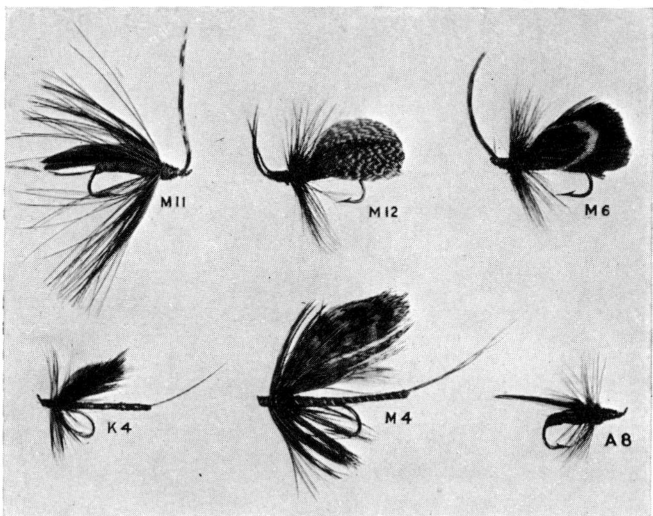

These Nature Flies are finely and strongly made. They are tied from patterns made by Mr. Rhead to imitate natural flies collected and painted by him while on the streams of New York and Pennsylvania.

Mr. Rhead states that the same varieties of flies are found on most of the trout streams of the United States and lower Canada, and that the forty patterns he submitted are the best out of hundreds of natural flies collected by him, and are the ones on which the trout feed freely.

April Patterns	**May Patterns**	**June Patterns**	**July Patterns**
A- 2 Brown Buzz	M- 1 Green Drake	J- 1 Female Greeneye	K- 1 Golden Drake
A- 4 March Brown	M- 2 Brown Drake	J- 2 Male Greeneye	K- 2 Pinktail Drake
A- 5 Long Tail	M- 4 Mottled Drake	J- 4 Greenback Drake	K- 4 Spottail
A- 8 Red Bug	M- 5 Cinnamon	J- 5 Yellow Tip	K- 6 Olive Drake
A- 9 Long Horn	M- 6 Sandy	J- 7 Lemontail	K- 7 Orange Stone
A-10 Cowdung	M- 8 Gray Drake	J- 9 Chocolate Drake	K- 9 Redhead Gnat
A-16 Shad, Male	M-10 Yellow Sally	J-14 Pointedtail Drake	K-10 White Miller
A-17 Shad, Female	M-11 Flathead	J-16 Emerald	K-12 Plume Spinner
A-18 Shad "with eggs"	M-12 Alder	J-19 Hairy Spinner	K-13 GoldenSpinner
(Shad flies also occur in May)	M-17 Golden Spinner	J-20 Gold Body Spinner	K-17 Orange Miller

Each pattern is tied on one size hook only, which is suitable for natural size of fly. Average size about No. 10.

Dozen **$2.00**

"Halford Pattern" Dry or Floating Flies

Dressed on highest quality 8, 10 and 12 turned-up eyed hooks, and have very hard body. Hackle and wings are tied so that fly will float. Tied strictly to the "Halford" patterns, with a few additional patterns for American waters, that have proved great "killers."

Blue Dun, Gray Hackle, Brown Hackle, Harlequin, Artful Dodger, Black Gnat, Coachman, Flight Fancy, Ginger Quill, Jenny Spinner, Silver Sedge, Stone, Cow Dung, Grizzly King, Beaverkill, Professor Sand.

Dozen **$1.25**

Leonard West, author of a British classic entomology, *The Natural Trout Fly and Its Imitation,* was not the only author who cashed in on his work by selling his endorsement. Halford did it with his series of numbered patterns and in this country Louis Rhead got a royalty on his "nature lures." A rather amusing attempt to do the same thing was also tried a few years ago. The inventors of an artificial, fluorescent fiber trade-named Gantron, which could be used for fishing-

MARSHALL FIELD & COMPANY 49

We are the exclusive Chicago agents for the

"Leonard West" Series of Imported Trout Flies

Each genuine fly sold by us is distinguished by a blue and white label bearing a facsimile of Leonard West's (registered trade-mark) autograph.

Patterns listed here have been carefully selected for American waters, from flies described and illustrated in Mr. West's work, "The Natural Trout Fly and Its Imitation." We show a few typical patterns. It is, however, impossible in black and white to do justice to the wonderful effects, both of color and design, obtained by Mr. West's unique dressing.

2 Orange Crane Fly	50 Stone Fly	81 Xyloto
85 Ruby Wasp	95 Red & Blk. Caterpillar	98 Green Caterpillar

Above, dozen..**$1.75**

3 Evening Crane Fly	4 Gravel Bed Fly	5 Sml. Yellow Crane Fly
7 Black Gnat	8 Green Gnat	9 Ruby Gnat
12 Hoverer Fly	13 Small Hoverer Fly	17 Green Beetle
24 Wood Fly	25 Speckles	38 Small Red Spinner
34 Brown Spinner	35 Brn. & Yellow Spinner	51 February Red
39 Red Spinner	45 Jenny Spinner	52 Yellow Sallow, Pale Quill Body
80 Alder	96 Black Ant	

Above, dozen..**$1.50**

14 Silver and Black	22 Small Oak Fly	32 Turkey Brown
19 Snipe Fly	26 Bronze Fly	36 March Brown
20 Hawthorn	28 Bloe Fly	37 Early Olive Dun
49 Whirling Blue Dun	63 Buff Sedge	73 Water Measurer
58 Corncrake Sedge	69 Sailor Beetle	87 Autumn Green

Above, dozen..**$1.25**

fly bodies as well as for many other products, tried to get a royalty out of every Gantron-bodied fly sold by anyone, anywhere. They sold a tiny paper slip imprinted "Gantron" for a nickel and announced that they would prosecute anyone who sold a Gantron fly without a slip attached. So few cared for Gantron flies that this addition of 60 cents a dozen to their price never came into court.

Tooley's Bunty Bait

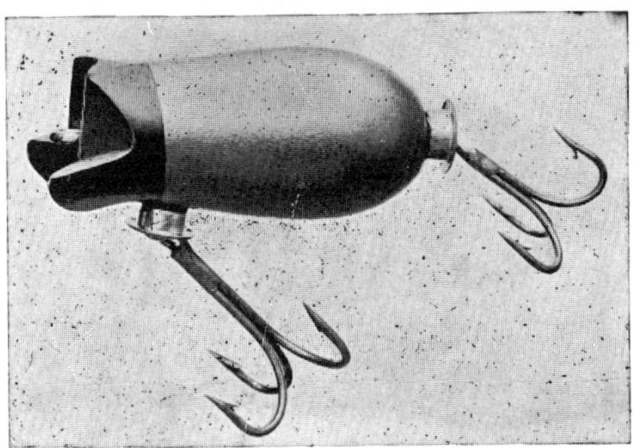

Was designed and is manufactured by a practical fisherman. It has proved a wonderful killer. Is the correct weight and size for bait casting. Two detachable treble hooks hung close together, but cannot tangle. Finished with waterproof celluloid enamel. Body 2⅛ inches long. Wiggles just under the surface of the water when reeled in at the proper speed.

No. 50. White head, red body.
No. 51. Red head, white body.
No. 54. Red head, gold body.
Each $0.75

"Jim-Dandy" Wobbler

It comes through the water like an object in great distress, making it a "sensational killer." Hooks cannot tangle.

No. 102. White with red face.
No. 101. All white.
Each $0.75

The South Bend Bass-Oreno

A new bait possessing all the combined merits of baits known as "wobbler" types. Is a very effective fish getter with a darting motion when reeled in. The faster it is reeled the deeper it will travel. Made of red cedar. Enamel will not crack. Equipped with three extra strong nickel plated treble hooks.

Body is 3½ inches long, just the right size and weight for critical anglers who do not wish to cast a clumsy bait. When not in motion it is a surface bait and floats.

Style No. 973RH. Red head with white body.
Style No. 973Rain. Rainbow color.
Each $0.50

The New Weedless Moonlight Floating Bait No. 2

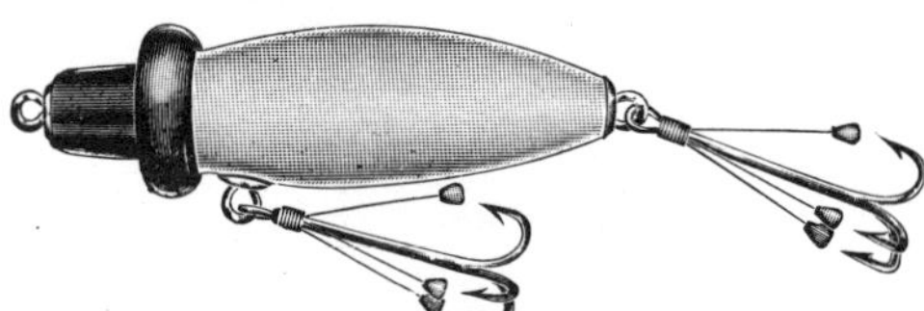

This bait is very similar in construction to the famous Moonlight Floating Bait No. 1. It is a LUMINOUS, SELF - GLOWING BAIT with a red head and is equipped with WEEDLESS treble hooks.

Length of body 3⅝ inches. Size of hooks 3/0. Hooks can be removed if desired. Weight ¾ oz.

No. 2—Weedless Moonlight bait. Each.................................... $0.60

Luminous and illuminated baits have long been an obsession with the angling inventor despite the fact that no one has ever seen a natural fish lit up. This luminous plug is one of a numerous clan. The luminous paint absorbed light during the day and at night emitted it at a rapidly diminishing rate. Thereafter, the fisherman had to revive his plug at short intervals with a flashlight. It didn't work very well.

MARSHALL FIELD & COMPANY 93

No. 7. Trolley Sinker

The best trolley made. Can be opened by steadily pressing lever in and then pushing sideways. Has three brass pulleys; the middle pulley catches line below when pulling up, thus preventing line from cutting in corner of fork. Weight 10 oz.
Each $0.25

No. 6 Trolley Sinker

Also a double trolley with brass forks and brass pulleys. Weight 7 oz.
Each $0.20

No. 1 Trolley Sinker

Has brass fork and brass pulley. Weight, 4½ oz.
Each $0.10

No. 2 Trolley Sinker

Is same design as No. 1, but is heavier and has larger brass pulley. Weight, 6 oz.
Each $0.15

No. 4 Trolley Sinker

Is a double trolley; has brass fork and brass pulleys; can be opened by pushing arms out. Weight, 7 oz.
Each $0.25

Fishing Alarm Bell

To be used for throw line or trolley fishing from a boat or pier. It is called the sleepy fisherman's friend.
Each $0.05

Automatic Anchors

Weighs about 1 pound and can be carried in pocket or tackle box. It is used for trolley fishing, anchoring small boats when hunting or fishing, also for anchoring decoys. Throwing out this anchor, it opens automatically, and if you wish to haul in, pull line tight and let go at once. This will loosen anchor and close it up automatically so you can land it easily.
Each $0.25

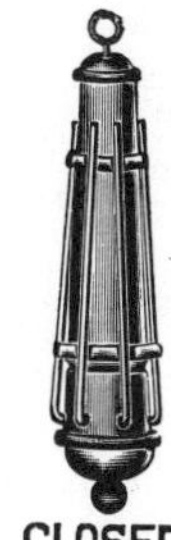

Even in 1917 a "pocket anchor" would have been such a bargain at 25 cents that one suspects a typographical error.

Redfield's Patent Adjustable Spring Cap Sinker

Nos.	2	3	4	5
Doz.	**$0.25**	**$0.30**	**$0.35**	**$0.40**

Nos.	6	7	8
Doz.	**$0.45**	**$0.50**	**$0.60**

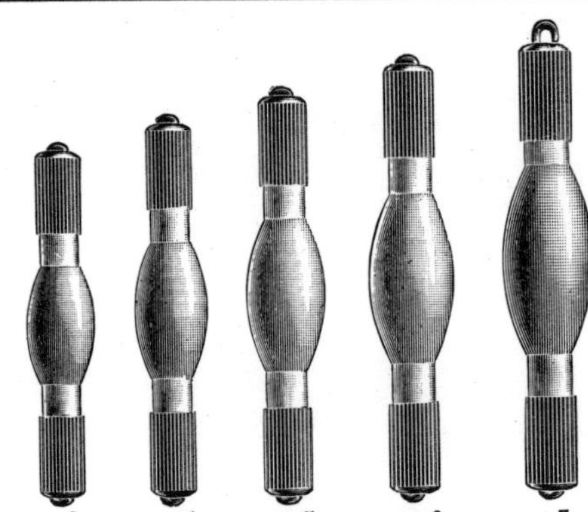

Plain Ringed Sinkers

Nos.	2	3	4	5
Weight, oz.	⅛	1/6	1/5	¼
Doz.	**$0.10**	**$0.10**	**$0.11**	**$0.12**
Nos.	6	7	8	9
Weight, oz.	1/3	½	¾	1
Doz.	**$0.13**	**$0.15**	**$0.23**	**$0.29**

Cut shows No. 8.

Official Tournament Casting Weights

As adopted and used by all Casting Clubs.

All official weights are stamped. Made of aluminum. Two sizes, ¼ oz. and ½ oz.
Each **$0.15**

Cooper's Safety Pin Snap Swivels

Cooper's Snap

The only practical snap. A boon to fishermen.

Will not catch weeds and are absolutely reliable for strength. Will carry 50 lbs. without opening.

Spring steel wire, with brass swivel. Three sizes.

With No. 1/0 Swivel, dozen **$0.60**
With No. 2 Swivel, dozen .... **.48**
With No. 4 Swivel, dozen .... **.48**

Cooper's Safety Pin Snap and Swivel Sinkers

Same as safety snap swivel, but has swivel sinker in place of brass swivel. Made in 3 sizes: With size 8, 10, 12 swivel sinkers.
Each **$0.10**

The Jamison Non-Kinking Sinker

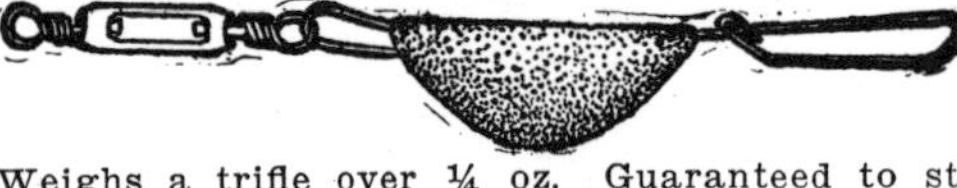

A combination of sinker, snap and swivel. Will hold any bait right side up, and positively prevents the line from kinking in either casting or trolling.
Weighs a trifle over ¼ oz. Guaranteed to stand at least 50 lbs. strain.
Each **$0.10**

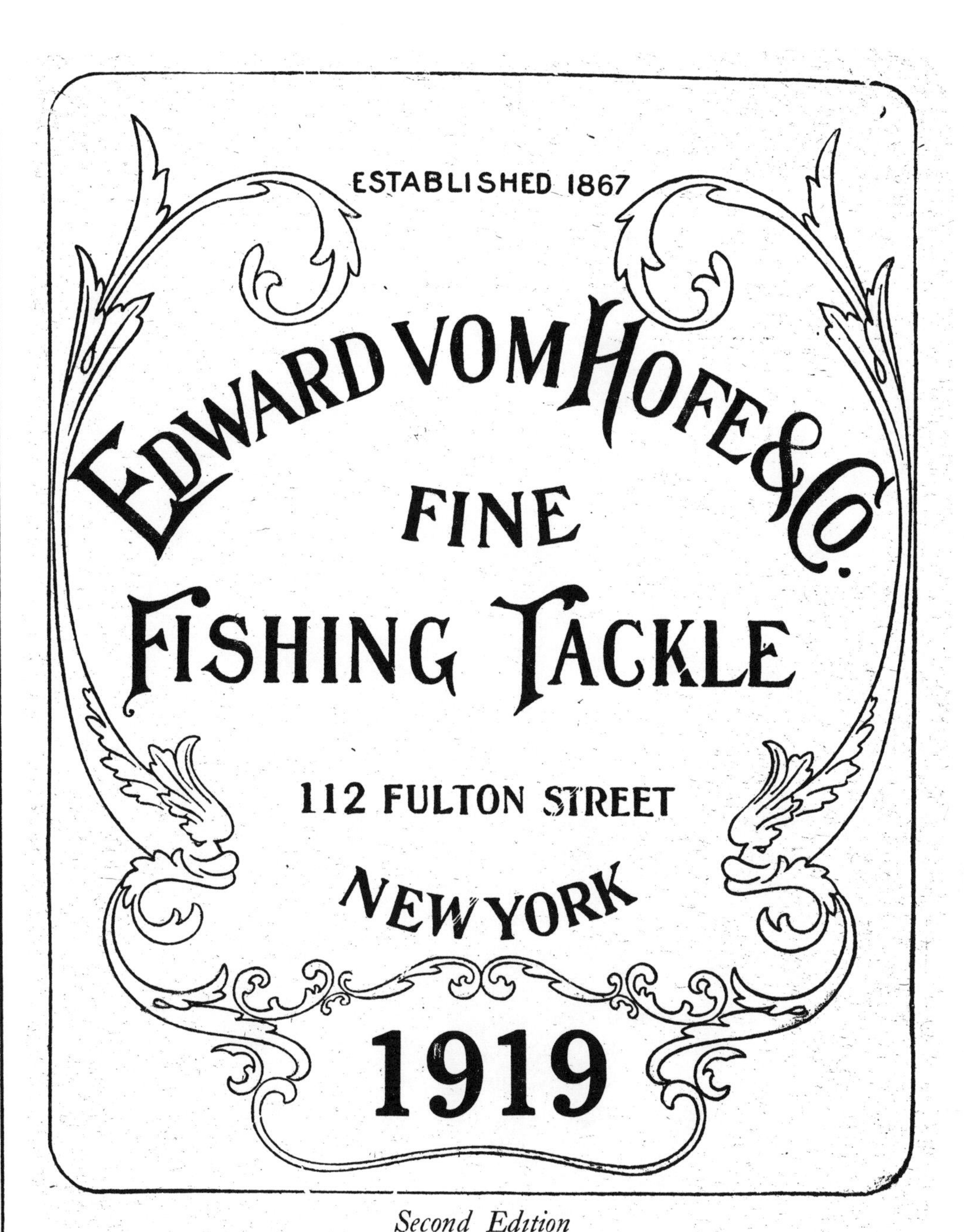

Second Edition

Julius and Edward vom Hofe were reel inventors and reel makers of much ingenuity and high skill. Their workmanship was of the highest quality and their expensive products dominated the field of flyrod salmon fishing and saltwater fishing. The star drag slipping clutch and the irreversible handle were invented in 1902, according to this text, but apparently did not become popular until saltwater game fishing came into vogue. Note that in 1919 the star drag still is not mentioned by that name except in the title of the reel. Maybe the robust prices deterred a great many potential customers.

A fisherman could always apply braking force by pressing a leather tab against the spinning spool, but only the irreversible handle could eliminate the knuckle-busting danger from the playing of a big fish. Properly used, the star drag is a fish-catching machine that virtually eliminates the loss of a fish by holding it too hard or by breaking the line.

EDWARD VOM HOFE & CO.'S

"UNIVERSAL STAR"

HAND-MADE TARPON, TUNA, DEEP SEA OR OCEAN REEL

Finest quality rubber, metal parts White Metal, full steel pivots, combination metal safety bands and re-inforced rubber disks, steel gear post, adjustable pivot cap, tobin bronze gear shaft, back sliding click, adjustable automatic tension drag (for description see page 38), "S" shaped balance handle, sliding oil cap, handle to screw off, solid reel seat, shouldered bars, bronze gears, countersunk screws, spring ball oiler over gear post, pilot wheel adjusted tension drag, all springs, pawls and tension parts of phosphor bronze, roller bearing under pilot, removable leather thumb pad, free spool arrangement, straight or pear shaped rubber knob is optional.

No.	Size	Capacity	Price
621	2/0,	300 yards No. 9, or 200 No. 15	$57.50 each
	3/0,	400 " " 9, " 200 " 18	60.00 "
	4/0,	500 " " 9, " 300 " 18 or 200 No. 24.........	62.50 "
	6/0,	300 " " 24, " 225 " 27 " 200 " 30.........	65.00 "
	9/0,	500 " " 24, " 350 " 30 " 300 " 39.........	75.00 "

In this, our latest model, we have made many alterations and improvements in details of mechanical features, but the fundamental principles remain the same, as patented in 1902, and are not to be improved upon as the experience of 15 years has proven.

ADVANTAGES OF THIS REEL

Under no circumstances can handle revolve backward; hence no injury to hands or fingers.

Bearings are all accessible for oiling without the use of tools or removing of any parts; danger of frozen pivots or gear post being entirely eliminated.

Free spool always at command of angler.

Drag easily and instantly regulated.

Both drags being automatic, will release under pressure. Breaking of lines, rods and other tackle is thereby avoided.

GALVANIZED FLOATING MINNOW BUCKET

Round

Oval

All our Buckets are made with an air tight compartment, making a floating pail. They are made of iron and galvanized to prevent rusting. Do not confound them with the ordinary tin pail.

12 quart, round	$2.75 each	12 quart oval	$3.00 each
16 quart, round	3.00 each	16 quart, oval	3.40 each

MINNOW OR LIVE BAIT CAR

Cylindrical body with conical ends, permits unimpeded passage through weeds. Will go through water easily when the boat is propelled, admitting plenty of fresh air and water the while and at the same time affording ample protection against injury to the minnows either from the motion of the boat or because of rough seas. Capacity 10 quarts.

Strongly built throughout. Finished in highest grade green baking enamel.

All metal galvanized iron ....$4.00 each

Any of above ordered by express add 25 cents for crate

REFRIGERATOR BASKETS

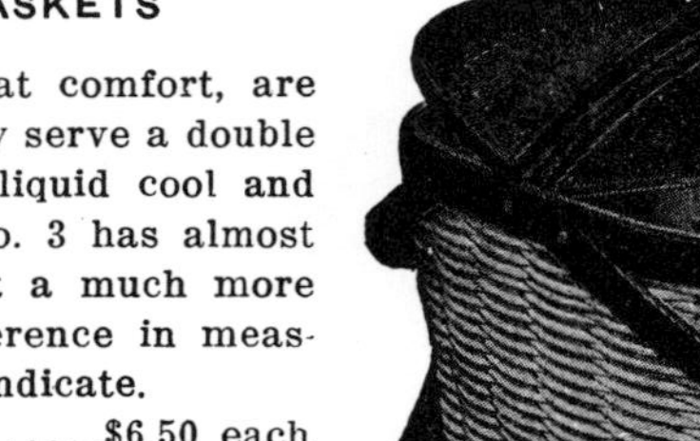

These Baskets are a great comfort, are well made and will last. They serve a double purpose, keep lunch fresh, liquid cool and fish fresh coming home. No. 3 has almost square ends thus making it a much more larger basket than the difference in measurement from No. 2 would indicate.

No. 0.	13x10x7½	inches	$6.50 each
No. 1.	18x12x8½	inches	7.25 each
No. 2.	20x13x10	inches	8.75 each
No. 3.	21x12x10	inches	11.50 each

CRAB TRAPS

Made of Galvanized wire and when not in use folds up flat, like a book.

Price .... 75 cents each

STRAPS

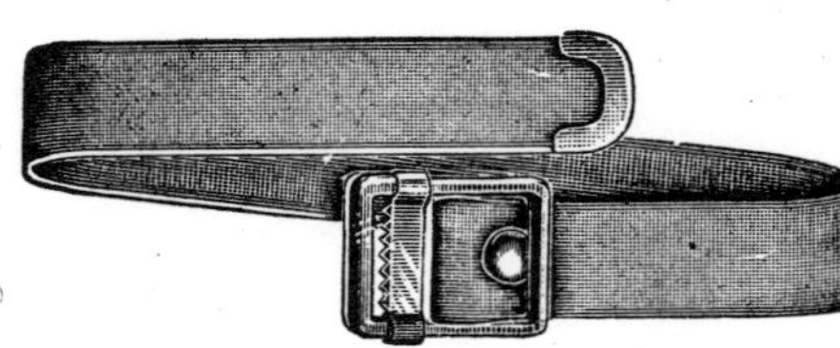

No. 1

No. 1. Plain web strap, 40x¾ inch with buckle..........................12c each

No. 2 and 3

No. 2. **Plain web strap,** with wide web center and buckle..................**30c each**

No. 3 **Plain leather strap,** with wide web center and buckle..................**40c each**

COMBINATION STRAPS

They are the best for the practical angler, for by their use the weight of the basket is thrown on the left shoulder leaving the right arm **free for casting.**

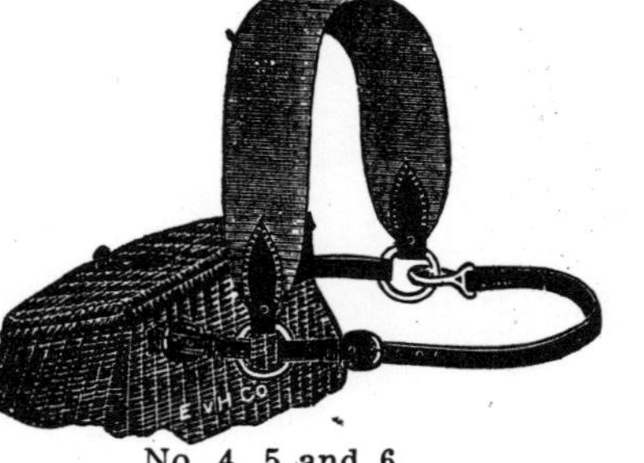

No. 4, 5 and 6.

No. 4. Made entirely of webbing ....**40c each**

No. 5. Made of leather with web center ....**60c each**

No. 6. Made of finest quality webbing, leather and brass buckles..........2.75 each

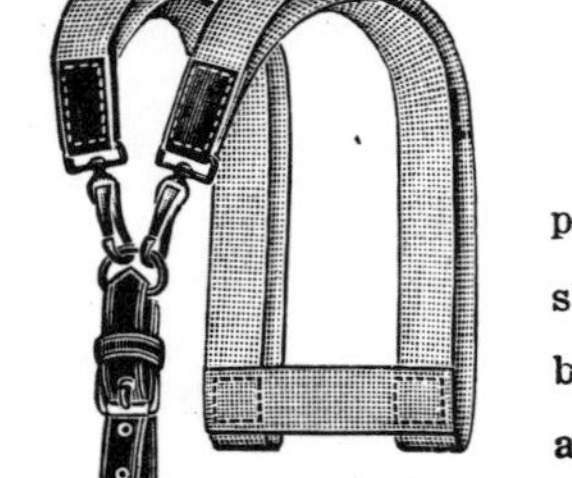

SHOULDER STRAPS

Used only for the taking of large fish, such as **Tuna, Tarpon,** Sharks and Swordfish. Strap **passes around both shoulders with hook in front to fasten on reel bar, made of** best quality webbing and leather, **and is a great relief to the arms.**

Price .... **$2.50 each**

INSECT REPELLANTS

We list several kinds of this material all of which we have tried and can recommend. They differ many in their method of application.

Wood's Lollacapop, a grease like cold cream, smelling strongly of tar. Put up in 2 oz cans ....30c each

Flyskeet, a liquid preparation in 4 oz bottles ....25c each

Bite-no-more, a liquid which dries on the skin, no insect will bite through it, and is perfectly harmless. In 2 oz cans........25c each

Mosquitone, put up in sticks in a glass tube, is practically odorless and has the soothing qualities of menthol ....20c each

HEAD NETS

No. 1-2

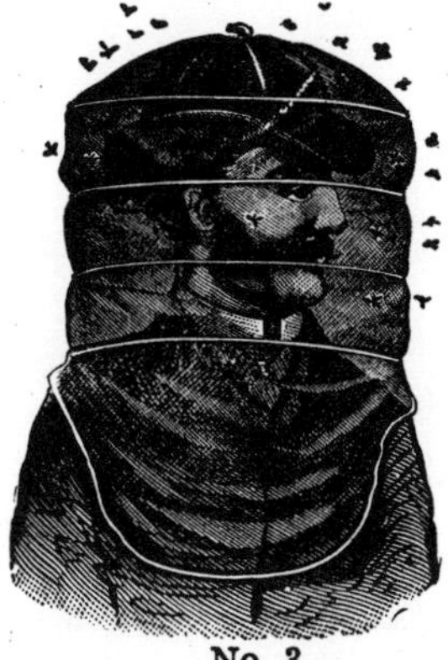

No. 3

No. 4-5

		Each
No. 1.	Made of fine green English netting, with light cloth top and worn over any wide brim hat. Fastens with draw string under collar.........	85c
No. 2.	Same as No. 1, cheaper material	50c
No. 3.	Made of green netting, has covered steel frame and rim of shot around lower edge	75c
No. 4.	Made of fine green English netting, fits around any hat, has horse-hair window which does not impair the vision and has self-closing aperture to admit of smoking. Weight 1 ounce	—
No. 5.	Same style as No. 3, but made of American cloth netting...............	—

The guide ("a little o' yer Fly Cream") and his "sport" in pith helmet and puggaree are old friends, and the three headnet wearers have not changed in a generation or more. But even fifty years ago, tackle catalogs were beginning to look modern. After all, the only major changes in half a century have been the advent of the fixed-spool spinning reel, the glass rod, and plastics—especially nylon leaders and lines.

LINE RELEASER

Ever have your fily in a tree? Got mad, of course. This little tool will **not save** your temper but it will save your line, leader, flies and possibly the tip **of your rod.** Set the tool on the tip of your rod at the side spurs, lift the tool with rod to **twig to** be cut, placing tool over same, now **keep** a steady pull on string and withdraw rod then by pulling the string the two **knife** edges swing to pass each other **closely,** the same as a pruning knife and down comes twig and your belongings.

Cut half size.

Cutter including leather case. . $1.35 each

SOLID BRASS CLEARING RINGS

Cut 1-3 size

For releasing line when caught on bottom of lake or stream.

Diameter 2¼ incnes.

Price .... $1.00 each

LINE WINDERS

Best quality, made of hard wood, good finish, revolve on handle.

No. 1. Size of frame, 8¼x4½ inches .... 25c each

No. 2. Size of frame, 10x5 inches .... 25c each

LEVEL REEL WINDER

Winds and spools your line without thumbing or fingering. Can be attached to any ordinary reel, and **prevents backlash snarls.**

You cast in the ordinary way, then simply turn your reel handle, the winder does the rest. The arm of the winder moves from side to side and spools the line evenly without bunching. The line passes through an agate rimmed eye in the arm of the winder, preventing friction. The winder does not interfere in the least with casting.

Price .... $1.50 each

DOCK BELLS

A Quality, Brass .... 15c each B Quality, Steel .... 6c each

It is impossible to see how the pictured gadget could possibly do what the text claims; I'll bet a red apple that it couldn't. Why should anyone make and sell a dingus like this when the level-winding casting reel had been on the market for years? The answer can only be, price; level-winders were relatively expensive in those days.

V

AFTER 1920

Abbey & Imbrie
1820
1920
Centennial
Abbey & Imbrie
Fishing Tackle
CENTENNIAL
CATALOG

(18) *Abbey & Imbrie, N. Y.* "Fishing Tackle that's Fit for Fishing." *Catalogue for 1920* 61

Fishing Outfit Built Especially for Boy Scouts (10)

Haversack Fishing Rod and complete angling outfit. Sanctioned by the Committee on Scout Supplies, Boy Scouts of America.

Everybody knows the motto of the Boy Scouts is "BE PREPARED." The Boy Scout who is fond of fishing needs one of these outfits to "be prepared" for Mr. Fish.

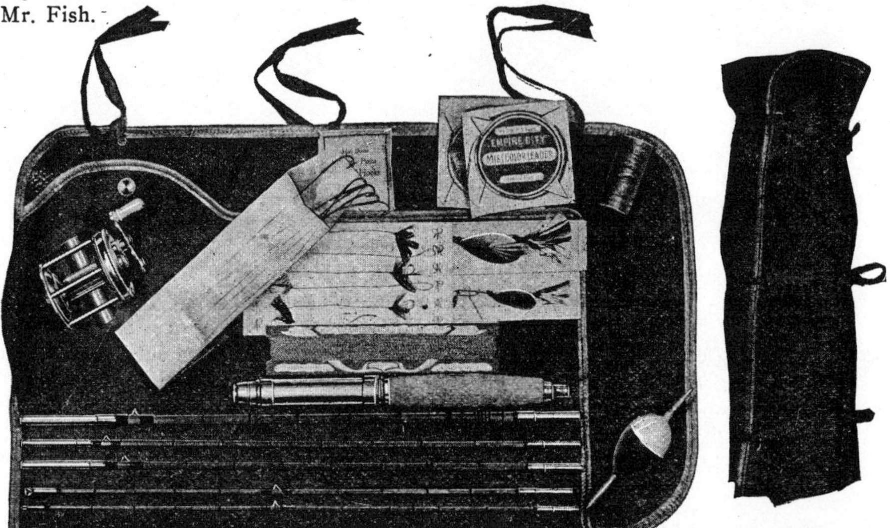

No. A **"Ready for the Hike"**

No. A—Split Bamboo Rod, with two tips, making a fly, bait or boat rod; quadruple multiplying, nickel-plated reel, sliding click and drag; 75 feet of pure braided silk line; half dozen hand tied selected flies; 1 dozen double snelled hooks; 2 three-foot double gut leaders; 2 nickel-plated trolling spoons; assortment of sinkers and two-color cork float; all in neat, leather bound carrying case. Made to attach to Boy Scout Haversack (101)..Price, **10.00**

No. B—Same as No. A described above, furnished with 4½-foot Steel Casting Rod with finger hook in place of split Bamboo Rod (102)..............Price, **$8.00**

No. C—Three-piece black enamel, cork handled steel rod, with nickel-plated reel seat; nickel-plated multiplying reel with click and drag; 75 feet of hard braided casting line; half dozen snelled spring steel hooks; one nickel-plated trolling spoon, half dozen assorted flies; assortment of sinkers; two-colored float—all in a neat carrying case, made to attach to Boy Scout Haversack (103)...........Price, **$5.00**

Almost as far back as trout flies have been offered for sale, they have been called "hand tied"; the term is still used today. But did anyone ever see an artificial fishing fly that was *not* hand tied?

During World War II a government representative who was buying recreational equipment for U.S. military personnel asked a well-known New York custom tier to quote a price on one million fishing flies. Jim Deren laughed heartily at this ignoramus and asked him if he had any idea of the magnitude of such a job. "Ah," said this genius, "you old-fashioned craftsmen must modernize. What you need is a machine with a lot of power-driven spindles each with its own supply of thread, body material . . ."

The world is still waiting for the power-driven, multiple spindle, electronically controlled by programmed computer, automatic flytieing machine that will create a solid stream of perfect flies untouched by human hands.

FORESTAND STREAM — MAY, 1921

JAMISON'S FLY ROD WIGGLER

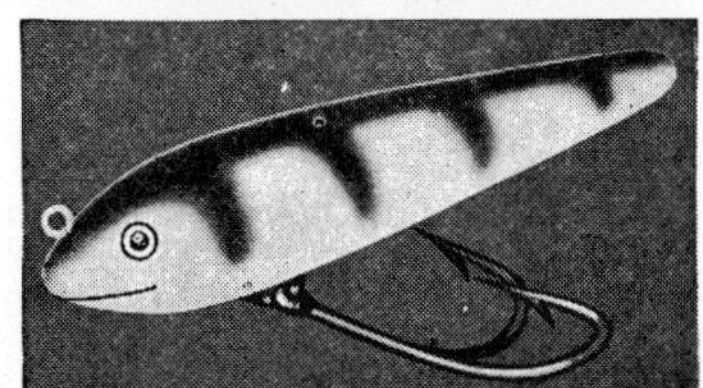

LOOKS LIKE A FISH ACTS LIKE A FISH

It catches more fish and bigger fish than any other fly rod lure known. Ask anyone who has used it. Exquisitely finished in beautiful designs that are exact imitations of real living minnows. Can hardly be told from one. Made in Silver Shiner, Golden Shiner, Red Side Minnow, Yellow Perch, Red Head with White Body, All White, All Yellow and All Red.

Large Bass size, 2⅛ in. long / Small Bass size, 1¾ in. long / Trout size, 1¼ in. long — 65c. each

Four in vest pocket compartment box, $2.60

Send stamp for catalog of Baits, Flies, Lines, Leaders, Etc.

W. J. JAMISON CO.
Dept. S 736 So. California Avenue, CHICAGO, ILL.

My New Blue Devil Darning Needle!

It's a Dry Fly—Trout and Bass Jump at It. You have known the Joe Welsh Leader for years—now make the acquaintance of the "Blue Devil."

Joe Welsh Leader in 6 breaking strains—a 3-ft. length by mail, 25c.; 6-ft. length, 50c.; 9-ft. for 75c.

A "Blue Devil" and 3-ft. Leader, 75c.

JOE WELSH
Pasadena, California
Distributor for
U. S. and CANADA

BENSON

Anti Back-lash
(Patented)

Requires no thumbing or spooling. DRYS THE LINE ON THE REEL. Instantly adjusted to any bait and force of cast. Throws bait into or with wind accurately and WITHOUT BACK-LASHING. Simply constructed—no gears to get out of order. Weighs but six ounces. Mechanically perfect. Direct drive "brass on steel" bearing. Takes up 15 inches. Beautifully built—smoothly finished in nickel. staunch, easily adjusted, free running. And the SPRING THUMBS THE REEL. It cannot back-lash. Instant take-apart.

Ask your dealer—or sent prepaid from manufacturers on receipt of $4.50. Address Dept. 21

Benson-Vaile Co.
KOKOMO, INDIANA

Price $4.50
WE PAY THE POSTAGE

TROUT FLIES
FROM THE EMERALD ISLE

Tied on best tested hooks; eyed or taper shank and looped gut (4½ inches). Any size from No. 8 to 12.

All the standard American patterns or any special pattern supplied.

Guaranteed Irish make and tied here on the premises.

PRICE, 60 CENTS PER DOZEN

Special terms to the trade. Immediate attention given to all orders. A trial solicited.

L. KEEGAN
(*Specialist in Fly Tying*)
3 INNS QUAY, DUBLIN, IRELAND

The rarest thing in angling, in 1921, was a foreign advertiser offering his wares direct to the consumer. There were lots of cheap British and other foreign flies coming here then, but through American dealers. One wonders how Keegan made out at 60 cents a dozen.

Billy and his first catch with the Little Egypt.

G. F. Rogers Billy Wood

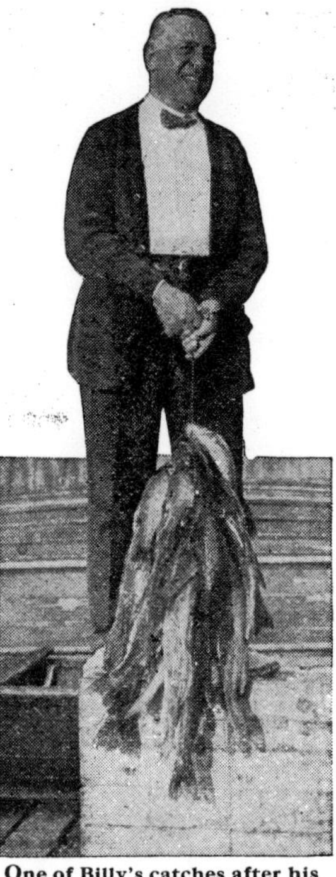

One of Billy's catches after his conversion.

The Conversion of Billy Wood

In response to one of our advertisements the following letter came in from Mr. William Wood, a total stranger:

April 2.

Dear Brother Al.:

I jest been a readin your Ad. in the Field and Stream where you was a speakin of them there Fishability Baits of yourn, an I sort a bounced my eyes erlong that list (of what the boys do be asaying) an she do read like a last years Almanac.

I guess though she is all to the mustard as I notice you have a Parson in the lineup, but it do get me sort of riled up when I think I was the only heman who could not work them critters of yourn an my Dollar gone.

Away last summer come June my runninmate G. F. Rogers caught me in an unguarded moment when my fingers wasn't crossed and whisked the above amount to couple with a like sum from his own diggins to buy a couple more Fish Chasers for our tackle boxes.

July 2nd found us up Georgian Bay way an fer all like two kids with a new toy we must try them there Egypt Wigglers, an I do fessup that when I got my lamps on them meanderin through the drink they did look good to me.

After tryin them this way and that, twix and between spells with other baits which we took along for two weeks we just histed the white flag and put them among some more souvenirs we was a keepin.

If those Bass (which were so thick that we had to lift a few before we could find room in the water for our anchor) refused the other baits I would not have kerred so much, but here we was a ketchin em with any thing from juicy Dew worms to homespun yarn, an quickern a cat could take a fit.

Now Al. I have been splashin baits with all them sure getem names sense I was big enough to gut a fish and I come clean when I says that I was a bit disapinted with the way them Bass overlooked Little Egypt.

Bless my soul Al. I do believe every word in your speel erbout them air baits o yourn, but from where I sit I would say there is some wrinkle such as spittin on your hook which we overlooked on the Directions an if you will put us hep to the game so as we might have our tintypes nailed on the wall with the rest of the Boys why we won't say any more about that dollar.

Yours truly,

Billy Wood.

SHIMMY WIGGLER, ½ or ⅝ oz., $1.00

ORIENTAL WIGGLER, ½ or ⅝ oz., $1.00.
All Red, All White, or Red and White.

LITTLE EGYPT WIGGLER, weight ½ oz., 75c.

SKIDDER, weight ½ oz., 75c.

Mr. Wood received an answer.—"If you can't catch bass with an Al Foss bait, better give up fishing and take up golf or checkers!" A circular was enclosed describing the "Oriental Wiggler" and telling of our $500 challenge to all other bait manufacturers. His next letter follows

April 11th.

Dear Brother Al.:

I do luv a rooster for tew things. Fust for the krow what am in him, and second for the spurs what am on him to bak up his krow with.

! ! Gee gosh all Hemlock ! ! Al. you do pint the finger of scorn at them orniary lo down Bait coiners in that there challinge of yourn, an jest to sick you on I do right here wrap up one mo William the which is payment for one of Little Egypts' brothers Oriental.

I don't jest feel that I will wear out morn two hook disgourgers sepratin little Oriental from the bowls of the finny tribe, but dog gone my hide if I don't give you an it a chance to add another star to your flag.

No sam-singin Parson can git his name on sich costly pages as you do buy, an me not be in the runnin. So send it along Al. an I'll zigzag little Oriental through the dampness till I set that spinner of hissen afire.

Bass-a-getably speakin the haw! haw! is on me so far, but, I am some ell commin down the back stretch an the hoss that noses me out at the wire will sure know he was in a race.

If me an Oriental fall down again you wont have any more friends than an alarm clock

Yours lurebly,

Billy Wood.

November 19th.

Dear Al.:

Tucked right ferninst the folds of this epistle you will diskiver a snapshot of yers truly an his runnin mate, G. F. Rogers.

Ashowin us hitched to the ends of a pike pole the which is strung with the results of teasin the walleyes with Little Egypt and Little Oriental for a little morn two hours (21 walleyes weighin 123 lbs).

Say! Al: if you know of some feller thet wants ter trade a settin hen fer a peck of wooden plugs jest kivered with hooks, jest you sick him on to me.

Fish-a-getably Yers,

St. Catherines, Ont., Can. Billy Wood.

Almost every dealer now has the Al Foss Pork Rind Minnows

45c—Bass, Musky and Fly Spinner sizes.

If yours is "dead from the neck up," either hunt up a new dealer or send us his name and we'll supply you direct.

AL FOSS, 1712 Columbus Road, Cleveland, Ohio

Watch for "The Conversion of Teenie Smith" in next month's magazines.

In Writing to Advertisers mention Forest and Stream. It will identify you.

222 FOREST AND STREAM

A COMPLETE CAMP ON WHEELS

KNOW the *complete* joy of a summer in the open—carefree and comfortable. Camp in the woods, revel in the fishing in those lakes and rivers where you've longed to cast a line. And take the family with you.

The "Auto-Kamp" Trailer

provides home comforts with camp life. Fully equipped tent, electric lights, two large beds with sagless springs and downy mattresses, big enough for four people. Auto-Kamp equipment also includes gasoline stove, ice box, food compartments, etc. Folds compactly and trails easily behind any car, over any road, at any speed.

Write TODAY for Auto-Kamp Catalog

Auto-Kamp Equipment Co.
2023 Sheridan Avenue
Saginaw Michigan

TENTOBED

A Tent and Bed Combined

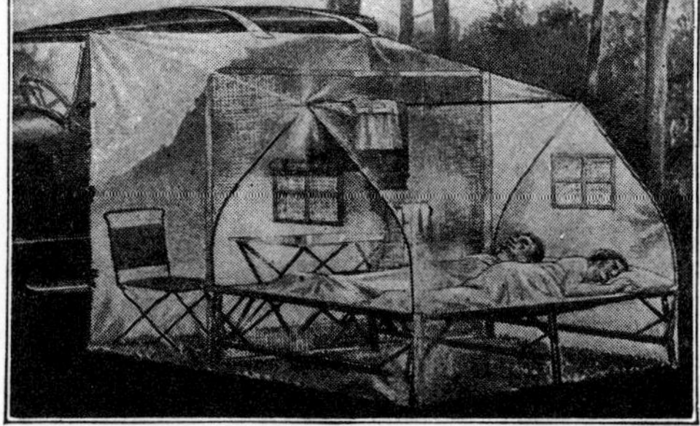

Tentobeds are the most practical for tourists and people desiring to camp. They are made in two sizes; one as shown is made especially to use with Auto. Other style is suitable for sleeping on porch or lawn. **Tentobeds roll up in a small package** very light in weight, can be put up in 5 minutes, require no stakes or poles. **Water-proof and Insect-proof.**

The beds are very comfortable to sleep in. They save the price they cost in hotel bills in a few days. You are independent and not obliged to pay the exorbitant prices often demanded of tourists.

On sale by reliable dealers. We will mail you, on request, literature fully describing Tentobeds, also our Autobed, made to use inside of auto.

TENTOBED COMPANY, Dept. 11, 3300 Jackson Boulevard, CHICAGO, ILL.

Here is a pioneer in the then little-known recreation of trailer-camping. Most trailers were homemade in those days; popular mechanical magazines abounded in plans and detailed instructions for building them. Campsites, either free or pay, were a rarity, and trailer-campers were called "tin-canners" and coldly regarded by boardinghouse- and innkeepers.

Page 306: The mass displays of fish have gone out of style but there are scores of good old names still in the catalogs even though many of them are now appendages of corporate conglomerates.

ART WILSON says, says he, that there must be a few really sizable bass still residin' in the waters of this here North America. Art allows also that he would kinda like to see the color of their hair. So he has rigged up a friendly little contest for all good bass fishermen. Fair field. Open to all. No strings. And darn little "tape" — red or otherwise.

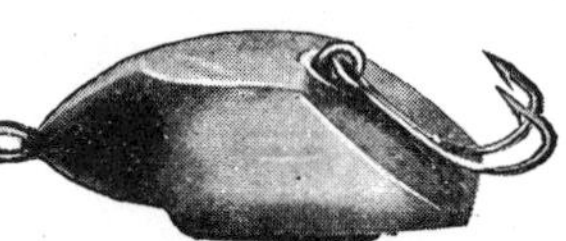

Wilson's Grass Widow

Weedless — but not fishless

75c

Here is the dope: A prize of $100 will be awarded to the man, woman or child who catches the biggest large-mouth bass this year on any one of the three new Wilson Wobbler Baits shown here, namely Bassmerizer, Grass Widow or Wilson's Sizzler. $100 will also be awarded to the person who catches the biggest small-mouth bass.

Please note carefully:— In order to qualify for this contest you must enter your name before July 1, 1921, and you must catch your large or small-mouth bass on one of the three Wilson Baits shown here.

If Your Dealer Does Not Carry These Baits in Stock, Order Direct from This Ad.

$1.00

Wilson's Bassmerizer

Bait shown on the left is a combination bait. Dives and wobbles—or, with lines attached to other end becomes a surface bait with a good husky wiggle.

$1.00

Wilson's Sizzler

Wilson's SIZZLER shown above is weedless until the fish strikes. Then the scissors, action bares the two sharp hooks.

MOST good dealers carry the old reliable Wilson Wobblers, but not all of them have stocked these three new numbers. If your dealer cannot supply you, simply mark a cross through the baits you want, enclosing check or money order to cover. We prefer to have you buy through your dealer, but we will ship you direct if your dealer cannot supply you.

WILSON WOBBLERS

The Baits That Taught Bass How to Fight

"TAKE a Wilson Wobbler with you—and you'll come back home with bass." If you are an old-time fisherman you know that statement is more than a catch phrase. *I is gospel truth!* These wiggling, wobbling, bass-alluring baits are dead-sure fish-getters —and the three new numbers shown above (the baits on which this contest is built) are worthy of their Wilson Wobbler parentage.

Enter Your Name Today

Simply drop us a line stating that you wish to be enrolled in this contest and your name will be registered. If you want any of the baits shown on this page just mark a cross through those you desire and send a check or money order.

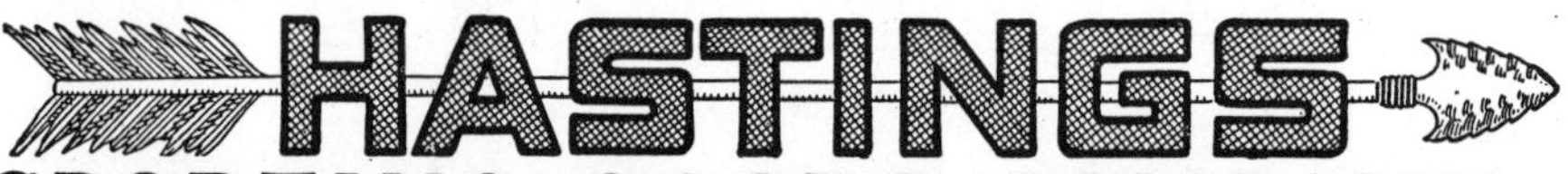

SPORTING GOODS COMPANY

418 Michigan Ave. HASTINGS, MICH.

Conditions of Biggest Bass Contest

Two Prizes — $100 Each

One will be awarded to the person catching the biggest large-mouth bass and one to the person catching the biggest small-mouth bass. In case of a tie in weight, greatest length over all will decide.

Should there be a tie as to both weight and length, girth measurement will be the deciding factor.

SHOULD THERE BE ONE OR MORE TIES IN WEIGHT, LENGTH AND GIRTH MEASUREMENT EACH TYING CONTESTANT WILL RECEIVE THE PRIZE OFFERED.

Contestants must furnish photograph of bass and bait—and sworn statement as to weight, length, girth and date of catch.

Contest open to all who use one of the three baits shown above. Contest closes November 1, 1921. Photos and statement must be mailed on or before that date.

Write today if you wish to enter. All contestants must be registered before July 1, 1921.

Offering money prizes "in gold" was very common until the U.S.A. went off gold coinage. It was intended to inspire confidence, one supposes; what other reason could there be—then?

Abbey & Imbrie

"Fishing Tackle that's Fit for Fishing"

Catalog 195
1923

Abbey & Imbrie

Division of Baker, Murray & Imbrie, Inc.

97 Chambers St., New York, N. Y.

THIS IS OUR 103rd YEAR

Spanish Silk-Worm Gut

For Leaders, Flies and Snelled Hooks

After being removed from the worm, the gut is drawn and then assorted according to quality, thickness and length.

We do not sell less than 100 strands of a kind.

Weight	Light Trout	Heavy Trout	Heavy Bass	Extra Heavy Bass	Salmon
First Quality—Stock Nos.	1	2	3	4	5
Per 100 strands	$0.70	$0.80	$1.00	$1.30	$2.80
Second Quality Stock Nos.	11	22	33	44	55
Per 100 strands	$0.60	$0.70	$0.80	$1.00	$1.80

Highest Quality Selected Mist Color Silk Worm Gut

The angler who makes his own leaders or ties his own flies may be sure that every strand of this gut is round, smooth, strong and free from flaws.

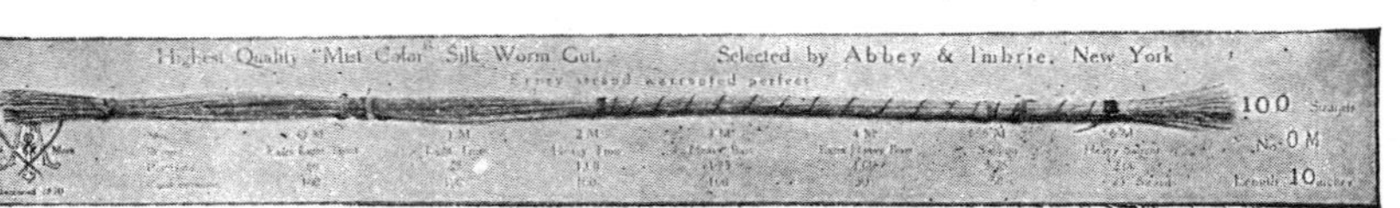

Stock Nos.	0M	1M	2M	3M	4M	5M	6M	
Weight	Extra Light Trout	Light Trout	Heavy Trout	Heavy Bass	Extra Heavy Bass	Salmon	Heavy Salmon	
Card contains	100	100	100	100	50	50	25	Strands, 10 in. long
Per card	$1.15	$1.35	$1.75	$2.25	$1.75	$3.00	$3.50	

Highest Quality Very Light Selected Silk Worm Gut—Mist Color

Half-drawn Gut (for Nos. 12 and 14 Hook Flies)..... Quarter-drawn Gut (for Nos. 10 and 12 Hook Flies)..	7	10	12	14	16	inches
	$1.50	$2.25	$3.00	$3.75	$4.50	per 100

Highest Quality Selected Mist Color Gut—Looped on One End

Ready for the angler who wishes to tie his own flies or snelled hooks or to attach to eyed hook flies. Length about 8½ inches over all.

Stock Nos.	0ML	1ML	2ML	3ML	4ML	5ML	6ML	
Weight	Extra Light Trout	Light Trout	Heavy Trout	Heavy Bass	Extra Heavy Bass	Salmon	Heavy Salmon	
Single Gut	$0.60	$0.70	$0.85	$1.10	$1.35	$2.25	$4.25	per card of 3 dozen
Double Gut	$1.20	$1.40	$1.70	$2.20	$2.70	$4.50	$8.50	per card of 3 dozen

Trout Fly Watch Charms

First Quality, Gold Filled. ½ doz. in display box.....Each **$1.00**

Second Quality, Gold Plated. One dozen on a card....Each **.75**

Spanish Silk-Worm Gut—How it is Made

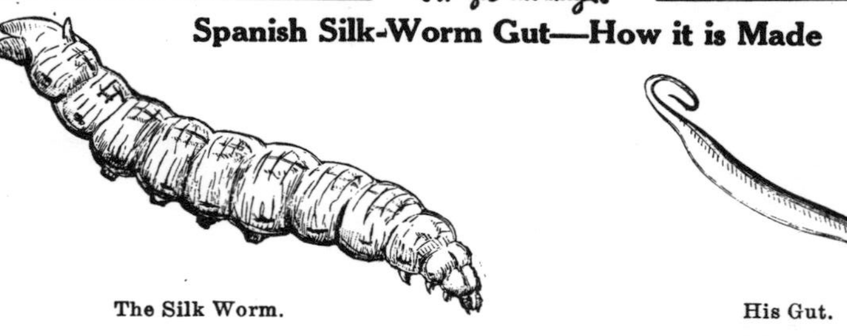

The Silk Worm. His Gut.

It is a common mistake even among otherwise well informed anglers, to speak of the gut of hooks, flies and leaders, as "cat gut." It is no discredit to that excellent domestic animal to say that her gut, if obtainable, is quite useless for fishing purposes. The gut familiar to all fishermen, is the gut of the silk worm, known to scientists as the "Bombyx Mori."

The earliest cultivation of the silk worm was in China, many centuries ago. Wherever mulberry trees grow in profusion, there one finds the prime requisite of successful silk worm culture. The best silk worm comes from the Province of Murcia in Southern Spain, and most of the gut which American and British anglers use is the product of that locality.

The silk worms of Murcia begin life early in March, and occupy about six weeks in coming to maturity, during which time they usually take four "Sleeps" in which state they lie dormant for three or four days at a time, then make a fresh start at consuming Mulberry leaves.

The silk worms are left in small buildings, mostly thatch-roofed, where they are spread out on low shelves. Mulberry leaves are brought in and scattered over them two or three times a day. They are hungry little beasts, and consume an enormous amount of food—except when taking one of their three or four day naps. The silk glands in the Bombyx Mori consists of two long thick-walled sacs, running along the sides of the body which open by a common orifice on the under lip of the worm. As the silk worm approaches maturity these sacs become gorged with a clear viscous fluid, which upon being exposed to the air immediately hardens to a solid mass. When the worms arrive at maturity those accustomed to their ways know by their appearance that they are fit either to spin themselves into a cocoon or to "make gut." If the price of gut is high as compared with silk, the owners (who are sensible business men) usually decide to "make gut." This decision, unfortunately for the worm, means murder and sudden death. The worm has no chance to turn. He is sacrificed forthwith to make an anglers holiday.

The process is simple but effective. The unsuspecting worms, having fed bountifully for six weeks on Murcia's choicest mulberry leaves, are gathered unceremoniously into baskets and emptied into tubs of vinegar and water. They are, indeed in a pickle, where they expire shortly. They are allowed to lie in this for some hours, which solidifies the "liquid silk" so that it may be drawn out in the form of "gut" in which all anglers know it.

These strands of gut are dried in the sun, when the surface film is either scraped off, or may be dissolved. The length of the strands can be regulated to a certain extent, but not altogether, as a strong "pickle" gives the silk sac a greater consistency than a weak pickle, and the gut will be shorter and thicker; but if this is overdone the strands pull out crooked, lumpy and cracked. The process of separating the gut—the long from the short, the thick from the thin, the high quality from the inferior—requires skill and long experience. There is no branch of the fishing tackle business that calls for greater devotion to the maintenance of reputation and high standards than in the selection of silk worm gut. To the novice all gut looks pretty much alike. But even the novice knows when the "biggest fish" gets away because a strand of gut broke at the crucial moment. And what he is likely to remember, the next time he buys his tackle, is to look for the name and trademark that guarantees to him a square deal even in so comparatively insignificant an item in his outfit as a strand of silk worm gut.

Page 310: More than a century ago, there was a determined effort to establish an American silk-growing industry in South Carolina by planting mulberry trees and utilizing the larvae of the Cecropia moth, an American cousin of the Asiatic silkworm. They look almost exactly alike—huge, fantastically shaped and colored insects of quite alarming appearance—but the sacs of the Cecropia larva are capable of being drawn into strands of great length, six feet and more. Apparently the Civil War removed even the vestiges of what was already a failing domestic industry.

Edwin T. Whiffen wrote a very interesting exposition of growing one's own leader material in an old how-to-do-it fishing book, *Trout Lore;* and an article about it was reproduced as an appendix to Dr. George Parker Holden's book on rodmaking, *The Idyl of the Split Bamboo.* Both books are long out of print but rare-book dealers turn them up occasionally.

Page 313: Here is our old friend "Steel Vine" again. This dealer at least has the grace to admit that it is bamboo, and that the corners are cut off the hexagonal construction to make a round rod. Fishermen would laugh at a round bamboo rod today, but they know more about rods than the fishermen of fifty years ago. Heddon still clings here to this design of a level-winder that apparently utilized some sort of cam action to waggle the line guide back and forth to spool the line. Note the short spool, 1½ inches; the waggler couldn't reach farther than that.

Underneath this item, see the competition—the South Bend conventional type of level-winder with the patented antibacklash braking bail; and surprisingly, the one without level wind but using the braking bail actuated by the line.

"Steel Vine" Bamboo Rods

"Steel Vine" cane is a light colored close grained variety of bamboo of strong fibre. It has great strength and elasticity, making it a durable rod of good action. Made of six strips of cane, glued, as in a split bamboo rod, and rounded. All are three pieces with extra tip.

The **"Fontinalis"**—A light and delicate fly rod for whipping streams, yet strong enough to stand the play of gamey fish when in the hands of a careful angler. It has a cork hand grasp and full Nickel Silver mountings, including the snake guides. Put up in a velvet covered wood form and bag. Weight, 4 ounces. Length, 8 feet ....Each $14.50

Steel Vine Stripping Rods With Reversible Handle

These rods are especially recommended for "stripping," viz.: the reel being used below the hand, and the line drawn from the reel by hand to make any length cast desired. Nickel Silver Mountings, Reversible Cork Grip, Hand-made Nickel Silver Bell Guides. Agate first Guide and Agate Tops. Put up in a velvet covered wood form and bag. Weight less than one ounce to the foot. Length, 9 or 9½ feet. Each $21.00

The "Abbey" Steel Vine Rods

With cork hand grasp, nickel plated mountings, welted ferrules and put up in a flannel covered form and bag. With "Chinchilla" pattern closely wound silk windings. **Strong, with good action. A dependable rod at a popular price.**

No. S. V. 9½ Fly—6½ oz., 9½ ft. (for river and lake fishing) Each $13.00

No. S. V. 8 Bait—7 oz., 8 ft. (for general black bass fishing) Each $13.00

Ordinary Quality Steel Vine Rods

With nickel plated mountings, welted ferrules, cork hand grasp, and put up in a flannel covered form and bag. Handsomely wound in two colors of silk.

Fly Rods (Snake Guides)

No. 3010. 5 oz., 8½ ft. (for stream and river fishing)...Each $10.25
No. 3011. 5½ oz., 9 ft. (for stream and river fishing)..Each 10.25
No. 3012. 6 oz., 9½ ft. (for river or lake fishing)......Each 10.25

Bait Rods (Two-Ring Guides)

No. 3015. 7 oz., 8 ft. (for general black bass fishing)...Each $10.25

Steel Vine "Fontinalis" Fly Rod

Good Quality Split Bamboo Rods

Swelled Butt Rods With Cedar Inlaid Butt, Three Pieces With Extra Tip

Nickel plated mountings. In flannel covered forms. Handsomely wound with clustered silk windings in several colors. With snake guides.

Trout and Black Bass Fly Rods

No. 3030. Cork grip, 4½ ounces, 8½ feet long (for stream fishing).......Each $14.50

No. 3032. Same as No. 3030, 6 ounces, 9½ feet long (for river or lake fishing) Each $14.50

No. 3132. Same as No. 3032, but with less expensive selection of material, 5½ ounces, 9 feet long (**for stream and river fishing**)..........................Each 9.50

Swelled Butt Trout Fly Rod With Cork Grip for Stream and River Fishing

No. 3060. Half swelled, cork grip, flannel covered form, 6 ounces, 9 feet long. Mounted **with snake guides.** Nickel mountings..........................Each $10.75

Heddon's New Auto-Spooler Reel No. 4-18 Each, $18.00

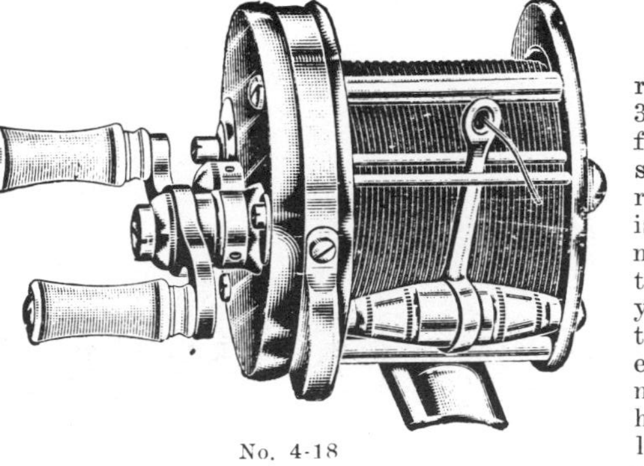
No. 4-18

A radical departure in self-spooling reels.

This reel is the same quality, material, workmanship and finish as the No. 3-15 reel — solid watch nickel silver frame, phosphor bronze gears, hardened steel pinion, helical spiral gears. Quadruple multiplying. The spooling device is of sturdy construction, producing minimum amount of friction and practically unlimited life. Spool holds 50 yds. of 20 lb. test and 75 yds. of 15 lb. test line. Length of spool 1¼ in., diameter 1⅝ in. It lays a kite-wind spool much the same as one would make by hand, but being always constant relieves the angler from attention to spooling. Like all Heddon reels it is completely oiled without taking down.

The South Bend Level-Winding Anti-Back-Lash Casting Reel

An attractive new Reel—A combination of the famous South Bend anti-back lash device and the popular level-winding feature—all in one reel. No thumbing—no spooling necessary.

Gives you instantly, without any previous practice, all joys and pleasures of bait-casting. Will not back-lash and is perfect in its level-winding or spooling device. The reel is of beautiful yet plain design. Strong and rigid in construction, but not heavy or clumsy. The frame and all component parts are made of nickel silver, satin finish. Agate jeweled spool caps of the screw-off pattern with adjustable spring tension grip. Gearing is quadruple multiplying. Equipped with click. The crank or handle has double grips, white Ivoroid. Capacity, 100 yards. A screw-driver, one extra pawl, and a practice casting weight is supplied with each reel. Complete with chamois bag. Price..Each, $25.00

The "South Bend" Anti-Back-Lash Casting Reel Nickel Silver with Jeweled Agate Bearings. Quadruple Multiplying

This reel is one that really works as if it were thumbed by an expert, the brake being automatically applied with the proper force as the line slackens at the end of the cast. The braking effect is adjustable in a moment, without the use of tools, to suit any weight bait. A half turn of the adjusting screw releases the brake and the reel can then be used and thumbed as an ordinary reel. Capacity, 60 yards. Price...........................Each, $12.50

"REDIFOR" NICKEL SILVER SELF-THUMBING REEL

When using the Redifor self-thumbing reel one has nothing to do with the delicate thumbing, because the automatic thumbing device takes care of that. Fitted with thumbers which are entirely automatic and needs no adjustments, being attached to the left flange of the spool **enclosed within the reel,** free from all possibilities of damage. Has Genuine Agate jeweled caps. Made of Nickel Silver treated to prevent tarnish, and with generated spiral tooth gears. **Has adjustable front sliding click and drag. Reel has a capacity of 60 to 100 yards according to size of line used. A highly satisfactory reel at** a low price, complete in leather hinge cover box, with oil can. Diameter disc, 2 inches; spool, 1⅞ inches wide............Each, $15.00

X-RAY VIEW ANTI-BACK-LASH DEVICE

Spoon Baits and Minnows—(Continued)

Percy Wadhams Nature Baits

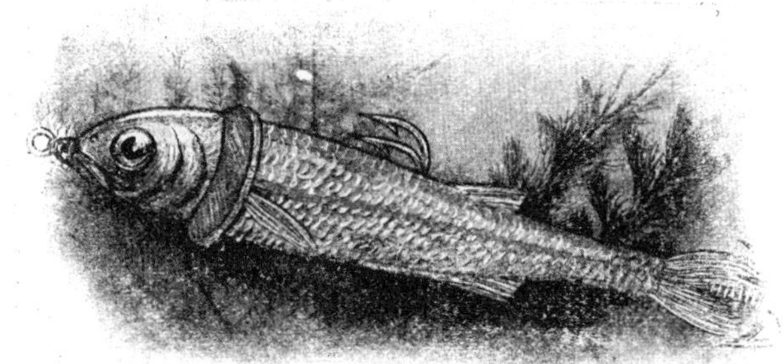

Smelt

A series of artificial lures which are a most life-like imitation of the fish they represent. They are practically indestructible, as the colors cannot be scratched or rubbed off. The weight has been carefully considered and varies according to size. The lighter the weight used the more natural the motion in the water. They are direct copies from "nature" and will be found a very attractive bait for Trout & Black Bass.

1½ Inches (For Trout) .... Each	$1.25	**Nos. 1 (Gudgeon) 2 (Dace) 3 (Smelt) 4 (Trout)**
2 Inches (For Trout)	1.50	
3 Inches (For Bass)	2.00	

"The Griffiths" Minnow

This Minnow is supplied with a body having a screwed head and several detachable fins of different colors, the object of which is to suit varying weather and water conditions. If the weather is bright and the water clear, a dark fin, such as copper, should be used; if the day is rather cloudy and dull, the brass fin should be used as it is a little brighter; but if it is a very dull day, or very colored water, the silver fin should be mounted, which will be found to be very deadly. The fin mounted on the body is already bent up to what is considered the best position, the others, however, are left flat for the angler to experiment with. It will be found that an angle of about 45° with the body will give the best results. It is a good plan to have one fin bent in the reverse direction to reverse the spin, and thus unkink the line should it become kinked. The fins are so constructed that they give the maximum spin with the minimum of motion through the water, and the advantage of this method of fixing them is that they can be adjusted to suit the volume and pressure of the water.

The 1 inch size is made with one treble hook (as illustrated), the larger sizes having 2 treble hooks, tandem style.

Inches		Each	Inches		Each
1	For Trout..................	$1.35	2½	Bass	2.25
2	Trout and Bass.............	2.00	3	Pickerel	2.70

Flexible Quill Eels

Made in a deep red color, and an excellent bait for trout and bass. They are mounted with one each treble side hook and tail hook and with swivel.

2½ Inches.	For Trout	Each,	$0.50
3 Inches.	Trout and Bass.......................	Each,	0.75
4 Inches.	Bass	Each,	1.00

Preserved Minnows

Preserved Minnows

Are indispensible when it is difficult to procure live bait. Are rigid enough to stay on the hook without splitting open. They have not lost the natural shape or shine of the live minnow.

Three Sizes.

Small size, for Trout and Perch (approx.) 60 in bottle, Per bottle $0.30

Medium size (approx.) 22 in bottle. Per bottle.............. .30

Large Size (approx.) 16 in bottle, for casting. Per bottle.... .30

(If sent by mail in special container, to conform with Postal Regulations, $0.25 extra per bottle.)

WHERE THE BLAZED TRAIL CROSSES THE BOULEVARD
ABERCROMBIE & FITCH CO.
MADISON AVE and FORTYFIFTH STREET
NEW YORK

Camping
45

Except for the bathing suit and the skirt, these gals would be reasonably in style today. Modern times were here in 1923.

Page 318: Hiram Hawes made superb rods and was a master craftsman, I have one of his little seven-footers, a delightful wisp of bamboo that casts an old-fashioned F tapered silk line astonishingly well.

Cross was bought up by Heddon and continued only as a name; they called their best handmade ferrules Cross. Double-building is merely a way of utilizing good cane that is too thin in the "enamel" (dense outer wall) to make up into big sticks.

Page 319: Modern times have put collar and necktie onto our headnet-wearing friends. But I still want to know how the smoker got the smoke out of his enclosure, and how he spat. After a long session with the pipe his face must have resembled a smoked salmon.

TROUT AND BASS FLY RODS

HAWES' RODS

These rods have the reputation of being the finest made in the world. Mr. Hawes has devoted a lifetime study to the selection of material and the finest hand construction. For 28 years he was associated with his uncle, H. L. Leonard, and helped to build the world-wide reputation of Leonard Rods. His practical experience as a fisherman and expert tournament caster, together with his thorough knowledge of all features of rod-making, have enabled him to produce what we believe to be the best rod ever built. All Hawes' Rods are made from the very best six-strip bamboo. They are mounted with special grade of German silver and the waterproof ferrules are of the famous split design. The fly and salmon rods have steel snake guides and metal reel seats.

These rods are hand-made and the output is, therefore, limited. We urge you to *anticipate* your wants if you contemplate the purchase of a Hawes' Rod. If any style, length or weight of rod is desired, other than those listed, prices will be quoted.

HAWES' TROUT, BASS AND DRY FLY RODS

Three Pieces and Extra Tip with Bamboo Tip Case

These rods are quicker in action and more powerful for their weight than any other rod made. They are extremely resilient and have the strength to lift a long, heavy line from the water and cast true and steady under all conditions. Their balance is so perfect that they have the "hang" of much lighter rods.

8 ft. long, weight about 3¾ oz....
9 ft. long, weight about 4¾ oz.... } Any length $50.00
9½ ft. long, weight about 5½ oz....
10 ft. long, weight about 6 oz....

We can furnish a detachable butt on any of these rods at an extra cost of $7.00

Rods fitted with one agate guide and two agate tips extra cost of $2.00

Extra Joints

Butt....$19.50 Middle....$15.00 Tip....$12.00

HAWES' "FEATHERWEIGHT" FLY RODS

Three Pieces and Extra Tip with Bamboo Tip Case

This rod is the most dainty piece of fishing tackle that the angler can hope to possess. The weight varies from 2 to 2¼ ozs. and fish have been taken on these rods up to 2 pounds.

These rods have wooden reel seats with metal band and hood; also English snake guides.

Lengths vary from 7 to 8 ft., any length......$70.00

Extra Joints

Butt....$25.00 Middle....$19.00 Tip....$14.00

HAWES' DRY FLY AND TOURNAMENT RODS

Three Pieces and Extra Tip with Bamboo Tip Case

Mr. Hawes' personal experience in tournament casting has taught him what the tournament caster needs for record making. Unusual power and speed will be found in all his rods for this class of work. In dry fly fishing it is necessary to keep the fly in the air to keep it dry. Consequently, you need a powerful rod. For this style of fishing, Hawes' rods are particularly suited owing to their unusual retrieving power. The 4¾ to 5¾ ounce rods are the weights most generally used for dry fly fishing. They have solid cork grips, snake guides and metal reel seats.

Light Tournament Class

Specially adapted to dry fly fishing

Length, 9 ft., weight, 4¾ oz.....
Length, 9½ ft., weight, 5¾ oz..... } Any length $60.00
Length, 10 ft., weight, 5¾ oz.....

Medium Tournament Class

Fine rods for swift water or large fish

Length, 10 ft., weight, 7¾ oz....
Length, 10½ ft., weight, 8½ oz.... } Either length $60.00

With one agate guide and two agate tips, extra, $2.00

Rods With Extra Joints

Any of the above rods can be supplied with two middle joints and three tips at................$90.00

Extra Joints

Butt....$22.00 Middle....$17.00 Tip....$13.00

HAWES' SALMON RODS—Six-Strip Bamboo

Three Pieces and Extra Tip with Bamboo Tip Case

These rods are made in keeping with the American idea of lightness and greater comfort in casting. They are extremely powerful and have that beautiful balance and action which all Hawes' Rods possess to a marked degree. These rods are gaining popularity every year for use on large salmon rivers and in the hands of an expert seem to have no difficulty in handling the largest fish.

Length over all	Handle lengths	Weight	
13 ft.	20 -in.	16 to 17 oz.......	$90.00
14 ft.	20½-in.	18 to 20 oz.......	90.00

Extra Joints

Butt....$33.00 Middle....$24.00 Tip....$18.00

HARDY BROS. DE LUXE FLY RODS

This is the latest design in Trout fly rods, and embodies all that is useful and practical with great elegance and refinement. Built from the finest grades of Bamboo, most carefully balanced to fish either dry or wet fly with great precision and delicacy, yet strong enough to kill either large Trout or small Salmon. The handle is of cork, covered and fitted with the No. 2 patent screw grip reel seat of special white metal. The joints are suction, perfectly fitted, bridge intermediate guides with agate butt and tip tops. We carry them in three lengths.

8½ ft. approximate weight, 4¾ oz........
9 ft. approximate weight, 5½ oz........ } Price, $65.00 Each
9½ ft. approximate weight, 5¾ oz........

CROSS RODS

The Cross rod is double built. Two strips of cane are cemented together, the inside of one strip to the enamel of the other strip, thus making a lamination of the very finest and toughest material. Six triangular strips cut from this laminated cane make a rod that has power in every fibre; the pithy part of the cane is completely eliminated. Rods made in this manner weigh less, for their strength will stand more abuse, and will cast better. It is almost impossible to set them under the most adverse conditions. The Cross rod is the "last word" in fine rod making. They are made of extra Tonkin cane, 12 strips built into six double sections. Fly rod tips, however, are single built; their diameter is so small that all the pith or soft wood is eliminated in planing. Cross rods are not made in Tournament models; they are first, last and all the time fishing rods. All Cross fly rods are in three joints with extra tip, furnished with heavy duck bag, and aluminum case of new design for entire rod. Can be produced in agate or

MARBLE'S TROUT KNIFE

A vest pocket knife for cleaning and cutting trout. Made of a high-grade steel and fitted with a metal-bound leather sheath.
Length, 5½ inches. Each.................... $0.55

AYENEFCO FISH KNIFE

The angler's all-around handy knife. Of good steel, carefully made with a sharp point at tip and a good cutting edge, black wood handle. In leather sheath. Price, each........................ $1.50

FISH SCALER AND SHREDDER

No trouble to scale the largest fish with this scaler. Just scrape the scales off. Is also the very best means of shredding fish meat..................$0.25

"SMOKER'S" HEAD PROTECTOR

Adjustable over hat band and around the neck. The material is a very fine gauze, into the front of which is inserted a net made of horse hair, which is strong, flexible and will not break. Into the horse hair net is set a button-shaped self-closing valve covered with slotted rubber; through this a pipe may be inserted.................................. $1.25

SPORTSMAN'S HEAD NET

It does not gather around the neck; the yoke holds the net well away from the face. It has a top of lightweight twill, the spread of which is held in shape by the hat. The material is all-over English net, and the bottom is fitted with a yoke which sets snugly over the shoulders and ties with lacing under the arms. We have this head net with green, brown and white netting.
Any color $1.50

GAUNTLET FISHING GLOVES

Offers best protection from bites of flies and mosquitoes and will retain softness and pliability regardless of repeated soakings. Tan color and open fingertips for handling trout flies, leaders, etc. Tanalite cloth above the wrist with elastic to clasp above the elbow. $3.50
Gloves without the Tanalite sleeves 2.50

FLY DOPE

No "North Woods toilet" for the spring and summer is complete without a generous supply of good "dope." The "Touradif" fly dope is compounded and put up by ourselves on our own original formula and none but the purest ingredients are used. As a protection against the bites of black flies and gnats it has no equal. As it has a good heavy base, it is more lasting in effects than most "dopes," and an occasional application is all that will be required. Clean and pleasant to handle and agreeably scented. It is also a most excellent skin softener. Excellent for chap or sunburn.
In Friction-Top Tins, 1 oz................. $0.25
In Collapsible Tubes, 2 oz................. .25

DARLING'S BLACK-FLY LOTION

This is not a preventive, but a cure for the bite of this merciless pest. It will be found most efficacious in practically all cases and should be included in the kit of every sportsman and tourist in "fly time." Its base is a pure, sweet oil and contains nothing to injure the most tender skin, but on the contrary is a skin emollient and an excellent remedy for sunburn.
Per 2 oz. vial.............................. $0.25

"MOSQUITO-FOE"

Mosquito-Foe is a short black stick, one-quarter of an inch thick, which is set into a holder and will burn for about one hour, giving off a fragrant odor of the woods. Two of the sticks allowed to burn for one hour in a closed tent or room will eliminate every mosquito. Its use will give positive relief, as mosquitoes clear out or die in contact with these fumes. Packed in box of 16 sticks with holder. $0.25

IDEAL FISHING FLOATS

More service in one "Ideal" than in dozens of old style floats. Metal band doesn't break and cannot come off. Metal ferrule at bottom—no getting out of order. Colors—red and green or white and green.

Length, 2½-inch	$0.15
Length, 3½-inch	.20
Length, 5 -inch	.40
Length, 5 -inch	.50

PORCUPINE QUILL FLOATS

Double tapered 4, 6, 8 in. long................ $0.15

CORK FLOATS

	Small	Medium	Large
Barrel shape, each......	$0.10	$0.15	$0.20
Egg shape, each......	.10	.15	.20

HEAD NETS AND FLOATS

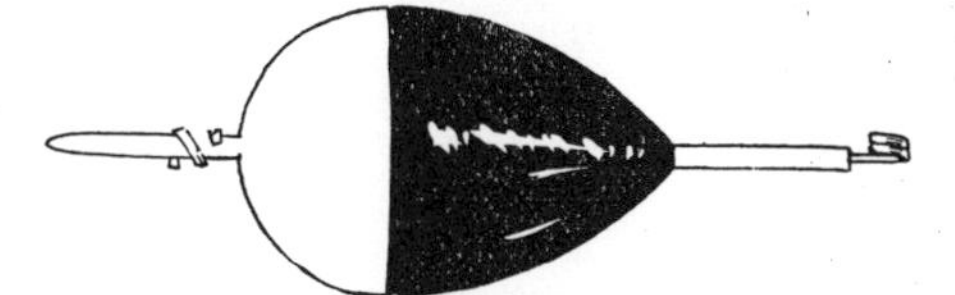
EGG CORK FLOAT

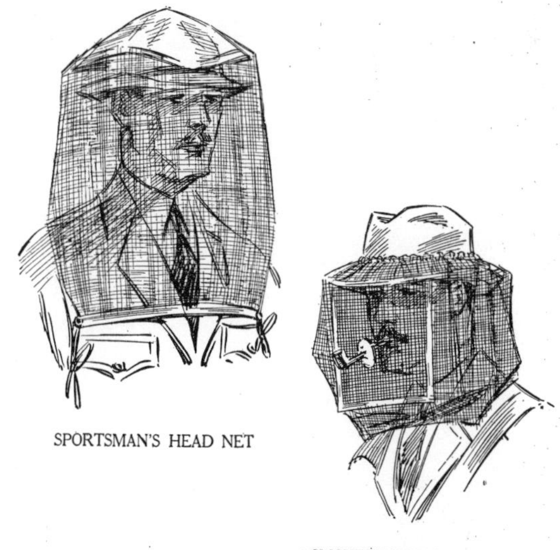
SPORTSMAN'S HEAD NET

"SMOKER'S" HEAD PROTECTOR

BARREL FLOAT

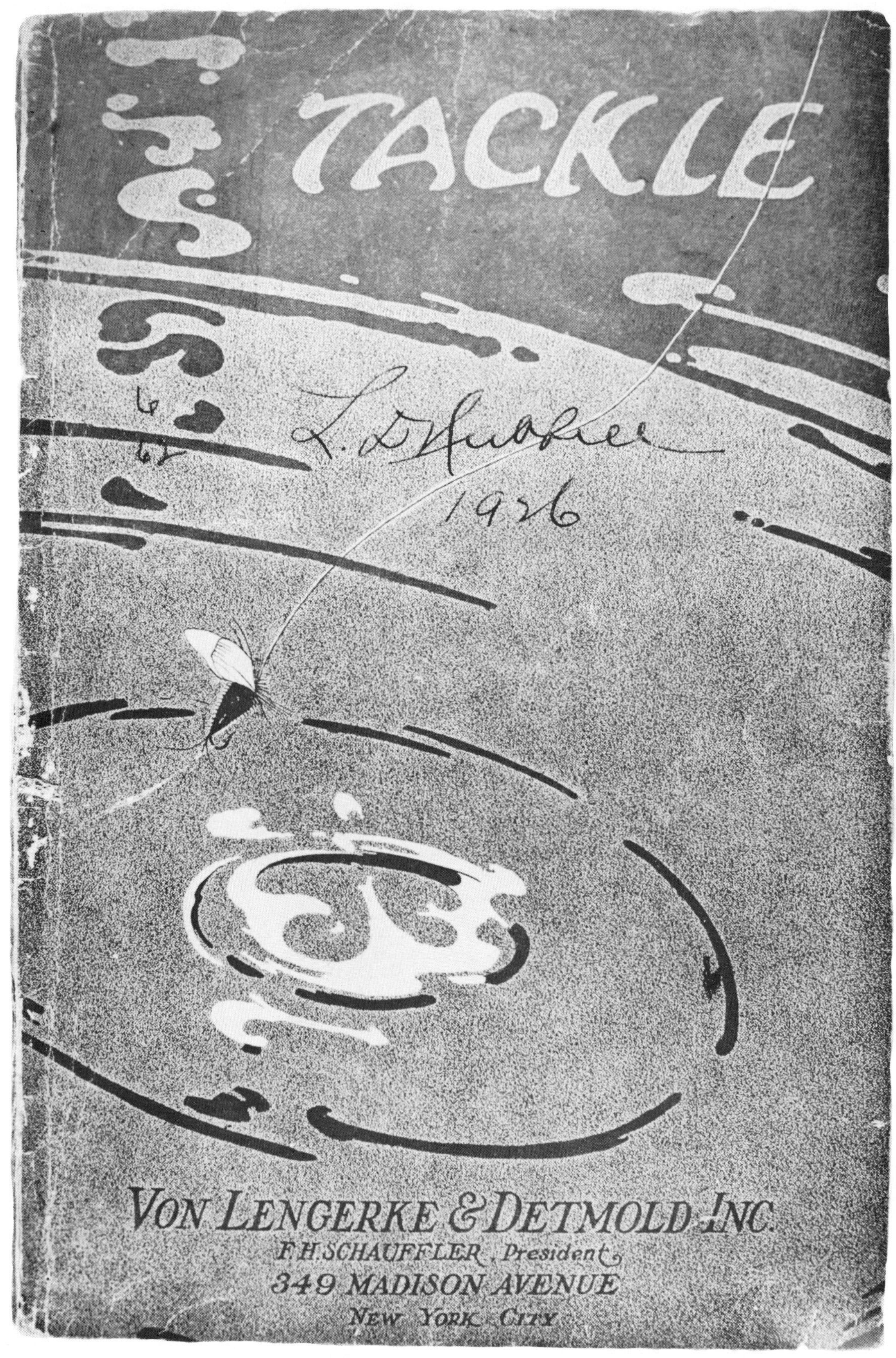
TACKLE
VON LENGERKE & DETMOLD INC.
F.H. SCHAUFFLER, President
349 MADISON AVENUE
NEW YORK CITY

FISHING TACKLE

RODS, REELS, LINES, FLIES
LEADERS, BAITS, FLY
AND TACKLE BOOKS
AND BOXES

...1926...

VON LENGERKE & DETMOLD INC.
F. H. SCHAUFFLER, President
349 MADISON AVENUE
NEW YORK CITY

Reels

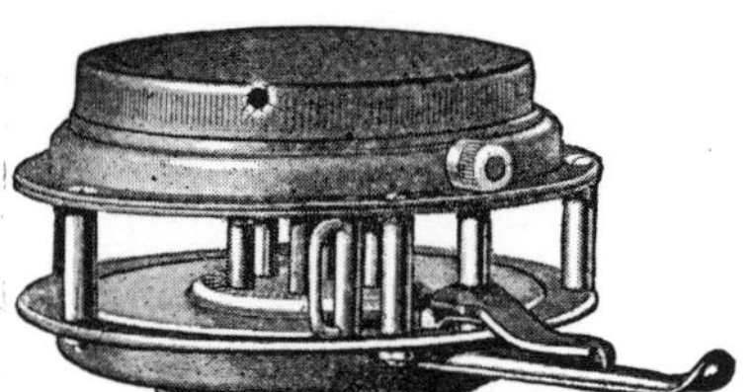

MARTIN AUTOMATIC REEL

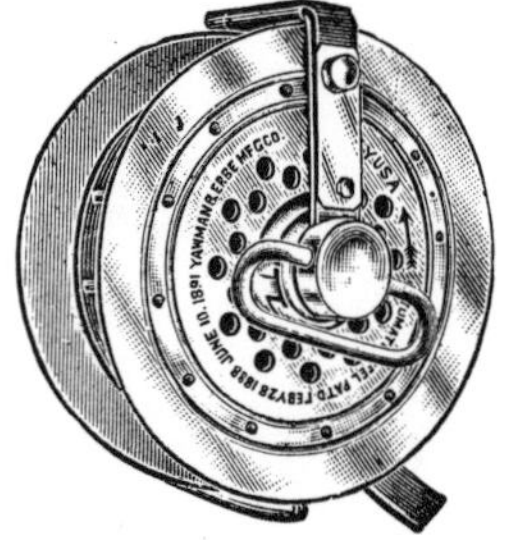

"Y & E" AUTOMATIC REEL A

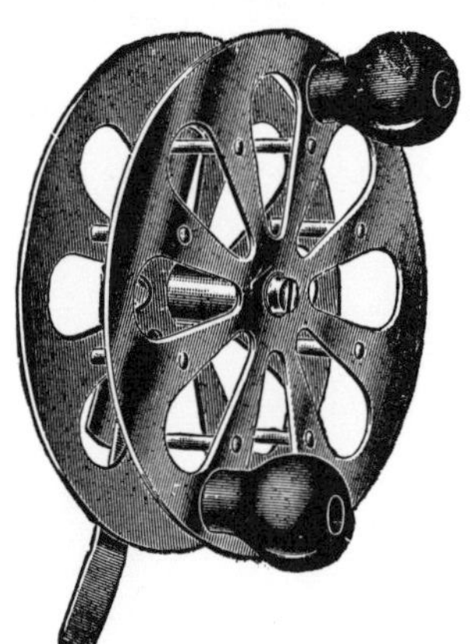

WIRE LINE REEL

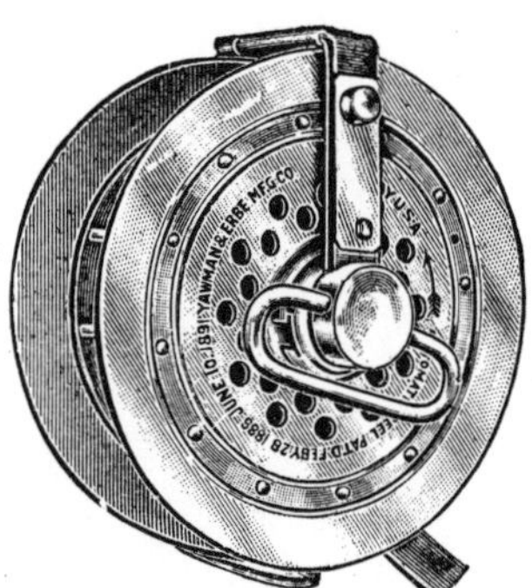

"Y & E" AUTOMATIC REEL B

WIRE LINE REEL WITH GUIDE

PROGRESS
Description on Page 50

VON LENGERKE & DETMOLD INC.
F. H. SCHAUFFLER President
349 MADISON AVENUE
NEW YORK CITY

All Prices Net and Subject to Change Without Notice.

73

Bass and Trout Bugs

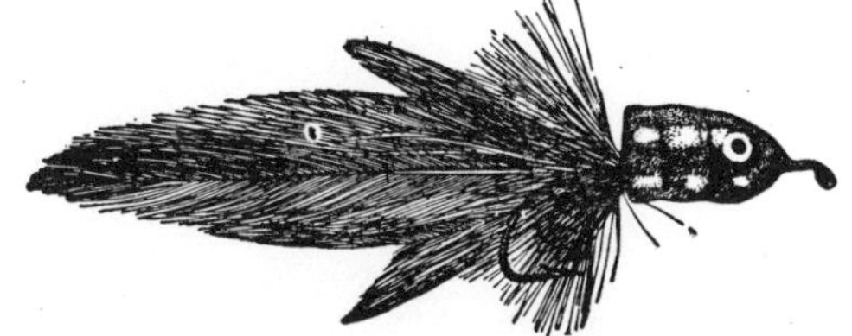

WILDER-DILG

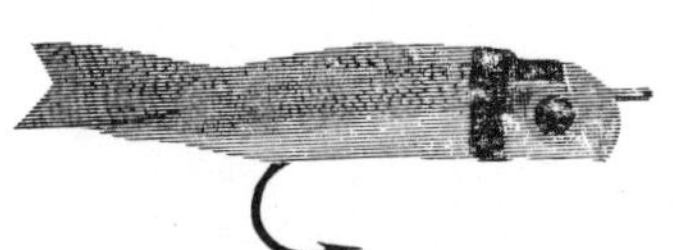

HAYES

TUTTLE'S MOUSE

TUTTLE'S DEVIL BASS BUG

TUTTLE'S TROUT BUG

CALLMAC BUGS

VON LENGERKE & DETMOLD INC.
F H SCHAUFFLER President
349 MADISON AVENUE
NEW YORK CITY

All Prices Net and Subject to Change Without Notice.

The CREEK CHUB BAIT CO.
GARRETT-INDIANA

The Wawasee Reel

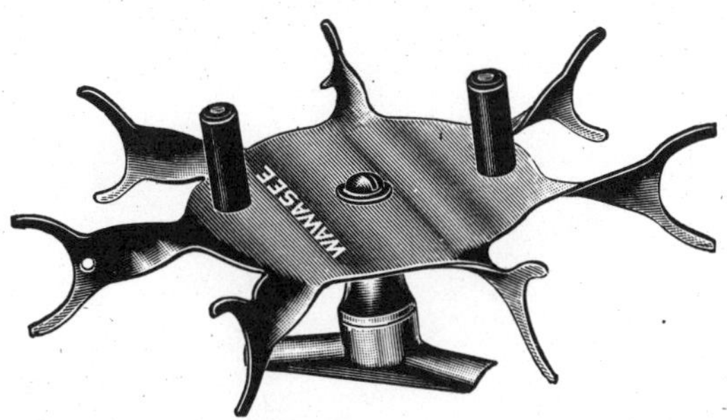

Price $3.50 Each

Here is a reel which has been used by a great many bait casters in Northern Indiana during the past fifteen years in various forms but all the same principle and the use of these reels is constantly increasing. It is a reel without gears and therefore very simple and strong in construction, has a diameter of 5¾ inches and weighs 4 ounces; is made of one piece of sheet metal on a hub and fastens to the rod the same as other reels. This type of reel has advantages all its own and is preferred by a great many bait casters, especially those who have more than ordinary trouble in reeling the line in level on the reel. The line when reeled in on the Wawasee Reel requires no attention, and there is no picking of backlashes out from between narrow bars. When there is any trouble with the line, which is very seldom, it is easy to correct as it is all out in the open. Another feature is that bait can be reeled in faster and more casts made (fast reeling with an underwater lure is O. K.), also the bait when cast is started faster than with the quadruple reel which better insures the hooking of the fish. With the Wawasee reel the breaking is done on the hub with the thumb or finger, which is an advantage, while on most other reels of this style the breaking is done on the side of the reel.

Close attention should be paid to the placing of the reel on the rod so it lines up properly with the first guide. We guarantee this reel to be well made and to give good satisfaction.

Perfection Hone

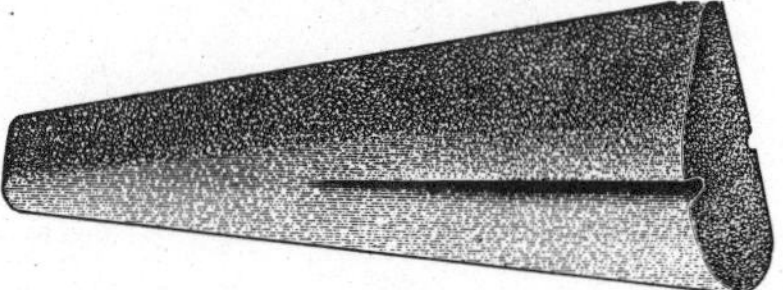

Price 50 Cents Each

It is important that hooks be kept with sharp points and with a little Perfection Hone in your kit you are always prepared to keep them sharp and have a reminder in front of you to do so. Made of Carborundum.

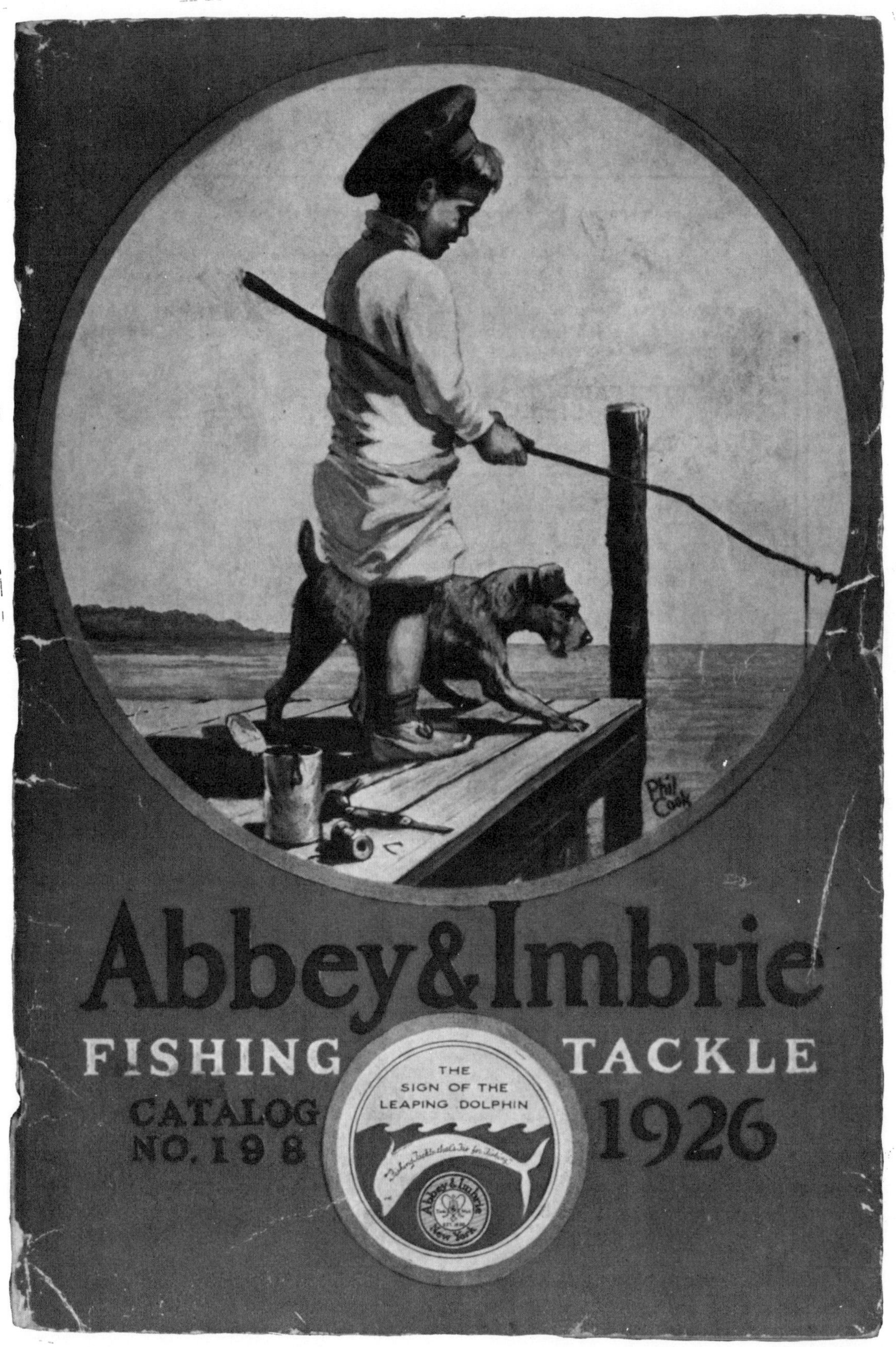
Phil Cook
Abbey & Imbrie
FISHING TACKLE
CATALOG NO. 198
THE SIGN OF THE LEAPING DOLPHIN
1926

THE CHOICE OF A BAIT

Yet it may be well to remember that an artificial bait serves other purposes than to imitate a tempting morsel to a hungry fish. It may represent an enemy trespassing upon a fish's feeding ground. And it may attract, by its color and gaudy appearance, for no other reason than its gaudiness. Fish are pugnacious when defending their rights, and have curiosity enough to investigate an attractive bait when they are not feeding.

Casting spoons are lighter than trolling spoons; and a spoon that revolves steadily upon its own axis—known as a "spinner"—is better in shallow water or for surface trolling; but a "darter" or a "wobbler" are usually preferred in deep water. Double-bladed spoons represent the movement of a live minnow more accurately than spoons with single blades.

When fish are seen jumping they will rarely take an artificial sinking bait. They may occasionally take a surface bait, but they are feeding on flies, and flies are then the bait to use.

The angler must study the mood of the fish. If the fish are recently from the spawning beds, they will fight anything that comes with a glitter to disturb their neighborhood; especially if their young are still clustered.

The best baits for this purpose are the large spoons and wood minnows. Surface baits are particularly killing in the early season.

Wood minnows are used almost exclusively for bait-casting, although some anglers use them for trolling.

Some artificial baits are frank imitations of insects or small animals. You will find quite an assortment in these pages. They are clever copies from life and serve well enough when live bait is scarce.

Your luck will vary with the day, the season, the locality, the mood of the fish. Do
... the "man on the spot." He is usually willing to give helpful
...w of the angling fraternity.

...BODY" MINNOW

...tly Luminous"

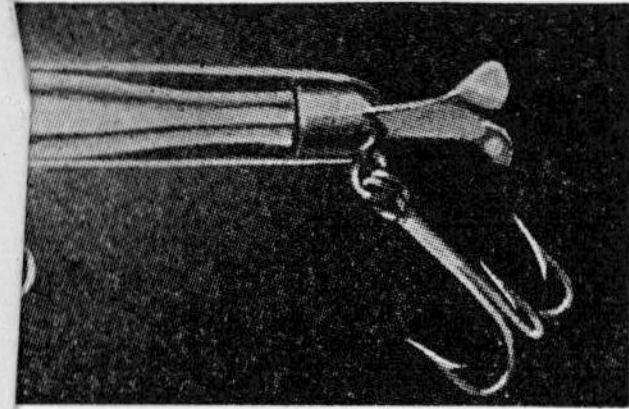

THIS SIDE OF CARD IS FOR ADDRESS

...ped especially as an Abbey & Imbrie Centen-
... success.
...rmanently luminous material which has every
...ruction causing it to spiral through the water
...ed to night or day fishing, as deep waters are

...ce so that the angler may use it to advantage
...hed to the line at a proper distance above the
...l.
... you introduce this brand new wriggling lumi-

...l plated head and tail, with fins and propeller,
... can be easily detached and single hook used
...ed top and bottom by wires to which the hooks
...ncluding head and tail, $3\frac{1}{4}$ to $3\frac{1}{2}$ inches.
..............................Each $0.75

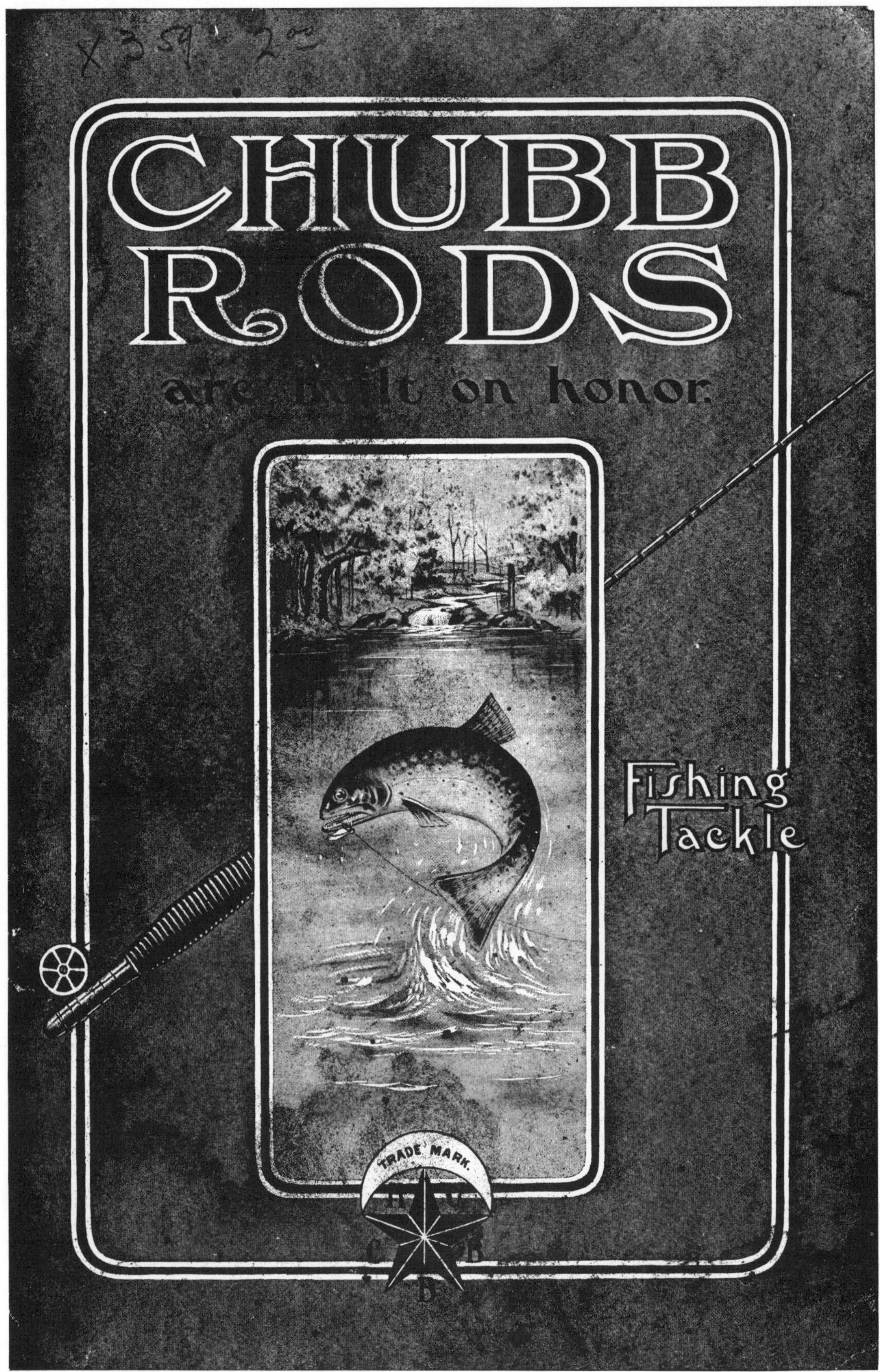
CHUBB RODS
are built on honor.
Fishing Tackle
TRADE MARK

Thomas H. Chubb

The Fishing Rod Manufacturer.

We hereby Guarantee to the purchaser of every Chubb Rod, which has stamped upon it our Trade Mark That it is made by skilled workmen out of the best material in all of its parts. And we do warrant it for the space of One Year. And will replace, free of charge, any part that proves defective or breaks while in actual service; if the breakage is in any way due to fault of material or workmanship.

Trade Mark. H U C B B

Signed T. H. Chubb Rod Co.

"BUILT ON HONOR"

LANCEWOOD AND GREENHEART RODS

CHUBB'S "TRADE MARK"

These Rods are hand made and guaranteed to be first-class in every respect. Cork or cane hand grasp, welted ferrules, closely wound with two colors fine silk and all rods have two tips. Nickel Silver or Bronze Steel Snake Guides, put up in grooved wood form covered with Canton flannel and in cloth case.

Rods made with waterproof ferrules, 20c per rod extra.

Rods equipped with Agate guide and Agate tops, $2.00 extra.

Solid cork grip, 50c; double, 85c.

TROUT FLY OR DRY FLY RODS

Description—Order by Letters or Numbers

No.	Length	Weight	Trimmings	Price
40¼	8 to 9 ft	3½ to 4½ oz.	Reel bands, Nickel	$ 8.00
40¾	8 to 9 ft.	3½ to 4½ oz.	Reel bands, Nickle Silver	9.00
A ½	8 to 9 ft.	5 to 5½ oz.	Reel bands, Nickel	8.00
B ½	8 to 9 ft.	5 to 5½ oz.	Reel seat, Nickle Silver	9.00
A¾	9½ feet	6 to 6½ oz.	Reel seat, Nickle	8.00
B ¼	10 feet	6½ to 7 oz.	Reel seat, Nickel Silver	9.00
40	9 feet	4 to 4½ oz.	Reel seat, Nickle	8.00
B ¾	9½ feet	6 to 6½ oz.	Reel seat, Nickel Silver	9.00
A ¼	10 feet	6½ to 7 oz.	Reel bands, Nickel	8.00
40½	9 feet	4 to 4½ oz.	Reel bands, Nickle Silver	9.00
A	10½ feet	6½ to 7 oz.	Reel seat, Nickle	8.00
B	10½ feet	6½ to 7 oz.	Reel seat, Nickel Silver	9.00

"UNION LEAGUE" TROUT FLY ROD

Four-joint, extra tip

No.	Length Weight	Price
41	10½ feet, 8 oz., reel seat, Nickel	$ 8.00
42½	10½ feet, 8 oz., reel seat, Nickle Silver	9.00

L.L. BEAN
Manufacturer
FREEPORT, MAINE

SPRING 1931

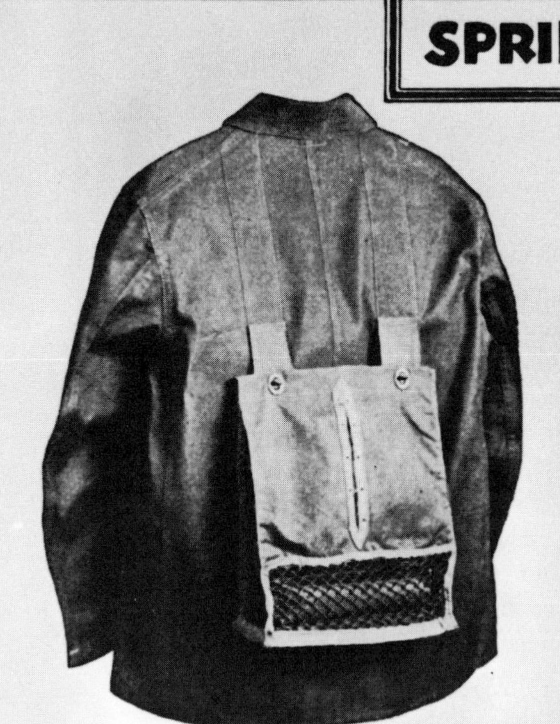

See Page 13

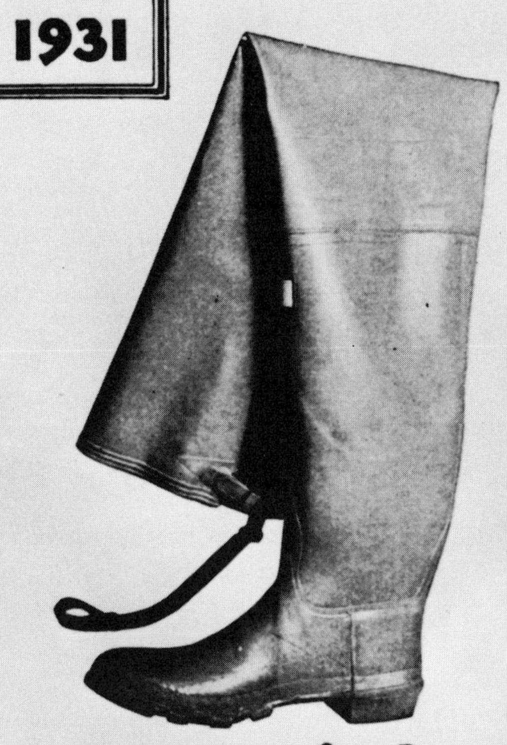

See Page 3

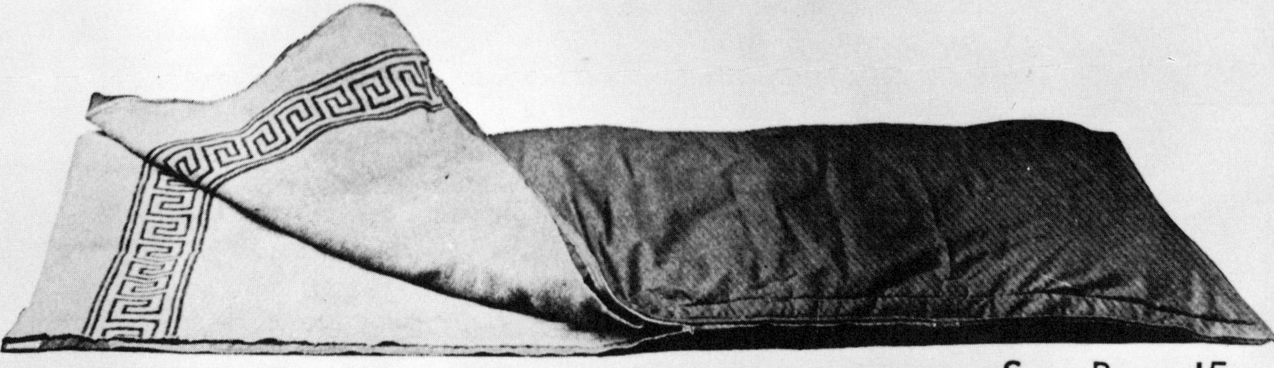

See Page 15

The famous house of L. L. Bean was supplying fishermen with clothing and footwear for many years before this 1931 catalog offered, for the first time, items of fishing tackle.

Leon Bean of Freeport, Maine, was a dedicated deer hunter. A lot of the Maine deer woods is close to being water-soaked muskeg, so the still-hunter, who needs to walk silently and far, requires footgear that is both waterproof and ventilated. Neither leather nor rubber were satisfactory but a combination of the two was, as Bean discovered when he cut the tops off a wornout pair of leather shoepacs and sewed them onto a pair of overshoes commonly called postman's rubbers. Soon he was making and selling what later were commonly called lumberman's rubbers. No one has yet devised as good a substitute.

Bean sold his wares through direct-mail catalogs, a marketing method then in considerable disrepute because of false or misleading product claims and the near impossibility of getting attention to claims for refunds or substitutions. Bean changed all that. If the goods aren't what you thought they were, or don't fit, he said, send them back and we'll return your money *by the next mail,* or send you a smaller size, etc., if that's what you prefer.

The revolutionary thing was that he did it, fast, accurately, and cheerfully. To avoid going broke in a hurry, he made his catalog descriptions complete, factual, and truthful, and offered free samples of materials so the buyer could judge for himself. In an era when the mail-order catalog (with meritorious exceptions) was half fanciful fiction and half glossed-over generalities, Leon Bean told the truth.

This policy became the foundation of what today is a very large and highly successful business. Bean kept his costs and prices down and his quality up, and built up a great backlog of fanatically faithful customers of whom I've been one myself for over forty years. He continually added well-tested and widely demanded new products to his line, and new services too. Early in the history of the business, one of the employees who lived above the plant got tired of being so often aroused from sleep to come down and let in some urgent customer, so he just kept the place open at night, during the rush season. For many years now, the Bean shop has been open twenty-four hours a day so that, for instance, deer-hunters from out of state can get hunting licenses and ammunition or other requirements on their way to the opening of the deer season at dawn.

One important thing Leon Bean did was to convince the military that some of the equipment developed and tested by millions of hunters and campers could be useful for soldiers in the field. The best publicized of these items and the one that got Bean his first national publicity outside of field sport magazines was his first product. Countless thousands of the lumberman's rubbers were worn gratefully by countless thousands of American troops. The soldier's framed backpack is just a copy of the Bergans-Meis mountaineering pack long used abroad and, for some years, here also; and the mummy-type sleeping bag is just a copy of the down or wool-"batt" insulated mummy bags that campers, mountain-sheep hunters, and the like have used for generations.

Bean also designed and I think made what was called a bombardier's bag—a sort of wire-framed canvas briefcase for an aviation bombardier's maps, booklets, papers, and odds-and-ends, that opened out flat by a three-side zipper and had also a zippered outside pocket on each side, the same length and width as the center compartment but shallower.

Copied in leather or plastic, this "carry-on bag" is now a popular item of traveler's luggage. But they've "improved" it by substituting four separate, small outside pockets for the original two big ones, thereby materially reducing the carrying capacity of the bag.

Bean's Fishing Shoe

A new 10″ shoe for early boat fishing, stream fishing, wet wading and fall hunting. Weight only 35 ounces per pair.

The top is made of special rubberized duck fabric that will not harden by wetting and drying.

The bottom is a light weight rubber same quality as used in our Maine Hunting Shoes, yet sole is heavy enough to protect feet from rough traveling.

The lowest priced and most practical all around shoe for hunters and fishermen we ever made.

Sizes: 5 to 12. Price $3.55 postpaid.

Send for free sample of canvas and rubber.

Shoes may be returned for full credit after one week's wear if not absolutely satisfactory.

$3.55 Postpaid

Manufactured and Sold by

L. L. BEAN, FREEPORT, MAINE

No. 24 Stocking

Price 59c

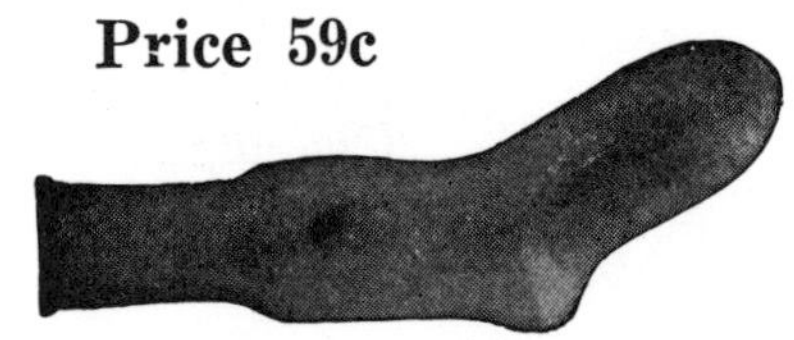

Is a fine, wool, very light gray cashmere. It is especially adapted as an understocking or for wet wading. Sizes 9½ to 12.

Maine Hiking Shoe

$2.77
Postpaid

For long tramps and general outing this is the most practical and comfortable summer shoe we ever offered.

While not a heavy shoe the sole is thick enough to protect the feet on an all-day tramp.

Designed particularly for everyday wear at summer camps and cottages, also early fall hunting.

Is made of good weight olive green duck with fairly thick, pure crepe rubber sole and heel that will not slip on any kind of traveling.

For canoe and fishing trips it cannot be beaten. It has a fiber shank to support the arch, a feature not found in any other rubber sole canvas shoe.

I am so enthusiastic over this shoe that I will refund the purchase price after ten days' wear to any dissatisfied customer.

Sizes: 5 to 12. Price, $2.77. Delivered free anywhere in the United States. Send for free sample of canvas and rubber.

(Spring 1931)

L. L. BEAN, FREEPORT, MAINE

Bean's Tan Trouting Boot

$6.85

Made of dark tan rubber twice as tough as that used in ordinary boots. Color, which is compounded especially for us, makes boots practically invisible when wading or duck hunting.

It is the lightest wading boot made, comes almost to the waist and when rolled will go in coat pocket.

A new feature is cleated sole as shown. A distinct help in preventing slipping while tramping or wading.

Perfectly adapted for stream fishing, duck hunting, washing car, swamp hunting, and general dull weather outing. Very easy to dry out, as tops can be rolled way down. Can fit all feet from A to EE.

With every pair we give a small repair outfit that will mend a snag or cut in three minutes. Send for free sample of rubber and try to puncture it with stick or pencil.

We have this boot in both Men's and Ladies.'

Price: Men's sizes 5 to 12, $6.85. Ladies' sizes 3 to 8, $5.85.
Extra long or extra large legs 25c extra. Delivered free east of Mississippi. If west, add 25c.

MAINE TROUTING BOOT GUARANTEE

We guarantee these boots to outwear two pairs of ordinary rubber boots and will give a new pair to any dissatisfied customer. If the rubber breaks return them together with this Guarantee tag and we will replace them free of charge.

L. L. BEAN
Freeport, Maine

Maine Arched Innersole

$1.00
Postpaid

After experimenting for years we find that it is just as necessary to have a stiffening in the shank of a rubber or moccasin as it is in a leather shoe. As a steel shank cannot be made in the rubber we have put it in the innersole, the value of which cannot be estimated until worn. Every hunter and fisherman should use them on long tramps. It takes away that flat-footed feeling, making your trouting boots feel the same as your every-day shoes.

Made of the very best genuine leather with virgin wool blanketing back.

The felt takes up the moisture while the leather keeps the feet off the rubber and prevents "drawing" that is so objectionable with most rubber boots and shoes.

Give size and description of shoe when ordering. Price $1.00 Delivered free.

High-grade, flat, leather Innersole 45c.

(Spring 1931)

Manufactured by L. L. BEAN, FREEPORT, MAINE

Bean's Fishing Coat

Back view showing Fish Bag, which is easily attached and detached with turn buttons.
Color: Dark Brown to match Coat. The Tabs near collar are for ease in carrying bag when returning from fishing ground.

Back view showing big back pocket supported by shoulder straps for carrying lunch, light rain shirt, etc.
Also game pocket for Fall hunting.

A light weight brown duck Coat with six pockets.

The big feature is the netting fish bag on back that keeps fish much better than basket as it allows free circulation of air. It has loose aluminum bottom that is easily cleaned. Carrying bag at back is big improvement over basket at side that is always in the way.

Four folding lunch boxes and four drinking cups free.

For fall bird shooting it is better than a heavy canvas hunting coat.

Price: Coat complete with all extras $5.75 postpaid.

Price: Coat, fly book and hook holder $4.50 postpaid.

Price: Fish bag with shoulder strap and hook holder in leather case $1.75 postpaid.

Order one of these coats and if not more than satisfied after one week's wear, return it and we will refund your money.

Send for free samples of coat and bag.

(Spring 1931)

Front view showing large double pockets for bait that can be turned for cleaning. Also two breast pockets and long inside pocket for fly book and license.

FREE

Fly Book and Hook Holder furnished free with every coat. This arrangement for carrying flies and gut hooks cannot be beaten.
Fly Book has transparent panels.
Hook Holder is a celluloid strip in leather case. The handiest little article you ever saw.

Manufactured by L. L. BEAN, FREEPORT, MAINE

Automatic Bottom Fishing Pant

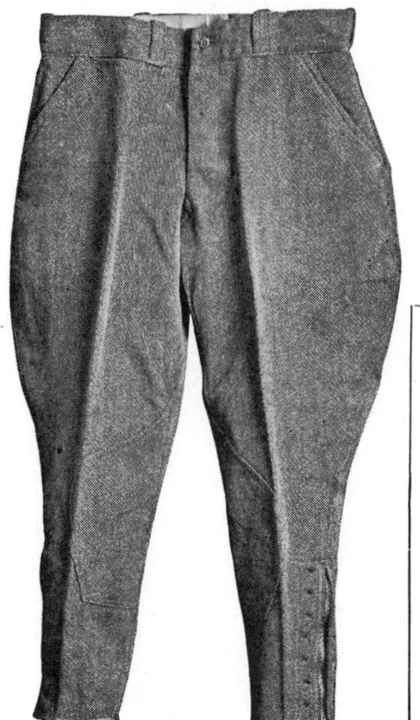

Is made of tough cotton whipcord with talon fastener at bottom as shown. Double stitched throughout with reinforced knees. Two front slash pockets, two back flap pockets and watch pocket.

This is the most practical, best value Fishing Pant we ever offered.

Sizes: 32 to 46. Price: $3.35 postpaid.

Send for free sample.

Bean's Fishing Hat

We have finally perfected a light gray khaki hat with veil that will keep off black flies and mosquitoes.

By occasionally sprinkling a little Maine Fly Dope on brim and back veil it will give almost perfect protection to face and neck. Then rub a little on back of hands and wrists and you will find fishing a pleasure instead of a torture.

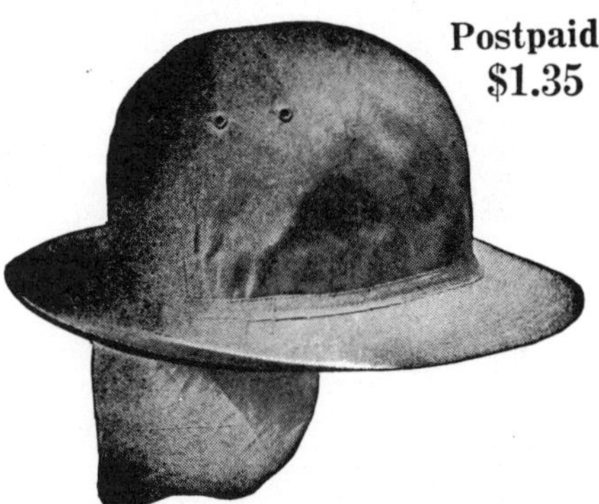

Postpaid $1.35

Price: Hat and small bottle Maine Fly Dope $1.35 postpaid. Extra Fly Dope 20c a bottle.

An automatic bottom pant is just one with zippers in the cuffs. With a slight change of silhouette and leather-trimmed pockets, this is the famous Bean Bird-Shooting Pant that has been the standby of upland bird shooters and fishermen for more than thirty years. They're made of whipcord, reversed. A posh breeches-maker who let out the waistline of one of the various pairs I have worn out was startled to note that the raised cords of the fabric were on the inside of the garment. "Why, they're made inside out!" he exclaimed. "If you'd ever tried hunting in a pair of whipcord breeches *not* reversed you'd know why these are made the other way. When you walk, whipcord 'whistles' almost as much as corduroy does," I told him.

Commentators outside the angling circle have found mirth in Bean's longtime characterization of this garment as a pant. But this is the accepted and universally used term in the garment trade and has been for more than a century. At worst, it is trade jargon, a contraction of pantaloons. I will note in passing that the garment industry carefully designated the nether garments once worn by little boys as "knee pants" and those for track athletes and the like as "short pants." Women's underwear is not, and has never been, called "pants" in the trade. To be a pant, the garment must reach to the ankles.

Bean's Rod and Reel Outfit

The handiest outfit a fisherman ever owned. Simply rig up Rod, Reel, Line and Hook, place in case and on reaching stream you are ready to fish in one minute. When through, telescope Rod and place complete outfit back in case where it is absolutely secure against catching hook or snarling line.

The Rod is a high grade $8\frac{3}{4}$ ft. steel, telescope style, with patent locking device that keeps guides in perfect alignment. This new feature in connection with the all agate guides, as shown at left, allows line to render 100% perfect.

Reel, as shown at right, is all nickel, level winding, quadruple action with a 100 yd. line capacity that is suitable for both trolling and stream fishing.

The Case is of our own manufacture, made of heavy hose duck, full leather bound and reinforced with calfskin at end to protect guides. Opens and closes instantly with automatic fastener as shown. Length over all, 38 inches.

For the average fisherman this outfit will take care of all his requirements. For lake fishing it is an excellent emergency rig. It takes up very little space and in a few seconds can be made ready for plugging or putting over an extra trolling line.

Price complete $4.85 postpaid.

L. L. BEAN, FREEPORT, MAINE

Even in 1931, a steel rod, level-wind reel and case for $4.85 was a bargain.

For generations of Maine boys who fished the brush-brooks and tiny feeders, this rod and reel outfit was standard operational equipment, as necessary as the worms themselves. Once telescoped and hooded in its case, this rod could be carried through the thickest moose cover without snagging the line. Once on the scene, a worm would be impaled on the snelled hook tied direct to the 12-pound test, soft silk bait-casting line, with a lead bullet of suitable weight clamped on just above the knot. The rod was poked cautiously through the bushes and lengthened by pulling out the joints until the worm was over the main current. Then the click on the reel was snapped off and the bullet was allowed to carry worm and line down into the water. If the weight was correct, the current would take the worm downstream, tumbling along the bottom, right into the mouth of the waiting trout.

Usually the fish wasn't played off the reel but by a curious country custom of stripping in line by hand, holding it in the fisherman's teeth while he reached out for another handful of line. The fish was derricked out without ceremony, if necessary by collapsing the rod to get him through the bushes. Then the line was rewound and the hook rebaited.

This rural custom of holding line in one's teeth has limitations. A man who tried it at the famous Fishermen's Paradise on Spring Creek at Bellefonte, Pennsylvania, had a big rainbow stocker haul his false teeth right out and into the river. Since wading is forbidden in this stretch, the fisherman had to endure the mirth and merriment of the innumerable other fishermen until a booted warden could be summoned to retrieve the phony choppers.

The Home of Payne Rods

E. F. Payne Rod Co. When the big breakup between Hiram L. Leonard and the Mills interest occurred in the 1890s, various skilled Leonard workmen quit to set up small custom rodmaking shops of their own. Fred Thomas went back to his native Bangor and made very fine rods right up to his death around 1930. Loman Hawes, H. L. Leonard's nephew and the mechanical genius who invented the "beveler" for sawing rod strips to any desired combination of tapers, died as he and another (Edwards?) were about to set up a shop. Loman's brother Hiram, the tournament caster, made the "Hawes-Leonard" rod for many years. (He could use the name because his wife was Leonard's daughter Cora; the others tried to, but Mills quickly stopped that.) They were very fine rods.

Billy Edwards set up rod shops, usually for some large sporting goods company, to finance his efforts to set up photograph galleries, of which he lost several through fire or financial anemia. In one of these rodmaking interludes, Edwards made (for Winchester, as I recall) a 7½-foot flyrod of perfect dry-fly action and handy size. It created a furor around New York in the 1920s, and the continuing popularity of this offbeat size even today is a tribute to Billy Edwards.

After Ed Payne's short-lived venture with the Kosmic company he and Frank Oram started the E. F. Payne Rod Co. in Highland Mills, New York. When Ed died, his son Jim, who had worked in the shop from the age of ten, inherited his father's half interest; and when Oram died, Mrs. Oram, who worked in the shop—she "wrapped" (wound) the rods—inherited her husband's half interest.

Except for a couple of years of war work for Wright Aeronautical, Jim stayed in that plant until his death several years ago. He made all types of flyrods and a few bait-casting rods, all so good that they command enormous prices at second hand now. But two patterns are distinctively Payne.

One was the Payne 8½-foot flyrod, an oddball size that became almost his trademark. The other was a 10-foot one-hand flyrod that he developed for Albert E. Hendrickson. "A. E." wanted it for the risky sport of fishing off the top of the Gatun Dam in the Panama Canal for the school tarpon gathered below the dam on their spawning run. But the rod proved to be just the thing for the then newly developed sport of low-water, dry-fly fishing for Atlantic salmon, and it became enormously popular for that use.

"A. E." was the rod company's best friend, best customer, longtime benefactor, and occasional financial savior. Jim once told me that he made 48 ten-footers before he suited "A. E.'s" taste, but I think that many of these and many other Payne rods as well were bought to give the company a little needed revenue from time to time. "A. E." was famous for giving away Payne rods. He also bought, one time when the company was hard up, 4 percent of its capital stock made up evenly by Jim and Mrs. Oram.

I note in passing that "A. E." is the Hendrickson in whose honor his fishing friend Roy Steenrod named the dry fly Roy originated on one of their fishing trips to imitate the *Ephemerella* invaria and subvaria female duns that were hatching. It is, I think, today the most popular dry fly in the East.

After Hendrickson's death, his Payne stock was sold to Abercrombie & Fitch, who thought it might help them to get the exclusive selling agency for Payne rods that Jim had always refused to give them. (My feeling is that he preferred to have old friends and new customers drop in to discuss their wants, place their orders, and swap the fishing news of the day.)

Some years after the Second World War, a retired capitalist who thought it would be fun to create a company which would make the best rod, the best reel, and the best shotgun in the world acquired the Abercrombie & Fitch holding and also bought Mrs. Oram's stock. But Jim refused to sell, and his intransigence defeated the plan. Eventually another capitalist, a knowledgeable rodman and fine angler himself, bought all the stock including Jim's and set up a company with Jim as president and, above all, in complete charge of production.

Competition for labor, and high wage scales, arising from the simultaneous construction of the State Thruway and various New York City waterworks, doomed the new owner's well-conceived plan to make Payne rods a top-quality, nationally distributed product. Ownership of the Payne Rod Co. ultimately passed into the hands of the Gladding Corporation.

All the old Leonard workmen who set up their own shops were notable for their rigid adherence to the highest standards of workmanship in spite of small incomes and, often, poverty. But I think Jim surpassed them all in his fanatical adherence to his own incredibly high standards of craftsmanship and his rigid determination to uphold the status of the Payne name as a tribute to his father. Jim was a king of craftsmen, a true friend, and a real gentleman.

The Payne Rod

The elder Payne was one of the pioneer makers of fine rods, and his son now carries on the Payne artistry with the same faithful skill that characterized his famous father. All of his work is done by his own hands with the aid of unique tools and contrivances originated by Edward Payne to expedite and give accuracy to the delicate operations.

Out of six bamboo strips is created a finished lance-like whole so unified that the naked eye cannot tell where they have been joined together.

When it comes to ferrules, once more the superiority of the Payne methods stand out. Factory ferrules are worked on machines and turned out in handfuls so that often their sharp shoulders cut into the bamboo and there's a split rod and a lost fish. But Payne's ferrule-making is different. He draws his by hand through a cunningly devised machine that his father originated. Each metal ferrule is drawn to just the right degree of hardness so as to make it fit and conform to the wood, and still have the right amount of elasticity to take up all shocks and strains of the rod, and still not break. There is no record of a Payne rod breaking at the ferrule.

When finally the butt of the finished rod rests comfortably in your hand, and you go down to your favorite stream for a cast, you know that you're holding nothing less than an exquisite piece of art. There is all the give and take, the balance, the thrilling sense of sturdiness that you've often dreamt about for your ideal rod. Along it the line flows out with that singing swish that is such sweet music in an angler's ear. Yards away the fly drops in easy grace upon the surface of the stream.

All your skill and craft can be thrown into the playing of the fish when you're angling with a Payne rod. Never once does that troublesome fear that the strain may be too great for your rod come in to spoil the sport. So that you may know the best there is in angling, Payne has given the best there is in him to the making of your rod.

Dry Fly Salmon Rod

Three piece with extra tip joint, dark finish, metal reel seat, independent handle to fit in bottom of grasp. Packed in aluminum tip case and heavy canvas bag.

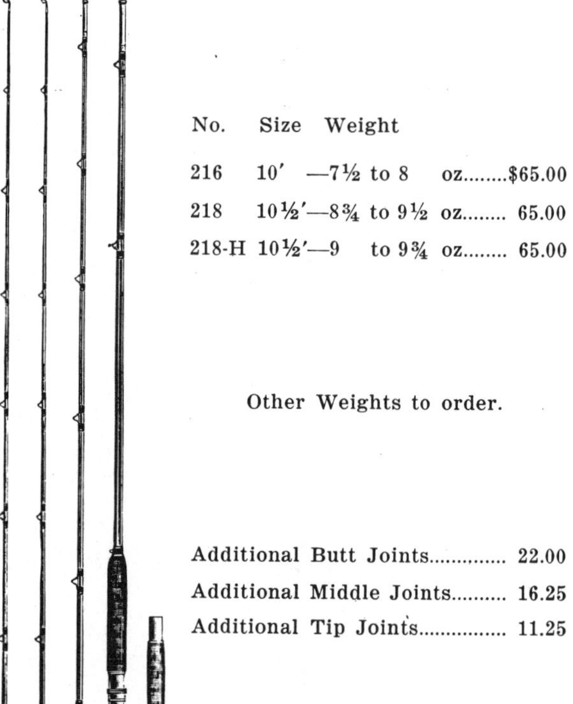

No.	Size	Weight	
216	10′	—7½ to 8 oz	$65.00
218	10½′	—8¾ to 9½ oz	65.00
218-H	10½′	—9 to 9¾ oz	65.00

Other Weights to order.

Additional Butt Joints	22.00
Additional Middle Joints	16.25
Additional Tip Joints	11.25

Payne's Handmade Rods

3-Piece Fly Rod

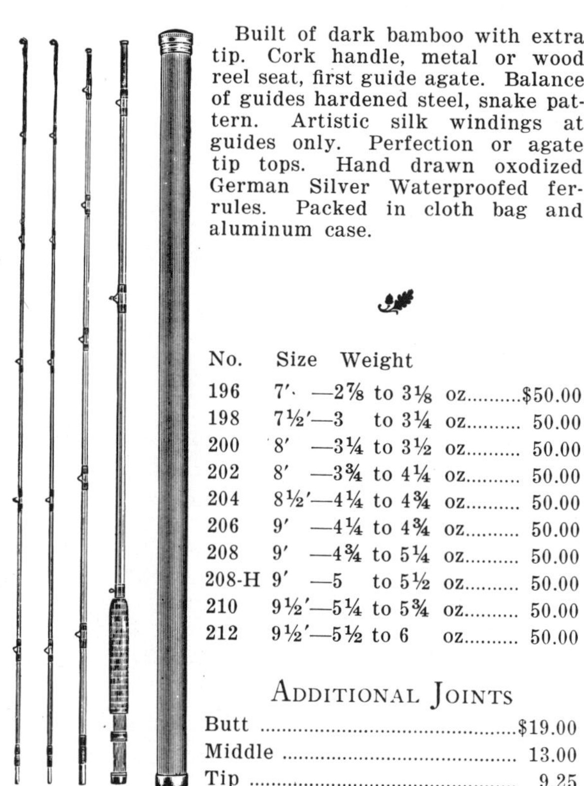

Built of dark bamboo with extra tip. Cork handle, metal or wood reel seat, first guide agate. Balance of guides hardened steel, snake pattern. Artistic silk windings at guides only. Perfection or agate tip tops. Hand drawn oxodized German Silver Waterproofed ferrules. Packed in cloth bag and aluminum case.

No.	Size	Weight	
196	7′	—2⅞ to 3⅛ oz	$50.00
198	7½′	—3 to 3¼ oz	50.00
200	8′	—3¼ to 3½ oz	50.00
202	8′	—3¾ to 4¼ oz	50.00
204	8½′	—4¼ to 4¾ oz	50.00
206	9′	—4¼ to 4¾ oz	50.00
208	9′	—4¾ to 5¼ oz	50.00
208-H	9′	—5 to 5½ oz	50.00
210	9½′	—5¼ to 5¾ oz	50.00
212	9½′	—5½ to 6 oz	50.00

Additional Joints

Butt	$19.00
Middle	13.00
Tip	9.25